The
Psychoanalytic
Study
of the
Child

VOLUME TWENTY-SIX

The Psychoanalytic Study of the Child

VOLUME TWENTY-SIX

QUADRANGLE BOOKS

NEW YORK / CHICAGO

A New York Times Book

DR. SEYMOUR L. LUSTMAN died in a tragic accident on August 5, 1971 at the age of 51. He had been one of the Managing Editors of *The Psychoanalytic Study of the Child* since 1968 and an important contributor since 1956. We mourn the death of a gifted researcher, a dedicated teacher, and a loyal friend and colleague. An appropriate commemoration of Dr. Lustman's scientific contributions and their significance for psychoanalysis will appear in Volume 27 in 1972.

Sorrowfully,

Ruth S. Eissler
Anna Freud
Marianne Kris
Lottie M. Newman
Albert J. Solnit

CONTENTS

CONTRIBUTIONS
TO PSYCHOANALYTIC THEORY

ASPECTS OF NORMAL
AND PATHOLOGICAL DEVELOPMENT

CLINICAL CONTRIBUTIONS

APPLIED PSYCHOANALYSIS

CONTRIBUTIONS TO PSYCHOANALYTIC THEORY

Ego Autonomy and Ego Pathology

DAVID BERES, M.D.

CONSIDERATION OF THE CONCEPT OF EGO AUTONOMY CALLS FOR A
survey of the concept of ego in psychoanalysis. I shall focus on
those points that are relevant to the development of my theme.

The Concept of Ego

Psychoanalytic psychology has developed gradually since Freud's
earliest writings and in great part by changes introduced by Freud
himself, and more recently by Heinz Hartmann, Ernst Kris, and
others. The changes are more evident in the increasing conceptualization of what has come to be called ego psychology.

In early psychoanalytic writings the concept of psychic activity
was based on the dichotomy of consciousness and unconsciousness.
Further, two different aspects of unconsciousness were postulated,

the one the so-called true, dynamic unconscious made unavailable to consciousness by the forces of repression; and the other, the momentarily unconscious, easily available to consciousness and named the preconscious. Three qualities of psychic activity were thus formulated as three systems, named the system *Cs.*, the system *Pcs.*, and the system *Ucs.* This formulation we recognize as the topographic theory.

In this formulation Freud equated ego with the system *Cs.* He further conceptualized that the conflict in neurosis was between unconscious sexual impulses of the system *Ucs.* and the conscious demands, standards, and prohibitions of the systems *Pcs.* and *Cs.* It was not till several decades later (1923) that he introduced the term "id" (p. 23) and designated the superego as a separate structure (p. 28).

In this work Freud recognized the inadequacy of the topographic theory on the basis of his clinical observations. He noted that the defensive and moral components of psychic activity which he had attributed to the system *Cs.* and which he equated with ego were not always conscious; that, in fact, they often were *Ucs.* in the true dynamic sense of the term. It was thus an error to equate *Cs.* with ego because some ego functions were clearly unconscious. Freud reformulated his concept of psychic structure, not in terms of the dichotomy *Cs.-Ucs.*, but in terms of the interrelationship of groups of mental functions, as they are observed to interact in states of conflict and in states of adaptation.

These groupings of mental functions—id, ego, superego—are abstractions which comprise the structural theory of psychoanalysis. We use the abstractions to codify our observations. The danger of treating the abstraction as a concrete entity, of reifying it, must constantly be kept in mind. Hartmann (1950) has said succinctly, "the ego . . . is a substructure of personality and is defined by its functions" (p. 114). The same approach applies to id and superego. As clinicians we observe behavior; we listen to the patient's verbal communications. From these we deduce functions and structure.

The functions ascribed to the ego, whether in the service of adaptation or coping with conflict, are in relation to outer and inner elements—in the case of outer elements with regard to the outside world, the environment; in the case of the inner elements, with regard to different functional aspects of the mind, instinctual drives, wishes, prohibitions, ideals. Nor can inner and outer elements be kept in separate compartments. There is always an outer world—even if it is the laboratory setting of sensory deprivation; there is always the activity of inner forces, and the two are in constant interaction with each other.[1]

I emphasize the concept of the human psyche as a dynamic interaction of functions, but at the same time I give equal emphasis to the organization of these functions into identifiable groups which, as our clinical observations indicate, operate as coherent entities identified as the substructures of the psyche.

The word "ego" predates the writings of Freud. It was, however, used not in the sense it now has in psychoanalysis, but in the sense of the self. In his "Project for a Scientific Psychology," which Freud wrote in 1895 but never published, he conceptualized ego as an organization of the psyche with certain specific functions, primarily an agency inhibiting the discharge of psychic energy, in that work termed "quantity" or "Q" (p. 323). In subsequent years Freud made frequent reference to ego, especially to defensive functions, but not as a subject of primary interest. Only with the publication of *The Ego and the Id* in 1923 was ego psychology placed on a firm foundation as part of the structural theory.

To define ego, as Hartmann suggests, is to list the functions and to describe their manifestations. There are many such lists, some shorter, some longer, but they are all elaborations of what Hartmann (1956) calls "the powerful triad of functions: adaptation, control, and integration (synthetic function)" (p. 290).[2] We have Freud's list:

> . . . in each individual there is a coherent organization of mental processes; and we call this his *ego*. It is to this ego that consciousness is attached; the ego controls the approaches to motility—that is, to the discharge of excitations into the external

---

[1] For a detailed discussion of the effects of sensory deprivation on autonomy of ego functions see Miller (1962).
[2] I have in an earlier paper (1956) proposed such a list of ego functions.

world; it is the mental agency which supervises all its own constituent processes, and which goes to sleep at night, though even then it exercises the censorship on dreams. From this ego proceed the repressions, too, by means of which it is sought to exclude certain trends in the mind not merely from consciousness but also from other forms of effectiveness and activity [1923, p. 17].

Autonomy of Ego Functions

What I have said so far serves as the basis of my discussion of autonomy. If it is agreed that the term "ego" is an abstraction defined only by its functions, it follows that we cannot speak of ego autonomy in a global sense; we can speak only of autonomy of specific and separate ego functions. In order to make the concept of autonomy meaningful in clinical work we must deal with specific ego functions and not with the "ego" as a whole.

The author most identified with the concept of autonomy is Heinz Hartmann, whose book, *Ego Psychology and the Problem of Adaptation,* in which the concept is introduced, is a psychoanalytic classic. Although Freud did not at any time speak of ego autonomy in specific terms, he indicated even in his early papers that ego functions were active in their operation (for example, 1911, p. 67; 1915, p. 134; 1923, p. 55); and in "Analysis Terminable and Interminable" (1937), he postulated the existence of "original, innate distinguishing characteristics of the ego" (p. 240), a concept which foreshadows that of primary autonomous ego functions.[3]

Hartmann (1955) defines autonomy as "stability of . . . ego function, or, more precisely, its resistivity to regression and instinctualization" (p. 229). To understand the concept of autonomy it thus becomes necessary to consider in some detail the development of ego functions and the role of regression in conflict.

Hartmann postulates an undifferentiated state in the neonate out of which there gradually develop the various psychic functions. The infant is not born with ego functions. He is born with

---

[3] See Hartmann (1956) for a detailed discussion of the development of Freud's concept of ego, especially the adumbration of later theories in his earlier writings.

the potential, the capacity to develop the functions which comprise not only ego, but also id and superego. Development takes place by the interaction of two factors: maturation and experience. For instance, the human infant has the capacity to develop speech and language, but the specific qualities of his speech and the language he speaks are determined by the environment to which he is exposed. Some ego functions develop predominantly by maturation; others predominantly by the effects of environmental factors, that is, by learning. The latter originate from identifications, primarily with the parents, and from situations of conflict, from the interaction of drives and defenses.

The concept that the infant is born with the capacity to develop ego functions implies a hereditary basis of ego mechanisms. Hartmann (1939a) has described inborn psychic apparatuses, assigned to the ego, such as perception and motility, which he designates as primary autonomous functions. These develop essentially by maturation but require what he calls an "average expectable environment" for their functional expression. The primary autonomous functions may subsequently be drawn into conflict and lose their autonomy, as we see in our clinical work in misperceptions and disturbances of motility.[4]

Other ego functions develop by identification and out of conflict situations. In the course of development these functions may achieve a degree of independence and stability which permits them to operate relatively divorced from conflict and to maintain their stability in later conflict situations, a state comprised of secondary autonomous functions. Activities originally involved in conflict of a narcissistic, libidinal, or aggressive nature thus achieve autonomy by what Hartmann (1950) calls "change of function." For example, the intellectualization which serves as a defense against sexual impulses in adolescence may in later life achieve autonomy and serve in scholarly pursuits in the so-called conflict-free sphere of the ego.

The loss of autonomy of an ego function results in regression to an earlier functional state; it may also involve drive regression, but not as parallel phenomena. Anna Freud (1965) notes:

[4] For a discussion of experimental psychophysical studies of primary autonomous ego functions see Weiner (1966).

In contrast to drive regression, the retrograde moves on the ego scale do not lead back to previously established positions, since no fixation points exist. Instead, they retrace the way, step by step, along the line which had been pursued during the forward course. This is borne out by the clinical finding that in ego regression it is invariably the most recent achievement which is lost first [p. 104].[5]

The role of conflict in the development of ego functions and their later manifestations has further implications. Since human beings have instinctual drives, expressed as needs and impulses which seek immediate gratification and which are forced to delay discharge, or limitation and distortion by reality, conflict is inevitable. In any civilization as far as we know conflict is not only inevitable—it is ubiquitous. Hartmann (1939b) reminds us that "conflicts are a part and parcel of human development, for which they provide the necessary stimulus" (p. 12).

Ego functions and conflict interact and influence each other. The individual copes with conflict by the activity of the ego, sometimes successfully, sometimes unsuccessfully. In the latter instance we have symptoms, inhibitions, perversions, character disturbances, or psychoses. But conflict also serves the development of ego functions, especially in the early stages of development. This calls for what Ernst Kris (1950) has described as the optimal balance between deprivation and gratification.

Multiple and complex factors enter into the development and autonomy of ego functions. Functions are modified by the experience of conflict—an aspect of learning—and may further, by

[5] See also Sandler and Joffe (1967) who distinguish between "functional autonomy" and "structural autonomy." They apply "concepts of function and structure to contrast activities and processes on the one hand with patterns of organization, schemata, agencies, apparatuses and mechanisms on the other." They assume that early structural organizations are never lost ("except under the influence of organic changes in the brain") but are inhibited in their function with later structural development (p. 260). With "functional regression" under the influence of stress there is loss of functional autonomy, but the "persistent" ego structures which have been inhibited in the course of development are reactivated and reemployed. These intriguing ideas deserve more consideration than I can give them within the scope of this paper. I would only say that my approach to the concepts of function and structure differ in some details (Beres, 1965).

"change of function," assume autonomous status outside of conflict.

I quoted earlier Hartmann's definition of autonomy as the
"stability of an ego function, or, more precisely, its resistivity to
regression and instinctualization." Regression and instinctualization are defensive measures in conflict situations, and autonomy
implies the capacity of ego functions to resist regression and instinctualization in the midst of conflict.

Loss of autonomy is a form of regression, but regression is, as
Anna Freud notes (1965, p. 93), "a principle in normal development." She says: "According to experience, the slow method of
trial and error, progression and temporary reversal is more appropriate [than instantaneous transformations of function and be-
havior] to healthy psychic growth" (p. 99). Regression of ego functions thus may be a normal defense mechanism, especially in
children. There is the further observation that infantile modes of
thought and action persist into adult life without being considered
pathological.[6] Normal psychic functioning must include the capacity to use defensive measures including regression and instinctualization under conditions of stress and conflict. In this sense
there can be no absolute autonomy. The crucial issue is whether
the loss of autonomy persists or is transient.

This point was emphasized by Ernst Kris (1952) who introduced and described the concept of regression in the service of
the ego, of controlled regression. Here we deal with a transient
loss of ego autonomy, which is followed by a reorganization of
primary process elements in the creation of a sublimated activity.
In this instance the synthetic function of the ego remains autonomous and "tames the chaos" of the regressed functions.[7] Normal
regression and transient loss of autonomy of some ego functions
also occur in play, whether in the child or adult, and in the au-

---

[6] See in this connection Brenner (1968). He writes: "Normal modes of ego functioning are not wholly free of the archaic, infantile features which characterize
pathological manifestations; the differences are relative, not absolute" (p. 428).

[7] Brenner (1968) and Weissman (1968) argue against the designation of regression
in this instance. It seems to me, however, that in the strict sense of the word
there is regression of ego functions, though it serves normal psychic activity. The
recognition of the role of regression does not denigrate the resulting sublimated
activity in art or science.

dience participation in a work of art. Where the regression is less
transient and more profound, there will be a corresponding impairment of autonomy of ego functions and loss of sublimatory
capacity.[8] The primary autonomous function of perception may,
for example, be involved in conflict in the primal scene experiences of the small child, lose its autonomy, and reappear in an
autonomous state in the characterological trait of curiosity of the
scientific investigator. The misperceptions and sexual fantasies of
the child indicate the loss of autonomy; the scientific work, the
restoration of the autonomy.

Hartmann has conceptualized a conflict-free sphere of the ego,
in which by definition the ego functions operate autonomously.
The ego functions may be facilitating gratification of id impulses,
but these would be impulses that are both ego-syntonic and reality-
syntonic. Gratification of impulse is, after all, a goal we all strive
for, though we may be forced to modify or divert the gratification.
Freedom from conflict does not mean independence from drives.

It is conceivable that ego functions may have a definite instinctual component and without conflict operate with autonomy. An
example would be the exhibitionism in the motility function of
the ballet dancer. Instinctualization does not of itself destroy autonomy; it does so only if it evokes conflict. Furthermore, autonomy and conflict may independently be variable and transient.
Hartmann (1950) stresses the importance of what he terms "ego
interests" in psychoanalytic psychology. Hartmann notes the
"closeness to id tendencies underlying them" (the ego interests),
but adds that they "follow not the laws of the id but of the ego"
(p. 136f.). In another paper Hartmann (1947) says:

> The ego interests are only one set of ego functions among others;
> and they do not coincide with the ego function that considers
> also the demands of the other psychic systems and that I have
> described as the ego's organizing function; their prevalence in

---

[8] For a comprehensive discussion of the concept of regression see Arlow and
Brenner (1964). They define regression as "the *re-emergence* of modes of mental
functioning which were characteristic of . . . earlier periods of development" (p.
71) and emphasize that "As a rule regressions are specific and discrete in nature
rather than global and total" (p. 75).

an individual does not warrant the assumption that the drives are harmoniously included in the ego, or that the superego demands have been integrated into it [p. 66].

It follows that ego interests may or may not involve conflict and may call on autonomous or nonautonomous ego functions to achieve gratification.

Conflict between impulses and reality is not a direct conflict between these two agencies. The conflict created by an environmental stimulus becomes a conflict because it evokes an instinctual drive and an unconscious wish or fantasy. This creates a danger situation—loss of love, loss of the love object, the danger of physical injury or mutilation—any of which is portended if the unconscious wish should be gratified. Ego defenses are brought into play by the anxiety which the danger situation arouses, and it is between the instinctual drives and the defenses that the conflict takes place. That is why in psychoanalytic theory we speak of conflict as between the substructures of the psyche—between id and ego, or between ego and superego. This metaphorical language is a short-hand description of clinical observations.

In summary, autonomy is a concept to be applied to specific and separate ego functions, not to the ego as a whole. Our clinical observations are never of the abstraction, ego, but of the manifestations of specific functions. Further, the functions of ego do not operate in isolation. They interact with instinctual drives and superego functions, and they mediate between these and reality. The ego functions are never independent of drives or reality; they operate in relation to them and facilitate drive discharge. Autonomy of ego function implies freedom—freedom from the distorting influence of conflict, and freedom to operate with appropriate efficiency according to the role of the specific function in the psyche's organization and in relation to id, superego, and the external world.[9]

---

[9] The freedom I speak of is not identical with the freedom Freud (1923) describes when he says: "after all, analysis does not set out to make pathological reactions impossible, but to give the patient's ego *freedom* to decide one way or the other" (p. 50n.). The latter is an expression of autonomy of the person, rather than autonomy of ego functions.

This approach is, in my opinion, entirely compatible with Hartman's definition: the resistivity of an ego function to regression and instinctualization. I grant that this approach has a teleological taint and suggests arbitrary judgments of health and morality, but I believe these cannot be avoided when we deal with clinical psychic phenomena.

Self Autonomy vis-à-vis Ego Autonomy

The distinction between ego autonomy and autonomy of the self or person is often lost in writings on autonomy and leads to confusion because different authors are dealing with different levels of autonomy, what logicians define as "mixed categories."

It is necessary to clarify what we mean by "self" and "person" as distinct from "ego" and to consider the role of autonomy in so-called "free choice." This involves the problem of determinism.

Ego and self are not synonymous terms, though Freud, especially in his early writings, used the word ego sometimes to indicate the self and sometimes to indicate a coherent organization of functions.[10] Self is a complex concept including sense of identity, body sensations, affective responses, cognitive processes, self representation and object representation, all involving a number of ego functions. Hartmann (1956) notes that, for Freud, "the subjective experience of one's self was a function of the ego, but not the ego" (p. 279).

We are in even greater difficulty when we speak of the "autonomy of man" or "autonomy of the person." These are concepts which must be distinguished from autonomy of ego functions.

The problem may be resolved, if only in part, when we recognize that we are dealing with different levels of conceptualization, each significant and valid in its own sphere. There is first the philosophical level with the vast philosophical and theological literature of free will, freedom of choice, man's responsibility for

---

[10] See, for example, Freud (1914), especially p. 75: "The libido that has been withdrawn from the external world has been directed to the *ego* and thus gives rise to an attitude which may be called narcissism" (my italics). Hartmann (1953) states clearly: "Narcissism is, strictly defined, libidinal cathexis of the self, not of the ego" (p. 192). Cf. also footnote 9 above.

his actions, and similar problems. The second level comprises the recent psychoanalytic and psychological studies on self and identity. The latter are closely related to the third level of conceptualization, the theories and clinical observations of ego functions.

We see as surface phenomena that in ordinary human activities man has to make choices between alternative possibilities. But when we apply the principle of psychic determinism, so basic in psychoanalytic theory, we recognize that the choice which the individual makes is the resultant of a chain of unconscious and conscious determinants. The "freedom to choose" is limited by both external factors and inner forces. Choice and decision are complex actions involving the multiple functions of all subdivisions of the psyche. We are familiar with the disturbance of the capacity to make choices and decisions, for example, clinically observable in obsessional patients with ruminative doubting.

I do not minimize the importance of the nonanalytic approach to the problem of conscious choice. The importance of the contribution that psychoanalysis makes to this problem is the demonstration of the role of unconscious factors in the process.

When we observe what appears to be conscious freedom of choice, we may in a descriptive and empirical way speak of a kind of autonomy, whether autonomy of the self, of the person, or autonomy of man. Our knowledge of ego psychology and of the functions of the ego permits us to go further in our explanatory efforts, even if not as far as we would wish.

We may say that unconscious factors bring the individual to a point where he has to choose between conscious alternative possibilities. He must exercise conscious judgment and thought. Here we can say the person has "freedom of choice"—in fact, we think of the goal of psychotherapy and psychoanalysis as the patient's becoming capable of choosing his own way of life when he has insight into his unconscious conflicts. But we may also say that the person's choice, even at this moment of conscious choice, is nevertheless also determined by deeper unconscious factors as well as by external forces. We are indeed in a dilemma, in danger of ignoring the complexity of the problem on the one hand, if we assume that man is wholly free, and the danger of infinite regress on the other, if we assume the total absence of free choice in human behavior.

Our approach will depend on the level on which we attack the problem, whether on the manifest level or on the level of deeper determinants. As Waelder (1963) points out, there is neither complete psychic determinism nor complete indeterminism.

The concepts of activity and passivity are peripheral to the concept of ego autonomy and more central to the concept of autonomy of the person. Freud's discussion of the passive aim of the masochist or the exhibitionist makes clear its dependence on the active role of ego functions (1915). In regard to reversal into the opposite and turning round upon the subject's self he says:

> The earlier active direction of the instinct persists to some degree side by side with its later *passive direction,* even when the process of its transformation has been very extensive. The only correct statement to make about the scopophilic instinct would be that all the stages of its development, its auto-erotic, preliminary stage as well as its final active or passive form, co-exist alongside one another; and the truth of this becomes obvious if we base our opinion, not on the actions to which the instinct leads, but on the mechanism of its satisfaction [p. 130; my italics].

Activity and passivity refer here to the totality of a psychic manifestation and leave unexplored the question of the autonomy of the ego functions involved in the manifestation.

In the same paper Freud wrote: "The relation of the ego to the external world is passive in so far as it receives stimuli from it and active when it reacts to these" (p. 134). "Ego" here appears in two different meanings. The passive ego is the self; the active ego comprises the ego functions. The latter, whether autonomous or not, are always active.[11] Whereas ego autonomy involves specific functions, autonomy of the self involves problems of freedom, choice, free will, responsibility, determinism, activity and passivity. Ego functions are involved in the autonomy of the self, and the two interact in the manifest behavior of the individual.

[11] Several authors have written papers on activity and passivity, but when they touch on the question of autonomy, seem to be concerned, as far as I understand them, only with the autonomy of the person. See Gray (1967), Holt (1965), Rapaport (1953), and Schafer (1968).

A related aspect of psychic functioning is automatism, first given detailed exposition by Hartmann (1939a). He defines automatism as automatic motor behavior, perception, or thought which he designates topographically as preconscious. They operate without the hypercathexis of consciousness and, in fact, may be disrupted if the attempt is made to execute them consciously. Emphasizing the important role of automatism in adaptation, he says: "Actually both flexibility and automatization are necessary to and characteristic of the ego; purposive achievements depend on some functions taking a flexible, others an automatized form, and still others combining these two forms in various proportions" (p. 92).

It follows that automatization is not synonymous with autonomy. Automatized action, perception, or thought may involve nonautonomous ego functions as well as autonomous ego functions. Only careful analytic investigation will determine the state of autonomy of the ego functions involved in an automatized activity. Hartmann lists compulsions, tics, and catatonias as "pathological automatisms" and notes that "sexualization of automatic functions plays a role in many neuroses" (p. 90).

Clinical Considerations

The following brief clinical example illustrates the interaction of environmental and inner forces in the manifestations of autonomy and the distinction between autonomy of the person and autonomy of ego functions.

The patient was a professional woman with the immediate problems of being distressed by the situation in the office where she worked. She was the only woman who functioned on a professional level; the other women in the office were secretaries. She felt exploited and subjected to indignities on account of her sex. She was given menial assignments below her capacities and, in her opinion, below that of the men in the office. She complained that she was ignored as a person.

This was the external situation as she described it. It appeared to be one of environmental stress that produced anxiety and depression.

What do we see from the viewpoint of autonomy?

First, what I would consider autonomy of the self. The patient was free to choose. She could resign and seek another position; she could assert herself and demand recognition and respect. But she remained passive. She complained bitterly to me and to her friends. She claimed she did not dare speak up, not only because she might lose her job, but: "I can't see myself doing that." She rationalized that she was well-paid and had heavy expenses—she was a divorcée and had a young daughter for whom she must provide.

The patient's passive attitude, her ineffectual complaints about her situation, along with her lack of action to correct it, all speak for a loss of autonomy of the *self* in relation to her environment. Further, she is dependent on outer approval for maintaining her self-esteem.

Somehow, the picture seems incomplete. Suppose then, we turn to the examination of inner forces and specific ego functions, that is, autonomy of the ego.

The patient had a masochistic character structure and much of the abuse she complained of was invited by her. This appeared in her sexual and personal relations as well as in her work situation. The passivity repeated an infantile pattern that she had experienced in her early relationship to her mother. Behind her passivity was the unconscious wish to be given without having to ask. To ask implied aggression and the danger of rejection. She was frightened by her aggressive impulses which she must repress and turn on herself. Her aggression was also fed by intense penis envy. She sought fulfillment of infantile wishes and unconscious fantasies of blissful dependence.

When we examine the autonomy of separate ego functions, we do not find a uniform state of affairs. Certain functions showed a loss of autonomy; her object relations were disturbed by her masochism, by her insatiable need for love and protection, and by her inhibited aggression. We see loss of affect control, poor judgment, and misperception where conflict intervened. The autonomy of these functions was affected by unresolved inner conflict in association with the stress of external forces.

But at the same time other functions operated well. The patient remained at her job and usually accomplished satisfactorily whatever she undertook. She was coping adequately with the care of her child and the maintenance of her home.

Her thought processes were most of the time unimpaired, but when, for example, she was distressed by some slight, real or imagined, she became confused, memory was disturbed, and she made gross errors in her work. Similarly, her reality function was essentially undisturbed, though she would at times misinterpret what was a colleague's preoccupation as a conscious wish to snub her, under the influence of her wish to be universally loved.

Autonomy of ego functions in this patient was subject to rapid disequilibrium in conflict situation, and this was a central aspect of her psychopathology. The instability of autonomy served here, as it does in other cases, as an index of pathology.[12] I would emphasize that this approach is applicable to separate ego functions, but it is not applicable to the ego as a whole. In any individual, as in this case, some functions are more stable and others less.

I believe that in our clinical work it is most useful to focus on the separate ego functions and to keep the abstract concept of ego as an organized structure in the background for our theoretical formulations. I suggest that it is the reification of the abstraction, ego, that leads to confusion of autonomy of self and ego autonomy.

The case I have described illustrates the clinical significance of the concept of autonomy.

One cannot conceive of an ego function independent of the external world. Insofar as psychic activity involves the interaction of instinctual drives, superego prohibitions and ideals, reality demands, and the integration of these by ego functions to resolve conflict and to achieve adaptation, there is no autonomy of ego functions in isolation, independent from either environment or drives.[13] Ego functions may control instinctual drives, but they may also permit instinctual gratification.

[12] See Hartmann (1952): "The degree of secondary autonomy, as I have called this resistivity of ego functions against regression, is a problem equally relevant for our clinical, theoretical, and technical work. It is closely linked up with what we call ego strength and probably is the best way to assess it" (p. 177).

[13] Miller (1962) defines "ego-autonomy as a capacity for self-government in relation to both the demanding and nondemanding aspects of id and environment" (p. 15).

Implicit in the concept of autonomy is the question of normality, more specifically, normal functioning. We are also concerned with age-appropriate behavior and its pathology as we see it, for example, in infantilism or prolonged adolescence. In mental illness we see regression of ego functions as a result of inadequate coping with conflicts which were caused by drive impulses or environmental stress—in either case a breakdown of ego autonomy.

Nor is the environment, when it enters into psychic activity, an independent entity. External situations, external stimuli, evoke conscious or unconscious impulses, wishes, and fantasies. As noted above, if these involve a danger situation, anxiety arises and defense mechanisms are brought into play. The conflict is not between the drive impulses and reality—it is between the drive impulses and the defenses, between id and ego in our metaphorical language.

Autonomy is not "independence *from,*" whether it be "from the id" or "from the environment." Autonomy is an index of function, more specifically of ego functions in relation to id and superego, the other structures of the psyche, and the external world.

Rapaport has proposed a theory of a reciprocal relationship between two autonomies, one from the id, the second from the environment (1951, 1958). According to his theory, the greater the autonomy from the id, the less the autonomy from the environment, and vice versa. Clinical facts, however, do not support this theory, as the case described above demonstrates. In this instance there was on the level of autonomy of the self loss of autonomy in relation to the environment, and concurrently loss of autonomy of ego functions in relation to id pressures and superego ideals and prohibitions. Rapaport's concept neither applies to nor elucidates the clinical observations.[14]

What Rapaport denotes as autonomy from the environment would be better designated as the capacity of ego functions to respond to environmental vicissitudes and demands in accordance with motivating drive impulses, superego demands, and reality limitations. The difficulty with Rapaport's formulation lies in the

[14] For a detailed critical discussion of Rapaport's theory see Miller (1962), Gill and Brenman (1959, p. 169ff.), and Holt (1965).

reification of the abstraction "ego" and the consequent mechanistic manipulation of the global ego to fit it into an elaborate and elegant theory.

Disturbed ego function may result from maldevelopment or from regression—the former caused by organic defect or by deprivation in early childhood; the latter, as response to conflict. In work with children it is especially important to recognize this distinction because the therapeutic approach is altogether different in each instance. It is a well-established observation that the ego functions in the small child are relatively unstable and regress under stress—a separation, the birth of a sibling, a change in the environment—and under favorable conditions may recover with equal speed and spontaneity. Autonomy, to the extent that it is established at all, is still fragile (Anna Freud, 1965, p. 93ff.).

Even in adults transient disturbances of autonomy of ego functions are everyday occurrences, in the so-called normal person as well as in the neurotic or psychotic. For example, a man leaving an assignation with a lady, not his wife, stands before the door of her apartment and hears the street noises as sounding his name. His ego functions of perception and reality testing are momentarily impaired under the impact of his guilt and anxiety. He recovers immediately.

Another example is a virtuoso musician who, auditioning before Toscanini, is unable to play a note on his instrument. Here a complex set of ego functions involved in his ability to play his instrument loses its autonomy under the influence of the castration anxiety evoked by the presence of the great Maestro.

These can hardly be called examples of ego pathology in view of their transient nature, but they illustrate that it is not only stability of autonomy that constitutes normality but also the recovery of autonomy when it is temporarily lost.

Let me turn briefly to some familiar clinical entities.

In another paper written some years ago (1956) I dealt in greater detail with the significance of ego pathology in schizophrenia. Then I said:

> The child in his development only gradually assumes those qualities which in time give him the unique status of a human

being. The capacity to form concepts; the use of language, symbols and tools; the capacity to form identifications; the distinctive thought processes, both primary and secondary process; the postponement of gratification; the organizing or synthetic function—these and other human functions develop in the child and are part of his ego. In the course of this development, whether normal or pathological, there will be manifestations of immature functioning which will be similar to the disturbances seen in schizophrenia. In fact, if one accepts the concept that schizophrenia is primarily the result of ego regression, then it may be said that it is the breakdown of these unique human qualities that comprises the schizophrenic process [p. 230f.].

Today I would restate what I said then in terms of ego autonomy as well as ego pathology.

In the schizophrenic patient certain ego functions have lost their autonomy, the capacity to operate optimally in mediating between the instinctual drives, superego demands, and the limits imposed by the environment. The functions suffering loss of autonomy include especially those involved in the relations to reality, the control of drives, thought processes, and the capacity to deal with personal relationships. At the same time other functions, such as memory and motility, may remain intact.[15]

It has been postulated that primitive inhibitory processes which are part of the primary autonomous equipment of the ego and forerunners of the subsequently developing defense mechanisms may be innately defective and so set up a predisposition to schizophrenia. Later on this may become manifest in specific vulnerabilities of the defenses used in coping with conflicts and lead to loss of autonomy of ego functions (Hartmann, 1953; Weiner, 1966). What we see in schizophrenia, then, from the viewpoint of ego autonomy is that crucial ego functions, whether by innate

---

[15] Arlow and Brenner (1964, p. 154) state: "the later concepts of Freud's structural theory, particularly the concept of regression of ego functions, explain the clinical phenomena of the psychoses better than do his earlier concepts of libidinal decathexis and recathexis." They emphasize the defensive function of the regression. The revision of the concepts of the psychopathology of the psychoses proposed by Arlow and Brenner is consonant with my thesis in this paper. See also Arlow and Brenner (1969).

deficiency or by regression imposed by conflict, fail in their autonomous capacity and are dominated by drive impulses.

This does not mean that concomitantly there is an increased autonomy from the environment. I cannot agree with Rapaport (1958) when he says, "the reduction of the ego's autonomy from the id (as by the intensification of drives) results in a loss of touch with reality, which amounts to a maximized autonomy from the environment" (p. 732). Loss of touch with reality is a regressive manifestation of a complex of ego functions, and, far from indicating increased autonomy, it signifies rather a severe loss of autonomy, not only in relation to the drives but also to the external world. Loss of touch with reality is an unsuccessful attempt to deal with conflict, with both inner and outer forces.

It is also useful to examine the neuroses from the viewpoint of ego autonomy. In the neuroses we find evidence of disturbed ego function, of disruption of autonomy of certain functions, as I have attempted to illustrate in the case presented above. I would further suggest that in the neuroses there is an increased tendency to loss of autonomy of ego functions.

It is an observable fact that a person will characteristically use the same defense mechanisms no matter what the conflict. This, I suggest, is not an example of autonomy. There is a difference between autonomous and repetitive or persistent phenomena (Sandler and Joffe, 1967). Defenses are used repetitively in conflict and so appear stable. Only by change of function and activity in the conflict-free sphere of the ego do defenses achieve autonomy, the secondary autonomy described by Hartmann.

The persistence of a psychic activity, whether of id, ego, or superego, does not signify autonomy. The rigidity of the obsessive-compulsive patient, his repetitive and persistent compulsive acts are not indicative of autonomous ego function. Nor is delay of response always indicative of autonomous ego function. Certain defensive patterns attempt to deal with unconscious, unresolved wishes and fantasies by specific mechanisms that characterize this clinical entity. Rapaport's statement (1958), "Obsessive-compulsive defense . . . maximizes the ego's autonomy from the id" (p. 732), is not supported by clinical experience. The obsessive-compulsive

patient, despite his defenses, is not free from the influence of his
drives or of his superego prohibitions.

The loss of autonomy by the sexualization or aggressivization
of an established ego function may be seen in all forms of psychopathology. I have given several examples in my comments so far.
We see this process clearly in hysterias both as symptoms and inhibitions. We see it in the regressions in our patients in the course
of the analytic situation. It is also a danger in the pitfalls of
countertransference.

To work well as therapists and analysts calls for autonomy of
a number of ego functions—judgment, memory, conceptualization, control of drives, and others. This autonomy may suffer
interference by libidinal forces—identification with the patient,
rather than empathy; the wish to be admired as a brilliant therapist; or the wish to protect and rescue the patient. Similarly, aggressive impulses may instinctualize the ego functions—the wish
to control the patient and to direct him; and, above all in the
form of therapeutic zeal, the demand that the patient get well at
the therapist's command. All this may, of course, go on unconsciously. As therapists and analysts we all experience the tendency
to instinctualize our dealings with patients, and to be good analysts and therapists we have to learn to counteract this tendency.

Conclusion

Ego psychology is not an isolated theoretical exercise. It is part of
the psychoanalytic approach to the study of the total personality,
whether normal or pathological, and it does not preclude consideration of drive impulses, superego functions, and the role of
the environment. Ego psychology serves both as a tool in clinical
psychoanalysis and as a base for a psychoanalytic psychology.

We seek to evaluate the autonomy of the different functions in
relation to the underlying conflicts and fantasies, and to determine, by the definition I prefer, the capacity of each specific
function to resist regression and instinctualization and to perform
optimally its role in coping with conflict and promoting adapta-

tion. From this point of view the aim of psychoanalysis is to restore the autonomy of ego functions which have been lost or diminished in conflict and by instinctualization and regression.

BIBLIOGRAPHY

ARLOW, J. A. & BRENNER, C. (1964), *Psychoanalytic Concepts and the Structural Theory.* New York: International Universities Press.
— — (1969). The Psychopathology of the Psychoses: A Proposed Revision. *Int. J. Psycho-Anal.,* 50:5–14.
BERES, D. (1956), Ego Deviation and the Concept of Schizophrenia. *This Annual,* 11:164–235.
— (1965), Structure and Function in Psycho-Analysis. *Int. J. Psycho-Anal.,* 46:53–63.
BRENNER, C. (1968), Archaic Features of Ego Functioning. *Int. J. Psycho-Anal.,* 49:426–429.
FREUD, A. (1965), *Normality and Pathology in Childhood.* New York: International Universities Press.
FREUD, S. (1895), Project for a Scientific Psychology. *Standard Edition,* 1:283–387. London: Hogarth Press, 1966.
— (1911), Psycho-Analytic Notes on an Autobiographical Account of a Case of Paranoia (Dementia Paranoides). *Standard Edition,* 12:3–82. London: Hogarth Press, 1958.
— (1914), On Narcissism: An Introduction. *Standard Edition,* 14:67–102. London: Hogarth Press, 1957.
— (1915), Instincts and Their Vicissitudes. *Standard Edition,* 14:109–140. London: Hogarth Press, 1957.
— (1923), The Ego and the Id. *Standard Edition,* 19:3–59. London: Hogarth Press, 1961.
— (1937), Analysis Terminable and Interminable. *Standard Edition,* 23:209–253. London: Hogarth Press, 1964.
GILL, M. M. & BRENMAN, M. (1959), *Hypnosis and Related States: Psychoanalytic Studies in Regression.* New York: International Universities Press.
GRAY, P. (1967), Panel Report: Activity-Passivity. *J Amer. Psychoanal. Assn.,* 15:709–728.
HARTMANN, H. (1939a), *Ego Psychology and the Problem of Adaptation,* tr. D. Rapaport. New York: International Universities Press, 1958.
— (1939b), Psychoanalysis and the Concept of Health. *Essays on Ego Psychology.* New York: International Universities Press, 1964, pp. 1–18.
— (1947), On Rational and Irrational Action. *Ibid.,* pp. 37–68.

— (1950), Comments on the Psychoanalytic Theory of the Ego. *Ibid.*, pp. 113–141.

— (1952), The Mutual Influences in the Development of Ego and Id. *Ibid.*, pp. 155–181.

— (1953), Contribution to the Metapsychology of Schizophrenia, *Ibid.*, pp. 182–206.

— (1955), Notes on the Theory of Sublimation. *Ibid.*, pp. 215–240.

— (1956), The Development of the Ego Concept in Freud's Work. *Ibid.*, pp. 268–296.

HOLT, R. R. (1965), Ego Autonomy Re-Evaluated. *Int. J. Psycho-Anal.*, 46:151–167.

KRIS, E. (1950), Notes on the Development and on Some Current Problems of Psychoanalytic Child Psychology. *This Annual*, 5:24–46.

— (1952), *Psychoanalytic Explorations in Art.* New York: International Universities Press.

MILLER, S. C. (1962), Ego-Autonomy in Sensory Deprivation, Isolation, and Stress. *Int. J. Psycho-Anal.*, 43:1–20.

RAPAPORT, D (1951), The Autonomy of the Ego. *The Collected Papers of David Rapaport,* ed. M. M. Gill. New York: Basic Books, 1967, pp. 357–367.

— (1953), Some Metapsychological Considerations Concerning Activity and Passivity. *Ibid.*, pp. 530–568.

— (1958), The Theory of Ego Autonomy: A Generalization. *Ibid.*, pp. 722–744.

SANDLER, J. & JOFFE, W. G. (1967), The Tendency to Persistence in Psychological Function and Development. *Bull. Menninger Clin.*, 31:257–271.

SCHAFER, R. (1968), On the Theoretical and Technical Conceptualization of Activity and Passivity. *Psychoanal. Quart.*, 37:173–198.

WAELDER, R. (1963), Psychic Determinism and the Possibility of Predictions. *Psychoanal. Quart.*, 32:15–42.

WEINER, H. A. (1966), Some Thoughts on the Concept of Primary Autonomous Ego Functions. In: *Psychoanalysis—A General Psychology: Essays in Honor of Heinz Hartmann,* ed. R. M. Loewenstein, L. M. Newman, M. Schur, & A. J. Solnit. New York: International Universities Press, pp. 583–600.

WEISSMAN, P. (1968), Psychological Concomitants of Ego Functioning in Creativity. *Int. J. Psycho-Anal.*, 49:464–469.

Death Drive, Ambivalence, and Narcissism

K. R. EISSLER, M.D., PH.D.

IN THIS PAPER, DATA WILL BE PRESENTED THAT APPEAR TO ME TO lend support to Freud's theory of a death drive. A brief discussion will follow, dealing with selected aspects of ambivalence and narcissism. I shall attempt to focus on the energic interplay between drives and ego at a primitive level, without considering such later complexities as conflict and superego. Moreover, in the instances to which I shall be referring, I shall instead try to stay within the simpler core of energic interplay. I shall then make an effort to determine the consequences that are produced by the joint action of death drive, ambivalence, and narcissism. At one point, I shall offer a view on orality that will be different from the prevailing view.

The Biological Basis of the Death Drive

One can see in the prepublished papers of the 27th International Psychoanalytic Congress in Vienna (*Intern. J. Psycho-Anal.,* 1971) a reaffirmation of the fact that Freud's final systematization of drives is still being rejected by the vast majority of psychoanalysts (cf. Brun, 1953). Just as Freud's classification of drives as libidinal and aggressive has become quite popular and just as that division is now well-nigh indispensable to psychoanalytic practice and theory, so most authors are highly critical of Freud's assumption of a death drive, which is basic to his final theory of drives. Since the arguments against it are so formidable and widespread, the question may be raised whether it is at all necessary to come to terms with this concept.

Brenner (1971, p. 138), for example, has suggested that psychological observation alone is at present sufficient to establish a psychoanalytically adequate classification of drives; clinical observation, he then goes on to note, clearly shows the presence of an aggressive drive, and therefore he suggests, following Hartmann (1949), that the last word with regard to the death drive should be left to the biologist, who will, at some point in the future, decide the merits of that concept. Yet the same sort of trouble now seems to be brewing with regard to the psychobiology of the aggressive drive, in that no aggressiogenic zones, equivalent to the erotogenic ones, are to be found (Brenner, p. 138).

Nevertheless, one could ask whether the rejection of a death drive really does serve a constructive purpose. Death is, after all, the most important event in man's life, after his birth, and a psychology that has nothing to say about it, that is unable to allocate to death a meaningful place in its overall structure, does not seem worth talking about.

One may or may not agree with Heidegger's philosophy, yet the basic principle on which his metaphysics rests, is correct: events must be explained by what precedes them—that is to say, in the precedent circumstances subsequent events must already be announced, if not actually contained, in one way or another; since man, without exception, will die, the various processes that precede death must make the outcome not only understandable but also inevitable. Man's existence is basically a continuous progression toward death and therefore the antecedents of the final stage of that progression must be demonstrable. The psychologist, however, may refuse any demand to make death part of his inquiry, and instead declare death to be per se an exclusively biological event, unrelated to any psychological context. That, in my opinion, would amount to sheer prevarication, even though death is, of course, enforced by biological processes.

Among the many objections that may be raised against such a stance, I shall refer only to the unlikelihood that the only event in man's life that is predictable with absolute certainty should be a completely nonpsychological one. The meaning and importance of this absolute certainty, unmatched by the certainty with which we can speak of any other event, are usually insufficiently acknowledged. Not even the rising of the sun can be predicted with that degree of certainty, insofar as it requires this addition: "unless cosmic conditions change"; the prediction of death, on the other hand, requires no such qualification.

In view of the subject's overriding importance, one might even say that a poor theory is better than none at all, and therefore decide to stick with Freud's concept of a death drive until a better theory has been devised. Those who reject the death drive are not aware that, when they do so without introducing another set of explanations for the phenomenon of death, they are simply scotomatizing the most relevant part of psychology, and then going on as if their theories still had some chance of being correct. That chance they certainly do not have, since these theories leave more things unexplained than the things they do explain.

The death drive, according to Freud, does its work silently within the organism. Some writers have described it as working "against" the self. All "against" phenomena of that sort, however, are secondary; they occur only after the death drive has been deflected toward external reality and then once again turned back against the subject. Since the work of the death drive not only is silent but proceeds *within* the self, no manifestations can be expected of the kind we are accustomed to encounter in cases of internalization. From Freud's theory one would have to conclude that by way of free associations no message can be obtained about a death drive, but only messages about aggression turned outward and its subsequent recoil.[1]

From the start of the 19th century, man's thinking was diverted from the subject of death, as is appropriate to a society that has been dazzled by an enormous leap forward of science and technology, and that believes in general progress. Medical thinking has since then been preoccupied with problems of the causes of individual death; as one consequence, our knowledge about all those diseases that lead to death has been enormously enlarged. But the fact was more or less overlooked that the same person would have had to die, even if he had not suffered from the particular disease that did fell him. Overshadowed by the wealth of knowledge that has been obtained through the study of individual death, death as a general phenomenon, which runs through all the forms of organic life, has evoked much less interest.

The most frequent causes of individual death are injuries and diseases. If death were to be regarded—as most biologists still do—either as an accident (a chance event, as it were) that befell a complicated machinery (*Betriebsunfall*), or as an event that had been enforced by wear and tear (*Abnützung*) of that same machinery, Freud's theory of a death instinct would be wrong. A discussion of why these two concepts do not explain the universal presence of death within the organic world, however, would lead too far afield.

It would be wrong to expect that much can be gleaned from current textbooks of physiology or pathology that can be used to establish a biological basis for Freud's death drive. The physiology or pathology of the death drive can be learned only from a biology that has approached the study of life under the aspect of death as the fundamental problem of life, regulating directly or indirectly all of life's manifestations. In other words, Freud's theory requires a biology that looks into the causes of physiological death—that is to say, one that sees death as a necessity of life, even under optimal conditions.

This was done with consistency and the gain of deep insight by Rudolf Ehrenberg, professor of physiology at the University of

[1] I shall omit any discussion of whether this also holds true of primary masochism (Freud, 1924).

Göttingen, who published in 1923 his *Theoretische Biologie.*
Bernfeld and Feitelberg (1930, p. 194) were the first, I believe,
to point out that Ehrenberg's views can be correlated with Freud's
theory of a death drive. Indeed, Ehrenberg's theoretical views
make Freud's theory appear to be far more probable than one
would gather from other publications. For Ehrenberg, the fact
that the passage of life per se (*der Ablauf des Lebens*) regularly
leads to death was the cardinal problem of life, as well as of pathology.

Life is, according to Ehrenberg, a process that takes place
within a vital space (*Vitalraum*) and is characterized by a gradient
of assimilation. This latter gradient is not constant; it varies during the course of an organism's life and is, moreover, not uniform
for all tissues and organs. Further, even with regard to the same
organ, it varies according to the particular circumstances. The
gradient of assimilation on the part of an individual organism
will nevertheless, in all instances, approach zero during the course
of its existence; when that point has been reached, physiological
death occurs. An organism usually dies its individual death, of
course, before it has reached the zero point.

Although the life of any organism does take a course that
brings it closer and closer to the zero point, some tissues, under
certain artificial conditions, do not take that same direction.
When some tissues are placed in appropriate conditions, in which
they can grow without restraint, they not only will not approach
the zero point of the assimilative gradient, but will instead go on
growing without interruption. The younger the tissues are, the
more effective will this process be. This is not, however, true of
all tissues. Brain cells, for example, cannot be made to grow *in
vitro.*

One may state in general terms that cells lose the ability to
divide, either because of aging or because they have reached a
certain degree or form of differentiation. When the ability to
divide has been lost, cells are doomed to die. Growth is, therefore, the problem of life and death. So long as the vital space
can be enlarged and growth thereby maintained, the assimilative
gradient will become steeper, and the reaching of the zero point
postponed.

As a matter of fact, Max Hartmann succeeded in developing

a technique that made it possible to establish such conditions under circumstances that were far less artificial than those involving tissue culture *in vitro*. He amputated *Tubularia,* a primitive organism that belongs to Hydrozoa; this amputation over and over again stimulated the regeneration of the lost organ. The amputation creates a void in the organism's potential vital space to be filled by growth. Biologists even speak of the potential immortality of Hydra, since, if one continues to enforce in them these processes of regeneration, the organism does not ever die. (In this discussion I have, for the sake of simplification, adhered to the old theory and disregarded the recent report that cells lose their capacity for growth after 80 to 100 years even when growing *in vitro*.)

There is a growth in volume and weight—external growth. Ehrenberg also speaks of *internal growth,* by which he means the structuralization of cells, tissues, and organs. In keeping with the psychoanalytic terminology, I shall refer to it as structuralization, or structural growth. External and internal (or structural) growth do not take place in separate phases, but at the same time. External growth, however, by and large comes to a standstill, whereas structural growth continues. Some biologists have equated life with external growth; yet it is evident that a differentiated organism goes on living after the phase of external growth has ended. In the life of man, for example, the span of existence after maturation is even longer than is the preceding span of external growth.

One could therefore say that everything that is given to the process of assimilation is alive, yet the end product of assimilation may be "actually dead" (Ehrenberg, 1923, p. 8). Structure, unless unusual circumstances arise, remains insusceptible to change and indissoluble within the cell, organ or organism. The older an organism becomes, the more of its vital space is taken up by structure. What is structured increases absolutely as well as relatively, during the course of life.

Structure is thus biologically irreversible—which is why life entails processes that are irreversible. This is the biological equivalent of the second law of thermodynamics. Gillespie (1971, p. 156) is quite right in emphasizing that organisms are not closed systems: if they were, man's existence would be of a very short duration. While the human organism starts out as an almost ideal open system, however, it does increasingly become a closed one.

At the beginning of life, cells are practically totipotential—a faculty that they more and more lose; they then become unipotential. In the state of totipotentiality, the vital gradient is very high, and the momentum of external growth is enormous. Aging, however, reduces both. In losing the faculty of totipotentiality, the cell thereby acquires its individuality, which cannot be other than limited and specific. Ehrenberg's biology is based on a general principle, formulated by the biologist, Karl Ernst von Baer, as follows: "The developmental history of the individual is the history of its growing individuality in every respect [*Die Entwicklungsgeschichte des Individuums ist die Geschichte der wachsenden Individualität in jeder Beziehung*]."

This is a principle that can be reapplied, without any change and without any loss of meaning, to the psychological history of the individual. From this it follows that when the possibility is created of forming new or higher forms of psychological structure, death is postponed. The "melting down" of structure, the excretion of structured substance, restores life—as was observed in the aforementioned amputation of some primitive organism.[2]

One may think of death as a side product, as it were, caused by something unavoidable, even though it is incidental or fortuitous, or by the retention of scoria or slag. Ehrenberg (1923, p. 25) turns—I think, rightly—against this conception of life, and emphasizes that it is structure that conditions the catastrophic end of the organism. Yet structure necessarily develops within the life process, and its pullulation constitutes the very process of life.

In the central nervous system, which is the highest regulator of life in the human organism, the structural changes include: increasing pigmentation; the shrinking and condensation of nuclei; conglobation of chromatin; and, finally, decrease of cell volume,

[2] I would like to add here that the feeling of rejuvenation that is experienced upon awakening out of a deep, subjectively dreamless sleep (which is not dreamless at all, as we now know) makes me certain that some dreams, if not indeed most of them, have the psychobiological function of dissolving psychic structure (cf. Bernfeld and Feitelberg 1930, p. 196).

vacuolization and reduction of the number of cells. Thus life can be seen as consisting of processes that are irreversible. The end products of these processes gradually accumulate in the cell, leading to a state that inhibits the continuation of assimilation. Only the removal of structure or the enlargement of vital space can then serve to extend the time of an organism's life.

A simple case of the bypassing of structuralization is the division of protozoa. In more differentiated organisms, those with great regenerative power, the melting down of structure reaches an equivalent goal. In still higher forms of differentiation, with a now reduced regenerative power, the separation of germ cells from the organism that is doomed to die becomes necessary as the only way to continue life processes.

The general physiological process that is correlated with structural growth is the increase of connective tissue, along with the decrease of water and plasma. The proteins of cell plasma in the young organism are hydrophilic; in aging, however, they become hydrophobic. This process then leads to a state of torpidity or rigidity. When external and structural growth have reached their end point, when further individualization is no longer possible, when unstructured or less structured substance can no longer be transformed into individualized forms of higher structure—then the structural configuration deteriorates, falls apart, dies.

The transformation of a biological system that consists of totipotential cells, with a high assimilative gradient and a potentially large vital space to be filled by extensive and structural growth, into one that consists of unipotential cells, with a low assimilative gradient and their vital space maximally structured—this is the equivalent of what is seen in physics, as the shift from an open to a closed system.

It should be unnecessary to state that this is only approximately true, so that the formulation should really read that "Life is marked by the transition from a more or less open system to a more or less closed one." From all this, one can learn that death is not an accidental event, or a "minus" event; neither is it a consequence of life, or of the using up of a life substance. Instead, it is necessary to life; without death, there is no life—or, as Ehrenberg puts it—death is the prerequisite of life.

One could therefore say that Ehrenberg's biology is a biological demonstration of Freud's psychological theory. The biological forces responsible for the transformation of the organism into a closed system are the equivalent of Freud's death drive. I do not feel prepared at this point to speculate whether the assimilative process should be viewed as equivalent to libidinal processes, by contrast with the structuralizing. The main point is the fact that the basic life process is constructed in such a way that it necessarily brings forth its own inhibition.

Whether or not the inhibitory biological forces are sufficient to serve as the substratum of a drive—that is to say, whether "death drive" was a misnomer, in that what we are dealing with here is a force that is not the equivalent of a drive—I would not dare try to decide. The main question is that death is demonstrated to be not imposed upon the organism against its will, as it were; instead, the life process in itself (not against itself), and exactly by way of fulfilling itself (the German term *vollenden* brings this out even more strongly), produces death. Yet, decisive as Ehrenberg's research may be for Freud's final drive classification, however much it may help to make that classification meaningful, I am far from wishing to say that it solves all the problems involved in the construct of a death drive.

Some of Ehrenberg's views may even seem to contradict basic psychoanalytic propositions. Ehrenberg's theory is compatible with the formulation that, during the course of the life process, free energy is converted into bound energy (1946, p. 34); and it is the total conversion of free energy into bound energy that results in death. This formulation raises an interesting theoretical issue: it suggests that the death drive reaches its goal through the conversion of free energy into bound energy. With regard to the libidinal drives, psychoanalytic theory assumes that they are able to reach their aim of direct physical gratification only so long as they are maintained in a free state. Libidinal energy that is permanently bound is irreversibly lost to drive gratification. The possibility that the counterpoise of the two drives is also achieved by a reversal of the form in which they finally come to rest, is a challenging one to consider.

When the death drive is prevented from doing its work by the

creation of structure—that is to say, when it remains free energy
—in what way, then, does it manifest itself? Here the answer seems
to be that it forces the cell to divide, and that this then deprives
the cell of its individual existence. Freud was, by and large, in
agreement with Weismann, who believed that unicellular organisms do not die so long as they have the opportunity to divide.
According to this view, death would be a late acquisition of organisms, making its earliest appearance only with the emergence of
metazoa. Max Hartmann raised objections to this view. In his
opinion, when an organism ceases to exist, yet makes a new appearance in two samples of its kind, one can hardly overlook the
fact that, in this instance, reproduction has been coincidental
with death. Freud (1920, p. 47) reported, without further comment, Hartmann's objection. (François Jacob [1970, p. 317] seems
to agree with Weismann.)

Thus, when the death drive is prevented from binding free
energy in the form of structure, this gives rise to the division of
the cell, which thereby shortens the cell's individual existence.
As to the points on which Ehrenberg's biology of death and
Freud's propositions may not be in full agreement, the following
should be mentioned. Freud's view that "a special physiological
process (of anabolism or catabolism) would be associated with each
of the two classes of instincts [drives]" (1923, p. 40), is not confirmed by Ehrenberg: catabolism serves assimilation. This, however, I believe to be a by no means serious obstacle to the reconciliation of the two theories, since Freud's main point that
both drives are active "in every particle of living substance,
though in unequal proportions" (p. 40) appears to come close to
Ehrenberg's basic view.

The foregoing outline may suffice as a demonstration that
Freud's theory of a death drive is by no means untenable within
a strictly biological frame of reference, so long as the latter aims
at an explanation of physiological death. Neither should it be
overlooked that Freud's theory of the death drive, when it is
taken in conjunction with Ehrenberg's biology, may lend itself to
historical application. Empires grow, mature, and decline, as some
historians, such as Spengler, have proposed. So long as they grow,
they are protected against death; once their expansion has come

to an end, however, they fall into the danger of declining. Their structuralization is speeded,[3] until finally they collapse under the combined impact of their own rigidity and an assault from without. For a long time, the history of China showed another type. That country survived by way of being destroyed in part by invading nomads; this amounted to a melting of structures and a subsequent filling out of the potential vital space with new structure. How far such observations should be taken as being only metaphorical, I shall not discuss here. At any rate, it seems to me quite probable that later research will show historical processes to be variants of basic psychobiological laws.

Death Drive and Structuralization of the Psychic Apparatus

Ehrenberg's view that, from the beginning of life, a tendency toward organic structuralization is observable raises the question of whether a psychic equivalent of this tendency can be recognized. As a matter of fact, the end stage of man's life can also be described psychologically as almost total rigidity, lack of elasticity. In the end, the psychic apparatus too loses the ability to assimilate new material; free energy is at that point at its disposal in only minimal quantities. The voice of the id has become muted; the ability to adapt to changes is lost; the efficacy of the perceptive organs has been increasingly diminished; by the end stage, irreversible processes have converted the psychic apparatus from one that began by being endowed with totipotentiality into one that is an almost closed system. It is particularly in the area of memory that Ehrenberg's view can be confirmed: while the early memories are preserved, no new structure can apparently be formed in old age; the present no longer leaves any memory traces. The regressive features that are so often observed in old age do not contravene this comparison of the end stage of psychic life with a closed system.

Between birth and old age, however, lie innumerable chains of

---

[3] Cf. Nietzsche (1884–1888, #254): "An old Chinese said that he heard that when empires are about to collapse, then they have many laws [*Ein alter Chinese sagte, wenn Reiche zugrunde gehen sollen, so hätten sie viele Gesetze*]."

structural processes. Psychic life is as little possible, as organic life is, without the steady formation of structure; man seems to perish likewise as a result of the total structuralization of the psychic apparatus.

Yet what is the psychic constellation at the beginning of life? The neonate's psychic situation is in many respects unique. I want here to point out only one. According to legend (quoted, following Christoffel 1939), the German Emperor Frederick II (1194–1250) wanted to know what language would be spoken by children who never heard a single word. He therefore entrusted the raising of orphaned neonates to nurses who were required to feed them and clean them, but forbidden to caress them or to utter a single word to them. Everyone of them died as an infant. The chronicler added: "They could certainly not live without the favor, the friendly features and the caresses of their attendants and wet-nurses." This legend is the mythic precursor of what von Pfaundler (1915, 1936) and later Glanzmann (1938) called "hospitalism" and the death attacks (*Sterbeanfälle*) (Christoffel, 1939, p. 453) of those neonates who have been brought up under the psychologically unsuitable circumstances that exist in foundling homes and hospitals. Von Pfaundler gives an impressive and very moving description of the severe psychic damage, so often leading to death, that is suffered by infants who are deprived of care and nursing at the hands of mothers or of their substitutes. Von Pfaundler's findings were fully confirmed, on the basis of psychological tests, by Spitz (1945, 1946).

All investigators are in agreement that the disastrous effect of hospitalism is not the consequence of failures in nutrition and hygiene. It can be proven clinically that libidinal gratifications are indispensable for the setting in motion of structural processes. A neonate who is not caressed or in some other way made the recipient of affection will not develop its psychological potential. It strikes me as being particularly significant that, according to von Pfaundler, severely idiotic children are less endangered by hospitalism than are sensitive children (Christoffel, p. 457). It seems that those infants who possess a large potential for differentiation are in greater need of maternal love than are the torpid ones. Apparently when the psychological vital space has been constitutionally reduced, the damage that is caused by the absence of maternal love is less than it would otherwise be.

As psychoanalysts and educators, our main preoccupation is with the repair of weakened or defective structure, or with initiating and stimulating its growth where it is lacking. This may be one reason for overlooking—or, at least, for paying less attention to—how much psychic structure is formed automatically, predominantly within the area of conflict-free development (Hartmann, 1952, p. 18). Such functions as perception, motility, and thinking develop in relative independence of external reality—that is to say, their structuralization progresses in accordance with laws that are inherent in the psychic apparatus itself, so long as the necessary minimum of libidinal influx and accretion is maintained. Processes of conflict-free development are ascribed to maturation, which is looked upon mainly as an organic, cerebral process; yet these cerebral processes have their psychic counterparts and the latter must consume enormous amounts of psychic energy. The question I am raising has to do with the kind of psychic energy that is consumed by structural processes that occur more or less automatically within the psychic apparatus under suitable libidinal conditions.

Clinical observation demonstrates that it is the libidinal inflow from external sources that initiates and maintains structuralization of the psychic apparatus; moreover, once psychic structuralization has been set into proper motion, it leads to an irreversible state of rigidity and inelasticity. The psychic equivalent of the organic necessity to form structure that accumulates and finally leads to death would be the innumerable chains of structural processes within the psychic self. According to this view, the "silent work" of the death drive would therefore show two aspects: one within the body, the other within the psychic self. Both aspects would be characterized by an accumulation of irreversible structure formation.

Aggression and the Fusion of Drives

According to Freud, the death drive is not limited to the internal domain of the organism, so that its energies are not exhausted by their work within the self. They are deflected toward, and partly drained off in the outer world, in the form of aggression and destruction. It is "through the agency of Eros that the destructive instincts . . . are directed towards the external world" (Freud, 1923, p. 46, n. 3). The death drive that is deflected in this way does not ever appear in its pure form; it is always mixed, to a varying proportion, with libido. The developmental process, according to Freud, favors an increasing admixture of libido with the aggression that is turned against the outer world. This theory of fusion has also been characterized recently as invalid (Brenner, 1971, p. 142). Yet once we undertake to discuss the fusion of the two basic drives, we enter the clinical field, and certain well-known data can be presented for consideration. Observation of the child's drive development appears to confirm the correctness of Freud's basic view of fusion.

As soon as a healthy newborn has been permitted to settle down—that is, as soon as the tribulations of birth and of the subsequent cleaning that is customary in our civilization have become matters of the past—the infant does not fall asleep, as one might expect, but remains awake. Without any sign of displeasure on his part, his tongue then starts to wander spontaneously along his lips. No physiological explanation has been offered for these tongue movements, so far as I know, and we must therefore evaluate them as the first behavioral manifestations that occur without external provocation but rather spontaneously. They cannot be regarded as reflexes, or as chains of reflexes. These spontaneous licking movements have never, to my knowledge, been used for purposes of psychoanalytic theory formation, although their importance should not be questioned. Since orality is the first and primary manifestation of the infant's drive development, all manifestations in that area have relevance for a theory of drives. I consider the regular spontaneous licking movements of the newborn to be as important as the newborn's sucking, which is regularly referred to by psychoanalytic researchers.

With a rather primitive and therefore not altogether reliable apparatus, I myself have measured the pressure relations of these movements (Eissler, 1938). The curve is an unorganized, vague one, as it were: in an irregular design, it goes slowly toward a peak, from which it again descends, irregularly and slowly, to a base line. It is when the lips are externally stimulated that the sucking reflex makes its appearance. Its rhythm is quite different, and the curve is well organized and repetitive, consisting of a succession of equal amplitudes. The pressure quickly increases to a maximum, and then decreases with the same rapidity to a base line, only to reach its maximum quickly once again.[4]

The sucking reflex leads, under the proper circumstances, to the incorporation of liquids, whereas the spontaneous tongue movements along the lips serve no function of self-preservation. The effect of the sucking reflex is the disappearance of the object at which it is aimed; this makes it easy, indeed unavoidable, to refer to it as the prototype of aggression. Never again will the death drive, among its many externalized forms, find a pattern in which objects are so profoundly destroyed; the spontaneous tongue movements, by contrast, appear to be exclusively in the service of pleasure gain.

Mitscherlich (1971, p. 161) raises the question of "whether one can speak of aggression in the sense of destructive intent in an infant that has not yet acquired motor control." There can be no doubt that there is no possibility for any intent of that sort to exist in the neonate. Yet the neonate's survival seems to make necessary an act that amounts objectively to the most complete destruction possible. Before this act has been initiated,[5] the same organ performs movements that carry all the earmarks one would expect to find in a libidinal gratification in the service of auto-erotism. Although neither pattern can be assigned the dignity of a psychological event, they may both be taken as psychologically paradigmatic—that is to say, one is justified in interpreting them in terms of drive psychology.

Freud probably anticipated this objection to his psychology of

---

[4] I do not know for how long the spontaneous licking movements persist. I would expect them to disappear rather soon and to be fused, so to speak, with the sucking reflex. I have observed the same slow licking movements in an adult who was suffering from a severe neurological disease, the diagnosis of which I was not able to determine for external reasons.

[5] The newborns I observed showed the spontaneous licking movements before they did the sucking reflex. Sucking reflexes have been reported in the fetus. The priority of types of movement, however, is of no relevance at this point.

drives. When discussing the infant's intake of nourishment, he warns: "physiology should not be confused with psychology" (1940, p. 154). It has to be admitted that no rules have yet been worked out that would tell us when biology may be legitimately called in to serve psychology. Freud was close to falling into the errors of a biologizing psychology; his disentanglement from biological encroachments was the true hour of birth of the new psychology. The same dilemma is met with vis-à-vis culture. It is impossible to meet the requirements of psychoanalytic theory formation without relying on some biological and cultural data. It is well known what happens when too much or too little is done in either respect. In view of the continuing absence of rules, the psychoanalyst must rely, in this area, on what may be called "scientific tact"—a rare quality, with which Freud was richly endowed. Therefore, it is quite possible that I have overrated the psychological meaning of events that can be observed in the oral zone of the newborn.

The act of devouring will become automatized and lose its cannibalistic implication during the course of development, yet devouring will still remain the model for an array of psychological processes. It is possible that all acts of destruction ultimately have, in the unconscious, the meaning of devouring. The libidinal manifestation that makes its appearance in the tongue movements is spontaneous and autoerotic, as is proper for the libido in its initial stages. The aggressive manifestation that is seen in the sucking reflex is elicited by stimulation from without, and shows a higher degree of structuralization than the libidinal one. Further, the libidinal and aggressive gratifications are distinct, even though they use roughly the same biological machinery.

In the next phase of the scheme of drive development—the anal phase—an essentially different situation is met with.[6] Libidinal and aggressive gratifications are no longer distinct but intermingled, and the aggressive-destructive drive is essentially modified. Now the goal is to manipulate, to hurt, even to torment

[6] I omit here a discussion of Abraham's (1924) subdivisions of the main pregenital phases. If anything, they would bring out even more succinctly the gradual decline of the aggressive components in succeeding phases of infantile drive development.

the loved object. Yet depriving the love object of its existence is no longer a prerequisite for drive gratification, and this constitutes an all-important progress in the reduction of destructiveness. In complete disregard of the object's pleasure and welfare, however, the child attempts to force it to serve his own wishes and pleasures. In this pursuit, the object may even lose its existence, since the anal child may try to take it apart. But whatever the damage to the object may be, the need for its total destruction —its being made to disappear altogether, which was the leading goal of the early oral phase—has vanished. Thus libidinal and aggressive gratifications are no longer separate but fused; at the same time, a great moderation of destructiveness is to be observed.

About the boy's phallic phase, Anna Freud (1949, p. 40f.) has written: "Boys on this level of development dominate but also protect their mothers, or other love objects." The primary goal is no longer to hurt the object, and the object's existence is therefore no longer endangered in that way; instead, the goal is to preserve the object and to be loved by it.

In the only too rarely achieved genital phase, which Abraham (1924, p. 496) calls postambivalent, the pleasure of both subject and object coincides. The subject places himself in the service of the object's welfare, and aggression is reduced to that minimum that is necessary to taking sexual possession of the love object.

The shortcomings of this outline will, I hope, be forgiven. Its only function has been to show that, within the development of the drives, the succession of psychobiological phases actually shows a step-by-step reduction of aggressive manifestations, in favor of proportionally increasing libidinal ones. It is therefore wrong, and the result of a confusion of conceptual frameworks, when the quite evident psychobiological fusion of the drives, which is accomplished under suitable conditions during the course of drive development, is argued against on the grounds of the clinical fact that, during the oedipal phase, the boy's ambivalence is heightened (Brenner, 1971). It was Diderot who probably was the first to recognize that the child is capable of almost unambivalent drive impulses: he said tersely (and Freud quoted him several times) that the child, if he possessed the violence of a man's passions, "tordrait le col à son père et coucherait avec sa mère [would strangle his father and lie with his mother]." Freud, of course, added that these two wishes are "the true representatives of the *uninhibited* life of the instincts" (1916–1917, p. 337; my italics).

The reasons for the boy's ambivalence during the oedipal phase are well known. I need to present here only three among the many reasons: castration fears, passive wishes toward the father, feelings of guilt. Thus one finds clinically a personality that is rather torn by ambivalence; yet the maturation of drives has progressed so far that now an impulse of what can be spoken of as unadulterated love is generated toward an individual love object, while aggression is directed against other objects, which stand in the way of the gratification of this one great instinctual longing.

Aggression and Aggressiogenic Zones

The psychobiology of the aggressive drive has not yet been adequately examined in the psychoanalytic literature. Many analysts have noted the absence of the equivalents of erotogenic zones with respect to aggression. From Freud's assumption that drive manifestations are a mixture of libidinal and aggressive drives, however, it is to be expected that there are no purely erotogenic zones.

A general remark must be interpolated here about the concept of erotogenic zones. Landmark (1935) has pointed to the ambiguity that is attached to this concept in Freud's writings, insofar as Freud sometimes defines it as referring to the organs that produce excitement, and then again as referring to such organs as are the receptors of external stimuli. The matter seems even more complicated in the search for aggressiogenic zones, for one might feel inclined at first to look at musculature as an aggressiogenic zone. Freud suggested this organ as the "instrumentality" through which "the destructive impulses [are] diverted on to the external world" (1923, p. 41; cf. Gillespie, 1971, p. 157). However, closer examination will show that what is considered an erotogenic zone contains in general a broad spectrum of functions. The oral cavity, because of its sensitive covering, may be stimulated by external stimuli and then function as a sensory receptive organ; yet it may also produce sensations that create a craving and thus put a demand on the psychic apparatus. It is also the apparatus that executes the act of gratification. Consequently, the fact that musculature is an instrument would not exclude its also having the function of a source of stimulation. As early as 1912, Sadger described musculature as an erotogenic organ, yet it is also an aggressiogenic one (see Stone, 1971). And this is true of practically all so-called erotogenic zones: the mouth may kiss or bite; the hand may stroke or choke.

To be sure, depending on its biological structure, an organ will be more suitable for the discharge of aggression or of libido. The genital apparatus per se is directed more toward libidinal gratification, yet it lends itself, under the appropriate conditions, to aggressive discharges. There are men who have the fantasy of hurting the woman through intercourse, and orgasm may require or elicit, as the case may be, the fantasy of murder. A not very rare type of woman experiences man's ejaculation and the subsequent diminution of the penis as a castration that has been carried out by the vagina—an experience that serves as the prerequisite for her own orgasm.

At one point, Freud described the skin as both an erotogenic and an aggressiogenic zone: "touching and physical contact are the immediate aim of the aggressive as well as the loving object-cathexes" (1926, p. 122). The eye, respiration, and many other such organs and functions have also been described in the psychoanalytic literature as serving both.

It is probably only under extreme conditions that an organ serves exclusively one group of drives, as musculature possibly does in the epileptic seizure (cf. Freud, 1923, p. 41). What are now called erotogenic or erogenous zones are probably misnamed: these places serve the energies of both drives. Their proportion will, of course, depend on constitutional and phase-specific factors, as well as on fixations and the child's personal experiences.

At any rate, when one searches for the biological substrata of aggression, it becomes evident that the organic substratum of libido is far more clearly visible than is the substratum of the death drive and its derivatives. There are special, well-defined hormonal glands that regulate sexual development, and the physical links between stimulation and gratification can be mapped out with relative ease. One also finds, as I have tried to show, equivalent psychobiological processes with regard to aggression; but it is evident that in that area the processes are not as well marked as they are with regard to libido.

As a matter of fact, Freud proposed his theory of the death drive and aggression in terms that were general enough to permit alternatives of biological determinants. His theory is not bound to a specific set of biological patterns: a variety of biological possibilities could serve well as underpinnings for his theory. With regard to drive-arousing zones and executive organs, it may be noted that Freud's psychological theory of aggression is not dependent on whether any specific biological apparatus is found that serves that purpose, or whether the aggressive drives make use of equipment that is primarily in the service of the component libidinal drives. I shall therefore take the liberty of interpolating at this point a piece of speculation with regard to the latter alternative.

The fact that the biology of libido can be worked out with so much greater ease than can the biology of the death drive and of aggression may in itself be meaningful. If Ehrenberg's and Freud's theories do have validity, then one is forced to conclude—as Ehrenberg openly states—that death came before life. The vital gradient had to be built up in the face of the tendency toward structuralization. At the beginning of life, the vital gradient led quickly to cell division; and it is not yet clear how it came about that the most complicated biological structures arose which are capable of tolerating high vital gradients, or that structuralization is able to take all the detours and delays that make the duration of life possible, in the form of individual organisms that do not "decay" by division as speedily as the protozoa do. Yet, in view of the death drive's evolutionary seniority, it would not be surprising if it turned out that all the libidinal accruements gained by way of evolution are also used by the death drive and its derivatives.

The death drive was there already, so to speak, at the time

when the channels of libidinal discharge evolved. It is because the life process per se serves the death drive that the latter did not need any special avenues of discharge. This is speculation; but it may serve nevertheless as a tentative explanation of why the biology of death poses a more difficult task than that of life. It may be just the omnipresence of the death drive within the organic realm that makes it so difficult for the biologist to give a satisfactory explanation for physiological death.

The part of Freud's theory of the death drive that serves to explain aggression does not find any counterpart in Ehrenberg's theoretical biology. If the concept of a death drive is accepted at all, then the supposed link between the death drive and aggression would fall within the orbit of psychology. But at this point one is confronting a contradictory situation brought about by Ehrenberg's biology, which served so well the purpose of justifying the concept of a death drive. If the death drive is identified as that biological force that leads to organic and psychic structuralization, then it would seem that aggression cannot be its derivative, since what aggression aims at is the destruction of structure.

When he offered his justification for the derivation of aggression, Freud was right in saying that, within a psychoanalytic theory, the assumption of a drive "turning from the ego to an object" (1920, p. 54) should not cause any difficulty. Such a turn, however, from the self to external reality could not ever change the drive's mode of gratification. Consequently, it looks as if one has to give up either Ehrenberg's biology, as a preliminary justification and explanation of the death drive, or the part of Freud's theory that derives aggression from the death drive. It is contradictory that a drive whose primary goal is to form structure converts this goal into its opposite, namely, the destruction of structure when turned away from the organism toward external reality.

If the notion is accepted, however, that sucking is the first manifestation of the deflected death drive, then in this instance it should be clear that aggression is placed fully in the service of the organism's self-preservation. It would round out the minimum requirements for making possible progressive structuralization of body and psyche. One may therefore say that the first manifestation of aggression—even though its objective effect is the destruction of an external object—fulfills what would be, within Ehrenberg's frame of reference, the death drive's primary aim. (At this point, however, the discussion of the troublesome problem of self-preservation cannot be continued, but must be postponed until later.)

A historical note may be in place at this point. When Freud (1920) introduced an aggressive drive into psychoanalytic theory, without citing Adler, he was reproached on the ground that Adler had already written a paper in 1908, on the aggressive drive in life and neurosis. In a footnote that Freud added in 1923 to the case history of Little Hans (1909), he made some comments on the question of historical precedent.

In that footnote, he asserted that his disagreement with Adler's 1908 paper remained unchanged even though "I have myself been obliged to assert the existence of an 'aggressive instinct'" (1909, p. 140, n. 2). A historical inquiry into the differences of conceptualization involved in aggressive drive postulated by Adler and Freud would have to go to the length of a paper in itself. For that reason, only a few remarks can be made here.

The discussion of Adler's concept is made difficult, to begin with, by the fact that his 1908 paper contains contradictory statements. At the beginning of the paper, Adler declares that sadism and masochism are the result "of two originally separated drives, which have later experienced a confluence." This sounds at first like a precursor of Freud's theory of fusion. But Adler regarded all drive manifestations as a result of the confluence of a variety of drives, not of two general drives—which is the principal point in Freud's fusion theory.

Further, Adler interpreted manifestations of the infant's behavior as aggressive; but he explained them as being the consequence of frustration (p. 581). Aggression is caused, in Adler's view, by the infant's difficulty in obtaining pleasure; this explanation would correspond to the now current frustration theory. Adler's definition of aggression as "the simplest and most frequent instance of affect displacement" would per se make it entirely different from Freud's concept. Yet on the very same page, as the definition just quoted, he writes of "the aggressive drive in its pure form."

When Adler wrote that "the aggressive drive dominates the entire motility," he seemed once again to anticipate one of Freud's later propositions; but then he went on to see in anxiety "a phase of the aggressive drive directed against the own person" (p. 58), and one is again forced to wonder whether his concept of aggression is in any way related to Freud's.

At any rate, there is no trace of Freud's comprehensive construction of a death drive to be found in Adler's paper. I believe that the future historian will find in precisely that aspect of Freud's view the measure of his greatness. Furthermore, Adler's concept of aggression is hardly related to destruction, but can rather be described as constituting an urge to *activity,* coupled with a tendency toward *cruelty.*

Nevertheless, it is still possible that the future historian of ideas will attach less importance to the differences which I enumerated in the foregoing and will evaluate Adler's paper as a valid precursor of Freud's final theory of drives. He may be less impressed than the contemporary inquirer by the central fact that Adler did not do justice to Freud's discovery of the libidinal drive, but instead continued to adhere to a plurality of drives, which by and large operate independently of one another and are correlated with the inferiority of single organs.

Ambivalence

Closely related to man's repertory of drives, in which two main drive forces with contrary goals participate, is the clinical fact of ambivalence. One should not, however, equate ambivalence with the presence of two opposing drive forces. Ambivalence is deeply rooted in man, and lies beyond the orbit of his drives. That is to say, even though ambivalence presupposes the presence of opposing drives, it is not sufficiently explained by their presence.

Animals also have at their disposal contrary drive impulses, and yet their relations with their environment are not interpenetrated by way of ambivalence, as can be observed in humans. The problem of ambivalence is more complex than has generally been observed. It is my feeling that the stimulus barrier already contains the seeds of ambivalence. After all, even though the stimulus barrier is a biological necessity for survival, it does drive a wedge between the subject and the world. Perception is the basic and most important link between subject and world; without perception, any sort of communication is made impossible. The interaction between drive and environment would be reduced—were it not for perceptual mediation—to reflexes that had been elicited by chance contacts between organism and external stimuli.

Nevertheless, the structure of the perceptual apparatus shows a peculiarity that is very consequential: the intensity of its response to an external stimulus weakens quickly, unless the stimulus changes. Pure colors lose their purity, and take on a grayish appearance; the sensation of taste quickly loses its intensity. It is definitely a biological property that weakens the perceptual ties to the object. It is as if nature did not wish man to linger too long with any one object, as if it wanted him constantly—perhaps, even incessantly—to scan his environment.

Man's early environment was characterized by the unbroken presence of dangers. The auditory apparatus, the functioning of which goes on without interruption, is able to receive stimuli from all directions and therefore to warn us of the movements of objects, whatever the direction from which they may be approaching. The visual apparatus, characteristically put out of functioning by the blinking reflex, should be ever-ready to discover those non-moving dangers that are not heard as well as to acknowledge the nature of auditory stimuli.

According to this view, the teleological function of the perceptual ambivalence would then be to prevent man from being attracted by objects solely as the result of their innate perceptual values. If an object is dangerous, then the additional anxiety signal will help to make man respond in an appropriate manner. Pleasure for its own sake, outside of a biologically useful context, can become a terrible danger, as has been shown by modern experiments, in which a monkey undergoes stimulation of the pleasure center in the central nervous system (cf. Brun, 1923). Man, too, should not dwell too long on pleasure and, in his case, this calls for ambivalence "across the board." The Homeric myth of the Sirens contains a deep psychobiological truth: while man can protect himself against visual stimulation, he remains at the mercy of the auditory stimulus. The stimulus barrier protects the psychic apparatus, not only against overexcitation by what may prove to be damaging quantities and intensities of stimuli (Freud, 1920), but also against an all-too-great closeness and fixation to objects.

A biological root of perceptual ambivalence may also be discovered in cathectic peculiarities of the perceptual system, such as Freud has proposed: "It is as though the unconscious stretches out feelers, through the medium of the system *Pcpt.-Cs.*, towards the external world and hastily withdraws them as soon as they have sampled the excitations coming from it" (1925a, p. 231). These supposed micro-oscillations would greatly support man's ambivalence toward objects.

Ambivalence is an important aid in the process by which the child outgrows the oedipal phase. The incest taboo is species-specific; the heightening of ambivalence that is, I believe, observable in man may be one of its prerequisites. It may turn out to be an evolutionary acquisition, necessary for the enforcement of the taboo. It is possible that, without the intensification of ambivalence, the incest taboo could never have been enforced and culture would never have developed. The least that can be said is that, without the tendency toward ambivalence that pervades the psychic apparatus, the danger of frequency with regard to incestuous acts would be far greater.[7]

Overt acts of seeming ambivalence may be the derivatives of strong positive ties to an object. This is also one of the reasons why the problem of human ambivalence is such a complex one. Shakespeare's Cleopatra is, with seeming justification, presented as a paradigm of female ambivalence: after all, she does cause the downfall of her lover, whom she once loved beyond anything else. And yet, on closer scrutiny, one is forced to admit that in order to obtain his full love, she had first to destroy him as a political figure. As long as his political entanglement had any chance of being carried to success, she had no chance of receiving as much of his love

---

[7] The clinical observation that the undoing of a conflict of ambivalence with regard to the mother contributes to a resolution of the oedipus complex does not constitute a valid objection to this proposition.

and affection as she, a loving female, was entitled to obtain and actually needed. Thus one discovers behind a seeming act of ambivalence an indomitable motive of "pure" love; one may therefore surmise that here ambivalence was put into the service of love.

Ambivalence is quite generally a prerequisite of cultural progress. Man loses his interest in anything that is repeated. Scientific solutions, art forms, ways of living, having become "stale," are rejected or at least appreciated with increasingly diminishing enthusiasm. Instead, the desire arises to replace them with new ones, even though what is heralded as "new" is often nothing but a variation of a previous structure, discarded a long time previously. Consequently, one may say that one part of that craving for change that is so characteristic of cultural development is produced by ambivalence toward the old.

Ambivalence pervades the psychic apparatus to such an extent, in fact, that the cultural demands of altruism and unambivalent love relations appear to infringe on certain basic principles of human nature. Putting oneself into the service of an object seems to have a chance of being fulfilled only in the mother-child relation, where it is of the utmost importance for the survival of the species. The one cultural area in which one might expect to find unambivalent attitudes is the professional relationship. It is well known how precarious even these relationships are.

Hypothetically, the following may be suggested: the saturation of cultural and individual life with ambivalence is the consequence of a principle that nature has wisely instituted. Nature strives for variety and for the further development of forms. The probability of variety and higher development increases, the more the members of a group intermingle. It would not be in the interest of growth and of the extension of organic life if members of a group were to remain attached to one another. Apparently, wherever it is possible, the maximum of pair relations should be enforced.[8] Yet what may be of the greatest benefit in the world of nature may become a bane in the world of culture.

[8] The examples that Lorenz (1963) describes as contradicting this principle are apparently exceptional; they would not necessarily disprove the existence of the principle I have postulated.

Narcissism

Narcissism is not easy to define. One appropriate way to do so might be to follow Cusanus, and say what it is not. It is *not* the energy that flows from the subject to the world. This general definition in the negative does, however, require qualification: even objects can be cathected with narcissistic energy.

The smooth functioning of the organism depends on its cohesiveness. Psychoanalytic theory assumes a strong cathexis of the body, which is the mainstay of man's existence. The infant learns to love his body, as the initial main source of pleasure, and he thereby develops an intensive body narcissism. Gradually, outer objects acquire psychological relevance. Initially, these objects are cathected with narcissistic energy. With ego formation and the development of a rudimentary conscience, the narcissistic cathexis of objects is gradually transformed into object libido. At the height of the oedipal phase, the child is capable of forming strong object relations, considerably reduced in the amount of narcissism. During the latency period, the narcissistic relationship increases; but with puberty and adolescence an intense growth of object relations sets in.

The healthy, mature person should be able to maintain constant, almost unambivalent object relations without any danger to the self arising out of narcissistic depletion. This danger actually does exist during adolescence, and in those acute phases of amorousness that are wrongly called, pejoratively, "infatuations." The acute state of the adolescent in love sometimes entails such quantities and intensities of passion that the ego's cohesiveness can no longer be maintained. It is my impression that this is the meaning of Shakespeare's *Romeo and Juliet*. The playwright allows his protagonists to perish as the result of complex external factors; yet the hidden meaning seems to be that, whatever might have happened in the external world, the two were destined to die because at that age the person is not yet sufficiently structured to cope with such enormous libidinal stirrings as they had been exposed to.

As Hartmann (1950, p. 84f.) has pointed out, one must distinguish which parts of the personality are narcissistically cathected. In a harmonious personality, the narcissistic cathexis is distributed in such a way as to guarantee optimal functioning. But narcissistic cathexis may also be unevenly distributed (Kohut, 1966). The superego may be preponderantly cathected, for example, as happens in melancholia; this leads to the defusion of drives, after which aggression is maximally released against the ego. Or else narcissistic cathexis may be concentrated on the ego, or on the self. However, there is one type of person known who enjoys steady object relationships, even though these are predominantly narcissistic. Such persons are usually very strong and efficient personalities. In their instance, loving has the effect of endowing an object with value. Whatever they come into positive contact with acquires for them—if only by virtue of its being worthy of their appreciation—a glow of ennoblement. A disappointment by the object would amount, in their case, to a narcissistic defeat of such gravity that they are quite ready to overlook or even to deny the object's defects.

Such object relationships are often surprisingly enduring. To the outer world, they appear to be true object relations, although psychologically they are not so (Kohut, 1966, p. 245). In such personalities, aggression has been separated from libido. They react with indifference to objects that they do not cathect narcissistically, and they can be—at times, excessively—aggressive and destructive, being uninhibited by any restraint in their relations with those objects that in some way constitute a hindrance to the attainment of their goals. Clinically, they are of interest because one can see in them, more clearly than usual, the vicissitudes of narcissistic libidinal and aggressive drive impulses.

Aside from the importance of narcissism for psychobiological reasons, it must be considered that it is the indispensable counterpoise to man's frightening irrelevance in the cosmos. Vis-à-vis the vastness of the globe which he inhabits, and the still greater vastness of the firmament to which he raises his gaze, without a healthy narcissism he would be crushed by the infinities that surround him. How else could man—who is the only one who is cognizant of death—endure the passing of time that brings him irretrievably closer to it? And thus man's narcissism has served to convert a world that is from a psychological point of view unlivable into an abode that was created by God expressly for his pleasure, well-nigh entertainment.

Freud's Theory of Drive Defusion

After this consideration of narcissism, an argument can be taken up that has been raised against Freud's fusion-defusion theory. Jacobson (1964, p. 16) calls it a "mystery"—for which this theory is, according to her, unable to account—that "drive defusions bring about libidinal impoverishment and absolute predominance of aggressive drive energy." The progression of drive development from orality to genitality is accompanied by a lessening of aggressive components, a fact that speaks strongly in favor of fusion. Yet Jacobson rightly asks what the vicissitudes of libido are in psychotic regressions where, so often, an excessive amount of crude aggression makes its appearance clinically. Even in less dramatic situations in which ambivalence precipitates aggression against an object, the aggression is all too visible; yet can one observe corresponding libidinal manifestations?

It is my impression, however, that such aggressive breakthroughs confirm, no less than dramatic psychotic regressions do, Freud's theory of defusion. For in all such instances an increase of narcissism also takes place. It is as if the libidinal component in the relationship to the external world or to a particular object were taken out of that relationship and added to the cathexis of the ego or self, with the aggression as a result remaining the only clinically observable manifestation.

Freud described this very process when he stated (1930, p. 121) that even in states of "the blindest fury of destructiveness, we cannot fail to recognize that the satisfaction of the instinct is accompanied by an extraordinarily high degree of narcissistic enjoyment." Bernfeld (1925) had pointed to the close relationship between narcissism and the destructive drive (see also Bernfeld and Feitelberg, 1930, p. 202). The same observation can be made in the psychoanalysis of delinquents: the greater their aggression, the greater their narcissism, and it is this that so often brings efforts of psychoanalytic intervention to naught.

Man cannot be aggressive, it seems, without narcissistic gratification (Rado, 1927)—an equation whose consequences are most fateful for individual and collective life.

The Interplay of Aggression, Ambivalence, and Narcissism

I have outlined, in a somewhat sketchy form, how wise nature went about developing an evolutionary process that led, in the end, to anthropogenesis. A death drive within the organism, by means of the life process, enforces differentiation—that is to say, structural growth. When this structuralization has reached its maximum, the psychobiological unit decays, yet not without having left an undetermined number of sprouts in which the same processes will be repeated.

Part of this death drive is deflected and, in the form of aggression, placed in the service of man's survival and his protection against dangers. Ambivalence stands in the way of fixations to objects—fixations that would be dangerous to his further development, and would cause stagnation in cultural development. Narcissism, by its enforcement of self-centeredness, is the first prerequisite of survival; it provides man with a firm platform from which he can venture forth into the adventure of living, without running the risk of squandering his valuable heritage.

As wise as evolution was in giving man each of these treasures, just so fateful is their interplay. Aggression, which is necessary and useful per se, also becomes the main tool by which to obtain narcissistic gratification. It is the lure of this sort of pleasure that prevents man from using his aggression wisely. An ambivalence in general toward objects that might weaken the possibility of establishing ties to particular objects, and thus enable man to enrich his world, through facilitating his free movement from object to object, is rarely used in that way; instead, ambivalence becomes a guide for the discharge of aggression against loved objects, and man becomes destructive precisely where he loves.

Man's problem is not his aggressive drive as such, but rather the fact that his aggression is steered not by self-preservation, but by narcissism and ambivalence. Animals have no less aggression at their disposal than man does, yet their aggression does not become a danger to animal life and to nature (Lorenz, 1963) in general. But man's aggression, just because it is directed by narcissism and ambivalence, constitutes a supreme danger to man and culture. It has been said that the lion and its potential prey are able to mingle peacefully together so long as the lion is satiated. With the first signs of the lion's need for food, however, its prospective victims disperse in a hurry. Here we observe aggression wisely distributed, limited to the area where it belongs—namely, self-preservation.

Such a pattern is incompatible with man's group life. Man's aggression actually goes far beyond the orbit of necessity, even though there are areas of self-preservation in which he acts—whatever his accompanying feelings and fantasies may be—with seeming rationality. This is shown, for example, in his intake of food, which I have postulated as the first and paradigmatic act of the aggressive drive. Yet, aside from those narrow areas of self-preservation that are mainly governed by well-defined physiological laws, man's aggressive behavior is far in excess of the dictates of self-preservation. It is injurious and destructive to others beyond such necessities; and it takes, more often than not, a turn that endangers man's own welfare and even leads to his downfall.

What is observed clinically in the individual is also confirmed historically. The narcissistic overvaluation of one's own group goes very far back in human history. In the Western orbit, we find it already fully developed in ancient Greece and Rome. The Christian churches were not able—it is questionable whether they even tried—to moderate its severity. If anything, the narcissism and ensuing aggression of the Christians seem to have vastly outdistanced those of the Western collectives of antiquity. Nationalism, the scourge of modern history, seems, in its turn, to have gone even beyond the preceding historical period with regard to group narcissism. Here, as in individual life, one can observe that group aggression goes far beyond the necessities of self-preservation.

In connection with the effect of differences in power and their influence upon man, Freud wrote about the "misuse" of aggression, which is usually not as harmless as what is provoked by "the narcissism of minor differences" (1930, p. 113f.). The misuse of collective aggression in the service of narcissistic gratification is one of the perennial themes in the history of mankind.

Man does not use his aggression mainly against the enemy or the prospective enemy; instead, ambivalence forces him, as mentioned before, to use it precisely against his love objects. Freud wrote of.the "unexpected regularity" with which love is accompanied by hate (1923, p. 43).

I am not here taking into account conflict, defense, or feelings of guilt. We know all too well how immeasurably man's existence is complicated by those later acquisitions. To mention only one of these complications, conflicts of ambivalence are frequently solved by the use of aggression as a defense against forbidden—so often homosexual—love objects, as a denial of feelings of guilt and anxiety. I am deliberately omitting, however, such complexities as are brought about mainly by the evolvement of a highly differentiated ego, such as is rendered necessary by a highly developed culture and civilization, but focus on a more primitive level of the psychic apparatus.

In the lives of the animals instances are known that, if they were to be translated into human terms, would have to be regarded as manifestations of extreme ambivalence. When the queen bee rises, the drone that can fly the highest becomes her lover. This is "rational" behavior, and it is in accordance with Darwin's law of selection of the fittest. The lover is then eviscerated and the germ plasma taken in by the queen, to be used for propagation. All other drones are killed. All this is also "rational" and necessary: it makes the continuation of bee life a highly probable event.

A pattern of that kind—aside from its biological impossibility and inappropriateness—would not last very long in man's history. I am here referring to the well-known and often-discussed breakdown of instincts in the human species, which made anthropogenesis possible, or which was brought about by anthropogenesis, as the case may be (cf. Hartmann, 1939; Hartmann, Kris, and Loewenstein, 1949, p. 13). What evidently happened was that certain mechanisms that had until then regulated the course, distribution, and discharge of energies were no longer at the disposal of man.

The instincts of animals had provided more or less automatic, or at least rigidly regulated, solutions to the problem of drive demands and reality necessities. Freedom from dominance by instinctual solutions was the great gift that evolution presented to man; at the same time, it was his doom. The queen bee pattern, if it were in fact to become the model of human propagation, would not endure: the male population in the human hive would interfere with such biological requirements, and thus endanger the functioning of this type of collective life.

The ability to say "No!" to rebel, to oppose successfully a biological demand was an evolutionary achievement that had been unknown to subhuman species; at the same time, this achievement brought grave dangers with it. Nietzsche (1884–1888) speaks of "the prerogative not to be an automaton; 'the freedom' even at the danger of taking the wrong step, of making the wrong choice [*das Privilegium, kein Automat zu sein; 'Freiheit' auf die Gefahr hin, sich zu vergreifen, falsch zu wählen*]" (#411). Man was given a chance for freedom; but still it was only a chance; freedom was not enforced, if one may be permitted this paradox. There are energic couplings and concatenations that make the attainment of rational goals an event of low expectation in the history of individuals and of collectives.

Yet the full effect of ambivalence on culture has, in most instances, escaped psychoanalytic observation. As a clinician, the psychoanalyst is able to observe the ongoing conflicts of ambivalence. At the time when a patient is being analyzed, the full effect of ambivalence can still be thwarted. The one area in which, in most instances, the clinician has an opportunity to observe something that comes close to the cultural effect of ambivalence is to be found in the parental relationship to the child. It is probably no exaggeration to say that more frequently than not parents are the undoing of their children, even though the children are, actually, in most instances, what lies closest to their hearts. It almost looks as if there were a secret tendency in man to destroy just what he loves most.

The cultural significance of ambivalence often becomes visible to its fullest extent, however, only after a man's life has come to an end. The famous "By their fruits shall ye know them" has to do with just this. I am referring here to the way in which a man may serve his ideals. Just as the impact of parental ambivalence is sometimes fully realized only after the parents' death—retrospectively, through a study of the effects that a man's actions have made on the collective—one may make the surprising observation that, by his own actions, he has himself left the seeds out of which would grow the destruction of that very cause to which he has devoted all his energies.

Napoleon may serve as a historical example of this; with regard to him, this secret ambivalence was already revealed during his lifetime. Faced with the unique opportunity of forming a European Republic, he instead directed his narcissistic aspirations to enhancing the glory of France. Here we observe a genius of organization using his talents in such a way as to bring the greatest damage on the very group in whose service and for whose benefit he had been professing to use his entire energy. In spite of all his apparent intentions, in the end he destroys the very country to whose "glory" he had for a time contributed so much.

In our own historical period, it is curious to observe how it was precisely two men who had devoted all their thinking to the preservation of the capitalist system and the protection of the West against communism who actually paved the way for the growth and expansion of communism beyond anything that any communist leader by himself would have been able to achieve. Herbert Hoover, by presiding at the initiation of the great economic depression, irretrievably destroyed the confidence that the West had until then had in the capitalist system; and Hitler, by starting the Second World War, made it possible for communism to become entrenched in Central Europe and Asia. Hitler's ambivalence is particularly noteworthy, inasmuch as he left Germany—which he had wanted to make great and powerful—defeated, truncated, and divided.

The historian, to be sure, will very likely not accept such implications. He will refer to miscalculations and human errors, and to an abundance of reality factors that brought about the downfall of the great planners. He will refuse to recognize the psychological implications of those terrible misfortunes that the great planners usher in on behalf of precisely those for whose welfare and aggrandizement they have ostensibly fought so hard. Psychology does not dispute the working of reality factors; but it is hardly possible for a psychologist to assume that a man can bring disaster—indirect as the psychological link between cause and effect may be—upon what he alleges to be closest to his heart and the center of his most intense concerns, without his having harbored a secret wish— deeply repressed as it may be—that just such a disaster would come to pass.

When Nietzsche (1884–1888) says: "Paul has once again strengthened, and on a large scale, exactly what Christ in his lifetime had annuled [*Paulus hat gerade Das im grossen Stil wieder aufgerichtet, was Christus durch sein Leben annulliert hatte*]" (#167), he is outlining one of the most outstanding historical examples of ambivalence in the religious history of the West—one that laid the foundations for an unprecedented religious intolerance and persecution, which degraded the teacher's ideal into its very opposite. One wonders who is the greater danger to mankind —the Judases or the Pauls? In both instances, aggression engages in an unholy alliance with ambivalence.

Discussion of Self-Preservation and Orality

It is not probable, in view of the almost universal aversion felt by psychoanalysts against the conception of a death drive, that calling attention to Ehrenberg's *Theoretische Biologie* will have any marked effect. Bernfeld and Feitelberg (1930) had already done so previously, but without success. However, their paper has not become well known in this country. Neither has Ehrenberg's theory, it seems to me, had any influence on the thinking of biologists in Europe. He did not become the founder of a school. Nevertheless, I can imagine his views fertilizing the thinking of later generations.

At this point, I should like to make a general comment on the psychoanalytic classification of the drives of self-preservation, which has long been a thorn in the side of psychoanalytic theory formation. As is well known, two contradictory statements are to be found in Freud's decisive paper of 1920. First, Freud classified them entirely as derivatives of the death drive: "They [the instincts of self-preservation] are component instincts whose function is to assure that the organism shall follow its own path to death, and to ward off any possible ways of returning to inorganic existence other than those which are immanent in the organism itself. . . . Thus these guardians of life, too, were originally the myrmidons of death" (p. 39). Yet a few pages later (p. 52), Freud stressed "the libidinal character of the self-preservative instincts," since Eros is the preserver of all things.

Indeed, many analysts have felt puzzled by the fact that drives which, after all, so frequently manifest themselves in the shape of aggressive acts should nevertheless be classified as libidinal; and, likewise, by the no less paradoxical alternative that the drives in the service of the preservation of life are derivatives of the death drive.

A consideration of Ehrenberg's differentiation between individual and physiological death solves this problem. The drives of self-preservation aim at the avoidance of individual death brought about by fate or accident, prior to the attainment of maximal structuralization; they do not protect against physiological death. The fact that drives work in support of a supraordinated drive is well known from the psychology of the libidinal drives, where one observes component drives placed in the service of genital gratification. The drives of self-preservation, although they cannot be called components of the death drive in the narrower sense of the word, function nevertheless in a manner equivalent to such component drives. If maximal structuralization is accepted as the aim of the death drive, then the self-preservative drives are "the myrmidons of death," but only of physiological death.

Thus Ehrenberg's differentiation would remove the paradox inherent in the view that self-preservation and death drive belong to the same group of drives. Freud found it characteristic of "purely instinctual as contrasted with intelligent efforts" that organisms defend themselves against events that "by a kind of short-circuit" would rapidly lead to death—that is to say, to an event which, according to the theory of the death drive, is life's aim. ". . . the organism wishes to die only in its own fashion," Freud concludes (1920, p. 39). In this instance, however, reason would have to agree with nature. Nature safeguards the principle of its basic dynamics. Since life is possible only because of death, and every organism owes its very existence to the death of its predecessors, each generation—if reasonable—can only agree with its own cessation once it has fulfilled the function of its existence. However, the organism should be protected as well as possible against accidental, contingent, and premature fatalities, a task that is accomplished by the self-preservatory drives. Reason would not object to death once maximal structuralization has been attained and the psychobiological unit—if anything—can only expect partial or complete breakdown of its vital agencies. Only individual death carries the mark of horror. It is but a truism when I say that the distance from physiological death is the decisive factor with regard to the evaluation of death: an infant's death is a disaster; a youth's death is a tragedy; the mature adult's death, a calamity; the death of the aging, a misfortune; the death of the very old, a release. I have observed in all instances of *dementia senilis simplex* a total absence of the fear of death; likewise, very old people in many instances lose almost all fear of death. The struggle between Eros and Thanatos has come to an end, and existence has become a passive waiting for the conclusion of life.

I should also like to add a few remarks here about orality. Lewin (1950), for example, although he wrote extensively about oral psychopathology and made a profound presentation of the aggressiveness it contains, nevertheless continued to look at orality as a libidinal organization. Simmel (1944) was the one who most succinctly outlined the contradiction that lies in Freud's assigning self-preservation to libido, yet speaking of a "cannibalistic" organization.[9] The prototype of self-preservation is the act of devouring that one feels compelled to ascribe to an aggressive-destructive drive. Furthermore, according to Freud, all later drive manifestations presuppose a progressive fusion of aggression and libido; this alone should be sufficient to interpret the incorporation of objects, which is the central event of the oral phase, as an act of destruction. In other words, according to Freud's theses on fusion and defusion, orality must necessarily be more destructive than anality.

Furthermore, when one observes a newborn and sees the playful autoerotic licking movements that seem to be connected with a

[9] Cf. Anna Freud (1949, p. 40): "In the oral stage the infant destroys what he appropriates (sucks the object dry, tries to take everything into himself)."

pressure peak, as my graphs would indicate, one can hardly fail to postulate a separate, so to speak, unfused discharge of libido and aggression during the earliest phase of drive development. This is also what might have been expected on theoretical grounds in accordance with one of Freud's formulations regarding the death drive—namely, "that the sadism which has been forced out of the ego has pointed the way for the libidinal components of the sexual instinct, and that these follow after it to the object" (1920, p. 54). This could perhaps also be asserted with regard to orality, if sucking movements are shown to occur *in utero* with some regularity. But there is another difficulty involved here. Aggression is associated in our minds with hatred, or at least with some expression of aversion against the object. Nothing of that kind, however, is to be observed in the infant's relationship to oral objects. The infant's positive relationship to them may well have been the main reason why Freud persisted in regarding orality as libidinal.

At one point, however, Freud did not hesitate to look upon orality as an aggressive manifestation. When he discussed the ego's response to the necessity of restricting its aggressions, he continued: "the ego does not feel happy in being thus sacrificed to the needs of society, in having to submit to the destructive trends of aggressiveness which it would have been glad to employ itself against others. It is like a prolongation in the mental sphere of the dilemma of *'eat or be eaten'* which dominates the organic animate world" (Freud, 1933, p. 111; my italics). This "eat or be eaten," however, implies an aggressively hateful relationship to the object that is to be devoured.[10]

In response to this clear-cut dilemma, it was proposed that we postulate two different kinds of aggression: objective and subjective (Lantos, 1958, p. 116). Objective aggression, according to Lantos, leads to the gratification of hunger; it is "a libidinal indulgence." Not being subjectively experienced as aggression, it is therefore without affect (Lantos, 1958, p. 116). Subjective aggression is, by contrast, directed against human beings; it is a reaction to frustration. Lorenz (1963) also distinguishes between inter- and

[10] Cf. Freud (1940, p. 149): "the act of eating is a destruction of the object with the final aim of incorporating it."

intraspecies aggression, maintaining that the prey arouses as little aggression in the animal that kills it as "the nice turkey which I have just seen hanging in the pantry arouses in me" (quoted after Lincke, 1968, p. 40.) He therefore considers interspecies and intraspecies aggression to be essentially different. Lincke (1968) accepts Lantos's and Lorenz's differentiation of the two aggressions.

The ethologists may be right, yet I think that this point of view should not be transferred to human psychology. There it obscures the entire issue. I still hold with Leonardo da Vinci, who was horrified by the thought of man's oral destructiveness and, with the greatest sadness, asked this question: "Does not nature produce enough [vegetarian food] for thee to satisfy thyself?" (Richter, Vol. II, p. 104; see also p. 341ff.).

Indeed, one wonders how Lorenz, considering his admirable empathy with such birds as geese, which took on, under the exquisite mastery of his pen, an almost humanlike life, could ever contemplate with pleasure the eating of a turkey. A wealth of cultural data makes it hardly possible to accept the intake of food as being a neutral, nonaggressive act, when hardly any culture is known that did not institutionalize food taboos. Even in our enlightened civilization there are few who would eat horsemeat and hardly any, the meat from a dog. It is reasonable to assume that, in most people, the cannibalistic meaning of food—even though it is deeply repressed—is still alive.

Fenichel (1939) has shown the oral quality of the trophy and its use in the gratification of a narcissistic feeling of omnipotence; his idea that man's greed and lust to subject his fellowman is genetically a derivative of the oral impulse will be accepted by most. Narcissism, by taking hold of aggression and using it for its own purposes, succeeds in carrying aggression into all fields of human contact. In my opinion, any inclination to view interspecies and intraspecies aggressions in human psychology as two more or less genetically independent variables must result in a denial of the formidable character of the problem that mankind is facing. But the differentiation of these two kinds of aggression has once again moved into full focus the fact that the gratification of prey aggression is not in any way connected with hatred, whereas that of rival aggression is. Indeed, the infant devours with pleasure and this is—as noted earlier—the reason why the intake of food is ascribed to a libidinal gratification.

In his paper on "Negation," Freud (1925b) described orality as having two sides: swallowing the pleasurable and spitting out the unpleasant. Later in the article, Freud compares the polarization "of the original process by which the ego took things into itself or expelled them from itself" (p. 239) with affirmation (Eros) and negation (instinct of destruction). I am not familiar with any examination of spitting out, from the developmental point of view, and would surmise that it makes its appearance later than sucking. It is therefore not yet certain whether swallowing and spitting out can be regarded as if they were equivalent, even though opposite processes. At any rate, since I have identified spontaneous auto-erotic movements as libidinal, I would tentatively propose that swallowing and spitting out be regarded as two aspects of aggressive orality.

Spitting out appears to be a radical rejection, an early spontaneous "no," a forerunner of hatred.[11] Spitting out is the equivalent of saying: "It does not exist any longer. I have killed it." It could also, however, be interpreted as a psychological forerunner of projection. Thus, on an archaic level, an object is either swallowed or totally rejected—that is to say, in both cases it is made to disappear, which may indicate that the two are functions of the same drive.

Furthermore, swallowing is, in a sense, pleasurable destruction. In this kind of destruction, the success of the action is anticipated; no obstacle is perceived between impulse and gratification: if the anticipated prey were to resort to successful resistance, prey aggression would instantly turn into rival aggression, just as rival aggression turns into prey aggression, as soon as the hated enemy's trophy or scalp is contemplated with pleasure by the victor. Thus one may say that, in the human species, there is no necessity to distinguish between two different kinds of aggression, even though the various degrees of fusion with libido, along with the interdependence of aggression and ego development, do create a huge

[11] For a different view, see Spitz (1957).

spectrum of manifestations which in turn must, of course, be sub-divided into groups.

Many writers have commented on the fact that there seems to be an element of insatiability in man's aggressive-destructive drives. It is difficult to gauge the pressure of the drives with which the psychic apparatus has to cope. What may appear on the surface as the insatiability of a drive may be revealed as having been determined by quite different causes. It has turned out, for instance, that a patient who habitually masturbated two to four times after intercourse performed that sort of ritual without being driven to it by any sexual urges. In this instance, the amount of sexual gratification obtained went far beyond the demands of a biological urge. The necessity for postcoital masturbation was enforced by needs of defense and for a reassurance of independence. A similar constellation may be encountered with regard to oral aggression in a bulemic patient. But eating as such becomes, under average circumstances, an ego activity and thereby loses most of its usefulness as an outlet for aggressive drive energy.

Aggression does not lead to a final consummatory action (Craig, 1918) comparable to orgasm, which leaves the organism, for the time being, free of drive demands. In view of the absence of such discharge channels, it is quite possible that the biological supply of aggression is extreme and capable of being curbed only by fatigue and exhaustion. It would be wrong, however, to postulate that the psychic apparatus has to cope continuously with the demands of enormous quantities of aggressive drives. One can say only that such quantities are ready, upon demand, to be activated. The fact that man's history, when it is compared with that of other species, makes it appear as if his aggression were insatiable, is the outcome of narcissism, which actually is insatiable. I am fully aware that I am at this point simplifying a far more complex situation, by limiting myself to the energic aspect.

It may appear that I have neglected the papers by Hartmann, Kris, and Loewenstein—particularly the one of 1949, in which it is proposed that self-preservation is an ego function (p. 13).[12] It is not clear to me whether or not this formulation implies that there

---

[12] Cf. Freud (1940, p. 145): "It [the ego] has the task of self-preservation."

are no drives of self-preservation. There is sufficient evidence to show that the bulk of self-preservation is indeed entrusted to the ego; but hunger and thirst alone prove, it seems to me, that the drives of self-preservation continue to be active, even in the face of a fully developed ego structure. This becomes particularly evident in situations of extreme danger. A drowning person, for example, or a person who is suddenly brought face to face with danger to his life, fights frantically for survival. He is almost literally overwhelmed by a passionate urge to escape. In such situations, a person is subjected to strong manifestations of the autonomic nervous system; as a consequence, he frequently manifests strength and skills that, under ordinary conditions, are not accessible to him.

In such states, it is well known, a person is subject to intense drive urges. The point that may remain debatable is the nature of the energy that is inherent in those ego functions that serve self-preservation under less dramatic circumstances. Do they not also presuppose a background of a strong drive for self-preservation? The ego, in order to achieve its aims, which are in fact dictated by a highly differentiated civilization, needs a huge array of subtle ego functions; but in activating these functions, it may—and usually does—serve a latent goal, which is highly cathected, narcissistically as well as aggressively (cf. Stone, 1971, p. 224). Without this background of drives, it might easily fall into lethargy, restricting itself to the narrow orbit that is physiologically given by hunger and thirst.

To summarize: the assumption of two aggressive energies seems superfluous. The genetic prototype of self-preservation is food incorporation, which is the epitome of destruction. In the course of drive development, other aggressiogenic zones are added. A progressive fusion of aggression with libido takes place both biologically and psychologically. Rival aggression is, in short, one phase in a line of development that started with the incorporation of food. With the development of the ego and the perception of an external world, aggression comes to serve the purpose of eliminating unpleasant and disturbing stimuli. Incorporation and spitting out may very well be two aspects of the same drive impulse. Self-preservation is increasingly entrusted to the ego; yet the drives of self-preservation still remain observable, if only under extreme conditions. Ego functions that operate without the involvement of drives may still be serving latent goals that are intensely cathected with narcissistic and aggressive energy.

Remarks on the Defenses against Aggressive Drives

In several papers that have had a profound impact on the thinking of psychoanalysts, Hartmann, Kris, and Loewenstein have, both singly and in cooperation, pursued in this country the work that Freud left unfinished with regard to the important area of the coping with aggression on the part of the ego and the self. It is now better known how it was possible, following the breakdown of regulation by instincts, for man to ward off a psychic force that, if it had been left untamed, might well have seriously endangered the survival of the species in the past.

The ego, apparently an evolutionary acquisition, is an instrument by means of which aggression, which aims primarily at the destruction of objects, can be converted into a force that works in the service, not only of further structuralization and differentiation of the ego itself, but also of the expansion, differentiation, and intensification of culture and civilization. It is the evolvement of ego structure that justifies man's conception of himself against the background of nature—indeed, ultimately, as apart from nature. Yet, despite the unquestionable potential, inherent in ego structure, to rarify, convert, transform, and, finally, discharge aggressive energy for constructive purposes, without at the same time causing destruction—in spite of all this, it is my impression that a longitudinal study of a completed life span would show that, more often than not, aggression has succeeded in reaching its goal, if only in a highly concealed—I would say, often distorted —way.

To be sure, man's existence requires a minimum of libidinal as well as aggressive gratifications, and these are already contained in the mere process of living. Restriction of drive discharge to these minima is extremely rare. It may have been accomplished occasionally by saints, endowed as they are with enormous willpower and devotion to the divinity to whose service they have felt consecrated.

I am thinking here, however, of the average man of good will. He may, if he is so motivated, be able to establish a fairly successful control of his libidinal relations. He may, of course, not be able to succeed in curbing his libidinal gratifications, when they occur in the form of narcissistic or psychosomatic symptoms; but as far as his direct relations with other people are concerned, he may be able to succeed in restricting the gratification of his libidinal drives to such an extent that they become concordant with the demands of his personal as well as his societal conscience.

That is hardly feasible, however, with regard to the gratification of aggression. Much as he may be determined not to harm others, scrupulously as he may stand guard over his actions, he will nevertheless inevitably harm and injure others, even though he himself may not notice it. The reason for this paradox—if it is a paradox —lies in the fact that the defense against forbidden libidinal wishes can prevent the gratification of such wishes within an object relation, but the defense against aggression per se harms others. Repudiation of an unconscious homosexual wish, for example, may lead to a phobia. As analysts, we know that symptoms entail, in a distorted way, the gratification of that very wish to defend against which the symptom was formed. What the symptom will rather successfully protect the person against is, in this case, manifest homosexuality.

In choosing an extreme example of an equivalent situation with regard to aggression, I would select melancholia, which constitutes an excessive defense against an aggression that has been aroused by an object that is loved ambivalently. Rather than discharge that aggression against the object, the ego submits to extreme pain and anguish. Yet even the layman is aware of the pain that is visited upon the other members of a family when one of them is suffering only from depression; all the more the melancholic brings suffering upon everyone who is in contact with him. To be sure, the suffering he causes is usually not as severe as the suffering he himself has to undergo (unless he commits suicide); yet the anguish of the melancholic patient's environment is far from inconsiderable but proportionate to that of the patient.

Defenses against aggression do not reach their goal in social reality, because the effect of these defenses on the environment is a destructive one. While they protect the melancholic patient against becoming a murderer, they do not leave the patient's environment unharmed. Even though I may have selected in this instance an extreme case, nevertheless clinical observation has demonstrated that the defensive apparatus is more proficient vis-à-vis the libidinal drives than it is with regard to the aggressive ones, if only for the reason that, in the majority of instances, the mere absence of an act of love already amounts to an aggression.

The pervasiveness of aggressive energy was mentioned earlier; here is its social equivalent. It may not be unnecessary to remind the reader of the hopelessness of man's struggle against those aggressive demands that are placed upon the psychic apparatus. Certainly, the average person manages to get through life without indulging in gross aggressive acts; murder is the exception during times of peace. But it is a fact of extraordinary importance that the vast majority of people are able and ready to destroy human lives when society sanctions their so doing, as happens in times of war. Evidently almost everyone's conscience is quite able to tolerate the daily death by starvation of 12,000 human beings, all over the world. When Benjamin Pasamanick (*Psychiatric News,* Washington, D.C., April 7, 1971) recently described as "murderous" a wealthy society's inability to take action with regard to the hunger to which its own members are being exposed, he may have been expressing a deep psychological truth, such as should be heeded by the psychologist, who daily observes how a patient will go out of his way to avert a manifestly aggressive collision with his environment. Pasamanick's formulation sounds almost like a confirmation of Freud's statement (1915, p. 296): "we spring from an endless series of generations of murderers, who had the lust for killing in their blood, as, perhaps, we ourselves have to-day."

The accomplishments produced by the formation of ego structure—for example, the ego's ability to neutralize aggression to the extent where nondefensive ego activities are also able to evolve—all these should not prevent us from perceiving that, despite such achievements of taming aggression and of placing it in the service of the greatest accomplishments, man still continues to participate, by commission or omission, in the gratification of the grossest sort of aggression and destruction. By means of a fine web of denial, he

blots out those feelings of guilt that would be only too commen-
surate with the misdeeds in which he has had a hand, either
directly or indirectly, and in that way he gratifies in full measure
his aggressive heritage which his ambivalence and narcissistic self-
aggrandizement demand.

Concluding Remarks: Collective Aggression and the Present

In the 1920s, August Aichhorn, after having analyzed delinquent
juveniles, called attention to the leading role that aggression plays
in their psychopathology. In 1930, Freud made aggression the
center of his psychocultural essay on *Civilization and Its Discontents*. If governments had been rational, the leading statesmen of
Europe might well have gathered around him at that time, and
asked him for his counsel as to how to meet the impending grave
danger. The Second World War confirmed Freud's ominous feelings. The problem of aggression has since then moved more and
more into the center of human concern; there is no doubt that,
almost all over the world, it has become the subject of debate.

Yet it seems that man's present preoccupation with his own
aggression has not been caused primarily by the tragic events of the
past. It is my impression that the horror of the Second World
War, with its concentration camps and its Hiroshima, would have
receded into the background, were it not for the fact, as everyone
now knows, that at some secret place an arsenal of deadly weapons
has been gathered that, if set into motion, will destroy all life on
the planet.

Mitscherlich's (1971, p. 166) call for interdisciplinary cooperation in the study of human aggression has to be welcomed and
supported, for there is no psychological phenomenon that can be
explained by the use of the psychoanalytic method alone. Much
as the psychoanalyst has been able to contribute to research in
homosexuality, nevertheless the pederasty of ancient Greece, along
with the fluctuation of homosexuality within one and the same
group, depending upon historical circumstances, poses questions
the answers to which lie outside the orbit of psychoanalysis. Even

neurosis, an area in which the psychoanalyst is so much at home, is not an exclusively psychoanalytic problem. Freud twice remarked that the rise of neurosis has rested on the decline of the power of religion (1910, p. 146; 1921, p. 142).

The implication of Mitscherlich's call is the same as that of the general hope—namely, that the increase of knowledge and insight, with regard to the very complex problem of aggression, may make it possible to prevent the threatening disaster. Although there is hardly any alternative for the profession to focusing its attention on this subject, I myself am doubtful whether one can afford to be too hopeful in one's expectations. It has been said too often—and it therefore does not need any elaboration here—that knowledge does not always increase man's field of action—as happens, for example, in seismology. Furthermore, human aggression and destructiveness cannot yet be examined with that freedom from moral prejudice with which the scientist in general approaches, or at least ought to approach, the subject of his research. Aggression remains for almost everyone of us a moral issue. It should also be noted that it is anxiety, almost despair, that is the main motivation for man's present concern with this grave problem. Dangers have, it is true, stirred man to search for knowledge in the past and they have even sharpened his ingenuity; yet one has to admit, regretfully, that anxiety and moral preconceptions greatly reduce the probability of attaining rational and reality-adequate solutions.

But all these obstacles shrink, as compared with the fact that the scientist's voice is at present heeded only within narrow and well-defined technical areas—and even there, only after a hard struggle against powerful irrational forces. In listening to the suggestions of social psychologists and sociologists as to what, in their opinion, is necessary for the prevention of collective aggression, one cannot help arriving at the conclusion that, correct as their suggestions may be, they have no chance of being realized, for two main reasons: they presuppose unattainable reorganizations in man's personality as well as changes in the social structure of a magnitude that cannot be expected to take place by way of the democratic process.

I further wonder whether even we analysts, who try so hard to be unprejudiced, to study human emotionality with objective coolness, are able to fathom the full depth of human hatred. When Mitscherlich (1968, p. 87) writes that "hatred does not gratify," I regard this as an implication of his refusal to acknowledge a frightening truth about hatred. Love per se does not gratify: it has to reach its aim, if it wishes to do so. In the same way, true hatred will not come to rest until it has been satisfied. Freud (1930, p. 110n.) quotes at length Heine's rustic idyl of simple country life, for which he longs. The poet adds, however: "If God wants to make my happiness complete, he will grant me the joy of seeing some six or seven of my enemies hanging from those trees." A formidable truth is there expressed, palliated somewhat by Heine's unquenchable wit. There probably is no more exquisite exultation than the one that is felt when a harsh and uncompromising hatred is gratified by the total destruction of an execrated enemy. The more terrible and humiliating the destruction, the greater the triumph.

This should be the lesson of history, since morality forbids us to revel consciously in such feelings. It is the message one obtains from a good many inscriptions on the *stelae* of ancient kings. What were the frustrations they had to suffer? Their sexual wishes were abundantly gratified, yet they did not take pride in them. What seems to have gratified them most, to have impressed them as their most significant experience, was the destruction of a mighty rival king—the mightier, the better. If it were simply a matter of gratifying an aggressive, destructive urge, the destruction of any enemy would have been sufficient. But the triumph that is glorified by the inscription is a narcissistic triumph of extraordinary dimensions, such as cannot be accomplished by love, since true love has the effect of reducing narcissism. A triumphant experience of hatred, narcissism, and ambivalence that together have been fulfilled can probably not be exceeded in intensity by any other experience. The self at that time experiences a boundless sense of omnipotence; for a considerable stretch of time, it will even be able to ignore the gnawing experience of the passage of time, which is always reminiscent of death. It is true that the avoidance of the time experience also takes place during orgasm; but there it is not accompanied by self-awareness. In orgasm, the ego has to step back: the time experience is done away with by way of a reduction in differentiation and consciousness.

In the aggressive-narcissistic triumph, however, the self achieves a higher degree of its own awareness, and its boundaries extend far to the horizons of space and time. At that time, too, time stands still—and longer than it does during orgasm—for no movement is experienced or perceived in a world that has become totally engulfed by the triumphant self. Once again, I find a deep truth expressed in the Homeric myth: Paris, having been deceived to accept love as the highest value, has to pay a heavy price for his error; he turns himself and his clan into the victims of his enemies' destructive-narcissistic triumph.

Experiences of far-reaching narcissistic triumphs, brought about by the crushing of an enemy, are all but unobtainable in a well-regulated community; instead, the screen, the stage, and literature provide substitute gratifications. The hope is often expressed that displacement upon nondestructive activities, such as sports and contests, will be able to provide sufficient outlets for such cravings, and others like them. The social success that is achieved, in all walks of life, however, by persons who evoke the image of ruthless, narcissistic aggressiveness makes me hesitate to place any faith in the permanence of the solution that is offered by peaceful substitute gratifications.

Let us return to the present historical moment, however; it undoubtedly requires more than insight into therapeutic solutions. Even if the analyst did know how to cure the variety of sociopathic syndromes—most of which still defy his therapeutic efforts—a different kind of knowledge is required in the struggle against what may be called "collective sociopathy." The work of analysts such as Brocher (1968), who is interested in the understanding of group processes, certainly constitutes significant progress; yet I wonder whether any science has ever produced the sort of knowledge that might in any way be used as a tool that could conceivably have any bearing on the merciless course of history.

It is also necessary to raise the question of whether we are really

sufficiently aware of the probability that the present state of civilization and culture would ever have been reached, unless certain
acts of the crudest aggression and destruction had first come to
pass. The Roman Empire would not have been formed, nor would
Europe ever have been Christianized, if some ruthless and brutal
individuals or groups had not resorted uncompromisingly to
aggression. The same thing holds true of the colonization of North
America and, to a lesser degree, of the United States' present
status as an independent nation. As Nietzsche said (1884–1888,
#602): "Beauty comes to an end when one thinks through the
processes of history [*hört die Schönheit auf beim Durchdenken
von Vorgängen der Geschichte*]." The topic of the role that force
has played in history—a role that has always involved some form
of destruction—is a comprehensive one and goes far beyond the
scope of this paper; yet this much may be said: it is necessary to
inquire whether or not "history" on this planet is actually possible
without collective aggression of some type. It may turn out to be an
illusion for anyone to expect that, under present conditions,
aggression could disappear from the intercourse of nations.

Some anthropologists assert—perhaps on good grounds—that
there are no signs that aggression by man against man, such as is
seen in killing, had any place in the early phases of man's history.
It may be that, in those early phases, human aggression was animal-
like, limited to the context of self-preservation. It was only after
man changed from a more or less nomadic form of existence to
one of settlements, after large collectives formed and became
stratified, that warfare arose. Even now, collectives characterized
by a surprising absence of aggression and living at low levels of
civilization have been observed in the East. My own guess is that
this remains possible as long as the individual group member has
not yet formed a solid ego boundary; instead his ego is confluent
with that of the other group members (cf. Mahler, 1968). This
may be compared with a syncitium—a tissue in which the cells
are not separated by walls but have fused. One has to keep in mind
that the degree of ego structure is relevant to pathways of aggressive discharge.

In order for a human being to kill in cold blood—or perhaps

even to be able at all to kill a fellow creature—the ego must have achieved a considerable development. It may be that the first murder constituted a great discovery: so long as man saw in his fellowman only a mirror image, he was unable to kill what was, after all, his own image. At any rate, the development of man's civilization and culture has rested on human beings who are capable of committing murder. If man had never acquired that capacity, it is almost certain that he would never have developed such cultural configurations as religion and art. Structures such as these presuppose the establishment of firm ego boundaries, of such solid structuralization that the self can experience itself as an autonomous entity. Yet this degree of structure also makes it possible for aggression to be carried to the maximum of social relevance —that is to say, for man to be able to become a killer of his fellow-man.

If this construction should prove to be correct, it would be highly instructive. It would show that a higher development of ego structure does not necessarily lead to a pacification of aggressive-destructive manifestations; it may even lead to their intensification. It is well known that a progress that is directed toward the elimination of conflict and defect in one area may generate severe difficulties in many others—and to such an extent that, in the end, it may become questionable whether the solution achieved was not more harmful than helpful.

Yet the present historical moment is characterized, as all agree, by the fact that mankind has reached the stage at which its technological advances have made it possible to destroy not only mankind but all life on this planet. This is the cardinal problem of our times. Independently of individual scientific convictions, and whether these convictions imply optimism or pessimism, the prevention of that disaster should be the chief goal for everyone.

At any rate, it is reasonable to ask what the history of mankind would have been thus far, if narcissism and ambivalence had not served as the steering wheels for aggression. Necessary and even indispensable as they may be singly, aggression, ambivalence, and narcissism become mankind's apocalyptic horsemen, when they ride together, as they have always seemed to do.

BIBLIOGRAPHY

ABRAHAM, K. (1924), A Short Study of the Development of the Libido, Viewed in the Light of Mental Disorders. *Selected Papers on Psycho-Analysis.* London: Hogarth Press, 1948, pp. 418–501.

ADLER, A. (1908), Der Aggressionstrieb im Leben und in der Neurose. *Fortsch. Med.*, 26:577–584.

BERNFELD, S. (1925), *Psychologie des Säuglings.* Wien: Springer.

— & FEITELBERG, S. (1930), Der Entropiesatz und der Todestrieb. *Imago*, 16:187–206.

BRENNER, C. (1971), The Psychoanalytic Concept of Aggression. *Int. J. Psycho-Anal.*, 52:137–144.

BROCHER, T. (1968), Anpassung und Aggression in Gruppen: Identität und Gruppen. In: *Bis hierher und nicht weiter,* ed. A. Mitscherlich. Munich: Piper, pp. 152–206.

BRUN, R. (1923), Selektionstheorie und Lustprinzip. *Int. Z. Psychoanal.*, 9:183–200.

— (1953), Über Freuds Hypothese vom Todestrieb, eine kritische Under-suchung. *Psyche,* 7:81–111.

CHRISTOFFEL, H. (1939), Einige fötale und frühstkindliche Verhaltensweisen. *Int. Z Psychoanal. & Imago,* 24:447–460.

CRAIG, W. (1918), Appetites and Aversions as Constituents of Instincts. *Biol. Bull.*, 34:91–107.

EHRENBERG, R. (1923), *Theoretische Biologie: Vom Standpunkt der Irrever-sibilität des elementaren Lebensvorganges.* Berlin: Julius Springer.

— (1946), *Der Lebensablauf: Eine biologisch-metabiologische Vorlesung.* Heidelberg: Lambert Schneider.

EISSLER, K. R. (1938), Zur genaueren Kenntnis des Geschehens an der Mund-zone Neugeborener. *Z Kinderpsychiat.*, 5:81–85.

FENICHEL, O. (1939), Trophy and Triumph. *The Collected Papers of Otto Fenichel,* Second Series. New York: Norton, 1954, pp. 141–162.

FREUD, A. (1949), Aggression in Relation to Emotional Development: Normal and Pathological. *This Annual,* 3/4:37–42.

FREUD, S. (1909), Analysis of a Phobia in a Five-Year-Old Boy. *Standard Edition,* 10:3–149. London: Hogarth Press, 1955.

— (1910), The Future Prospects of Psycho-Analytic Therapy. *Standard Edition,* 11:139–151. London: Hogarth Press, 1957.

— (1915), Thoughts for the Times on War and Death. *Standard Edition,* 14:273–302. London: Hogarth Press, 1957.

— (1916–1917), Introductory Lectures on Psycho-Analysis. *Standard Edition,* 15 & 16. London: Hogarth Press, 1963.

— (1920), Beyond the Pleasure Principle. *Standard Edition,* 18:3–64. London: Hogarth Press, 1955.

— (1921), Group Psychology and the Analysis of the Ego. *Standard Edition,* 18:67–143. London: Hogarth Press, 1955.

— (1923), The Ego and the Id. *Standard Edition,* 19:3–66. London: Hogarth Press, 1961.

— (1924), The Economic Problem of Masochism. *Standard Edition,* 19:157–170. London: Hogarth Press, 1961.

— (1925a), A Note upon the 'Mystic Writing-Pad.' *Standard Edition,* 19:227–232. London: Hogarth Press, 1961.

— (1925b), Negation. *Standard Edition,* 19:235–239. London: Hogarth Press, 1961.

— (1926), Inhibitions, Symptoms and Anxiety. *Standard Edition,* 20:77–175. London: Hogarth Press, 1959.

— (1930), Civilization and Its Discontents. *Standard Edition,* 21:59–145. London: Hogarth Press, 1961.

— (1933), New Introductory Lectures on Psycho-Analysis. *Standard Edition,* 22:3–182. London: Hogarth Press, 1964.

— (1940), An Outline of Psycho-Analysis. *Standard Edition,* 23:141–207. London: Hogarth Press, 1964.

GILLESPIE, W. H. (1971). Aggression and Instinct Theory. *Int. J. Psycho-Anal.,* 52:155–160.

GLANZMANN, E. (1938), Fragebeantwortung (Hospitalismus, Sterbeanfälle). *Z. Kinderpsychiat.,* 5:64.

HARTMANN, H. (1939), *Ego Psychology and the Problem of Adaptation.* New York: International Universities Press, 1958.

— (1950), Comments on the Psychoanalytic Theory of the Ego. *This Annual,* 5:74–96.

— (1952), The Mutual Influences on the Development of Ego and Id. *This Annual,* 7:155–181.

— KRIS, E., & LOEWENSTEIN, R. M. (1949), Notes on the Theory of Aggression. *This Annual,* 3/4:9–36.

HEIDEGGER, M. (1927), *Sein und Zeit.* Tübingen: Neomarius Verlag.

JACOB, F. (1970), *La logique du vivant.* Paris: Gallimard.

JACOBSON, E. (1964), *The Self and the Object World.* New York: International Universities Press.

KOHUT, H. (1966), Forms and Transformations of Narcissism. *J. Amer. Psychoanal. Assn.,* 14:243–272.

LANDMARK, J. (1935), Der Freud'sche Triebbegriff und die erogenen Zonen. *Imago,* 21:345–351.

LANTOS, B. (1958), The Two Genetic Derivations of Aggression with Reference to Sublimation and Neutralization. *Int. J. Psycho-Anal.,* 39:116–120.

LEWIN, B. D. (1950), *The Psychoanalysis of Elation.* New York: Norton.

LINCKE, H. (1968), Aggression und Selbsterhaltung. In: *Bis hierher und nicht weiter,* ed. A. Mitscherlich. Munich: Piper, pp. 39–49.

LORENZ, K. (1963), *On Aggression*. New York: Harcourt, Brace & World, 1966.

MAHLER, M. S. (1968), *On Human Symbiosis and the Vicissitudes of Individualism*. New York: International Universities Press.

MITSCHERLICH, A. (1968), Aggression-Spontaneität-Gehorsam. In: *Bis hierher und nicht weiter*, ed. A. Mitscherlich. Munich: Piper, pp. 66–103.

— (1971), Psychoanalysis and the Aggression of Large Groups. *Int. J. Psycho-Anal.*, 52:161–167.

NIETZSCHE, F. (1884–1888), *Der Wille zur Macht*. Leipzig: Kröner.

PFAUNDLER, M. VON (1915), Physiologie des Neugeborenen. *Döderleins Handbuch der Geburtshilfe*, I. Wiesbaden: Bergmann.

— (1936), Fragekasten (Hospitalismus, Sterbeanfälle). *Münch. med. Wschr.*, 29:1183.

RADO, S. (1927), An Anxious Mother. *Int. J. Psycho-Anal.*, 9:219–226, 1928.

RICHTER, J.-P. (1939), *The Literary Works of Leonardo da Vinci*, 2 Vols. London, New York, Toronto: Oxford University Press.

SADGER, I. (1912), Haut-, Schleimhaut- und Muskelerotik. *Jb. psychoanal. psychopath. Forsch.*, 3:525–556.

SIMMEL, E. (1944), Self-Preservation and the Death Instinct. *Psychoanal. Quart.*, 13:160–185.

SPITZ, R. A. (1945), Hospitalism: An Inquiry into the Genesis of Psychiatric Conditions in Early Childhood. *This Annual*, 1:53–74.

— (1946), Hospitalism: A Follow-up Report. *This Annual*, 2:113–117.

— (1957), *No and Yes*. New York: International Universities Press.

STONE, L. (1971), Reflections on the Psychoanalytic Concept of Aggression. *Psychoanal. Quart.*, 40:195–244.

WOLFF, P. H. (1966), *The Causes, Controls, and Organization of Behavior in the Neonate* [*Psychological Issues*, Monogr. 17]. New York: International Universities Press.

The Infantile Neurosis
Genetic and Dynamic Considerations

ANNA FREUD, LL.D., D.Sc.

I WELCOME MY PARTICIPATION IN THIS SYMPOSIUM AND EXPECTED that it would be a straightforward task to compare the analysts' present ideas about the infantile neurosis with those which were formulated half a century ago.

Nevertheless, when I began to approach the subject more closely, I began to be doubtful about its legitimacy and appropriateness. I felt that I was setting out to compare two sets of propositions which had arisen on different grounds, fitted into different

Contribution to a weekend conference of English-speaking members of European Societies, organized by the British Psycho-Analytical Society and held on October 3 and 4, 1970, in London. The theme of the conference was "Changing Concepts of Infantile Neuroses and Their Effect on Theory and Technique." This paper was published in *Problems of Psychoanalytic Training, Diagnosis, and Technique of Therapy* [*The Writings of Anna Freud*, Volume VII]. New York: International Universities Press, 1971, pp. 189–203.

conceptions, and, in short, had not enough in common to be treated as if they were on a par.

The Conception of the Infantile
Neurosis at the Time of Little
Hans and the Wolf Man

I assume that we take the case histories of Little Hans (1909) and the Wolf Man (1918) as outstanding examples of infantile neuroses, and the discussion of the processes involved in their disturbances as evidence of the then-reigning conceptions concerning this pathological manifestation.

When doing so, I suggest that we do not neglect in our evaluation one overridingly important difference between past and present. Psychoanalysis, at that period, was not concerned with infantile psychopathology as such. Interest and study were concentrated on the neuroses of adult life, their genesis, their dynamics, their relationship to normal character formation, their difference from the psychoses, etc. Infantile neurosis came within the focus of this interest only since it was one of the new findings, made by means of the new technique, that what is relevant for the formation of the adult disturbance are the underlying childhood experiences; i.e., that there is no adult neurosis, whether conversion hysteria, phobia, or obsessional neurosis, which does not have a neurosis in infantile life as its forerunner. Moreover, what was demonstrated in the case histories named above was the fact that both, the adult and the infantile disorder, shared the same motivation by conflict, the same construction, the employment of the same mechanisms, and that their symptoms represented identical attempts at conflict solutions, inadequate as the latter may be if viewed from the aspect of reality adaptation. What I am describing here is, of course, the well-known formula which covers the formation of neuroses in general: conflict, followed by regression; regressive aims arousing anxiety; anxiety warded off by means of defense; conflict solution via compromise; symptom formation.

It was assumed (though not proved at the time, since there were no longitudinal studies) that the finding that every adult neurosis is preceded by an infantile one is not reversible; not every infantile neurosis is followed by neurotic illness in later life. This was taken to have a number of implications such as the following:

that the infantile neurosis is *more frequent,* i.e., more "normal," as an occurrence than its adult counterpart;

that many infantile neuroses are open to a *spontaneous cure* which takes place at the point when the emotional upheavals of early childhood are lightened by entry into the latency period;

that it depends on the *experiences of adult* life whether the childhood conflicts will be reactivated, i.e., whether a new neurosis will be formed.

It is well known that the precipitating events for the adult neurosis were seen in the conflicts between active and passive sexual strivings; between heterosexuality and homosexuality; between object love and death wishes against the same persons; between crude instinctual trends of all kinds and opposing superego demands. The corresponding constellations for the infantile neurosis were found in the stormy events of the phallic-oedipal period where conflicts are likewise going on—conflicts between the positive and the negative oedipal attitudes; the masculine and feminine identifications; the ambivalences in the attitude to the parents; the castration wishes and castration fears of the male child; the conflicts between the different aims in life represented by the different structures within the personality (id, ego, superego). It was natural to assign the infantile neurosis, and especially its peak, to the phallic-oedipal period since full structuralization of the personality, full strength and independence of the superego, and accordingly full ability to develop conflicts resembling those of later life were not expected to exist before that time.

It would be a grave mistake, nevertheless, to assume that the infantile neurosis was ever taken to be the only representative of infantile psychopathology. It was merely that, at the time, it was the only one of great import for the analyst concerned with the adult neuroses. What remained outside this focal point were the intellectual defects, so far as they were not of a pseudonature, i.e., neurotic; the clinical pictures, then known under different terms, which are now labeled "autistic"; and the many failures of early physical or mental functioning which precede the oedipal period, are not due to conflict, and seemed of lesser relevance for the adult neurosis, even though their description was included in every analytic case history where they were treated as playing the role of preparatory or facilitating factors.

The Present Scene

There is a world of difference between these studies of the past and the present scene. What we are pursuing at present are not evaluations undertaken from the viewpoint of any later mental disorder but an elaborate map of infantile mental difficulties as such, or, to express it more succinctly, an enumeration, description, and explanation of any interference with optimal mental growth and development. On the basis of our knowledge of developmental phases, as established by reconstruction from adult analysis, by child analysis, by direct observation of infants and young children, we attempt to do this from birth onward, with the phallic-oedipal phase placed not at the lower but at the upper end of our investigation.

I contend that, due to these developmental considerations, we have stepped outside the realm of psychopathology in the usual sense of the term and have entered instead into a new area with new complexities: namely, into the study of early personality development. It appears almost as a by-product that, while doing so, we also assemble those developmental aspects which, in due course, will lend themselves to the production of conflicts and may even determine beforehand which among the available defense mechanisms the individual's ego will choose to employ and, accordingly, which forms of compromise and symptom formation will be open to him.

The Psychosomatic Reactions of Infancy

The distinction between personality background on the one hand and conflict-determined psychopathology on the other is illustrated by what follows here concerning the earliest difficulties of an infant in the areas of breathing, feeding, elimination, sleeping, skin sensitivity, etc. These difficulties, so far as they have no discernible organic cause, are physical as manifestations, and emotional as regards origin. They result on the one hand from interaction between inborn modes of functioning and the mother's handling of these potentialities, on the other hand from a kind of emotional infection emanating from her, i.e., from the infant's response to her moods, her anxieties, her preferences, and her avoidances. The affects engendered in the infant are discharged through the body; his physical experiences may find expression in his affective states. This easy access from mind to body and vice versa is known to be normal during the first year of life and becomes pathological only if it is maintained beyond this period after new pathways for discharge via thought, speech, and action have been opened up.

What is important to us here is that these early "psychosomatic" events make basic contributions to the building up of an individual's personality, especially by way of the pleasure-unpleasure, satisfaction-frustration experiences. It is an old finding that the satisfaction of early body needs opens up the way to object attachment and following this to the individual's general capacity for object relationships. In more recent times, observations and reconstructions concerning the first year of life have established that a lack of balance between pleasure and unpleasure, and especially a predominance of pain and frustration at this time, may prevent ego building and/or lead to lasting ego distortion and ego deviations from the norm; that a mother's failure to comfort her infant adequately may have lasting results for the individual's later general ability or inability to cope with even normal amounts of unpleasure, pain or anxiety.

What is primarily a personal attribute will then, secondarily, make its contribution to the child's psychopathology. That the form and strength of object attachments are decisive in the choice of neurosis is well known. Ego distortions may render the ego quite unfit to play its role in an infantile neurosis and may lead to the much more abnormal borderline states. A heightened intolerance for unpleasure leads almost inevitably to an exaggerated use of the ego's defense mechanisms and, consequently, to special severity of inhibitions and other neurotic manifestations.

There is, further, an even more direct manner in which the early psychosomatic events contribute to the later infantile neurosis. Whatever organ systems, physical functions or body parts (skin, intestinal tract, breathing, limbs, etc.) are involved in them, remain more vulnerable ever after than the rest of the child's physique and this creates the so-called "somatic compliance" of which later hysterical conversion will make use.

The Early Mother-Infant Relationship

The same difference between primary effect on personality development and secondary consequences for psychopathology are again met with in that area of the mother-infant relationship which is wholly psychological. The ingredients here are, on the mother's side, the manner in which she cathects the child's body and person, narcissistically or with object libido; with libido or aggression; positively or negatively; with or without significant changes and interruptions. On the infant's side, there is—subject to his inborn capacities—his reaction to her involvement, passive or active; pleasurable or painful; satisfied and comfortable or frustrated and demanding; loving, hating, ambivalent, etc. What arises on the basis of this highly complex mixture is the individual child's general attitude to himself and to the world around him. It is an old psychoanalytic assumption that the experience of being well loved in infancy creates for all later life a feeling of security and self-confidence. We meet this again in the more modern literature under the terms of basic trust, self-regard and self-esteem. This determines on the one hand the balance between narcissism and object relatedness, on the other hand such personal characteristics as optimism or pessimism, courage or cowardice, outgoing or withdrawn attitudes. The relevance of these for psychopathology is obvious; they will be decisive for or against the occurrence of depression; for or against the choice of phobic mechanisms, etc. The constancy and strength of early object ties also facilitates internalizations and identifications, and these in turn enrich the personality on the one hand, and prepare the ground for conflict between the inner agencies, i.e., for neurosis, on the other hand.

The Component Instincts (Prephallic)

It may seem illogical to the listener or reader if the child's pleasure-pain, satisfaction-frustration experiences with his objects are viewed separately from those determined by orality and anality. This runs counter to our analytic experience that these two lines of development are intertwined and inseparable—that phase development depends for its normal unfolding on the presence of objects toward whom the component instincts can be directed; and vice versa, that object relations, even though shaped by the ego, derive their power and intensity from the libidinal and aggressive energies of the component instincts and reflect in their quality the dominant attributes of these early stages of drive development: greedy, demanding, dependent, incorporating during the dominance of the oral zone; clinging, possessive, torturing during the dominance of the anal one.

Nevertheless, the contributions toward both personality development and infantile neurosis made by the prephallic component instincts are different from those described previously, and this, I believe, merits a separate discussion. So far as personal attributes and character formation are concerned, they are, of course, well known; they enter into these either as residues of their original appearance or transformed into their opposites. But over and above this, they are of the greatest import for the formation of the infantile neurosis in two respects: (1) by preparing the way for regressions; and (2) by producing the base for neurotic compromise formations which can be considered to be the true forerunners of the infantile neurosis proper.

1. As regards regression: if we regard it as characteristic for the onset of a neurotic process that the individual's ego retreats from an ongoing conflict, danger or frustration to a previous, safer form of satisfaction, then the component instincts assume the special significance of being the agents which open up the opportunity for such returns. It is true that on the side of the ego, there also may exist tendencies to return to the past, based on inclinations to persevere, to maintain former modes of functioning and expression. But the latter, even where they are in evidence,

fail to account for the powerful attraction which is exerted by the past, i.e., the force which propels an individual child backward, causes him to lose important developmental gains, and involves him once more in the pursuit of primitive wish fulfillments which he had outgrown previously. Such happenings become plausible only if we think in terms of amounts of instinctual energy which are latent on the early levels and can be reactivated according to need, i.e., in terms of fixation points to which regression takes place. It is implied in this assumption that the energy amounts left behind are those derived from the component instincts.

2. As regards symptom formation preceding the infantile neurosis: even more to the point is the fact that it is the area of the component instincts, i.e., the oral and anal sexual trends and their frustrations, which produce early, unmistakably neurotic symptoms. These may be hysterical, phobic, or obsessional in nature, such as the affliction of limbs; phobic reactions toward food intake and elimination, sleep or bath, loneliness; inhibitions of touch or motility; rigid insistance on regularity and absence of change; obsessional intolerance of dirt, cruelty, etc. Overtly, these manifestations are identical with the symptoms of a full-blown infantile neurosis; but, on closer scrutiny, a number of important differences between the two become apparent.

The *conflicts* on which this early symptomatology is based are not between internal agencies, but represent in the main clashes between an instinctual wish within the child and a prohibiting or inhibiting influence in the external world, the only exceptions in this respect being those caused by ambivalence, which arise as soon as the ego has developed sufficiently to take notice of conflicting trends and to be intolerant toward them. The *dangers* by which the child's ego feels threatened at this time are attributable not to fear of the superego, i.e., guilt, but to fear of the object world, i.e., either of punishment or loss of love. *Regression* from the forbidden wish of the moment to former satisfactions may or may not take place; if it does, and if no protest is raised by the environment, it is frequently accepted as ego-syntonic by the child. The *symptoms* themselves are not interconnected and organized into syndromes, as they will be later, but isolated and independent of each other. Further, they are transitory, i.e., subject to changes in the environment, changes in the ups and downs of object relations, and above all subject to developmental alterations in the importance and dominance of the instinctual trends concerned. We may say that these early compromise formations represent first attempts of the developing ego to come to terms with frustration. But, compared with the complexity of the later neuroses, this neurotic symptomatology is diffuse, unstable, and unorganized.[1]

The Phallic Phase

With the child's further progress through the next developmental stage, whatever psychopathology he will display assumes its final shape. What we expect from development are decisive advances in structuralization, in every aspect of ego and superego functioning and in the ego's ability to hold its own. Where these moves occur, ongoing wishes and fear of their disapproval by the object world lose their role as direct pathogenic influences. Their place is taken by regression when the wishes are frustrated, and this reactivation of developmentally earlier forms of satisfaction now arouses internal disapproval, i.e., guilt. Accordingly, the whole inner turmoil and the compromise solutions found for its relief are removed from external influence, become immovable through environmental changes, and may inhibit, distort or block further growth instead of profiting from progressive development.

Unlike its forerunners, what is now the infantile neurosis is no longer the ego's answer to the frustration of single trends, but is an elaborate attempt to deal with the whole upheaval caused by the action of conflicting drive derivatives; conflicting, exciting, pleasurable or painful affects; mutually exclusive attitudes toward objects—i.e., with the whole range of the oedipus complex and castration complex, set against the background of personal qualities and characteristics which have been established from infancy onward, and shaped by the fixation points which have been left behind during development.

Insight into these complex interactions between past and present, background and actuality, ego qualities and instinctual trends,

---

[1] A fuller description of this preparatory phase is given by Nagera (1966).

conflicting identifications, opposite id tendencies, etc., are revealed to us in every analysis of an infantile neurosis. This does not mean that they are also easy to describe in their entirety. To enumerate and to integrate with each other whatever enters into the neurotic structure is no mean task, as shown, for example, in the final summing up of the Wolf Man case where we are presented by the author with a whole imposing array and sequence of contributing factors: a primal scene observation which leaves consequences for masculine or feminine identification; contributions from orality in the form of disturbances of food intake and fears of being devoured; urethral erotism in the service of identification with the father's masculinity; the experience of seduction which arouses early castration fears; contributions from the anal phase, on the one hand in the form of receptive-passive trends, on the other hand promoting aggressive strivings which predominate over anal erotism; earlier fears giving way to guilt which transforms sadism into masochism; passive-homosexual trends which succumb to the ego's fear of castration on the phallic stage. We are also shown how the comparatively simple anxiety hysteria with some features of conversion hysteria acquired an obsessional overlay, and how finally the whole upheaval subsides spontaneously with some residues left behind: inhibitions toward women which change to dependency toward them, some repetitive tendencies, a powerful "not entirely unconscious" inclination toward men, and an intolerance for narcissistic frustration which led to the reactivation of the infantile disorder in adult life.

Beyond the Infantile Neurosis

As mentioned before, not every child's psychopathology assumes the form of an infantile neurosis. The construction of the latter presupposes that various important developmental steps have been negotiated successfully and, as we know, this is not always the case. Due to constitutional defects, early deprivations, lack of suitable objects, wrong environmental handling, etc., the capacity for object relatedness may have remained inferior; identifications and internalizations may be weak; structuralization may be incomplete; the id-ego borders may be permeable; the ego itself may emerge from its early experiences as immature, deformed, distorted, etc. Where such developmental failures dominate the scene, the child will present clinical pictures on the border to much more severe pathology such as psychosis or mental deficiency; or he will remain arrested on the described lower level of disjointed neurotic symptom formation which corresponds to a preoedipal organization of the personality.

As analysts we hold a multiple view of the infantile neurosis. On the one hand, we regard it as belonging to the realm of psychopathology and realize that in its excessive forms it can be severe and crippling. On the other hand, we also know that it has a regular place in the childhood of many individuals whose future adaptation to life is successful, and that the conflicts underlying it are normal ones. Looked at from the developmental point of view, the infantile neurosis doubtless represents a positive sign of personality growth; a progression from primitive to more sophisticated reaction patterns and as such the consequence and, perhaps, the price which has to be paid for higher human development.

Technique

If, in the context of this paper, nothing has been said about the implications for therapy, the omission is intentional. The subject needs more space than could be given to it here, where I confine myself to one remark:

The psychoanalytic technique, including the technique of child analysis, was originally devised for, and has proved its worth in, the application to the neuroses proper, i.e., to the states of internal conflict where the ego needs assistance to widen its sphere of influence, and where this help can be provided via interpretation of the unconscious elements which are beyond its reach. In our times, the analysts' therapeutic ambition goes beyond the realm of conflict and the improvement of inadequate conflict solutions. It now embraces the basic faults, failures, defects, and deprivations, i.e., the whole range of adverse external and internal factors, and it aims at the correction of their consequences. Personally, I cannot help feeling that there are significant differences between the two therapeutic tasks and that every discussion of technique will need to take account of these.

BIBLIOGRAPHY

FREUD, A. (1965), *Normality and Pathology in Childhood: Assessments of Development* [*The Writings of Anna Freud*, Vol. VI]. New York: International Universities Press.

FREUD, S. (1909), Analysis of a Phobia in a Five-Year-Old Boy. *Standard Edition*, 10:3–149. London: Hogarth Press, 1955.

— (1918), From the History of an Infantile Neurosis. *Standard Edition*, 17:3–123. London: Hogarth Press, 1955.

NAGERA, H. (1966), *Early Childhood Disturbances, the Infantile Neurosis, and the Adulthood Disturbances* [*Monograph Series of the Psychoanalytic Study of the Child*, No. 2]. New York: International Universities Press.

On Motivation and Instinct Theory

HANS W. LOEWALD, M.D.

I

PSYCHOANALYSIS IS INTERPRETATION. FREUD CALLED HIS BASIC WORK *The Interpretation of Dreams.* The essential activity of the psychoanalyst is to interpret. The psychic life of the individual is interpreted in new ways whereby it assumes meanings and an inner coherence which heretofore were not apparent. Consequently,

Associate Clinical Professor of Psychiatry, Yale University Medical School, New Haven, Conn.

I gratefully acknowledge the help for this work provided by a grant from the Robert P. Knight Fund.

In this paper I have condensed the first three chapters of a projected book which is concerned with aspects of psychoanalytic theory. While my views should ultimately be judged within that wider context, I offer them at this stage of work in progress as a contribution to the ongoing discussion of the psychoanalytic concept of instinct.

the meaning of what we call psychical or mental has changed. Man has gained a new power of understanding, and of thereby influencing, human life, by the observation and discovery of phenomena and events hitherto unknown or unheeded, by interpreting them in a manner which so far had not been applied to psychic life, and by bringing known psychological observations and activities within the context of that new interpretation, i.e., by understanding them differently.

Interpretation—we have no other way of applying our mind, whether in observation and understanding or in action. It is only when a context of meanings, when interpretations have become commonplace that we speak of the material in question as "facts." Then we tend to deal with the material in the manner of our dealings with chairs and tables, forgetting or disregarding the mental activity of interpretation which is embodied in it but is now hidden. Even chairs and tables are such only within the context of our understanding use of them and are oddly shaped and assembled pieces of stuff outside this context.

Psychoanalysis is, however, a special case. Its essence is interpretation. The psychoanalyst interprets dreams, slips of the tongue, symptoms, fantasies, thoughts, behavior, moods, emotions, memories, plans, actions, decisions, choices made or contemplated, physical illness, life circumstance—in principle anything and everything the patient lets be known or that can be deduced from what he reveals. The psychoanalyst's interpretations are based on and make use of a fundamental assumption: that whatever transpires is personally motivated. This assumption is the all-embracing interpretation which constitutes the foundation for all individual interpretations.

This founding interpretation has components which are condensed in the expression "personally motivated": (1) What the patient reveals is motivated within and not simply chance occurrence or merely determined by forces external to him. (2) The fact of his revealing it to the analyst and the time at which he does so are personally motivated; personal motivation is involved in the past and current events he reveals, as well as in his present activity of revealing them. (3) We must also hear something else that is evoked in the expression "personally motivated," namely that motivations, while residing in the person motivated, have something to do with relations with other persons who themselves are centers of motivation. These others involved in the motivational network are the important persons in the patient's past and current life, pre-eminently including his psychoanalyst.

Such an interpretative assumption or set of assumptions as a new organizing principle has a power, a tendency, a tension of its own. This tension can be yielded to and made his own, step by step, by the "object" under consideration, i.e., by the person being analyzed, since he has organizing power of the same order as that of the analyst. This is what happens in the course of a successful analysis (as, on a much different level, in the successful upbringing of a child). The fact that the patient can make this interpretation his own is unique for psychoanalysis as a scientific endeavor; there is no other field of scientific activity where the order of organizing potential is the same in the "object" and the "investigator." In nonpsychoanalytic psychology the object of psychological investigation is never the individual in his full range of potentialities. This is also the reason that psychoanalysis is more than a science in the classical sense, calling forth, as it does, the investigator in the one investigated. But it also makes for one of the intrinsic problems of psychoanalysis: the "object" of investigation can never truly be made to stand still and be an object. Thus it seems that psychoanalysis also cannot help being less than a science in the classical sense.

I have implied that the object of psychoanalysis is the individual human person. Only in this entity do we encounter what psychoanalysis calls psychic life and psychic reality. It is the unit with which we deal. This, of course, does not mean that no general statements and propositions can be made about this reality. But it does mean that psychoanalytic statements and propositions are valid specifically in respect to this entity as conceived in the basic interpretative assumption mentioned and as apprehended in the psychoanalytic method which is determined by this assumption. Psychoanalytic statements are not necessarily valid in respect to other units, such as for instance family or society, even though these are composed of individuals; nor are they necessarily valid or pertinent for psychological phenomena taken out of the context of the unit constituted by the individual, as is the case in experimental or general psychology.

That the individual's life is, in principle, personally motivated is an interpretation which flows from a particular understanding of man implied in monotheism—the belief in a personal God as exemplified in Western Judaeo-Christian religion and civilization; but this self-understanding has been radicalized and modified by the decline of that belief. Psychoanalysis is an exponent and promoter of this decline. Freud's uncompromising strong stand against Judaeo-Christian religion is certainly not incidental to his lifework, but I shall not go into these matters here.

That the life of the human individual is personally motivated does, of course, not mean that it is initiated, brought into existence by the individual. It does mean that it has the potential of being conducted by the person himself, that the course and conduct of one's life, within certain limits, can be, or can be helped to be, in one's own hands.

The interpretation, fundamental to all specific psychoanalytic interpretations, that anything occurring in one's life is personally motivated, has a momentum that tends to transform what is being interpreted. This is, in a sense, true for any interpretation: it has the tendency to transform, to restructure that which is subject to the interpretation. The theories of modern physics and their results and consequences show this clearly. A statement of fact restates something in known and accepted terms; an interpretation changes the terms, declares that which is being interpreted to be differently structured, to have a different meaning, and to be in a different context.

The momentum, the dynamic power of an interpretation, in psychoanalysis manifests itself as personal influence.[1] The interpretation of personal motivation is a statement about potentiality rather than actuality insofar as unconscious motivation is concerned; thereby it tends to render actual what has been potential. We make a woman, plagued by the compulsion to murder her child, understand that she harbors feelings of hate against the child which are related, for example, to a disturbed relationship

[1] Interpretation in psychoanalysis must be seen in the context of the personal relationship which the psychoanalytic situation represents.

with her husband, which in turn is connected with certain feelings toward her father. While in the actuality of this woman's psychic life such motivational concatenations have previously not been apparent, they now are discovered due to a certain kind of psychic work she performs in conjunction with the analyst. What was an impersonal, unrelated compelling force becomes inserted in a linkage of personal motivation; that is: it becomes open to the dynamics of personal motivation.

The psychic work performed by the patient has one of its sources of motivation in the psychic work of the analyst, in his work of understanding and interpretation, which is a motivating force when it is directed toward the patient as another center of motivational activity. It is a kind of facilitation within a constellation or field of motivational activity composed of two centers of such activity. The interpretation, then, through its own motivational momentum and the expression this takes in content and manner of interpretation, assists the patient in making a motivational concatenation actual, while previously it existed only "in the Unconscious."

The concept "unconscious," as a negative term, refers to potentiality: something is not what it might (or might not) be or become. This something is considered from the standpoint of what it might be but is not. The interpretation of personal motivation, by making statements about unconscious motivation, tends to raise the level and complexity of psychic organization, by "speaking to the Unconscious," as we say, from the standpoint of a higher organizational level, from the standpoint of what it might become. As analysts we speak, in interpretations of unconscious motivation, from the level of consciousness to the unconscious.

The term "id," as a positive term, denotes what is signified by it directly, not from the viewpoint of consciousness. Apart from other reasons for its choice, the term makes it more feasible to visualize the coexistence of mental processes of different organizational levels, without the implication, suggested by the negative term "unconscious," of mutual exclusion or of the active removal of consciousness (repression). On the other hand, the term unconscious is indispensable since it points to consciousness and indicates potential mutual transformation from one into the other.

What was (pre)conscious can become unconscious—the phenomenon of repression. Repression itself is a term which speaks from the level of (pre)conscious mental organization and, as initially conceived, of an activity performed on that level. By initially equating the unconscious and the repressed, and by tending to equate repression and (pre)conscious mental activity, great difficulties were created. The concept of repression, which had its origin and justification in a circumscribed area of observation, became overextended (as did the concept of defense) and was given more duties than it could perform. The unconscious, on the other hand, was forced into a bed of Procrustes where only what was repressed was allowed to be part of it. Furthermore, it became apparent that the repressive motivational forces themselves could be unconscious (not merely preconscious), and this could not be accounted for by the equation of the unconscious and the repressed. Nor could it be understood how "unconscious mental contents" could become conscious (as in psychosis), i.e., return from repression, without losing those characteristics which were supposed to be theirs by virtue of their being repressed. Freud's shift to the subdivision id-ego-superego undoubtedly made things easier. But when we are concerned with the mutual relations between these substructures and with the mental processes involved in these relations and in the substructures themselves, much remains to be understood and conceptualized differently.

I have mentioned these issues here in a preliminary way because repression and defense, and the conceptualization of, and the very term, the Unconscious, are crucially, although not exclusively, determined by the basic psychoanalytic interpretation of personal motivation. Freud originally (i.e., before he distinguished between preconscious and conscious) saw repression and defense as conscious motivations in the sense of conscious acts of will. For example, in "The Neuro-Psychoses of Defence" (Freud, 1894) he wrote:

> . . . the splitting of the contents of consciousness [in one form of conversion hysteria] is the result of an act of will on the part of the patient; that is to say, it is initiated by an effort of will whose motive can be specified [p. 46]. [Or:] the most unambigu-

ous statements by the patients [suffering from obsessions and phobias] give proof of the effort of will, the attempt at defence, upon which the theory lays emphasis [p. 52].

This clearly was Freud's starting point, and he contrasted this (as far as hysteria is concerned) with the etiological notions of "an innate weakness of the capacity for psychical synthesis" (Janet) and of a hypnoid state (Breuer) (p. 46), in other words with etiological factors conceived as nonmotivational in nature. Freud also was at that time still inclined to doubt whether unconscious processes should be called psychic processes at all.[2] This means, in the present context, that personal motivation was still to be understood as conscious motivation insofar as psychical processes and consciousness were still considered to be coterminous. On the other hand it also means that unconscious processes, if they were to be interpreted in psychological terms, to be inserted in a psychological nexus, should—to the extent to which this is possible—be interpreted in terms of personal motivation.

Not enough attention has been paid to the intriguing fact that in psychoanalysis unconscious processes and phenomena are interpreted in terms of personal motivation, while conscious processes, and especially also volitional acts—whether of thought or deed—tend to be viewed as less personally motivated than superficially appears to be the case but as determined by instinctual-unconscious forces. It is as though what counts in mental life takes place on a kind of middle ground between two poles, and the two poles are being interpreted in terms of each other. Interpretation of unconscious mental life in terms of personal motivation has, under favorable circumstances, a power to move organization of

[2] "The separation of the sexual idea from its affect and the attachment of the latter to another, suitable but not incompatible idea [the 'false connection' operative in obsessions]—these are processes which occur without consciousness. Their existence can only be presumed, but cannot be proved by any clinico-psychological analysis. Perhaps it would be more correct to say that these processes are not of a psychical nature at all, that they are physical processes whose psychical consequences present themselves as if what is expressed by the terms 'separation of the idea from its affect' and 'false connection' of the latter had really taken place" (p. 53). It should be noted that Freud in these sentences by implication speaks of interpretation (the existence of these processes can only be "presumed") and of potentiality ("as if" they "had really taken place").

mental processes in the direction of consciousness. Interpretation of conscious-volitional mental life in terms of unconscious-instinctual motivation has a power to move organization of mental processes in the opposite direction, the direction of unconscious-instinctual life. In clinical psychoanalysis this is clearly visible and made use of by the analyst. The analyst oscillates between "id interpretations" and "ego interpretations," between interpretations downward and interpretations upward (to use and extend a term employed by Bornstein [1949] and Loewenstein [1951]). The overall direction of a psychoanalytic investigation seems to be not so much toward consciousness per se, but toward an optimal communication, an interpenetration and balance of the two forms of mental processes and of the psychic structures their activities bring about.

But we now must attempt to clarify what is meant by personal motivation and how it operates. Freud's model for personal motivation, at least as far as repression and defense are concerned, was, as we have seen, conscious will. In contrast to "wish," it is a concept which he rarely considered or used subsequently.[3] Later a distinction was made between repression, an unconscious "mechanism," and suppression connoting conscious intent. But of course it is instinct which moved into the center of the psychoanalytic consideration of motivation, instincts as unconsciously motivating forces.[4] Instincts, the Unconscious, the id—these words evoke the impersonal, the depth hidden beneath the surface, concealed by the surface mask of the person as an organized, conscious human being (the Latin *persona* = mask of an actor). They also suggest involuntary action, innate impulse, elementary and untamed forces, compelling, irrational, unreasoning. The id is called daemonic. A

[3] The concept of will, however, is implied whenever Freud speaks of choices the patient is able to make once the unconscious sources of his behavior are understood by him, i.e., have become conscious, so that gratification of a wish may be sought or renounced by the ego.

[4] As in the *Standard Edition*, the German *Trieb* is here translated as "instinct" and not as "instinctual drive" or "drive." The arguments advanced by Strachey (1966) in his "Notes on Some Technical Terms Whose Translation Calls for Comment" in favor of "instinct" have persuaded me to adopt that translation. Besides, the fact that the English standard text of Freud's writings now uses the term, for better or worse, weighs heavily in favor of it.

daemon is something that possesses us, that has power in us or over us; in Greek religion it is a divine power, not definitely personified, a power of lesser stature than a personal god, yet more personal than the forces of nature.

Once repression and other "mechanisms" of defense were no longer acts of will, once their unconscious nature was acknowledged, they too moved into the area of the impersonal or less-than-personal and became manifestations of the ego-instincts.[5] Later the distinction between ego-instincts and sexual instincts (libido) was given up in favor of a classification which used different criteria, whereby a share of ego-instincts and sexual instincts joined forces in the concept of narcissism (ego libido or narcissistic libido versus object libido) to become a much widened libido; while another share of what formerly had been subsumed under ego-instincts and libido (in the forms of self-preservative instincts, repression, and sadism) became the aggressive instinct; and various kinds of fusion and defusion of sexual and aggressive instincts accounted for a variety of instinctual manifestations.

Nevertheless, motivation had become instinctual, as had repression and defense, in contrast to the early notion of personal will. Psychic life is motivated by sometimes conflicting, sometimes confluent, sometimes fused, sometimes defused, instinctual forces. There seems to be no room for *personal* motivation. Yet I have claimed that personal motivation is the fundamental assumption of psychoanalysis. We now seem to see that, on the contrary, psychoanalytic psychology postulates instinctual, unconscious, impersonal forces as the motives of our psychic life. Where is the person? Where is the ego or self that would be the source and mainstay of personal motivation?

The problem is not resolved by hypotheses about a primary autonomy of the ego, primary ego apparatuses, and the like (Hartmann, 1939). They make the psychoanalytic ego into a biological

---

[5] Strachey (Editor's Note to "Instincts and Their Vicissitudes," Freud, 1915a, p. 115) states that "Freud introduced the term 'ego-instincts' and identified these on the one hand with the self-preservative instincts and on the other with the repressive function." He refers to Freud's introduction of the term in "The Psycho-Analytic View of Psychogenic Disturbance of Vision" (1910), where Freud clearly speaks of repression as a function of the ego-instincts which oppose the sexual instincts (p. 213).

entity with a psychological superstructure and make use of an energy concept which is biological or physical. The energy postulated in such hypotheses, while called psychic energy, is nonpsychic, i.e., nonmotivational, and instinctual motivation becomes secondary where it counts most: in the understanding of the structuring of the personality by the organization and transformation of instincts. Inborn apparatuses are nothing but a euphemism for neurophysiological and neuroanatomical substrates, they have no psychological status. Instinct (*Trieb*) does have psychological meaning and the term has its legitimate use in psychoanalysis only as a psychological concept, and not as a biological or ethological one. Nobody of course denies neurophysiological processes and neurological structures, or the maturation of such structures. But to speak of inborn ego apparatuses is speaking of a Hamlet who is not the Prince of Denmark. In psychoanalytic psychology the ego is a psychic structure which cannot be found anywhere in biology or neurology, just as an organism cannot be found anywhere in physics, or a superego in sociology. It makes sense to speak of the development of the id and the ego out of an undifferentiated phase, in which there is as yet no differentiation of id, ego, and environment, as long as the concept of the undifferentiated phase is not biologized and it is recognized that as psychoanalysts we cannot go back beyond that limit.

Ego and id are psychoanalytic constructs which do not make use of the distinction conscious-unconscious, although they must, of course, be considered in juxtaposition to that distinction. But they do make use of the concept of instinctual energy (as the first or most primitive form of psychic energy in general) by postulating free or mobile and bound energies as well as gradations in the degree and complexity of mobility and binding. They also make use of the conception of the equivalence of energy and structure (structure is bound energy and energy is unbound or potential structure), a conception which has been used in physics and has revolutionized it. Psychology has been no less revolutionized by the use of that conception in psychoanalysis, which is not to say that Freud was clearly aware of using it. It is an idea that was "in the air" and was made use of in various contexts, among them physics and psychoanalysis. In itself it is an idea which does not derive from physics as an established body of knowledge and observations but which, when applied in its investigations, restructures the whole field (compare Freud's introductory paragraph to "Instincts and Their Vicissitudes" which, with good reason, is praised as a lucid statement about such matters). That the same conception has been used in psychoanalysis does not mean that psychoanalysis has taken it over from physics or that it is physical in nature and thus not really applicable in psychological discourse. Neither do the concepts of energy and structure have of necessity physical connotations. They became conventional scientific concepts with specific physical connotations through their use in physics, but they are not by nature physical concepts or entities. Even less so is instinct by nature a biological concept or entity. On the other hand, something like myelinization or neutron or superego are terms invented within contexts of specific sciences, and they cannot be used elsewhere except by metaphor.[6]

Ego and id, conceived as psychic structures, come into being, within the psychic unit the neonate is about to become, by intricate interaction processes between conflicting, converging, and merging psychic energy currents surrounding and within the emerging psychic system; such interactions result in the organization of psychic structure. It cannot be stressed enough that such organization is most vitally codetermined by the fact of the far higher complexity and organization of psychic energy obtaining in the—for the observer—surrounding or environmental psychic systems. It is by the interaction with them that motivational forces of various orders of complexity and integration, and stable motivational structures of any kind, come into being within the newly emerging psychic unit, the child. On that basis, but never without maintaining further interaction with psychic forces of the environment, interactional processes within the new psychic system can be built into various forms of structured organization, whereby higher levels of motivation come about. Structures are understood as more or less systematic and stable organizations of psychic energy; they bring their higher potential to bear on mobile instinctual energy, thus transforming its currents into higher

[6] See Schur's brief discussion of the concept of psychic energy and his references (1966, p. 42f.).

orders of motivational energy. Freud's use of the concept of hyper-cathexis in "The Unconscious" is, I believe, in keeping with such a formulation. To my understanding he described such a course of events, with a view on memory and perception and within the topographic framework, when he writes: "The system *Ucs.* contains the thing-cathexes of the objects, the first and true object-cathexes ['first and true' because instinctual]; the system *Pcs.* comes about by this thing-presentation being hypercathected through being linked with the word-presentations corresponding to it [words as symbols, as higher-order 'presentations' originally provided by the environment]. It is these hypercathexes, we may suppose, that bring about a higher psychical organization and make it possible for the primary process to be succeeded by the secondary process which is dominant in the *Pcs.*" (1915b, p. 201f.). Freud clearly speaks here of both higher-order structures (systems) and higher-order processes.

We are now prepared to give a preliminary answer to the question about personal motivation. Motivation, in the course of psychic organization, becomes increasingly personalized. The higher forms into which instinctual motivations become transformed, and the more highly organized instinctual energy conformations which we call higher psychic structures, assume dominance—to a greater or less degree—within the developing individual. But instincts as the original motive forces never become extinct, nor do the structures corresponding more closely to these primitive forces. Thus the id is never superseded by the ego's increasing dominance, whereas the ego may "regress," decrease in organization to a state closer to that level of psychic energy organization which we call id. It may be noted that the concepts of sublimation and instinctualization and of controlled regression conform to this picture of things.

The interpretation of personal motivation restructures what is less organized, or kept out of the overall organizational context of the person (repression), into a higher, more individually centered order of motivational energy and structuralization of such energy. This can occur only to the extent to which the organizational process of psychic development can be laid bare and revived, for no reorganization takes place by mere superimposition. The latter, on the contrary, should be taken as a method of defense against reorganization (for instance, in many obsessional and "normal" characters). In the context of the just-quoted passage from "The Unconscious" Freud (1915b) writes: "Now, too, we are in a position to state precisely what it is that repression denies to the rejected presentation in the tranference neuroses: what it denies to the presentation is translation into words *which shall remain attached to the object*" (p. 202; my italics). Superimposition is this lack of "attachment" of words to objects, lack of the link between the unconscious and the preconscious presentation in Freud's language, a form of insulation where hypercathexis has not taken place. What Freud describes here as attachment or link is the same phenomenon, although viewed in a different context, which he calls transference in Chapter VII of *The Interpretation of Dreams*: "an unconscious idea is as such quite incapable of entering the preconscious and . . . it can only exercise any effect there by establishing a connection with an idea which already belongs to the preconscious, by transferring its intensity on to it and by getting itself 'covered' by it. Here we have the fact of 'transference', which provides an explanation of so many striking phenomena in the mental life of neurotics" (1900, p. 562f.).

To lay bare the organizational process of psychic development means to enter into the organizational process as a new factor, to become a new factor in the process. The disorganizational and reorganizational movements taking place in the analytic process are codetermined by a new motivational factor, the analyst; and his activity is governed by his interpretation and integration of himself as personally motivated.

The interpretation of personal motivation, basic to the whole conception of psychoanalysis, is founded on a specific, though most comprehensive, self-interpretation of man. It has motivational impact on oneself and others. It tends to restructure lower-order motivational forces (such as instincts), by making possible the transformation of a share of them into forces of greater complexity which can then be redeployed within the nexus of higher levels of motivational organization. But only by the constant or repeated "transference" (of the intensity, as Freud puts it) from lower to higher levels can the viability and vitality of higher structures and higher motivational forces themselves be guaranteed and maintained.

It would seem that the redeployment I spoke of makes it understandable that unconscious motivating forces and "contents," i.e., their manner of representation, are by no means absent from the ego (which thus is not equivalent to the *Pcs.*) but are there rearranged in a different nexus. In the course of ontogenetic development, then, instincts, while also remaining active as such, become transmuted into higher forms of that psychic excitation which we describe as motivation, such as for instance "will." [7] And further, all motivational forces, including unmodified, unreconstructed instincts, enter into new, higher-level organizational formations which are conceptualized as psychic substructures.

II

In the preceding section I started with personal motivation, worked my way toward instinctual motivation, and back again to the personal—all this to introduce these matters; they have not yet been thoroughly discussed. Let me now start at the other end, instincts, and enter into things more fully and in detail. Two issues are of particular interest: (1) What is the status of the instincts in relation to the total organization we call the psyche? (2) What is the relation of instincts to objects?

The consideration of both questions involves fundamental aspects of psychoanalytic theory. In the course of their discussions I shall refer to specific theoretical formulations and examine their

---

[7] In "The Neuro-Psychoses of Defence" (1894) Freud says that it is "a peculiarity of all states resembling sleep that they suspend the distribution of excitation on which the 'will' of the conscious personality is based" (p. 50). What we call will is, according to this terminology, a particular distribution or form of psychic excitation, and instinct is a less developed form or distribution of such excitation in the hierarchy of psychic organization. The term "excitation" (like the terms "energy" and "instinct"), although used here by Freud in analogy to physiological processes, can and must be divested of its physiologic-biological connotations, which it did not have from the start but which it acquired by being used in specific sciences. "Excitation" has a perfectly legitimate general meaning which becomes specified in and for a specific science. "To be excited" in ordinary language is used for a state of mind or mood or feeling tone. The word was not taken from physiology but given to it, or appropriated by it.

explicit content and their implications as I understand them, without losing sight of the fact that terms and concepts frequently have much richer meanings and connotations than is readily apparent when they are used in highly theoretical formulations— formulations which are much determined by certain theoretical-scientific preconceptions and "conventions," as Freud calls them (1915a, p. 117), and which in any event, as definitions and elaborations of definitions, cannot avoid a certain rigidity. But such formulations are precisely the ones which become enshrined in the body of psychoanalytic knowledge and theory, with a resulting shrinkage and impoverishment of its compass and depth.

What is the status of instincts in relation to the total psychic organization? Are instincts to be understood as elemental component forces of the psyche, or are they forces impinging on the psyche and thus, by definition, themselves nonmental? The problem, I believe, is analogous to the question whether the unconscious is to be understood as psychical, part of mental life, or not. Freud, after initial doubts (see footnote 2 above), became unalterably committed to viewing unconscious processes as mental processes—which was a decision to establish psychoanalysis as a psychological science—regardless of the nature of their correlation to physical processes, a correlation which is to be presumed as well in regard to conscious processes in any event. But he appears to have wavered in this respect when it comes to instincts. I have already stated that I consider instinct a psychoanalytic psychological concept, which should be kept free of biological and ethological connotations (although the relations between the psychoanalytic concept and nonanalytic instinct concepts may, of course, be profitably discussed). It has to be borne in mind that in such matters a decision is involved to assign the status of phenomena, processes, and events having a grammar and logic of their own— in short, the status of an autonomous field of science—to sequences and relations previously unknown or not systematically investigated; these were previously considered only in respect to their being concomitant with other sequences and relations of a different order.[8] Perhaps we will be able to gain some understanding

---

[8] For some of the epistemological-philosophical issues pertinent here compare Michael Polanyi's book *Personal Knowledge* (1958).

of the reasons for Freud's indecision in regard to instincts in the course of the ensuing discussion.

In "Instincts and Their Vicissitudes" (1915a) an instinct is said to be "a stimulus applied to the mind." The concept "stimulus" is taken from physiology in this context. Instinct is a stimulus which "does not arise from the external world but from within the organism itself." Freud says an instinctual stimulus might better be called a need. "What does away with a need is 'satisfaction'." Instinct here is seen as a factor which operates upon the mind, from within the organism, to be sure; it is called internal here in contrast to the external world of the organism's environment, but is operating from outside of that mind. Freud finds it important to call attention to the fact that "postulates" concerning the properties of the system which is being stimulated are implied in his discussion of instincts as organic stimuli (for instance, in the sentence: "What does away with a need is 'satisfaction'"). The most important postulate "runs as follows: the nervous system is an apparatus which has the function of getting rid of the stimuli that reach it, or of reducing them to the lowest possible level; or which, if it were feasible, would maintain itself in an altogether unstimulated condition" (the constancy principle). And he appears to describe something like the evolution from such a physiological system to a "psychic apparatus" when he says that instinctual stimuli "oblige the nervous system to renounce its ideal intention of keeping off stimuli" and to "cause it to undertake involved and interconnected activities by which the external world is so changed as to afford satisfaction to the internal source of stimulation" (p. 118ff.).

But we obtain a somewhat different picture of "instinct" if we consider mental life from what Freud here calls a biological point of view. "If now we apply ourselves to considering mental life from a *biological* point of view, an 'instinct' appears to us as a concept on the frontier between the mental and the somatic, as the psychical representative of the stimuli originating from within the organism and reaching the mind, as a measure of the demand made upon the mind for work in consequence of its connection with the body" (p. 121f.). Instinct now is not a physiological stimulus but is the "psychical representative" of the latter. The

meaning of the term "representative" is left open, and the nature
of the connection of the mind with the body is left undetermined.
Instinct, understood as a psychical representative (Repräsentant),
is not a stimulus impinging on the psychic apparatus but is a
force within or of the psychic apparatus; a force which represents
stimuli originating in the body in a different, i.e., psychical, form.
While organismic stimuli "reach the mind," in this version instincts are not these stimuli themselves, but they represent such
stimuli. If we wish to call instincts stimuli, they would be mental
stimuli, stimuli which form part, are elements, of the mind. They
act as dynamic forces *of* the mind and not *upon* it from the outside.

The concepts "representative" and "representation" will have
to concern us at considerable length on a later occasion, but two
points should be mentioned here: (1) We must distinguish between psychic representative (Repräsentant and Repräsentanz)
and representation in the sense of idea (Vorstellung). The meaning
of representation, as used in the word representative, is wider
than that of representation as idea. Psychical representation in
the wider sense includes, for instance, such nonideational phenomena as affects and, of course, as we have seen, instincts.
(2) Mental or psychical representatives are hierarchically structured
in such a way that representatives of a lower order can be re-
represented—not *necessarily* in the form of ideas—on higher
mental levels. This is implied when we speak of primary and
secondary process and when Freud speaks of thing presentations
and word presentations and of the hypercathexis of the former
by the latter (1915b, p. 201ff.).[9]

Instincts then, considered from a so-called biological point of
view, are mental stimuli. The system in which physiological
stimuli are represented as instincts is capable of representing.
What may be said to be stimulated by physiological, organic
stimuli (and, we may assume, by other kinds of physical stimuli
as well) is this faculty of representing, an activity which is then

[9] Compare Strachey's discussion on the "ambiguity in Freud's use of the term
'Trieb' ('instinct') and 'Triebrepräsentanz' ('instinctual representative')" (1915a, p.
111ff.). In "The Unconscious" (Freud, 1915b), Vorstellung is translated as "idea"
or "presentation."

seen as inherent in the mind and not brought to it from the organismic needs. The organismic needs may stimulate this activity, they do not introduce it into the mind. The property of the system which is being stimulated, according to our discussion, is no longer the one Freud postulated when he considered instinct from a physiological point of view (the function of getting rid of organic stimuli), but is the property or function of representing (in the wide sense of representation). Whether or how in the course of evolution mental activity has developed out of physiological activity, is another matter.

A crude analogy may help to clarify the state of affairs: the fact that a transformer is capable of transforming electric currents of a certain frequency into currents of another frequency is not explained by the frequency or the force of the incoming current. That mental, "representing" activity is in some way correlated with (or powered by) neurophysiological activity also is not denied. A radio, in order to perform its function, has to have a power supply which is precisely independent of the stimuli that reach it and that stimulate the radio to perform its work. The neurophysiological activity in the nervous system which we assume to underlie or power mental activity is something quite different from the somatic needs which Freud calls instincts in his first ("physiological") formulation and which are said to be represented by instincts in his second ("biological") formulation. In terms of Freud's model, the organismic needs or stimuli reach the mind and demand work from it. The mind's work consists in "representing" (in the wide sense of representation), in generating mental representatives, and not in "getting rid," of the stimuli that reach it; and this work, the functioning of the mind, may be said to be powered by neurophysiological activity. The mind's "connection with the body" (1915a, p. 122) is therefore twofold: (1) the mind's work is *powered* by neurophysiological activity; and (2) this work is *stimulated* by the organismic needs. The work itself, on this level, consists in instinctual activity, which is defined as representing organismic needs.

Let me emphasize once more: the basic postulate concerning the general function of the psychic apparatus is no longer that of getting rid of the (organismic) stimuli which reach it, but that of generating mental representatives of these stimuli, i.e., generating instinctual activity. And my accent is not on the fact that instincts are mental representatives of organismic stimuli, but on the fact that they are mental representatives. Freud perhaps gave a hint of his being uneasy about the idea that the mental apparatus has the function of getting rid of stimulation when he redefined, in that same passage, its task more broadly as that of stimulus-mastery [*Reizbewältigung*], an expression which is less prejudicial as to the manner of dealing with stimuli (1915a, p. 120).

We come to the conclusion that instinct in psychoanalysis, following Freud's definition of it as a mental representative of organismic stimuli, is a mental force or stimulus and may be described as the most primitive element or unit of motivation. It is a motivational stimulus, constituent of the stream of mental life, and not a biological stimulus operating upon that stream.[10] But it must be admitted that Freud was not consistent in using instinct as a strictly psychological concept, in part because of the equivocal meaning of the term representation throughout psychoanalytic theory.

Let us now briefly consider a particular, but central aspect of the apparatus model. An instrument or apparatus, like a microscope, telescope, or camera is a tool or a machine made use of by some other agency or agencies for certain purposes which are defined by that other agency. The apparatus itself is at rest unless used by another agency. The mind, in this respect to be compared to an organism, is itself a center of activity, has purposes of its own, as it were.[11] An organism is embedded in its environment in such a way that it is in living contact and interchange with it; it modulates and influences the environment by its own activity, and its activity is modulated and influenced by the environment. Although misleading in some crucial respects, to compare the mind with an organism is much more appropriate than to compare it with a tool or machine (or, for that matter, than to use

[10] For a discussion of the definition of instinct (instinctual drive) as a psychic representative versus the definition as somatic stimulus, and of the conception of instinct as motivational force in a hierarchy of motivational forces, see Schur (1966, especially pp. 29–46).

[11] In reference to this question, as well as to the whole problem of motivation and of instincts as motives, see Rapaport (1960).

the reflex arc model); not only because an organism is a center
of activity in its own right, differentiated from but in continuous
active interchange with its environment, but also because its activity is of the same or a similar order as that of the living environment. I shall have occasion to refer to the organism analogy
at various times, but it must be kept in mind that it is an analogy
from another field which, while closer to our field than physiology, physics, mechanics, and optics, has a different conceptual
framework, is structured by different founding postulates, and
deals with a different order of "data." The degree of objectivation
possible in biology—since we apply our mind to something which
by definition of the field has no mind, is not mental—is far greater
than that possible in psychoanalysis as a psychological science.

I believe that the structural model, in contrast to the topographic one, is a model built in analogy to an organism; this is
one of the reasons why it is, in many respects, more usable in
psychoanalysis.[12] The structural model does not conceive of instincts as organic stimuli which are extraneous to the mind and
impinge on it, and it does not conceive of the mind as an instrument—however complex—which processes incoming stimuli to
discharge them again in some modified form and whose operations are simply set in motion and determined by another agency.

To avoid misunderstanding I wish to state that such schematic
descriptions, machine model and organism model, apply to the
conceptual models used and not to the flesh and blood of Freud's
discoveries and formulations which much of the time far tran-
scend the models used or even disregard them. In introducing
the topographic model and the simile of a microscope or camera
in *The Interpretation of Dreams,* Freud writes:

> I see no necessity to apologize for the imperfections of this or
> of any similar imagery. Analogies of this kind are only intended
> to assist us in our attempt to make the complications of mental
> functioning intelligible by dissecting the function and assigning
> its different constituents to different component parts of the ap-

---

[12] For detailed discussions of the two models or "theories" see Merton Gill (1963)
and Arlow and Brenner (1964). See also my review of the latter work (Loewald,
1966).

paratus. . . . We are justified, in my view, in giving free reign
to our speculations so long as we retain the coolness of our
judgement and do not mistake the scaffolding for the building
[1900, p. 536].

Freud's reminder is important for any such undertaking and
applies to his later metapsychological writings and to the structural model as well. But it must also be said that the general
nature of the scaffolding used indicates something about the plan
and standpoint adopted for erecting the building and delimits
its extension and scope of function. In other words, the theory or
model does not always do justice to the discoveries and insights of
psychoanalysis, and theory may have to be brought to conform to
them more closely and to understand them differently, by something more than mere additions and refinements. Freud's new
conception of the structural theory is one example; another example is provided by his continued attempts to revise and change
his instinct theory.

With the formulation of the structural theory the conceptualization of instincts and of the mind changed. This change did not
come about suddenly, and it was not consistently adhered to after
its culmination in *The Ego and the Id*. In some respects the change
may even have been more apparent than real. If one tries to look
at Freud's work as an organic whole, similar perhaps to the organization of the psyche itself, comparisons come to mind with
the interplay and conflict of active forces and between various
organizational layers, with progressive and regressive directions
and movements and influences, as they occur during the lifetime
of an individual. Nevertheless, in an overall way one can say that
in the structural theory the psyche is conceptualized as consisting
in and constituted by an interplay of psychic forces and structural
layers in a manner that could not be achieved by the apparatus
model. The view of the relations between the inside and the outside of the psyche, of the relations between the inner forces and
the forces external to the psyche, changed quite radically and had
much to do with the emergence of the structural theory, as will
become clearer in the next section.

The conceptualization of instincts changed in a number of

ways. Since the psyche was now being conceived more like an organism (this is exemplified in Freud's comparisons of it with an amoeba and its pseudopodia, and in his description of the ego as an outer layer of the id which has been modified by the external medium on which it borders), instincts tended to become forces within this organism. But there was no longer any particular emphasis on an instinct's being a psychical representative. In fact, in "The Unconscious" (1915b), especially in the discussion of unconscious emotions, it becomes doubtful whether Freud continued to adhere to this view (p. 177ff.). In *Beyond the Pleasure Principle* (1920) instinct became a more global concept for *"an urge inherent in organic life to restore an earlier state of things"* (1920, p. 36). This harks back to the constancy principle. In the "physiological" view of instincts in "Instincts and Their Vicissitudes," the psychic apparatus dealt with instincts, understood as organic stimuli, in accordance with this principle; the psychic apparatus had the function to restore that earlier state of things, namely, the state of rest, nonexcitation. Now, however, instincts themselves have become expressions of this principle; they are no longer forces which interfere with it or call it into operation. This means that they are forces, urges *of* an organism, whether biological or psychical, *manifesting* the constancy principle, not stirring it into action. The gain, from the present point of view, was that instincts and the psyche were no longer at loggerheads with each other, as they had been when instincts were seen as disturbing an apparatus which wanted to be unstimulated and was intrinsically inactive and opposed to activity; instincts now were active forces constituting the dynamic elements of the psyche. But the emphasis on their being psychical representatives was lost.

Since 1920, instincts are conceived as broad polar forces of living matter, the life or love instinct, Eros, and the death instinct, Thanatos. They lose their distinction as psychic forces, although they also manifest themselves in psychic form. This conforms to a tendency, always present in Freud, to view and implement psychoanalysis as a biological science. But it is one thing to consider the correlations and illuminating analogies between psychoanalysis and biology, or to put psychoanalytic findings within an overall framework of biological or even cosmic evolution. It is quite another thing to reduce psychoanalytic data and concepts to biological ones, as though a psychology were possible without postulating psychic life and psychic reality, without being committed to the mind's existence (whatever form or meaning of existence may be involved from a philosophical point of view). Freud, like many before and after him, did not always avoid the fallacy of thinking that the switch from psychological to biological or physical concept formation could make psychology more objective. But such a switch only dissolves psychology. As long as the human individual is apprehended by himself and by other individuals as a center of activity distinct from other centers of different kinds of activity—be they stars or nebulas, atoms, plants, or animals— psychology as an understanding of the mind as mind will then have to be re-created. To the extent to which Freud, in *Beyond the Pleasure Principle,* places psychoanalysis in a continuum whose referent is not mind but living matter, he loses the subject of psychoanalysis.

It is now possible to answer the first question I raised at the beginning of this section: what is the status of instincts in relation to the total psychic organization? Instincts, whether defined as psychic representatives of organismic stimuli or needs, or, much more broadly, as urges inherent in organic life (including psychic life as a special case), are forces within the psychic organization and not stimuli which operate on that system from without. The system itself is conceived as something akin to or analogous to an organism, and not as an apparatus made use of by an organism. A duality of instincts in their interplay, confluence and conflict, constitutes the activity of this organization. It is assumed that the system is a center of endogenous activity (whatever the ultimate reason for that activity may be) which consists, in its primitive form, in what we call instinctual activity. True, there is, according to Freud, the death instinct, the tendency to die, to return to a state of rest. But the opposing tendency to live, the life instinct, also is an intrinsic motive force; it is not imposed upon the system by forces outside of it.

From this point of view, insofar as the death instinct can be equated with the constancy-inertia-unpleasure principle,[13] the death instinct is nothing startlingly new in Freud's theory. The constancy or unpleasure principle always regulated the psychic apparatus and in that sense was intrinsic to it, in contrast to the instincts conceived as stimuli extrinsic to it. But in an apparatus such a principle could not be conceptualized as an instinct. When the psyche was conceived of as an organic entity, as a living structure, the abstract principle became an instinct. What *is* new in Freud's new instinct theory and in the structural theory is the life instinct as an intrinsic motive force of the psyche paired with the death instinct.[14]

III

Before going on to a discussion of the second question, the relations of instincts to objects, some more general remarks about instincts and an "instinct psychology" (*Trieb-Psychologie*) are in order. They will also serve as a corrective to the preceding discussion in respect to instincts as biological forces. One concern of Freud's, especially in the beginning, was to free psychology of its intellectualistic orientation; of its bias in favor of consciousness; and, from the point of view of then-current morality, its preoccupation with the "higher," rational, and morally acceptable reaches of the mind. He was not alone in his interest in and emphasis on the irrational in life and human nature, the importance of primordial, archaic, infantile, and primitive forces in human life and the life of the mind, including those existing "in consequence of its connection with the body." But he was the one to bring these matters most forcefully within the compass of psychiatry and psychology, and to penetrate and articulate them with the methods of scientific investigation and conceptualization.

[13] This equation, in my opinion, is valid only up to a point. Freud's conception of the death instinct also contains other elements which are not under discussion here (see footnote 14).

[14] For brief discussions of the connections between the constancy-unpleasure principle and the death instinct, and between a separate pleasure principle and the life instinct, see Freud (1924, p. 159ff.), and Schur (1966, especially pp. 146–152). For comments on the regulatory principles and the death instinct, see Loewald (1971).

Triebe were, however, not just abstract constructs or concepts in a theory of motivation or personality, to be sorted out from other forces of motivation, to be classified and distinguished from affects, perceptual and cognitive processes, and somatic needs. *Triebe,* instincts, were—much more than scientists, doctors, ministers, judges ("the educated circles") wanted to admit or know—what made the human world go around, what drove people to act and think and feel the way they do, in excess as well as in self-constriction, inhibition, and fear, in their daily lives in the family and with others, and in their civilized and professional occupations and preoccupations as well. They dominated their love life and influenced their behavior with children and authorities. They made people sick and made them mad. They drove people to perversion and crimes, made them into hypocrites and liars as well as into fanatics for truth and other virtues, or into prissy, bigoted, prejudiced, or anxious creatures. And their sexual needs, preoccupations, and inhibitions turned out to be at the root of much of all this. Rational, civilized, measured, "good" behavior, the noble and kind deeds and thoughts and feelings so highly valued, much of the time were postures and gestures, self-denials, rationalizations, distortions, and hideouts—a thin surface mask covering and embellishing the true life and the real power of the instincts.

The life of the body, of bodily needs and habits and functions, kisses and excrements and intercourse, tastes and smells and sights, body noises and sensations, caresses and punishments, tics and gait and movements, facial expression, the penis and the vagina and the tongue and arms and hands and feet and legs and hair, pain and pleasure, physical excitement and lassitude, violence and bliss—all this is the body in the context of human life. The body is not primarily the organism with its organs and physiological functions, anatomical structures, nerve pathways, and chemical processes.

If Freud had not had all this in view, and the vagaries and foibles of people, his own and those of his patients, he would never have been able to write his case histories and to create a scientific psychoanalysis as distinct from both neurology and academic psychiatry and psychology. He would not have been able to understand dreams and jokes and neurosis and the psychopathology of everyday life. He created, partly in spite of his inclinations and not without grave misgivings, an entirely new method and standard of scientific investigation which went counter to scientific principles and methods derived from or devised for a different realm of reality—principles and methods which stultified an appropriate approach to and grasp of psychic life. He could do this because he was unwilling to accept the narrow limitations imposed on science by the science of his day, whose child he remained nevertheless. He broke out of those limits and widened the field of scientific action, while loath to accept the consequences of such a venture in all its implications. But had he not in such a way brought science and life as it is lived together again, psychoanalysis would never have had the impact on modern life and scientific thought that we see today.

Instincts and the life of the body, seen in the perspective sketched above, are one and the same. They become separate only when we begin to distinguish between soma and psyche. But once this is done—and without this distinction there is neither physiology-anatomy nor psychology—instinct in psychoanalysis must be understood as a psychological concept. I believe it means reintroducing the psyche into biology and physics if one speaks of Eros and Thanatos as universal cosmic tendencies. Whether this is legitimate or not remains, in my opinion, an open question; this psyche, however, would in any event not be psyche or mind in terms of human psychology. Within the framework of psychoanalysis as a science of the human mind we must, if we accept the Eros-Thanatos conception (or its less "metaphysical" form, the duality of libido and aggression), speak of instincts as psychic representatives, and of life and death instincts as such representatives.

IV

I turn now to the second question raised about instincts: *What is the relation of instincts to objects?* This is possibly the most complex and most important problem for psychoanalytic theory today, and perhaps one of the most controversial issues as well. In this paper I shall approach the problem only from a few selected angles. In its wider implications it is the problem of object relations and of what has been termed object-relations theory (for a recent extensive discussion see Modell, 1968). My limited treatment of this broad issue here is intended as a first approach toward it.

The status of objects in psychoanalytic theory has undergone a gradual and profound change in the course of time. In broad outline, one may say that objects were first conceptualized predominantly as means for providing satisfaction of instinctual needs, i.e., as possible sources of "pleasure" and, by the same token, possible sources of unpleasure and frustration of such needs. Satisfaction, be it noted again, was understood as that process which, in conformity with the pleasure-unpleasure principle, leads to the elimination or reduction of excitation (stimulation), or is the result of such a process. Objects were taken as givens and no psychoanalytic questions were raised about them and their status in psychoanalytic theory. Such a psychoanalytically naïve conception of objects, despite subsequent changes, still pervades much of psychoanalytic theory.

But gradually it became apparent that, at least in regard to early psychic stages—and these are of specific importance for instinct theory—objects are not givens. On the contrary, a highly complex course of psychic development is required for environmental and body-surface stimuli to become organized and experienced as external, in contrast to internal, and for such sources of stimulation, gratification, and frustration eventually to become objects, in any acceptable sense of that word, for a subject or self. Hand in hand with this came a growing recognition of the fact that, what from an external (i.e., nonpsychoanalytic) observer's point of view are called objects, are indispensable and crucial factors in the organization of psychic functioning and psychic structure. In other words, what is naïvely called objects plays an essential part in the constitution of the subject, including the organization of instincts as psychic phenomena and of the subject's developing "object relations"; and what is naïvely called subject plays an essential part in the organization of objects (not merely of object representations). A detailed reconsideration of the concepts of object and object representation in psychoanalysis must be reserved for a later occasion. At that time the relation of instincts to objects will have to be re-examined.

In order to provide a focus of orientation the following thesis is proposed: *instincts, understood as psychic, motivational, forces, become organized as such through interactions within a psychic field consisting originally of the mother-child (psychic) unit.* (This formulation implies that neither objects nor instincts are any longer taken as givens, or as concepts simply appropriated from other sciences.)

When Freud (1915a) undertook "to discuss certain terms which are used in reference to the concept of an instinct," he significantly included, together with "pressure," "aim," and "source" of an instinct, the term "object." While he thus acknowledged that the object of an instinct is something intrinsic to instinct, he immediately gave the object a special status by saying that it "is not originally connected with" the instinct, "but becomes assigned [*zugeordnet*] to it only in consequence of being peculiarly fitted to make satisfaction possible." And by defining object as "the thing in regard to which or through which the instinct is able to achieve its aim," by saying that "the aim of an instinct is in every instance satisfaction," by specifying that satisfaction "can only be obtained by removing the state of stimulation at the source of the instinct" —the source being "the somatic process which occurs in an organ or part of the body" (p. 122f.)—he remains with or reverts to a somatic instinct concept, remains within the purview of the constancy principle (satisfaction or pleasure equals reduction or abolition of stimulation), and narrows down the object to a means of satisfying somatic needs which primarily have nothing to do with the environment. It must be left to biologists to decide whether the closed system model is really serviceable in their field; it certainly is not in psychology.

With the introduction of the concepts of narcissim, narcissistic identification, and "introjection" (in the sense in which Freud [1915a, p. 136] uses the term), the problem of the development and organization of intrapsychic processes and structures was definitely raised and approached, mainly in terms of ego and superego development. But the instinct concept, and id theory by and large, were left out of consideration in this new approach. I do not mean to say, of course, that Freud did not consider the relations of narcissism to the instinct problem. The concept of narcissism was in fact introduced mainly to gain an understanding of the instinctual processes subsumed under the term narcissistic libido (in contra-distinction to object libido). But this did not lead Freud to a re-consideration of the instinct *concept* in terms of the relationship between instinct and environment ("object"). By and large, he continued to operate—despite his definition of instinct as psychic representative—with a somatic and "innate" instinct concept, and he discussed instincts psychoanalytically only when he took up what he called their vicissitudes.[15] If instincts are resolutely con-ceptualized as psychic forces, these vicissitudes are not something that happens to instincts (once they are there, as it were) but are the processes by which they become organized as instincts, by which, we might say, somatic processes become transformed into psychic processes, into psychic representatives.

This transformation, the organization of instincts *qua* psychic forces, comes to pass, I maintain, through interactions within the mother-child psychic field. If one views the problem from the van-tage point of the organization of psychic reality, the question whether objects are or are not "originally connected" with in-stincts is nonsensical. Phenomena such as instincts and objects gradually become constituted, by differentiation and integration, in those interaction processes. Neither instinct nor object, to begin with, is there to become or not to become connected with the other. Once each can be differentiated from the other as an in-ternal or external phenomenon, because of the interactions by which they come into being, each, so to speak, "contains" elements of the other. Saying that an object is primarily, psychoanalytically understood, a libidinal object, implies this situation.

---

[15] As late as 1938 he wrote: "The forces which we assume to exist behind the [need-]tensions of the id are called *instincts*. They represent the somatic demands upon the mind" (1940, p. 148). (I have slightly modified Strachey's translation in the interest of precision; Freud does not speak of "tensions caused by the needs of the id," as Strachey translates, but of need-tensions [*Bedürfnisspannungen*].) No cause-effect relationship is implied between the needs of the id and the ten-sions; needs of the id *are* tensions for Freud, they do not *cause* tensions. It is true that the word "represent" is used ("they represent the somatic demands upon the mind"), but the whole passage makes it clear that instinct itself is conceived as somatic force *behind* the need-tensions of the id. Since the id is a province of the mind (not a biological-somatic entity or concept), forces behind the id act *upon* the mind, not *within* it as mental processes, so that Freud reverts here to his "physiological" approach to instincts (see section II above).

If we use the language of the fully developed adult objective reality to which we are accustomed in ordinary scientific terminology,[16] we would have to say that the object does not become "assigned" to the instinct (understood as psychic force) but contributes crucially to the organization of instincts *qua* instincts, just as instinctual forces crucially contribute to the organization of objects *qua* objects. In this sense the object is no less an original element of the instinct than its pressure, aim, or source.

Speaking in terms of the ontogenesis of psychic reality, I would say that the neonate's incoherent urges, thrashings, and reflex activities become coordinated and organized into instincts and assume aims and direction by activities and responses coming from the environment. And here we should include in our consideration the meaning of "satisfaction." The responsive, attuned activity of the primary caring person does not simply provide satisfaction in the sense of being a means for abolishing excitation. The experience of satisfaction, I believe, is a "creative" process in which appropriate environmental activity does not necessarily or only reduce or abolish excitation but also *engenders* and organizes excitation processes. So-called "mnemic images" are thus created, which are not additions to but constituents of instincts. Mnemic image must be understood here in the sense in which Freud speaks of motor or kinesthetic images (*Bewegungsbild*) in his discussion of satisfaction in the "Project" (1895, p. 318).[17] In the "Project" Freud barely mentions instincts, but his discussion of the "Experience of Satisfaction" (p. 317ff.), with its emphasis on the "specific

[16] I regret that a very much needed clarification of the meanings and ramifications of the term "objective" would lead us too far afield in the present context. In any psychoanalytic investigation the subject-object antithesis creates great methodological and terminological difficulties. It should be noted that Freud mentions this problem (1915a, p. 134): "The antithesis ego—non-ego (external), i.e. subject—object, is . . . thrust upon the individual organism at an early stage. . . . This antithesis remains, above all, sovereign in our intellectual activity and creates for research the basic situation which no efforts can alter." I do not believe, however, that this latter dictum can be taken as the last word on the matter.

[17] Mnemic "images" of this kind are neither visual images nor ideas, but action patterns comparable to those in hysterical "reminiscences" (Breuer and Freud, 1893–1895, p. 7). "Acting out" is a higher form of this type of mnemic process-structure. These mnemic activities are of utmost importance for the psychoanalytic theory of memory and especially of unconscious memory and so-called "memory traces." In another connection they are the prototypes of identification processes.

action" brought about by the "extraneous help" on the part of an "experienced person," adumbrates this understanding of the psychological genesis of instincts as psychic representatives.

The fact that such mnemic action patterns become established as constituents of instincts does not mean, however, that at this stage a differentiation of internal (intrapsychic) and external has already occurred. In the mnemic action pattern, urge and response, environmental engenderment, and the subject's excitation are not differentiated from one another, so that a repetition of such action patterns remains at first a re-enactment of a global event. Only repeated occurrences of such re-enactments, due to the combined effects of recurring need-tensions, environmental responsive actions, and satisfaction events (in the sense outlined above), in alternation with delays and temporary absences of the experience of satisfaction by virtue of differentials between—objectively speaking—subject and environment, lead eventually to a subjective differentiation of mnemic "image" and "actual satisfaction." In such a way, that is, differentiations between something like an internal action pattern (a "memory") and an external factor operating in the effective reinforcement, perpetuation, and revival of that action pattern come about.[18]

In the process of a mother's caring activities, which consist of spontaneous stimulations as well as responses, instincts come into being in the child. The pressure [*Drang*] of the uncoordinated urges which become instincts results from separation events, particularly and most prominently from the event of birth, of physical separation from the mother organism. Rapaport, I believe, has ideas similar to mine when he writes that *"Motives* are characterized by appetitiveness implying a coordination of the instinctual drive discharge [what I would call uncoordinated urges biologically determined] with a definite (even if broad) range of objects," while *"Causes* [nonmotivational] have only a direction which does not change, that is, causes do not 'home' appetitively on the object by changing the direction and path as the place or conditions of the object change." He also emphasizes that "the role of the object

---

[18] An original nondifferentiation of cognitive-memorial and instinctual processes is implied here, as is the view that cognitive-memorial processes are instinctually based.

in instinctual drive discharge also involves the 'summation' of the excitation provided by the object as a stimulus and the excitation provided by instinctual drive energy. When the accumulation of instinctual drive energy has not yet reached threshold intensity, this 'summation' may raise it to that intensity and thus bring about discharge" (1960, p. 878). I differ with him inasmuch as I hold that the summation of these two sources of excitation creates the instinct (*qua* psychic, motivational force), and is generated or mediated by the stimulating-responsive activity of the "object" which gathers, sums up, something for the infant. While Rapaport speaks of instinctual drive *discharge*, I stress, in keeping with my view of the psychological organization of instincts, not the conditions for discharge of instinctual drive energy but the conditions for the formation of instincts as psychic phenomena.[19]

In my view, then, based on the definition of instinct as a psychic representative, the neonate's incoherent urges and thrashings, of which I spoke, are not instinctual. They, like bowel movements or breathing or the crying of the neonate, are not psychic representatives; they are as yet no more than somatic manifestations of stimulation and organic need. In this connection it may be questioned whether the stimulation which becomes psychically represented as instinct can be confined to "inner," organismic stimulation, if "external" stimulation by the mother enters into the formation of instinct. Inasmuch as the entire psychic life of the baby is in the early stages apt to be characterized as instinctual [*triebhaft*], in response to organic as well as "external" stimulations, what we call instinctual in psychoanalysis seems at that stage to have more to do with the primitive character of motivation, of psychic organization, than with "organic" versus "environmental." Everything is still close to the body and its "language" and expression, not just organic needs. This would be in contradiction to Freud's distinction between instinctual and "physiological" stimuli (1915a, p. 118). This problem as well as Freud's emphasis on the difference between

---

[19] In his paper "On the Psychoanalytic Theory of Motivation," from which the quotations in the text are taken, Rapaport discusses many problems of the instinct concept which are of great importance but must be left out of consideration here. The term "synergic action" perhaps would be preferable to "summation."

the constant force of an instinctual stimulus and the momentary impact of an external stimulus cannot be discussed in this paper.

A few words need to be said about the concept of primary narcissism in relation to the concept of instinct advanced here. In "Instincts and Their Vicissitudes" Freud writes:

> Originally, at the very beginning of mental life, the ego is cathected with instincts and is to some extent capable of satisfying them on itself. We call this condition 'narcissism' and this way of obtaining satisfaction 'auto-erotic'. At this time the external world is not cathected with interest . . . and is indifferent for purposes of satisfaction. During this period, therefore, the ego-subject coincides with what is pleasurable and the external world with what is indifferent (or possibly unpleasurable, as being a source of stimulation). [Thus, there is an original situation] in which the ego loves itself only and is indifferent to the external world [p. 134f.]. [On the basis of this view of primary narcissism the distinction is made between a "purely narcissistic stage" and an "object-stage" (p. 137). The latter is an advance which is said to come about in the following way:] Those sexual instincts which from the outset require an object [i.e., are not capable of autoerotic satisfaction], and the needs of the ego-instincts, which are never capable of auto-erotic satisfaction, naturally disturb this state and so pave the way for an advance from it [p. 134f., n.].

Our present conception of the original situation of mental life called primary narcissism is different. We no longer understand it as a stage where "the external world is not cathected with interest" and is indifferent or hostile (unpleasurable), but as a stage which Freud in *Civilization and Its Discontents* (1930) described as follows:

> An infant at the breast does not as yet distinguish his ego from the external world as the source of the sensations flowing in upon him. . . . He must be very strongly impressed by the fact that some sources of excitation, *which he will later recognize as his own bodily organs,* can provide him with sensations at any moment, whereas other sources evade him from time to time—

among them what he desires most of all, his mother's breast—
and only reappear as a result of his screaming for help. *In this
way there is for the first time set over against the ego an 'object',
in the form of something which exists 'outside'*. . . . In this way,
then, the ego detaches itself from the external world. Or, to put
it more correctly, originally the ego includes everything, later it
separates off an external world from itself. Our present ego-feeling is, therefore, only a shrunken residue of a much more inclusive—indeed, an all-embracing—feeling which corresponded to
a more intimate bond between the ego and the world about it
[p. 66ff.; my italics].

In the "primal psychical situation" [*psychische Ursituation*]
(Freud, 1915a, p. 134) of primary narcissism, understood in this
new light, ego and external world, ego and "object" are still one
undifferentiated psychic field. And it would not be correct to describe this primal situation as though the external world were
not cathected with interest and were indifferent (or unpleasurable) while the ego-subject would coincide with what is pleasurable.
Pleasure and unpleasure, at this stage at any rate, are not distributed between inside and outside, or pleasure attributed to
what is internal and unpleasure to what is external. Pleasure and
unpleasure, at this stage, are global states of being. And an adequately empathic mother is, as a matter of fact, a participant in
this state of being, no less or hardly less than the infant.[20]
  What are the implications of the revised conception of primary

---

[20] Any sufficiently empathic observer of the mother-infant relationship and interaction can see (and can learn from perceptive mothers) that this is the case; that
there is a mutual correspondence and responsiveness, a reciprocal heightening and
decrease of states of pleasure and unpleasure, including physical pleasurable and
unpleasurable sensations in the mother. In somewhat later stages we tend to describe such phenomena as emotional contagion or identification, as for instance in
the nonverbal transmission of anxiety from mother to child or vice versa. Any
competent psychotherapist is aware of similar events in the treatment of sensitive
or "regressed" patients. It therefore remains an important question to what extent
an investigation and understanding of early psychic stages is at all possible if the
focus of observation does not encompass the mother together with the infant. If
this is done, we are, I believe, much less at the mercy of reconstructive *speculations* in regard to early stages than is often assumed. Compare Winnicott's paper
on "Primary Maternal Preoccupation" (1956).

narcissism for the instinct concept? What indeed is the ego of which we speak at such a stage? It clearly is not the structure we have in mind when we think of the mental structures id, ego, superego. In the passage I quoted from "Instincts and Their Vicissitudes" the word ego is used in the sense of "the whole subject"; at one point Freud uses the term "ego-subject" to make this clear.[21] The word ego is used in the same sense in Chapter I of *Civilization and Its Discontents* from which I quoted. A reading of the whole first chapter of that book makes it clear that Freud is not dealing with the ego as a mental substructure. To put it another way, the meaning of ego as a mental substructure dissolves when we concern ourselves with early "ego states" and with their later equivalents. When, in "Instincts and Their Vicissitudes" Freud writes that "at the very beginning of mental life the ego is cathected with instincts [*triebbesetzt*]," or when he speaks of a body-ego or pleasure-ego, a distinction between what he later would call id and ego clearly could not be intended, given the stage of mental development to which he refers. The ego-subject (to use Freud's specifying term) at this stage *is* an instinctual one.[22]

Due to "various promptings" (Freud, 1930, p. 67), by gradual development (see above) there is an "object" being set over against the ego or—and this is saying the same thing—an instinctual ego over against the "object." That Freud describes the ego's primal state as narcissism is in itself a fact which makes it clear that instinctual life is the referent here. (The introduction of the concept of primary narcissism is an "extension of the libido theory"

[21] I advisedly avoid using the term "self" in this connection and at this psychic stage. "Self" denotes a "Person's or thing's own individuality or essence, person or thing as object of introspection or reflexive action" (*The Concise Oxford Dictionary*, 1938); see also Webster (1958) under: *self*, n.; especially 3. In psychoanalytic literature the term is used far too loosely and equivocally. Accordingly, I cannot agree with a definition, as proposed by Hartmann (1950), of narcissism as cathexis of the self in contradistinction to cathexis of the ego.

[22] Winnicott (1956, p. 305) writes: "In reconstructing the early development of an infant there is no point at all in talking of instincts, except on a basis of ego development. There is a watershed: Ego maturity—instinctual experiences strengthen ego. Ego immaturity—instinctual experiences disrupt ego. Ego here implies a summation of experience."

[Freud, 1914, p. 75].) We cannot have one theory in regard to the constitution or organization of the ego, and another one in regard to the organization of instincts. The early development of the ego, as adumbrated by Freud in *Civilization and Its Discontents, is* the organization and development of instincts understood as psychic representatives. Freud did not make this explicit and did not revise his instinct concept in accordance with the new insights into early mental development. Among the reasons for his not doing so are his theoretical bias in favor of a biological instinct concept, and his reluctance, amounting to an aversion, to involve himself deeply in the investigation of mental stages and states where the subject-object polarity does not hold.[23]

In this context Freud's concepts of the original reality-ego and the purified pleasure-ego (1915a) should be reconsidered, but I can state only that in the light of the revised conception of primary narcissism neither concept can be retained in its original form.

As a preliminary conclusion, the following may be said about the relation of instincts to objects: objects are "originally connected" with instincts in such a way that the problem is not how they become connected in the course of time and development, or why they become connected. Rather, seen from the standpoint of instinctual life, the problem is: how what later is distinguished as object from subject, becomes differentiated, in the course of mental development, from instincts. Only if instincts are conceptualized as organismic, biological stimuli impinging on a preordained "psychic apparatus" which is not itself instinctual but stimulated by such instincts, and if instincts are conceived merely as biological urges pressing for discharge—only then can the idea arise that the "object" is not an original element of "instinct." At the same time, I have suggested that, in order to speak of the relation of instinct to object in a truly psychoanalytic discourse, the object concept itself must be freed of its naïve connotations rooted in nonanalytic epistemological preconceptions.

[23] See Freud's comments on the oceanic feeling (1930, p. 64f., p. 72f.). Compare also his letter to Hollos (written in 1928) which clearly shows such an aversion and Schur's discussion (1966). Cf. my paper "Ego and Reality" (1951, especially p. 13), which deals with this problem from another angle.

BIBLIOGRAPHY

ARLOW, J. A. & BRENNER, C. (1964), *Psychoanalytic Concepts and the Structural Theory*. New York: International Universities Press.

BORNSTEIN, B. (1949), The Analysis of a Phobic Child: Some Problems of Theory and Technique in Child Analysis. *This Annual*, 3/4:181–226.

BREUER, J. & FREUD, S. (1893–1895), Studies on Hysteria. *Standard Edition*, 2. London: Hogarth Press, 1955.

FREUD, S. (1894), The Neuro-Psychoses of Defence. *Standard Edition*, 3:43–68. London: Hogarth Press, 1962.

— (1895), Project for a Scientific Psychology. *Standard Edition*, 1:281–397. London: Hogarth Press, 1966.

— (1900), The Interpretation of Dreams. *Standard Edition*, 4 & 5. London: Hogarth Press, 1953.

— (1910), The Psycho-Analytic View of Psychogenic Disturbance of Vision. *Standard Edition*, 11:209–218. London: Hogarth Press, 1957.

— (1914), On Narcissism: An Introduction. *Standard Edition*, 14:69–102. London: Hogarth Press, 1957.

— (1915a), Instincts and Their Vicissitudes. *Standard Edition*, 14:109–140. London: Hogarth Press, 1957.

— (1915b), The Unconscious. *Standard Edition*, 14:159–215. London: Hogarth Press, 1957.

— (1920), Beyond the Pleasure Principle. *Standard Edition*, 18:3–64. London: Hogarth Press, 1955.

— (1923), The Ego and the Id. *Standard Edition*, 19:3–66. London: Hogarth Press, 1961.

— (1924), The Economic Problem of Masochism. *Standard Edition*, 19:157–170. London: Hogarth Press, 1961.

— (1930), Civilization and Its Discontents. *Standard Edition*, 21:59–145. London: Hogarth Press, 1961.

— (1940 [1938]), An Outline of Psycho-Analysis. *Standard Edition*, 23:141–207. London: Hogarth Press, 1964.

GILL, M. M. (1963), *Topography and Systems in Psychoanalytic Theory* [*Psychological Issues*, Monogr. 10]. New York: International Universities Press.

HARTMANN, H. (1939), *Ego Psychology and the Problem of Adaptation*. New York: International Universities Press, 1958.

— (1950), Comments on the Psychoanalytic Theory of the Ego. *This Annual*, 5:74–96.

LOEWALD, H. W. (1951), Ego and Reality. *Int. J. Psycho-Anal.*, 32:10–18.

— (1966), Review of: *Psychoanalytic Concepts and the Structural Theory*, by J. A. Arlow and C. Brenner. *Psychoanal. Quart.*, 35:430–436.

— (1971), Discussion of *The Id and the Regulatory Principles of Mental Functioning*, by M. Schur. In: *The Unconscious Today: Essays in Honor of Max Schur,* ed. M. Kanzer. New York: International Universities Press (in press).

LOEWENSTEIN, R. M. (1951), The Problem of Interpretation. *Psychoanal. Quart.,* 20:1–14.

MODELL, A. H. (1968), *Object Love and Reality.* New York: International Universities Press.

POLANYI, M. (1958), *Personal Knowledge: Towards a Post-Critical Philosophy.* London: Oxford University Press.

RAPAPORT, D. (1960), On the Psychoanalytic Theory of Motivation. In: *The Collected Papers of David Rapaport,* ed. M. M. Gill. New York: Basic Books, 1967, pp. 853–915.

SCHUR, M. (1966), *The Id and the Regulatory Principles of Mental Functioning.* New York: International Universities Press.

STRACHEY, J. (1966), Notes on Some Technical Terms Whose Translation Calls for Comment. *Standard Edition,* 1:xxiii-xxvi. London: Hogarth Press, 1966.

WINNICOTT, D. W. (1956), Primary Maternal Preoccupation. *Collected Papers.* New York: Basic Books, 1958, pp. 300–305.

Some Suggestions
for a Critique
of Kleinian Psychology

CLIFFORD YORKE, M.R.C.S., L.R.C.P.,
M.R.C. Psych., D.P.M.

JUST OVER 50 YEARS AGO MELANIE KLEIN BECAME MUCH OCCUPIED
with a little boy called Fritz (see 1955). She had often given advice
on his upbringing and when, at the age of 4¾ years, Fritz began
to ask a series of questions closely concerned with his own origins,
Klein found herself involved in assuaging his curiosity. Six
months later, the relationship became an analytic one, and in
1921 accounts of each phase of her contact with him were com-

Psychiatrist in Charge, Hampstead Child-Therapy Clinic, an organization which
is at present supported by the Field Foundation, Inc., New York: the Foundation
for Research in Psychoanalysis, Beverly Hills, California; the Freud Centenary
Fund, London; the Anna Freud Foundation, New York; the Grant Foundation,
Inc., New York; the Andrew W. Mellon Foundation, New York; the National
Institute for Mental Health, Bethesda, Maryland; the New-Land Foundation, Inc.,
New York; and a number of private supporters.

bined to form her first published paper—an event of undeniable historical importance.

The first part of her paper, which deals with the first period of observation, education, and sexual enlightenment, shows great sensitivity and perceptiveness, and is charmingly told. The same can be said for the second part, which is subtitled "Early Analysis." In the first part, Klein is content to let the material speak for itself, which it does with eloquence. In the second part, she introduces interpretations, though sparingly in comparison with her later analyses, based largely on the content of anxiety dreams. The child's oedipus complex as well as the homosexual aspects of his difficulties come under scrutiny. Aggressive wishes are brought to consciousness, and in all these matters Klein's skill seems undeniable.

From this one analysis she draws two conclusions. The first is that it should be possible to analyze children of 3 years or even younger, an assertion which, with qualifications, has long ceased to be a matter of controversy. The second is the suggestion that every child, whether normal or not, might benefit from analysis. This quickly matured into the conviction that *every* child should have analysis as part of its normal upbringing, a view which Klein continued to hold throughout her life.

Some 10 years after her treatment of Fritz began, a 4-year-old boy called Dick was brought to Klein and was plainly severely ill. His intellectual attainment was on the level of a 15- or 18-month-old child. He showed little affect of any kind, was "indifferent to the presence or absence of mother or nurse," had no significant interests, "rarely displayed anxiety, . . . strung sounds together in a meaningless way," and constantly repeated certain noises (p. 238f.). His scanty vocabulary was used incorrectly, but in any case he showed no wish to be understood. Klein, in her first session with him, found his behavior quite different from that of a neurotic child. He let his nurse go with no trace of emotion, showed complete indifference to Klein, ran about in an aimless way, and treated his therapist as if she were a piece of furniture. His movements were poorly coordinated, and he had a fixed expression and faraway look. His behavior appeared to have neither meaning nor purpose. The history included: fruitless attempts to suckle him on the part of the mother, persisting to the point where the child almost died from starvation; digestive disturbances, rectal prolapse and hemorrhoids; and a loveless environment.

During Dick's first session, which began in the way described, Klein tried to interest the boy in the toys she had made ready, but without success; and we can take up her own account at this point:

> I took a big train and put it beside a smaller one and called them 'Daddy-train' and 'Dick-train'. Thereupon he picked up the train I called 'Dick' and made it roll to the window and said 'Station'. I explained: 'The station is mummy; Dick is going into mummy.' He left the train, ran into the space between the outer and inner doors of the room, shut himself in, saying 'dark' and ran out again directly. He went through this performance several times. I explained to him: 'It is dark inside mummy. Dick is inside dark mummy.' Meantime he picked up the train again, but soon ran back into the space between the doors. While I was saying that he was going into dark mummy, he said twice in a questioning way: 'Nurse?' I answered: 'Nurse is soon coming,' and this he repeated and used the words later quite correctly, retaining *them* in his mind [p. 242].

The second and third sessions were apparently similar, but he began to show apprehension and constantly asked, "Nurse coming?" At the end of the third session, he greeted the nurse with quite unusual delight. During the third session he showed for the first time some interest in the toys, pointed to a coal cart and said, "Cut." Klein continues her account of this session as follows:

> I gave him a pair of scissors, and he tried to scratch the little pieces of black wood which represented coal, but he could not hold the scissors. Acting on a glance which he gave me, I cut the pieces of wood out of the cart, whereupon he threw the damaged cart and its contents into the drawer and said, 'Gone'. I told him that this meant that Dick was cutting faeces out of his mother. He then ran into the space between the doors and scratched on the doors a little with his nails, thus showing that he identified the space with the cart and both with the mother's body, which he was attacking. He immediately ran back from the space between the doors, found the cupboard and crept into it [p. 243].

I have omitted nothing material from Klein's account of these sessions, which are described in her paper on symbol formation (1930). It is quite clear, to say no more, that a great deal had happened in 10 years.

Since Freud's death, and even during his lifetime, his fertile contributions have inspired many to extend his studies in a number of directions, both theoretically and clinically. It was, perhaps, only to be expected that the genetic point of view would be of particular interest, and that analysts should seek to understand more clearly the less accessible regions of the young child's mind. In particular, the need to throw more light on the preverbal phase of development was always pressing, since the very young child is unable to communicate with words, is not accessible to direct analysis, and can be understood only through analytically informed observation. Among the developmental problems which have required more detailed elucidation we may name, as examples, the development of psychic structure and, more specifically, the early phases of ego formation; the early history and antecedents of the superego; and the forerunners of the oedipus complex. Any hope of exploring more thoroughly the early history of the child's mental development was bound to be seized with avidity.

Melanie Klein has claimed to extend our knowledge in precisely these directions, and for these reasons alone her views must be studied with the closest attention. From the beginning, her opinions were lent unusual prestige by virtue of her pioneering work in child analysis; she was preceded only by Freud's vicarious treatment of Little Hans (1909) and by the work of Hug-Hellmuth, and she was the first to advocate and undertake the analysis of children under 5. Such courageous steps were bound to lend weight to her words and to bring her a ready and receptive audience.

The questions which immediately raise themselves, and to which this discussion is addressed, can be put very briefly. How far do her claims appear to be justified in the light of the evidence she presents? To what degree do her views present a legitimate extension of psychoanalytic understanding and methodology, and how far, if at all, do they present a departure from this? What sacrifices, in terms of other useful clinical and theoretical concepts, have to be made for their acceptance? And, since science is indivisible, how far are Klein's views compatible with the claims of other sciences?

The Early Development of Melanie Klein's Theories

It is not generally recognized that the development of Klein's thinking falls into three phases. In published form, the first of these extends from 1921, when she described her treatment of Fritz, to 1932, when she published her book on *The Psycho-Analysis of Children*. The second phase begins with the publication, in 1934, of her paper on the psychogenesis of manic-depressive states, which introduces her concept of the "depressive position." The final phase, beginning with the paper on the emotional life of the infant in 1952, is introduced by the concept of a "paranoid-schizoid position" and, continuing until her death, includes the elaboration of her concepts of envy and gratitude.

A detailed analysis of the first phase would form a fascinating study, especially if attempted chronologically. Both the treatment of Fritz and the analysis of Dick fall within it; and the intervening changes in theory and technique are sufficiently remarkable to warrant closer attention to the transitional stages by which they were brought about. Some of these were subtle or involved a mere matter of emphasis, especially in theoretical discussions; while others, such as the equation of children's play with free association, were more obviously fundamental and quickly became well known, especially in the field of technique. Glover's summary of the main conclusions of this phase (1945), while succinct and very useful, is not concerned with its evolution. All that can be said on this occasion is that, during this period, Klein (1926, 1927a, 1927b, 1929a, 1930, 1932) developed her play technique hand in hand with certain theoretical innovations; introduced new concepts of symbol formation which influenced that technique (1923b, 1927a, 1930); began the elaboration of a broader concept of transference (1926, 1927a, 1927b, 1929a, 1932); and revised the theory of inhibition and sublimation (1923a, 1923b,

1931). She produced new views on infantile curiosity (1928, 1930, 1931). At the same time she introduced the concept of a phase of maximal infantile sadism, directed largely at the child's objects—the mother's body contents, the father's penis, and the parental couple in intercourse (1928, 1929b, 1930, 1932). This phase was originally believed to arise at the *end* of the first year, but was later advanced to the *middle* of that year. The phase was associated with the concept of an early superego and the beginnings of an oedipus complex. Anxiety was derived from aggression, which was seen *par excellence* as the principal source of conflict. Toward the end of this phase the concept of an aggressive drive was replaced by the death instinct (1932).

These comments are cursory, and can only indicate some of Klein's main interests at the time. A full historical account is badly needed.

Major Kleinian Tenets

A historical approach to the second and third phases would equally be of interest, though possibly less rewarding; and I propose now to give a rough outline of the main conclusions which Klein had reached at the time of her death. It is more convenient to describe these views from an ontogenetic standpoint. I shall use, for the present, Kleinian terminology.

The ego exists from birth. Unconscious fantasy is present from the beginning. Fantasy is the mental representative of an instinct. Every instinctual impulse, therefore, has its corresponding fantasy. As an example, it can be said that the impulse to suck can be experienced only through the concomitant fantasy of a breast. The ego, however poorly organized it may otherwise be in its early stages, is, nevertheless, capable of forming object relationships; it can experience anxiety; and it can use defense mechanisms. Defense mechanisms, like instincts, can be experienced only as fantasies: for example, projection is experienced as a fantasy of pushing something out; and introjection, as taking something in—that is, as incorporation. It may at once be said that introjection is the only form of identification accepted by the

Kleinian school, with the exception of *projective identification,* a special concept to be described later.

The prototype, and indeed the basis, for *all* conflict is the struggle between the life and death instincts, and this is already operative during birth. This is stated quite explicitly by Klein in her paper on anxiety and guilt (1948). The trauma of birth is experienced as an overwhelming attack and therefore gives rise to persecutory anxiety in relation to the external world. The child's first object, the mother's breast, is correspondingly felt to be hostile.

This feeling of persecution is reinforced from another quarter. Part of the death instinct is, from the first, directed outward and therefore, in fantasy, destructively attacks the mother's breast. Frustration by the breast is experienced as a retaliatory attack for the baby's destructive impulses, thus reinforcing the part of the death instinct which has remained directed internally. The attacked breast—the "bad breast" in Kleinian shorthand—is now an attacking breast, and is "the external representative of the death instinct."

This bad breast is introjected—that is, it is taken into the ego in an attempt to control it—but this simply means that the ego is now menaced from inside. This further intensifies the internal danger situation, since that part of the death instinct which was externally deflected once again threatens the ego from within. This leads to the reprojection of the dangerous bad breast back into the external world, but this in turn simply re-establishes the menace from outside. As Klein herself puts it (1948), there is "a constant fluctuation between the fear of internal and external bad objects" (p. 118).

Let us leave the death instinct for the moment and return to the life instinct. The life instinct (the libido), too, attaches itself to the breast as its first external object, which therefore becomes a gratifying breast—a "good" breast. The good breast is also internalized through introjection and, as a gratifying internal source of bounty and goodness, reinforces the life instinct. This life-giving internal object reinforces the ego and lends it strength. The struggle between the life and death instincts is now repre-

sented, internally, by an ideal breast on the one hand and a devouring breast on the other. The two breasts "form the core of
the super-ego in its good and bad aspects" (p. 118), and represent
the clash of instincts within that structure.

Part of the libido is again projected outward, in order to maintain a good external life-giving breast. As with the death instinct,
part of the libido is retained to strengthen a libidinal relationship
with the good and gratifying *internal* breast, thus reinforcing the
feeling of an internal ideal object. The breast is thus split, whether
externally or internally, into an ideal breast on the one hand and
a persecuting breast on the other. The mechanism by which this
is achieved is known as "splitting." Good reality experiences reinforce the feeling of security, while bad, depriving experiences
add to the feelings of persecution (1946, 1952a, 1952b).

Thus we arrive at the main characteristics of the first 3 months
of life which Melanie Klein called the *paranoid-schizoid* position:
"paranoid," because of the persecution fear, and "schizoid," because of the splitting. During this phase the most characteristic
fear is that the bad persecuting object will get inside the ego and
not only destroy the ideal internal breast, but annihilate the self
as well. Under the influence of this persecutory anxiety, it is
therefore essential to preserve the good object within by keeping
out the persecutor. Incidentally, the breast is regarded as a *part
object* since the infant is still unaware of the whole person who
both mothers and frustrates him.

What are the defense mechanisms of the paranoid-schizoid
phase? Projection and introjection have already been mentioned,
but they may work in various ways. The good breast, for example,
may be projected to preserve it from a bad internal persecutor.
It is the splitting process which is really the core of the matter;
whatever the means used to attain it, the first requirement is to
keep the ideal objects and the persecutors apart.

Splitting may be accompanied by idealization. Sometimes, when
the persecution feels too great to be tolerated, an omnipotent
denial of persecution may be introduced through the attempted
idealization of the bad object. Sometimes the bad object, too, is
introjected in an attempt to control it and master it. On the other

hand, the introjection of the persecutor may result in hypochondriasis or even in disintegration of the ego.

A few words must be said about projective identification. Klein's first discussion of this appears in her paper on the emotional life of the infant (1952a), but Joan Riviere's definition (1952) is comparatively short and to the point. She says: " 'projective identification' . . . represents the fantasy of forcing the self in part or as a whole into the inside of the object in order to obtain possession and control of it, whether in love or in hate" (p. 33).

The ultimate defense available to the ego in reducing the anxiety of the paranoid-schizoid position is disintegration. This is a desperate measure in which the ego falls to pieces in an attempt to avoid persecution.

The defense mechanisms may subserve valuable functions in healthy development. Projective identification is a primitive basis for empathy; splitting, for discrimination. Even persecutory anxiety is held to be a necessary preparation for the capacity to deal with situations of danger.

How does the paranoid-schizoid position stand in relation to normality? This depends on a relative preponderance of "good" over "bad" experience, so that the ego is more closely identified with the ideal object and thereby develops a sense of its own goodness as well as of the goodness of the object.

Before turning to the depressive position it is necessary to say a little about the Kleinian concept of envy, since envy is held to be capable of affecting the earliest infantile experiences and is thus a potentially disrupting factor in development (1957, 1960). Envy antedates jealousy, since the latter can operate only within three-person relationships. Envy, on the contrary, exists from birth. Since the ideal breast is held to be the fountain of all love, goodness, and bounty, the ego strives to emulate the breast and to be like it. Where this attainment seems impossible, the ego desires to attack the breast and to ruin it, so that the source of painful feelings of envy can be removed. Here, much depends on the balance between the wish to preserve the marvelous source of comfort and love and the envious wish to destroy it.

Projection often operates in the service of envy, and this is most notable when the infant tries to ruin the breast by projecting into it all his badness. In fantasy, the breast is messed up with excrement, urinated on, attacked by all the sadism at the child's command, including an evil and penetrating scoptophilia ("the evil eye"). Later, when the oedipus complex sets in, envy may operate in a similar manner against the parental couple.

Since envy is painful, defenses against it may be brought into operation. Paradoxically, spoliation appears to be one of these, since, although it fulfills the aims of envy, a spoiled or ruined object ceases to arouse it. Idealization is also a defense, but, since it merely serves to increase the envy, it can scarcely be said to be very successful. More effective, it seems, is a splitting off of the painful affect. Most important, perhaps, are the love, affection, admiration, and hence gratitude, which come into conflict with the envy. If the latter is not too great, the gratitude, introjected into the ideal breast, will overcome the envy, and the breast enrich and strengthen the ego (1957).

We can now deal briefly with the concept of the *depressive position* (1934, 1940, 1946, 1952a, 1952b). Assuming that development has been favorable, that good experiences have outweighed the bad, and that identification with the good breast has been strengthened, the infant begins to tolerate his death instinct much better, and to resort much less to splitting and projection. Ego integration is increased as paranoid feelings lessen. According to Klein, a phase of development now begins in which relations to part objects are succeeded by the recognition of, and relation to, whole ones. The infant now recognizes his mother as well as other people with whom he comes into contact as whole persons. This means that sources of badness and goodness are no longer felt to be separate and split off from one another. The mother is now seen as both the source and the recipient of good *and* bad feelings and experiences, and the child now has to face his own ambivalence. The deepest anxiety of the depressive position is the child's fear that his destructiveness will have damaged or destroyed the object of his love and his dependence.

The child now resorts increasingly to oral introjective mechanisms in order to internalize the mother in an attempt to protect her from his own destructiveness. But oral omnipotence increases the fear that the good external object as well as the good internal one will be devoured and destroyed in spite of his love for her. This leads to guilt, depressive suffering, and despair. Hence, even the attempt to preserve the object is experienced as destructive, so that in fantasy the dead, devoured mother lies in pieces inside him. Feelings of loss and hopelessness therefore characterize the early part of this phase, which begins in the second quarter of the first year.

Nevertheless, these very experiences of depression act as a spur to further development through the mobilization of reparative drives. The child longs to repair and restore the lost or damaged object, through his love for her, in an attempt to overcome his destructive drives. Once again the libido is at war with the death instinct. Depressive anxieties are resolved as, internally in fantasy and externally in reality, the good object is restored. The capacity to love and to differentiate between objects now means, in addition, a considerable gain in reality testing.

Superego changes ensue. In the paranoid-schizoid position the twin roots of the superego are to be found in the introjections of the good and bad part objects. The ideal breast is the root of the ego ideal, while the persecuting breast is the root of the menacing and punitive superego. As splitting is lessened, the superego is more integrated, and comes to be experienced as a whole object, which is now the recipient of ambivalent love. Injurious attitudes to the superego occasion guilt; but as an object of love the superego is an ally of libidinal trends in their struggle against destructiveness.

At this phase of development reparation becomes linked with the giving up or inhibition of instinctual aims—that is, with sublimation. (According to Segal [1964], psychotic mechanisms, such as splitting and projection, are gradually replaced by so-called "neurotic ones," such as repression.) The displacement of instincts onto substitutes heralds the onset of symbol formation.

Reparation may be considered, in part, a defense against the depressive position. But often the really painful quality of this phase can be dealt with only through the operation of the so-called *manic defenses*. Any feelings of dependence on the object are denied or reversed. The whole of psychic reality is denied. Objects are felt to be manically controlled, triumphed over, and treated with contempt. In this way the object ceases to be felt as valued, and dependence is reversed. In favorable circumstances, manic defenses may yet give way to reparation and successful resolution of the depressive position.

Space permits only brief reference to the early stages of the oedipus complex, which Klein (1946, 1952a) believes to be an integral part of the depressive position. In his fantasies, the infant feels that the parents are in constant intercourse, and he projects onto them all his impulses—oral, urethral, anal, and genital. The parents are felt to be enjoying mutual gratifications of all these desires, while the child himself is excluded. Jealousy, envy, and deprivation feelings are activated or reactivated, and aggressive wishes and fantasies are remobilized as the child wants to attack the parents by every sadistic means at his disposal. In fantasy, the mutilated and murdered parents are introjected and form part of his depressive internal world.

The fantasy of a combined parental figure is regarded as a defense against the recognition of differentiated parental objects having intercourse together. The concept of the phallic woman likewise has a defensive function as a combined parental object. Awareness of both the penis and the female genitals is present from earliest times, though to begin with these, like the breast, are "part objects."

Under the influence of persecutory and depressive anxieties, both boy and girl turn from the mother and her breast to the father's penis as the new object of oral desire. For the girl, feminine receptivity is an important element in this shift and is therefore heterosexual, but the wish to incorporate the father's penis and have it as her own implies a homosexual component. For the boy, there is a passive homosexual component in his wish for the father's penis, but in his fantasied incorporation his heterosexuality is strengthened. Suffice it to say, for the present, that as genital trends come to the fore, heterosexuality is strengthened. Earlier wishes to deprive the mother of penises, body contents, and babies now come under the reparative trends of the depressive position so that, in fantasy, these are restored to the mother. In the boy, this happens through his fantasied intercourse with her, and his wish to give her babies; in the girl, through identification with the mother in intercourse with the father. It should be noted that, in Kleinian theory, a phallic phase as such does not exist in girls.

Differences between Kleinian and Classical Viewpoints

However imperfect and oversimplified this outline may be, it is, I believe, a fair and accurate summary of the overall Kleinian position. On the other hand, it is one thing to present such a statement as an expository introduction to Kleinian thinking, but quite a different matter to use it as a text on which to build a detailed critique. That is why this paper does no more than indicate the lines such a critique might follow and to suggest why, in spite of such recent papers as Kernberg's (1969), such a critique is still called for.

Nevertheless, I hope that enough has been said to indicate some of the enormous differences which exist between the Kleinian and the classical viewpoints. One of the most striking is surely the concept of conflict. In Kleinian thinking, the fundamental conflict is between the life and death instincts; and since this is present from birth onward, it is unaffected, except perhaps in form, by subsequent development. The Freudian, on the other hand, thinks of conflict as it occurs between different agencies: id versus ego; ego versus superego, and ego versus external reality; though he still takes account of conflicts of an intrasystemic kind. But since, at first sight, the Kleinian system uses the *language* of structural theory, this matter must be dealt with. For even a brief examination is enough to establish substantial differences in connotation; and the most obvious concern the term "ego."

It seems quite plain that, by and large, Klein uses this term to mean "the self." There are exceptions to this: in her pamphlet "Our Adult World and Its Roots in Infancy" (1959) she defines the ego as the "organized part of the self" and takes the self to include, in addition, the id. But such a use is rare.

With the development of the structural theory in 1923 the "ego," for the vast majority of analysts, has come to mean the executive apparatus of the mind, engaged in the task of meeting the triple requirements of the id, the superego, and external reality, with varying degress of success. Among the ego's important functions are its unconscious operations of defense, its synthesizing activity, and its role in adaptation to reality. We would also add, to quote Freud (1923), that "By virtue of its relation to the perceptual system it gives mental processes an order in time and submits them to 'reality-testing'. By interposing the processes of thinking, it secures a postponement of motor discharges and controls the access to motility" (p. 55). It is necessary to add that the ego is responsible for the organization of its mental content, from the most primitive memory traces to self and object representations.

This list is not complete and, in different circumstances, would call for elaboration; but it should suffice for the present purposes. As I understand it, the Kleinians have no term for the "ego" in the sense outlined. Insofar as they accept any of the functions listed they are compelled to attribute them to the "self." Freud's structural triad is therefore replaced by a "self"—which from the earliest times contains a superego—and life and death instincts which impinge upon it in the form of fantasy representatives. Furthermore, it should be noted that, without a clear concept of the "ego" in the Freudian sense, all distinction between the "self" and its representation disappears, just as no distinction is drawn between an object and an object representation. This was bound to happen since, for all practical purposes, *the concept of a mental apparatus, as something distinct from its contents, has virtually disappeared.*

The consequences appear to be drastic, and attention can be focused immediately on one of them. Objects and self take on a new concreteness. Each can be put into, or expelled from, the other in the most literal manner. This appears to be responsible for the view that, if a patient projects anger onto the analyst, the latter is bound to feel it. This literal tendency appears, if anything, to be even more pronounced in some South American circles, but the tendency to concrete thinking was necessarily encouraged by the new formulations, in spite of the emphasis on fantasy.

Before exploring these consequences further it is necessary to return for a moment to differences in terminological usage, in particular, to the term *fantasy*. This matter has already been dealt with in detail by Glover (1945) and only brief consideration is called for here. The standard Kleinian definition of fantasy was first used in the controversial series of discussions in the British Society and was first put forward in published form by Susan Isaacs (1948): "Phantasy," she said, "is (in the first instance) the mental corollary, the psychic representative, of instinct" (p. 83); and that definition has been quoted and requoted ever since. In her summary Isaacs reaffirmed that "Phantasies are the primary content of unconscious mental processes" (p. 112). In the main body of the text, however, her argument clearly implies that fantasy is the basis of all mentation, whether conscious or not. To give but one example, she links early fantasy formation so closely with the capacity to hallucinate (Freud's hallucinatory wish fulfillment) that the two are virtually identical.

It is quite obvious that the adoption of such a definition of fantasy explicitly does away with all distinctions between different forms of mental content. A fantasy is not only indistinguishable from a hallucination—and presumably a delusion—but memory traces, and their organization into representations, images, various forms of ideational content, thing presentations, word presentations, identifications and introjections, concepts and precepts, are all subsumed under the term "fantasy," and doubly so, since any of them can become, under certain conditions, psychic representatives of an instinct.

But all this says nothing of the Freudian meaning of fantasy, which has recently been explored in detail by Sandler and Nagera (1963). Only the relevant points of their conclusions will be summarized. In particular, a careful distinction is drawn between conscious fantasies (daydreams), fantasies which are descriptively unconscious (preconscious), and fantasies which have been repressed into the system *Ucs*. (It should be added that these comments concern themselves entirely with fantasy as discussed by Freud; I shall make no mention of the extension of Freud's views proposed by the authors.)

The dating of fantasy is particularly important in the present context. Freud (1911) links the emergence of fantasy quite specifically with the development of the reality principle. As the reality principle develops, and objects, aims, and desires have to be modified, given up, or postponed, fantasy begins to compensate for what, in many instances, is felt as intolerable loss. In general, fantasies bring together different mental contents, not previously associated as representatives of reality, in a wish-fulfilling way. They have to be distinguished from memories, though the relation between the two was a concern of Freud's throughout his analytic writings. (Witness *remembered* versus *fantasied* seductions in childhood.)

Little need be said here about daydreams apart from the fact that Freud thought they could be tolerated in the *Pcs.* and *Cs.* as long as their instinctual cathexis did not rise above a certain level. If this happened, repression into the *Ucs.* ensued, and the fantasy thus became subject to primary process functioning. Preconscious fantasies differed from the daydream only insofar as they did not possess the quality of consciousness. They were descriptively, but not dynamically, unconscious. But once a fantasy has been repressed it "functions exactly like a *memory of instinctual satisfaction* and can provide the ideational content of the instinctual drives" (Sandler and Nagera, 1963, p. 180). Repressed preconscious fantasies can be distinguished from other forms of ideational content which have an instinctual cathexis. Incidentally, it should be noted that distinctions between *Pcs.* and *Ucs.* systems are rarely made by Kleinians.

I hope these comments on fantasy give some indication of the kind of conceptual clarity which has, from the Kleinian viewpoint, to be surrendered in favor of Susan Isaacs's portmanteau term. But there is one further aspect of the Kleinian view of fantasy which must be touched on; namely, its relationship to defense activity. To get this in perspective, a word must first be said about the classical view of defense. As indicated, drives cathect mental representatives, and these have further derivatives. Where entrance into the *Pcs.* is denied, organized systems of anticathexis oppose the derivative, since the latter has the pressure of instinct behind it. These systems of anticathexis form an important part of defense activity and use energies derived from the ego. To describe the defenses in detail would involve further consideration of mental representations: for example, we could not discuss projection without considering the ways in which the object representation and self representation are modified in the process. But the point to be established is this. The Kleinian view of defense is necessarily different from the Freudian one because internal representations of objects and self in relation to one another are not accepted, and because the whole theory of ego cathexes and anticathexis, with its concept of ego energies, has no place in Klein's schema. Segal recently confirmed this in discussion, and added that, in the Kleinian view, all mental energy is and remains instinctual.

The classical view of defense is therefore replaced by a concept of *processes* which are considered to be quite inseparable from *concomitant fantasy*. The concept of the id and ego defenses against it (a concept at the heart of the Freudian theory of conflict) gives way to a concept of fantasy operating against fantasy—or would do so if followed to its logical conclusion (Kernberg, 1969). This would iron out all mental content and make the concept of conflict irrelevant. Nevertheless, it must be repeated that Klein *did* introduce a *new* theory of conflict—the concept of the constant fight between the life instinct on the one hand and the death instinct on the other. Since these drives are said to be detectable only through their representative fantasies, however, we have not moved very much further forward. Fantasy still fights fantasy.

A few additional comments on the Kleinian concept of defense seem called for. A thorough critique would have to explore the concepts of projection, introjection, splitting, projective identification, idealization, disintegration, and the manic defenses, to say no more. What impresses me about these defenses is that they rarely seem to work. No sooner has one dealt with an internal persecutor by, say, projection, than one is persecuted by it from outside. In saying this, I am not trying to score a debating point, but wish to draw attention to the fact that the term "defense" cannot be understood by Klein in the sense in which Freud used it. I think we should look to the Kleinians themselves for clarification on this point. On the whole, their view seems to indicate that preponderance of "good" experience over "bad" is more important in maintaining some degree of internal harmony than successful "defense" in the Freudian sense.

It should not be thought that the use of the same terms by Kleinians and other analysts in discussing defenses implies any closer agreement. Projection is a case in point. While the majority of analysts understand projection in terms of an impulse externalized onto an object and then experienced as if it were directed against the self, the position is complicated for the Kleinians by their failure to distinguish between externalization and the classical view of projection, and by their belief that an instinct cannot operate without an associated fantasy. In any case, the concept of projective identification seems more important in practice than the concept of projection.

A few words need to be said about the Kleinian instinct theory. This preserves the Freudian duality of instinct; but the primary destructive or aggressive instinct is conceptualized in terms of the death instinct, though this latter term did not appear in Klein's writings until 12 years after Freud first introduced it in *Beyond the Pleasure Principle* (1920). It is sometimes said that this is no longer much of an issue, but it was evidently important to Klein both for her "depressive position" and her "paranoid-schizoid position." Insofar as it may remain an issue (and in practice I think it does), it is important to emphasize that the "death instinct" is not a psychological concept, but a biological one, or, perhaps more correctly, a philosophical speculation. Freud (1920) introduced it as "often far-fetched . . . , which the reader will consider or dismiss according to his individual predilection" (p. 24). It is certainly not a *clinical* concept. What we observe in clinical practice are the vagaries of *aggression*. Clinically, none of us has any doubt of the importance of aggressive instincts since we see them constantly at work. By contrast, the death instinct was thought of as operating silently and was therefore undetectable, a point which Freud repeatedly emphasized.

It is of some interest to note that the Kleinian concept of envy, introduced during the third stage of Klein's thinking, rivals the death instinct in importance since it is described as such a powerful and motivating force *from the very beginning of life* that it has all the status of a drive and can no longer be considered an affect in any conventional sense. This seems an unavoidable conclusion from the discussion of the concept in *Envy and Gratitude* (1957).

Perhaps the most fundamental change in Kleinian instinct theory concerns the concept of phase development. Freudian theory has always allowed that phases overlap, that residues of earlier phases are found in later ones, and that regression is easily set in train; indeed, in many respects, regression in children is an everyday phenomenon, as at bedtime. But what is cardinal in psychoanalytic theory is the concept of phase dominance. Furthermore, the concept of an instinct as a psychical force which originates somewhere in the hinterland between soma and psyche does not do away with Freud's conviction that links must somewhere exist with a somatic source; nor does it do away with the notion that such a source confers on each part instinct whatever quality it may possess. The concept of erotogenic zones is still vital to instinct theory. As far as I know, this aspect of psychoanalysis is nowhere specifically abandoned by Klein, but its importance is greatly diminished by putting the phases closer and closer together. Thus in the very first months of life the infant, in fantasy, attacks, first the breast, and later the mother's body, with teeth, nails, excrement, urine, and every sadistic weapon at his command.

The genital phase also begins very early, and knowledge of the genitals is said to be there from the first. The early oedipus complex is so closely tied to the "depressive position" that it must be assumed to have its roots in the second quarter of the first year. This telescoping of phase development is justified on the grounds that the analysis of children of 2 years upward makes such assumptions incontrovertible. Kleinian child observation is also adduced in support. It has already been mentioned that other fundamental changes in Freudian theory have been made—for example, the repudiation of a phallic phase in girls; while even in boys, the phallic phase is consistently called a genital one.

It seems likely that, when Melanie Klein started to elaborate her concept of a "depressive position," instinctual phases became of less interest to her. The stage for this was already set, in the first phase of her thinking, when she postulated a point at which in-fantile sadism of all kind was at its height; and, well before she had postulated a depressive position, this point was advanced to the middle of the first year of life. It is also probable that, to begin with, Klein did not intend to overthrow the existing concept of phase sequences, but rather wanted to show that each phase had earlier roots than had so far been contemplated. If matters had remained there, the outcome might have been rather different; but since new findings (or assertions) take the lion's share of the inter-est, the older formulations rapidly become vestigial.

One casualty of this process is the concept of fixation; the re-lated concept of regression likewise undergoes a sweeping change. Both these concepts are related to the concept of phase develop-ment. It is of some interest that Klein, even in the 1920s, used the term "fixation" in a variety of senses—for example, she speaks of fixation of affects, sexual-symbolic fixation, and so forth. In the third phase of her thinking, regression can be only to the paranoid-schizoid or to the depressive position, which in any case hold the central places in pathology as well as in normal development. (Indeed, she asserted that the depressive position is *never* fully resolved.) Regression is understood as coming about at a point where the libido fails to overcome and master the death instinct. Factors which in classical theory tend to bring about regression to an earlier phase no longer hold, which means that *inter alia* the Freudian theory of symptom formation goes by the board. Few Kleinians would, today, dispute this. As for fixation, it was always the psychoanalytic view that various factors could predispose to this: overindulgence, deprivation, constitutional factors, and so forth. These last might still be important in Kleinian theory, and the role allotted to good and bad experiences might conceivably stem from a similar framework; but if so, this is minimized, in my view, by the enormous importance given to "fantasy" as well as the question of phase contraction. Fixation can now be considered only in terms of "positions."

I turn now to some related problems, though space permits no more than the scantiest references. A study of Klein's paper on anxiety and guilt (1948) shows that she largely ignores Freud's second theory of anxiety (signal anxiety), in spite of reference to it. She also condenses all of Freud's basic danger situations, so that, in effect, these become the dangers of the paranoid-schizoid and depressive positions. All anxiety is depressive or persecutory. Anxiety, in Klein's view, is directly derived from the death instinct: as she puts it, "anxiety is aroused by the danger which threatens the organism from the death instinct" (p. 116).

As for guilt, Melanie Klein does not commit herself whether this is an element in depressive anxiety. In my view it would not be logical for it to be otherwise, but Klein is content to say that, "I would suggest that depressive anxiety, guilt and the reparative urge are often experienced simultaneously" (p. 120).

This formulation of anxiety underlines further important problems. Why, in the Kleinian view, is there never any fear of the libido? It is of course a fundamental postulate of the Kleinian standpoint that everything about the libido is life-giving and good, and everything about the death instinct dangerous, destructive, and bad. This is not the way Freud saw it. Anxiety as a danger signal could be called forth by any basic *danger situation*. Of these, one of the most important was the danger of castration. This was considered to be particularly important in relation to the oedipus complex and the oedipal masturbatory fantasies (in the boy). In Klein's formulations this seems to have been radically modified. No longer is there anxiety in relation to libidinal incestuous impulses or erotic drives as such, except via concomitant aggressive wishes, and these have themselves been modified in the new schema. Fear of aim-inhibited impulses, fear of love and tenderness, so often a feature of non-Kleinian analyses, no longer seems of any importance. Likewise, such concepts as the erotization of anxiety no longer exist. Incidentally, it may be added that the range of affects considered by the Kleinians seems uncommonly restricted.

It is worth noting that, in the Kleinian view of sexual development in children, the shift to heterosexuality and full oedipal love springs from the wish to make reparation. There appears no indication that fantasied oedipal satisfactions result from direct sexual wishes as such. It is difficult to avoid the conclusion that, for all the stress on the life instinct, the libido in Freud's sense (and therefore sexuality) is greatly diminished in prominence. If this is so, the implications for libido theory of these particular formulations require further study.

I hope I have said enough to indicate that a thorough and comprehensive critique of the Kleinian viewpoint would have a lot of ground to cover. In particular, it would need to follow the fate of metapsychology in Klein's work. If it is believed that metapsychology is neither more nor less than the language of psychoanalytic theory, there is much to be accounted for. Metapsychology is simply the description of mental events from the dynamic, economic, structural, topographic, and developmental points of view. In Klein's work all these viewpoints have undergone radical changes.

The topographic point of view has vanished altogether, and the economic point of view survives only in the quantitative question of the predominance of one instinct over another. With the changed meaning of the term "ego" the structural viewpoint loses its original clarity. The developmental point of view is, to my mind, entirely recast. To this must be added the fact that the Freudian theory of symptom formation has been replaced by a totally different theory in which the boundaries between normality and pathology are obscured, with so-called psychotic "positions" playing the predominant part in each and every case.

If I have said little about the early dating of psychic events as such, this is not because I feel this is unimportant. Indeed, the question comes into its own when we ask ourselves how far Klein's formulations are compatible with the findings of other sciences, particularly neuroanatomy and neurophysiology. This question was raised by Augusta Bonnard many years ago in an unpublished paper read to the British Society, while Brenner (1968), in his Presidential address to the American Society, gave an unequivocal and negative answer. But on the whole it seems advisable to leave, in the present outline, the further discussion of divergencies which are very well known; I want to refer only to a comment made by W. H. Gillespie during a discussion of a Kleinian paper. Why is the origin of the ego fixed arbitrarily at the time of birth? Is it not logical to go even further, as one South American has done, and fix it at the time of conception?

Differences in Technique

The important question remains: why do such wide theoretical differences persist in spite of frequent exchanges of opinion and discussion? Part of the answer must surely lie in clinical practice and technique, including the perpetuation of these techniques through the analysis of candidates. In this connection, only a very few points may be mentioned.

One of the major differences, in both adults and children, concerns defense interpretation. Since the classical view is that an impulse cannot be made conscious before the defenses against it are accessible, defense interpretation tends to precede that of id content and its various derivatives. In general such an analysis works at the most accessible derivatives and defenses against them, gradually deepening the work as treatment progresses. On the other hand, the Kleinians do not appear concerned with defense interpretation as such—a logical conclusion if their theoretical premises are granted. The alleged *fantasy content* of a defense in the Kleinian sense is often interpreted; while what Freudians would call id content is always interpreted directly. This is true with both children and adults.

Symbol translation appears to play a very large part in Kleinian analysis. The examples given from Dick's early session are entirely typical; and readers of the much more recent *Narrative of a Child Analysis* (1961) can see for themselves what an enormous part it has continued to play. It is also clear, as Klein frequently pointed out, that play is regarded as the equivalent of free association. Readers of her early papers will also discover that Klein regarded play as analogous with the dream. Even if anomalies of this kind are overlooked (that the dream is synonymous with free association), and even if play *is* the child's form of free association, such communications are rarely followed in a way which is at all comparable with classical technique. Incidentally, symbol translation also plays a large part in the Kleinian analysis of adults.

In my view, free association is discouraged in adult analysis by constant intervention and by so-called "deep" interpretations. Such a technique by-passes instinctual derivatives and is based on the assumption that the unconscious is immediately and directly accessible. This is an important technical consequence of an impaired conceptual distinction between preconscious and unconscious content, and is at odds with the more generally accepted view. Interpretations often appear to stem from theoretical assumptions rather than from the patient's material.

The question of transference is a vexing one. All analysts try to be sensitive to transference and to use it as a technical tool in their clinical practice. But they also distinguish between different *forms* of transference—for example, spontaneous transference and transference neurosis. The Kleinian view is that a transference neurosis (or psychosis) is, in all cases, there from the beginning and is to be found in all child analyses. Yet, there cannot be a transference neurosis if the case is not a neurotic one. But since the Kleinian view of neurosis is so radically changed from the Freudian, such a point can scarcely be expected to carry any very great weight. Incidentally, reality factors often appear to be somewhat neglected, and such problems as forming a treatment alliance, whether in adults or children, rarely receive much attention.

Lastly, the possibility that the Kleinian patient learns a special language from the analyst, of rather a concrete kind, has been stressed by many, most recently by Michael Balint (1968). A much more detailed examination of all these technical questions is urgently required.

Conclusion

The question is bound to be asked: why give consideration to yet a further critique of the Kleinian school when there already exists a literature which includes papers by Waelder (1936), Glover (1945), Bibring (1947), Brierley (1951), Zetzel (1953, 1956a, 1956b), and, most recently, Otto Kernberg (1969)? Personally, I find Glover's criticisms very telling, but he carries less weight than he deserves in view of his former involvement in some of the bitter and acrimonious disputes of the '40s. Furthermore, the paranoid-schizoid position had not then been elaborated. Some of the other papers, valuable though they are, also concern only the earlier Kleinian views and need updating. In my opinion, neither Zetzel nor Brierley go far enough in their criticisms and tend to invite a compromise which could result in the sacrifice of important Freudian concepts. Lastly, Kernberg's paper, for all its detailed work and survey of the literature, is not to my mind satisfactory. It indicates the possibility of a greater degree of rapprochement than seems either likely or desirable; it credits the Kleinian school with contributions to theory and technique which are doubtful, to say the least; and it persists in calling itself an "ego-psychological" critique for reasons which seem to me baffling.

I think the time has come for a really thoroughgoing examination of the Kleinian literature, its theory and its practice, and for a very careful and detailed comparison with the Freudian view. Many contributions to such a study may already exist—for example, Joffe's excellent paper on envy (1969)—and others could soon be added.[1] I suspect that we would then be able to answer, with conviction, the questions put forward in the introduction to this paper, and to establish a firm foundation for the view that the two approaches have little in common beyond one or two technical parameters and a language which serves only to blur some very important distinctions.

BIBLIOGRAPHY

BALINT, M. (1968), *The Basic Fault: Therapeutic Aspects of Regression.* London: Tavistock.

BIBRING, E. (1947), The So-Called English School of Psychoanalysis. *Psychoanal. Quart.,* 16:69–93.

BRENNER, C. (1968), Psychoanalysis and Science. *J. Amer. Psychoanal. Assn.,* 16:675–696.

BRIERLEY, M. (1951), *Trends in Psycho-Analysis.* London: Hogarth Press.

FREUD, S. (1909), Analysis of a Phobia in a Five-Year-Old Boy. *Standard Edition,* 10:153–318. London: Hogarth Press, 1955.

— (1911), Formulations on the Two Principles of Mental Functioning. *Standard Edition,* 12:213–226. London: Hogarth Press, 1958.

[1] Since the above was written, a study group has been formed at the Hampstead Child-Therapy Course and Clinic, where this paper was first read, to foster these aims.

— (1920), Beyond the Pleasure Principle. *Standard Edition*, 8:7–64. London: Hogarth Press, 1955.

— (1923), The Ego and the Id. *Standard Edition*, 19:3–66. London: Hogarth Press, 1961.

GLOVER, E. (1945), Examination of the Klein System of Child Psychology. *This Annual*, 1:75–118.

ISAACS, S. (1948), The Nature and Function of Phantasy. In: *Developments in Psycho-Analysis*, ed. J. Riviere. London: Hogarth Press, 1952, pp. 67–121.

JOFFE, W. G. (1969), A Critical Review of the Status of the Envy Concept. *Int. J. Psycho-Anal.*, 50:533–545.

KERNBERG, O. F. (1969), A Contribution to the Ego-Psychological Critique of the Kleinian School. *Int. J. Psycho-Anal.*, 50:317–333.

KLEIN, M. (1921), The Development of a Child. *Contributions to Psycho-Analysis*. London: *Hogarth Press*, 1948, pp. 13–67.

— (1923a), The Role of the School in the Libidinal Development of the Child. *Ibid.*, pp. 68–86.

— (1923b), Infant Analysis. *Ibid.*, pp. 87–116.

— (1926), The Psychological Principles of Infant Analysis. *Ibid.*, pp. 140–151.

— (1927a), Symposium on Child Analysis. *Ibid.*, pp. 152–184.

— (1927b), Criminal Tendencies in Normal Children. *Ibid.*, pp. 185–201.

— (1928), Early Stages of the Oedipus Conflict. *Ibid.*, pp. 202–214.

— (1929a), Personification in the Play of Children. *Ibid.*, pp. 215–226.

— (1929b), Infantile Anxiety-Situations Reflected in a Work of Art and in the Creative Impulse. *Ibid.*, pp. 227–235.

— (1930), The Importance of Symbol-Formation in the Development of the Ego. *Ibid.*, pp. 236–250.

— (1931), A Contribution to the Theory of Intellectual Inhibition. *Ibid.*, pp. 254–266.

— (1932), *The Psycho-Analysis of Children*. London: Hogarth Press.

— (1934), A Contribution to the Psychogenesis of Manic-Depressive States. *Contributions to Psycho-Analysis*. London: Hogarth Press, 1948, pp. 282–310.

— (1940), Mourning and Its Relation to Manic-Depressive States. *Ibid.*, pp. 311–338.

— (1945), The Oedipus Complex in the Light of Early Anxieties. *Ibid.*, pp. 339–390.

— (1946), Notes on Some Schizoid Mechanisms. In: *Developments in Psycho-Analysis*, ed. J. Riviere. London: Hogarth Press, 1952, pp. 292–320.

— (1948), A Contribution to the Theory of Anxiety and Guilt. *Int. J. Psycho-Anal.*, 29:114–123.

— (1952a), Some Theoretical Conclusions Regarding the Emotional Life of the Infant. In: *Developments in Psycho-Analysis*, ed. J. Riviere. London: Hogarth Press, pp. 198–236.

— (1952b), On Observing the Behaviour of Young Infants. *Ibid.*, pp. 237–270.

— (1955), The Psychoanalytic Play Technique. *Amer. J. Orthopsychiat.*, 25: 223–237.

— (1957), *Envy and Gratitude: A Study of Unconscious Sources.* London: Tavistock; New York: Basic Books.

— (1959), Our Adult World and Its Roots in Infancy. *Human Relations,* Vol. 12, No. 4.

— (1961), *Narrative of a Child Analysis.* London: Hogarth Press; New York: Basic Books.

— HEIMANN, P., ISAACS, S., & RIVIERE, J. (1952), *Developments in Psycho-Analysis,* ed. J. Riviere. London: Hogarth Press.

RIVIERE, J. (1952), General Introduction to: *Developments in Psycho-Analysis.* London: Hogarth Press, pp. 1–36.

SANDLER, J. & NAGERA, H. (1963), Aspects of the Metapsychology of Fantasy. *This Annual,* 18:159–194.

SEGAL, H. (1964), *Introduction to the Work of Melanie Klein.* London: Heinemann.

WAELDER, R. (1936), The Problem of the Genesis of Psychical Conflict in Earliest Infancy. *Int. J. Psycho-Anal.*, 18:406–473, 1937.

ZETZEL, E. R. (1953), "The Depressive Position." In: *Affective Disorders,* ed. P. Greenacre. New York: International Universities Press, pp. 84–116.

— (1956a), An Approach to the Relation between Concept and Content in Psychoanalytic Theory: With Special Reference to the Work of Melanie Klein and Her Followers. *This Annual,* 11:99–121.

— (1956b), Current Concepts of Transference. *Int. J. Psycho-Anal.*, 37:369–376.

ASPECTS OF NORMAL

AND PATHOLOGICAL

DEVELOPMENT

Notes on Some Imaginary Companions

SHELDON BACH, PH.D.

SEVERAL YEARS AGO I HAD OCCASION TO OBSERVE TWO TODDLERS who invented an imaginary companion that grew, briefly flourished, and eventually was completely forgotten. The subsequent development of the children suggested that this had been a normal developmental fantasy used to cope with certain difficulties of the anal stage, and that it had some special relationship to the formation of gender identity.

Intrigued by this observation, I later came across two female patients who, even as adults, retained vivid memories of their childhood companions. In these cases, where a distinctly deviant development had brought the women to analysis, the companion

From the Division of Psychiatry, Montefiore Hospital and Medical Center and Albert Einstein College of Medicine.

had been neither forgotten nor internalized, and it proved to be the focal point of problems with accepting the feminine identity.

In both normal and pathological development the fantasy companion appeared as an element in the displacement series of nipple-feces-penis-child, and its survival or disappearance seemed related to how successfully this series was integrated.

Thus, in the two analyzed cases, one of the major problems for these women was how to be actively feminine. Because unresolved conflicts with the preoedipal mother had been displaced onto the father, they experienced unusual difficulties in solving the oedipus complex with the father and in accepting the feminine identity. These issues presented themselves on one level as a conflict around the fantasy of introjecting the paternal phallus. In both cases the imaginary companion came to represent an envied and idealized phallus, and was used defensively to perpetuate a regressive, narcissistic solution of the oedipus conflict. Before elaborating on this further, I would like to turn to some clinical material.

Doodoo: An Imaginary Companion

A brother and sister, aged 2 years and 3 years 4 months, created an imaginary companion named Doodoo. Although Doodoo originated in the children's private play, he soon began to appear in the presence of adults where he indulged in merry pranks like those of Eulenspiegel. He defied authority, righted wrongs, and was held responsible for every breach of regulations, for whenever something happened in the nursery that might incur censure, the children would respond to the habitual "Who did that?" by blandly maintaining that "Doodoo did it!"

For each infraction Doodoo was harshly punished by the children, in mock-serious and all-too-faithful imitation of their elders, but while lip service was given to his naughtiness, it was also abundantly clear that he was the object of considerable admiration.

A description of Doodoo, obtained from both youngsters, ran as follows: Doodoo is a boy who is very dirty and very bad. He is about two to five inches long, although he grows bigger when he eats carrots and meat and vegetables. At this point the connection with the scybalum was spontaneously made by the children, for whom "doodoo" was a distinct, though infrequently used, nursery word for bowel movement. It seemed that Doodoo had originated with the younger sibling, who at that time was in the throes of toilet training.

Doodoo's fortunes fluctuated with the ebb and flow of nursery discipline until, about a year later, he was joined by an imaginary sibling named Good Doodoo. It appeared that the elder sister had originated this new addition and that a surprising metamorphosis had taken place in the process. For the sister, Good Doodoo had become a neat, obedient, and very intelligent little girl, dressed in a pinafore that resembled a man's shirt. For the brother, on the other hand, Good Doodoo remained a boy, but purged in this reincarnation of the dirtier and more refractory aspects of his predecessor while still retaining his heroic qualities. Thus, Good Doodoo could climb fences and do amazing gymnastic feats, surpassing even the father in his daring, ingenuity, and prowess. And so the two Doodoos coexisted for a while, but less and less was heard from them as the children came of school age until, finally, the Doodoos vanished completely from memory.

This observation raises a number of interesting questions about the function of the companion, the different aspects it assumes for the two sexes, its subsequent fate, and the significance of its shared development. We may presume that when two people share a fantasy or transitional object, they are brought together by a shared unconscious wish and that the fantasy is a resolution of the wish and its prohibition, a resolution which they might not have been able to achieve or to enjoy separately (Sachs, 1942).

This little girl had reacted to the birth of her younger brother with a remarkable lack of rivalry and had handled her jealousy by sharing with her mother in the care of the new baby. The advent of the oedipal conflict, coupled with the brother's growing independence, may have threatened a revival of hostile feelings toward sibling and mother, feelings which the brother, engaged in his own struggle for autonomy, might share.

We might suppose that for both children Doodoo represented some prohibited expression of hostility toward the mother as well as an attempted solution of the sibling conflict by turning the rival into a partner and making an anal baby, as the fantasied grownups did. The significance of this for the little girl in particular will be discussed later. But for both children it would mean a shared alleviation of guilt and a fantasied or "artistic" resolution of a problem of omnipotence and control.[1]

Doodoo, of course, had made his appearance around the time of the 2-year-old brother's toilet training. This suggests that we may be dealing with a primitive ego-ideal precursor from the anal stage, formed around the nucleus of a prohibited and projected anal-sadistic impulse (Sperling, 1954). It is interesting to note that Doodoo, who originates as a split-off fragment of omnipotence in response to parental restrictions, begins in the course of his development to assume the realistic aspects of mastery associated with the anal phase. We seem to be witnessing a two-stage process, in the first of which the child says: "Maybe I can't mess and disobey, but Doodoo can." In this stage the companion still has the experiential quality of the child's own projected impulse.

In the second stage the impulse seems to have been subjected to a reaction formation, with the companion assuming some of the anal and phallic prerogatives of the idealized father. Now there are direct comparisons with the father's clothing, athletic abilities, and intelligence. We might say that in the first stage Doodoo represents those activities that are forbidden, while in the second stage he represents those activities that are aspired to.

At this point the fate of the companion may be important, for he seems to be the carrier of certain anal-phallic impulses connected with mastery and symbolically linked to the paternal phallus. In the case of Doodoo these impulses may have been transformed and reintegrated by the children, for the companion soon became unnecessary and was indeed forgotten. But perhaps we can gain a better understanding of the process by looking at some material gathered from the analytic therapy of two women who maintained vivid memories of their companions well into adult life.

[1] Compare the secretly shared imaginary son in Edward Albee's *Who's Afraid of Virginia Woolf?* I am grateful to Drs. Kurt and Ruth Eissler for drawing my attention to this aspect of the material.

Robin: An Imaginary Alter Ego

Margaret, a 24-year-old woman, had the following dream early in treatment: "I dreamed I was a twin. I met my twin sister on the street. When we were born my father gave the other twin away because it was too much trouble for mother. So she had been deprived of all the material things I had, but she grew up to be far more self-reliant than I."

The patient felt this dream expressed anger at her parents for rejecting the independent part of her personality, as well as a hope that through analysis she might one day be able to find and integrate it again.

This girl had grown up in a scrupulous and restrictive Catholic environment in which hostile and sensuous feelings were strictly suppressed and women confined to a domestic role. The father was an active and successful man, but his wife had been depressed ever since the birth of Margaret's elder brother who was crippled. The mother's controlling and overly solicitous attitude toward this boy had extended to her daughter, who was confined to a playpen until she escaped and thereafter was rarely allowed to play outside the house. This confinement contributed to Margaret's guilty identification with her handicapped brother, which she experienced as an actual physical inhibition inversely proportional to her psychological distance from home.

When Margaret was born her mother became acutely depressed, and the maternal grandmother, a strong and assertive old woman, moved in to care for her daughter and took over complete responsibility for raising her grandchild. She dominated the household and developed an extremely close relationship with the little girl until she suddenly died when Margaret was 4½ years old.

The mother then turned toward her daughter with a frantic demand to be sustained. Margaret remembered feeling that she must either take care of her mother or lose her, and resenting the sudden burden of maturity this placed on her. She herself was unable to experience a grief reaction and sometime thereafter, in a kind of desperate insurance against merging and ego destruction, she invented a double named Robin.

Robin was permitted to wander in the woods and fields adjoining the house and to experience all the adventures that were forbidden to Margaret. When engaged in these adventures, the little girl *became* Robin; that is, she deliberately assumed an alter ego that completely replaced her self. Late in the evening, when the father would return to the gloomy household bringing fascinating stories of the world outside, Margaret would dress up in her best clothes and become Robin. Then she would tell her father of her own imaginary adventures in a ritual which they shared for many years.

In the analysis it became clear that the primary function of Robin was to escape from the hostile eye of the mother, who was experienced as having murderous intentions toward this other part of her. A secondary function was to enable Margaret to dress up and please her father without guilt, for the mother was still depressed and could neither take care of herself nor leave the house. To Margaret she was like an older sister, "a rival into whose hands I had fallen after grandmother died, and I felt that she wanted to destroy a part of me."

It seemed that what had occurred was a split in the ego, one part of which was identified with the crippled brother and depressed mother and was, like them, confined to the house. With grandmother alive, the little girl had apparently been able to integrate her active and passive strivings, but after the grandmother's death, the mother could tolerate only a regressive and symbiotic attachment. Then the active and aggressive impulses were projected onto Robin, whose name apparently derived from a TV show about "a woman who ran away and changed her name and wrote on the mirror with lipstick: I am Robin!"

Robin was the active, aggressive, and guilt-free ego, built on an identification with the dead grandmother and a part of Margaret that her mother seemed unable to accept. As the little girl turned toward her father, Robin also was equated with the anal child and the paternal phallus and became the carrier of Margaret's sexual and incestuous wishes. The integration of this component, that is, the introjection of the active paternal phallus, was blocked by oedipal guilt expressed as fear of penetration by men and a regressive masochistic wish to merge with the mother. An equilibrium was found in a halfway position. Margaret clung passively to her mother while hating her, and she idealized the active father while desexualizing him, meanwhile maintaining a secret life and splitting off the active identification.

Thus, unable to live in the mother's world and afraid to enter the father's, Margaret retained Robin as a kind of transitional identity. But she had not disappeared, for she played an important role in Margaret's subsequent object choice. When Margaret first came to analysis, 20 years later, she was involved in a series of unhappy affairs with two types of men, one of them clearly representing the depressed mother with whom she kept trying to merge in an attempt to "turn her on." The other men all had idealized adventuresome qualities that directly reflected the split-off part of herself, but her attempts to solve this conflict with the help of the object always foundered on the same oedipal guilt and fear of destruction that had prevented the original solution.

Crumber: An Imaginary Male Twin

A female patient, Phyllis, had from the age of 2½ developed an imaginary identical male twin named Crumber. This little girl was the child of an elderly, rigid, and withdrawn couple who had placed severe restrictions on her emotional and physical expression. In the course of a long automobile trip during which the mother had refused to stop for the child to relieve herself, Phyllis took up a matchbox and, pretending that it was a telephone, made a call to Crumber, an identical twin brother whom she invented on the spot. Crumber was "myself folded outward," the anal child, and his derivation is attested to by the physical pressures of the moment. This incident, which had never been forgotten, was corroborated by the parents.

We may note here several similarities between Crumber and Doodoo. He appears in response to an anal restriction, experienced as a narcissistic blow. He is clearly a projection of the scybalum and a preserved fragment of the shattered omnipotence. He comes to the aid of the child in distress to console her in denying her separation and helplessness, and to help in the mastery of aggressive and sadistic impulses that have been split off as too dangerous. This projection of the powerful scybalum or fecal stick tends to become phallicized and is retrospectively conceived of by the patient as "myself folded outward," an exvagination equivalent to the possession of an imaginary penis. While in some cases this may predominantly be a defense against the perception of separation or castration, the companion may also come to represent the paternal phallus conceived as a support in the struggle to confront and separate from the phallic mother.

The patient I am discussing, who came for analysis at 30 because she was unable to marry, had difficulties in relating to men that centered around her inability to separate from her rigid and controlling mother. The father was a mild, withdrawn, and passively resentful man who was insidiously dominated by his wife. Since the patient had never resolved her separation and activity conflicts with the mother, much of the aggression inherent in these conflicts had been displaced onto the father. Thus the definitive change of object from mother to father became especially difficult because the incorporation of the paternal phallus had acquired the significance of a sadistic and castrative attack that aroused considerable guilt. One of the presenting problems was frigidity; it is noteworthy that for a long time Phyllis was unable to pronounce the word "penis" aloud until the sadistic fantasies and concomitant guilt had been analyzed.

The material that follows derives from a phase of therapy during which the patient had married, borne a daughter, and was considering terminating treatment. While discussing her difficulties in separating from the therapist, she related these to her daughter, who was learning to walk and whom she tended to restrain for fear that she might fall. She remembered a dream:

> My friend Phyllis seduces me. As we are lying in bed together, I feel her testicles between my legs and then she changes into my husband.
>
> When I told this dream to my husband, for a moment I fantasied taking away his penis. My friend and I have the same name. She reminds me of Janet Leigh whom I once saw in a dance . . . as if she had a third leg. There was really someone tied behind her, tied back to back, like Siamese twins; if one

dies, then the other does. That dream reminds me of Crumber
. . . an extension of myself. Phyllis my friend and Phyllis myself, . . . a man and woman tied together like Siamese twins.
They might as well make love.

I'm leaving my mother, I'm leaving therapy, and I'm leaving
you. It's as if you were my penis that I depend on for control,
like a kangaroo balances himself with his tail. Crumber was
really an imaginary penis because in the dream the penis wasn't
there.

Crumber . . . Crumba . . . Columbia . . . my father went
to Columbia and we were brought up on Columbia songs. . . .
Rig-a-jig-jig and away we go! . . . He was a solemn man, but
when he sang these songs, he could be gay. He would hold me
on his lap and sing, Rig-a-jig-jig and away we go! Hurrah!—
and then open his legs and let me slip through. Or he would
whirl me in the air! I find I've been doing the same thing with
my daughter recently, singing the same song, but I hadn't understood why I felt so strongly.

The man has it and he entrusts it to the woman . . . he de-
posits something . . . a baby full-formed . . . a penis . . . a
crumb.

Columbia was a secret society for Dad, a separate way of life
away from home . . . dinner with his fraternity brothers. He
stopped it all when I went to college, that was the story they
told me; he gave up his Columbia so that they could afford to
send me to school. I took away his Columbia like I wanted to do
to my husband in the fantasy after the dream. Then he began
collecting coins in jars, dirty little things that we sold after he
died. . . .

I guess this is all coming up because we're in the process of
tearing away from each other.

It feels very strange to have a hidden thing like this revealed. . . .

Although the immediate reference is to the imaginary penis, in
subsequent hours it became clear that what was revealed was a
feeling of castration stemming from an experience of powerlessness in relation to the preoedipal mother. The history of this
feeling and its defensive vicissitudes seemed closely paralleled by
the development of the material in the hour. The alter ego in
the dream is a complementary narcissistic imago possessing the

imaginary penis, originally the phallic mother and later the imaginary identical twin, Crumber. Here the imaginary companion
seems to serve as a kind of transitional object in the shift from
the mother to the father, although with this patient the position
has clearly not been stabilized.

In recounting the dream to her husband, the awareness of
separation once again activated castration fears, penis envy, and
castration wishes. In reaction to this she speculated on the existence of the phallic woman and was reminded of Crumber, an
extension of herself. She concluded that Crumber was really only
an imaginary penis, which then reminded her of her father.

"Once," she seemed to say, "I believed that my father was a
creative and powerful man and that I could assimilate this power
from him through our 'romping activities.' He was going to give
me something . . . a crumb(er), a penis, a baby. . . . But I
couldn't accept it, and I felt guilty about hurting and depriving
him. Finally, I became disillusioned in him and saw his power
as anally degraded.

"If we separate now, will I tear it away from you and hurt
you? Or, if I don't steal it away from you, will I be revealed as
empty?"

Discussion

In his recent illuminating review of the phenomenon of the
imaginary companion, Nagera (1969) observes that it plays a relatively small role in the analysis of children and is often not recovered in the analysis of adults. He says:

> Perhaps the answer lies (in the case of the very young child) in
> the fact that what is important is not the content of the fantasy
> associated with the imaginary companion but the developmental
> purpose it is designed to fulfill. In this sense it has to be consid-
> ered part of a developmental process and that is not the type of
> thing that is recovered by the lifting of the infantile amnesia.
> Furthermore, what cannot be recovered has to be reconstructed,
> and there are obvious difficulties in reconstructing the early ex-
> istence of an imaginary companion. Another possible reason is

that in the analyses of adults we do not pay as much attention to this phenomenon as we should [p. 166].

I would like to suggest that in the case of Doodoo, the developmental purpose of the fantasy was fulfilled, and therefore the companion was forgotten. In the cases of Crumber and Robin the process was not as successful, and consequently the existence of the companion can be taken as an indication of maturational lag.

To begin with, in each instance the companion appears in response to a narcissistic blow, the main ingredient of which is a loss of omnipotent control over reality. With Doodoo and Crumber, the blow was an anal restriction, and the resulting companion was a projection of the omnipotent scybalum. By this means a fragment of the shattered omnipotence was preserved and used both to deny separation and helplessness and to master and contain the aggressive impulses. I also noted that in the course of development the original anal homunculus tends to become phallicized and to acquire attributes of the father imago.

In the case of Robin, the narcissistic blow was the death of the child's grandmother, the mothering figure, and the resultant threat was a regressive symbiosis with the depressed mother. To counter this, the little girl invented an active double as a kind of insurance against merging and ego destruction.

In fact, one of the most striking similarities of these three companions is that for each child they represented some vital aspect of mastery or competence, a core element of the active spontaneous self. As might be expected, this self appeared primarily under the guise of opposition to the mother and seemed to draw its support in some measure from aspects of the idealized father imago.

For we know that as differentiation from the mother advances, the child may be caught in a conflict between his growth processes, his desire to recapture the lost omnipotence of the earlier symbiosis, and his fear of a regressive engulfment. At this point the father assumes importance as an object that is cathected in accordance with the nature of the conflicts in relation to the mother.

The idealization of the father occurs in reaction to the loss of the mother and normally takes place on a more reality-oriented level.

Greenacre (1966) has stressed the importance at this time of the "romping" games commonly played with the father and the illusion they may foster in the child of being large, powerful, and active through participation with the father. One might say that the father is being asked to share his omnipotent phallus with the child, partially as a support in the struggle to separate from the archaic mother. In this respect, an imaginary companion of the type I have been discussing may be considered a kind of transitional phenomenon, for it becomes implicated in the displacement series of nipple-feces-penis-child, and should tend to disappear with the successful integration of this series through the internalization of the superego and the sexual role.

Presumably these functions were fulfilled in the case of Doodoo, for in following his vicissitudes we note that his final incarnation is a perfect ego ideal: a clean, obedient, intelligent little girl for the sister; and an active, heroic, and relatively amenable little boy for the brother. It is at this point that the need for him disappears; he becomes structuralized, as it were, and is covered by the infantile amnesia.

In the other two cases the process appears to be somewhat less successful. Here the companion can be neither completely integrated into the ego nor completely abandoned, for to abandon him would be to lose an important part of the self, while to integrate him is too conflictive and beyond the synthetic capacity at this time.

Thus the companion continues to exist in memory as an external rather than an internal object and proved, in these two cases, to be the focal point of difficulties with establishing the feminine identity.

BIBLIOGRAPHY

GREENACRE, P. (1966), Problems of Overidealization of the Analyst and of Analysis. *This Annual,* 21:193–212.

NAGERA, H. (1969), The Imaginary Companion. *This Annual*, 24:165–196.

SACHS, H. (1942), The Community of Daydreams. *The Creative Unconscious.* Cambridge: Sci-Art Publishers, pp. 11–54.

SPERLING, O. E. (1954), An Imaginary Companion, Representing a Prestage of the Superego. *This Annual*, 9:252–258.

The Baby Profile

Part II

W. ERNEST FREUD

> I learnt to restrain speculative tend-
> encies and to follow the unforgotten
> advice of my master, Charcot: to look
> at the same things again and again un-
> til they themselves begin to speak.—
> FREUD (1914, p. 22)

Introduction

IN HIS RECENT SEARCHING INQUIRY INTO THE SCIENTIFIC ACTIVITIES
of the American Psychoanalytic Association, Heinz Kohut (1970)
emphasized Anna Freud's statement that "the most important contributions which institutes can make to the maintenance of genu-

This paper is part of a study, entitled "Assessment of Pathology in Childhood,"
which is financed by the National Institute of Mental Health, Bethesda, Maryland
(N.I.M.H. Grant M-5683). The study is conducted at the Hampstead Child-
Therapy Clinic, London, where Mr. Freud is a research psychoanalyst.

The views expressed in this paper have been arrived at by the author as a result
of discussions in the Well-Baby Research Group of the Hampstead Child-Therapy
Clinic. The members of this group are: Dorothy Burlingham, Liselotte Frankl,
Anna Freud, Irene Freud, W. Ernest Freud, Hanna Kennedy, E. Model, Humberto
Nagera, Marjorie Sprince, and the Well-Baby Clinic's pediatrician, Josefine Stross.
Also collaborating on the project were Phyllis Cordell and Kerry Kelly Novick. I am
greatly indebted to all of them for their enthusiastic support and interchange of
ideas; without them the project would not have been possible.

ine psychoanalytic research is through the enhancement of the students' capacity to think metapsychologically . . . , [implying] that the secure possession of this basic mode of thinking was a crucial precondition for the preservation of psychoanalytic research as such" (p. 472f.). Fortunately for all concerned, she also provided the best systematic teaching aid for the implementation of her ideas in the form of the Metapsychological Profile (Anna Freud, 1962). From the assessment of children it was extended to the evaluation of adolescents (Laufer, 1965) and adults (Anna Freud, H. Nagera, and W. E. Freud, 1965).

The further extension of the Profile to early infancy was undertaken by the Well-Baby Research Group of the Hampstead Child-Therapy Clinic, which set itself the task of working out a *Baby Profile*. The background of this project was outlined in an earlier paper (W. E. Freud, 1967), as were the environmental sections of the Profile, now referred to as Baby Profile, Part I. This paper, Part II, attempts to complete the Baby Profile.

The design of the metapsychological sections required another thirty meetings extending over a period of nearly two years. It resulted in a paper entitled "Baby Profile II" (W. E. Freud, 1969), which consisted of the metapsychological sections, illustrated by clinical examples, with comments on the problems and difficulties encountered in the design of each section. In it I also discussed some general problems the project had raised.

In order to provide extensive clinical documentation we are now engaged in working out a series of Baby Profiles. Profile-making is, however, a time-consuming art and requires skilled observers who can work together as a team. In the meantime it seemed advisable to make the whole schema available in its present form. The term "schema" refers to both the environmental sections, I–VII (outlined by W. E. Freud, 1967) and the metapsychological sections, VIII–XV, discussed below.

As was stated earlier (W. E. Freud, 1968), the general idea of the Baby Profile is to convey a global, overall picture of an infant's personality from the impressions of one or more observers (hence the importance of an overall final summary in section XV). As on a photograph, it should at least adumbrate areas of actual and potential strength and weakness. Of necessity, the younger the infant, the more of the mother will be in view; we have tried to put this to advantage in section VII, 1 (Auxiliary Ego), where provision is made for commenting on the nature of the mother's defenses, fixation points, unresolved conflicts, and anxieties (W. E. Freud, 1967).[1]

We had originally aimed at perfecting the schema before publishing it, but it soon became apparent that revision and improvement had better be viewed in terms of ongoing rather than finite tasks.[2] This not only is in keeping with the conception of Profiles as vehicles for open-ended metapsychological research but also takes account of the special conditions pertaining to the Baby Profile, where we are frequently dealing with manifestations at the point of emergence from biological and physiological into psychological phenomenology.

Opinions were divided on whether one single schema would suffice to do justice to the profusion and complexity of the many ongoing changes that occur during the first 12 to 18 months of life[3] or whether a number of different schemas should be devised to take account of chronological diversity. Be that as it may, the overriding need was for a method that could, in a preverbal setting, simultaneously view manifestations from an observational and from a conceptual point of view. Many of the phenomena confronting us are due to internal stimuli that cannot be observed and must therefore be inferred. Normally we can see what is there, but if we look closer and receive some help, we can see more; and here Sigmund Freud's simile is relevant: "a student who is looking through a microscope for the first time is instructed by his teacher as to what he will see; otherwise he does not see it at all, though it is there and visible" (1916–1917, p. 437). One of the aims of the Baby Profile is to achieve just that—to point to facets and manifestations of early development which might other-

---

[1] Such assessment of the mother's personality (or, for that matter, of the father's) can of course be supplemented with the aid of the Adult Profile (Anna Freud et al., 1965).

[2] It is understood that categories should not be multiplied beyond necessity. The sequence of sections, however, may remain open to debate.

[3] At this stage we have left open the actual age range for the applicability of the Baby Profile and the specific age at which it might be preferable to begin to use the Child Profile.

wise be overlooked or escape attention (Anna Freud, 1953, p. 9).

One of the consequences of seeing more has been an increased awareness of what still remains to be understood. Those relatively uncharted areas highlighted by the Baby Profile probably merely reflect what has occupied most psychoanalytic thinkers at one time or another. There is the challenge of understanding the intricate processes of ego formation (section IX), especially the unfolding development of defenses (section IX, D). In section IX, C, on the State and Functioning of the Mental Apparatus, we have been unable to do much more than list a number of aspects that contribute to ego building and eventually will develop into ego functioning. Many representative, meaningful, and convincing clinical examples are needed to illustrate these processes and to clarify precisely when a phenomenon should cease to be regarded as a forerunner or antecedent and can be recognized as a function, however precariously established. The following example illustrates this dilemma.

Observation: Don (age 6¾ months): In the course of a well-baby clinic visit the mother (a highly intelligent professional woman) told us that Don had got the knack of bringing empty cardboard boxes within reach of his grasp by hitting their tops with his hands until they turned over toward him. In the bath he tried to do the same to a plastic floating duck, but there the duck floated further away. He then became very angry and hit the water. This has happened several times.

Comment: We infer that on the basis of memory Don has established a firm and reliable connection between actions performed by him leading to specific results. Should his understanding of cause and effect be regarded as a forerunner of the synthetic function, or should it be viewed as an example of integrative thinking?

Similar problems were encountered in other areas, e.g., aggression (VIII, C, 2). For purposes of mental health the directional aspect seems the most important one, but can one speak of direction inward or outward before a distinction between the two has been established? The implications of too much inward-directed aggression are far-reaching. The primitive fear of one's own aggressive impulses forms the basis for a cruel superego in the adult, who as a result may be crippled by self-punitive tendencies that may also interfere with analytic treatment (Lampl-de Groot, 1967). When, how, and why are quantities of aggression, which should find an outlet toward the object world, deflected and directed toward the body (section VIII, C, 2, a, ii), and at what age does an infant stop responding primarily with his body and begin to respond with changes of mood and his mind? Many other areas of uncertainty could be cited.

We believe that systematic, metapsychologically sophisticated infant observation holds the key to a deeper understanding of many of the unsolved problems, although we realize that some of these and other questions can in the last resort be answered only through *longitudinal* studies. But precisely because of these considerations the Baby Profile is tremendously important in that it records a baseline of observations in a systematic schema that can be linked to comparable psychological tools designed for later ages, even though the "docking device" with the Child Profile may not yet have clicked perfectly into place. With the addition of the Baby Profile to the already existing Child, Adolescent, and Adult Profiles, we now have a continuous series of metapsychological instruments which permit, on the one hand, overall monitoring of unfolding development from the very beginning of life and, on the other, retrospective assessment of observational data.[4] It is obvious that the systematic correlation of manifestations from earliest infancy with those encountered in the later stages of development and in adulthood should yield rich findings, the implications of which for prediction, prophylaxis, and therapy need not be elaborated.

While the detailing of these correlations will have to await the outcome of further research, the short-term applications of the Baby Profile have already shown a number of welcome and encouraging results. As a teaching aid the schema has decisively influenced both the orientation and the organization of our infant observations, which in turn enhanced the quality of Baby Profiles

---

[4] We have not overlooked that adequate validation and verification of these metapsychological tools may have to await the completion of a sufficient number of representative longitudinal studies.

that are currently being discussed. The comprehensiveness of the schema has affected the observations of normal, disturbed, and handicapped (blind) babies in their homes as well as in the Well-Baby Clinic. The schema attracted the interest of other research groups of the Clinic similarly engaged in work with very young infants, such as the Blind Group and the Borderline Group.

In addition to monitoring normal development, the Baby Profile is ideally suited for the earliest spotting of incipient pathology, an area with enormous research possibilities (E. Kris, 1950, 1951). By explicitly drawing attention to the many aspects that can be involved in a disturbance, the schema has proved no less useful in helping to sort out transient difficulties (e.g., in the areas of feeding and sleep, and of providing optimal conditions for speech development). In addition, it has led to more sophisticated formulations of predictions (cf. M. Kris, 1957). It is probably fair to say that the availability of the Baby Profile has subtly revolutionized the way in which we ask questions, which in turn has had a beneficial influence on our research work.

The Baby Profile has facilitated the quest for much more detailed knowledge about the infinitesimal and scarcely perceptible developmental sequences, which should in time lead to a refinement of our thinking on "critical" phases, so that optimal states of readiness for inevitable events, such as weaning, can be pinpointed more easily and matched with optimal timing of intervention. Conversely, and even more important, the application of the Baby Profile has spotlighted phases of minimal readiness when interference must at all cost be avoided.

Furthermore, the Baby Profile offers the prospect of more accurately dating when certain manifestations first emerge in different infants, thus highlighting the wide range of variations in individual differences. It should also teach us more about the development of affects, as the following observation of an infant (12 days old) illustrates.

During a pause in the breast feeding, the mother sat the baby girl up, facing her, and spoke to her in a very soft sing-song voice, smiling at her, and saying, "Is that good, is that what you want? Ye-es, ye-es," and as she crooned the word, the baby seemed to mimic her with a head movement and mouth movements of her own, never taking her eyes off her mother's. (Soon after she had a bowel movement.)

There is much that the Baby Profile can help us understand about the so-called prognostic pointers (section XIV), to find out how reliable and how phase-specific they are. How early and in which form can they be picked up, and under what conditions are they liable to change?

Lastly, enlarging on any section of the Baby Profile will lead to an increase in knowledge, as is currently experienced through more extensive work on the auxiliary ego (section VII) and on The Infant's Reaction to His Perception of Other People's Affective State (section X, F).

In summary, our experiences with the schema have proved it to be unique as a teaching aid and invaluable for organizing infant observations in a systematic way. Even if it cannot be expected to answer all questions, it is usually instrumental in helping one see problems in better perspective. It is an ideal foundation for longitudinal studies and has brought welcome results in short-term applications. It should remain open to revision and modification.

If science can be thought of as a method by which we are leap-frogging into new discoveries, then the Baby Profile is offered as one more stepping stone into the unknown.

Baby Profile

Part I

The headings forming Part I of the Profile were described in detail by W. E. Freud (1967, pp. 222–238).

I. REASON AND CIRCUMSTANCES FOR APPROACHING WELL-BABY CLINIC

II. DESCRIPTION OF PARENTS OR PARENT SUBSTITUTES

III. DESCRIPTION OF THE INFANT

IV. FAMILY BACKGROUND (PAST AND PRESENT)

V. BEFORE BIRTH—MOTHER

Physical (conception and pregnancy)
Psychological (anxieties, expectations, aspirations)

VI. HISTORY OF BIRTH (PHYSICAL AND EMOTIONAL) —THE NEWBORN PERIOD UP TO 6 WEEKS (PEDIATRICIAN'S IMPRESSION)

Details of labor and birth
Separation of the baby from the mother after delivery
Father's behavior

VII. PRESENT ENVIRONMENTAL CIRCUMSTANCES AND MANAGEMENT

In the areas of feeding, cleanliness, comfort, motility, positioning, general contact, sound contact, smiling contact—fostering pleasure or unpleasure

> *Note:* Some aspects of management should be evaluated in greater detail in the context of the Mother-Infant Interaction during Feedings (VIII, A, 2, c).

1. AUXILIARY EGO—Assessment of Mother's *manifest* responses to the baby

2. AUXILIARY EGO—Assessment of Mother's *latent* attitudes

Part II

VIII. ASSESSMENTS OF DEVELOPMENT

(Assessments at time of observation. Note changes in relation to earlier observations.)

A. BODY NEEDS AND FUNCTIONS

1. SLEEP

Sleeping arrangements (location, clothing)
Favorite sleeping position

Sleeping pattern (length, quality, and times of sleep)—note age-adequateness or otherwise

Falling asleep (peaceful, restless, difficulties)

Waking from sleep (e.g., peaceful, grizzly, etc.)—note especially behavior after waking up in the morning

Vulnerability of sleep (state reasons, if possible)

Parents' attitude(s) toward sleep

2. FEEDING

(a) *Mother*

Physical condition (breasts, nipples, difference between breasts)

Attitude to feeding (manifest and latent)

Physical and mental complications, as they might affect feeding before, during, and after delivery

Food Supply

Breast milk—supply (sufficient or otherwise)

Formula—specify

Mixed feeding—specify

Demand feeding vs. schedule feeding—state approximate times

Reasons for delay in feeding (was it avoidable or unavoidable?)

Underfeeding, overfeeding, forcing food against the baby's needs

Consistency or inconsistency in handling in the feeding situation

(b) *Infant*

Note reactions anticipatory to feeding, to delays, to food intake, and the age-specific changes in all of them.

Signs of Hunger or Thirst

Crying

Distress

Tension[1]

Absence of signs

---

[1] See also *Signs of Tension Reduction, Pleasure, and Unpleasure during and after the Feeding Process,* below.

Patterns of Food Intake
Sucking reflex, its history from birth
Chewing and biting, etc.
Hints at Congenital Activity Pattern[2]
Passive or active feeder
Beginnings of self-feeding
Differentiation: emerging likes and dislikes (note also the
    mother's preferences and dislikes)

Activities during Feeding
Rooting
Crying or pleasurable sounds
Eyes (on what do they focus during feeding?)
Legs
Hands and fingers
Body movements
Sucking—reaction to interference (e.g., when finger is re-
    moved)

*Signs of Tension Reduction, Pleasure, and Unpleasure
during and after the Feeding Process*[3]
In the mouth area (specify, if possible)
Relaxation—body (specify, if possible)
Sounds that convey pleasure
Note any signs of unpleasure in connection with alleviation
    of hunger or thirst

Reactions to Interruptions of Feeding
Interrelations between Feeding and Sleeping[4]
Interrelations between Feeding and Elimination[5]
*Major and Minor Interferences in the Infant's Feeding
Process*
Immaturity at birth
Deformities (e.g., cleft palate, harelip)

[2] "The Congenital Activity Type is a descriptive term, referring to the amount of activity a newborn infant shows in response to certain stimuli" (Fries and Woolf, 1953, p. 48).
[3] See also *Signs of Hunger or Thirst*, above.
[4] See also VIII, A, 1, above.
[5] See also VIII, A, 3, below.

Illness (e.g., pyloric stenosis)
Sore gums or thrush
Teething
Sucking
Biting
Wind
Vomiting
Others

(c) *Mother-Infant Interaction during Feeding*
This whole section should include observations of the ways in which mother and infant are in tune or out of tune with each other's needs and rhythms. Allowance should be made for the child's changing states of maturity.

(i) Physical
Note the manner in which the mother handles and holds the infant (comfortably or awkwardly), the amount of skin contact, and the scope for independent movement that is allowed. Note also the infant's position as regards comfort and distance from the mother as well as his reactions to being held or not held.

(ii) Psychological (Dialogue)
Note the extent to which the feeding situation is a very intimate and special occasion between mother and infant. If the feeding situation is colored by ambivalence on the mother's part, and by something like rejection of food or handling on the infant's part, note the partner's reaction.

(d) *Retrospective Assessment regarding Food Intake, and Prediction*
From your knowledge of the infant's development up to the time of observation, what do you think accounts for his present reactions in the feeding situation?
From your assessment of the present feeding situation, attempt a prediction of its effects on later development.[6]

---

[6] In this context, see M. Kris (1957).

3. ELIMINATION
Consistency
Frequency and regularity
Physical interferences
Interventions (necessary and unnecessary)
Mother's attitude (manifest and latent)

4. OTHER NEEDS
Note how the following needs are met:
   Protection against inappropriate stimuli
   Provision of adequate stimulation
   Provision of comfort and methods of comforting, holding, cud-
     dling, rocking[7]
   Stability and flexibility of routine and arrangements
   Maintenance of appropriate body temperature
   Skin contact and stimulation
   Unrestricted movement and exercise
   Needs for other physical comfort
   Other needs (not mentioned above)
Comment on the general success or failure of fulfillment of the
infant's body needs.

B. PLEASURE-UNPLEASURE INDICATIONS[8]
Note manifestations and give reasons for considering them as
either pleasurable or unpleasurable.

Examine them according to:
   Sources
   Reactions
   Intelligibility
   Overall balance or imbalance

C. DRIVE DEVELOPMENT

1. LIBIDO
   (a) *Regarding Oral Zone and Phase*

      (i) Oral excitation in the feeding process
         Sucking, biting, chewing, tasting, etc.
         Oral greed or disinterest

[7] See also VIII, A, 2, c, above.
[8] Further elaboration will be found in section X, AFFECTIVE STATES.

(ii) Pleasure sucking

Finger and/or hand sucking
  onset
  finding
  mode
  time and frequency
Tongue sucking
  first noted
  frequency
  exclusive or complementary
Other objects for sucking
  dummy, bedclothes, etc.
Related activities
  drooling
  blowing bubbles
  other mouth play
Reaction to interference with sucking

The following two sections are viewed more as a sideline to actual libidinization.

(iii) Pleasurable use of the mouth for approach, grasping, "perceiving," and exploring
Comment on the presence or absence of these manifestations, as well as on any other significant circumstances in this area.

(iv) Sound production for pleasure
Add a general comment on orality, with reference to the *intensity* and *extent* of observed manifestations (e.g., are they evenly spread, or have you noted anything excessive?).

(b) *Regarding Manifestations from Other Zones*

(i) Anal zone
Signs of anal excitation
Pleasure-unpleasure

(ii) Phallic zone
Masturbation, erections

(c) *Regarding Libido Distribution*

    (i) Prestages of self-cathexis

The notion of primary narcissism (investment of the individual's body and/or self, and/or parts of the self, with libidinal cathexis) is a theoretical concept derived from the analysis of adults. It is not easy to find evidence for it from direct observation of the infant. All that can be observed at this stage are the outward manifestations of fluctuating states having positive and negative qualities, i.e., signs of well-being, contentment, pleasure from gratification, etc., or their opposite, i.e., signs of restlessness, discomfort, unpleasure, and pain.

We assume that the preponderance of the first-named states leads to a gradually increasing investment of the body and of the emerging self with positive libido, i.e., to primary narcissism, whereas the preponderance of the latter states interferes with this outcome. Popularly, these are summarized under the headings of "happy" or "fractious" baby.

The Profile-maker should note manifestations of either category and draw conclusions from them.

    (ii) Prestages of object relationship

We assume that at the beginning of life no distinction is made between the experience of gratification and comfort and its provider, i.e., that what is cathected libidinally is the pleasurable experience as such. This would be borne out by observations that there is a stage in which most infants indiscriminately accept ministrations so long as the manner in which they are given remains the same. We call the relationship created on this basis anaclitic, i.e., a libidinal relationship based on need satisfaction.

What begins in this way as purely internal experiences within the child changes gradually into experiences occurring as interactions between the child (or parts of him) and agencies in the external world (or part of them—breast, bottle, the mother's body parts, etc.). From then onward the libidinal importance of gratifying experiences (their investment) is transferred increasingly to the person(s) who provide(s) them.

The Profile-maker should note, therefore, when and how the infant reacts to all changes—whether in the prevailing mood of the familiar caretaking person, or a change to another caretaking person, or changes in their manner of handling him and dealing with routine ministrations, or any other changes. If possible, an attempt should be made to indicate the main aspect of change to which the infant responds.

(iii) Further steps in object relatedness

We expect such precursors of object relatedness to lead in due course to constancy of object relationships. The term "constancy" has by now acquired two separate connotations: in one sense it denotes the ego's ability to maintain and retain an internal representation of the object, or part object, independently of the object's presence or absence in the external world; in the other sense it denotes the ability to retain the libidinal cathexis of this internal representation, independent of the presence or absence of needs.

Once object constancy in both senses has been achieved, the relationship to the object is not undone by temporary experiences of frustration, separation, loss, disappointment, etc., but merely changed in quality. For several years in the course of development there will be a considerable overlap between the anaclitic prestage of object love (step 1) and object-love proper (step 2). There will also be frequent regressions from the higher to the lower level.

The Profile-maker should at all times note the quality of the observed object relationship as well as its fluctuations between the two levels.

2. AGGRESSION

Description of observed manifestations is most important for this section.

(a) *Definition*

Manifestations of the discharge of aggression can appear in the service of angry or unpleasurable tendencies and affects. Although such manifestations contain a fusion of libidinal and aggressive components, we are, in this part of the Profile, focusing on aggressive aspects only.

Discharge of angry or unpleasurable affects may show itself in various ways:

(i) Nondirected:
as restlessness, sleeplessness, fractiousness, etc.

(ii) Directed toward the body:
in external self-injury (biting, scratching, pulling own hair)
in internal "psychosomatic" disturbances, such as gastrointestinal, respiratory, vascular, urinary, dermatological, neuromuscular (spasms, convulsions). The organic etiology of such disturbances has to be considered side by side with the nonorganic causes.

(iii) Directed toward the object world:
as anger, rage, or motor attack (such as biting, hitting, kicking, scratching)
where external discharge of angry or destructive affects is blocked, we should look for repercussions elsewhere.[9]

(b) *Examination of the Circumstances in Which Aggressive Manifestations Occur*

Examination of the *total* setting usually facilitates clarification of precipitating causes. The aggressive manifestations may be triggered off by tiredness, boredom, unpleasure, pain, anxiety, teasing, response to the caretaking adult, or by something else.

Where aggressive manifestations are thought to be reactions to *frustration,* evaluate the capacity to delay urgency of gratification, i.e., comment on the minimum amount of frustration or interference required to trigger off intense manifestations of aggression.

[9] Further elaboration will be found in section X, AFFECTIVE STATES.

Usually the mother, who is familiar with the infant and acquainted with the circumstances, will know with a high degree of certainty what is likely to be involved. In the Well-Baby Clinic reactions to interferences such as undressing, examination, dressing are instructive.

(c) *Study of the Range of Expressions of Aggression at the Disposal of the Infant*
Global reactions (involving the whole body) [10]
Localized and psychosomatic expressions
Vocal expressions
Mimic facial expressions[11]

(d) *Rate of Recovery from the Effect(s) of Build-up and Discharge of Aggression*
(Note any aftereffects)

IX. EGO DEVELOPMENT

A. STATE AND FUNCTIONING OF THE SENSORY APPARATUS
Visual, auditory, tactile, taste, olfactory, skin sensations, proprioceptors, kinesthetic

B. STATE AND FUNCTIONING OF THE MOTOR APPARATUS

1. REFLEX AND RANDOM

2. DIRECTED COORDINATED MOTILITY (DISTINCTION BETWEEN ID CONTROL AND EGO CONTROL)
Initially, in the absence of a functioning ego, motility appears to be exclusively under id control in the service of fulfilling body needs and id impulses. With advancing ego functioning, motility gradually comes under ego control, although this is still in the service of direct gratification of instinctual needs.
Note what aims motor activity serves.

C. STATE AND FUNCTIONING OF THE MENTAL APPARATUS
Many mental activities contribute to the emergence of the gradually unfolding ego and its adaptation to the external and internal world.

[10] See E. Kris (1939).
[11] See Darwin (1872).

Comment on the following aspects of *ego building* which eventually develop into ego functioning: perception; attention (intensity and span); exploration and responding; laying down of memory traces—recognition, thinking, memory (recognition and recall); distinction between self and nonself; reality orientation, linking up of psychic experience (forerunner of synthetic function?); forerunner of speech (babbling, comprehension), speech, etc.

D. Primitive Reactions to Unpleasure (Precursors of Defenses?)

Reactions to unpleasure foreshadow later defense. We are therefore interested in noting reactions to unpleasure from whatever source. It is difficult to discern defense activity, or even to assume its existence, before the emergence of a rudimentary ego. The baby's manner of reacting may, however, suggest or foreshadow the kind of defense he is likely to adopt in the future.

Such reactions are, e.g., protest, avoidance, withdrawal, regression, somatization, etc.

E. Forerunners of Identification

Imitation, introjection, passive into active, etc.[12]

X. AFFECTIVE STATES

In the first few weeks of life we expect to see no more than the variations of mood which reflect either pleasurable or unpleasurable states (as described in section VIII, B). Gradually these widen into discernible expressions of other affects.

What appears in the pleasure range are affects, such as contentment, serenity, joyfulness; their counterparts in the unpleasure range are anxiety, unhappiness, anger, and rage. The chronological appearance of these various affects may differ widely from infant to infant.

A. Range of Affects

Note how many different affects can be observed at each stage of development.

B. Situations in Which Affects Appear

Note which experiences of the infant give rise to an affective re-

---

[12] See also X, F.

sponse. Examples are: reactions to fulfillment or frustrations of needs and to disappointments in objects, changes of position, handling by strangers, etc.

C. AVAILABILITY OR ACCESSIBILITY OF AFFECTIVE RESPONSES

Describe whether the infant can, or cannot, experience and react with the appropriate affect in specific situations. Where applicable, note which affects are not available to the infant. Note whether affects are expressed via the body or in other ways.

D. APPROPRIATENESS OF AFFECTIVE RESPONSES

Describe whether the affective response seems appropriate in intensity to the stimulus that provokes it, i.e., whether it seems excessive or too weak. As regards quality, note whether affective responses are inappropriate, such as when joy appears where the normal reaction should be sadness, etc.

E. TRANSIENCE OR PERSISTENCE OF THE AFFECTIVE RESPONSES

Describe whether there is recovery from the affective state within a reasonable time after an affective response has been triggered off or if there is a tendency for the affect to persist and linger on excessively.

F. THE INFANT'S REACTION TO HIS PERCEPTION OF OTHER PEOPLE'S AFFECTIVE STATE

Note the infant's tendency to perceive and respond to affective states in the mother, such as happiness, impatience, worry, unhappiness, depression, anxiety, anger, etc. Note also whether such empathy extends to other people besides the mother. Consider such reactions as possible forerunners of later imitation and identification.

XI. FORERUNNERS OF FIXATION POINTS (VULNERABLE AREAS OR SPECIFIC LIBIDINIZATIONS)

In this section consider anything that can be regarded as setting up something like a greater readiness, sensitivity, or potential for vulnerability, i.e., anything that is thought to create "specially sensitized areas which may become potentially particularly fertile grounds for later fixations." [13]

[13] See W. E. Freud (1967, p. 234).

Examples may be found either in very early and persistent auto-erotic activities (sometimes carried on via a transitional object), or in physically overstimulating experiences affecting the skin, the mucous membranes, the intestines, etc. Note especially any painful illnesses in early life and nursing, medical, or surgical interventions.

XII. FORERUNNERS OF TENDENCIES TO REGRESSION

Some oscillation between forward and backward developmental moves can already be discerned at a very early age, at which time they are to be viewed as within the range of normality. Note their frequency, rate, the occasions which give rise to them (if any), and the recovery rate from regressive moves.

Note also whether an established pattern in these alternating moves can be discerned and look for changes in this.

XIII. FORERUNNERS OF CONFLICTS

In considering the very young infant we do not think in terms of either external or internal conflicts. The question of *external* conflicts does not arise before the infant has learned to distinguish between himself and the outer world. *Internal* conflicts are not expected to occur before a personality structure has been established, i.e., before the inner agencies have been separated off from each other. Nevertheless, forerunners of both types of conflict can be discerned even at these early stages.

With regard to the external world, note the manner in which the infant responds to the type of maternal care and handling to which he is subjected. We distinguish in this respect between "compliant," "determined" or "difficult" babies. Naturally, in early infancy these modes of behavior are primarily the infant's means for the expression of object relationship. Nevertheless, they allow for some speculation regarding the tendency toward peaceful acceptance of or opposition to environmental influences.

As regards the internal world, we find clashes between competing needs, such as finger sucking and feeding, simultaneous anger and rejection of the object with clinging to it, etc.

XIV. GENERAL CHARACTERISTICS, WITH SPECIAL PROGNOSTIC RELEVANCE FOR FUTURE PATHOLOGICAL OR NORMAL DEVELOPMENT

When dealing analytically with older children, we have learned to look out for certain general characteristics in their personalities which seem to be significant for their establishing, maintaining, or regaining mental health. We do not know at present whether these characteristics are inborn or acquired early in life; nor do we know whether they are open to influence either by life experience or by analytic treatment. In any case, it seems important to us, wherever they appear, to trace them back to their first appearance within the personality.

A. THE INFANT'S THRESHOLD OF TOLERANCE FOR THE FRUSTRATION OF NEEDS AND WISHES

Individual infants differ remarkably with regard to the degree to which they can tolerate frustration. What is reacted to violently by some, such as postponement of fulfillment, disappointment, is taken in stride by others. A low threshold in this respect exposes the child to greater quantities of unpleasure. This leads to increased pressure toward the immediate discharge of tension which in the long run will militate against the gradual modification and taming of instinctual drives.

B. THE INFANT'S THRESHOLD OF TOLERANCE FOR ANXIETY

Note here how easily anxiety is released and whether or not, or to which degree, the infant is devastated by the experience of anxiety. Note also the rate of recovery from any experience of anxiety; i.e., whether and for how long the anxiety state outlasts its causation. This is of specific importance with regard to later neurotic development. The more anxiety an individual produces, and the less he can tolerate, the quicker he will resort to defensive measures and symptom formation, once his ego has acquired the capacity to ward off dangers.

C. THE INFANT'S ABILITY TO ACCEPT SUBSTITUTE GRATIFICATION

While some infants cannot be satisfied except by the direct fulfillment of their unmodified wishes, others will be content with substitutes which are offered to them. This latter capacity is important because it foreshadows the individual's later *sublimation potential,* which opens up innumerable pathways for discharge, reduces unpleasure, and facilitates aim-inhibited gratification, contentment, and achievement. Where an individual does not develop beyond primitive, crude instinctual and material needs and wishes, he is exposed to increased disappointments with markedly decreased opportunity for the relief of tension.

D. BALANCE BETWEEN PROGRESSIVE AND REGRESSIVE TENDENCIES

While noting the oscillations between forward and backward developmental moves (see XII), the observer is asked to pay special attention to any imbalance between them. The child's further normal development depends to a large degree on the intactness of the progressive tendencies, i.e., on his wish and ability "to move forward and complete development." [14]

Where this force is outweighed by the clinging to early pleasures and by moving back to them whenever difficulties arise at later stages, normal growth can be severely interfered with.

XV. SUMMING UP OF THE DEVELOPMENTAL STATUS

In this final summing up of impressions convey a concise and clinically meaningful opinion which will be of use for later comparison and reference. Comment on the personality picture of the child, and on the salient features in his development, such as precocity or retardations in any directions. Also take special note of any unevenness in development. Infants may be either uniformly well developed or forward in some respects and lagging behind in others.

From your assessment attempt a prediction of later development. If applicable, include recommendations for influencing discernible traits of adverse development.

BIBLIOGRAPHY

BIBRING, E. (1937), On the Theory of the Therapeutic Results of Psycho-Analysis. *Int. J. Psycho-Anal.*, 18:170–189.
DARWIN, C. (1872), *The Expression of the Emotions in Man and Animal.* Chicago: University of Chicago Press, 1897.

[14] See E. Bibring (1937) and Anna Freud (1965).

FREUD, A. (1953), Some Remarks on Infant Observation. *This Annual*, 8:9–19.
— (1962), Assessment of Childhood Disturbances. *This Annual*, 17:149–158.
— (1965), *Normality and Pathology in Childhood*. New York: International Universities Press.
— Nagera, H., & Freud, W. E. (1965), Metapsychological Assessment of the Adult Personality: The Adult Profile. *This Annual*, 20:9–41.
FREUD, S. (1914), On the History of the Psycho-Analytic Movement. *Standard Edition*, 14:3–66. London: Hogarth Press, 1957.
— (1916–1917), Introductory Lectures on Psycho-Analysis. *Standard Edition*, 15 & 16. London: Hogarth Press, 1963.
FREUD, W. E. (1967), Assessment of Early Infancy: Problems and Considerations. *This Annual*, 22:216–238.
— (1968), Some General Reflections on the Metapsychological Profile. *Int. J. Psycho-Anal.*, 49:498–501.
— (1969), Baby Profile II. Presented at the Pre-Congress Meeting of the Well-Baby Research Group at the Hampstead Child-Therapy Clinic.
FRIES, M. E. & WOOLF, P. J. (1953), Some Hypotheses on the Role of the Congenital Activity Type in Personality Development. *This Annual*, 8:48–62.
KOHUT, H. (1970), Scientific Activities of the American Psychoanalytic Association: An Inquiry. *J. Amer. Psychoanal. Assn.*, 18:462–484.
KRIS, E. (1939), Laughter as an Expressive Process. *Psychoanalytic Explorations in Art*. New York: International Universities Press, 1952, pp. 217–239.
— (1950), Notes on the Development and on Some Current Problems of Psychoanalytic Child Psychology. *This Annual*, 5:24–46.
— (1951), Opening Remarks on Psychoanalytic Child Psychology. *This Annual*, 6:9–17.
KRIS, M. (1957), The Use of Prediction in a Longitudinal Study. *This Annual*, 12:175–189.
LAMPL-DE GROOT, J. (1967), On Obstacles Standing in the Way of Psychoanalytic Cure. *This Annual*, 22:20–35.
LAUFER, M. (1965), Assessment of Adolescent Disturbances: The Application of Anna Freud's Diagnostic Profile. *This Annual*, 20:99–123.

The Impact of Early Sexual Discovery on Mood, Defensive Organization, and Symbolization

ELEANOR GALENSON, M.D.

AND HERMAN ROIPHE, M.D.

THE GIRL WHOSE EARLY DEVELOPMENT WILL BE DESCRIBED IN THIS paper is one of a group of infants who have been studied in a research nursery established at The Albert Einstein College of Medicine. We have been engaged in an investigation of genital development during the second year of life and the interrelationship of this genital development with other areas of personality formation. We deliberately included in our infant group a number of infants who experienced certain somatic disturbances dur-

Dr. Galenson is Associate Clinical Professor of Psychiatry, and Dr. Roiphe, Assistant Clinical Professor of Psychiatry, Albert Einstein College of Medicine.

This research on early sexual development has been supported by the Department of Child Psychiatry of The Albert Einstein College of Medicine. We would like to express our indebtedness to the entire research staff whose dedicated work and rich contributions have been vital for our project, and to Mrs. Helen Vizzini for her untiring assistance in the preparation of this manuscript.

ing their first year of life. In Ruth, an infant with such an early somatic problem, we were able to observe the impact of her awareness of the genital difference in relation to several areas of her subsequent development—the establishment of a basic mood, her particular type of defensive organization, her level of play behavior and symbolization, and the quality of her developing object relations.

The contributions of Greenacre and Mahler to very early development, their theoretical formulations and clinical material, have served as the foundation upon which our own work has rested. We have selected, from the larger body of their work, a few specific statements which we consider particularly relevant to the infant we are describing.

Greenacre (1953) alluded to the effect of certain disruptive influences occurring during the first 18 months or so of life. She distinguished two groups: infants who suffered from early physical disturbances, and infants who experienced disturbances in the mother-child relationship. Greenacre stressed the interference with the developing sense of the infant's own body, the effect upon the emerging ego, and the possible consequences for later sexual development. Many of her later publications further amplified this early proposition.

Mahler (1966) described the particular vulnerability of the child during the period from about 14 to 16 months of age, a period characterized by ambivalence toward the parents and hostile dependence on them. These seem to call forth both the early pathological defense mechanism of splitting the good and bad mother images and the mechanism of turning aggression against the self.

Mahler (1966) mentioned two developmental events that take place at this age period: "I must emphasize the importance of the double trauma of toilet training and of the discovery (at a much earlier age than we have thought) of the anatomical sexual difference as contributory factors in the genesis of the propensity of girls to depressive moods. . . . [The depressive reaction] has been observed in girls definitely more often than in boys. Their anger toward and disappointment with the mother for not having given them the penis could be traced convincingly in several cases" (p. 164). We shall discuss these seminal observations in relation to the influence of such developmental events upon the establishment of mood and defensive organization.

Some details of this early period of normal sexual interest and activity as well as certain distortions in development were described by Roiphe (1968a). He proposed that this sexual interest is a normal developmental sequence which occurs sometime between the ages of 16 and 24 months. Roiphe also singled out a group of children who show castration reactions or distorted development during this period of early genital discovery, provided that they earlier had had experiences which resulted either in an unstable body schema or in an unstable mental representation of the maternal object. Such experiences included physical disturbances or poor or absent mothering.

Our research was designed to investigate and document the existence of this early phase of sexual interest and activity proposed by Roiphe. We assume that this phase begins sometime between the ages of 16 and 24 months and is characterized by certain primary behaviors, including frank masturbation and the expression of intense curiosity about the anatomical differences between the sexes, both in relation to other children and adults. Moreover, we planned to consider other changes in behavior, particularly the child's play and behavior toward the mother, which occur within the temporal context of this phase and which may be affected by this early sexual activity.

In addition to objectively verifying the occurrence of these behaviors, we proposed to document the existence of a set of mutilation anxiety reactions occurring in children who experienced, during their first year of life, a major birth defect, severe illness, surgical intervention, orthopedic corrections and immobilizations, loss of a parent, or depression or other gross emotional neglect by the mothering figure. The mutilation reactions were expected to occur in such predisposed children when they arrive at the phase of early genital awareness. They would be characterized, in boys, by verbal expression of the fear of losing the penis, and, in girls, that they already have lost the penis. Other evidences of this reaction were expected to consist of a variety of fears and aversions, hypochondria, regression in toilet training, and abrupt changes in eating or sleeping patterns.

A final hypothesis of our research design concerned the existence of a genetic continuity between some forms of early play and the nonverbal type of symbolism which characterizes musical and other artistic forms. In an earlier paper, Galenson (1971) proposed this genetic continuity, and described a type of data analysis which might be particularly suitable for demonstrating this development of complex nonverbal symbols from the primitive symbolism of the infant.

Methodology

The psychoanalytic proposition that the direction and force of instinctual pressures, the nature of mother-child relationship, and body schematization exert molding and distorting effects upon one another is by now a basic frame of reference for direct infant observational research carried out by psychoanalysts. It has been extremely difficult, however, to document the facts and details of this reciprocal interdependence from the data of direct infant observation. These data consist of a variety of observable behaviors—motoric, affective, play—from which we deduce the status of underlying drive development, object ties, body schematization, and the developing mental representation of self and object. Since the infant still lacks speech, the task of interpreting these data is enormously difficult.

In the earlier paper concerned with precisely this dilemma of understanding infant behavior characteristic of this essentially preverbal era, Galenson attempted to demonstrate the genetic continuity between early play and later artistic nonverbal symbolism by calling attention to certain structural similarities between these seemingly very different forms of behavior and thought. Werner and Kaplan's (1963) work on symbolism offered considerable support for this point of view. These authors compare the dynamic-vectorial nature of patterns of early psychic functioning with the qualities of direction, force, balance, rhythm, and enclosingness which are easily distinguishable in the early patterns of sensorimotor development. Werner and Kaplan propose that these dynamic-vectorial properties have relevance for later symbol formation, in that these qualities "reflect the fact that there is an early experience of dynamic similarities obtaining between entities—here body parts—that are materially different" (p. 86).

Galenson proposed that this "structural" or "dynamic-vectorial" type of analysis could be useful in studying the behavior of young infants in order to identify the original body zone from which a particular bit of observed behavior was derived. For example, thumb sucking is a zonal activity which has a characteristic pattern of rhythm, quality, form, etc. This oral pattern should aid in identifying behaviors which are currently located elsewhere, but were originally oral in nature. The current site might be the own body of the child, his mother's body, or inanimate objects. The point is that such derivatives of body sensation or self-exploration, although displaced from the original zone, are not represented or symbolized by a fixed or socially agreed-upon symbol, the word, and perhaps never will be. It is interesting that these early forms of infant play share many attributes with the symbolism of musical and visual art forms, in that there are no independent units with fixed meanings, apart from the contextual meaning; there is no dictionary construction; they cannot be translated into other symbols; and their meaning is understood only through relations within the total structure. Galenson proposed, therefore, that there is a genetic connection between early body-derived play and the symbolism of the creative arts.

Structural analysis based upon the foregoing propositions has been a basic part of our methodological approach. We follow the process of displacement from the original zonal site to another body area. The next step is externalization to outside objects which are then utilized as concrete semisymbolic representatives of the bodily experience. It is through this link with the original zonal area that we hope to document, from the data of direct infant observation, the assumption that play, as all other infant behavior, is patterned by the instinctual drives. In addition, we hope to follow the development of some of these open-ended and very plastic early symbols of infant play as they become more complex. We suspect that in certain infants the early symbols will be integrated and utilized for the nonverbal symbolism of artistic forms, whereas other infants will show a greater proclivity for acting out the earlier symbolic play.

In the case material which follows, some structural or pattern analyses of clusters of infant behavior will be included, to demonstrate this aspect of our research methodology.

The Setting

Our data are collected in the nursery, which was established in 1967, according to the model at The Master's Children Center developed by Mahler (1963; see also Pine and Furer, 1963). A large room, with a small kitchen and bathroom immediately adjoining it, is furnished at one end with an informal grouping of sofas for the mothers, while small tables and chairs, open toy shelves provided with toys appropriate for this age group, two rocking horses, a large-sized doll's bed and several doll carriages occupy the remainder of the room. A diapering table is set against the wall next to the bathroom, and a one-way screen which is used for video-taping occupies part of the wall immediately adjacent to the toy area. Infants have free access to both the bathroom and kitchen. Our research population is a self-selected upper-middle-class group. Nine mothers attend with their infants 4 mornings each week, for a 2-hour session from September, when the infants are between 12 and 15 months of age, through June of each year. Although our nursery is offered as a kind of indoor play ground, the parents are informed that we are engaged in research concerning normal development during the second year of life. The mothers are expected to take care of their own children, although our two nursery teachers act as additional supervisors.

Each mother-child pair is assigned to a pair of observers consisting of a senior staff member and a junior member, either a psychiatric resident or child psychiatry fellow who has elected to work in the nursery during the entire year. Each observer attends at least one session each week, while several senior observers attend two or more. Developmental data concerning the first year of life are gathered at the beginning of each nursery year (although more recently we are visiting prospective babies at home during their first year of life, prior to entrance in our program, and obtain this early material at that time). Ongoing data are gathered in the following manner: the observer questions the mother about the child's behavior at home during the preceding week, making certain that a group of behavioral categories selected in advance are covered. The observer spends the remainder of the nursery session directly observing the child. A 10-minute period is recorded directly in the form of a narrative record, while the rest is dictated after the session as an impressionistic account. All material is reproduced and circulated to the two observers as well as the two directors.

The data for each mother-child pair are summarized every 2 months, again according to preselected categories, and these summaries are then presented for staff discussions at the weekly staff conference. Formulations of the material already gathered as well as predictions concerning future development are developed out of these presentations. Although follow-ups have been obtained on only a portion of our research population thus far, systematic follow-up is now included in our research design.

Ruth's Early Development

The data which follow were collected over a period of 10 months, starting when Ruth was 12 months old, while she and her mother attended our nursery during 4 mornings each week.

The First Year

Developmental details of Ruth's first year of life were difficult to elicit from her mother, who had been anxiously preoccupied with the future fate of a congenital defect in Ruth. A corrective device, applied in the perineal area, was worn by Ruth from the 3rd through the 12th month of life. (Details of this defect and the corrective measures applied cannot be offered here for reasons of confidentiality.) Following a normal pregnancy and delivery, Ruth had been bottle-fed until age 6 months, when she began to spit out solids. Her mother, feeling this signaled a need for self-sufficiency in the whole feeding area, responded by allowing Ruth to feed herself and by abruptly withdrawing all bottle feeding. No particular sequelae were noted by the mother, although there was a large variety of oral behaviors including mouthing and licking of objects and tongue protrusion and pulling when Ruth entered our nursery during her 12th month. The less-than-optimum recognition of Ruth's cues, as evidenced in the abrupt, probably traumatic weaning, proved to be characteristic of this mother's relationship with her child, and lent a particular quality to the developing object ties.

The device applied for correction of the congenital deformity was worn at all times, except during bathing and diapering; it placed a mild restriction upon leg motion, but had only slightly delayed motoric development. Ruth stood with support at 7 months, crawled at 8 months, and walked with support at 14 months, and without support at 16 months. Ruth had made a remarkable accommodation to the corrective device as she crawled about most efficiently.

Yet in spite of a fairly smooth development in the motoric, perceptual, and other areas, her developing object relations were of a peculiar nature. From her 6th month on, Ruth had suffered intense "stranger anxiety," the most striking elements of which were her visual hypervigilance and her clinging to her mother's body. At about the same time she had developed a fear of the noise of a vacuum cleaner, of lying down in the tub for hair washing, and of her periodic physical examination for her congenital deformity. All but the fear of strangers and the fear of her pediatrician had disappeared when she entered our nursery at age 12 months. Her stranger anxiety was still so intense that it took several days before her staff observer could approach without eliciting intense distress, even as Ruth sat on her mother's lap. We learned from her mother that Ruth's way of mastering her separation anxiety was to fall asleep immediately when left with a neighbor for baby-sitting.

We feel that the persistent separation and stranger anxiety derived from several sources: first, the periodic removal of the corrective device was perceived as an intermittent loss of a body part; secondly, the partial motor restriction added to the difficulties of her developing body schematization and limited aggressive motor discharge; and thirdly, the mother's anxious concern about the body deformity and its future fate along with her less than adequate mothering resulted in some disturbance in Ruth's developing object relationships. In short, Ruth was experiencing more than the ordinary difficulty in the establishment of the mental representation of the maternal object and of the self, the symptomatic expression of which was her intense separation and stranger anxiety which continued well beyond the average period. Therefore, according to Roiphe's (1968a) hypothesis, Ruth would be expected to demonstrate a major distortion in development when she arrives at the period of genital discovery.

Ruth's 14th through 16th Months

From about 14 months of age Ruth began to practice many varieties of "object-disappearance" games, including the usual peek-a-boo, mirror peek-a-boo, repetitive toilet flushing, and repetitive use of the mail-box toy (in which forms are dropped through cut-out slats and then retrieved).

In her relationships with people, modest frustration evoked mild temper tantrums as well as focused hostility directed to other persons or herself. She would, for example, scratch, bite, and tease her mother and her favorite staff member, or bite her own fingers. Focused affectionate behavior also appeared as Ruth kissed and hugged people, dolls, and other objects. In relation to certain aspects of ego functioning, we witnessed an interesting spurt in her use of symbolic speech. Ruth acquired names for her parents and dolls which she soon used even in the absence of these objects. Semisymbolic play also began to appear when she placed dolls in bed, on the play toilet, etc. Ruth attained this level of symbolic play at 16 months, at least 2 months later than many of her peers.

From the group of behaviors just described, we infer that more distinct and stable mental self as well as object representations were becoming established. As self and object differentiation proceeded, object-directed aggressive and affectionate behavior emerged, as well as a certain amount of self-directed aggression in the form of self-biting. (We have come to regard the balance between self- and object-directed aggression as a crucial determinant for later development.) The spurt in symbolic functioning as evidenced both in speech and in semisymbolic play appeared to accompany the increasing self and object differentiation.

The increasing individuation was, however, accompanied by manifest anxiety, as indicated by an intensification of oral behavior. This included eating, as well as her earlier forms of thumb and object sucking, and tongue licking, pulling, and protrusion. Furthermore, Ruth's engaging in any new activity was contingent on a specific condition—the maintenance of direct visual contact with her mother at all times, which her peers of 16 months no longer needed. Yet, in spite of these evidences of more than usual anxiety, her chronically "anxious" searching look, with eyes slightly narrowed and gaze soon averted, now gradually gave way to a more open, bright expression, often with a trace of playful teasing. We infer from this that some greater stability of the mental self and object representations had been achieved.

Body Exploration

We were particularly interested in following those behaviors dealing with the identification of body parts. At 14 months, Ruth could name her own facial features and appendages as well as those of her parents. She had been exposed to her mother's naked body from the beginning, but it was not until her 14th month, at the same time as focused hostile aggression and affection emerged, that she began to stare intently at her mother's breasts and pubic hair, as yet without attempting to touch them. It should be mentioned that her father, unlike her mother, had avoided undressing in Ruth's presence from her 6th month onward.

At about 14½ months, the umbilicus became the focus of Ruth's attention as part of a highly exciting, reciprocal umbilicus-touching game with her mother. Soon afterward interest in anal functioning became evident as Ruth insisted upon being in the bathroom during her mother's toileting procedures, a common occurrence in all the families we have studied. She pointed to and developed a distinctive name for the stool in the toilet, and flushed the toilet repetitively both at home and in the nursery. All of this took place in the absence of any effort at toilet training by the mother. At 16 months, when she had just begun independent walking, Ruth gestured that she wanted to see her stool in the soiled diaper which had just been removed from her. She then proceeded to sit on the toidy seat in the nursery while clothed. Shortly thereafter she acquired a distinctive word for urination, a step following the usual developmental progression from anal to urinary zone.

These behaviors indicated to us that there was increasingly stable mental representation of her own body. New themes appeared in her play activities. She stacked blocks to build high towers, piled toys into carriages and other receptacles, repetitively emptied drawers and shelves of their contents and then refilled them, performing all this in an orderly and deliberate manner, in contrast to her previous "throwing style." She insisted that her toys remain just where she had put them, and now was able to take toys away from her peers and defend her own possessions.

The new organizational level of her play was, we inferred, related to the ongoing anal and urinary schematization in that the anal and urinary areas and functions were evidently achieving more solid mental representation. Anal traits of possessiveness as well as some degree of elementary organization, demonstrated in Ruth's orderly arrangement of concrete objects and her interest in their spatial relationships, seemed to reflect the new level of personality organization.

The enormous surge in almost all areas of development which had begun at 14 months reached a climax during Ruth's 17th month, just one month after she had finally attained unaided locomotion. She could now maintain distance from her mother as she engaged in social interchange; and her oral activities subsided remarkably; she held her own cup alone for the first time. Her sleep which had been disturbed for several months became peaceful, and she developed an attachment to a transitional object in the form of a "fuzzy dog" which was her constant nighttime companion. For the first time since the initial development of stranger anxiety during her 6th month, Ruth now greeted strangers without a trace of her former apprehension. This remarkable qualitative change in the nature of her object relations indicated to us that there was increasing reliability of the mental object representation, as a result of which her separation anxiety almost completely disappeared.

In the midst of the new-found pleasure and freedom of her early 17th month, evidence of Ruth's first focused genital interest was observed in the nursery and simultaneously reported by her mother. Her occasional fleeting gesture toward the genital area during diapering in the preceding month or so was now, at 17½ months, replaced by intentional genital handling during every diapering as she inserted two fingers between her labia. She crouched down and peered up between her widespread legs; undressed dolls, calling some of them "boy" for the first time; examined their perineal areas; and smilingly used the family word which had been offered her for both genital and anal areas (again a common practice in the families we have studied). She tried to lift and peer beneath her mother's skirt and that of her favorite staff member. Her interest in the reciprocal umbilicus game dwindled, but the diapering of other nursery children, which Ruth had previously ignored, now became of great interest to her. She hovered about the toilet, pushed the potty seat about the nursery, and shadowed her mother whenever she entered the bathroom. From this behavior, we confirmed that mental representation of the genital area and of the anatomical genital difference was being established as we had had earlier evidence that she had been aware of urinary and anal functions and sensations.

Intensification of Genital Awareness and Mutilation Reaction between 18¼ and 19 Months

Some 3 weeks after the onset of her genital curiosity, that is at 18¼ months of age, subtle but pervasive changes in mood, in the nature of her object relationships, and in other aspects of ego functioning began to appear. On one occasion Ruth was watching with her usual interest the diapering of a boy in the nursery. Fully clothed, she then sat down on a toidy seat, holding a long xylophone stick perpendicularly against her perineal area, and displaying an odd look of uneasiness on her face. The toilet flush handle became of increasing interest to her as she fondled and licked it whenever she was near it. We could follow the pathway of displacement from the visual percept of the offending male genital itself to a variety of sites away from the body (by utilizing the structural type of analysis previously described), as Ruth insistently and repetitively fingered knobs, car handles, and a variety of other protruding objects, which she now named "flush," a word previously reserved exclusively for the toilet handle.

Under the impact of her increasing anxiety about the observed sexual difference, distortion in verbal symbolization had occurred. The single attribute of phallic shape now united otherwise dissimilar objects under the common symbolic word "flush." She was visibly disturbed by all broken toys, refusing to use broken crayons which had previously been entirely acceptable. We felt this behavior indicated that these toys had become invested with the significance of the two body zones with which she was now most concerned, the genital and anal, and a defect in the concrete external inanimate object which was thus invested could no longer be tolerated. It appeared that these two areas of ego functioning, play and speech, had suffered distortion through the increasing use of denial as she tried to cope with mounting anxiety. In the same manner, the toilet handle which through displacement had come to represent the offending male genital now evoked so much anxiety that its symbolic word designation was no longer maintained in a discrete form. Instead, the word "flush" was generalized to other phalliclike objects. Thus this particular word symbol lost some of the specificity it had previously attained.

We have witnessed many instances of such invasions of ego functioning in connection with instinctual development and on-going body schematization. Although these states are usually temporary, there is of course the possibility of a subtle and permanent influence on precisely those areas of ego functioning which are in the process of rapid development during the latter half of the second year of life: namely, developing symbolization both in the verbal and in the nonverbal areas. Visual symbolization in particular undergoes developmental elaboration at this age. One would therefore expect that stressful events occurring during this critical developmental period would leave permanent traces in the visual-perceptive area of functioning. Moreover, in this particular child, the development of visual perception was probably even more complex than is usual in view of the visual fixation which had been so impressive in her earlier stranger anxiety.

Ruth now engaged in new visual activities. She ran to look at any baby being diapered in the nursery, immediately thereafter glanced down at her own perineal area, and spoke her word for urination, indicating that the visual inspection involved a direct comparison. She became an intent window gazer in the nursery, and was overheard murmuring "Daddy" on several occasions as she stared out at an empty street, seemingly occupied with fantasy. Her obvious concern with the genital differences exerted pressure on her parents, who now allowed her to witness her father's urination on several occasions. She was fascinated by the sight.

Her intense visual sexual curiosity seemed to combine with the sensations of genital arousal that she experienced as she witnessed diaperings and urinations. From this constellation an interesting group of phenomena emerged. Whenever she found someone looking at her, she blushed a deep red color and tried to hide her face. Simultaneously, she developed a new interest in all forms of fire such as her father's matches, her grandfather's barbecue, and fire engines. She repeated the words "hot" and "fire" in all these situations, and looked at the "hot" events with obvious fascination and clear signs of erotic excitement.

First, as to her "fiery" interest; Ruth had experienced genital sensations of localized arousal and warmth as she masturbated, sensations now retrospectively connected with her earlier oral perceptions of warmth. (Ruth's first word had been "hot," a warning used by her mother against burning her mouth with hot food.) In addition to the internal associative link, there was an external one in that the local genital warmth found an equivalent perceptual quality in the fires she observed and whose warmth she felt; and these fires in turn became linked with fire engines. All fiery events were thus equated with genital arousal, leading to the emergence of a new symbol: fire stood for sexual arousal!

The connections between looking, sexual arousal, interest in fires, and the word "hot" had become established.

These interesting phenomena of blushing and hiding her face on being looked at appear to relate to the matter of the developing sense of identity. Greenacre (1958) has emphasized the crucial role of the face and genitals, in contrast to other body areas, in establishing individual recognition of the own body self. Ruth's facial inspection had earlier been an important aspect of what we inferred to be her primitive attempts at self-object differentiation. As she now tackled this same task on a more complex level she avidly inspected genitals and objects to which genital displacement had taken place. It must be emphasized, however, that her earlier experiences had contributed a less than optimally firm body basis.

The corrective device worn against the perineal area during the first year had surely aroused genital sensations, resulting in greater than average instability of genital schematization. Now, at 1½ years, her new and acute awareness of genital arousal, and the confusing comparisons of her own genitals with those of others, constituted a new threat to the already distorted genital schematization. We speculate, therefore, that displacement occurred from genital area to the face which had been the site of the earlier efforts at identity establishment. Having become aroused as she visually inspected her father's genitals, she now became aroused when she was visually inspected herself. Genital blushing and facial blushing were, for the time being, simultaneous phenomena, although we assumed that the genital aspect would soon become inhibited and eventually repressed. (The ready displacement from genital to face as well as the extensive employment of introjective-projective mechanisms are, of course, characteristic of psychic functioning during this developmental period.)

Toward the end of her 18th month, Ruth's comparisons and inspections of the genital area began to decrease; simultaneously a slow deterioration in her mood set in. The cheerfulness of her 17th month was replaced by irritability and decreasing frustration tolerance, but this time the aggression was not directed against the mother, as it had been at 15 months. Instead she teased and provoked other adults and again began to bite her own fingers in a renewed emergence of self-directed aggression. The earlier fear of strangers and the clinging to her mother returned in ever increasing intensity.

The Use of Displacement Following an Earlier Developmental Pathway

The mechanism of gradual displacement was evident as Ruth's attention turned upward from the offending genital zone to her former interest in her umbilicus. She repeatedly pushed her finger into it, lifted the clothing of our nursery dolls, and pointed at and named a nonexistent umbilicus, using the word "button," which was not the name her parents had used to designate this area. Many inanimate protuberances also became "buttons" in the same type of symbolic distortion we had observed during the period when she had first scrutinized the anatomical genital differences. As part of this effort to deny the genital difference by affirming the ubiquitous umbilicus in its place, Ruth tried to pin a safety pin on the abdomen of her favorite Teddy.

In the midst of Ruth's mounting distress her mother discovered that she was in the earliest months of a new pregnancy. Although we assume that this new event influenced Ruth's future development profoundly, her original distress had begun well in advance of any possible awareness of the pregnancy.

Crisis at 19½ Months

During one of her usual nursery sessions, Ruth bit ferociously on her own fingers, and then chewed on the ear of a toy bear after she had witnessed the diapering of an infant girl. She had chewed and macerated a similar toy bear's ear at home a few days previously. On yet another morning, she was being supported in the arms of her staff observer for a better view of an infant boy's diapering which she had rushed to observe. Suddenly she averted her gaze, pulled off first one of the observer's earrings, and then the other, and gestured her wish to be put down on the floor. Running into the adjacent bathroom, she tore off toilet paper, dropped it into the toilet, and then tried to flush it away as she simultaneously licked at the flush handle.

All these behaviors indicate a wish to dispose of protrusions. Avoidance and displacement mechanisms were increasingly in evidence as her gaze avoided the perineal areas of dolls whose abdomens she diligently examined for the "button." She was more and more distressed by broken or imperfect toys, pointing at their defects and actually using the word "broken." And a new fear of falling objects, particularly if they caused spattering or splashing, emphasized her awareness of the urinary aspect of the male genital. Temper tantrums returned, her sleep was once again disturbed, and the "toy dog" transitional object, which had been her obligatory nighttime companion, now became a daytime necessity as well. In addition, a new obligatory object made its appearance in the form of a doll which Ruth called "boy." She insisted that this doll, which resembled her other usual girl dolls in every way, be seated next to her at all meals, and that "he" receive a mouthful of food each time she fed herself.

In attempting to understand the meaning of these new developments, we assumed that Ruth had arrived at only marginal stability in the maternal object representation, compromised during her early months by the sudden weaning, the less than optimum mother-child relationship, and the limitation of aggressive motor discharge in consequence of the corrective device she wore. Now her awareness of the genital difference and the additional burden of anger and disappointment at her genital state resulted in a split in the maternal image, with projection of the bad object. Recrudescence of the fear of strangers indicated a renewed fear of object loss which followed the weakening of the maternal object representation through splitting. Simultaneously, a split in the mental self representation seemed to have occurred, with the obligatory toy dog and the doll "boy" representing split-off portions of Ruth's mental self image.

As this critical period continued, inhibition of genital curiosity was soon reflected in a narrowing of her recently enlarged area of general curiosity. Ruth turned from her recent rich doll play to play with toys which involved the solution of tasks related to spatial relationships as well as anal functioning. The use of such toys had been the most prominent aspect of her early play. Now she again began to stack blocks, pile toys on top of one another within all kinds of receptacles, and use the "shape box" repetitively. This restriction of general curiosity paralleled the growing inhibition of Ruth's interest in toileting. She lost interest in the toilet and conspicuously avoided all references to the genital, anal, and urinary functions and areas. In sharp contrast, her interest in the toilet flush handle itself intensified, and she now used the word "flush" to designate the entire toilet, the opening and closing of doors, the electric light switch, and the brake of her carriage. All of these objects and situations shared the element of control rather than that of phallic shape, which had characterized her earlier symbolic distortion.

Her favorite inanimate companions were no longer the toy dog, but a number of dolls which she carried along without using them in play, one of which she named "baby." It seemed that Ruth had begun to use the concrete doll to take the place of the longed-for phallus. Her use of the name "baby" for this doll-phallus signals the establishment of a very early phallus-baby equation.

The Turning Point

Ruth's worsening sleep disturbance reached its peak during her father's unusual absence from home over a period of several nights. She wept bitterly as she called for her mother, repeating her distinctive words for urination and defecation. She was inconsolable throughout the night. The following morning she deposited a stool in her newly acquired toidy seat for the first time, after which she stood up, gazed at the stool in amazement, and promptly urinated on the floor.

This acute reaction to the father's absence must be viewed against the background of the severe early stranger and separation anxiety which had waned and now had returned again. With the temporary loss of the father, the fear of maternal loss was rekindled, and Ruth's defecation in the toidy on this fateful morn-

ing seemed to represent a final surrender to her mother's wishes
as she parted with the stool-phallus.

As if in vague recognition of the meaning of Ruth's gift of her
stool, her frantic parents decided to purchase on that day a carriage and baby doll which she had been requesting for some time.
With the carriage at her bedside and the doll in her arms Ruth
had her first quiet night in several weeks. Her last audible word
as she fell asleep was "flush!"

Ruth's use of dolls at this critical time suggests that they now
served in part as infantile fetishistic objects in an effort to repair
her sense of the defective genital. We have come to realize that
the doll has a complicated series of meanings, some deriving from
early stages of development when they have a "transitional object"
quality, while others serve a much more advanced state of symbolization. We have noted regression in semisymbolic play with
dolls, just as in other areas of symbolization, and consider this to
be important evidence of disturbed development.

Ruth's dramatic first surrender of her stool ushered in a period
of relative "submission" in other areas of behavior, although Ruth
refused to use the toidy seat itself for many weeks thereafter. Sub-
dued and even sad at times, she was no longer interested in the
toidy seat, the toilet and its flush, or in her father's showering to
which she had rushed excitedly at every opportunity. All genital,
anal, and urinary exploration and curiosity had ceased in relation
to her own body, the diapering of other children, and her parents.

The toys she now played with were small toy horses which she
placed at either side of her as she sat rocking in a small chair.
She clung to the baby doll and its carriage. Broken toys and
crayons continued to distress her and she refused to use them.

At 22 months Ruth was a quiet child whose constant eating
companions were the two dolls at her sides, as Ruth insisted that
they be fed while she fed herself. Her former anxious look of the
narrowed eyes and tense face in the presence of strangers had returned, and her curiosity had become definitely limited in scope.
The recognition of a definitive change in mood was her mother's
first clear statement that Ruth would probably always be a "quiet"
one who would be "afraid of strangers."

Comment

We are unable to assess the importance of the mother's new pregnancy and of the father's absence from home at such a crucial period of development in this child's life, although we were able to verify that the castration reaction itself had begun well before the mother's conscious knowledge of her pregnancy. The effect of pregnancies as well as of brief and prolonged paternal absences has been studied in detail in several infants in our project. We plan to report this material at a later date.

Summary

In this paper we reported observations on the development of a child with a congenital defect that required repeated medical examinations and the constant wearing of a corrective device during her first year of life. The resulting early disturbance in body schematization and in the developing mother-child relationship distorted and delayed the separation-individuation process and interfered with the establishment of an optimally stable maternal mental representation. Yet, with the development of free locomotion, there was a spurt in individuation and in symbolic development between Ruth's 14th and 17th months, as evident in the disappearance of stranger anxiety, the emergence of symbolic play, and in her enlarging verbal capacity. This ongoing individuation process brought her in due time to the awareness of anal, urinary, and genital anatomy and function, along with their appropriate sensations.

In this already vulnerable child, however, the discovery of the sexual anatomical difference and sexual sensations brought with it overwhelming disappointment and anger at the mother, with loss of self-esteem and the marked inhibited and depressive reaction which continues to characterize her. The incomplete and unstable fusion of the good and bad maternal images gave way under the impact of her anger; the maternal images were split and the bad image was projected onto other figures. A basic mistrust prevails, and it is likely that she will continue to have difficulties in separating from her mother. Another consequence of the distorted development of body schematization and object relations was a concurrent split in the mental representation of her own body (the boy doll and eating companion) and a weakening of several aspects of ego functioning (such as general curiosity, play, and symbolization).

Ruth's very early object relations, self identity, and other ego functions appear to have been indelibly affected by bodily experiences in her first year. We observed the impact of the discovery of the sexual anatomical difference during her second year and attempted to delineate the fateful consequences for defensive organization, object relations, mood, and style of play behavior.

Follow-up at 31 Months

A sister was born when Ruth was 26½ months old. Ruth seemed fond of the new baby and initially showed no hostility toward her. Just after the baby returned home, Ruth showed a spurt in doll play, but soon she abandoned it almost completely. Blocks became her favorite toy and the Empire State Building her favorite block-building project.

Toilet training had been accomplished before the baby sister was born. Although speech was advanced, the use of the personal pronoun "I" had not yet been achieved. Ruth continued to show marked anxiety in relation to even minor injuries. On one occasion she insisted on wearing long trousers to cover her scraped knee, long after the bandage had been removed. Following an injury to her lip she refused to eat for 3 days and made persistent attempts to hide her face from the view of others. And her tolerance of separation continues to be well below the expected level.

In summary, Ruth's earlier difficulties in the areas of self-esteem, object relations, and other aspects of ego functioning, such as nonverbal and verbal symbolization, were still in evidence as she entered the oedipal period; and the castration anxiety of her second year of life had never disappeared.

BIBLIOGRAPHY

GALENSON, E. (1971), A Consideration of the Nature of Thought in Child-hood Play. In: *Separation-Individuation,* ed. J. B. McDevitt & C. F. Settlage. New York: International Universities Press, pp. 41–59.

GREENACRE, P. (1953), Certain Relationships between Fetishism and the Faulty Development of the Body Image. *This Annual,* 8:79–98.

— (1958), Early Physical Determinants in the Development of the Sense of Identity. *J. Amer. Psychoanal. Assn.,* 6:612–627.

MAHLER, M. S. (1963), Thoughts about Development and Individuation. *This Annual,* 18:307–324.

— (1966), Notes on the Development of Basic Moods: The Depressive Affect. In: *Psychoanalysis—A General Psychology: Essays in Honor of Heinz Hartmann,* ed. R. M. Loewenstein, L. M. Newman, M. Schur & A. J. Solnit. New York: International Universities Press, pp. 152–168.

PINE, F. & FURER, M. (1963), Studies of the Separation-Individuation Phase. *This Annual,* 18:325–342.

ROIPHE, H. (1968a), On an Early Genital Phase: With an Addendum on Genesis. *This Annual,* 23:348–365.

— (1968b), Castration Complex and Object Loss (in preparation).

WERNER, H. & KAPLAN, B. (1963), *Symbol Formation.* New York: Wiley.

On the Development
of the Experience of Mental
Self, the Bodily Self, and
Self Conciousness

ERNEST KAFKA, M.D.

IN THIS PAPER I DESCRIBE SOME MATERIAL FROM ANALYTIC PATIENTS that presents a specific pattern of imagery and symptomatology. Using the method of reconstruction, I attempt to demonstrate that this pattern reflects what seems to me to be an underlying archaic body experience which occurs initially as a consequence of separation from mother representatives and which, in similar situations later in life, is regressively activated. I intend to trace its evolution from its beginning in the first year of life to a somewhat less archaic organization indicating some individuation. I hope to add to our "insufficient knowledge" (Freud, 1937) of the early developmental period, when self-object and bodily self-psychic self distinctions appear, and place this addition in the larger framework of the development of consciousness.

(217)

Clinical Material

Patient 1

A woman in her 30s suffered from multiple phobias. She could not tolerate buses, trains, tunnels, heights, crowded places, or eating in the presence of others. When she exposed herself to the situations she feared, she felt a confusion that she interpreted as meaning that she was losing her mind. She said she felt she could not control her thoughts. Her greatest fear was that she might vomit. Once she began to vomit she expected to continue to do so, unable to stop, until she died. While having such thoughts, she felt nausea. She could not separate thoughts about nausea and the experience of nausea.

In describing how she felt, she did not often use words such as sad, angry, or embarrassed. Rather, she felt "like a fragile empty bag." Such experiences repeatedly appeared in her dreams. In one, she wandered over a countryside, searching for a place to be alone, but always other people appeared. She found herself in a bathroom, but people wandered in and out. In another, she was driving a car. She drove into a tunnel, the lights went out, she feared she might crash into something, she stopped, someone ran into her car from behind.

In these dreams she seemed to be trying to establish boundaries, attempting to be alone, surrounding herself with bathroom walls, a car, a tunnel—but the need for objects overcame this trend, and she was intruded upon by others. She could not separate herself from objects, yet she feared they would control her and injure her. In fact, she felt she had no will of her own, couldn't initiate things, depended entirely on her husband, following all his suggestions and sharing all his opinions. Yet she feared him and regarded him as a cruel tyrant. She attempted to deal with her problems by isolating herself in her house and, when she was at her worst, in her bedroom in her bed. In her analysis, she tried to contain and control her words and feared she might leak out feces, urine, tears, or vomitus. To her, all these contents were equivalent.

Her symptoms had appeared when she, her husband, and two

children established their own home. Prior to this time, they had lived with in-laws, before that with her parents, before that, toward the end of the war, as fugitives. In childhood she had been closely attached to her mother and had regarded her father as an ideal man who could do no wrong. During a temporary separation of her parents (age 9), she had developed a transitory agoraphobia. Earlier (age 5) she had night terrors when her parents went out for the evening.

As an infant she had suffered from an impetigo, which was treated with salves and baths. Toilet training was accomplished by the age of 14 months. The parents were stringent in demanding self-control. When they took her on visits to friends, she was not permitted to indicate a need for a bathroom because her parents regarded this as an unseemly reference to things of which one did not speak. Often she had to restrain herself, painfully and anxiously. Sometimes she failed to do so. "Accidents" were punished by whippings. Tears, expressions of anger or of personal wishes were anathema.

She slept in her parents' bedroom until she was 8 years old. Her father frequently appeared nude, and made the patient sleep nude "for her health." He was seductive with her, both in exciting physical games (wrestling and throwing her in the air), and later, during her mother's frequent depressions, in substituting her for her mother as a companion on walks, theater trips, and café afternoons.

In the analysis, her fears of separation were related to her mother's depressions and the discords between her parents, which gave rise to fears of abandonment. Her response to separation was clarified: it took the form of increased clinging and identification with the abandoning object, accompanied by trends to further regression with fears of explosion, draining, and loss of sense of self. It was proposed that in addition to her uncertain relation to objects, she had experienced skin stimulation that heightened her sense of the surface of her body, in infancy because of her impetigo, later because of beatings and erotic play. It was suggested that excessive stimulation together with early and excessive demands that she contain bodily contents as well as affects led to experiences of painful inner pressure that later reappeared in her experiences of herself as a mass of dangerous contents, held in check by a fragile container. In adult life, the loss of maternal objects that occurred when she felt she must become the mother had been an important factor in precipitating the regressive attempt to recover the object. This reactivated an early state organized in terms of poorly differentiated body surface and interchangeable, dangerous contents, accompanied by absence of feelings of identity and mastery.

Patient 2

A man in his 30s came into analysis shortly after he moved from a job that had clearly defined directives and rigid rules to one that required spontaneity, inventiveness, and an outgoing self-revealing attitude. His success as a bureaucrat had led to his promotion to the position of administrator-consultant. At about the same time, his mother developed heart disease and underwent an operation. He was not aware that this meant something to him. He attempted to attach himself to a superior but failed. Severe anxiety and a moderate depersonalization soon followed. Work became an ordeal. He said he felt that few thoughts or feelings originated with him. In describing his experience of himself, he used such images as feeling like a clam. Someone could reach into his mouth, grab his tongue, and pull out his insides. There he would be, a soft mush. In associating to this imagery, he remembered that in childhood he had felt that his mother knew all his ideas and feelings.

On another day, he said he felt as though encased in armor. He imagined that messages or dagger thrusts could be passed in and out through a chink which was at the same time a source of danger. He felt false—on the surface he was a mask of friendliness; within, a Cassius, hiding in the shadows with a knife.

It became apparent that practically every suggestion or criticism by another person was an intrusion and a blow. This man was always on his guard. Subways and sidewalks were battlegrounds where he constantly risked infringement of his sphere of control. Spontaneity and friendliness were impossible. He feared he might be ridiculed for his friendliness, or his ideas might be taken and used by others. He said he felt like an "insatiably gnawing rat; hiding in a dark corner of [his] interior, ready to spring out when others were not looking, ready to devour what [he] could." He was terrified of injections and rectal examinations. Premature ejaculation or loss of erection sometimes interfered with his ability to penetrate in the sexual act. There was a mild train phobia. Exercising and muscle-conditioning were important because, for him, strong muscles were a protection; they made him feel he had "a casing of cement." He feared crying lest, once started, he be unable to stop; his shell would melt.

Often, at work, he was unable to reveal his ideas and opinions. He feared he had a limited supply of them and might be used and, when empty, discarded. He feared influence and was extremely suggestible. He felt easily exploited. The ideas others had sometimes made him feel "real and warm"; at other times they made him feel he was bursting. Mondays were most difficult because he wanted to stay home, which he said was like being "hidden, protected, warm," as in his childhood when he avoided school.

When he was a child, his mother could always seduce him and arouse him with sexual play. She bathed him until he was 7 or 8. She made him "feel alive." He could not long remain angry with her, even when she hurt or humiliated him. The outside world was "cold and cruel." Mother revealed her body to him, complained to him about his father, kissed him with soft lips. In later life he realized that his desires to perform cunnilingus had to do with these remembered lips. But with his mother he had to respond with sexless affection. Often her friendliness turned to ridicule. Then, he felt "withered," "shrunken," his mind "dried up as though all the juice had dried out of my system." With his mother there was a tremendous temptation to "relax, reveal, loosen." Until the age of 8 or 9, she inspected his bowel movements and praised or derided them as she praised or derided his school performance. He wet himself often. He had had childhood nightmares of being under water, of drowning or suffocating. When excited, he could not control his feelings. Even now, sometimes, as though a switch had flipped, he still changed from "good boy to bad boy, like an erection appearing, from mask to rat."

As an infant he was fed on a rigid schedule, which did not suit him; according to family tradition, he cried in rage for 2 hours before every feeding. Toilet training was undertaken early, but little is known about it. Later he retained stool. Between the ages of 1 and 3, there were almost daily temper tantrums in which he lay screaming and kicking on the floor. He held his breath till he felt he would burst. His mother handled this by letting him tire and get it out of his system. When the patient was 3, his sister was born. For years he had fantasies of killing her. Shortly after her birth, he underwent a tonsillectomy, for which he was unprepared. The sensations of ether anesthesia were included in many subsequent dreams and appeared in waking feelings of suffocation. After this operation the patient was tractable, fearful, and unspontaneous. He imitated others, adapted himself to their standards, and did not create an independent character of his own.

In this case, too, it was evident that the patient's representation of his mother had been disrupted when she fell ill—a disruption that was accentuated with his loss of the maternal elements represented by the large corporation, which provided goals, punishments, nourishment. In response, he first tried to attach himself to a superior; failing in this, he regressed to a level in which an earlier relationship with his mother was partially recaptured. He became unproductive, stayed home, developed a premature ejaculation reminiscent of his enuresis. Tendencies toward more primitive wishes for union with the object appeared. These were evidenced by his fear of and susceptibility to influence. At the same time, there was a reappearance of primitive self experiences involving absence of control and defensively emphasizing the body boundary as a container of undifferentiated internal contents. Feelings, thoughts, secretions were experienced as equivalent. The threat of further dedifferentiation brought about a tendency toward further withdrawal. He felt threatened when "entering" work, trains, or wife, as he felt threatened by others intruding on him, in subways, streets, or competitive situations.

This patient's history revealed, as had that of case 1, events that may have emphasized his sense of surface. There were many references to the erotic relation with mother, the remembered baths, bursting feelings associated with breath holding and stool retention, and banging, kicking, rageful temper tantrums.

Patient 3

Another patient sought reanalysis in his early 40s. He complained of feelings of failure and depression. He said that he had led, and was leading, a false life as a heterosexual because secretly he had homosexual wishes. He experienced strong longings for care and nourishment and rivalrous anger and fear. Meanwhile, he said, he played the role of a human being. He compared his experience of life with the siege of Troy. He wanted to be like an invincible walled city but found himself a hollow Trojan horse as well as susceptible to invasion by one. Troy itself was an imperfect shell, concealing evil. As Troy, as Helen, were entered and controlled, he was easily seduced. A few kind words made him mushy, defenseless. On another occasion he said he felt like an empty paper bag, full of air. A fond hope was one day to be driven in a limousine. This would make him feel safe and protected.

On the analytic couch, he had a number of curious experiences. In one, he felt pressed down, crushed, unable to move. He said it felt as though he were pushed down by a teacup. In association he described tightening feelings in the lips and cheeks and a feeling of pressure on the tongue. During sessions his mouth sometimes began to water as though he were about to eat. He had an urge to pick the skin from his lips, and felt like kicking his feet. A bookcase facing him seemed to swing like a pendulum. He felt sleepy. He was only aware of sensations of surfaces.

He described how, as a child, he had crushed bugs, listening to their shells crack. He had a dream in which, as an oarsman of a shell, he caught a crab. He had a distaste for lobster, and a mild spider phobia. Humpty Dumpty had fascinated him, he remembered, in childhood. He had hoped analysis would be like plastic surgery. He wanted a cosmetic result, an improved surface appearance. He feared anything more extensive than an alteration in the mask because it would involve revealing the worms, the feces inside. There was no experience of solid internal structure, physical or mental. These skeletonless thoughts and feelings seemed to him to represent his real character. Change would involve death. He was reminded of his fear of his mother's anger when he made errors, and this thought reminded him of his fantasy, at age 5, upon hearing her cry in the bathroom, that she had just aborted. He could not imagine change otherwise than in connection with loss of control and death, and this was frightening.

In the transference, he looked for a chink in my armor; he talked of his fear of my rage, which must lie, "like the molten iron beneath the crust of the earth, ready to erupt." In an accident he broke a leg—a strange experience since he had no sense of himself as skeletal. He feared he might soil the couch. On the other hand, he had a wishful fantasy that a hole might be made in his head to let out the pressure of rage, conceived of as a gas or hot liquid. But then, nothing would be left. In sex, he said, the woman sucks the man dry. He becomes an inanimate figure, a dummy. The tea-cup that pressed him was like the sensation of his mouth around his tongue. Someone could reach into the mouth and take out what he had, or stuff in what he did not want.

This man had had an infantile feeding schedule that was said to have brought him to screams of rage, and a meticulous mother who kept the schedule with iron rigidity. As might be expected, cleanliness, containment of feelings, determined suppression of sexual expressions were demanded. At the same time, the patient slept on a porch adjacent to his parents' bedroom and was over-stimulated and seduced by his mother. He was her intimate, the hearer of her marital complaints, the receiver of her descriptions of the father's inadequacies. Often he felt he would burst with tension and excitement and, until the age of 2½, with the enemas his mother frequently administered.

In this case, too, separation was an important precipitating event in bringing about symptomatology. The first analysis began shortly after his marriage, when he set up his own home, away from his mother. The second analysis came about some years after his mother's death, which he had largely disregarded at the time. Around an anniversary of her death he began to wish for a second child, but his wife refused. This coincided with a change in his work situation, which required him to shift jobs, and his wife's receiving a promotion.

Again, there was a regressive activation of a state in which maintaining a sense of separation and a sense of control were threatened by powerful tendencies toward reunion with an archaic maternal object. In the resultant self experience there was an emphasis on both the surface and a rather undifferentiated interior.

Cases Described in the Literature

Other examples of such self experiences appear in the literature. After Stanley, the 7-year-old patient reported by Elkisch and Mahler (1959), ate some unusually long string beans, he had a delusional obsession in which his body became a sewer as well as the sewer's contents. Teddy, another child, was "preoccupied with the delusion that father, grandfather, and he himself were a communicating system of glass tubes which competed at draining the life fluid from each other during the night" (p. 229). These may represent more primitive variants of the phenomena described by my patients.

A. Reich (1960) reported several cases characterized by a body-phallus equation and pathological self consciousness; one in particular: "When he was little more than six months old, Robert's obsessional mother started toilet training by means of regularly given enemas. For years to come, this interfered with his development of the sense of being a person separate from his mother: it was she who had power over his body. At the same time he experienced himself as an open bag full of excrement" (p. 277). This sense of self as container full of excrement was later included in a body-anal-phallus equation. The later stage was regressively experienced in earlier terms.

Isakower (1938) described certain experiences associated with falling asleep. Among these are sensations particularly in mouth, skin, and hands; sensations of floating, sinking, and giddiness; blurring of the distinction between quite different regions of the body and between internal and external; and visual impressions of an approaching shadowy mass. "The sensations in the oral cavity . . . are diffused over the whole skin, the outermost frontier of the body, which, indeed, is scarcely yet recognized as such. . . . At all events it represents the surface on which contact is made with the world" (p. 338).

One of Woodbury's patients (1966) felt "hollow," "empty," "without content," "like a person who has lost all his collagen and falls in a puddle" (p. 276).

Winnicott (1962) wrote of a point in the child's developing experience of the self when the surface is experienced as a "limiting membrane" (p. 59). This occurs at a stage in which self-nonself differentiation is taking place.

Lewin (1946, 1953, 1968), Hoffer (1949), Anthony (1961), and Woodbury (1966) also described what they considered to be experiences of reactivated archaic ego states, experiential organizations in which the body experience is mainly centered around the mouth and self-nonself differentiation is incomplete.

Greenacre (1950) reported a comparable case. I excerpt from it briefly.

> A woman of thirty sought treatment for severe inhibitions and emotional disturbances invading practically all phases of her life. Extremely shy, sensitive to the point of constant flight from others, she was unable to work for any length of time, and spent much time in idleness, becoming irritable whenever prodded by her family to do anything. [When she was 10, a man lifted her so that she could see the movement of the little hands upon the dials of the gas meter. In doing so] he put his hand under her dress and stimulated her genitals. [Later she allowed herself to be tied up in mock torture. She utilized a technique of masturbating in the bathtub.] . . . she seemed to be in an unusual state of chronic tension . . . in almost any situation involving appearance in public, . . . any special sadomasochistic stimulation (fights or accidents), she would "go to pieces." This meant that she had some sudden spontaneous bodily discharge: a vaginal orgasm, a burst of uncontrolled weeping, loss of control of the bladder, an unexpected diarrhea, or, during her menstrual period, an extreme degree of flooding. . . . at the age of six she was constantly with the mother . . . as though appersonated by the mother. . . . [She] clung to her bottle until she was about three. . . . She was "successfully" toilet trained extremely early. [She later] lived in a state of fear of toilet accidents. . . . Severe outbursts of temper . . . were ultimately controlled by whippings. . . . [She experienced] vigorous romping and tickling by her father, and the stimulation of early primal scenes. [Some-

times she] got into states of almost frantic exhilaration. [Dreams revived a memory of (at age 4 or 5) finding her mother doing something to her father's genitals while he was in a plaster cast. Her mother was evidently helping him with a bottle-shaped white-enameled urinal. In kindergarten she had enemas given her in the bathtub. When she had whooping cough, her parents decided to go on vacation anyway, but she was warned not to embarrass the family by coughing or vomiting. A dream in analysis involved getting off a bus in fear of being sick, entering a movie theatre through swinging doors, and going to the toilet. In another part, a little boy put money in a slot machine. Out came hundreds of packages of little cigarettes, and the patient became frightened because the machine was emptying itself] [pp. 206–218].

Kestenberg (1970) and Bornstein (1931) have described similar cases.

Discussion

The material of these patients reveals striking similarities. In their regressed states, they all experienced themselves as what I suggest may be conceptualized as containers and contents. Mental and physical were not distinguished from each other. Instead, thoughts, feelings, concepts were experienced in bodily terms. These patients felt that their bodies consisted of surfaces with openings, through which materials could pass in or out, and of liquid or semiliquid contents. The surface, often shell-like, was described in terms of armor, cement, Troy, the Trojan horse, bugs, the earth's crust, a urinal, bathtub, slot machine, and so on.

The contents—vomitus, flatus, feces, tears, blood, urine, semen, water—were evidently felt and treated as equivalent to crude emotions such as anger and tension, although even as emotions they were still poorly defined, to thoughts, and also to some sense of essence of life. In fantasies incorporating these experiences, drainage could take place and provide relief of tension, but they also threatened dangerous attacks on objects and risks of uncontrolled leakage and death. On the other hand, dangerous fluids, in the form of unwanted foods or injectable substances, and controlling commands arousing dangerous stimuli could be instilled into the container.

An experience of control over input and outflow of these contents was present, but the control was a rudimentary one. The experience of body was not distinct from the experience of mind. Spontaneous activity of all sorts was potentially dangerous and had to be profoundly inhibited. Experiences of falseness were frequent. Strong, undifferentiated attachment to their mothers and precipitation of regression by separation from maternal organizing influences also characterized these patients. Mothers or mother substitutes had to be at least in the background for these patients to feel comfort and personal integrity. The regressive pull involved the wish to recover the maternal object.

The histories of these individuals reveal early influences that evidently brought about intense feelings of body surface and body contents confined by the surface. These early influences, occurring during infancy and the first year of life, included excessive surface and skin stimulation, as described by Greenacre, Hoffer, Winnicott, and others, and, in addition, hollow emptiness due to hunger, and bursting inner pressure due to held breath, or retained feces, and enema fluids. Later in life the parents of these patients exposed them to experiences of the same type, among them seduction and stimulation of feelings and thoughts, especially rage, together with stringent demands for the containment of these mental qualities; similar demands relating to body contents, which thus perpetuated the equation of mental and physical body contents. Separation from mother figures, experienced as abandonment, with the consequent feelings of helplessness and anger, as well as opportunities for spontaneous expression, equated with draining and soiling, resulted in exacerbation of symptomatology. Thinking was in extremes, with rapid switches of attitudes, usually occurring in relation to experiences of hard surface or soft and liquid contents.

These experiences may therefore be thought of as aspects of regressions to fixation points at a stage during which in normal development self-awareness, self-object separation, and mental self-bodily self distinctions begin to occur. The adult phenomenology and observable manifestations reflect the incomplete differentiation of mental and bodily self experience as well as the archaic ties to the object.

Changes in Self Experience in Analysis

In what follows I shall describe the changes of the bodily self and mental self experiences that occurred during the analyses in my three patients. While many important conflicts and trends were identified and analyzed in the course of these patients' treatment, I restrict myself to the vicissitudes of the organization of early experience and to certain aspects of their relationship to maternal objects.

In patient 1, the phobic woman, the analysis achieved a partial remission of her disabling symptoms. She became able to entertain friends and eat in their company, and, later, even to eat in public. Her sexual interest increased, and her growing sense of control was revealed in an ability to relinquish control in achieving orgasm. The changes in her body experience are of special interest in the present context. She revealed that she had a mild urinary incontinence, a dribbling with sneezing and coughing, which had so frightened her that she had been unable to talk, and even to think, about it. She now decided this might have some anatomic basis, and consulted a physician. She felt she had discovered her anatomy. Her body now felt solid, yet had parts. She had little fear about the vaginal examination and cystoscopy. An uncomplicated operation resulted in a gratifying remission of her symptom, evidently due to parturitional anatomic damage. Later, she adopted a diet and changed her ways of dressing. She became flirtatious in the analysis. Her perception of her body, its functioning, structure, and beauty were expressed in a new hobby. She took up furniture repair and refinishing. She had reached a new stage of self awareness. She began to have sexual daydreams. She became aware of underlying motivations in herself and in others, and recognized a certain degree of complexity in her thoughts. She came to understand, in more than the schematic form she initially had, some of the inner motivations behind her parents' attitudes and behavior. These changes thus brought about a new self

awareness and self consciousness, a sense of control and separateness, appreciation of complex motivation in herself and others,
and an altered experience of her body.

Patient 2 discovered one day that his attitude about his musculature had changed. He now derived pleasure from the roundness
and suppleness of his muscles. Their hardness and armoring
quality seemed to him to have lost significance. Subsequently, his
golf game became much better as he felt "my body move harmoniously in my swing." Later, he mentioned that he was neglecting
a ledger he had carefully kept to record and detail every item of
his income and expenses. "After all," he joked, "it's only money."
He found himself mentioning ideas to people at work and joking
with them, even telling sexual jokes, with a certain retrospective
surprise that he had given away something without sense of loss
or fear. As one would suppose, his concern about bowels and his
worry about adequate sexual performance had markedly diminished. He took to fairly heavy drinking, partly in a spirit
of vengeful independence, and partly in a pleasurable exercise of
his ability to get high and lose control, as well as for other reasons.
His drinking subsided after a while.

Patient 3 presented a complicated analytic development characterized by great variability and changeability. In the context of
this paper, one point is noteworthy: the patient repeatedly had
tongue-in-mouth experiences reminiscent of the Isakower phenomenon, as well as of Spitz's and Woodbury's comments about the
mouth as primal cavity and primal object.

Spitz (1965) says, "all perception begins in the oral cavity" (p.
62), and agrees with Isakower's opinion that sensations in the oral
cavity, possibly merged with sensations of the external cutaneous
covering, constitute the model for the earliest postnatal ego
structure.

Woodbury wrote, "the tongue-in-mouth complex acts not only
as a 'screen' but more precisely as a metamorphic framework, ref-
erential system, and *perceptual organizer*" (p. 298).

In this patient, the experience of tongue-in-mouth seemed later
to have been extended to the total body. It may have contributed
to the container-contained experience in the feeling of the body

within the teacup and the mind in mental imprisonment, with thought and feeling restriction.

In his analysis, he developed hostile and competitive fantasies frankly put in anal terms. I became shit, and shit less beautiful, less well-formed, and of poorer color than his. He was, he said, frightened by his temerity and elated about his independence in bringing up this thought. He made phallic comparisons, which at that time he assumed would be less favorable to him and consequently more pleasing to me. Often, his manner was one of throwing stones (or fecal pellets) and ducking the response. He separated his thoughts into what he regarded as "good, well-formed ones" and others that were "too liquid, too compressed, or too thrusting." He wondered how to turn his thoughts into money, which he would not spend but store in the bank. He worried that I might become enraged, hurt, intruded upon by his competitiveness. He remembered childhood ideas about his bowel movements. He had daydreams in which, after they were flushed down the toilet, they went into the ground, where they became part of an animated world of little people, serving as furniture, food, and as the little people themselves. In these thoughts the body-cavern was more complex than it had been earlier in his analysis. The intrauterine and anal birth fantasies involved in this thinking became clear to him.

Gradually there appeared an early childhood memory of an enema bag hanging in the bathroom, then memories of baths with mother, enemas, his fear he might not be able to hold in the water and thus anger his mother, her coldness, his need for closeness. He competed with me in the area of interpretations, tried to make them first, and read analytic literature. Fears of separation and of the effects of his anger led to tearful thoughts about accidents, his son's health, dreams involving dismemberment and blood, and a variety of phallic castration anxiety components, as well as to frequent returns to the earlier, simpler shell in which the interior was undifferentiated.

At this stage, the similarity of this case to classical descriptions of anal conflict seen as regressions from phallic conflicts stands out. The anatomic and concurrent mental experience and the transference relationship were obviously interrelated. The patient's thinking style and other mental organizations showed a clear relationship to the associated organization of body experience and object relationships.

To sum up the clinical evidence: these patients initially demonstrated a container-containment self experience which in the course of analysis changed. In two cases, a differentiation of the surface and the interior of the body appeared. Patient 2 came to feel his muscles, which developed volume and synergism. He lost his sense that things taken in or let out were directly, quantitatively related to the extent to which he was alive and powerful. As his body surface came to be experienced as subdivided, no longer uniform, so did what went in and out.

The woman patient became aware of a liquid-containing cavern within her body. A bladder appeared as a part of her body. Her sense of her body now included curves and volumes as well as surfaces, pleasure-giving orifices and subdivisions of organs as well as inlets and outlets. She played with anatomy in her furniture restorations. Her thoughts and feelings became more separated from each other and from early body experience, and could be dealt with as things apart, abstracted, to be played with or allowed to have existences of their own, so to speak, just as the body and its contents were subdivided, more subtly experienced, something possessed.

Play with the body in golf, sexual relations, and with the mind in having an alcoholic high, or a daydream, appeared in these patients' lives, together with the experience of a superordinate sense of control of the self which was separable into bodily self and mental self components.

Coincidentally with the developments just mentioned, both patients noticed a certain separation from their archaic mothers and maternal representatives. With this separation came a sense of independence and the capacity to think about their mothers in a more abstract, observant way. Both patients showed a new awareness of their mothers as individuals with minds and consciousnesses. Regressions, terrors, and rages in relation to these figures diminished, to be replaced by less automatic (in Hartmann's sense [1939]) responses. Of course, fluctuations and regressions continued to occur. Spiegel (1970) discusses comparable changes in analytic patients and terms them developments from "perceptual" to "cognitive ego." Modell (1968) believes that such behavior in analysis reflects mental organizations characteristic of the development period of the "transitional object," which precedes that of "the sense of identity."

The third patient showed a number of levels of organization, including tongue-in-mouth, container-contained, organ and mental differentiation, and more subtle awarenesses on a phallic level. In this case the patient's analytic experience seemed to recapitulate and rework stages in his ontogenesis.

The Early Organization in the Sequence of Development

I think it is reasonable to suggest that the two main organizations just described—the container-contained, and the segmented, partly differentiated body—and their associated experiences of mental activity can be located within a larger ontogenetic sequence. The body sequence would be: (1) a hypothetical undifferentiated stage such as that described by Bak;[1] (2) the mouth, or mouth-tongue organization; (3) the container-contained stage; (4) the period of developing experience of organ, orifice, and surface differentiation. In the container-contained stage, there begins to be an awareness of the body, separate from diffuse mental experience. This is followed by an awareness of more differentiated thoughts and feelings separate from concrete body experience. Eventually, there appear thoughts divorced from body experience as well as the capacity to distinguish between different types of mental experience. For example, a child in the early phallic phase can identify a dream and distinguish it from other thoughts or real events.

A 3½-year-old child's dog died.[2] Days later, she awoke in the

---

[1] Bak (1939, 1943) reviewed a number of phenomena encountered in schizophrenics. These included experiences of cosmic significance, fusion, self-object confusions, and temperature sensitivity. He suggested that rapid cooling of the baby after delivery might contribute to the thermal orientation of schizophrenics, and that temperature sensations may be the earliest body experiences, before self-nonself differentiation occurs. Separation from the object reactivates the early experiences of separation from mother, and loss of warmth leads to a subsequent frozen world feeling.

[2] For a further discussion of the development of dream recognition, see Greenacre (1964), especially pp. 12–14.

morning and told her mother that she had dreamed that she and
her nurse had gone to buy another dog. Some hours later, the
child asked the nurse if she remembered going to buy the dog.
When the nurse looked puzzled, the child brightened and remembered, "Oh yes, it was a dream." There was a suspension of what
Schafer (1968) calls the reflective self representation, that is, of the
distinction between mental and bodily self experience with a
superordinate self-observer, and its later reinstitution. A capacity
for awareness of dream experience, involving a self-observation
and a distinction between mental self, bodily self, and nonself was
at this time becoming established in this little girl. This may be
called self consciousness. The dream within the dream is a representation, in the dream, of the waking experience of dream
recognition. The dream within the dream means one has recognized a dream as a dream, in the waking state. It is a late occurrence and constitutes evidence of an experience of mind. In this
case there is thought about thought, consciousness of consciousness. This is self-self consciousness, an aspect of a relatively advanced organizational stage.

A dream reported by patient 2 late in his analysis contained
representations of a number of self and object experiences he had
previously described at various times. It can serve to illustrate
a model of ontogenetic experiences eventually leading to self-self
consciousness. In this dream, the patient observed an execution.
A queen ordered the condemned criminal to stand. He did, and
an executioner struck him on the back with an axe. The patient
(as observer in the dream) experienced both a feeling that this
was inevitable and amazement that the criminal had no awareness
or understanding of the meaning of this fate, that is, of the permanence of death. In analyzing this dream, the patient recalled
that his mother had punished transgressions in a ritualistic manner, commanding him to get the hairbrush, lower his trousers,
and bend over her knees. Then the punishment was meted out. It
never occurred to him to rebel. He could not conceive of the idea,
"I can prevent her doing this to me." It was inevitable. Now he
could look back on himself at this period, from a new viewpoint,
that of the amazed observer.

The representation of the robotlike prisoner who has almost
no self experience is a representation of a "reminiscence" of the

early organizational stage in which separation from mother is incomplete. All things come from her. The object's commands equal the subject's response.

The patient as amazed dream observer is a representation of an organization that includes an experience of a mental self separate from and controlling a bodily self. Bodily pain and passivity are experienced as different from mental pain and passivity. This organization developed later in the patient's life than the early organization, referred to in the dream, to which it is contrasted. In the analytic hour the patient was a waking observer who described the dream observer, who in turn, from a separated viewpoint, observed the queen who controlled the mindless, acquiescent prisoner.

Another association was the idea that he and his mother had both wished he were, and thought of him as, her phallus. This wishful fantasy of the phallic stage combined the phallic wish with the archaic wishes for union with mother, and was expressed in the regressive terms of early experience. It included the experience the patient had of himself as a container, attached to his mother. As with A. Reich's patients, very early experiences entered into a much later body-phallus fantasy. Schuster (1969) reported a patient with a body-phallus identification who on the couch experienced a feeling of increasing size. This patient traced the feeling back only as far as latency when it had entered into the body-phallus identification. A much earlier origin is likely.

The dream and its treatment in the analysis thus include representations from a developmental series of experiences of the self. These are: (1) an un-self experiencing mind-body almost equated with the object, the prisoner; (2) the experiencing prisoner in his containerlike, blood-containing aspect, experiencing crude emotions, and being controlled by the queen; (3) the dream observer of this situation experiencing the subtler emotion, amazement, and recognizing the separation between the prisoner and the queen; (4) the self-conscious patient aware of his role as inventor and reporter of the dream; and (5) the self-self-conscious, waking observer of the dream inventor and invention. (In the last, the patient is aware of himself as observer of his and his mother's mutually shared fantasy of being mother's phallus.)

These are organizations that involve increasingly general, ab-

stract, and inclusive self and object experiences. The most subtle
includes self consciousnesses of the mental self. They represent
steps in the history of the patient's self-self consciousness development. A further abstraction took place later on, when the patient
imagined himself as the analyst observing all this. Spiegel (1970)
termed this a development to "the cognitive self."

A parallel development sequence of body-self experience might
be: (1) primal state of undifferentiation; (2) container-contained;
(3) orifice and some organ awareness with differentiated surface
and interior separate from waste products and secretions and with
some sense of control over the liquid contents; (4) mind awareness,
with mind differentiated as a psychic organ controlling differentiated body organs and their contained materials; (5) consciousness of awareness of mind.

A parallel object relation sequence can also be constructed: (1)
fusion; (2) self and object distinction, in which the self remains
attached, appendagelike to the object, which is in control; (3)
objects including organs are distinguished, persist in memory in
the absence of external stimuli, and are manipulable in fantasy;
(4) awareness of (3) as in the controlled daydream; and (5) consciousness of the object's and the self's awareness and fantasies.

These sequences are consistent with Mahler's views. Mahler
(1968) describes two subphases within the phase of primary narcissism, absolute primary narcissism followed in the third month by
the symbiotic stage. The first phase "is marked by the infant's
lack of awareness of a mothering agent." In the second, "the
infant begins dimly to perceive need satisfaction as coming from
a need-satisfying part object—albeit still from within the orbit of
his omnipotent symbiotic dual unity with a mothering agency"
(p. 10). In this second substage the "body ego contains two kinds of
self representations: there is an inner core of the body image, with
a boundary that is turned toward the inside of the body and
divides it from the ego; and an outer layer of sensoriperceptive
engrams, which contributes to the boundaries of the 'body self.'
. . . the shift of predominantly proprioceptive-enteroceptive cathexis toward sensoriperceptive cathexis of the periphery is a major
step in development" (p. 11).

Later in this symbiotic subphase (overlapping with the separation-individuation phase at about 12 to 18 months), the "body is taken as object . . . with the well-known focal concentration on the libidinal zones" (Elkisch and Mahler, 1959, p. 219). Greenacre (1953) feels that until the age of about 6 months, "the mouth and lips," "tactile sensations," "superficial kinesthetic responses," and "smell" furnish the bulk of the sensory life of the infant, with hearing and vision playing extremely variable roles. With the development of sitting up, focusing of the eyes, and more precise arm and hand movements, much of the infant's exploratory activity is switched from mother to prehensile vision and arm-hand activity. Mahler's "hatching period" beginning in the last quarter of the first year of life blends with Greenacre's stage after 6 months. There is a shift, Mahler writes, toward "sensoriperceptive cathexis" involving concentration on the libidinal zones and the body experiences occurring with more precise arm and hand movements. The patterns and transitions regressively re-experienced by the patients described presumably appear in this period and can be considered aspects of it.

Greenacre (1964), as noted before, discusses the age at which a child recognizes his dreams as such; upon reviewing the data of others as well as her own, she concluded this may occur in the 4th year. Greenacre also quotes a 4½-year-old child saying of God, "He is *not real*. God is just thinking" (p. 13). God's thoughts are apparently equivalent to dream reality, and distinguished from waking reality.

My example supports the view that children of this age distinguish between psychic reality and external reality. I have no data to suggest the normal age at which self-self consciousness may first appear.

Summary

There are understandable doubts that conclusions drawn about early development from phenomena of later life are correct, and that normal development can be deduced from pathological manifestations. Nevertheless, numerous authors have made plausible suggestions about early development based on observations of phenomena seen in analytic patients in later life. Certain patients respond to the loss of real or internal objects with a regressive dedifferentiation characterized by the loss of a clear sense of self. They feel controlled by others and have self experiences in which mind-body distinctions are weakened, and in which affects and physical elements are crudely and not separately experienced. At the same time, their regressive response involves an attempt to regain the object on a more primitive level and to maintain the separated self. This new balance is unstable, containing the threat of further regression to a still more dedifferentiated state in which self-object distinctions may be lost.

In their imagery, these patients reveal a self experience in which the self is composed of a potentially permeable container, rather uniform, sometimes hard or brittle, and sometimes fragile, and contents made up of thoughts, feelings, and fluids that are poorly distinguished from each other. This container with its contents threatens to become attached to and controlled by an object similarly poorly defined and differentiated. This self experience seems to involve the reactivation of early sensations caused by skin stimulation, breath holding, fecal and enema fluid retention, and feelings of rage and tension. The history given by these patients includes numerous occasions when such experiences must have occurred.

This organization seems more developed than the oral state discussed by Spitz and Woodbury, but clinically one may observe the fear of further regressions, particularly the fear of an objectless selfless state.

In the course of analysis a more differentiated experience of self and objects appears. The experience of a uniform body surface and contents is replaced by an experience of a body made up of organs having distinct and differing characters. Mental contents are also more clearly distinguished from body experiences and from each other. Affects are more differentiated and motives and thoughts are separately perceived. In addition, an experience of observation appears. Objects as well as body and mental self are observed. Spiegel (1970, p. 688) describes this as the establishment of a "cognitive self" which reaches "beyond the present into the past . . . yet retaining the present" and that includes self and object perceptions. This development may be viewed as a part of normal development taking place between 12 and 18 months of age in the evolution from the archaic objectless state to the mature organization when self-self consciousness is established.

BIBLIOGRAPHY

ANTHONY, E. J. (1961), A Study of "Screen Sensations." *This Annual*, 16:211–245.

BAK, R. C. (1939), Regression of Ego-Orientation and Libido in Schizophrenia. *Int. J. Psycho-Anal.*, 20:64–71.

— (1943), Dissolution of the Ego, Mannerism, and Delusion of Grandeur. *J. Nerv. Ment. Dis.*, 98:457–463.

BORNSTEIN, B. (1931), Phobia in a Two-and-a-Half-Year-Old Child. *Psychoanal. Quart.*, 4:93–119, 1935.

ELKISCH, P. & MAHLER, M. S. (1959), On the Infantile Precursors of the "Influencing Machine" (Tausk). *This Annual*, 14:219–235.

FREUD, S. (1905), Jokes and Their Relation to the Unconscious. *Standard Edition*, 8. London: Hogarth Press, 1960.

— (1937), Constructions in Analysis. *Standard Edition*, 23:255–269. London: Hogarth Press, 1964.

GREENACRE, P. (1941), The Predisposition to Anxiety. In: *Trauma, Growth and Personality*. New York: International Universities Press, 1969, pp. 27–82.

— (1945), The Biological Economy of Birth. *Ibid.*, pp. 3–26.

— (1948), Anatomical Structure and Superego Development. *Ibid.*, pp. 149–164.

— (1950), The Prepuberty Trauma in Girls. *Ibid.*, pp. 204–223.

— (1953), Certain Relationships between Fetishism and the Faulty Development of the Body Image. *This Annual*, 8:79–98.

— (1964), A Study on the Nature of Inspiration. *J. Amer. Psychoanal. Assn.*, 13:6–31.

HARTMANN, H. (1939), *Ego Psychology and the Problem of Adaptation.* New York: International Universities Press, 1958.

— (1950), Comments on the Psychoanalytic Theory of the Ego. *This Annual*, 5:74–96.

HOFFER, W. (1949), Mouth, Hand and Ego-Integration. *This Annual*, 3/4:49–56.

ISAKOWER, O. (1938), A Contribution to the Patho-Psychology of Phenomena Associated with Falling Asleep. *Int. J. Psycho-Anal.*, 19:331–345.

JACOBSON, E. (1954), The Self and the Object World. *This Annual*, 9:75–127.

— (1964), *The Self and the Object World.* New York: International Universities Press.

KESTENBERG, J. S. (1970), Discussion of "The Transitional Object and the Fetish" by Phyllis Greenacre, New York Psychoanalytic Society.

LEWIN, B. D. (1946), Sleep, the Mouth, and the Dream Screen. *Psychoanal. Quart.*, 15:419–434.

— (1953), Reconsideration of the Dream Screen. *Psychoanal. Quart.*, 22:174–199.

— (1968), *The Image and the Past.* New York: International Universities Press.

MAHLER, M. S. (& FURER, M.) (1968), *On Human Symbiosis and the Vicissitudes of Individuation.* New York: International Universities Press.

MODELL, A. H. (1968), *Object Love and Reality.* New York: International Universities Press.

REICH, A. (1960), Pathologic Forms of Self-Esteem Regulation. *This Annual,* 15:215–232.

SCHAFER, R. (1968), *Aspects of Internalization.* New York: International Universities Press.

SCHILDER, P. (1935), *The Image and Appearance of the Human Body.* New York: International Universities Press, 1950.

— (1942), *Mind: Perception and Thought in Their Constructive Aspects.* New York: Columbia University Press.

SCHUSTER, D. B. (1969), Bisexuality and Body as Phallus. *Psychoanal. Quart.*, 38:72–80.

SPIEGEL, L. A. (1970), The Self, Reality and Perception. *Ann. N.Y. Acad. Sci.*, 169:683–694.

SPITZ, R. A. (& COBLINER, W. G.) (1965), *The First Year of Life.* New York: International Universities Press.

WINNICOTT, D. W. (1962), The Aims of Psycho-Analytical Treatment. In: *The Maturational Processes and the Facilitating Environment.* New York: International Universities Press, 1965, pp. 166–170.

WOODBURY, M. A. (1966), Altered Body-Ego Experiences: A Contribution to the Study of Regression, Perception, and Early Development. *J. Amer. Psychoanal. Assn.*, 14:273–303.

Late Adolescence

Developmental and Clinical Considerations

SAMUEL RITVO, M.D.

PUBERTY AND ADOLESCENCE USHER IN A PERIOD OF RAPID PHYSIO-
logical, morphological, and psychological change normally lasting
6 to 8 years. The psychoanalytic elucidation of this kaleidoscopic
period has gained enormously from the approach of dividing
adolescence into stages and defining each phase by its phenomenological characteristics and the corresponding metapsychological
conceptualizations. In this way we have progressed in our knowledge of the instinctual upheaval, the shifts in object relations,
alternations between regression and progression, and the restructuring of the psychic apparatus, all of which underlie the otherwise baffling phenomenology of adolescence.

This paper was presented as the Brill Memorial Lecture at the New York
Academy of Medicine, on November 24, 1970.

From the Child Study Center, Yale University, New Haven, Conn.

Late adolescence is important to distinguish as a stage because it defines that period at the end of adolescence when the last major spontaneous integration and structuring of the personality take place as the adolescent enters upon the psychological and reality tasks of adult life. Blos (1962) stresses that unlike puberty and early adolescence when rapid morphological and physiological changes occur, the closing phase of adolescence can be defined only by its psychological features. It is a period of development in which no new intrinsic maturational or biological energies enter the picture. But the psychological features of late adolescence do reflect the fact that this is the age when the biologically mature individual must take steps defining who he is in relation to his society. The duration and style of adolescence are influenced more by cultural and social factors than any other developmental period. The start is determined biologically by puberty; but it may be prolonged by internal psychic conditions in the individual and by the conditions of society. This period spans what Erikson (1956) has described as the psychosocial moratorium. In our post-industrial technological society this period is more prolonged for more individuals who comprise a greater segment of society than in previous historical periods. The transition to work and love in the realistic world is a longer process.

As psychoanalysts we probably have our largest and most in-tensive experience with that segment of the youth population which is most affected by the conditions which prolong adolescence —the subsidized, dependent student group. With the vastly in-creased size of this group it seems likely that more persons are drawn into this group who are not suited to a life in which inner organization and motivation are at a premium and in which im-mediate reality demands closer to self-preservation do not support the ego in its autonomy from the instinctual drives.

What are the main developmental issues of late adolescence? Blos (1962) stresses that late adolescence is primarily a phase of consolidation in which there is an "elaboration of: 1) a highly idiosyncratic and stable arrangement of ego functions and interests; 2) an extension of the conflict-free sphere of the ego (secondary autonomy); 3) an irreversible sexual position (identity con-stancy) . . . ; 4) a relatively constant cathexis of object- and self-representations; and 5) the stabilization of mental apparatuses which automatically safeguard the integrity of the psychic organism" (p. 129). In a later paper (1967), Blos examines further the relationship between the consolidation of psychic structure and character formation as a normative integrative process aimed at the elimination of conflict and anxiety arousal. He assigns to this process primarily a regulatory function in the maintenance of homeostasis in patterned self-esteem regulation, in the stabilization of ego identity (Erikson, 1956), in the automatization of threshold and barrier levels to internal and external stimuli, and in the containment of affective fluctuations, including depression, within a tolerable range.

Jacobson (1964) lays great stress on the changes in the ego and superego identifications of the adolescent. In late adolescence, an unmistakable shift of power to the ego occurs which gives it increasing influence on id and superego. The ego acquires the role of an active mediator. The adolescent's worldly strivings and his identifications with the realistic images of his parents are used as aids for the readjustments of the superego and its moral codes. The superego enters into a new equilibrium with the id and ego in which the id is restricted and more mature ego goals and standards of achievement are adopted. The formation and structuralization of the ego ideal are crucial developmental steps in adolescence.

The modifications in the psychic systems in late adolescence stem from a confluence of social and reality pressures on the one hand and internal strivings on the other. The crises of late adolescence arise because of the failure to achieve the earlier developmental tasks, especially the failure to resolve the effects of childhood neuroses and other developmental disturbances which have distorted the ego and hampered the development of object relations. The increasing demands on the ego toward the end of adolescence to take the ascendancy in the last spontaneous integration and consolidation of the personality may bring long-standing, latent vulnerabilities of the ego into open clinical manifestation. The clinical crises of this period span the full range of character disorders, psychoneuroses, and borderline conditions. It is also the age of greatest liability to the severest failures of the ego, the psychoses. The crises of personality integration present themselves in terms of the life issues of the period: the difficulties in approaching the new heterosexual object; the concerns about homosexuality; the reactions to the inexorable processes of self-definition as these go forward in choices and decisions determined by the past as well as the present and the visions of the future.

The individual in crisis responds intrapsychically to the conflict over these issues along the pathways prepared by his earlier development in terms of anxiety, regression, defense, and symptom formation. The dynamics of these conflicts do not change basically from generation to generation and follow the basic psychological laws that govern intrapsychic phenomena. Yet the manifest expression of these conflicts does change because a person can use only the vehicles at hand in the contemporary historical period of his society and culture or those which he invents using the modalities at hand in his environment. When the vehicles at hand include drugs, new methods of contraception, worldwide instant communications, jet-age mobility, the threat of nuclear explosions, and a technological society in which adolescence is prolonged, the conditions exist for such kaleidoscopic shifts in available life styles and such distorted or apparently novel behavioral expressions of basic psychological conflicts that their recognition as variations of basic themes may be hampered for a time. There still remains the possibility that such extensive external changes and the changing moral attitudes which are internalized bring about more than "apparent" change. Furthermore, in treating individuals the analyst always deals with the variations rather than the basic theme.

Of the many factors entering into the crises of late adolescence I would like to examine in more detail two which play an important part in this period—object relations and ego-ideal formation—and therefore also have an impact on the technique of psychoanalysis during this period. My discussion is limited to the male because my analytic experience in recent years has been preponderantly with males. I hope that the advent of coeducation at Yale will help to correct this and teach us more about the salient differences between male and female adolescent development.

Object Relations

In early adolescence the reawakened pregenital urges and the newly acquired genital urges are in danger of making contact with the libidinal cathexes of the original objects from the oedipal and preoedipal past (Anna Freud, 1958). This lends a new and threatening reality to hitherto repressed fantasies. The anxiety which arises becomes a motive force in the efforts to loosen or break the ties to the infantile objects. The breaking of the object ties and the return of the libido to the self and the ego result in the increased narcissism of the adolescent. The heightened narcissistic libido manifests itself in the bodily preoccupations, the hypochondriacal tendencies, and the prominence of somatizations in the psychoneurotic symptoms of adolescence. The quickly established and often equally quickly broken attachments to peers and adults are formed on the basis of idealizations which are externalizations and projections of the adolescent's own narcissism. These relationships are the basis for new identifications and are initial steps in the reversal of libidinal cathexis from the self to the object but do not yet constitute lasting new object ties.

The late adolescent must leave his narcissistic retreat and turn more to the external world for gratification and self-realization, a process that has major consequences for his relationship to the external world. Paradoxically, with the establishment of genital primacy, the individual becomes directly dependent on the body of the object in a way that has not existed since infancy. This can be seen in the strong bodily and emotional ties that the individual has to the person with whom he experiences the genital sexual gratification. The greater dependence for gratification upon the external object brings about a shift in the relations or balance between the reality principle and the pleasure principle. Reality now assumes a relatively greater role in the attainment of pleasure than it previously had. The role of fantasy is relatively lessened and assumes more preparatory and anticipatory functions.

With the progress of adolescence the individual shifts from gratification or discharge largely in connection with fantasy about the object to gratification more directly in activity with the object.

The adolescent is impelled in this shift by his own more intense erotic arousal and object hunger which press him to function according to the reality principle in the service of the pleasure principle. Attempts at gratification through fantasy prove disappointing to the adolescent just as attempts toward hallucinatory gratification proved disappointing in the past. Unlike the infant who does not know at first that the external object is necessary and responds with crying and helplessness, the adolescent knows that the external object is necessary and seeks the object. In both there is no fully adequate substitute for the external object.

The younger child is predominantly in a passive position in relation to the object, whereas the adolescent is much more in an active role. The necessary and phase-specific turn to activity with the external object means that the sexual excitement which was previously discharged in fantasy and the autoplastic activity of masturbation now has to seek gratification in the context of the alloplastic relationship to the external object. For the adolescent this constitutes a new and strange reality element to be mastered. One consequence of the turn toward greater activity is the increased possibility of anxiety and conflict over the discharge of aggression upon the object, requiring the institution of vigorous defenses or avoidance or flight from the object.

Another consequence of the turn toward the external object in the move toward the genital sexual relationship is that the conditions of pleasure gain for the individual become more manifest and more specific. As the conditions of pleasure gain dictate the situations and practices which enhance or inhibit sexual excitement and responsiveness, the adolescent becomes aware of the limitations and distortions of his sexual life over which he has little or no control. The conditions of pleasure gain have multiple internal sources. They arise from the conditions of infantile sexual life (Freud, 1914): from the quantitative aspect of the component instincts, indicating the fixation points of earlier libidinal and aggressive development; from object relations, dictating the characteristics of the partner; or from the superego, necessitating guilt and self-punitive or self-damaging behavior.

When the adolescent turns to the external object, the fantasies which were a source of pleasure in connection with masturbation may become a source of acute conflict when the gratification has to be sought directly with the object and not exclusively in fantasy. Early in adolescence when the new genital urges and the re-awakened pregenital strivings connect with the oedipal and pre-oedipal objects, the fantasies were a source of anxiety because they threatened to become too realistic. In later adolescence when the realistic relationship with the new object is taken up, the individual has to cope with the revival of the libidinal cathexes of the old objects as they appear now in the context of the realistic relationship. The necessity to *act upon* the old oedipal and pre-oedipal fantasies becomes a source of increased anxiety. The nuclear infantile conflicts come up for final resolution, so to speak, with the difference that there is a greater element of reality to conflicts which earlier had existed largely in fantasy.

Eissler (1958) has examined the function of orgasm in adolescence in the fusion of the unconscious representation of reality with the specific external circumstances. He emphasizes the first orgasm in puberty and the establishment of orgasm in a permanent place in the life of the adolescent as crucial experiences in the long developmental process by which the reality principle is installed and maintained in psychic life.

To the ego already distorted, restricted or split by infantile and childhood conflict and experience; to the superego which has not been modified by influence from a normally functioning ego, the situation becomes acute and may assume critical proportions. The time to choose a life work and make a commitment cannot be staved off further, the young man's measure will finally be taken for all the world to know. The oedipal conflict comes to life in earnest for the time has actually come to take the man's place. The issue may become particularly transparent in those young men who enter their father's profession or vocation, and a frequent point of breakdown is on taking this step in school. The unconscious death wishes against the oedipal rival regain a poignancy absent since the height of the oedipal period. The shift of influence to the ego also means that the ego reacts more intensely to these dystonic elements in the form of anxiety, symptom formation, and concern for the future of the work life and love relationships. This is often the point at which the adolescent comes for treatment.

The path from the first new approaches to the object in adolescence to the adult love relationship involving lasting intimacy and care is a developmental process extending over a period of years. Although the pleasure principle impels the adolescent to turn actively to the new object for gratification, the object choice and the object relationship have at first *both* narcissistic and anaclitic elements. In his approach to the new object the adolescent starts from the position of ego regression described by Geleerd (1961) in which he gives signs of regression to the undifferentiated phase of object relations with wishes and fantasies of merging with the object and blurring of the ego boundaries.

Geleerd viewed this regression as necessary for later healthy ego integration in the adolescent. I am interested here in the steps by which the adolescent emerges from this regressed position. Even in the heterosexual object the male adolescent can love what he once was or would like to be. The object is often seen as embodying ideals he has for himself in qualities of mind and body and the incandescent passion may flicker and go out when she does not live up to an ideal he has for himself. She may be regarded as a possession or attribute of the self which can be a source of pride and satisfaction if she is seen as perfect or a source of shame and self-criticism if she is viewed as flawed or defective. The initial steps toward the new object contain elements of the adolescent's own narcissism which can be discerned in the attitudes and behavior toward the new object.

Clinical psychoanalytic observation suggests that for the adolescent the new object serves functions that in some ways resemble those the object had in infancy and early childhood (Kris, 1955). At that time the central love object acts as a stabilizer of physiological and affective processes. Where the central love object is absent as in institutionalized children, Kris hypothesized that the neutralization of instinctual energy does not take place to the usual degree and the ego is not invested with the energies which lead to the normally expected developmental steps such as the organization of action and problem solving even if the noninstinctual energies connected with the maturational processes are available. This old pathway is used again by the adolescent who has retreated to a narcissistic position in the course of loosening the ties to the infantile objects and who is absorbed in himself, his body, his feelings, his thought processes. In this condition he is likely to have somatic and hypochondriacal symptoms, to be preoccupied with existential ruminations about the absurdity of life, to be without a sense of purpose, and to shift rapidly from exalted feelings to feeling worthless. He may be unable to organize himself for action or work if there is no immediate or urgent reality demand, and even this may fail to activate him.

This state may change with dramatic swiftness with the cathexis of the external object. Not only do the manifestations of the narcissistic investment of the self abate with the cathexis of the object, but the capacity to organize for action and work and the sense of purpose and being in touch with the real world are strengthened. The sequence from narcissistic investment to cathexis of the object and then to improved functioning in activities requiring increased supplies of neutralized instinctual energies can be observed repeatedly in the same individual. At these times the object serves again as the mother once served—as an organizer with whom the child identifies, thus making neutralized energies available for development in the direction of sublimation and work.

Although the adolescent turns actively to the object for gratification, he does so with a resurgence of old passive, anaclitic aims toward the object. They take the form of a revival of the old dependent, clinging, possessive demands toward the object with abrupt outbursts of the negative, hostile side of the ambivalence at the slightest rebuff or frustration, which is experienced as a painful, narcissistic wound. During the period of emergence from the narcissistic retreat of earlier adolescence, the relationship to the object shows some of the features of the infantile relationship to the need-satisfying object.

A central narcissistic concern related to the castration anxiety of the phallic-oedipal phase is the concern over genital potency (Deutsch, 1967). Frequently, it is only after this concern subsides with the establishment of potency that the passive, infantile strivings toward the object come into the foreground. The passive strivings and the need for the object as organizer were expressed succinctly by a sophomore at a time when he was experiencing an insatiable sexual curiosity and desire for everyone he encountered, man or woman. He said, "Wanting girls so much is a weakness because of why I want them. I need a girl for physical stability. I need the warmth, the flesh. I want to be taken in the warm insides of the girl. But I know that aggressive courting is necessary for that and I don't feel up to it at the moment. Smoking marijuana is a good substitute for a girl. It gives me the same feeling of calm fulfillment."

In another hour during the same period of the analysis when he felt that his activities had no significance and that life had no meaning for him he spoke again of his longing for a girl. "A girl is my link with the world. I can't touch anything until I touch a girl. The world becomes real that way. If I can control the girl's body, it makes my body whole. It is a way to get from my own body to the world. My own body becomes a tool rather than a reflection."

The first approaches to the new object start from a strongly narcissistic position and the active turning to the object is accompanied by an intensification of passive aims. The intensified passive wishes to merge and be taken close revive former anxieties connected with fantasies and fears of engulfment. Through the projection of the aggressive components onto the object and reversal of the passive and dependent strivings the male adolescent views the woman again as a phallic woman who threatens him in a variety of ways still related to the strongly narcissistic investment of his body and his self-image. He is tortured by concerns that she will not find him adequate, that she will deplete him physically, that she will offer temptations which will undermine his resolve to commit himself to a goal. These concerns also contain the hostile and punitive reactions of the superego against the oedipal content of the masturbation fantasies of the antecedent adolescent period. Under these influences the attitude toward the new object oscillates between a feeling of urgent need for a close, exclusive possessive relationship with the heterosexual object and an anxious apprehension that the girl clings to him, makes demands on him, and threatens his freedom and integrity.

The willingness of the girl to enter into such a relationship is for the male adolescent a gratifying and reassuring, though often transitory confirmation of his consolidating realistic sense of his own worth as he moves developmentally from the self image which has been distorted by the narcissistic retreat and the exaggerated intellectual and ascetic defenses of the earlier period of adolescence. The object plays a crucial role as an external referent for the internal reorganization which takes place.

The eventual steps toward lasting intimacy and care are dependent on the ability to progress from the predominantly narcissistic relationship to the object and to tolerate the anaclitic dependence on the object which otherwise has to be avoided by many adolescents because of the painful affects and aggression connected with it from childhood frustrations and disappointments. Normally, both the narcissistic satisfactions and the object-libidinal gratifications which can be gained from the new object raise the self-regard of the ego and contribute both to the consolidation of the ego in late adolescence and to a change in the ego ideal in the direction of deriving gratification from being able to realize some parts of the ideal and of being the one to provide for the loved person in a variety of ways. This contributes an element of pleasure gain to the work functions. Genetically the change draws upon oedipal and preoedipal ideals but is also realistically rooted in the new developmental capacity to provide genital sexual pleasure, itself an important source of narcissistic gratification.

The strong impression gained from clinical psychoanalytic observation that passive aims are prominent in the initial approaches to the new object may be colored by a selection factor, since it is quite likely that the more passive adolescents gravitate toward analysis. Nevertheless, this may be an instance again in which the study of pathology or one sector of normal variation may contribute to the understanding of development. When the adolescent takes the first steps in turning actively toward the new object in the developmental move toward the assumption of the adult sexual role and the mature love relationship, he does so only partly in identification with the ideal of the phallic-oedipal period. In large measure he turns to the new object with passive needs as he did to the earlier external object so that the object again functions as an organizer and stabilizer crucial to the consolidation of late adolescence. The interplay between drive and object is essential to the emergence from the narcissistic retreat.

Although the relationship to the new object may have a large narcissistic element in the beginning and this may be a prerequisite for daring to take the step so risky to his self-esteem, other developmental issues in the resolution of which the object has a role are carried along in this step. The object is also an immediate portion of reality to which the adolescent turns for the nutriment he needs in the looming struggle over what will be his place in life. The object's interest and love are the needed replacements for the blows to his narcissism which the adolescent anticipates and sustains as he makes his choices. His decisions eventually transform the omnipotentiality of the youth (Pumpian-Mindlin, 1965) into the specific, individual, delimited identity of the adult. In this the object functions for the individual in a manner synergistic with and complementary to the ego ideal. As one 19-year-old expressed it, "Sometimes I wonder how good I am compared to the others around me. Most of the time I know I'm pretty good, but I would like to have someone who would be interested enough in me or care enough about me to share what I think and what I feel."

It is well known that identification with the parents in their adult role plays a large part in the shift of power to the ego in late adolescence. But it is important to realize fully the role of the new object in this process of consolidation of the ego because the object offers the possibility both of gratifying the instinctual drives and, via identification with the object as a repetition of the early central love object, making available to the ego increased resources of neutralized instinctual energies for its adaptive functioning.

The actual experience with the object in infancy and early childhood has a profound effect on the outcome of adolescence. The object stands in a pivotal position between the instinctual drives and reality in the reorganization of the drives under the hegemony of the ego in late adolescence. The outcome of this developmental process in adolescence is therefore critically affected by the history, the characteristics, and the experiences of the earlier object relations. This is the time when the effects of deprivation, loss, separation, deficiencies, and peculiarities of mothering which resulted in the developmental disturbances of infancy and early childhood become operative again. Sleep and eating disturbances, somatic complaints and bodily concerns become frequent and are prominent in the symptom formation of this period. The earlier disturbances in object relations may have impaired the development from the need-satisfying object to object constancy with resulting deviations and distortions in the ego. These may have a particularly strong impact on children with constitutional vulnerabilities. In the face of the new demands of genital sexuality, of the need to make realistic commitments in the irreversible process of self-definition which threatens the narcissistic self image, the adolescent makes use of old object representations and looks for new objects in the external world who can be merged and blended with the old object representations in the search for the necessary accommodation of both instinctual drives and external reality. The adolescent with early impairment of ego and object relations has severe difficulty making his way back from the ego regression of earlier adolescence.

The recognition of the widening chasm between the defensively aggrandized self image and the desperately struggling self produces intense anxiety and heightened feelings of guilt and shame. The excessive ambivalence and hostility which accompanied the early unsatisfactory object relations now interfere with the capacity to identify with the parental objects in their adult roles and with the new objects on the model of the earlier central love object as stabilizer and organizer. This is after all the age of greatest incidence of schizophrenic psychosis in which there is a break with reality. It is also the time of greatest need for the therapies which provide direct support for the ego through supplying an object, often through specialized communities in institutions.

The Ego Ideal

The consolidation and integration of the ego toward the end of adolescence also occur in consonance with changes in the ego ideal.

Because the ego ideal is the substitute for the lost narcissism of the individual's childhood it remains throughout life an agency of the mind which is most closely connected with the regulation and maintenance of self-esteem and therefore also with need satisfaction and wish fulfillment (Lampl-de Groot, 1962). What is idealized at each period of the child's development is linked to the source and nature of the injury to the child's narcissism at that period (Kohut, 1966).

The adolescent is in the situation where he experiences the new genital strivings and capacities when his libidinal ties are still to the oedipal and preoedipal objects. The ego experiences this as a danger, and the anxiety and the guilt engendered by this situation become the impelling forces for breaking the tie with the infantile objects. The libido which he withdraws from the infantile object is turned on the ego and the self, resulting in the increased narcissism which so regularly follows upon the breaking of the infantile object ties. It also goes into the idealization of abstractions and moral and ethical values and concepts, for example, asceticism, religious beliefs, philosophies, and intellectuality in general. These idealizations and the new identifications with contemporaries and adults free energies which are neutralized by the ego and in that form are available for aim-inhibited pursuits.

This economic formulation accounts for the bursts of sublimations and achievements in adolescence. The stability and the extent of the sublimation also depend on the capacity of the ego to maintain the activity in the conflict-free sphere. This may be facilitated when the sublimated activity also serves a defensive function in relation to the drives and the superego. With the stabilization of the ego and with the shift from the narcissistic cathexis of the self of early adolescence to the greater object-libidinal cathexis of late adolescence the idealizations and identifications provide the directions for the displacements to aim-inhibited goals, and form the basis for choice of work and the mastery of a portion of reality.

For example, the sophomore mentioned earlier remained at the top of his class in college and turned to his work as a haven even at the times of his most acute unhappiness. His family had no intellectual interests and provided no stimulation in this direction during his childhood. Because of his small size he could not fulfill his father's athletic ideals. He was humiliated by his older sister's athletic superiority over him. His intellectual and literary interests started when he idealized a high school English teacher who inspired him and took an interest in his work. Literature and writing also represented something clean, pure, and perfect, in complete contrast to his own dirty, flawed, deteriorating body and his revolting, frank or thinly disguised, incestuous fantasies.

The ego ideal as a structuralized institution of the mind is a development of adolescence. The later stages in the formation of the ego ideal which occur at the end of adolescence illustrate the hierarchical organization and mutual interrelations between ego, ego ideal, and superego, with the ego in the role of active mediator. The adolescent's worldly strivings, his identifications with the realistic images of his parents become aids in the toning down and readjustment of the superego demands, while at the same time the ego calls on the superego for support in restricting the id and in developing mature ego goals and adult achievement standards.

Jacobson (1964) distinguishes between the ego ideal and what she terms the wishful self image, that grandiose, glorified, heroic fantasy figure which may have elements of the ego ideal in the details of its contents, but which is primarily the inflated self image cathected with the libido withdrawn from the infantile object ties at a time when psychological independence from parental objects has not been established and when intolerable anxiety is easily aroused by the hazards of failure if the attempt is made. At the end of adolescence these images tend to become increasingly ego-dystonic, and their persistence beyond their appropriate and useful time precipitates the crises of late adolescence.

One of the main genetic roots of the ego ideal is in the passive-feminine homosexual orientation of the negative oedipus complex. In the paper "On Narcissism" Freud (1914) pointed out that it is mainly homosexual libido which is bound in the formation of the ego ideal. This aspect of the ego ideal is very useful in understanding the problems of homosexuality that occur in late adolescence in connection with the approach to the new object and with taking steps in the realistic world which have a crucial quality for the individual in relation to his self-esteem. Conscious homosexual fantasies and episodes of homosexual activity may appear simultaneously with or in alternation with approaches to the heterosexual object. They may have a multiple and shifting meaning in the same individual. They can function as a defense against the fears of being engulfed by the castrated or castrating phallic woman because of the intense passive strivings which arise from the revived preoedipal object ties and the pregenital strivings related to them. They can also represent an identification with the woman in the passive-feminine defense against the oedipal strivings which are stirred up by the approach to the new object. They also appear at times when the main threat is to the vulnerable self-esteem of the adolescent. This especially is the case in those who cling to a grandiose, inflated self image in a compensatory fashion at a time when they are unable to tolerate failure and further narcissistic wounds to an already hard-pressed ego. The threat of failure stems from the pressure to take the steps and make the choices which will define the individual and his place in the community.

At such a point the adolescent may turn to someone who represents his own ideal. The ego is threatened for falling so far short of the narcissistic ideal and the demands of the superego, and is attacked by feelings of guilt and shame. Under these conditions the ego is in desperate need to restore its self-regard. The homosexual libido hitherto bound and neutralized in the ego ideal is reinstinctualized and seeks gratification in the perverse fantasies or activities with the immediately idealized homosexual object, with the idea, "I love and am loved by the kind of person I would like to be." The ego ideal is repersonified in the homosexual object and the process of ego-ideal formation, including the vicissitudes of homosexual libido, may be repeated a number of times. There is also at that point an identification with the idealized qualities of the narcissistic homosexual object.

Two brief clinical vignettes will furnish an illustration. A 19-year-old youth suffered acute anxiety when he was to leave home for college. He dreaded the prospect that he would not be able to make the grade, let alone not live up to his grandiose and inflated expectations. During this period he had a rush of erotic feeling toward two young men each of whom had qualities which he prized and idealized in his grandiose self image.

A 20-year-old youth was constantly "testing himself" for homosexual feelings by monitoring his reactions to older men and contemporaries to whom he was attracted. At the time he was concerned whether he would be able to establish his potency in a relationship with a girl who was quite hostile and cutting to him at times. Simultaneously, he developed a new friendship with a young man whom he admired. He devoted himself to this relationship with almost equal fervor. At one point he had to fend off erotic feelings toward his friend when they had a long and searching discussion of their relationship with one another while they were sharing the patient's father's bed on a visit to the city. When the immediate issue of potency was resolved for the time being, the friendship cooled considerably. Just as "the evolution of conscience is reproduced regressively [in paranoia]" (Freud, 1914, p. 96), the evolution of the ego ideal may be regressively reproduced in the homosexual attachments of adolescence.

Psychoanalytic Treatment in Adolescence

Psychoanalysts have sounded warnings about the difficulties in the way of psychoanalysis at the height of the adolescent upheaval (e.g., Spiegel, 1961). Anna Freud (1958) gave the most succinct of these when she drew the parallel between the reactions to treatment during unhappy love affairs or periods of mourning and the adolescent's reaction to treatment when his libido is at the point of detaching itself from the parents and cathecting new objects. At such a time the preoccupation is with the present, and little or no libido is available for investment in either the past or the analyst. The later adolescent period, more specifically the college-age period, becomes a feasible and even an advantageous time for psychoanalysis. Although he may have been unsuccessful in adequately detaching his libido from the parental objects and still may have no investment in the past, he may make a libidinal investment in the analyst because he seeks relief from his anxiety, depression, and ego-dystonic symptoms. He may also have an increasing awareness that his future love and work life may be threatened. At this time there is normally a change in the ego ideal by which the individual relinquishes the grandiose, heroic, inflated self image for an ideal which can function as a guide to realizable life aims and goals in terms of object choice, career, and role in society. When the ego finds itself in conflict with this ideal and begins to recognize that life goals are threatened and compromised by forces over which the adolescent has no control, he is likely to turn to someone for help. These factors may strengthen the motivation for sustaining the analytic situation and establishing a therapeutic alliance.

Since the older adolescent in crisis who comes to analysis is usually the one who has had a prolonged and difficult struggle over the establishment of his psychological independence from his parents, it is not surprising that this issue and related ones play a central role in the transference, especially in the early part of the analysis. This may take the form of shunning and denying dependence on the analyst as on the parents. At the same time the adolescent tends to regard the analyst as a new and more powerful ally in his search for independence, for the establishment of sexual identity, for finding a new object, and for the definition and achievement of life goals. This threatens to heighten the passive, homosexual strivings toward the analyst, to increase the transference resistance in the analysis, and to augment the tendency to act out transference-related feelings outside the analysis. The passivity and regressive pull of the analytic situation also contribute to the revival and intensification of the preoedipal object cathexes and the pregenital urges which are connected with them. When these threaten to appear in the transference, they may do so as somatic symptoms involving the autonomic nervous system and may be the initial symptoms of the transference neurosis.

One adolescent described in effect how he split the transference between the transference to the preoedipal infantile object and the transference to the analyst as the guiding, protective father figure, who will watch over his development as a man during this time of instability. He spoke of needing a girl as a break from work, to relax and relieve him, to hold onto and scream at it if he felt like it, whereas the analyst represented "long-term established or establishment help," founded on the assumption that life is really important or significant. As the latter the analyst, by his presence, interest, and attention also functions as an auxiliary ego augmenting the patient's ability to tolerate and recognize infantile strivings without having to resort to action, flight, or immediate gratification so characteristic of adolescence. In this sense analysis tries to ride the wave of progressive stabilization of the ego, which is the normal development of this period and contributes to this stabilization. A consequence for the analysis is a greater tolerance for the appearance and recognition of the transference neurosis and the analysis of it. With these steps the late adolescent shows a greater investment in memory and the past in relation to the conflicts of the present. The analysis loses the quality of merely a communication of current happenings. Analysis of the transference and reconstruction with affective validity become possible.

Analysis provides an opportunity to study the way in which adolescents use drugs in relation to the state of internal conflict, quite apart from their being an established feature of the everyday social scene. Generally, marijuana is used as an institutionalized way of making social contact, and for overcoming inhibitions against them. As observed in the psychoanalytic situation, marijuana and the psychedelic drugs are likely to be used at times of great loneliness, object hunger, narcissistic wounds to the ego, that is, when preoedipal strivings are intensified. The effect of the drug varies with the affective state and the state of ego organization at the time. The existing mood is intensified and reflects the instability of the ego, but the element of seeking for contact with the object is always discernible. Anxiety and loneliness can become a black, empty, frightening despair with the most intense craving for contact with another person. Taking the drug represents an attempt to gratify the wish for relief or reunion with the love object. In this representation the drugtaker assumes both roles, the one in need as well as the one who satisfies the need. The recognition that anyone who is "tripping" should have someone with him is not simply a reasonable precaution. For the drugtaker it constitutes a valid claim on the immediate interest of another person.

The psychoanalytic situation and psychoanalytic process always have to be considered in relation to the life setting and life circumstances in which they are taking place. From child analysis we know the influence that the developmental level of the child has on indications for analysis, on transference phenomena, and on the motivations for analysis. From training analysis we are familiar with another group of problems linked to the life setting of the analysis. So far as I am aware analysis in the older adolescent age group has been limited almost entirely to college students and those who have dropped out of college. The present-day American college, particularly the residential college, is the major institution provided by our society for the transition from childhood to adulthood where he can find, in Erikson's terms (1956): "a psychosocial moratorium during which extremes of *subjective experience,* alternatives of *ideological choice,* and potentialities of *realistic commitment* can become the subject of social play and joint mastery" (p. 119). This is often a world without work other than academic; limited to a group who are all the same age. The analyst may be the only person outside this age range with whom the youth has any significant human contact for months at a time unless he exerts considerable initiative to do so.

The student status is a mixed blessing for the analysis. At the start it may be a factor in overcoming the fear of passivity and dependence because it can be viewed as another school or college course, like an individual tutorial which meets five times a week. We are prone to assume that the adolescent who comes into an analysis supported by his parents is unequivocally the more passive one. There is clinical evidence to suggest that he may rather be the one who can tolerate this degree of actual dependence without feeling it as a threat to surrender.

With college students there is also the problem of whether the analytic work will be geared to the academic year with its examination periods, long holidays, and frequent interruptions or to a schedule geared more to the needs of the analytic work. If the analyst imposes an immediate intransigent set of conditions, the adolescent may respond as to a parent who forces on him the regressive dependence which still has a strong and dangerous attraction for him and he may be impelled to respond with defiance and flight. On the other hand the analyst may at the start recognize the conflict between the need of continuity in the analytic work and the reality situation of the student who may have no work, no home, no social life, and no community if he stays on for analysis during a long vacation. This approach can enlist the cooperation of the adolescent at the start and leave for later analysis the transference-resistance aspects of remaining alone with the analyst with little or nothing else to do, the condition that frequently threatens to intensify the infantile object ties which need to be loosened and relinquished. Adopting this attitude I have found repeatedly that with the progressive analysis of this particular source of resistance the student patient is able to shorten the vacations or remain through them. The normal vacation time is used frequently for significant self-examination without the feeling of being watched, and without the privacy, which is so necessary for adolescents, being intruded upon. The patient frequently returns on a distinctly new level of organization and consolidation.

Summary

Ideally, late adolescence is the time of the last spontaneous developmental consolidation and integration of the personality. In this restructuring of the psychic apparatus the ego gains in power and increases its influence on the id, superego, and ego ideal.

The inevitable moves toward love and work in the realistic world alter the balance between fantasy and reality in the mental life of the individual and make the conditions of pleasure gain more manifest to the adolescent himself. This awareness may become a motivation for treatment. The crises of late adolescence arise when the individual who has not been successful in breaking or loosening oedipal and preoedipal object cathexes is under pressure internally and externally to find a new object and to make self-defining commitments in the realistic world. The reliance of the older adolescent on the new object enables us to study the process by which he makes the transition from the increased narcissistic cathexis of the self so characteristic of earlier adolescence to the object cathexis required for the adult love relationship—a process which is discernible in analysis but which I believe takes place in all male adolescents. In this process the adolescent follows again old pathways from early childhood when the central love object became the stabilizer and organizer for the immature ego.

The formation of an ego ideal that is attuned to reality is a development of late adolescence which is necessary for the adaptive tasks of adult life. The crises of late adolescence are marked by failures of adequate ego-ideal formation and by insufficiently reality-attuned ego ideals which lead to disturbances of sublimation and the capacity for work. Homosexual fantasies and feelings in this age often bring about a fragmentation of the ego ideal as well as regressive efforts to reconstitute it.

The shift of influence to the ego results in anxiety and neurotic symptom formation and increased awareness by the older adolescent that he is in the grip of unconscious forces. This becomes a reliable motivation for entering into and sustaining the psychoanalytic situation.

The life situation of being still dependent on his parents and the setting in which he lives, usually the student status, have an influence on the transference and on technique. But in the neurotic adolescent no basic modification of the analytic situation is necessary.

BIBLIOGRAPHY

BLOS, P. (1962), *On Adolescence.* New York: Free Press of Glencoe, Ill.
— (1967), The Second Individuation Process of Adolescence. *This Annual,* 22:162–186.
DEUTSCH, H. (1967), *Selected Problems of Adolescence.* New York: International Universities Press.
EISSLER, K. R. (1958), Notes on Problems of Technique in the Psychoanalytic Treatment of Adolescents. *This Annual,* 13:223–254.
ERIKSON, E. H. (1956), The Problem of Ego Identity. *J. Amer. Psychoanal. Assn.,* 4:56–121.
FREUD, A. (1936), *The Ego and the Mechanisms of Defense.* New York: International Universities Press, rev. ed., 1966.
— (1958), Adolescence. *This Annual,* 13:255–278.

FREUD, S. (1914), On Narcissism. *Standard Edition,* 14:67–102. London: Hogarth Press, 1957.

GELEERD, E. R. (1961), Some Aspects of Ego Vicissitudes in Adolescence. *J. Amer. Psychoanal. Assn.,* 9:394–405.

JACOBSON, E. (1964), *The Self and the Object World.* New York: International Universities Press.

KOHUT, H. (1966), Forms and Transformations of Narcissism. *J. Amer. Psychoanal. Assn.,* 14:243–272.

KRIS, E. (1955), Neutralization and Sublimation. *This Annual,* 10:30–46.

LAMPL-DE GROOT, J. (1962), Ego Ideal and Superego. *This Annual,* 17:48–57.

PUMPIAN-MINDLIN, E. (1965), Omnipotentiality, Youth, and Commitment. *J. Amer. Acad. Child Psychiat.,* 4:1–18.

SPIEGEL, L. A. (1961), Disorder and Consolidation in Adolescence. *J. Amer. Psychoanal. Assn.,* 9:406–416.

Young Children in Brief Separation

A Fresh Look

JAMES AND JOYCE ROBERTSON

DURING THE LAST QUARTER OF A CENTURY MUCH HAS BEEN PUBLISHED about the effects of separation from the mother in early childhood, mostly in the form of retrospective or follow-up studies. The few direct observational studies appear to have been done exclusively in hospitals and other residential institutions (Burlingham and A. Freud, 1942, 1944; Heinicke and Westheimer, 1965; Micic, 1962; Prugh et al., 1953; James Robertson, 1952, 1953, 1970; Schaffer and Callender, 1959; Spitz, 1945; Spitz and Wolf, 1946; Vaughan, 1957). These provide a consensus that young children admitted to institutional care usually respond with acute distress followed by a slow and painful process of adaptation. James

---

The study of "Young Children in Brief Separation" is supported by the British National Health Service, The Tavistock Institute of Human Relations, and The Grant Foundation, Inc., of New York. To all of these our thanks are due.

Robertson (1953, 1970) described the phases of Protest, Despair, and Denial (later termed "Detachment").

Institution-based studies have been valuable in many ways, but have the limitation that the data they provide do not permit the responses to separation from the mother to be reliably differentiated from the influence of associated adverse factors such as illness, pain, cot confinement, multiple caretakers, and the confusion which follows transfer from home into a strange environment. Writers routinely caution the influence of associated factors, but without being able to indicate their relative importance. For lack of means of differentiation the literature on early separation therefore remains substantially a literature on an assortment of factors of unknown weight among which loss of the mother is only one.

But Bowlby (1960, 1961), theorizing principally on institutional data collected by James Robertson, makes generalizations which can be summarized as follows:

(a) that acute distress is a usual response of young children (between about 6 months and 3 to 4 years of age) to separation from the mother, regardless of circumstance and quality of substitute care; and, by implication, that there is no differentiation between the responses of these infants at varying levels of development;

(b) that the distress shown is the same in content and manifestation as the mourning of bereaved adults.[1]

Anna Freud (1960), commenting on Bowlby's grief and mourning theories, said: "Neither the Hampstead Nurseries nor hospitals and other residential homes have offered ideal conditions [for the study of separation per se]. . . . We, as well as Dr. Bowlby,

---

[1] "In this [paper] my principal aim will be to demonstrate that the responses to be observed in young children on loss of the mother figure differ in no material respect (apart probably from certain consequences) from those observed in adults on loss of a loved object" (Bowlby, 1960, p. 10).

". . . young children, even when they remain in their own homes and have familiar substitutes immediately available, nonetheless respond to loss of a loved figure with despair and mourning" (1960, p. 21).

"All that has been said [about adult mourning] applies equally to infants and young children of over six months. When for any reason they lose their loved object the three phases of mourning described are experienced. At all ages, we now see, the first phase of mourning is one of Protest, the second one of Despair, and the third one of Detachment" (1961, p. 338).

used data collected under circumstances where the children had to adapt not only to the loss of the mother but also to the change from family to group life, a transition very difficult to achieve for any young child. Whereas the mother herself had been the undisputed possession of the child, . . . the nurse as substitute mother had to be shared inevitably with a number of contemporaries; also, inevitably, it is never one single nurse who substitutes for the all-day and all-night care of the mother" (p. 59).

Although Anna Freud agreed that the overt manifestations of (institutional) separated infants resemble those of bereaved adults, she doubted that from 6 months of age there is an identity between the underlying processes. Her view is based on the one hand upon the theoretical ground that the capacity to mourn is a function of object constancy and ego maturity: "the nearer to object constancy, the longer the duration of grief reactions with corresponding approximation to the adult internal process of mourning." On the other hand she stresses the lack of relevant data: "we need to supplement our observations, excluding group or ward conditions. . . . From direct observation we know little or nothing about the duration of grief in those instances where the mother has to leave temporarily or permanently while the child remains at home" (p. 59).

Yarrow (1961) in a definitive review of research in this area showed that "Maternal separation has never been studied under pure conditions" (p. 471).

In Bowlby's most recent book (1969) there is passing reference to the complexities of the institutional situation, but emphasis remains on the assertion that regardless of age and conditions of care the young child's response to separation from the mother will be acute distress initiating the mourning sequence:

> The subjects of the various studies differ in many respects. For example, they differ in age, in the type of home from which they come, in the type of institution to which they go and the care they receive there, and in the length of time they are away. They differ, too, in whether they are healthy or sick. Despite all these variations, however, and despite the different backgrounds and expectations of the observers, there is a remarkable uniformity in the findings. Once a child is over the age of six

months he tends to respond to the event of separation from
mother in certain typical ways [p. 26].

Heinicke and Westheimer (1965), discussing their observations on young children in residential nurseries, acknowledge that
their data cannot determine the influence of institutional factors,
including that of multiple caretakers. In consonance with Anna
Freud they speculate:

> If it were possible to contrast a minimal care situation with one
> involving highly individualized care, . . . then one might well
> get quite different results [p. 196].
> . . . would suggest that if substitutes could adequately perform
> these [the parents'] functions, then the child would not experi-
> ence stress. The most rigorous test of this expectation would be
> to provide such substitutes and then study the child's response
> [p. 325].

Purpose and Special Requirements of the Study

In the attempt to get closer to separation per se we sought to
create a separation situation from which many of the factors that
complicate institutional studies were eliminated; and in which
the emotional needs of the children would be met as far as possible
by a fully available substitute mother. This would also give us an
opportunity to observe the influence of such variables as level of
ego maturity and object constancy, previous parent-child relationship, length of separation.

A. *Foster Care.* An implication of this approach was that we
ourselves should undertake the total care of the children, thus
insuring consistency of handling and high coverage of observation. We therefore combined the roles of foster parents and observers, and ordinary family life went on during each child's stay.

A previous fostering provided a basis for realistic anticipation
of the time and effort that would be required for total care, observation, and regular writing up.

It was decided that four children, taken one at a time, were as
many as could be coped with. According to studies published up
to that point, a 10-day period was presumed to be long enough to

allow Protest and Despair to show, but only the beginning of Detachment, if at all.

B. *Residential Nursery Care.* In a contrast study intended to obtain comprehensive naturalistic observations within the well-established patterns of response to institutional care, one child of comparable status to those fostered was observed in extended coverage during a 9-day stay in a residential nursery.

Selection of Children

Suitable subjects were defined as first and only children:
  (a) of between about 1½ years to 2½ years of age (the age range upon which much of the separation literature is based);
  (b) who lived with both parents;
  (c) who had not previously been separated from the mother except for an occasional few hours in the care of a familiar person;
  (d) whose mothers were going into the hospital for about 10 days to have a second baby. (Since there must always be a reason for a separation, it seemed best that this should be the same in each instance—mother going to have a second baby in a hospital which still kept mothers in for 10 days and did not allow visiting by children. Many hospitals, of course, discharge mothers after much shorter periods.)

The fostered children were found through hospital maternity units and child welfare centers, and were the first four offered who met the criteria. In the event two of the children stayed longer than the expected 10 days, for 19 and 27 days respectively, because of complications in the births.

Features of the Two Forms of Substitute Care

A. *Foster Care.* During the month or so prior to the separation, the child was introduced to the foster home and foster family so that he would transfer to a setting with which he was already familiar. This was done by a series of interchange visits between the families. Our family consisted of the foster parents, a 15-year-old schoolgirl daughter, and a 20-year-old daughter who came in occasionally from University.

The substitute-mother-to-be discussed with the parents the child's characteristics, toilet habits, food fads, sleeping pattern, comfort habits, and by observation and discussion gained some idea of the parents' ways of handling the child—so that many features of the home could be brought into the separation setting and by their familiarity contribute to the child's security.

On coming into foster care the child brought with him his own bed and blankets, toys and cuddlies, and a photograph of his mother. The foster mother sought to keep alive the image of the mother by talking about her and showing the photograph.

Fathers were free to visit as much as they wished and commonly came in the early evening after work, sometimes to share a meal with their child.

At the end of the separation each child was reunited with his mother in the presence of the foster mother. During the ensuing weeks and months the foster mother visited a number of times to help the child transfer from foster mother back to mother and, incidentally, to test the child's reactions to the foster mother as a separation-linked person.

B. *Residential Nursery Care.* Contact with this child, John, was obtained only a few days before his admission to the residential nursery and after the parents had taken him there on a visit. The parents had chosen this form of care in consultation with the family physician.

John was admitted to a toddlers' room with five other children of about the same age. Most of the others had been in the institution from birth. The young nurses were not assigned to individual children; they did whatever jobs came to hand and changed frequently because of times off and being posted to other duties. There was therefore no continuity of mothering care.

Methods of Observations and Recording

A. *Foster Care.* A primary consideration was the well-being of each child—to give the best possible care—and, while doing so, to observe to what extent and by what means the child coped.

The foster mother, Joyce Robertson, was also the principal observer. Her observations were direct, clinical, ongoing, a running account on a freely available pad, and filled out when time allowed; some use was made of a tape recorder. The full day's record was written up each evening, together with an assessment of the day, and checklists were completed.

The foster father, James Robertson, used a hand-held cine camera at intervals each day to capture special events and shifts of behavior around regular happenings such as meals, bedtime, and father's visits. Principal rooms (living room, child's bedroom, bathroom, kitchen) had sufficient indirect lighting to allow high-speed film to be used. As had already been established, a small cine camera in the hands of a trusted person is quickly ignored by young children and does not appear to affect their behavior (James Robertson, 1960). Filming took no more than 20 minutes on any day. The full written data have yet to be published, but the first four of a series of five films based on our assessment of the data have already been released (J. and J. Robertson, 1967, 1968, 1969, 1971).

B. *Residential Nursery Care.* On being advised of the pending admission, we paid one short visit to the family to gain an impression of the developmental status of the child and his relationship to the mother. During the separation we were able to observe most of the child's waking hours and to make written and film records comparable to those done on the fostered children.

In order not to be too conspicuous Joyce Robertson wore a nurse's overall and, without becoming involved in the tending of children, gave some assistance to the nurses at mealtimes.

Case Histories

We shall first present the case histories of five children, four in foster care and one, John, in residential care.

Kate, 2 years, 5 months

Kate was in foster care for 27 days. The expected duration of her stay had to be extended when the mother was detained in the hos-

pital due to complications in the birth of her second child (J. and J. Robertson, 1967; Kennedy, 1969).

Kate was the first and much-loved child of an immigrant Irish Catholic family. She had lived quietly with her parents in a small apartment on the fifth floor of a working-class tenement, and was unused to spending time away from her mother.

We first met Kate in her own home. She was a bright attractive child who, after a few minutes' initial shyness, made contact easily and talked well. During subsequent visits to our home Kate was increasingly relaxed and friendly. There was sometimes an over-excitedness in her manner, which perhaps denoted her awareness of the part that Joyce Robertson was to play.

Kate's upbringing had been on the rigid side. Her father employed smacks, but relied as much on prohibitions couched in quiet but threatening tones. Although the mother was softer and Kate had more latitude with her, the mother's demands were high.

Kate was more self-controlled than is usual for a child of her age, yet she was lively and spontaneous. The natural bond between mother and child was close and intensified because of their isolation together on the top-floor apartment. There was little body contact between them, but a close relationship was maintained by looking and talking.

The parents explained to Kate why she was to stay with us, and she was included in many of the discussions of arrangements, but it is improbable that she could really anticipate what being away from parents and home would be like.

The mother was at home waiting to be taken to the hospital when the foster mother collected Kate late in the afternoon. Kate left her mother quietly with the words: "Kate come back soon." For the rest of the day she was friendly and cheerful in the foster home, ate a good supper, and slept throughout the night.

First Week of Separation

During the first 5 days of the separation Kate was unusually cheerful, cooperative, and active. She laughed a great deal, talked loudly and rapidly, and moved about in an excited, exaggerated way. She showed no distress or bad humor, and was heard repeating to herself the parents' instructions and prohibitions: "Be a good girl, don't cry." "Eat up your potatoes." "Don't make a mess." She was reserved and tried to maintain herself on the basis of the remembered parental relationships and codes. The father's daily visits helped her in this.

Second Week

But by the end of the first week the defensive activity lessened. She related well to all the foster family, ate and slept well, and managed her own toileting—even during the night. There was much good humor and spontaneous natural laughter. But anxiety often broke through. Kate was less independent and often turned to the foster mother. She became fearful of getting lost and began to cling to the foster mother, especially when they were out in the street. She was less able to tolerate frustrations, could not always be the "good girl" who behaved as she remembered her parents wanted her to, and she wanted more bottles and sweets.

During this second week Kate often looked pensive and drawn, her eyes dark as though she needed sleep, and she cried more easily. When her mother was mentioned, she sometimes seemed not to hear, or she would point to the foster mother and say, "That's my Mummy." She played less constructively and was aware that sometimes she managed her body less well, occasionally falling over. Sometimes she did not comprehend what was said to her and answered vaguely as though preoccupied. Or she walked about dreamily, calling for the foster mother to rescue her from her fog. "What is Kate looking for?" she pleaded.

But this behavior was episodic, and for most of the time Kate was alert and cheerful. Colleagues who saw her were surprised by the good impression she made more than a week after losing her mother.

On the 10th day the hospital allowed Kate to visit her mother. She was at first distant, and only gradually warmed up to her mother. But throughout the visit she was like a rag doll, allowing herself to be cuddled and kissed but not responding. After half an hour she left with the same bland smiling acquiescence. But when she was back in the foster home, her feeling broke through: "I found my Mummy. Take me to see my Mummy. Kate get in Mummy's bed." And she threw her first temper tantrum.

For several days afterward Kate was often negative and aggressive, particularly to the foster mother but also to the other Robertsons. She was intensely aware of everyone's movements and needed to know where members of the foster family were, where they were going, and when they would return. Although for much of the time she was bright and cheerful, there were some grizzling spells and tears were often near the surface.

Third Week

During the third week Kate often said directly and with sadness: "I want my Mummy and Daddy." But sometimes, just a few minutes later, her sadness changed to crossness and she denied that she wanted them. She said: "I don't like my Mummy. Mummy is naughty." She paid less attention to her father during his visits, to his growing discomfiture, and on the 17th day pushed him prematurely to the door, saying, "You go." The father began to visit less often, ostensibly because he had a heavy job to do and his wife to visit, and because he knew that Kate was well settled;

but undoubtedly he was saddened and hurt by Kate's growing coolness toward him.

On a second visit to the hospital on the 17th day Kate chatted nonstop to her mother, but still kept a distance. She left without resistance, but in the street outside she looked tense and smacked at the foster mother's face.

Between the two hospital visits she had been affectionate and clinging, often calling the foster mother "Mummy" and showing jealousy when Jean, the 15-year-old daughter, made legitimate claims on her parents' attentions.

In the third week Kate was greatly at ease in the foster family and appeared to be finding a niche for herself. Much of her behavior was natural and spontaneous, showing the range of affect associated with a child in a secure setting. Her general competence and ability to play were returning. She no longer held on to the foster mother's hand in the street; and on an occasion when she was angry, she hung back and allowed the foster mother to get out of sight before she followed.

Fourth Week

During the fourth week Kate's dominant wish was still to be reunited with her parents. She was in constant danger of being overwhelmed by the feeling that they did not love her, did not want her back. The foster mother tried to keep Kate aware of the reality situation, that her parents *did* love her and wanted her back. This seemed to help counteract the projection of her feelings.

Kate became still more demanding of the foster mother's attentions, and her friendliness to others often gave way to angry scowling when they went near the foster mother. But for long periods she was relaxed and happy with the foster mother.

Throughout the separation Kate's relationship to the foster father reflected her changing feelings toward her father. Her initial pleasure in his visits gave way during the second week to disappointment, and during the third week to anger that he did not take her home. The more angry and disappointed she became with her father, the more she turned toward the foster father as a substitute.

As preparations were made to take Kate home on the 27th day there was an upsurge of anxiety. She vomited and had to be held. She resorted again to hyperactivity and mirthless laughter. All the way across London by car she denied she was going home and sang gay nonsense songs. But when she recognized her street, all pretense disappeared. In a strong voice she said, "That's my Mummy's house." Once across the threshold Kate disengaged from the foster mother's hand, which she had been gripping tightly, and for the next hour completely ignored the foster mother while she set about courting her mother with smiles and sweet talk.

After Reunion

The foster mother visited occasionally during the next month, and Kate was predominantly friendly and even affectionate—although excitement, quick speech, and heightened color sometimes betrayed unease. Six months later she was able to revisit the foster home in a relaxed and pleasurable way, with easy recall for her stay there.

During the first week at home Kate showed only slight upset. She slept restlessly, wet her bed, wanted more bottles, and cried more than she had previously. She warmed up to her father, and kept close to her mother by looking and talking as she had done before.

Her frustration tolerance was lowered and her demands more urgent and more frequent. She was resistive to her parents' demands, and despite explanations from the foster mother the parents could not tolerate this departure from her former good behavior. Kate was forced into submission by the father's smacks —actual and threatened—and by his firm disapproval. Her aggression became displaced onto an unoffending aunt.

Fourteen days after returning home Kate was taken by her mother to be enrolled for school two years in advance, as was necessary in a district with few Catholic places. That night she screamed as with nightmares, and in the morning was acutely breathless. The family doctor diagnosed bronchial asthma, the first attack Kate had ever had, and inquired about stress. With hindsight the mother realized that at the school there had been talk of Kate being "taken," etc., so it seemed that the first (and only) attack of breathlessness was a reaction to the threat of another separation—and to the parents' intolerance of direct expression of feeling, particularly of aggression. Denied this outlet, Kate had no other outlet than the psychosomatic one.

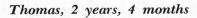

Thomas, 2 years, 4 months

Thomas was in foster care for 10 days (J. and J. Robertson, 1971).

His parents were in their middle 20s. The family lived in a small, but comfortable apartment over the family business. The father was a warm and outgoing man, a keen rugby footballer. He was family-oriented, proud of his son, and very ready to consider his needs. There was boisterous affection and quiet understanding in their relationship, with an occasional tinge of irritation when their needs clashed.

The mother was a gentle, affectionate person, who showed a lot of empathy and understanding for Thomas; but she was rather more controlling than at first appeared from her quiet, easy manner. She rarely compelled obedience, but instead pleaded or disapproved. Usually, if he did not comply, she withdrew interest with an "Oh, Thomas!" and this quickly brought him into line with her wishes.

Thomas was a well-developed, manly little boy who had a friendly, confident manner and talked very well. He was not reliably toilet-trained, and had a strong resistance to going to bed. The relationship to his parents was secure and demonstrably affectionate.

The parents had talked a lot to Thomas about the new baby and the coming separation, and were fairly confident that, if cared for well and visited every day by his father, he would be all right.

During several preseparation visits, mostly at our home, Thomas maintained a friendly, but reserved manner. He interacted with all members of our family on the basis of his books and toys, and talked of the time when he would stay with us.

First Week

Thomas went with his father to take the mother to the hospital and then was brought to us. He solemnly waved good-bye to his father, acknowledging with a quiet nod the promise of a visit later in the day.

Like the other children in the study, Thomas did not break down upon separation, but for the first 2 days defended against the anxiety by overactivity and pseudocheerfulness. He was never still. Then more appropriate feeling emerged—longing for his parents and home, and sadness when his father left after visits. But for most of the time he was in good humor, in friendly contact with his caretakers, and able to enjoy play and activities offered. He ate well and resisted sleep as he had done before separation.

Thomas asked about his mother and talked spontaneously about her; mingled among the comments were recollections of times when his mother was angry with him, as though wondering whether her going away was related to his having been naughty. Sometimes he cuddled his mother's photograph to him and kissed it. At other times the photograph made him uneasy; he would take a quick glance and turn away with pink cheeks. He thought a lot about his parents, and momentary sadness often overcame him. He would say, "Thomas is thinking."

The highlight of each day was his father's visit, and at first these visits were totally enjoyable with brief tears afterward. But soon Thomas's grasp of the situation made him unhappily aware that visits were temporary and that a good-bye was inevitable. He pleaded with his father not to go back to work but to "stay with Thomas," and after a few days visits were punctuated by tears. He cried bitterly, but briefly, when his father left.

Thomas held tightly to the pen his father gave him to look after. He would not allow us to sit on the chair his father sat on, and would not even sit on it himself: "No! That is my Daddy's chair. I want to sit on my Daddy's lap."

The parents had suggested that Thomas would need plenty of activity and this proved to be right. He welcomed every diversion, and unhappiness could always be averted by going shopping or playing in the garden. On one occasion when tiredness was combined with inactivity he became very unhappy, crying, "Where's my Mummy? I want my Daddy."

On the 5th morning, his voice bold and his mood cheerful, he said, "My Mummy is sitting in the hospital bed. Daddy has gone to work. Daddy has big boots. Thomas has little boots. The baby has bootees." Letting his hand move over his chair from home, he said, "This is a nice chair, Mummy bought it." He stroked the foster mother's arm and face with gentleness, "Nice Mrs. Robertson." He cuddled his mother's photo under his arm and then asked to have it pinned on the wall and told us all to look at it. He had a realistic view of the total situation and, though under strain, was coping well.

Thomas fluctuated between wanting the foster mother's affection and strongly resisting it; his need of mothering and his growing attachment conflicted increasingly with his love for his mother. Late on the 6th day, when he sat on the foster mother's knee tired and wanting his parents, he pushed away her encircling arms. "Don't cuddle me! My Mummy cuddles me." At other times he lay on the floor near the foster mother chatting in a relaxed friendly way about his parents, what they said, and what they did with Thomas.

Second Week

Thomas was affectionate, but often from the 6th day onward the affectionate gestures would without warning or provocation change to aggression. This highlighted the mixed feelings that Thomas was coping with. Sometimes the foster mother could avert the aggression by accepting but not returning the affection. Sometimes, especially just after a visit by the father, it was our daughter Jean to whom Thomas turned for comforting. There was no conflict, because Jean did not perform the caretaking functions associated with his mother.

In respect of ego development and level of object constancy Thomas was the most mature child in the sample. He was able to express his anxieties verbally, and it was therefore easier to help him maintain the understanding of the situation as given him by the parents. He used the temporary foster relationship adequately, while maintaining a clear memory of his mother.

The father's daily visits were very important for Thomas. He anticipated them with longing, experienced them with intense feelings of pleasure and sadness, and was openly unhappy for a brief period afterward. Toward the end of the separation it took Thomas several minutes before he warmed to the father. They then became enveloped in a quiet sadness. On the 9th day the father said, "We've both had enough."

On the 9th day Thomas showed more signs that he was less able to contain the strain. He was impatient, slower to respond to the foster mother's requests; he spoke in a whining voice, and chewed his clothing.

In interaction with the foster mother he was warm, affectionate, demanding, and aggressive. Sometimes he angrily pushed off her care: "Not you do it. My Mummy do it," he shouted.

In the afternoon of the 9th day he played a new game, that of being a baby. "I a baby. Got no teeth. Can't walk. Want a rattle. I get in a pram." The game went on and on, and his usual boyish constructive games were set aside.

Thomas knew he was to go home the next day. He awoke in lively good humor and announced, "I thinking about my rocking horse at home. Mummy says, 'No. Mustn't climb,' makes Mummy very cross."

When the parents arrived, Thomas looked uneasily at his mother for about 30 seconds, then went toward her with gentle affectionate gestures, stroking her hair, touching her face, and taking her in with his eyes. He dutifully greeted his father, but quickly returned to his mother. His first concern was to rediscover her physical characteristics by looking and touching; his next, that her "rest" in the hospital was finished. He made "pretend" tea for his mother, and several times broke off the game to kiss her. His caresses were gentle and his voice soft and affectionate.

Thomas's full attention had moved to his parents; and after bestowing a perfunctory kiss, he left the foster mother with every sign of urgency to get home.

After Reunion

Thomas returned to his family in much the same state as he had arrived in the foster home—untrained toiletwise, with a dislike of bedtime, and with easy expression of aggression and affection. He had been well supported by the foster mother and by his father, and returned home to parents who continued to handle him with empathy and understanding.

During visits over the next few weeks he was friendly to the foster mother, but cautious. He stayed close to his mother.

Thomas came through the separation better than any other child in the study. But afterward he was less easy to control than before, and in his relationship to his mother there was a defiant and aggressive element that was new. This was still prominent when the observations finished 2 months later. He was then also very aggressive toward the new baby.

Jane, 17 months

Jane was in foster care for 10 days (J. and J. Robertson, 1967; Kennedy, 1969).

She was a lively, attractive child of young parents in modest circumstances. They lived in the same block as we did, but the two families were on no more than smiling terms before we were brought together by the research project.

Jane had lived a quiet life with a minimum of outside contacts. The mother was entirely devoted to Jane's care, and provided activities in an imaginative way. Fussing and crying were discouraged, and high standards of obedience set. Jane's father gave a good deal of time to his professional studies, but made his presence felt by disciplinary interventions. At 17 months Jane understood many of her parents' prohibitions.

Familiarizing Jane with the foster family was more difficult than with the older children in the study. While the mother was available Jane had only fleeting interest in the foster mother. It was therefore several weeks before the rudiments of a relationship were established.

There were unexpected difficulties in acquainting Jane with the layout of our home, mainly because she transferred her parents' prohibitions to the new setting; she would not, for instance, enter the bathroom because it contained a washing machine like her mother's which she had been painfully taught not to touch. However, by the time the separation began, Jane was fairly at ease and had briefly visited us without her mother.

Jane was awake when the parents went to the hospital in the

middle of the night. But the foster mother, by then a familiar figure, was in the apartment before they left. After lying awake for an hour in her cot Jane fell asleep. The foster mother stayed until Jane awoke at 8 in the morning, showed her round the empty apartment, then carried Jane to the foster home. She ran with pleasure to the box of toys.

First Week of Separation

Jane immediately accepted full mothering care from the substitute mother and entered into a warm and pleasurable relationship. During the first few days she functioned well, feeding herself, sleeping and playing well, and did not cry.

She was gay and lively and directed intense, purposeful smiles at her caretakers. These grimaces were clearly intended to elicit answering smiles from those about her, and in this she was successful. (Some of the laughing-grimacing episodes have been captured on film, and the masklike artificiality is most apparent.) The gay overactivity and the intense smiling were understood as defensive, a means of combating anxiety. When a smile stopped, it was replaced by a blank, tense expression.

After the first few days the smiling behavior lessened and was then seen only immediately after sleep, as though at each awakening Jane had to assure herself that this was a friendly and safe place. The mother, on seeing the film record of these first days, commented, "Jane smiles a lot like that after I have been angry with her and she's trying to placate me."

By the 4th day gaiety had given way to restlessness and lowered frustration tolerance. More appropriate cross, negative behavior appeared. Jane played less well, sucked her thumb more, and wanted to be nursed. None of these changes were very marked, but they combined to give an impression of a child who was under stress and was at times bewildered. There was no crying, but increasingly she wanted attention and company.

On the 5th day there was less smiling and some irritable crying. She wanted to be held more, and resisted routine handling. For the first 4 days she had played in the communal garden without going to her own garden gate, or even appearing to notice it, although the setting was very familiar to her. On this morning she went to the gate and tried to open it, but failed. She looked over the low wall into the empty garden where she had played with her mother, shook her head in a negative gesture, then turned away with a wide smile filling her face. She ran a few yards into the communal garden, then stood as if uncertain which way to go.

On the 6th day Jane again went to her garden gate, and this time it pushed open. She ran down the path and tried the handle of the door into the apartment. Then she turned and hurried back to the garden gate with a distorted expression on her face. She closed the gate very carefully, but for some minutes hovered nearby. She strained to look over the garden wall, and peered through the bars of the garden gate at the empty house.

Then for the first time she resisted going into the foster home; and for the first time during the separation she spoke the word, "Mama."

Jane's father visited for an hour each day. At first she played happily with him, and cried when he left. Then, as her general frustration tolerance declined, she got angry with him. Later she would pointedly ignore him throughout a visit, but cling and cry when he made to leave.

Second Week

In the second week Jane continued to relate warmly to all members of our family. She had gained a new word—"Fflower," associated with the flowers on her foster mother's apron. Although she was quieter and ready to cry at minor frustrations, she continued to eat and sleep well.

On a visit to a weekly playgroup run by the foster mother Jane was completely at ease, interacting competently with the other children.

By the 10th day Jane was firmly attached to the foster mother and called her "Fflower." That morning she was lacking in energy, and became upset when the foster mother moved away from her. When her mother came to take her home, Jane recognized and responded to her with only slight hesitation. Initially there was uncertainty and shyness; but then sweet, smiling, placating behavior came to the fore—a remembered way of getting her mother's attention and approval. Mutely she invited her mother to take over; first she wanted her "potty," then she fetched her hairbrush, then her dress needed attention.

When the mother arrived, Jane and the foster mother had been playing a familiar game of putting pennies into a purse. But the game was transferred to the mother, and in a teasing way Jane avoided the foster mother with whom she had been so intimate.

After Reunion

During the first two days the placating behavior toward both parents alternated with its opposite—doing what she knew would bring their disapproval. Smacks and frustrations now led to outbursts of severe crying, which was a new feature. This was very different from the obedient Jane of preseparation days who at a clap of the hand or a sharp call would heed their prohibitions.

It was several weeks before there was a lessening of the provocation toward her mother. But the easy obedience did not return, and with a second child in the family the parents no longer pressed as hard.

Although Jane had responded to her mother with recognition and pleasure, she was reluctant to give up the foster mother.

In order that the child should not suffer the sudden ending of a good substitute relationship the foster mother visited several times in the next few weeks. She was at first warmly welcomed by Jane, and not willingly parted from. Then, as the relationship to her mother became more established, Jane hovered uncomfortably between the two mother figures. A week after her return home she ran toward the foster mother, but the mother put out an inviting hand and caused her to change course. Jane reached neither mother nor substitute mother, but fell between them and cut her mouth.

Two weeks later Jane had weaned herself from the foster mother. But although the foster relationship had lost importance, it remained friendly and warm.

Lucy, 21 months

Lucy was in foster care for 19 days because complications in the birth detained her mother in the hospital (J. and J. Robertson, 1973).

Lucy's parents were graduates, intelligent and extroverted. The father was an outgoing, optimistic young man; although he was married and his second child was nearing birth, he still managed to indulge his active bachelor hobbies. He was warm and demonstrative to Lucy, but their interactions tended to occur when it suited him and not when Lucy asked for them. The mother was cheerful and lively in the last weeks of pregnancy, but some of this liveliness revealed itself as a defense against anxiety about the birth; she responded appropriately to Lucy, but did not prolong the contacts.

Lucy's early developmental history was normal, reflecting the adequate mothering she had received. At 21 months her body control was excellent, and she played intelligently and constructively. But there were also less satisfactory aspects. Lucy did not talk, she slept a great deal, had an eating problem, and tended to withdraw when frustrated. Her expression was somber, and she dribbled. These features possibly related to a withdrawal of cathexis by the mother during pregnancy.

During the first few familiarizing visits Lucy was often glum, her face puckered and her brows drawn together to give a disgruntled expression. Even when she had warmed up, there remained a great deal of reserve and caution. On later visits she became quietly friendly, using her toys to make contact. She showed little variation in mood.

The foster mother collected Lucy from home an hour before the mother went to the hospital. The parting of mother and child was as undemonstrative as if Lucy had been going for an outing to the park. That first evening she interacted quietly with all of us, singling out the foster mother as the most familiar. At the first attempt she objected to going to bed, but after a period of play with the family she returned to bed and slept soundly throughout the night.

First Week of Separation

Lucy left her mother without protest and without a change of facial expression. In common with the other children she was active and cheerful for the first few days. This gave way to turbulent behavior—anger, petulance, gaiety, and affection toward the foster mother. Her expression lost its flatness and now reflected changing feelings. The father commented that Lucy's laughter had a new artificial quality about it.

During the first 2 days Lucy cried only when she was put into her cot and when her father left after visits. She was affectionate to the foster mother, often running to bury her head in the foster mother's lap.

By the 5th day Lucy presented a very different picture from the preseparation one. Descriptively there was a marked improvement, contrary to what is expected of young children during separation. Lucy looked bright and happy, and only occasionally withdrew. She was eating proper meals, and the dribbling had stopped. Solitary play had given way to interaction with the foster mother, who was followed about or pushed and pulled into Lucy's chosen direction.

The father's daily visit was pleasurable to both, and Lucy cried when he left. On the 6th day the father commented on her improved physical appearance, and the greater animation and responsiveness.

Second Week

In the middle of the second week Lucy became cross and negativistic, and could not accept comforting. She refused food and threw everything away from her, including her own cuddly toys. The feeding disturbance, which had been observed at home prior to separation, was now transferred to the foster mother with all its anger and provocation.

A few days later the mood was different again. Tears rose quickly. Sometimes Lucy sought comforting and could accept it, but at other times she isolated herself by crawling under a table or behind furniture out of reach. Ultimately she came to the foster mother to recover in her arms.

On the 10th day Lucy's father took her to a park where she had often been with her mother, and on return she was unsettled and aggressive toward the foster mother, screaming and scratching.

As the range of feeling became more richly expressed within the foster family, Lucy was less involved with her father during visits. On the 11th day he was disturbed that she was distant and that he could not get into their former warm relationship. That night Lucy slept badly.

Third Week

Friendly distance continued to characterize Lucy's attitude to her attentive father, but within our family she was most often relaxed and responsive. She sought more attention from the foster father. In her relationship to the foster mother she was affectionate, could tolerate prohibitions, could accept comforting, and could play quietly apart while remaining in contact. But without warning she would for a few hours be negative and defiant. Lucy was in a highly sensitive state and needed careful handling.

On the 17th day the father again took Lucy to the park near her home. She returned in a good mood and greeted us affectionately. But after the father had left, she threw herself on the floor and rolled about miserably, refusing to be comforted. After a time she allowed herself to be picked up, and at bedtime she clung tearfully to the foster mother and could not be put down.

On the 19th day Lucy's mother came to collect her. With

hardly any hesitation Lucy withdrew from the foster mother and responded to her mother's overtures. She looked intently at her mother, then smiled; after piling all her toys onto mother's lap, she climbed on top with a pleased expression. Without words Lucy had shown where she and they belonged. But before leaving for home she ran affectionately to the foster mother.

After Reunion

After two days of serene behavior the changing moods and demands which had manifested themselves during the separation reappeared and were focused on the mother. With the pregnancy safely behind her the mother now responded fully to Lucy's new demands. This richer interchange between them was maintained, as were many of the improvements that occurred during the fostering.

But Lucy had great difficulty in weaning herself from the foster mother. During a visit by the foster mother 3 days after reunion Lucy oscillated between affection and apprehension, smiling and frowning, clinging to her mother yet crying bitterly when the foster mother left. Several visits over the next 3 weeks were necessary to enable Lucy gradually to re-establish the relationship to her own mother and to decathect the substitute relationship.

John, 17 months

John was in a residential nursery for 9 days (J. and J. Robertson, 1969; Elkan, 1969; A. Freud, 1969; Rosenfeld, 1970).

John and his mother had a quiet harmonious relationship. He was an easy, undemanding child, and the mother was competent and unfussy in her handling. Toilet training had not begun. He was a sturdy, good-looking boy who ate and slept well and said a few words.

The father, a young professional man, was at a critical point in his training, and it was impractical for him to look after John while the mother was in the hospital. The family doctor recommended that he be put into the local residential nursery, an institution used by local authorities and approved for the training of nursery nurses.

John accompanied his parents when they went to see the nursery. The parents were reassured by the liveliness of the group of five toddlers that John was to join and by the friendliness of the young nurses. They anticipated that John would show some upset after the separation, but that they would be able to handle this. At 17 months John had of course no understanding of the preliminary visit.

The mother's labor began in the night, and John was left at the nursery when she was en route to the maternity hospital. John cried for half an hour, then fell asleep. When he awoke he found himself in a strange setting, a room with five other cots and in each a child of his own age clamoring to be dressed. He watched as they were attended to, and when 18-year-old nurse Mary approached him with a smile, he responded in a friendly way and interacted as she dressed him.

At breakfast it was another young nurse, Christine, who fed him and to her he was also friendly, as he was to two others who gave part of his care during the day. Any one of these could have become a substitute mother, but this the system of nursing did not allow. The young nurses were not assigned to individual children but turned to whatever duties came to hand. Although John found the nurses friendly, the contacts were fleeting and unsatisfactory to a child who tried hard to find one who would stay by him.

The other children had been in the institution from birth and were noisy, aggressive, self-assertive, and demanding; they had never known stable relationships and in many ways fended for themselves in a violent little community. They knew from experience that they could not expect their needs to be anticipated and met. John was bewildered by the noise, occasionally putting his hands to his ears, and as a family child was no match for the aggression of the other children.

When his father walked into this strange environment, John looked blankly before widening into a smile of recognition. He made no objection when his father left.

It was Mary, the nurse who had dressed him in the morning, who put John to bed. He was again ready to make a relationship. But Mary had to move on to other duties, and John gave a shout of protest and disappointment.

On the 2nd day John still coped quite well. While the institutional children rushed about, snatching and fighting, he played constructively as he had done at home—in a corner away from the commotions. Occasionally he still sought to find a nurse who would mother him. But usually his tentative approaches were overlooked as the nurses responded to the more clamorous children; or if he got a nurse's attention, he was either displaced by a more assertive child or the nurse dropped him to do other tasks. The young nurses were not concerned about John; he ate well, was quiet and undemanding, and cried only when he was put in his cot.

When his father made to leave after visiting, John's quiet uncomplaining manner changed to crying and struggling to go home with him. Nurse Mary comforted John, and he soon emerged into a smiling exchange and expectation of play. But again the young nurse could not linger, and John shouted in tearful complaint as she walked away from his cot.

From the 3rd day John was increasingly distressed. His overtures to the nurses did not bring him the care and affection he was used to. His needs were overlooked, and he was assailed by the noisy clamor and attacks of the other children. He still cried little, but either stood forlornly at the end of the room or played quietly in a corner with his back to the group. When his father visited, John smacked him crossly and pulled at his glasses.

On the 4th day there was marked deterioration. There were lengthy spells of sad crying which merged with the din of the other children and went unattended by the nurses. His play was listless, he sucked more, and his fingers often strayed over his face and eyes. He ate and drank hardly at all, and walked with a slow shambling gait.

He still tried, though with less effort, to get close to one or another of the changing nurses. But in this he was generally unsuccessful, and several times crawled under a table to cry alone.

On the 5th day his constant misery attracted some attention from the nurses. But they could not comfort him or interest him in toys, and he ate nothing all day. And as no nurse had direct responsibility for him, their concern was dispersed and ineffectual. His face was drawn and his eyes swollen. He cried in quiet despair, sometimes rolling about and wringing his hands. Occasionally he shouted angrily at no one in particular, and in a brief contact smacked nurse Mary's face.

John now made fewer direct approaches to the nurses; and as if defeated in his attempts to get comfort from them, he turned to a teddy bear that was larger than himself. While the other children were rushing about or clambering over the young nurses, John would be sitting somewhere burrowed into the teddy bear. Sometimes he stood looking around at the adults as though searching for one who would cuddle him. Nurse Mary made herself more available than did the other nurses, but she came and went according to the duty rota and not according to John's need of her. So she was not much help to him.

John's father had been unable to visit for two days.

On the 6th day John was miserable and inactive. When nurse Mary was on duty, her face registered concern for him, but the system of group care frustrated them both and her concern was lost in the babel of the other toddlers. John's mouth trembled with tears held in check. In contrast to the beginning of his stay when he stood out as the brightest and bonniest of the children, he was now unhappy and forlorn. Nurses picked him up briefly and put him down when other children needed attention. He cried a great deal. He manipulated the big teddy bear, twisting it this way and that in desperate attempts to find comfort.

When his father came, John pinched and smacked. Then his face lightened, and hopefully he went to the door to show mutely his wish to go home. He fetched his outdoor shoes, and as the father humored John by putting on the shoes, the child's face broke into a little smile as if thinking this presaged going home. But when the father did not move, John's face became overcast. He went to Mary, looking back at his father with an anguished expression. Then he turned away from Mary, too, and sat apart clutching his cuddly blanket.

On the 7th day John cried weakly but continually all day long. He did not play, did not eat, did not make demands, did not respond for more than a few seconds to the fleeting attempts of the young nurses to cheer him. He stumbled as he walked, unhappy and whimpering. His expression was dull and blank, not like the lively good-looking boy who had been admitted a week earlier.

John got some comfort from being held, it did not matter by whom. But always he was put down within a short time. Toward the end of the day he would walk toward an adult, then either turn away to cry in a corner, or stop short and fall on his face on the floor in a gesture of despair. He huddled up against the large teddy bear.

The father came late and John was asleep.

On the 8th day he was even more miserable. There was an angry note to his cries when another child sought to oust him from a nurse's knee. But there was no respite to his unhappiness. For long times he lay in apathetic silence on the floor, his head on the large teddy bear, and was impassive when other children came to him.

He still ate little. When his father came at teatime and tried to help, John was so distraught that he could neither eat nor drink. He cried convulsively over his cup. At the end of the visit John was abandoned to despair, and no one could comfort him, not even his favorite nurse Mary. When she tried to take him on her knee, he squirmed down on the floor and crawled into a corner beside the teddy bear. There he lay crying, completely unresponsive to the troubled young nurse.

On the 9th day he cried from the moment he awoke, hanging over his cot and shaking with sobs. All but one of the nurses were new to him, and he was slumped motionless on her lap when his mother came to take him home. At the sight of his mother John was galvanized into action. He threw himself about crying loudly, and after stealing a glance at his mother looked away from her. Several times he looked, then turned away over the nurse's shoulder with loud cries and a distraught expression.

After a few minutes the mother took him on her knee, but John continued to struggle and scream, arching his back away from his mother, and eventually got down and ran crying desperately to the observer. She calmed him down, gave him a drink, and passed him back to his mother. He lay cuddled into her, clutching his cuddly blanket but not looking at her.

A few minutes later the father entered the room and John struggled away from the mother into the father's arms. His crying stopped, and for the first time he looked at his mother directly. It was a long hard look. His mother said, "He has never looked at me like that before."

In the discussion with nursery staff afterward, they agreed among themselves that "we have had many children like John."

After Reunion

In the first week John had many temper tantrums. He rejected his parents at all levels—would not accept affection or comforting, would not play with them, and removed himself physically by shutting himself up in his room. He cried a great deal, and could not cope with the slightest delay in having his wishes met. He was aggressive and destructive in his play. Instead of carefully manipulating his toys, he now scattered them angrily.

During the second week the tantrums stopped and he was undemanding. For much of the time he played quietly in his room. But in the third week there was a dramatic change. His behavior became more extreme than in the first week. The tantrums returned; he refused food so resolutely that he lost some pounds in weight; he slept badly at night, did not rest during the day, and became clinging. The parents were shocked by this deterioration, particularly by the gulf that had appeared between them and their son. They reorganized family life around the task of supporting John and giving him maximum attention in an attempt to help him regain whatever had been lost.

A month after returning home John had a much better relationship to his mother. But his "good" state was precariously held, and a visit by the observer threw him back into the original state in which he refused food and all attentions from his parents. He recovered after a few days, but 3 weeks later (7 weeks after returning home) another visit by the observer again elicited extreme disturbance which this time lasted for 5 days and included a new feature of aggression against his mother. Presumably the observer's visits reactivated anxieties and fears related to the separation experience.

Three years after his stay in the residential nursery, when John was 4½ years old, he was a handsome, lively boy who gave much pleasure to his parents. But there were two marked features which troubled them. He was fearful of losing his mother, and got upset if she was not where he thought she would be. And every few months he had bouts of provocative aggression against her which came out of the blue and lasted for several days. These features seemed to be legacies of the traumatic experience of being for 9 days in a residential nursery which did not meet his emotional needs.

John's story is in the well-established pattern of institutional separations: "The infant is at the mercy of the compliance of its environment, and of the ability of the institution to provide an adequate substitute object" (Spitz and Wolf, 1946, p. 338).

The Influence of Variables

The four children who were given adequate substitute mothering in a supportive setting showed with a clarity not previously reported the influence of variations in

(a) level of ego maturity and object constancy;

(b) previous parent-child relationship and/or defensive behavior;

(c) length of separation;

while the contrast study of John, who was observed in a residential nursery, brought out more clearly the weight to be attached to additional stress factors such as

(d) inadequate substitute mothering, multiple caretakers;

(e) strange environment.

Level of Ego Maturity and Object Constancy

Since ego maturity and object constancy bear some relation to age, certain effects of these variables can be illustrated by comparing the over-2-year-olds (Kate and Thomas) with the under-2-year-olds (Lucy and Jane).

Thomas (2.4 years), comparatively advanced in ego maturity and object constancy, thought and talked a great deal about his mother; he pinned up her photo in a prominent place, kissed it, and got angry with it.

Thomas expressed verbally his difficulty in leaning emotionally on his foster mother while remaining true to his mother. While edging near to sit on the foster mother's knee he warned, "Don't kiss me, my Mummy kisses me." Comparing her grey hair with his recall of his mother's black hair, he said, "Your hair is the wrong color"; and later, looking at her blue eyes, he remarked that his mother had brown eyes.

Thomas spent long periods expressing his thoughts and concerns about his parents. In a tearful mood he said, "I'm thinking of my rocking horse at home. My Mummy says, 'It's a nice day, Thomas.' I like my Mummy best." And after a thoughtful pause, "Mummy says, 'Thomas is a naughty boy.' Sometimes my Daddy's eyes are angry." Talking and thinking about his parents kept feelings uncomfortably at surface level and Thomas's behavior reflected this.

His growing closeness to the foster mother and need of her attentions conflicted with his remembered love of his mother and resulted in aggressive outbursts toward the foster mother.

Kate (2.5 years), too, could remember and talk about her own home and parents. She spoke of the preparations she and her mother had made for the new baby and how she was going to help her mother look after it. She compared her mother's domestic equipment with that of the foster mother, noting what was like and what was unlike.

She asked often, "Where is my Mummy?" Kate explained that the foster mother was Jean's mummy and not Kate's mummy. But as the separation became extended into a third week, there were times when Kate said loudly and with emphasis to the foster mother, "*You* are my Mummy" and prefaced every remark with "Mummy."

Both Kate and Thomas were reserved during the first few days and kept the foster mother at a distance because the relationship to their own mothers was vivid and real. Then their need of mothering and their growing attachment to the foster mother sometimes brought conflicts of loyalty and provoked negative or aggressive episodes with the foster mother.

Because Thomas and Kate had clear memories of mother and home they could be helped to maintain these memories and anticipate eventual reunion. When Kate in unhappy spells said, "My Mummy doesn't love me, she won't come to take me home," it was possible to help her separate fantasy from reality. This helped to reduce the buildup of hostility against the mother and to keep alive the memories of a mother who cared.

There was no doubt that these two children missed their mothers and were under stress; but there was no desperate unhappiness. Memories of the absent mother, their understanding of the reality situation, reinforced by the ability to play out their preoccupations through the doll family, the support they got from their fathers, and the emotional interaction and ego support provided by the substitute caretaker combined to enable them to weather the experience without being overwhelmed.

· Both Thomas and Kate were able to drop the foster relationship as soon as the real mother returned.

Jane (1.5 years) and Lucy (1.9 years), a year younger than Thomas and Kate, did not have the sophistication in ego development of the older children; nor had they reached the older children's level of object constancy (Fraiberg, 1969). They were more dependent on the adult for physical survival, and their needs were more urgent.

Jane and Lucy could therefore not be helped to the same extent as the two older children to keep the absent mother in mind. Because of this and the intensity of their physical and emotional needs these two younger children accepted the mother substitute without the loyalty conflicts of the two older children. Almost immediately they related warmly and wholeheartedly to her.

It seemed that at their level of development the two younger ones did not carry a clear image of the absent mother, and did not have the older children's ability of spontaneous recall. Specific reminders were needed to bring the mother into mind, and for simultaneous resistance to the foster mother to be felt. For instance, after Jane saw her own garden gate, and Lucy had been taken by her father to a park near her home, both children for a brief period pulled away from the foster mother.

But these explicit feelings for the mother, and the related resistance to handling by the foster mother, could not be sustained because Jane and Lucy had not reached the level of object constancy that Thomas and Kate had obtained.

At reunion Jane and Lucy greeted their mothers with spontaneous pleasure, but they had more difficulty than did the older ones in re-establishing the relationship with the mother and in disengaging from the substitute mother.

Previous Parent-Child Relationship and/or Defensive Behavior

With children so young it was not always possible to differentiate between defensive behavior and precursors to defenses which were still very dependent on remembered parental attitudes.

During the first week Kate was obedient, reasonable, and very easy to handle. She recalled vividly her parents' disciplines and instructions: "Kate must be a good girl, musn't make a mess. Kate musn't touch your books. Must eat my potatoes first," she instructed herself. She recalled that her mother smacked her when she was naughty.

Kate was indeed a "good" girl who did not cry and who always did as she was asked. Her upbringing had been strict; angry feelings had to be controlled, crying was "naughty."

Kate was overactive and overcheerful, making tremendous efforts to maintain herself without her parents. "Look, I'm a good girl, I'm laughing," she repeatedly told the foster parents, laughing artificially. She kept herself busy, cleaning windows and sweeping floors, activities she had shared with her mother.

For 5 days this defensive behavior served Kate well. But when on the 6th day she was taken for an hour into a strange setting among strange people, the precarious balance was lost and she cried for the first time since leaving her mother.

For most of the first week Kate behaved in line with her parents' expectations. Then she found it difficult to maintain that standard of behavior without their support and demands. Her defensive behavior fell away and she became more openly anxious and clinging.

Thomas was so overactive that it was well-nigh impossible to keep him in the house. He needed to run, jump, and kick balls about nonstop. But the overactive behavior was short-lived. By the 3rd day he was expressing his sadness and anxiety with almost adult understanding of the situation.

Thomas showed his feelings more freely than any of the other children. He was more overtly aggressive and affectionate. This was in line with his preseparation behavior and with his parents' expectations of him.

Thomas and Kate were very different in their ability to control and express feeling, and their separation behavior reflected this.

During the first 3 days, Jane smiled a great deal, in obvious need to get answering smiles from her caretakers. Her smiles gradually took on an intense grimacing quality which would suddenly disappear and leave her with a confused unhappy expression. This lessened after the first 3 days, but for some further days the soliciting smiles were seen immediately after sleep.

At home Jane had been expected to be a smiling child, and crying was discouraged. To smile was to be "good." The mother reported that Jane always smiled more when she had been naughty and wanted to placate the mother.

Jane had been an obedient child who could be stopped from doing forbidden activities by a handclap and a "No" from her parents. She could even deter herself. Within reach of her father's cabbage patch she would stop, clap her own hands, shake her head, and thus stop herself from plucking them.

But this behavior was still dependent upon her parents' demands and withdrawal of approval, and in their absence she could not hold on to it for long. After the first few days of separation minor prohibitions from the foster mother went unheeded.

Lucy, a solemn child, became more active and animated during the first 2 days of the separation. This then gave way to turbulent behavior—affectionate and controlling at one moment, angry turning away from contact at another. This did not abate for more than a week. During the second week she transferred to her relationship with the foster mother the feeding disturbance which had been part of her relationship to her mother. By the end of the second week Lucy had become more relaxed and predominantly affectionate, and the feeding disturbance had disappeared.

Lucy's behavior was unexpected. This could be understood only in light of Lucy's experience of her mother's withdrawal of cathexis during pregnancy and her response to regaining fully responsive mothering during the separation.

Length of Separation

None of the four fostered children showed acute distress or despair. Lucy and Kate, whose separation became extended to 19 and 27 days, adapted increasingly well to the situation and with deepening attachment to the foster home and foster family. This was very different from the superficial relating described in institutional studies.

The 2½-year-old Kate, separated for the longest period (27 days), continued to verbalize longing for her mother increasingly intermingled with anger. But she, as well as the other three children, greeted her mother with pleasure and affection on reunion and without the avoidance and/or nonrecognition which occurs after a traumatic separation characterized by the protest-despair syndrome.

Inadequate Substitute Mothering, Multiple Caretakers

In ordinary family life there is always some awareness of the changing needs and moods of a younger member. There is a measure of certainty that unhappiness, hunger, tiredness, playfulness will be answered more or less appropriately and without too much delay.

For the young child in a family there are some known and expected responses because the same one or two people will be tending him. Even if his first cry is not taken too seriously, a real need is unlikely to go unanswered. Not so in the majority of institutions with their changing caretakers.

These respond in varying ways to what they see, if and when they see it. They are unlikely to see or understand the subtleties of the new child's gestures, language, needs, and anxieties. Just when he most needs to be understood, protected, reassured, he is most likely to be overlooked or handled without empathy and understanding. Several strange people will deal with him, one after another, and no one of them will share his anxieties or support him through the maze of new experiences.

John, accustomed to turning with confidence to his mother or father, found no consistency of response from his many caretakers. He tried again and again to get a response, to relate to his new caretakers, at first by asking for play, by giving gifts, then by asking for comfort by tears. But to no avail. No one person was sufficiently aware of his experience; the nurses came and went according to their duties, not according to his need of them. They busied themselves with other children, with other tasks.

Multiple caretaking meant for John that his previous methods of communicating his needs and of getting a response did not bring results. He tried, but withdrew eventually in the face of repeated failures. It was not just that he was cared for by many people, but that the many people all failed to meet his needs. His confusion and despair were partly a result of this.

In contrast, the fostered children continued to use their usual methods of communication and demand and were answered in ways which approximated the responses they were accustomed to. There was, of course, some variation; but not more than the fostered children could accommodate to.

Strange Environment

"Strange environment" is a vague term which is commonly used in the literature with a facility that conceals how complex and gross the factor may be. It is perhaps thought of as having to do with change of building, color scheme, furniture.

But for the young child a strange institutional environment is a multitude of harsh experiences, deprivations, and demands, which place a great burden on him. He will be offered strange foods, strange implements with which to eat. He may be helped too much, or too little. The noise and movement during mealtimes are likely to impose strain.

His toileting will be fitted into the institution's routine, not geared to his particular rhythm as happens at home. His special signs or calls will probably not be seen or heard. Toileting accidents will happen; recent gains will be lost. The child who is toilet-trained may be put back into diapers, or the child used to diapers may find himself without them. Had we not intervened, John, an untrained child, would have been toilet-trained by strangers at a time of stress.

"Strange environment" may mean the sudden withdrawal of a comforting "dummy" or bottle just when the child has most need of comfort. It may mean the unavailability of his special cuddly blanket or toy, not deliberately but by the accidents of institutional life.

The child used to sleeping for several hours in the morning and having a late lunch may find himself too tired to eat lunch, wakeful when others sleep, and ready for sleep just as the rest wake up. His sleeping rhythm will be disturbed.

John was a child used to sleeping until he woke in the morning, then having a day rest when he needed it, but his rhythm was not

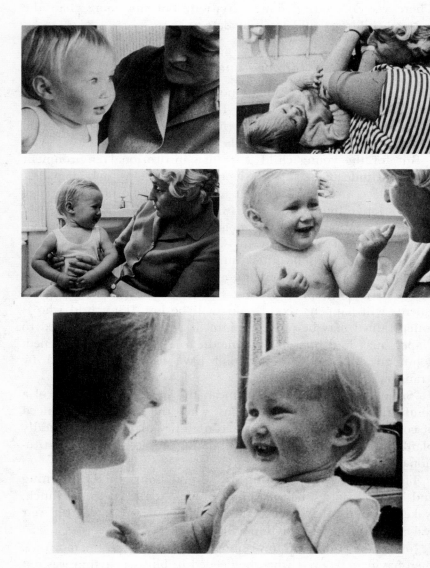

JANE, 17 months, given warm substitute mothering in a supportive environment, copes well and reunites warmly with her mother.

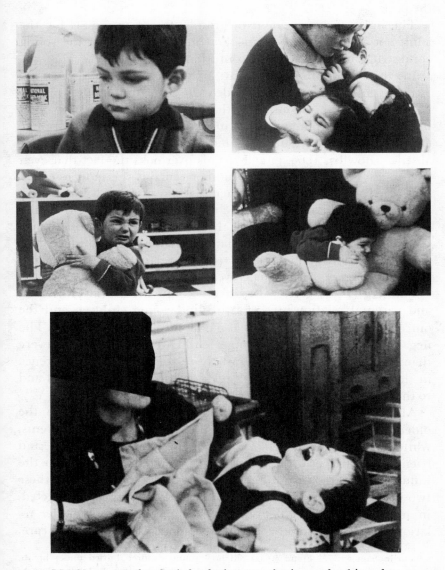

JOHN, 17 months, denied substitute mothering and subjected to the stresses of institutional life, is overwhelmed and at reunion rejects his mother.

that of the institution. He was most distressed when woken up from sleep because the clock had struck the hour for walks in the park.

The noise and movement of group life are strenuous for the adult not accustomed to them—how much more so for the young child struggling with so many confusions.

In the literature insufficient attention has been given to "strange environment" and "inadequate substitute mothering." It has been implied, for instance, that if a young child is not upset by a strange environment while his mother is present, the strange environment can have little significance if he shows distress in her absence (Bowlby, 1969, p. 29ff.). This overlooks the fact that even in a totally strange setting the mother remains the most essential part of a young child's environment,[2] whereas if she is absent and there is no familiar substitute he not only loses her but is totally exposed to the impingement of the environment. The mother is the person who "helps to mediate the environment, to keep it within his limits of tolerance" (Murphy, 1964, p. 41; see also James Robertson, 1958, 1962; Joyce Robertson, 1956, 1962).

Fraiberg (1971) gives a sensitive account of the early histories and parental relationships of two blind young children and the outcomes of brief separations at 14 months and 19 months. The negative responses of the younger child were much more severe than those of the older one. Fraiberg relates this to the difference in the quality of the children's relationship to their mothers and to the difference in developmental phase and abilities.

Although Fraiberg mentions that during the separation the older child was cared for by familiar and well-loved grandparents, while the younger was looked after by "various relations and friends who helped out," only passing reference is made to the influence of the vastly different separation experiences of these two blind young children. In fact, the child who was less affected, in addition to being older, better developed, and in a better relationship with his mother, also had much better substitute care.

---

[2] Burlingham and A. Freud (1942) tell how young children buried under bomb-damaged buildings emerged emotionally unscathed because they had been close to their mothers throughout.

Discussion

It has been shown that when the stress factors which complicate institutional studies had been eliminated, and adequate substitute mothering provided, four young children separated from their mothers for 10 to 27 days did not respond with the acute distress and despair described in the literature. In varying degree, reflecting their differing levels of object constancy and ego maturity, all four transferred cathexis to the substitute mother. Because they were not overwhelmed, as children admitted to institutions commonly are, their inner resources were available to cope with the loss of the mother. Individual differences in response, which are obscured by the severity of institutional separation, became apparent. None of these followed the sequence protest, despair, and denial/detachment described of institutionalized children.

During the first few days all four showed an increase in laughter and activity, which were understood as defensive against anxiety. The crying which occurred was mainly when the fathers left after visits and lasted no more than one or two minutes.

By the time the children might have been expected to show despair (according to earlier studies), that is, on the 2nd, 3rd or 4th day, there was some sadness, a lowered frustration tolerance, and some aggression. But this did not have the quality of despair. By that point each child had developed a relationship to the foster mother sufficient to sustain him, and had begun to cling to her. The relationship to the foster mother then held these children in a state of manageable anxiety. They used her increasingly and with growing intimacy.

Although under considerable strain throughout, all four children cared for in our supportive foster situation functioned and related well, learned new skills and new words, and at reunion greeted their mothers warmly. The separations had not been traumatic. The children had not been overwhelmed.[3]

---

[3] In a complementary study our social worker colleague, Katrin Stroh, investigated the behavior of nine small children who, while the mothers were in the hospital to have a second baby, remained in their own homes in the care of a

This was in contrast to John, the 17-month-old child observed in the residential nursery. Denied responsive substitute mothering, and exposed to the multiple stresses of the institutional environment, John protested and was in despair. He deteriorated in all areas, and at reunion rejected his mother with struggles and desperate crying. At the beginning of the separation John had shown himself ready to accept substitute mothering. It was stress factors additional to the loss of the mother which converted separation anxiety into trauma. In our view, the difference between the responses of the fostered children and those of John was qualitative, not merely of degree.

But that our foster children came through so well does not mean that the hazards attached to early separation can be eliminated entirely. At that early and vulnerable phase of development even the best of substitute care is not a certain prescription for neutralizing the risks. It will be recalled that after return home there was in all four children an increase of hostility against the mother which, although infinitely less than with John, carried some potential for disharmony in the mother-child relationship. Kate's initial aggression, for instance, was mishandled by her parents and but for our intervention could have developed into a buildup of recriminatory interaction. Although Jane had had optimal care, the discontinuity of relationship with her mother appeared to have resulted in a subtle disturbance of her superego development; it cannot be ruled out that other unobservable

familiar relative such as father, aunt, grandmother. This study was intended primarily to check in a general way the findings of the small foster sample being studied more intensively, including the extent to which we had succeeded in eliminating the factors of strange environment and multiple caretakers.

At least three preseparation home visits were made, two each week during separation, and two after separation, to make observations on the children and to interview parents and caretakers.

In important ways the behavior of these nine children who stayed in their own homes was similar to that of the four who were fostered. There was no immediate distress. After delays of 2 to 4 days they became clinging to the substitute caretakers and more irritable. But all continued to eat as before, and all learned new words. Reunion with the mothers was smooth and pleasant, with only short delay. This complementary study therefore supports in broad terms the findings of the more intensive foster-care study.

We hope to publish this material as part of a survey of how 100 families provided for the care of their young children while the mothers were in the hospital.

processes had been interfered with. The two younger children, Jane and Lucy, faced the additional hazard of a second experience of loss of a loved person because in their immaturity they had related wholeheartedly to the substitute mother.

These risks to well-being arose despite the children having been highly protected by conditions of care which were optimally structured and which would not always be replicated in the exigencies of everyday living. The children were healthy, had never been separated from their mothers, had plenty of time for familiarization with the foster family, and were put into the care of a fully available substitute mother who by reason of training and experience was specially competent to understand and meet their needs.

In everyday life young children face separations in emergencies, in illness and pain, often having previous histories of separation and family upset, and with still more factors complicating their situation even if stable substitute mothering is provided. It is not a simple opposition between foster care and institutional care. In addition to the loss of the mother, foster care can include many stresses due either to mishap or bad planning. Even in an ostensibly appropriate foster situation there may be a balance of adverse factors which can produce acute distress and despair (Cook, 1962; Deutsch, 1919). The complexities which commonly affect substitute care are such as to reinforce the view that separation is dangerous and should wherever possible be avoided.

There is an occasional child to whom a well-managed supportive separation appears to bring some benefits, as happened to Lucy, who was afterward able to initiate a richer interaction with her mother. In that instance the improvement resulted from a positive balance of factors such as those listed below, and from there having been a recent and remediable detriment to an essentially good mother-child relationship.

It will be clear that we do not subscribe to a simple view of responses to separation from the mother. There are individual differences resulting from a balance of factors—some working in the child's favor; some working against him; some making the actual separation easier, but the return home more difficult; some doing the reverse, making the separation more difficult, but the return home easier. How a particular young child reacts to separation can be understood as a product of the interplay of these factors.

Chart I suggests how some of these factors influence the separation experience of a child (see pp. 310–311).

The differences in response by John and Thomas, for instance, can be understood with reference to the chart. John suffered many stresses in addition to the loss of his mother: abrupt transfer to a strange environment; strange, inadequate, and multiple caretaking; strange food and routines; unusual demands and disciplines (see column A). There were few factors which might have reduced stress (see columns B and C). The balance between stress and support operated against John. His immature ego was overwhelmed and trauma resulted.

Thomas, on the other hand, had everything in his favor. He lost his mother, but suffered only minimally from other stresses; he benefited by factors (in columns B and C) which reduce stress. His relative ego maturity aided understanding of the reality situation, and his level of object constancy made it possible to help him keep alive the image of a caring mother who would return.

The above chart has particular reference to the age group of 18 months to 2½ years upon which much of the separation literature is based. But with modifications it is applicable to younger children down to the first months of life. For older children of about 3 to 5 years it would be necessary to incorporate additional factors associated with more advanced development.

This study has thrown no light on reasons for separation as variables influencing behavior during separation, since all the children were separated for the same reason—the birth of a second child. It is sometimes said that the prospect of a new and rivalrous sibling must be an additional stress. We had no access to fantasies, but the manifest behavior of the four fostered children suggested that the expected babies impinged hardly at all until they were physically present and taking their share of the parents' attention.

Kate, for instance, knew there was to be a new baby; but, as with the other children, did not appear to have the capacity to anticipate this as a threat. She took a little girl's pleasure in seeing babies in their prams in the street, and talked freely of the coming baby who would cry and sleep in a cradle. But when she was given a family of dolls as an aid to expressing her feelings, she did not use the baby doll. It did not appear to us that she avoided the baby. Rather, with the mother, father, and little girl dolls, she played out her immediate concerns about herself and her parents.

As always happens in research, questions answered discover still more questions to be asked. Kate, Thomas, Lucy, and Jane did not show acute distress and despair, and in the third and fourth weeks Kate and Lucy even appeared to be adapting and finding secure niches in the foster family. But what would have happened had the separations gone on indefinitely?

Would the two younger children, Jane and Lucy, with their slender object constancy and ego immaturity, have merged the memory traces of the mother with the image of the foster mother and have achieved a complete transference of cathexis? If so, would this have been a progressively smooth transition with no more manifest upset than had been shown during the duration of this study? Our data suggest that Jane and Lucy, two children of 21 months and under, would have transferred cathexis from mother to substitute mother without a phase of grief and mourning. This would be consistent with Anna Freud's view that the capacity to mourn is a function of the level of object constancy and ego maturity (1960, p. 59).

But even if Jane and Lucy had changed mothers without extreme upset, what might have been the consequences for their subsequent development—bearing in mind the indications of disturbance to superego development in Jane? From birth, internal structures including precursors to object relationships are in the process of increasingly refined development, and these are endangered by interference with or interruptions of the affective interactions unique to the particular mother-infant couple (Joyce Robertson, 1965). Infants from birth to about 2 years may show less upset than those over 2, but the level of overt upset is not a true indicator of the damage that may be occurring (Yarrow, 1964).

CHART I

Factors Which Combine to Determine Individual Differences in Young Children's Responses to Separation from the Mother

A	B	C
Factors in addition to loss of the mother which are likely to cause stress.	Factors likely to reduce stress.	Child's psychological status which may increase or reduce overt distress during separation, may increase or decrease the overt upset after separation, may increase or decrease the long-term effects.
(1) Strange environment	(1) Familiar substitute caretaker	(1) Ego maturity, level of
(2) Inadequate substitute caretaker	(2) Known foods and routines	(2) Object constancy, level of
(3) Strange caretaker	(3) Toilet demands unaltered	(3) Quality of mother-child relationship, facets of
(4) Multiple caretakers	(4) Own belongings	(4) Defense organization
(5) Cues/language not understood and responded to	(5) Unrestricted body movement	(5) Fantasies about illness, pain, physical interference, disappearance of mother, etc.
(6) Unfamiliar food and routines	(6) Familiar environment	(6) Preseparation experience of illness/separation

CHART I *(cont'd)*

A	B	C
(7) Unusual demands and disciplines	(7) Reassurance of eventual reunion	
(8) Illness, pain, bodily interference	(8) Keeping apart fantasy and fact ("My Mummy doesn't love me")	
(9) Bodily restriction	(9) Reminding child of parental disciplines	
	(10) Support from father	
	(11) Willingness of caretakers to talk about parents and previous life	

In a longer or permanent separation would the two older children have reached a point at which the acute distress and despair that are characteristic of mourning would have broken through? Or would they, too, as hypothesized for Jane and Lucy, have shed their mothers, more slowly, but with no more distress than they had shown during the project? In the third and fourth week of her separation Kate was becoming more and more attached to the foster mother and at ease within the foster family, but was still directing positive and negative affect toward the absent mother.

These are questions for another study.[4]

[4] Wolfenstein (1969), studying the reactions of school-age children to the death of a parent, found that mourning did not take place. An adaptive substitute for mourning was possible when there was an available and acceptable parent substitute to whom the child could transfer piecemeal the libido he gradually detached from the lost parent (p. 458).

Summary

The work reported in this paper extends and refines the observations by James Robertson (1953) on which his concepts of protest, despair, and denial were based. These phases were explicitly attached to separation from the mother when aggravated by strange environment, confinement to cot, multiple caretakers, and other stress factors associated with institutional care.

This paper describes how a total sample of 13 young children (17 months to 2 years 5 months) coped with separation from the mother when cared for in conditions from which the adverse factors which complicate institutional studies were absent. Four were fostered by the Robertsons and 9 were looked after in their own homes by a familiar relative. Separations ranged from 10 to 27 days.

None of the 13 children responded with protest and despair. In the authors' view, the difference between their responses and those of children observed in institutional settings was qualitative and not merely of degree. All were able to use the substitute for the absent mother.

The four fostered children, who were observed in special detail in the Robertson family, showed variations in response which were related to age, levels of ego maturity and object constancy, previous mother-child relationship, length of separation, and defense organization. Their behavior conformed to the psychoanalytic view that the capacity to mourn is a function of ego maturity and object constancy.

In a single contrast study, John, who in addition to loss of his mother was subjected to the inadequacies of residential nursery care, displayed the acute distress and despair commonly described of institutionalized children.

In 1960 this Annual carried a paper by Bowlby on "Grief and Mourning in Infancy and Early Childhood," together with critical essays on it by Anna Freud and others. In that paper, and in subsequent writings, Bowlby acknowledges that he draws mainly upon James Robertson's institutional data. But in developing his grief and mourning theory, Bowlby, without adducing noninstitutional data, has generalized Robertson's concept of protest, despair, and denial beyond the context from which it was derived. He asserts that these are the usual responses of young children to separation from the mother regardless of circumstance, and on this basis equates the separation responses of young children with the bereavement responses of adults in both form and content (Bowlby, 1960, 1961, 1969; Bowlby and Parkes, 1970).

Our findings do not support Bowlby's generalizations about the responses of young children to loss of the mother per se; nor do they support his theory on grief and mourning in infancy and early childhood. But we continue to share his concern about the potential harm associated with early separation from the mother.

BIBLIOGRAPHY

BOWLBY, J. (1960), Grief and Mourning in Infancy and Early Childhood. *This Annual*, 15:9–52.

— (1961), Processes of Mourning. *Int. J. Psycho-Anal.*, 42:317–340.

— (1969), *Attachment and Loss*, Volume I: *Attachment*. London: Hogarth Press; New York: Basic Books.

— & PARKES, C. M. (1970), Separation and Loss. In: *International Yearbook for Child Psychiatry and Allied Disciplines*, Volume I: *The Child and His Family*, ed. E. J. Anthony & C. Koupernik. New York: Wiley, pp. 197–216.

BURLINGHAM, D. & FREUD, A. (1942), *Young Children in Wartime*. London: Allen & Unwin.

— — (1944), *Infants Without Families*. London: Allen & Unwin.

COOK, P. S. (1962), A Two-Year-Old's Mother Goes to a Maternity Hospital. *New Zealand Med. J.*, 61:605–608.

DEUTSCH, H. (1919), A Two Year Old Boy's First Love Comes to Grief. In: *Dynamic Psychopathology in Childhood*, ed. L. Jessner & E. Pavenstedt. New York: Grune & Stratton, 1959, pp. 1–5.

ELKAN, I. (1969), Film Review: *John, Seventeen Months: For Nine Days in a Residential Nursery. J. Child Psychother.*, 2:82–84.

FRAIBERG, S. (1969), Libidinal Object Constancy and Mental Representation. *This Annual*, 24:9–47.

— (1971), Separation Crisis in Two Blind Children. *This Annual*, 26:355–371.

FREUD, A. (1960), Discussion of Dr. John Bowlby's paper [1960]. *This Annual*, 15:53–62.

— (1969), Film Review: *John, Seventeen Months: Nine Days in a Residential Nursery*. *This Annual*, 24:138–143.

HEINICKE, C. M. & WESTHEIMER, I. J. (1965), *Brief Separations*. New York: International Universities Press.

KENNEDY, H. (1969), Film Review: 1. *Kate, 2 Years 5 Months: In Foster Care for 27 Days*. 2. *Jane, 17 Months: In Foster Care for 10 Days*. *Brit. J. Med. Psychol.*, 42:191–193.

MICIC, Z. (1962), Psychological Stress in Children in Hospital. *Int. Nursing Rev.*, 9:23–31.

MURPHY, L. B. (1964), Some Aspects of the First Relationship. *Int. J. Psycho-Anal.*, 45:31–46.

PRUGH, D., ET AL. (1953), Study of Emotional Reactions of Children and Families to Hospitalization and Illness. *Amer. J. Orthopsychiat.*, 23:70–106.

ROBERTSON, JAMES (1952), Film: *A Two-Year-Old Goes to Hospital* [16mm, b & w, Sound, 45 and 30 minute versions; English/French; Guide booklet]. London: Tavistock Child Development Research Unit; New York: New York University Film Library.

— (1953), Some Responses of Young Children to Loss of Maternal Care. *Nursing Times*, 49:382–386.

— (1958), Film: *Going to Hospital with Mother* [16mm, b & w, Sound, 40 minutes; English/French; Guide booklet]. London: Tavistock Child Development Research Unit; New York: New York University Film Library.

— (1960), On the Making of Two Mental Health Films. *International Catalogue of Mental Health Films*. London: World Federation for Mental Health. And as: Nothing But the Truth. *Film User* (1960), 14.

— (1962), *Hospitals and Children: A Parent's-Eye View*. London: Gollancz.

— (1970), *Young Children in Hospital*. Second edition, with a Postscript. London: Tavistock Publications; New York: Barnes & Noble.

— & ROBERTSON, JOYCE (1967), *Young Children in Brief Separation*, Film No. 1: *Kate, 2 Years 5 Months: In Foster Care for 27 Days* [16mm, b & w, Sound, 33 minutes; Guide booklet]. London: Tavistock Child Development Research Unit; New York: New York University Film Library.

— — (1968), Film No. 2: *Jane, 17 Months: In Foster Care for 10 Days* [16mm, b & w, Sound, 37 minutes; Guide booklet] *Ibid.*

— — (1969), Film No. 3: *John, 17 Months: For 9 Days in a Residential Nursery* [16mm, b & w, Sound, 45 minutes; Guide booklet]. *Ibid.*

— — (1971), Film No. 4: *Thomas, 2 Years 4 Months: In Foster Care for 10 Days* [16 mm, b & w, Sound, 38 minutes; Guide booklet]. *Ibid.*

— — (1973), Film No. 5: *Lucy, 21 Months: In Foster Care for 19 Days* (in preparation).

Robertson, Joyce (1956), A Mother's Observations on the Tonsillectomy of Her Four-Year-Old Daughter. With Comments by Anna Freud. *This Annual*, 11:410–433.

— (1962), Mothering as an Influence on Early Development: A Study of Well-Baby Clinic Records. *This Annual*, 17:245–264.

— (1965), Mother-Infant Interaction from Birth to Twelve Months: Two Case Studies. In: *Determinants of Infant Behaviour*, ed. B. M. Foss. London: Methuen, 3:111–124.

Rosenfeld, S. (1970), Film Review: *John, 17 Months: For 9 Days in a Residential Nursery. Brit. J. Med. Psychol.*, 18:105–108.

Schaffer, H. R. & Callender, W. M. (1959), Psychological Effects of Hospitalization in Infancy. *Pediatrics*, 24:528–539.

Spitz, R. A. (1945), Hospitalism. *This Annual*, 1:53–74.

— & Wolf, K. M. (1946), Anaclitic Depression. *This Annual*, 2:313–342.

Vaughan, G. F. (1957), Children in Hospital. *Lancet* (June 1): 1117–1120.

Wolfenstein, M. (1969), Loss, Rage, and Repetition. *This Annual*, 24:432–460.

Yarrow, L. (1961), Maternal Deprivation: Toward an Empirical and Conceptual Re-evaluation. *Psychol. Bull.*, 58:459–490.

— (1964), Separation from Parents during Early Childhood. *Rev. Child Dev. Res.*, 1:89–136.

On the Beginnings of a Cohesive Self

An Application of the Concept of Transmuting Internalization to the Study of the Transitional Object and Signal Anxiety

MARIAN TOLPIN, M.D.

THIS PAPER FOCUSES ON THE FORMATION OF PSYCHIC STRUCTURE which enters into the beginnings of a "cohesive self" (Kohut, 1971) during the separation-individuation phase of development. On the basis of her extensive and fundamental research over the past two decades Mahler has delineated the complexities of this stage and deepened our understanding of its importance in normal and pathological development. Nevertheless, Mahler (1966) stated clearly that we know relatively little about the ego's developmental tasks during this critical developmental stage and about the precise

I want to thank Drs. George Pollock, Ernest S. Wolf, and Paul Tolpin for their valuable suggestions. I particularly want to express my appreciation to Dr. Heinz Kohut. His teaching at the Chicago Institute for Psychoanalysis has afforded a unique opportunity to study and to attempt to integrate his important recent contributions to psychoanalytic theory and practice.

nature of the structuralizations of the child's ego that must occur if further development is to proceed normally. Moreover, searching for etiological and genetic explanations of the severe personality disturbances in which structural defects are in the center of the psychopathology, numerous psychoanalytic investigations found this phase to be significantly implicated. Although Mahler's research has focused mainly on the genesis of certain psychotic disorders, the preponderance of psychoanalytic evidence suggests that the latter may be the most gross forms of a variety of disorders that have their origins in this phase (Anna Freud, 1965, 1971). For all these reasons Mahler recommended the "minute study" of the separation-individuation phase.

This paper is an initial attempt to undertake such a "minute study." As the subtitle implies, Heinz Kohut's concept of "transmuting internalization" provides the conceptual framework for this investigation (1966, 1968, 1971; see also Kohut and Seitz, 1963). This recently introduced explanation of structure formation adds another dimension to Freud's (1923) paradigmatic conceptualization (cf. Eissler, 1969) of the process involved in the formation of the ego—"the character of the ego is a precipitate of abandoned object-cathexes and . . . it contains the history of these object-choices" (p. 29). In the process described by Freud, Kohut also includes the narcissistic instinctual cathexes of the object imago and certain functions carried out by the object for the child, i.e., those discrete functions which promote and sustain narcissistic homeostasis. (The calming, soothing, and anxiety-regulating activities of the mother that maintain the infant's and toddler's equilibrium are particularly relevant to my discussion.)

When a "tolerable" phase-appropriate loss of some discrete function that the object carried out for the child is experienced ("optimal frustration"), the psyche does not resign itself to the loss; instead, it preserves the function of the object by internalization. When "effective internalization" replaces a function of the auxiliary ego by an internal structure that carries out the same function, a process has taken place that can be described as a structural "leap." For example, what the mother does for the baby when she rocks him to sleep, or later for the toddler when she reads him a story, is eventually replaced by a structure that enables the child to go to sleep by himself. This "leap" is accomplished by transmuting internalization, an intrapsychic process that involves "a depersonalizing . . . of the object, mainly in the form of a shift . . . from the total human context of the personality of the object to certain of its specific functions" (1971, p. 50). Thus, when narcissistic object cathexes are withdrawn ("abandoned") from the lost function of the object imago because of optimal frustration, the object's function is preserved ("precipitated") as "a particle of inner psychological structure [that] now performs the functions which the object used to perform for the child" (1971, pp. 64, 50).

This additional paradigm of bit-by-bit accretion of psychic structure from innumerable fractionated internalizations of specific maternal functions carried out for the child during infancy and the preoedipal period has led to new insights. These concern the drive-regulating, tension-reducing psychic structure which contributes to the neutralization of the drives, forms the "matrix" of the ego, and ultimately maintains the cohesiveness of ego and self. The application of the concept of transmuting internalization to the problem of ego formation during the phase when separation and individuation of necessity proceed hand in hand with the gradual loss of the previously experienced symbiosis illuminates the developmental tasks of this stage. These tasks are, in essence, another form of *psychic work* (see below). When this "work" is successfully accomplished by the infant-mother pair, the child acquires *"the normal workings of the mind"* (Freud, 1926, p. 150; my italics) which are necessary for a successful conclusion of the separation-individuation phase.

I shall describe two of the developmental tasks which confront the infant and toddler, and the ego "precipitate" that is their "expectable" (Hartmann, 1939) outcome. I have chosen two everyday aspects of infant behavior—the infant's attachment to the typical transitional object (Winnicott, 1953), and the infant behavior subsumed under stranger anxiety (Spitz, 1950). These are particularly well suited to demonstrate how the infant acquires the phase-appropriate capacity to soothe and calm himself and to mitigate his anxiety experience: innumerable minute internalizations of the maternal functions that first structure the original infant-mother "field" (Loewald, 1960, 1970) or symbiotic unity lead during separation-individuation to that degree of unification of the personality (self) which on the one hand permits expectable progression, and on the other prevents those deficits in the organization of the self with such adverse consequences for subsequent development. In Part I of this paper I shall discuss the infant's attachment to the transitional object, with special emphasis on the fate of the transitional object as a self-soothing psychic structure. My discussion also applies to the less striking transitional phenomena of which the infant's "blanket" is an especially visible example. Part II deals with the infant's anxiety experience in a stranger's presence and focuses on the acquisition of anxiety-regulating psychic structure. This leads to a formulation of the origin and phase-appropriate development of signal anxiety which, as far as I know, has not been explicitly proposed in the psychoanalytic literature on anxiety (for a recent review of this subject see Rangell, 1968).

The phenomenology of the transitional object and of stranger anxiety has been chosen for illustrative purposes because both are so readily accessible to the observer of the baby's behavior. Their deeper common denominator, which is most relevant to the study of structure formation during separation-individuation, is that separation from the transitional object when it is needed, and exposure to the stranger without the adequate mothering presence, both precipitate very similar reactions of acute distress.[1] The infant's distress is relieved only by reunion with the transitional object or by appropriate mothering intervention. I shall try to demonstrate that when the data of observation are approached with the psychoanalytic tool of empathic observation (Kohut, 1959) and the concept of transmuting internalization, the observable functions of the transitional object for the baby, in the first case, and of the mother, in the second, provide a *transitional form of mental structure* that then is destined to become a part of the child's own structure which maintain his cohesiveness.

---

[1] Since the precise differentiation between the precursors of the anxiety experience and the anxiety experience per se is not essential to my thesis I shall simply refer to the infant's "anxiety" or "distress." See Benjamin's (1961) thoughtful discussion of the importance of this distinction and the difficulties inherent in making it.

I. The Fate of the Transitional Object—
Soothing Psychic Structure

> . . . in health the transitional object does not 'go inside'. . . .
> It loses meaning . . . because the transitional phenomena have
> become diffused . . . over the whole intermediate territory be-
> tween 'inner psychic reality' and 'the external world as perceived
> by two persons in common', that is to say, over the whole cul-
> tural field [Winnicott, 1953, p. 233].

In my discussion of the acquisition of self-soothing psychic structure that enters into the formation of a cohesive self I shall
focus on a circumscribed aspect of the typical transitional object of
infancy: the "blanket" as a soother.[2] Differing from Winnicott, I
am proposing that the *soothing functions* of the transitional object
do, in fact, *"go inside" as mental structure;* and precisely because
of this the treasured possession is neither missed, mourned, repressed, nor forgotten. It is no longer needed.

Winnicott called attention first to what is now, by virtue of his
contribution, self-evident to us—that the blanket has a very soothing effect on its owner, and is most particularly sought and used
when the infant is most in need of soothing. Failure to find the
blanket at such times heightens the already existing state of distress, to which is then added the child's acute anguish over the
missing blanket. Reunion with the lost blanket replaces anguish
with joy, and facilitates recovery from the state of tension that
made the need for the blanket so imperative. Yet, in the face of
these clearly observable facts, John Bowlby (1969) has recently
made the assertion that the transitional object has no psychic significance whatsoever and that the blanket is merely a substitute
for the unavailable mother. This statement cannot be taken seri-

---

[2] I am using "blanket" as a generic word to cover all of the soft objects used by
infants. When I discussed the transitional object with my 13-year-old son, he asked,
"Why can't psychoanalysts use people language?" Blanket is "people language" for
the transitional object. It is not possible to integrate all of Winnicott's complex
ideas regarding the "intermediate territory" into this special focus on the blanket
as soother. Their relevance to "the 'puzzling leap' from the mental [sphere] . . .
to the physical embodiment of cultural values [human civilization]" (Eissler, 1969,
p. 477) deserves separate consideration.

ously. The child is as likely to use the blanket when the mother is also available to comfort him, and, in fact, does so. Many a mother has soothed her infant to sleep or calmed him in various ways when he is cranky while *he also soothes himself with his blanket*. Both common sense and empathic observations of the child and his blanket also lead me to disagree with Winnicott's statement that the blanket becomes more important as a soother than the mother. I think he, too, disagrees when he emphasizes that the illusion depends on the mother's "good enough" adaptation to her infant; and that without this adaptation the blanket would lose its meaning.

When the infant begins to use his blanket to soothe himself, he has created something—that is, he has endowed an inconsequential bit of the "external world" with a capacity to restore or improve his inner equilibrium. He usually creates this object when he has emerged sufficiently from the symbiotic state to begin to perceive his mother as the chief instrument of his sense of well-being and of his relief from distress. This observation certainly suggests that he has endowed his blanket with her soothing and tension-relieving functions. The formation of the transitional object thus enables the infant at an early age to begin to achieve a certain degree of independence from the mother by virtue of his own mental activities—he has at hand a means to calm himself. (This important developmental shift from passivity to increasing activity will be stressed in the discussion of the developmental lines of soothing and anxiety-regulating structure formation.)

Winnicott (1953) described the fate of the transitional object as a "decathexis" that occurs "especially as cultural interests develop" (p. 233).[3] In connection with Winnicott's formulation Kahne (1967) asked how the object with such vital importance to the child can undergo a process of decathexis without mourning. I believe that this question reflects a misunderstanding of the role of the transitional object in infantile development. As soon as the child has created the illusion for himself that the blanket soothes, he uses it in the characteristic manner that ultimately determines its psychic fate. I would emphasize that phenomenologically the

---

[3] Coppolillo (1967) has pursued this line of reasoning in a clinical application.

behavior with the blanket is like an addiction. (The phase-appropriate attachment to the mother as the "need-satisfying object" can also be conceptualized as addictionlike. Although the transitional object is not a substitute for the mother, it does concretely embody an aspect of the mother essential to need satisfaction.) The infant seeks and uses the blanket mainly when he needs to soothe himself. At other times the treasured possession which he cannot do without when he needs it is carelessly left behind and temporarily "forgotten" as soon as it has served its purpose. In fact, the child often does not know where the blanket is when he needs it most, and he regards it as his mother's duty to restore it to him.

The empathic mother accepts her "duty" even though it often enough involves a time-consuming search. Most mothers soon learn to take the blanket along on an outing, anticipating the time when the tired child in strange surroundings will need it. And sooner or later many children acquire, via their experience with the blanket, this anticipatory function for themselves and make certain that the blanket is brought along.[4] This typical behavior suggests that over the normal course of the attachment to the blanket the child *repeatedly* "cathects" and "decathects" it. His creation is there, so to speak, when he needs it, and it has little importance when he does not need it, providing, of course, that he knows that it can be found again. As Winnicott (1953) points out, however, "some abrogation of omnipotence is a feature from the start" (p. 233). That is to say, no matter how attached the normal child is to his blanket, he cannot always find it as soon as he wants it, and there are inevitable delays in his "refinding" it. The optimal loss of the blanket that this implies has important intrapsychic consequences which differ significantly from the effects of permanent (traumatic) loss.

[4] The framework of this study suggests the beginnings of the developmental line of the anticipatory function. Although this function has been stressed particularly in connection with signal anxiety, it undoubtedly enters into all inner regulations which avert psychoeconomic imbalance (traumatic states). The mother's exercise of the anticipatory function forestalls traumatic states of tension and anxiety throughout infancy and early childhood. Although the capacity for this cognitive activity is a part of the autonomous "givens," transmuting internalization of this maternal function is necessary for its effective organization as it undergoes maturation.

The Developmental Line
of the Transitional Object As Soother

In spite of the child's addictionlike attachment to the blanket this developmental configuration seems to "pass away" because its "time is over" (Freud [1919] was referring to the best known example of a developmental "passing"—that of the oedipus complex). The process of innumerable, repeated alternations between need for the blanket and relative disinterest in it ends in the blanket losing its vital importance for the child. This occurs because normally the soothing functions of the transitional object have entered into the formation of the matrix of the child's ego. The genuine "passing" of the transitional object marks a developmental milestone in early development. During its time of ascendancy a whole class of maternal regulatory functions undergo the fate described as transmuting internalization. It is these, then, that enable the child to maintain his cohesiveness (temporarily at least) apart from the mother by the end of the lengthy separation-individuation phase. The essential "leap" from maternal regulation to self-regulation is *illustrated* by the phenomenon of the transitional object. The special "leap" from soothing inanimate object to self-soothing capacity will be elucidated in the theoretical discussion of the formation, function, and fate of the transitional object—an application of Anna Freud's (1965) concept of developmental lines. My reconsideration of the transitional object has led me to the conclusion that the *self-object bond,* which it illustrates, replaces the physiological attachment of intrauterine life and the merger experience of the symbiotic phase, which are essential to the normal growth and development of the fetus and neonate.

The Formation and Function of the "Blanket"

The inanimate object acquires its unique soothing function because of its libidinal investment (A. Freud, 1965) during that *transitional phase* when normal growth propels the infant from body-mind symbiosis to beginning physical and psychic separateness. Mahler (1963, 1966) has repeatedly stressed that the newly "hatched infant separated from the common symbiotic membrane" is still psychically unequipped for separation. Although developmentally programmed, separation from "good enough" symbiotic oneness necessarily entails progressive, minute losses for the infant. Above all, the unique calming effects that the very young infant's physical merging with his mother has cannot be recaptured even in the "good enough" partnership of the next phase. It is simply impossible for the mother to hold and calm the larger, more active, and alert infant of the second half of the first year in exactly the same way that she held and cradled the physically more immature infant with whom an almost complete sense of physical merging is possible.

Physical growth thus automatically brings with it a minute alteration of the symbiotic unity and the blissful state connected with it. The infant who has now begun to associate soothing with what the mother does, withdraws cathexis from the imago of the lost soothing experience with the mother. For example, the mother has tried and failed to soothe the fussy, restless baby and puts him down in his crib for a time to see whether he is just tired and will go off to sleep if left to his own devices. In order to preserve the soothing experience of the previous merger which the infant is still unprepared to forgo, the cathexis of the mother's function is "transferred" to whatever is at hand and lends itself to such a "transference" [5] by virtue of its warmth, softness, pliability, odor, immediate availability, etc.—the object that in its inseparable commingling of aspects of infant and mother will continue the illusion of their merger and the physical-mental soothing to which it gave rise.

The transitional object is thus heir to a part of the infant's original narcissism that is preserved when it is assigned to the idealized parent imago (Kohut, 1966, 1971)—the metapsychological basis for its unique role in mental development and for its distinction from the "pacifier." (The pacifier belongs to the auto-

[5] Although I use the term "transference," this process does not involve transference in its strict metapsychological sense. There is a transferencelike process, however, when instinctual cathexis is withdrawn from the soothing effects of the merger experience with the mother and invested in a suitable "carrier." For a clinical example of such an investment at the time of normal progression from symbiosis to increasing separateness, see Kleeman (1967, p. 246).

erotic stage of mental organization; the blanket, to the stage of mental organization which develops when the idealized maternal imago's functions are cathected with narcissistic libido.) Innumerable circumscribed losses of the merger experience and numerous "transferences" occur before one particular object acquires this special status. The transitional phenomena described by Winnicott differ mainly quantitatively. For many infants one soft object becomes the main repository of cathexes. For others, the cathexes are "spread out" over many soft objects and other soothing experiences.

By thus re-creating the lost symbiosis and its soothing effects in a new form, while at the same time soothing continues to be experienced with the mother, the infant "artist" (Kohut, 1966) has at his command a concrete embodiment of a transitional self-object imago; with it he can temporarily regress to the lost symbiosis with which *he can dose himself when his need for more soothing than even the "good enough" mother can provide is imperative*. This type of regression may, on the one hand, be the successor of hallucinatory wish fulfillment as a detour to refinding the object in reality and, on the other, form the precursor of manifest regression in fantasy. In any event such temporary regressions provide a respite for the infant and enable him to return to the exigencies of separate existence.[6]

The transitional object is a "better soother" than the mother only in the sense that it can re-evoke the lost soothing of symbiotic fusion. No matter how good her soothing capacity, the mother cannot re-create the earlier state which the infant provides for himself by his own creation.

With the ongoing advances in development during the separation phase, however, the mother is progressively perceived as the "real" source of soothing. When her discretely perceived soothing functions are lost in small doses during the whole of separation-individuation, the narcissistic cathexis of the lost function is also "added" to the blanket via the cathectic shifts described above. This additional investment of the blanket *sustains the illusion of soothing*. The transitional object, like the infant himself, thus

---

[6] I have previously discussed (1968) the "existential" anxiety of separation as a spur to the artistic creation that is one of man's means for overcoming it.

undergoes a process of continued accretion. The younger infant (roughly between 4 to 8 months) who creates the blanket in the borderland between separation and symbiosis perhaps initially re-creates more of the original symbiosis than does the older infant who is well into the separation phase and who has used a variety of transitional phenomena for soothing before creating the special object. These differences in timing probably also account for the differences in intensity of attachment, in the way the blanket is used, in the duration of its use, all of which have not yet been studied. The wide range of differences that Winnicott purposely stressed probably reflect individual variations in the timing of true "hatching" from symbiosis as well as differences in the infants' reaction to loss of the merged state and to the stresses of the on-going separation process.

For example, I observed a 20-month-old toddler forming a transitional object from a flannel Halloween costume. His separation anxiety (see Part II) stimulated his need for more soothing than the "good enough" mother and the various transitional phenomena he had used previously could provide. Stevenson (1954) described instances in which the transitional object was "carried along" to subsequent developmental phases and acquired additional meanings and functions. Although my focus is restricted to the paramount importance of the blanket as a soother during separation-individuation and to its most *typical fate,* the later accretions clearly warrant further metapsychological study.

The mental feat (i.e., the transferencelike process) which results in the formation of the transitional object depends on inherent mental activity which unfolds when the infant experiences the consistently soothing "good enough mothering" during the symbiotic and early separation phases. The relative independence from maternal care achieved with the creation of the soothing imago which is neither self nor mother but which combines features of both has an earlier parallel. Almost from birth the infant is equipped for a degree of independence by virtue of his original autoerotic endowment. Although this endowment is the necessary precursor for the formation of the blanket, it does not provide sustained soothing for the normal infant. Sustained soothing is dependent on what the mother does for the infant. The "addition"

of narcissism to autoerotism (Freud, 1914) during the mental transitions of the first year leads to the narcissistic cathexis of the
mother's functions, which accounts for their inclusion in the rudimentary self system. Although the infant begins to perceive the
mother as a "not me" (Winnicott, 1953) or an admired and needed
"you" (Kohut, 1966, 1968) by the time the transitional object is
formed, her soothing functions are nonetheless perceived as a
part of the self by virtue of their narcissistic cathexis. When this
cathexis is withdrawn and invested in the blanket, a maternal
function perceived as belonging to the self is thus "added" to the
original autoerotic propensity, and the infant's own capacity for
sustained self-soothing is thereby augmented.

The essential point I wished to stress above is that the developmental shifts from passivity to increasing activity which enables
the infant to do for himself something that previously depended
almost wholly on the mother originate in the autonomous "givens"
(Hartmann, 1939; A. Freud, 1965) and develop in relation to experiences with the mother. The same is true with regard to the
development of the capacity for signal anxiety, which will be discussed in Part II. When the infant's own mental activity equips
him to soothe himself, he demonstrates with his blanket a special
case of a *transitional form of mental structure* that results from
narcissistic cathexis of the idealized parent imago. Developing as
it does when the "I"-"you," internal-external distinction is only
in the process of being made, this phase-appropriate "mental structure" is neither wholly internalized nor wholly external. There
is little doubt, however, that the transitional self-object in the
form of the blanket provides mental structure when we see the
infant calm himself with it; on the other hand, seeing the infant
"fall apart" (fragment) when he is deprived of it leaves little doubt
that the structure that it provides is not yet "inside."

Internalization of the Functions of the "Blanket"

The normal human infant requires a long period of time to
accomplish the shift to inner regulation. Genuine psychic separation depends on this mental transition. On the basis of studying
the transitional object I would suggest that it provides an additional psychic way station or necessary mental detour to the in-

ternalization of soothing structure for the infant who is "hatched" from symbiotic merger while still so vulnerable to disequilibrium. By prolonging the soothing and calming experiences originally provided by the mother in a concrete, sensual form, the blanket as a way station both prepares and bolsters the psyche for the bit-by-bit internalization and stable organization of the maternal functions that have been "transferred" to the inanimate object at a time when the psyche is still too immature to make the trans-muting internalization of these functions directly. Winnicott origi-nally noted that some infants use the mother herself as a transi-tional object. In the metapsychological sense the "good enough" mother's "holding" care provides the transitional form of mental structure which the infant needs throughout his early develop-ment. Winnicott's transitional object is a unique form of this structure. Since it "bolsters" the functions that are so wearing for the mother to perform it is not surprising that she too accepts the restorative powers of the blanket with relief and cooperates with her child's need for it.

The blanket thus functions as a psychic "preserve" analogous to the realm of fantasy in later development (Freud, 1911). By pre-serving the mental organization associated with the "good enough" mother who mediates structure while it is lacking "inside," the blanket eases the stress of transition to object constancy. (Green-acre [1969, 1970] also highlights this facilitating role.) At the same time it promotes internalization of the mental structure on which object constancy depends—the inner structure now performs for the self some of the equilibrium-maintaining regulations which depended at first on the need-satisfying object. Circumscribed losses of the mother in her role as need-satisfying (structure-medi-ating) soother and regulator not only are inevitable and unavoid-able during infancy; they are also necessary in optimal doses if mastery of separation from her and individuation of the psyche are to occur. I have explained how repeated, minute experiences of loss lead to the narcissistic cathexis of the blanket that creates the illusion of soothing symbiotic merger. Repeated experiences of losing and refinding the auxiliary soother when it is needed to restore equilibrium assist the psyche in the phase-specific task of replacing maternal soothing with tension-reducing mental activity

—the same process that eventually leads to the replacement of the soothing possession itself with the inner mechanisms that produce the same effect.

As the psychic way station that is the "repository" for cathexes and that re-creates the illusion of symbiotic merger, the transitional object is finally decathected when the cathexes are "abandoned" (i.e., withdrawn from the soothing transitional self-object imago) and "precipitated" as psychic structure (Freud, 1923), which has the same capacity to soothe, calm, and restore equilibrium. That is to say, the blanket is "decathected" little by little as its soothing functions undergo internalization. These functions contribute to the formation of the matrix of an ego that is now partially equipped (by virtue of that internalization) to perform soothing operations for itself, but now without the need for the illusory external soother. The leaving behind of the transitional object resembles metapsychologically the child's later transition from play with external props to fantasy, which is similarly independent of the inanimate objects in the external world and which similarly makes the daydreamer temporarily independent of reality.

Phenomenological observations of the child and his blanket do not suffice to indicate whether the blanket has really "passed" or is merely left behind. Metapsychological assessment of the total personality is necessary for this crucial distinction. When the process of effective internalization of maternal regulatory functions is impaired, fixations on the transitional form of mental structure or regressions to earlier autoerotic mechanisms are the result. To discuss this form of psychopathology *in statu nascendi* would take me far beyond the normal fate of the transitional object and the main thesis of this presentation, which is concerned with optimal internalization during the separation-individuation phase.

When the blanket "passes," it is shed as the cicada sheds its skin—when a new one has already formed and the old structure is therefore superfluous. Naturally there are wide individual variations in the use of the blanket and the timing of the final shedding. Although many toddlers discard it at the end of the period of its natural ascendancy (separation-individuation), some children continue to keep it around "just in case" and give themselves an additional boost with it at bedtime or other times of stress, for longer or shorter periods of time.

The transitional object is thus normally neither missed, mourned, nor repressed because it is not really lost. Its functions have been internalized. In that internalization process it is only the concrete attributes of the blanket (its texture, odor, warmth, etc.) which are left behind; the tension-regulating and tension-reducing effects of the mother as soother that were first invested in the blanket undergo transmuting internalization and are preserved as a part of the child's own capacity to avert traumatic intensities—i.e., "to calm himself down."

The underlying mental mechanism by which this self-sustaining capacity is acquired—fractionated (hyper)cathexis and decathexis (cf. Freud, 1917)—is analogous to the work of mourning, as well as to the work of analysis, "working through," and to the "work" of structure formation that proceeds throughout childhood via transmuting internalization. The specific history of the blanket by virtue of its visibility and externality thus provides a particularly illuminating example *in vitro,* as it were, of the optimal psychic mechanism for the mastery of loss of maternal regulatory functions which promote the infant's development. As I have already indicated, the transitional object in the form of the blanket is a special case of phase-appropriate mental structure formed when narcissistic cathexis of maternal functions enables the infant to perceive these functions as belonging to the self. The *special case* of the blanket as a transitional self-object imago thus illustrates the *general psychic tendency* to preserve the lost psychic effects and functions of an imago needed for inner regulation. When optimal (minute) loss occurs, an inherent intrapsychic process transmutes actual functions carried out by the human object into regulating psychic activity. (The mother's activities—e.g., her smiling, talking, crooning, rocking, patting, gazing, and so forth in ways too numerous to list—which promote inner equilibrium are central during the early stages on which I have focused.) This process is particularly evident in the analogous change in the transitional object. From the soft, furry, smelly, pliable, warm, concretely available blanket the psyche acquires inner regulatory functions which eventually enable the child to *calm and soothe himself with "the normal workings of the mind."*

As a striking example of the transitional mental structure formed by cathexis of the idealized maternal imago I would include the transitional object among the phenomena Spitz (1959) designates as psychic organizers. The smiling response, separation anxiety, and the acquisition of language also depend on autonomous endowment which unfolds when supported by "good enough" mothering. In order to avoid overemphasis on the blanket per se I want to stress again that it is the cathexis, optimal loss, and internalization of supporting maternal functions which build the ego during infancy. The blanket is a special way station for maternal soothing functions which the infantile psyche "distills out in pure culture." The normal infants who never create the special possession cathect and internalize the less visible soothing transitional phenomena. These then serve as multiple pathways to structure formation—like the mother herself. The infants who suffer maternal deprivation cannot re-create "good enough" mothering experiences because they have never experienced them. They are thus doubly deprived. They too are thrust into growth without the intermediate pathway that provides sustained soothing and promotes internalization of soothing functions for the self.[7]

Kohut has shown how the early foundations of a cohesive self depend on the formation of the transitional psychic structure that

[7] It is beyond the scope of this paper to discuss the metapsychological differences between the typical transitional object and a "patch" needed to enhance a defective sense of intactness (Greenacre, 1969, 1970). When a structural deficit is incurred during the period of infancy that I have discussed, a fixation on the need for the functions of the idealized parent imago occurs, and the personality is "addicted" to the functions of an external regulator. The clarification of the transitional object may assist in understanding disorders like addiction and fetishism in which this is the case. The question of whether the typical transitional object is really outgrown and what role it plays in psychopathology resides in the metapsychological understanding of its structure and fate in the psyche.

I would like to mention that it is not surprising that Wulff (1946) concluded that the infant who soothed himself with his mother's lingerie demonstrated a pathological phenomenon. The structure of an object created with the mother's pathological participation differs from the transitional object of the infant "left to his own devices."

I have described in connection with the blanket. The ability to perform soothing functions for himself firms or strengthens the infant's emerging self, and so forth, in a circular process. Hartmann (1952), from the vantage point of neutralization, described a similar circular process in connection with the development of object constancy. Object constancy depends on some degree of drive neutralization; neutralization is a necessary condition for the development of object constancy. The point of view of this study suggests an expansion of Hartmann's formulation: transmuting internalization of regulatory functions mediated by the "good enough" mother of the separation phase (the narcissistically perceived maternal imago and its functions) and the "assistant" (the transitional object) gradually leads to psychic structure which enables the child to satisfy some of his own needs; the freedom from exclusive dependence on the need-satisfying object conferred by this structure is indispensable for the achievement of object constancy.

The replacement of maternal functions by psychic structure is relative, of course. This process goes on gradually throughout "growing up" and the mother's continuing support of the child is essential for the maintenance of his developmental achievements. (The father's role in developmental acquisitions figures more prominently in later stages.) The optimal growth of particular structures is phase-specific, however. The superego and ego ideal are the phase-specific additions to the psyche with the passing of the oedipus complex. They will ultimately play an essential role in maintaining the intactness of the personality. The self-regulating activities described in both parts of this paper belong to a class of phase-specific acquisitions of the separation-individuation phase. Because these mental operations enter into the formation of a cohesive self their effective internalization during this phase is the necessary basis for optimal growth of the self in subsequent stages when further differentiation of the personality occurs.

Summary

This view of the infant's capacity to create for himself an auxiliary soother which ultimately becomes part of an inner regulatory structure suggests that despite the human infant's prolonged dependence his mental equipment includes innate factors which, sufficiently supported by mothering, potentially guarantee development into a self-regulating separate psychic entity with partial independence from external regulations. "Transference" of narcissistic cathexis from the lost soothing functions of the idealized maternal imago to the blanket creates a transitional self-object imago which serves as a detour to transmuting internalizations of maternal functions which promote cohesiveness. By contrast, *traumatic disappointments* in the mother as the psychic regulator leave a structural deficit and "an archaic, transitional self-object . . . is [still] required for the maintenance of narcissistic homeostasis" (Kohut, 1971, p. 28). When the soothing functions of the mother and the blanket are effectively internalized, a normal phase of relative structural insufficiency has passed. The fate of the outgrown transitional object is to "pass away" because it does "go inside" as soothing psychic structure.

II. The Infantile Origins of Signal Anxiety

What we need and cannot lay our finger on is some factor which will explain why some people are able to subject the affect of anxiety, in spite of its peculiar quality, to the normal workings of the mind, or which decides who is doomed to come to grief over that task [Freud, 1926, p. 150].

In what follows I shall try to demonstrate that the necessary foundations for what Freud called the ability "to subject the affect of anxiety . . . to the normal workings of the mind" are laid when the mother "subjects" the infant's anxiety experiences (or what may be more precisely considered their precursors [Benjamin, 1961]) to "the normal workings" of the infant-mother relationship of the preoedipal years. I am proposing that from the earliest developmental phases onward the infant experiences a phase-appropriate form of signal anxiety if the infant-mother unit is "good enough"; and that these signallike anxiety experiences which depend for their occurrence on the mother's "expedient" (Freud, 1926) interventions are the infantile precursors of the signal anxiety experience in the mature, separately functioning psyche.

I use the term "good enough" infant-mother unit—a variation on Winnicott's (1953) "good enough mothering" or "holding"— because it includes more explicitly the factors innate in the infant which affect the mother's mothering capacity. For an extreme example see Engel and Reichsman (1956). The discussion of what is intended by this term began with Freud's (1926) paradigm of the "psychical relation" to the mother who satisfies all needs at a time when the maternal object as such does not exist for the baby (p. 138). Extensive psychoanalytic exploration of this relation has continued. It has been discussed as the symbiotic relationship (Benedek, 1938, 1956; Mahler, 1968); the average expectable environment (Hartmann, 1939); the maternal shield (Khan, 1964); the auxiliary ego (A. Freud, 1965); attachment behavior (Bowlby, 1969), etc.

The metapsychological definition of "good enough" infant-mother unit suggested by the conceptual framework of this study is intended to elaborate the paradigm in *Inhibitions, Symptoms, and Anxiety*. The "caesura" of birth interrupts the *physiological attachment* of the fetus to the mother's body. This attachment is replaced by the neonatal symbiotic merger which continues to satisfy the needs of the biologically immature baby. When normal growth processes interrupt the merger experience, it is replaced, in its turn, by the transitional self-object bond (described in Part I in connection with the formation of the blanket) which continues a *"psychical" infant-mother attachment* necessary for optimal psychological growth. At the same time that this developing tie provides "a means to allay the anxiety of the infant in arms conditioned by separation from the mother," it provides the means for another "leap" normally accomplished during the separation-individuation phase: transmuting internalization of the anxiety-mitigating effects of the transitional bond equips the infant with the "precipitate" of ego functions which is the structural basis for "the transition from automatic to signal anxiety." This "first great step forward in the provision made for self-preservation" is a first great step forward in the organization of a cohesive self.

Signal anxiety is usually thought of as an anxiety experience that occurs developmentally late because it is dependent on such complex structures as the superego, the repression barrier, and the "strong" ego (Freud, 1926), which carries out such complex cognitive activities as experimenting in thought (remembering, anticipating, comparing, judging, choosing). My emphasis in this paper is restricted to the expectable development of the infant's "rescue signal" by virtue of those optimal anxiety experiences and their corresponding mental organization that occur during "good enough" separation-individuation. This development lays the necessary groundwork for further personality differentiation in later stages and further development of effective mental operations which first signal danger and then act to master it. Although early disturbances in the mother-child relationship have been broadly implicated in many forms of psychopathology, the specific structural acquisitions and corresponding deficits postulated here have not been explicitly formulated in the psychoanalytic literature despite the fact that the developmental line to be presented was suggested by Freud in *Inhibitions, Symptoms, and Anxiety.*

The Model of the Infant on His Mother's Knee

Bowlby's (1969) description of the phenomenology of stranger anxiety provides a model for the discussion of the early form of signal anxiety that I regard as the necessary (though not sufficient) condition for the development of the mature form.

> . . . in any one infant, the occurrence of fear of strangers [once it develops] varies greatly according to conditions. . . . both occurrence and intensity depend in large measure on how far distant the stranger is, whether he approaches the infant and what else he does; they probably depend also on whether the infant is in familiar or strange surroundings and on whether he is ill or well, fatigued or fresh. Yet another variable, studied especially by Morgan and Ricciuti (1969), is *whether an infant is on his mother's knee or away from her.* From the age of eight months onwards this makes a big difference, an infant sitting four feet from his mother showing much more fear than when sitting on her knee; this finding is no doubt related to the fact that from eight months onwards an infant begins to use his

mother as a secure base from which to explore [p. 326; my italics].

These familiar data of infant observation suggest that in the presence of a stranger the infant who is "close enough" to his mother experiences only a minute or mitigated form of stranger anxiety. It is obvious that "close enough" depends not merely on the mother's presence but on her whole way of sensing and responding to her baby's fear. The small anxiety responses are in sharp contrast to the overwhelming paniclike reactions to the stranger (the massive automatic anxiety experience or its precursor) that the infant experiences in the absence of the mother's alleviating behavior (Bowlby, 1969; Benjamin, 1961; Spitz, 1950; Mahler, 1968).

Using the infant on his mother's knee as a model we can empathically identify the infant's psychic state as an early form of signal anxiety. What is internal for the infant at such times is a minimal anxiety experience that is not disrupting. The minuteness of the infant's anxiety during this stage, however, depends entirely on the mother's structure-mediating response (Loewald, 1960, 1970) to his distress signals; or, put another way, the infant experiences signallike anxiety when the mother's buffering functions operate optimally at a time when the infant's own anxiety-reducing psychic structure is almost wholly lacking.

If we consider that inoculations of attenuated doses of anxiety ultimately lead to the capacity to master the anxiety experience itself and the experiences that give rise to it (using Freud's [1926] physiological analogy), the model of the infant on his mother's knee also suggests that we can regard the infant's minimal experience of anxiety as the optimal amount that promotes the process of internalization of the anxiety-reducing functions of the mother. When the infant is not "close enough" to his mother—i.e., when her anxiety-attenuating function is either consistently not sufficiently available or consistently fails—he is vulnerable to the overwhelming and disrupting anxiety experiences of the early phases from which he cannot recover adequately with his own limited resources. Under these circumstances the infantile psyche begins early to resort to the pathogenic mechanisms (A. Freud, 1965) that

are inexpedient substitutes for maternal buffering. In later childhood and adulthood when the mental structure that makes for a
"good enough" signal function is lacking, the psyche has recourse
only to the less expedient mental mechanisms that are associated
with severe forms of psychopathology.

Perhaps because this model is such a commonplace of everyday
life it has been overlooked that the infant's incipient anxiety and
the mother's anxiety-reducing response are the prototype of what
eventually occurs intrapsychically when the beginning anxiety experience acts as a signal to initiate the complex regulatory activities
that keep the anxiety experience to the expedient minimum. The
experiences of the infant in the situation of the model also are undoubtedly the infantile precursors of the capacity of the ego to take
itself (or *the self*) as an object, to treat itself like other objects, to
"observe itself, criticize itself, and do Heaven knows what with
itself" (Freud, 1933, p. 58).

I am postulating that the mother's anxiety-relieving responses to
the infant's distress signals are ultimately preserved as psychic structure as long as the inevitable anxiety experiences to which the
child is exposed usually are kept to minimal, manageable, bite-
sized doses by virtue of what she does until the child's own mental
workings can do the same thing. In fact, the main thesis of this
paper is that the successful outcome of the separation-individuation phase depends precisely on the gradual internalization of
equilibrium maintaining maternal functions that lead to a separate
(or "separated") self-regulating self.

The Developmental Line of Signal Anxiety

First Stages

What was originally carried out for the infant by the mother
comes, in the course of normal development, to be performed by
the psyche to cope with the anxiety experience and to preserve its
own integrity. This crucial change from symbiotic to separate
mental organization involves what can be considered the developmental line of signal anxiety. The following discussion focuses
only on the critical initial stages of this line—on the origins in the
"good enough" preoedipal infant-mother unit. The critical dis-

turbances in the unit (from the side of both infant and mother) which may occur, whatever their nature, may distort the normal developmental line and interfere with the phase-appropriate structuralization of the signal function. The capacity of the infant to "give the signal of anxiety, before the dreaded economic situation has set in" is an autonomous given with which the normal infant is endowed from birth. Like the propensity for automatic anxiety, anxiety "as a rescuing signal . . . is seen to be a product of the infant's mental helplessness which is a natural counterpart of its biological helplessness" (Freud, 1926, p. 138). This given of the apparatus is, however, guaranteed structuralization and effective operation only when the mother consistently carries out her role of anxiety reduction in response to the signal. The anxiety signal that consistently fails in its purpose during the stages of greatest biological and psychic helplessness atrophies or withers, as it were, from lack of support.

The Undifferentiated and Symbiotic Phases

The formulation of what might be called *primary signal anxiety* is based on the conceptualization implicit in the concept of primary narcissism—namely, that the infantile state depends on the mother's optimal functioning in place of the infant's not-yet-developed psychic structure; and on the conceptualization of the earliest mental organization that is congruent with the concept of primary narcissism—the hypothetical purified pleasure ego of the infant (Freud, 1915).

Although the traumatic state (psychic helplessness—the precursor of the massive automatic anxiety experience) is the unavoidable phase-appropriate experience of the earliest phases, there has been insufficient emphasis on the fact that in the "good enough" unit the infant also regularly experiences mothering interventions that mitigate the magnitude and duration of these states. Even more important, there has been insufficient emphasis on "what every mother knows"—besides the traumatic states, small to moderate forms of bodily-mental distress that never reach traumatic proportions are also typically experienced during the early phases as long as the mother's adaptation to her infant is "good enough."

The psychoanalytic literature has tended to emphasize the extreme polarities—the traumatic state and the experience of satisfaction—and their corresponding memory traces and mental structures. Valuable as the conceptualizations of these basic mental events and their associated mental configurations are—e.g., the depressive core (Benedek, 1956) and confidence or trust (Erikson, 1950)—their somewhat global emphasis has led to the relative neglect of those mental events which Kohut and Seitz (1963) have conceptualized as optimal frustration. Yet it is precisely that which leads to the gradual accretion of drive-regulating and tension-reducing psychic structure. This concept, coupled with those mentioned above, is particularly relevant to the discussion of the normal developmental process during which the psychic structure that reduces anxiety is acquired.

Since we assume that at first self-object differentiation is wholly lacking in the infantile psyche, we can also assume that states of minimal (nontraumatic) distress and quickly following states associated with pleasurable relief-bringing ministrations are both originally a part of the archaic or rudimentary self experience of the infant. I am emphasizing here that the infant does not merely experience pleasurable relief following his distress signals; he also experiences in a direct bodily form the whole variety of maternal activities that effect relief, and these experienced activities are also included in the self experiences of this stage.

The oceanic feeling and the Isakower phenomenon are usually understood as a form of re-experiencing the infant-mother unity of the earliest phase. Many other mental experiences are derived from this stage, although their later childhood and adult form depends on components added in subsequent phases. For example, the pleasurable, anxiety-relieving dream and fantasy experience of effortless flying probably has its archaic roots in the very young infant's experience of being lifted and carried around in the mother's arms.

As indicated above, when the infant-mother unit is "good enough," prolonged states of unrelieved traumatic frustration are relatively infrequent. Rather, the states of beginning minimal anxiety that prompts the "rescue signal," followed by pleasurable maternal intervention and relief, are the expectable experience. Both the signal and its consequence then, because they yield pleasure, are included in the early organization of the pleasure ego. That is to say, repeated experiences of small amounts of distress which is promptly relieved lead to the infant's perception of beginning distress as the forerunner of the activities that bring relief. This is probably the infantile basis for the mature personality's capacity to respond to situations that provoke mild anxiety as a pleasurable challenge. The optimistic expectation that the challenge can be overcome by appropriate means is grounded in the infantile experiences I am discussing.

On the other hand, if the infant-mother unit is not "good enough," beginning distress regularly signals, instead of rescue, the onset of the unrelieved traumatic state—the psychic situation *par excellence* that interferes with the inclusion of the signal of anxiety in the early psychic organization. The signal, like the traumatic state it heralds, then also follows the dictates of the pleasure principle, and is therefore excluded from the dominant ego organization of this phase.

I regard the twofold experiential state that is included in the infantile ego organization of the undifferentiated and symbiotic phases as the primary form of what is later experienced intrapsychically when a minute amount of anxiety initiates regulatory activities that avert a greater anxiety experience. This aspect of the purified pleasure ego is not superseded by the reality ego. On the contrary, it is the persisting and necessary basis for the psyche's capacity to tame and master the anxiety experience—a capacity that, although grounded in the pleasure principle, eventually serves the reality principle.

The Phase of Self-Object Differentiation

When the infant has learned that his mother's activities prevent the traumatic state, and that his distress signals directed to her have the same effect, the psyche has taken "a first great step forward" and is prepared for the beginning internalization of the mother's anxiety-reducing function. These internalizations provide the structural basis for the "transition" from automatic to signal anxiety.

The advance in self-object discrimination implicit in the perception of the mother is accompanied by advances in the infant's ability to perceive the various and discrete aspects of the mother's activities. The maternal activities that were previously included in the archaic body-mind-self are progressively perceived as originating in the needed and longed-for "you." The corollary of this advance in mental development is the increasing possibility of loss of one or another of these functions (when the mother is temporarily unavailable, tired, out of sorts, unempathic, etc.).

Until recently the emphasis on the phase-specific dangers of this stage—object loss and, later, loss of the object's love—has not sufficiently included the psychic consequences of optimal, phase-appropriate losses of discretely perceived and experienced aspects of the mother's anxiety-relieving functions. The continuing narcissistic perception of the mother and her functions during this phase enables the infant to continue to experience what the mother does to relieve anxiety as a part of himself. This experience, however, differs markedly from the more passive experiencing of her activity which characterizes the less differentiated earlier stages.

With his increasingly sophisticated repertoire of motor, mental, and verbal skills the older infant responds to the beginning anxiety experience with the vigorous efforts to get his mother to relieve his anxiety that earn him his reputation of being so demanding. In other words, the beginning anxiety experience now acts more and more as a signal to the infant to turn actively and intentionally to his "possession" (the mother) with the expectation that her activity will bring relief. The well-known demanding and possessive behavior of the child during the separation-individuation phase is thus seen as the expression of the phase-appropriate psychic organization that treats the mother's activities and functions as the child's own until they can be acquired from her to form the emerging self. Kohut (1966) has described how the infant experiences the activity of the mother more like the adult experiences the activity of his own arm than like the experience of a truly separate object. Casual observation of the infant's behavior with his mother at this stage establishes the truth of this assertion.

It is evident that as far as anxiety regulation is concerned the child treats his mother like he treats his other treasured possession —his blanket. The transitional mental structure provided by both accounts for this similarity. The mother, however, is not under the child's exclusive control. She has multiple, sometimes contradictory, roles, meanings, and functions for the child, in contrast to the relatively discrete meaning and function of the transitional object. The complex functioning of the mother necessary for effective anxiety regulation cannot be "transferred" to an inanimate object. There are limits to human inventiveness.

When the sequence—beginning anxiety, anxiety signals, maternal activity, relief from anxiety—has been repeatedly experienced during the preceding phases and the early separation-individuation phase, the memory traces of this sequence form enduring mental structure. When this structure is firmly established and when other aspects of mental maturation and development have unfolded according to the "ground plan" (Erikson, 1950)—e.g., the infant's ability to seek actively what he needs to reduce his anxiety—then the psyche is prepared for the bit-by-bit loss of discrete anxiety-reducing maternal functions—the optimal form of loss that leads to internalization of these functions as psychic structure.

A simple and typical clinical vignette from the separation-individuation phase illustrates *in statu nascendi* the acquisition of a bit of the psychic structure that is ultimately included in the organization of the cohesive ego and its operations which "subject the affect of anxiety . . . to the normal workings of the mind." Johnny, age 16 months, had been experiencing separation anxiety when his mother left him with a sitter. His awakenings several times a night during this stage were attributed to the separation anxiety, since his mother's appearance in response to his cries easily soothed him and promptly induced his going back to sleep.

One evening as she prepared to go out with his father and leave him with his grandmother (whom he dearly loved) she reassured the tearful little boy that she would be back later that same night. As an afterthought (prompted by his nighttime wakefulness that disturbed her sleep) she added hopefully, "I'll see you in the morning when the clock rings." When she returned Johnny's grandmother reported that he had awakened brightly around midnight and had called out cheerfully, "Clock ring!" The longed-for reunion was hastened, at least for the moment, by the wish-fulfilling dream. The dream on this occasion was especially notable because it was the first dream experience that the child had put into words. His capacity to expect that his mother would appear "later," the dream anticipation of her reappearance when the "clock ring" (for a 16-month-old a complex mental operation that involves a judgment regarding time and its passage, and the idea of future satisfaction), and his verbalization of the dream were clearly in the service of reducing the anxiety occasioned by the separation.

This example suggests that the infant's expedient use of his own ego functions in response to his separation anxiety was fostered by the manageable phase-appropriate frustration imposed by the brief separation that was coupled with the mother's structure-mediating message. The message meant, "I will be back later, but I would like to see you in the morning!" Not unexpectedly the pleasure principle made use of the latter part of the message for its own purposes, not the mother's. Naturally, this was not the first time that the mother had exercised the functions involved in verbalizing the reassurance that she would soon return, and in anticipating for the child that if he could wait a little while, all would be well. It is noteworthy, however, that these are the very functions that operated intrapsychically in the child to produce the dream of reunion in his mother's absence.

As with other psychoanalytic propositions concerning processes of internalization and structure formation, it is assumed that the psyche can preserve a lost maternal function because of its inherent endowment. I stressed this point in Part I. The mental structure necessary for the signal function is an inherent potential that undergoes development and achieves structural organization in the "good enough" infant-mother unit. For example, the cognitive components of the mature signal function cannot be thought of as acquired solely from internalizations since they are a part of the autonomous endowment.

It is the intent of this presentation, however, to show that the organization and expedient operation of all of the complex and hierarchical components of the signal function which accrue in the course of later development depend on the early developmental processes during which the mother's cohesive psychic organization provides the nutriment for, and is the organizer of, the infant's inherent endowment. This endowment unfolds in the optimal situation, for which the infant on his mother's knee provided the model, until the signal of anxiety that originally turned the child toward his mother acts instead as the instigator of the ego activities that are the "precipitates" of her functions.

The processes of internalization and structuralization are in the center of psychic development throughout the separation-individu-ation phase. As I indicated previously, the successful separation and individuation of the child's psyche from that of the mother— the genuine separation of self and object, of the child's ego from the maternal auxiliary ego—depends upon these processes. From the time that he is able on his own initiative to crawl or toddle away from his mother the infant uses his mother "as a secure base from which to explore." When he goes too far, even though now it is on his own initiative that he separates from his mother, he is likely to be overwhelmed by anxiety when his "base" disappears. The tuned-in mother knows this and usually remains within her young toddler's sight or hearing as he moves away. When he moves out of her range, as he is wont to do (e.g., he crawls off into another room), and suddenly panics when he realizes that his mother is nowhere to be seen, she also knows how to restore his equilibrium. She quickly reappears. For the normal infant of this stage her reap-pearance is usually all that is necessary for his prompt recovery (just as her "good enough" presence is usually sufficient to keep his stranger anxiety within tolerable bounds).

Kohut (1971) has illustrated how the empathic mother titrates the dose of anxiety to which she exposes her baby by her behavior with him in the peek-a-boo game—the phase-appropriate game during the beginning of this phase (the stage of the infant in the model)—when the infant's empathically perceived experience of joy, delight, and relief is heightened by the reappearance of his mother's face from behind her fingers which partially covered it.

The story of Goldilocks and the Three Bears illustrates my propositions regarding the mother's dosing function and its fail-ures later in this phase when the older infant and toddler is en-gaged in the process of actively separating himself from his mother on his own initiative and is still vulnerable to being over-whelmed by anxiety if her anxiety-mitigating functions are not "good enough" or "just right," to borrow the repeated theme of the Three Bears.

When Goldilocks first enters the strange but familiar house of the three bears (familiar because there is the familiar evidence that a mother, father, and baby live in the house in the woods), the dose of anxiety is "just right." Although Mama Bear's porridge is too cold and Papa Bear's porridge is too hot, Baby Bear's porridge is "just right" and Goldilocks eats it all up. But even though she finds that Baby Bear's chair is "just right," after Papa Bear's is too hard and Mama Bear's is too soft, Baby Bear's chair breaks all to pieces. The anxiety experience is no longer "just right" (as Goldilocks has strayed too far or stayed too long without the mother's intervention), and the beginning of the shattering fragmentation process that ends in being helplessly overwhelmed is foreshadowed. And so when Goldilocks goes to sleep, Baby Bear's bed cannot protect her from the overwhelming panic she experiences when the three bears return home and she flees, never to return again. The stranger in the absence of the mother appears in the story at the very time when the toddler's insufficiently stabilized self-soothing and anxiety-reducing functions usually need the mother's temporary augmentation, without which he is particularly liable to being overwhelmed.

Although Goldilocks and the Three Bears could be considered a cautionary tale for latency-aged children, it is not read to, or by, children of that age. It is the phase-appropriate tale for the toddler, to whom it is read (over and over again) at a time when he is engaged in the process of internalizing his mother's function of soothing him and reducing his anxiety states while he negotiates the developmental phase of separating himself from her. I suppose it could be considered a cautionary tale for the toddler's mother, who empathically attempts to keep the anxiety experience "just right" so that the strange and stranger experiences of separation stimulate the internalizations that effectively and expediently mitigate anxiety. Kleeman (1967, p. 249) provides a clinical example of the empathic response which makes the anxiety experience "just right." His data illustrate the "normal workings" of the infant-mother unit: when growth propels the baby girl he describes into the strange and exciting experience of increasing separateness from her mother, she needs to "check" back to the "base" for the empathic response which keeps her separation anxiety within tolerable bounds. When the mother's mitigating functions are lost in phase-appropriate doses which are "just right," the child's psyche internalizes the maternal functions and acquires for itself the expedient responses to the signal of anxiety that maintain its cohesiveness and the cohesiveness of a self separate from the mother. When the mother's interventions, or lack of them, fail to protect the child sufficiently from the overwhelming massive anxiety experiences of the separation-individuation phase, the psyche remains permanently vulnerable to the Goldilocks experience and may resort to the mental mechanisms that, although they are employed in an attempt to curb the anxiety experience, do not lead to its mastery.

Summary and Conclusions

This detailed study of two typical aspects of infant behavior leads me to propose that the phase-specific developmental task of the separation-individuation phase—the acquisition of the psychological structure that is the foundation for a cohesive self and for true psychic separation—is accomplished by the process that Kohut has designated as transmuting internalization. Re-examination of the transitional object and early signallike forms of the anxiety experience has served to demonstrate the psychic "work" that is effected by this process during this phase. In connection with the infant's "creation" of the "blanket" and his minute experience of stranger anxiety "on his mother's knee," I have demonstrated that the mother's soothing and anxiety-relieving functions "belong" to the infant's archaic self experience; and I have described the steps by which the "leap" to the inner capacity to manage tension and anxiety is effected by bit-by-bit internalization of these functions when the infant experiences their loss in phase-appropriate ("just right") doses. I concluded that when the infant is "hatched" from symbiosis and begins to perceive discrete mothering activities which afford satisfaction, his instinctual investment in these activities creates a transitional form of psychological structure which replaces the need-satisfying attachment of intrauterine existence and symbiotic merger. This *psychological attachment* enables the infant to bridge the developmental phase which spans the lengthy transition from psychic symbiosis to psychic separation.

My examination of the formation, function, and fate of the transitional object in Part I of this paper led me to the following proposition. When the infantile psyche "transfers" the mother's narcissistically cathected soothing functions to the blanket, this inanimate object becomes the treasured "not-me" possession that preserves the soothing effects of the lost symbiotic merger. With the blanket formed by this transferencelike process the child can dose himself with more soothing than even the "good enough" mother can provide. By re-creating the merger and the maternal functions on which it depends the psyche establishes an auxiliary pathway for the acquisition of tension-reducing mental structure. As soothing experiences with the mother are first prolonged and then gradually internalized with the help of the auxiliary soother, by the process of fractionated cathexis and decathexis which characterizes its use, the functions of the transitional object also "go inside"—the metapsychological basis for the fate of the "outgrown" blanket.

In Part II, using the model of the infant on his mother's knee in the stranger's presence, I proposed that the infant experiences a *primary form of signal anxiety* if the infant-mother unit is "good enough." The early forms of phase-appropriate signallike anxiety and their corresponding mental organization provide the necessary foundation for the subsequent development of more complex inner operations on which the mature function of signal anxiety depends.

The initial stages of the optimal developmental line of signal anxiety were described. When the inborn "rescue signal" and its anxiety-relieving consequences are included in the pleasure-ego organization of the undifferentiated and symbiotic phases, the infantile psyche is thereby prepared for the bit-by-bit internalization of the mother's anxiety-relieving ministrations. These internalizations build up the ego functions which gradually replace the needed functions of the auxiliary ego. The signal of distress which originally turned the infant toward his mother for relief now acts instead to initiate inner regulatory activities which effectively mitigate the anxiety experience. A "precipitate" of new ego functions is the basis for "the 'transition' from automatic anxiety to anxiety as a signal, and for a first great step forward toward preservation of the self."

My study of these phenomena leads to the following conclusions:

The work accomplished by transmuting internalization during separation-individuation lays the groundwork for several inter-related developmental achievements of great magnitude. The transition from need-satisfying object to object constancy, from automatic anxiety to anxiety as an effective signal, and from self-object merger to separate self is an expectable outcome of this phase. When new ego functions begin to regulate tension and anxiety, the child's own workings gradually replace what the mother does to satisfy his need for "narcissistic homeostasis." With a rudimentary capacity to satisfy this fundamental need, the infant has acquired the means for his separation and individuation from the mother and for the step which is its corollary—the transition to object constancy.

The transitional object deserves particular emphasis as an example of the phase-appropriate transitional mental structure which provides the immature psyche with a necessary detour to the internalization and organization of a whole class of equilibrium-maintaining ego functions. As a special case it illustrates the general psychic tendency to preserve the needed functions of a narcissistically cathected object imago by transmuting internalization. Since the blanket is such a visible indicator of the structure-mediating, growth-facilitating mother-infant bond appropriate to the separation phase, I have suggested that the transitional object (and phemonena) be included among the other visible signs which Spitz described as psychic organizers. As a psychic "preserve" of an older form of (self-object, need-satisfying) mental organization and an additional pathway for the acquisition of new (self-sustaining) structure, the transitional object assists the infant in the work of the separation process. When this process proceeds according to the normal timetable, the transitional bond between mother and infant will "pass away" like the transitional object itself—the functions of the self-object tie "go inside" as "the mysterious knot" of the personality which binds isolated parts into a whole unit (see Eissler, 1953, p. 119).

I believe that such processes of structure formation as I described in this paper are the metapsychological basis for the successful conclusion of the separation-individuation phase of development. The "separated" child is partially equipped to respond to mounting tension with the mental activities which replace the mother's buffering functions, and to respond to the beginning anxiety experience as to a signal and initiate the complex self-regulating activities which "subject the affect of anxiety . . . to the normal workings of the mind." And he is equipped to respond to his parents' total personality and complex meanings to him because he no longer perceives them exclusively for need satisfaction. Traumatic loss and disappointment in the mother as the psychic regulator leave deficits, in the achievements that I have discussed, of varying severity and consequence for further development. Inexpedient (pathogenic) mechanisms must then serve in place of the "hidden knot" and "normal workings" which have failed in their development.

Like the passing of the oedipus complex, the passing of the separation-individuation phase has fateful consequences for the developing personality. When the "normal workings" of the infant-mother unit has laid the foundation for a separate mental organization and a cohesive self, the child can progress to the later developmental phases and their tasks and further differentiation of the personality can continue.

BIBLIOGRAPHY

BENEDEK, T. (1938), Adaptation to Reality in Early Infancy. *Psychoanal. Quart.*, 7:200–215.

— (1956), Toward the Biology of the Depressive Constellation. *J. Amer. Psychoanal. Assn.*, 4:389–427.

BENJAMIN, J. (1961), Some Developmental Observations Relating to the Theory of Anxiety. *J. Amer. Psychoanal. Assn.*, 9:652–657.

Bowlby, J. (1969), *Attachment and Loss,* Volume I: *Attachment.* New York: Basic Books.

Brody, S. & Axelrad, S. (1966), Anxiety, Socialization, and Ego Formation in Infancy. *Int. J. Psycho-Anal.,* 47:218–235.

Coppolillo, H. (1967), Maturational Aspects of the Transitional Phenomenon. *Int. J. Psycho-Anal.,* 48:237–246.

Eissler, K. R. (1953), The Effect of the Structure of the Ego on Psychoanalytic Technique. *J. Amer. Psychoanal. Assn.,* 1:104–143.

— (1969), Irreverent Remarks about the Present and Future of Psychoanalysis. *Int. J. Psycho-Anal.,* 50:461–472.

Engel, G. & Reichsman, F. (1956), Spontaneous and Experimentally Induced Depression in an Infant with a Gastric Fistula: A Contribution to the Problem of Depression. *J. Amer. Psychoanal. Assn.,* 4:428–452.

Erikson, E. H. (1950), *Childhood and Society.* New York: Norton.

Freud, A. (1965), *Normality and Pathology in Childhood.* New York: International Universities Press.

— (1971), The Infantile Neurosis: Genetic and Dynamic Considerations. *The Writings of Anna Freud,* 7:300–325. New York: International Universities Press; and *This Annual,* 26:79–90.

Freud, S. (1911), Formulations on the Two Principles of Mental Functioning. *Standard Edition,* 12:218–226. London: Hogarth Press, 1958.

— (1914), On Narcissism. *Standard Edition,* 14:67–102. London: Hogarth Press, 1957.

— (1915), Instincts and Their Vicissitudes. *Standard Edition,* 14:117–140. London: Hogarth Press, 1957.

— (1917), Mourning and Melancholia. *Standard Edition,* 14:243–258. London: Hogarth Press, 1957.

— (1919), 'A Child Is Being Beaten': A Contribution to the Study of the Origin of Sexual Perversions. *Standard Edition,* 17:179–204. London: Hogarth Press, 1955.

— (1923), The Ego and the Id. *Standard Edition,* 19:3–66. London: Hogarth Press, 1961.

— (1926), Inhibitions, Symptoms and Anxiety. *Standard Edition,* 20:77–175. London: Hogarth Press, 1959.

— (1933), New Introductory Lectures on Psycho-Analysis. *Standard Edition,* 22:7–182. London: Hogarth Press, 1964.

Greenacre, P. (1953), Certain Relationships between Fetishism and the Faulty Development of the Body Image. *This Annual,* 8:79–98.

— (1960), Further Notes on Fetishism. *This Annual,* 15:191–207.

— (1966), Problems of Overidealization of the Analyst and of Analysis: Their Manifestations in the Transference and Countertransference Relationship. *This Annual,* 21:193–212.

— (1969), The Fetish and the Transitional Object. *This Annual,* 24:144–164.

— (1970), The Transitional Object and the Fetish with a Special Reference to the Role of Illusion. *Int. J. Psycho-Anal.*, 51:447–456.

GREENSON, R. R. (1969), The Origin and Fate of New Ideas in Psychoanalysis. *Int. J. Psycho-Anal.*, 50:503–515.

HARTMANN, H. (1939), *Ego Psychology and the Problem of Adaptation.* New York: International Universities Press, 1958.

— (1952), The Mutual Influence in the Development of Ego and Id. *Essays on Ego Psychology.* New York: International Universities Press, 1964, pp. 155–181.

KAHNE, M. (1967), On the Persistence of Transitional Phenomena into Adult Life. *Int. J. Psycho-Anal.*, 48:247–258.

KHAN, M. M. (1964), Ego Distortion, Cumulative Trauma, and the Role of Reconstruction in the Analytic Situation. *Int. J. Psycho-Anal.*, 45:272–277.

KLEEMAN, J. A. (1967), The Peek-a-Boo Game: Part I. Its Origins, Meanings, and Related Phenomena in the First Year. *This Annual*, 22:239–273.

KOHUT, H. (1959), Introspection, Empathy, and Psychoanalysis. *J. Amer. Psychoanal. Assn.*, 7:459–483.

— (1966), Forms and Transformations of Narcissism. *J. Amer. Psychoanal. Assn.*, 14:243–272.

— (1968), The Psychoanalytic Treatment of Narcissistic Personality Disorders: Outline of a Systematic Approach. *This Annual*, 23:86–113.

— (1971), *The Analysis of the Self: A Systematic Approach to the Psychoanalytic Treatment of Narcissistic Personality Disorders.* New York: International Universities Press.

— & SEITZ, P. F. D. (1963), Concepts and Theories of Psychoanalysis. In: *Concepts of Personality,* ed. G. M. Wepman & R. Heine. Chicago: Aldine, pp. 113–141.

LOEWALD, H. W. (1960), On the Therapeutic Action of Psychoanalysis. *Int. J. Psycho-Anal.*, 41:16–33.

— (1970), Psychoanalytic Theory and the Psychoanalytic Process. *This Annual*, 25:45–68.

MAHLER, M. S. (1963), Thoughts about Development and Individuation. *This Annual*, 18:307–324.

— (1966), Notes on the Development of Basic Moods: The Depressive Affect. In: *Psychoanalysis—A General Psychology,* ed. R. M. Loewenstein, L. M. Newman, M. Schur, & A. J. Solnit. New York: International Universities Press, pp. 152–168.

— (1968), *On Human Symbiosis and the Vicissitudes of Individuation.* New York: International Universities Press.

NAGERA, H. (1964), Autoerotism, Autoerotic Activities, and Ego Development. *This Annual*, 19:240–255.

RANGELL, L. (1955), On the Psychoanalytic Theory of Anxiety: A Statement of a Unitary Theory. *J. Amer. Psychoanal. Assn.*, 3:389–414.

— (1968), A Further Attempt to Resolve the "Problem of Anxiety." *J. Amer. Psychoanal. Assn.*, 16:371–403.

SPITZ, R. A. (1950), Anxiety in Infancy: A Study of Its Manifestations in the First Year of Life. *Int. J. Psycho-Anal.*, 31:138–143.

— (1959), *A Genetic Field Theory of Ego Formation.* New York: International Universities Press.

— EMDE, R. N., & METCALF, D. R. (1970), Further Prototypes of Ego Formation: A Working Paper from a Research Project on Early Development. *This Annual,* 25:417–441.

STEVENSON, O. (1954), The First Treasured Possession. *This Annual,* 9:199–217.

TOLPIN, M. (1968), Eugene Ionesco's *The Chairs* and The Theater of the Absurd. *Imago,* 25:119–139.

WINNICOTT, D. W. (1953), Transitional Objects and Transitional Phenomena. In: *Collected Papers,* London: Tavistock, 1958.

WULFF, M. (1946), Fetishism and Object Choice in Early Childhood. *Psychoanal. Quart.,* 15:450–471.

CLINICAL

CONTRIBUTIONS

Separation Crisis
in Two Blind Children

SELMA FRAIBERG

IN THIS ESSAY I PROPOSE TO BRING TOGETHER SOME OBSERVATIONS OF separation anxiety in blind children in the second year. The children in each case have been followed in our longitudinal studies of infants blind from birth. The twice monthly observations by clinically trained researchers have given us the opportunity to study the reactions to brief and prolonged separations within the context of a larger study of the developmental characteristics of blind infants.

Selma Fraiberg is Professor of Child Psychoanalysis and Director of the Child Development Project, University of Michigan, Ann Arbor.

This research has been supported since 1966 by Grant #HD01-444 from the National Institute of Child Health and Development and since 1969 by Grant #OEG-0-9-322108-2469(032) from the Office of Education. Support also came from the Grand Aerie Fraternal Order of Eagles and the Earhardt Foundation.

(355)

I am primarily concerned in this paper with the developmental crisis as an event that is experienced by both mother and child, one in which the adaptive tendencies of the child and the adaptive modes of the mother are united as the two partners work toward solution and restoration of harmony. We have learned that if we can trace the threads in the intricate pattern, the adaptive solution "found" by the baby represents both his own modes of dealing with tension and external danger and those that were offered by his mother, out of her own repertoire of action and defense. What is selected, borrowed, and integrated into a stable adaptation is, of course, not the mother's coherent language of personality, but elements of her style or the small vocabulary of defense that can be assimilated by a very young child. If we use the developmental crisis as a model, we know that within a very short time after crisis is resolved in infancy, we may see the product in personality with a clinical lens—a new characteristic in personality, or new variations on an old theme, but we can no longer trace the component themes.

For these reasons, longitudinal studies of infants provide a most favorable condition for the study of interlocking factors in mother-child interaction. Our own observations in our research sample are made through twice monthly home visits. Continuous narrative recording and a once monthly film sample provide us with detailed observations of mother-child interaction and a context in which the behavior of mother and child can be fairly assessed.

For this essay, I have selected two cases from our sample in which a blind baby experienced conflict in separation. Before discussing these specific cases it may be useful briefly to examine the characteristics of separation anxiety in blind infants and the meaning of separation to a child who cannot see.

Blindness and the Experience of Separation

In the case of the blind infant under one year it is difficult to isolate those conditions which mean mother is "absent" in everyday experience. In the case of the sighted child, mother is absent when she is not seen. Vision permits the sighted child to give meaning to the "goings and comings" of his mother since he can track her with his eyes to the point at which she leaves his visual field (goes to another room, closes a door, etc.).

For the blind child, mother can be present in the room, and if she refrains from talking or moving, she has left the child's perceptual field. Yet, we have rare examples in the first year which show that these moments of "not being in touch" with the mother created distress or anxiety in the child.

For the blind child in the last third of the first year, cessation of mother's voice or movements cannot be equivalent to disappearance of the mother for the sighted child. Vision, by its nature, is continuous; visual tracking confers temporal order to events, and a break or closure of the visual record is read as the sign of "gone." Sound is discontinuous, and for long periods in a blind child's day, things and people do not manifest themselves to him through sound (or touch). Since there is no stability or predictability in events that are experienced through intermittent sound, the breaking or closure of a sound sequence need not connote "separation" or "loss" or "absence."

It is of considerable interest that the largest number of our observations on separation anxiety occurs in the second year in our sample. Using unambiguous criteria such as "crying," "inability to be comforted by others," "clinging to mother upon return," we have *no* examples in the first year for 10 children in our sample. For 9 children who have completed their second year we have 8 cases in which the first occurrence of separation anxiety was recorded in the second and third years. A nearly identical pattern is found in the emergence of stranger anxiety in our blind sample (Fraiberg, 1970). In both stranger anxiety and separation anxiety there are marked differences in age of onset and peaks between our blind children and sighted children. Specifically, in the case of separation anxiety in sighted children, there is a consensus among investigators that separation anxiety emerges at 7 to 8 months of age and peaks at approximately 12 months of age with manifestations throughout the second year (Tennes and Lampl, 1964; Schaffer and Emerson, 1964; Ainsworth, 1967; Morgan and Ricciuti, 1969).

Among sighted infants, the ability to tolerate momentary or brief separations in the second and third years of life is probably related to the capacity for evocative memory (Piaget, 1937), which emerges in the second year and achieves some degree of stabilization by the middle of the third year (Yarrow, 1967; Ainsworth, 1967; Fraiberg, 1969). This means, of course, that the child's earliest measure for sustaining separation from the loved person is the evocation of the image of the mother (Spitz, 1965). We have reason to believe that the capacity to sustain this image in the second year is brief and fluctuating (Fraiberg, 1969). The sighted child in his second year still demonstrates a need to get visual, tactile, and auditory affirmation of the existence of his mother after brief intervals of separation. His tolerance can be shattered by a rise in need tensions or by the experience of external dangers without the protection of the mother—all of which suggests that "belief in permanence" is provisional in the second year and, while there is increasing stabilization of this concept in the course of development, it remains vulnerable throughout the early years, as we know from clinical studies of separation and loss. Mahler (1965) suggests that the capacity of the child at 25 months to tolerate absence of the mother for an extended period in nursery school, for example, testifies to the capacity of the child to sustain a mental image of the mother under normal circumstances. We know that at the same age, however, prolonged absence of the mother can create intolerable anxiety in a normal child.

In the case of the blind child, the capacity for evocative memory is markedly delayed by sighted child standards. If we assume that the demonstration on a Piaget scale of evocative memory for the "thing" correlates with evocative memory for human objects (Décarie, 1963; Fraiberg, 1969), there is at least a one-year delay in our blind subjects in the achievement of Stage VI for "things" and "persons." This means that for much of the second and third years of life, the blind child lives in a world in which his human partners evaporate in some mysterious way when they do not manifest themselves to the child and reconstitute themselves in some mysterious way when they return. Where evocation of the absent object provides a measure of tolerance for loss in the sighted child, there is no cognitive measure open to the blind child in the second year of life to sustain loss at a period in his development when his attachment to his mother can be adduced through stranger reactions and anxiety at loss.

If we move, now, to a discussion of cases, these differences between blind and sighted children in the second and third years need to be underscored: (1) We have a child whose own adaptive capacity to sustain loss is diminished by blindness. (2) We have a mother who must deal with a developmental crisis in her blind child's experience without anything in her own experience which can help her understand the extraordinary significance of loss to a blind child.

Case Illustrations

Jackie

Jackie Olson has been blind from birth due to retrolental fibroplasia. He was 3 months premature and weighed 2 pounds 3 ounces at birth.

When Jackie was 14 months of age, his mother was called away suddenly when her father died. She was gone for 3 days. During that time Jackie was in the care of various friends and relatives who helped out in the emergency. Soon after the mother returned, Jackie showed alarming symptoms, which I shall shortly describe, and began to regress in nearly all areas of development.

Pertinent Developmental Data

Prior to separation, Jackie's development would have placed him well within the middle range for blind children. He was sitting well unsupported, bridging, not yet creeping. He was able to stand alone at 13 months. If a correction were made for prematurity, these motor achievements for a blind infant are good. (In spite of demonstrated postural readiness for creeping and walking, there is a typical delay in blind infants in the achievement of mobility [Fraiberg, 1968; Fraiberg et al., 1964, 1966].) Jackie's adaptive hand behavior was good. He was using his hands capably to get information and to make fine discriminations. He had demonstrated his first reach on sound cue alone at 11 months 27 days, which is in the low range for our sample (modal age 10 months), but a correction for prematurity would modify this assessment. At 13 months, he had begun to solve simple barrier problems (a sound toy placed under a screen), a very good achievement judged within our own sample. He had the words "Dada" and "Dog" and a jargon for making his needs known.

There was a demonstrated attachment to his mother and preference for her in spite of a considerable instability in the mother's own personality and depressive tendencies, which showed themselves in occasional withdrawal from both Jackie and his 4-year-old brother, Allen. When Mrs. Olson was employed evenings for some weeks, Jackie (then 10 months old) grew more demanding of her time, which the mother understood. Interruptions of his playtime with mother led to screams of protest when she left the room.

When we now consider the events which followed separation from mother at the time of her father's death, it is important to place these reactions within the context of the level of human attachment, the cognitive level of this blind child, and the adaptive possibilities open to a blind child.

There was, then, valuation and preference for the mother, which we would see in a sighted child in the second half of the first year. There was no capacity to evoke the image of an object that had been removed from tactile or auditory experience. (Jackie's performance on screened object tests would place him at Stage IV on a Piaget scale. He could recover the object under one screen only; he could account for further displacements. The substantiality of the object was linked to the sign of the screen and to place.) From this we may infer that loved persons, too, are subjected to a kind of capricious fate when they do not manifest themselves to him. They affirm their substantiality through touch and sound primarily. When they do not or cannot manifest themselves to the child, they cease to exist. And while Jackie can recover a sound toy under a single screen, he is still immobile, another irony of blindness, and immobility robs him of the possibility of conducting a simple search for a mother who can be lost a hundred times a day within the desert of one's own home. What constitutes an adaptive solution to loss for the young blind child?

The Separation Crisis

Soon after the mother returned from her 3-day visit, Jackie showed alarming symptoms and began to regress in nearly all areas of development.

Jackie had screaming fits which lasted for hours. Our own observers found them nearly indescribable. These were screams or shouts of a repetitive, chanting character, and were practically unceasing for most of his waking hours. During these attacks the child's face was curiously immobile and expressionless. When the mother held Jackie, there was a brief respite, but at these times he would crawl desperately all over her body as if trying to get as much as possible of his own body surface in touch with his mother's body. This frenzied crawling was as nerve-wracking to the mother as the shouting. Meantime, Jackie abandoned his toys and showed no interest in games or any of his former activities. He was wakeful for long periods at night. He lost interest in food and, after a few mouthfuls, would vomit. In short, there was a pathological regression in nearly every sector of development, and the stereotyped shouts were themselves of a highly pathological type.

This situation had persisted for nearly two weeks before Mrs. Olson sought our help. We can hardly blame the mother for her inability to find a solution in this crisis. While she understood very well that the screaming and regression were related to her absence, that the baby was afraid to lose her, all the ordinary measures available to a mother and a baby coping with separation and loss were not available to this mother and baby because the baby was blind.

If this had been a sighted baby of 14 months reacting to a traumatic separation from his mother, the baby would have sought continuous affirmation of his mother's existence. As long as he could see mother, he could be reassured; and the really difficult times of the reunion period would probably occur around naptime or bedtime. The sighted baby at 14 months would be mobile, could follow mother around, check her whereabouts, make sure she didn't sneak off again. Vision would afford him anticipatory experience associated with separation. Seeing mother in a coat and hat means mother is going out. Anticipating separation allows him to protest, to cry, to build up anxiety which, however troublesome it may be, is a measure of defense against danger and diminishes the traumatic effect of ordinary separations. In short, the baby can be active in the face of danger.

For the blind baby there is no possibility of tracking mother. One cannot substitute hearing for vision in seeking reassurance. Unless we can find a mother who is a nonstop talker, we cannot provide equivalence here. The blind baby can only be assured through body contact with his mother, the only substantial proof of existence. Jackie (and this is true of most blind babies) was not mobile at 14 months, which meant that he could not act upon the danger of loss through active seeking. Jackie had no means of anticipating the ordinary goings and comings of his mother. Each loss, in the course of an ordinary day, was experienced as a repetition of the trauma. In the absence of any of the adaptive measures open to an intact baby at 14 months, Jackie had only one defense —regression.

If we turn to the mother, we see that the partner who must aid resolution in this crisis is also gravely disabled because of grief. She knows that the baby's clinging to her is connected with her absence, but she cannot comfort. Perhaps she herself is yearning for comfort and mothering. The screaming fits, which might be tolerable if she were not mourning, are infuriating to the mother who may be experiencing them as an intrusion and violation of her own grief and seclusion. And while it is true that a mother with larger resources than Jackie's mother might have felt her child's needs greater than her own, this mother did not. When things got too much for her, she shut the baby in his room and left.

We believe that the risks were very great at this point, that this crisis might have led to a deepening of pathological regression in Jackie and a fatal rupture in the mother-child relationship. In the retrospective histories of many older blind children we learn of traumatic separations, regression, and a failure to recover. For many years, before I had studied blind infant development, I was actually skeptical of these reports in the records of blind children. Jackie and other young blind children helped us understand this.

We helped the mother find a solution. It was a happy solution, as it turned out. Yet, the solution we offered came from our clinical insights and was one that a mother might not have discovered for herself. The question may be raised whether an ordinary mother, with or without the extraordinary problems Mrs. Olson faced at this time, would have been able to find the solution unaided. The message in the screaming was a very complicated one, a tough one for the clinicians, too.

A Clinical Intervention

This is what happened at our end at the Child Development Project. When Marguerite Smith reported her own observations of Jackie's screaming, she confessed that what she heard was nearly indescribable. Finally, straining for a descriptive phrase, she said, "It is something between terror and rage." This, as it turned out, was a very astute clinical observation. It was the component of "rage" that no one had identified in the repetitive hoarse screaming. It is very probable, too, that only a clinician who knew blind infants would have identified this component. There is a very good reason for this. A sighted child of 14 months can express rage vocally *and* through the motor patterns of fighting. He will kick; he will strike out with his hands and fists. Any mother can read these motor signs as "aggression," "rage," "anger," "mad." And, since the motor patterns of fighting can be directed toward a target at this age, we can read the signs and say, "He is mad *at* his mother" or "He is mad *at* his brother."

Many blind children in the second year do not have the motor patterns of "fighting." Jackie was among them. In my own experience with blind children I had been stunned by my first encounters with certain children who could express anger and rage only through the mouth, through screaming or biting. In our longitudinal studies of blind infants we came to understand this. In the last quarter of the first year, when aggression normally finds discharge through the external skeletal muscles, aggression in blind infants remains mouth-centered. All of our blind children eventually found the motor patterns of fighting at sometime in the second or third year (often with our help), but the slow and uncertain route which led to the achievement of discharge and defensive action told us clearly that blindness was a major impediment.

"To fight" requires a target, and the blind child has few targets
in the first and second years. Typically, even adaptive hand behavior is impeded by the absence of a target that can be localized
and attained. In Jackie's world of evanescent objects there were,
properly speaking, few targets, and if tactile encounter brought the
human target close, an aggressive action would cause the human
target to remove himself, escape, or retaliate, any one of which will
reduce him to helplessness once again. Moreover, the conceptual
development of a blind child at 14 months does not provide him
an "object," as it does for the sighted child of the same age. Since
the blind child is slow to acquire notions of substantiality and permanence, we cannot say that his anger is "object-directed." We
cannot say that his anger is directed toward the mother who has
left him, because his notions of causality cannot yet take into account the comings and goings of persons and things. I would see
aggression or rage in Jackie's case as a primitive defense against
danger and helplessness on this developmental level. He is not
mad *at* his mother or *at* the world. Helplessness triggers the need
for defensive action—"fighting." The motor patterns for fighting
are not available to Jackie; the targets for aggression are not accessible to him.

With all this in mind we made a suggestion to Jackie's mother.
We asked Mrs. Olson to try something and to report to us how
Jackie responded. We suggested that each time when Jackie began
his shouting, she provide him with pots and pans or banging toys
and encourage him to pound and bang with his hands and his fists.
Within a few days the mother called us. The banging games, she
said, "worked like magic." The shouting-screaming had stopped,
and Jackie had taken to pounding and banging with an enthusiasm
that surprised her. And while the pot-banging created its own
noise, this was a kind of noise that this mother could tolerate.
Moreover, banging provided adequate discharge of tension; it was
not necessary, for example, for Jackie to bang pots all day in the
same way that he had shouted all day. He used his pot-banging
when he needed it. Within a few days, Jackie began to show signs

of improvement in all areas. The shouting was now rare, the desperate clinging to the mother had disappeared, he was playing actively again and seemed to be his old self, according to the mother and our observers. Several weeks later the mother once again reported her amazement that the banging games had worked so well. Incidentally, too, Jackie became one of the blind children in our group who acquired the means for defending himself in the second year.

If we now return to the central problem, there are several points that emerge from this story of a crisis. Apart from the fact that in this instance we have a mother who is, under the best circumstances, not one who intuitively gets signs and signals from her children, it is doubtful that anyone without clinical experience could have made the crucial inferences from Jackie's behavior. To act upon a child's suffering, a mother must be able to read the sign language, must have intelligible signs. In the case of blind infants and young children, a very large vocabulary of sign language is either absent or delayed in appearance. (In the simplest terms we need only think of the vocabulary of facial signs that are differentiated through vision and which are not available to the blind child at all.) Further, if we consider that adaptation is a mutual process in the mother-infant relationship, the baby's own repertoire of adaptive behavior must play as large a role in crisis resolution as the mother's own repertoire. Jackie himself, 14 months old and blind, had no defense against helplessness except regression. There were no progressive forces working for an adaptive solution that could be encouraged and supported by the mother.

The story of Jackie and his mother was very instructive to us. We began to understand that something that we speak of as a mother's intuition is, after all, a reading of signs, and since a blind baby lacks the sign vocabulary of a sighted baby, the mother becomes a helpless partner in crisis. In this case, too, we had a mother who was perfectly able to recognize and tolerate aggression and anger when the motor patterns of aggression were available as signs, or when anger was articulated in recognizable forms, but neither she nor any other mother could easily identify the component of rage in the stereotyped shouting.

In this instance we were struck by another aspect of mother-infant reciprocity in crisis solution. Normally, there are adaptive tendencies at work for the baby even in crisis. A healthy sighted baby might cling to his mother and demand proof of her whereabouts after a traumatic separation. But he might also discover, quite on his own, that when he socked his Teddy Bear or threw his toys out of the crib, he felt better. And if his mother was "intuitive," that is, good at reading signs, she would have recognized that her baby was "letting off steam" in a healthy way and would have encouraged it, in which case she would be using something from the baby's repertoire of defensive action to help him find solutions. A mother can, of course, support socking the Teddy Bear or throwing toys out of the crib only if this kind of aggressive action is compatible with her own adaptive modes. We know one mother in our group who would say, "Now that isn't nice! Don't throw your dolly," and her blind daughter in the second and third years had to find a mode of discharging anger that was more congenial to mother, which happened to be verbal aggression. The possibilities are infinitely variable, of course, but in each case the mother does not simply offer a solution to crisis, she selects items from the baby's repertoire of adaptive behavior, and her selection represents a kind of screening of possibilities for compatibility with her own style.

Jamie

Our second example of separation crisis in the second year provides some interesting points of comparison with Jackie.

Jamie was blind from birth (hypoplasia of the optic nerves). When Jamie was 19 months old, a baby brother was born. The mother's confinement was the first separation he had ever experienced.

Pertinent Developmental Data

At 19 months, Jamie was one of the most precocious blind children in our group. His language achievements would have placed him in the superior range for sighted children, with good simple sentences and the use of a grammatically correct "I" and "you."

(The acquisition of "I" and "you" is typically delayed in blind young children.) He had begun to take independent steps at 14 months and was walking freely at 17 months. Adaptive hand behavior was excellent; he used his hands expertly to get information, he was able to execute simple mechanical tasks that are ordinarily difficult for blind children (winding a Jack-in-the-box, for example).

Jamie was the first child of two teen-age parents who were themselves extraordinary in their ability to understand a blind baby's experience. As members of large extended families, both parents were at ease with babies and young children. The mother, at 17, was expert; she had been caring for babies all her life.

Jamie's affection for his parents and his deep attachment to his mother were evident from the time we first met Jamie at 7 months. And while special affection for grandparents and cousins was also demonstrated, there was no question that mother was valued over all other persons. We began to get clear demonstrations of stranger anxiety at 9 months. He had a fair amount of independence and an ability to occupy himself well in periods when his mother was busy or out of the room, but he "touched base" with her frequently at such times, either calling for her in a questioning voice or exploring the house until he found her.

The Separation

While his mother was in the hospital Jamie was in the care of his favorite grandparents during the day and spent his nights at home with his father. During the stay at the grandparents Jamie, who had begun to walk independently, regressed to creeping. No other regressive behavior or reactions to mother's absence were reported to us.

Upon reunion with his mother, Jamie was at first very happy to see her, then moved from her side of the car and put his arms around his father. For 3 or 4 days following his mother's return, Jamie clung to his father and was reported to be "stand-offish" with his mother. When grandmother came into the house, Jamie began to cry each time and would have little to do with her. The parents understood that Jamie associated grandmother with the absence of his mother.

In our first observation following separation, when the new baby was 2 weeks old, Jamie alternated between affectionate overtures to his mother and striking her with his hands and fists when she held him. (The observer recorded that she had never seen such an outbreak of rage in Jamie.) Once, while the mother was holding the baby, Jamie touched the baby gently and said, "New baby, new baby." In the next moment he lost control and began an aggressive reach for the baby and poked him. When his mother gently intervened, Jamie had another tantrum and struck his mother. His mother did not retaliate, but again gently diverted him.

In the visits that followed we observed a number of occasions in which Jamie's anger toward his mother or anger toward the baby was handled by the mother. Typically, she intervened before the anger got out of control by suggesting an alternative "to work off steam." The most acceptable alternative was Buffy, Jamie's rocking horse. We have pictures of Jamie during this period, furiously riding his horse, until his rage was exhausted and he fell into easy rhythms.

Within a few months, Jamie's tantrums subsided. His jealousy of as well as affection for the baby were manifest throughout. His mother offered comforting, closeness, and generous amounts of babying when he needed it. There were no regressions during this period, and Jamie's development moved ahead without impediments. Jamie's independence and self-sufficiency at 2 years of age distinguished him as a blind child. There were few occasions recorded in which Jamie was reduced to helplessness in the second and third years. He was by no means a hostile child, but when he needed to, he could fight back. This in itself is of considerable interest because many blind children in the preschool years seem unable to protect themselves, to fight back, or even to possess the motor patterns for fighting.

Discussion

If we now compare the experience of Jamie and his mother and Jackie and his mother in a separation crisis, we see these interesting differences and similarities.

Both babies are blind, of course, which means that they share the common perils of the blind infant in the experience of loss. There are very large differences in the capacities of the two mothers to deal with critical events and to empathize with a blind child's experience. Furthermore, as Joyce Robertson and other correspondents have mentioned to me, the substitute care afforded to Jackie contrasted greatly with that which Jamie had, which must have contributed largely to his sense of helplessness and to his regression. If we were dealing with the problem of circumstance and reactions to loss of the mother, this paper would need to pursue other questions and we would probably need a range of cases to seek the answers for blind infants. But in this essay, I am primarily concerned with the adaptive *capability* in two blind children and the role of the mothers in facilitating adaptive solutions. From this point of view there are very important differences in the adaptive potentials of these two babies, and these appeared clearly in the developmental characteristics I have outlined.

First of all, Jamie's precocious language development tells us that he must have the capacity to evoke the image of a mother who is not present in reality. This in itself provides him with a measure of defense against loss. (Jackie at 14 months could not demonstrate in our observations or through objective tests that he had a concept of permanence.) While "permanence" is still provisional in the second and third years, Jamie can accept the proof, as it were, which means that his mother can give him the necessary reassurance. A child, even a blind child, who can evoke some kind of image of mother when she does not manifest herself, does not have to fasten himself to his mother's body, which Jackie needed to do.

Then, too, Jamie was mobile. In the course of an ordinary day, when he needed confirmation of his mother's existence, he could track her on sound and get to her under his own steam, or he could conduct a search because he had the conceptual equipment to deal with loss—"Mother must be *some* place." Moreover, mobility provided the possibility of *acting* upon the problem, conducting a search, while Jackie who was immobile was reduced to helplessness.

And last, Jamie had the capacity to discharge anger and to direct his anger against appropriate targets, something that is common-place in the development of every sighted child in the second year, and rare in the blind child. When Jamie hit his mother or hit the baby, the intention was clear. He was mad *at* his mother; he was mad *at* the baby. To be mad *at* an object one must have an object, in the strict sense of the word. The diffuse rage of Jackie had no object, in this sense. And Jackie, as we saw, did not even have the motor patterns for fighting which reduced him to helpless scream-ing.

In short, Jamie's reactions to separation provided intelligible signs and messages to a mother who was expert anyway in translat-ing the language of babies. The ambivalence of her child, hugging her and striking out at her, appeared in a language that she could easily understand. "He missed me when I was gone. He's afraid now. He's angry at me. He's angry at the baby." The mother pro-vided help for these conflicts. She gave assurance and closeness for the love needs and the anxiety; she did not retaliate for the anger but tactfully provided alternatives which directed the motor ex-pression away from her person.

On the one hand, then, Jamie provided the adaptive route through his own behavior, his own attempts at recovery. His mother, who understood love and understood anger, did not need to close these pathways; she only needed to strengthen the loosened bond and to redirect the anger so that there was adequacy in dis-charge, with a target removed from herself and the baby.

A nice story with a good ending. Yet we must not conclude from this story that the mother's expertness alone brought about this successful resolution of crisis. She was not only a good mother, but this was a baby with everything working for him. A question comes to mind, which may be a foolish question: if Jamie had been 12 months old, at the time of the birth of his brother, he would have had no capacity for evocative memory, no mobility, no targets for anger, not even the motor patterns for fighting. He would experi-ence loss as total helplessness. Under such circumstances a blind baby may regress, as Jackie did. And under these circumstances the conflicts of the child may be expressed in an unintelligible lan-guage as we saw in Jackie. How well might Jamie's expert mother fare in such a crisis?

BIBLIOGRAPHY

AINSWORTH, M. D. (1967), *Infancy in Uganda: Infant Care and the Growth of Love*. Baltimore: Johns Hopkins Press.

DÉCARIE, T. GOUIN (1963), *Intelligence and Affectivity in Early Childhood*. New York: International Universities Press, 1965.

FRAIBERG, S. (1968), Parallel and Divergent Patterns in Blind and Sighted Infants. *This Annual*, 23:264–300.

— (1969), Libidinal Object Constancy and Mental Representation. *This Annual*, 24:9–47.

— (1970), Smiling and Stranger Reaction in Blind Infants. In: *Exceptional Infant*, ed. J. Hellmuth. New York: Brunner/Mazel, 2:110–127.

— & FREEDMAN, D. A. (1964), Studies in the Ego Development of the Congenitally Blind Child. *This Annual*, 19:113–169.

— SIEGEL, B. L., & GIBSON, R. (1966), The Role of Sound in the Search Behavior of a Blind Infant. *This Annual*, 21:327–357.

MAHLER, M. S. (1965), On the Significance of the Normal Separation-Individuation Phase. In: *Drives, Affects, Behavior*, ed. M. Schur. New York: International Universities Press, 2:161–169.

MORGAN, G. A. & RICCIUTI, H. N. (1969). Infants' Responses to Strangers during the First Year. In: *Determinants of Infant Behaviour*, ed. B. M. Foss. London: Methuen, 4:253–272.

PIAGET, J. (1937), *The Construction of Reality in the Child*. New York: Basic Books, 1954.

SCHAFFER, H. R. & EMERSON, P. E. (1964), *The Development of Social Attachments in Infancy*. Monogr. Soc. Res. Child Develpm., Vol. 29, No. 3, Serial No. 94.

SPITZ, R. A. (& COBLINER, W. G.) (1965), *The First Year of Life*. New York: International Universities Press.

TENNES, K. H. & LAMPL, E. E. (1964), Stranger and Separation Anxiety in Infancy. *J. Nerv. Ment. Dis.,* 139:247–254.

YARROW, L. (1967), The Development of Focused Relationships during Infancy. In: *Exceptional Infant*, ed. J. Hellmuth. New York: Brunner/Mazel, 1969, 1:427–442.

Some Thoughts on Reconstruction in Child Analysis

EDNA FURMAN

ERNST KRIS (1956) DISCUSSED RECONSTRUCTION IN PSYCHOANALYSIS thoroughly and beautifully. He traced the concept and technique of reconstruction from their origins in Freud's early work, through the vicissitudes of their later development, to the present trends in the framework of psychoanalytic theory and practice. In doing so he highlighted the general change from the emphases on content to that on the ego state. Kris's understanding and insight were further augmented by his great technical skill, demonstrated in those parts of his article which so deftly outline and discuss the

From the Cleveland Center for Research in Child Development and the Department of Psychiatry, Case Western Reserve University, Cleveland, Ohio.

The clinical part of this paper was presented at the 6th Annual Scientific Meetings of the American Association for Child Psychoanalysis, in Williamsburg, Virginia, April, 1971.

clinical techniques. He described the many pitfalls encountered by the analyst, especially when he works on reconstructions with patients of widely varied pathology and personality make-up. For both adult and child analysts his work has been a basis for our thinking about reconstruction and an ongoing source of learning. Since then several articles have been published on this topic; among them M. Katan's (1969) has been of particular value to me. In this article M. Katan restates his earlier views (1939) on the therapeutic value of reconstruction, stressing that some memories related to the original event enable us to understand the pretraumatic state of the patient's ego. In my clinical work I have seen this as providing an important avenue to tracing the genetic origins of certain defenses and characterological solutions which helped to shape a patient's pathology.

The findings from child analysis and analytic observations of children have greatly contributed to the changes in the concept and role of reconstruction (A. Freud, 1951). There are also many papers demonstrating reconstructions in analytic work with children, among them such classics as Little Hans (Freud, 1909) and the cases of B. Bornstein (1931, 1946, 1949, 1953) and J. Waelder Hall (1946). I am not aware of publications which deal with the problems of reconstruction specific to child analysis. This gap was filled to some extent by the formal (Kennedy, 1971) and informal contributions of other child analysts to this topic at the 6th Annual Scientific Meetings of the American Association for Child Psychoanalysis (1971).

The following brief remarks summarize some of my own tentative thinking on the topic of reconstruction in child analysis and serve to introduce an illustrative clinical example.

Reconstructive Work with Children

In assessing his reconstructive work with his patient, the child analyst has two special sets of circumstances to take into account: (1) the child's parents, and (2) the immaturity of the child's personality. Inevitably one is closely linked with the other, but for purposes of clarity I shall attempt to discuss them under separate headings.

The Child's Parents

As a part of the very beginning of every child's analysis we are in contact with his parents. At that time we already form our impressions of them as parents and usually obtain a developmental history, either through a more systematic inquiry or through their own spontaneous remarks as they describe their life with the child. Although we are well aware that our initial impressions of the parents may be faulty and that their account of the child's personal history inevitably suffers from omissions, distortions, and even outright untruths, we do receive all this information and it becomes a part of our mental model of the child patient. In contrast to the adult analyst, we learn about the child patient from the start through outside sources, and we personally meet his most important early love objects.

There are, of course, many good reasons for seeing the parents. For the purposes of this discussion one of the main reasons for seeing them is the fact that the parents function in many areas as their child's ego. Much of the information which they give us could not be related by the child himself. Some young children cannot even state their correct age and home address, i.e., many realistic details which the adult patient knows and relates himself. In gathering initial information from the parents the child analyst does not necessarily obtain more information than the adult analyst, but he obtains it from persons outside the analytic situation and it is filtered through an ego other than his patient's.

Unless a child analyst adopts the theoretical and technical approaches of M. Klein and her followers, he continues to see his young patient's parents at more or less frequent intervals throughout the child's treatment. The many advantages of, and indeed imperatives for, ongoing contact with the parents have been discussed by several authors (Burlingham, 1951; Buxbaum, 1954; Furman, 1969). From the point of view of reconstruction in the analysis these interviews add a great deal to the analyst's knowledge of the child's past, be it the past of years ago or the past of yesterday. In any case, it is always a past gained from outside sources and viewed through eyes other than the patient's. This factor, foreign to adult analysis, has a definite bearing on the analyst's thinking and on his reconstructive technique.

Even some non-Kleinian child analysts try to avoid this "complication" by maintaining no contact with the parents. This approach does not bring child analysis closer to adult analysis. Quite apart from wider considerations of the parent-child relationship, from the point of view of reconstruction the exclusion of the parent entails an exclusion of those of the child's ego functions which are still partly vested with the parent and which the child cannot suddenly use independently in his analysis. Sufficiently developed secondary process thinking, so necessary for the reporting of daily events in the analysis, is often one of these functions. Furthermore, the transference neurosis is known to manifest itself differently in child analysis, as important cathexes remain with, or are reattached to, the parents during the course of the treatment. Thus, two of the analyst's main sources for reconstructive work— current life experiences and transference reactions—are only partly accessible within the analytic situation, certainly less so than is customary in the analysis of adults.

This unique situation poses the problem of whether, how, when, and to what extent the child analyst uses his "outside" information in the reconstructive work.

There are occasional instances when a mother's intuitive closeness with her young child enables her to recall a pertinent past event at the time when her child's analysis focuses on a certain current difficulty and its historical antecedents. In such a situation the analyst may feel it correct and helpful to use the mother's memory directly in the reconstruction with the patient. In the case of Randy, discussed below, the mother unfortunately lacked such available positive insight. She could at best occasionally confirm earlier events after they had been reconstructed in the analysis and after Randy's own memories and feelings had come to light.

Much more often the opposite is helpful, namely, to set aside earlier parental information because it is not pertinent to the child's experience. With Randy I had known from the beginning that his mother had started to work full-time when he was 18 months old. To him this was not as significant as her depressed emotional withdrawal which had preceded and followed her working year, the fact that she left and returned daily with the father, his experiences with the sitters who had taken mother's place, to mention but some of many aspects.

More frequently, of course, we deal with situations between these two extremes; i.e., we are able to utilize some aspects of the parental information at a point when the child's material coincides with it. At such times the analyst does not confront the child with the parent's account. He integrates the parental information into his own thinking and uses appropriate aspects of it within the context of the analytic reconstructive work. Kennedy (1971) addressed herself to this form of using parental information.

The Immaturity of the Child's Personality

The second circumstance unique to child analysis, especially with very young patients, is the immaturity of the child's personality. I am referring now to functions other than those already mentioned. Kris pointed out that the value of reconstructive work lies in its capacity to free the energy previously used in the cathexis of repressed experiences, thus making it available for neutralization. The greater the ego's ability to neutralize, the greater are the potential benefits of the lifting of repression. Kris (1956) further stated that the success of the reconstructive work and its value for the patient depend, among other things, on repression being the central defense, and on the lifting of repression lessening the investment of the subsidiary defenses, which in turn frees energy for insight and integration. M. Katan's work is helpful here in pointing a way toward understanding the ego, including the defense mechanisms at its disposal, just prior to the time of the traumatic event or period.

In child analysis we deem ourselves fortunate in having an ally in the maturational forces active within the child's personality. This ally helps in the task of decathecting the past and investing the present and the immediate future, a task so crucial to the shift of energy which we hope to achieve through reconstructive work. Other aspects of the child's personality, however, would appear as potential obstacles: the young child's ego is less capable of neutralization. Instinctual cathexes absorb much of his available energy, and his ego readily "sides" with the demands of the drives. Neutral interests are less developed, are usually still partly instinctual, and secondary autonomy is not yet fully established. The ego's capacity to use freed energy for its "own" purposes, for neutralization or sublimation, is relatively weak. In coping with conflictual situations the child still relies heavily on earlier defense mechanisms. Repression may sometimes not play a central role in the countercathectic process. The immature ego's synthetic function, so essential in the working through period of the reconstructive work, is not yet adequate to handle major mental tasks. Last, but not least, the young child still lives in, and depends on, the very environment in which earlier upheavals took place. Often enough he is still exposed to repetitions, or traces, of the same interactions or impressions which disturbed him earlier. This further complicates his ability to face them consciously and to integrate them without resorting to the use of defensive maneuvers.

Undoubtedly these factors vary enormously from child to child. The capacities for neutralization and integration vary in individuals as well as in different developmental phases. The nature and intensity of earlier defenses vary. The past traumatic experiences vary as well as the child's current home situation. In the case of Randy, illustrated in this paper, all the above factors were unfavorable. To some extent this was due to the particular nature of his disturbance. Kris pointed to the prominent use of obsessional defenses always being an obstacle, apparently regardless of age. To some extent, however, my patient's difficulties in profiting from reconstruction were considerably augmented by the fact that he was a young child. This did not make it more difficult to help him with his obsessional symptoms or, later, with his phobia, but it did handicap him in finding healthy adaptive solutions to his conflicts. Randy's analysis is not yet concluded. He may accomplish a good deal more. I am thinking of other patients, however, with whom it seemed indicated to resume analytic work at a later age, when the stressful past was more distant and when the ego's capacities for neutralization and integration were further developed.

Clinical Example: Reconstruction of Early Phallic Conflicts in an Obsessional Young Boy

Randy entered the Hanna Perkins Nursery School at 4 years 8 months. Our observations and work with the parents during the initial months led to the diagnosis of obsessional neurosis. Randy's large build, topped by a big shock of dark hair and menacing facial distortions accentuated his frequent yells, threats, and physical attacks. These outbursts occurred whenever he felt himself threatened by people or events, whenever his obsessional defenses were interfered with, and when he externalized his conflicts to involve an adult. His ego activities were severely restricted in the areas of motility, perception, and learning. Much of his thinking consisted of obsessional ruminations. His compulsions were most manifest around daily routines, preventing his compliance with simple demands; e.g., Randy would not dress himself and engaged his mother in a struggle of forcibly putting on his clothes. When this fight was interpreted as an externalization, Randy was pathetically reduced to endless doing and undoing, repeatedly putting on, then taking off, a boot or jacket, unable to control or foresee the outcome of his efforts. At such times the babyish softness of his body and face was noticeable and he would gratefully accept sympathy with his inner despair. In general, his relationships lacked signs of warmth and love. Essentially a loner, he interacted by controlling people and establishing his own superiority. By contrast, he thoughtfully protected and cared for inanimate objects.

The first child of young professional middle-class parents, Randy had not suffered physical deprivation and had generally enjoyed good health. His father had severe neurotic difficulties in his relationship with his son but was capable of feelingful relationships and was genuinely fond of Randy. The mother was severely ambivalent in all relationships and brittlely sensitive to narcissistic injury. Her son represented some of the most feared and hated aspects of herself, but she also endowed him with her highest aspirations, especially in the intellectual area. She admired his clever talking so much that she had not noticed the increasing restriction and pathology of his thought processes. Both parents lacked empathy with Randy's feelings and were often oblivious to his childhood needs. They could not conceive that he might react to physical punishment, open door bathroom and bedroom stimulation, sudden separations and changes of plans, frightening incidents or attacks by older children.

Randy's analysis started when he was 5 years 3 months. He has by now been seen five times weekly for nearly 4 years. Most of Randy's early life had to be reconstructed in the analysis since the parents were either ignorant of the genetically important events or so intimately involved in them that their own anxieties forced them to ward off accurate recall.

The first 18 months of the analytic work dealt primarily with what Randy aptly termed the "sad, bad, mad troubles," namely, his life as a toddler. When Randy was 18 months old his mother went into full-time teaching for one year, leaving Randy and his then 6-month-old sister to a succession of sitters. Randy had to cope with the mother's absence, her partial emotional withdrawal, her insistent toilet-training demands, as well as with the sadistic threats and handling by at least one sitter. We learned that he had warded off helplessness by angry omnipotent control; and narcissistic depletion, by introjecting unintegrated aspects of the ambivalent reprimanding mother and the fiercely menacing sitter. Both defenses contributed much to his ongoing behavior and lessened with insight. Increasingly, phallic concerns dominated the analysis and his functioning.

The period on which I shall briefly report here occurred in the latter half of Randy's second year of treatment and focused on the reconstruction of some of his early phallic conflicts during his third year of life.

Randy's prominent defense of isolation, the impairment of his synthetic function, and difficulty in instinctual fusion were a part of his symptomatology and affected the analytic material so as to make it difficult to follow. They influenced his memory of the past in such a way as to disconnect events and ideas from the related affects. We were often able to recover a lost memory long before the accompanying affect could be recognized and joined to it. For

the benefit of the reader I have supplied some of the lacking integration, but in condensing the material I have had to omit much
that related to current events and transference reactions.

At the time of the analytic period to be reported Randy had
improved sufficiently to have entered the first grade of public
school and was soon transferred to the second grade because of
his advanced academic achievement. The new exposure to the bigger boys accentuated his fears of and excitement with them, manifested in boasting and provocations. Although there had already
been much material on Randy's awe, envy, and excitement in connection with his father's bodily and mental exhibitionism, he did
not link this with his behavior with the boys. In addition, my absence during the summer vacation and his lonely walks to and
from school intensified his fears of being unsafe. There was a
marked exacerbation of his dressing symptom. Randy had reported
"doing nothing and thinking nothing" when it was time to dress.
I had begun to relate this to his struggles against masturbatory
activity and against excited and angry fantasies which he acted out
during the day.

Randy now opened the sessions with, "Let's talk about the fighting trouble," but then refused to associate. I suggested there were
two parts of him, one wanted to get over the trouble, the other
wanted to hold on to it, to which he replied, "But then I might
have an accident and tell it all when I don't even want to." "That
sounds like talking about wetting or soiling, rather than about
troubles. Could the two be mixed up for you?" I wondered. At
the same time Randy was also preoccupied with looking at, but
not seeing, evidence of other patients and of my family. He played
games in which I was to watch him and guess whether something
was there or not. When I interpreted his denial and his turning
passive-into-active mechanism, making me the confused watcher,
Randy leaned under the chair and seriously studied its legs. He
could not make out, he said, whether there were four or five legs,
the fifth leg belonging to the adjacent table. Randy's behavior
deteriorated. He made "messes," as he called it. His refusals to
dress and do necessary little chores appeared calculated to provoke
an angry manhandling. Once when I approached him to help, he
yelled, "Don't touch me, don't get your hands on me or I'll cut

them off." I suggested that he was so provocative and scared because a part of him wanted to be touched, perhaps even hurt, to be like a girl. "You're crazy." "Such ideas are so scary that boys sometimes feel they must be crazy to think them," I replied. Randy calmed down at once. The next day he asked me to help him undo a stuck zipper. As I worked on it Randy leaned back with an ecstatic expression. Later he muttered, "Piz-zip, piz-zip" and touched his fly. I told him that the zipper on his jacket seems to be mixed up with the zipper on his pants, that there must have been a time when he felt excited by mommy touching his penis in zipping up his pants. Randy promptly spilled some water, berating himself. I wondered whether this accident gave us another clue, namely, that mommy's exciting zipping and touching had occurred after he had wet himself as a little boy, when she was very angry, rough, and scary. Later Randy told of his dressing trouble that morning, how he had suddenly lost control, chased around, throwing things, and yelling. He added, "I never know when the trouble will come and then suddenly the piss is out." I pointed out how again dressing and pissing were brought together and suggested that, as a little boy, he used to hold back his urine. It must have scared him when it came out as it now scared him when troubled feelings overwhelmed him. Randy replied, "Mommy always put me on the pot *after* the piss was out. Janet was a good girl, she always let her piss go because she didn't have trouble holding it back. I remember Janet in our bedroom, sitting down on the potty and letting it go and mommy was nice to her." I reminded Randy how he had looked under the chair some time ago for four or five legs, like he must have searched anxiously to see whether Janet did or did not have a penis. A little boy would have thought that Janet let her piss go because she had no penis, rather than no trouble. Randy replied matter-of-factly, "No penis—no plug." He elaborated how he had always thought of the inside of the body as a big bathtub. Losing the plug empties one out and all goes down the drain. Later I could sympathize with Randy's early terrible dilemma of wanting to keep his penis-plug, yet also wanting to be good like his sister to be loved by his mother.

All this material was interwoven with evidence of an opposite instinctual trend: Randy continued his provocative boasting with

the boys. As his visual denial lessened he belittled other patients'
work and excitedly threatened to destroy it. I interpreted his defenses against feeling little and stupid. One day Randy suddenly
blurted out, "He's the biggest one I ever saw." He could not connect his statement to anything. I wondered whether, at the time of
his observing Janet's toileting, he had also watched his daddy urinate. Perhaps he felt very impressed by his father's size and performance, angry as well as too small by comparison. In response
Randy concentrated his provocative angry outbursts on his mother
and me. Why was it so important for him to make us angry? He
told me, "I did a bad thing yesterday, I threw a shoe and pencils
around and got mommy mad. I can always make her *mad*." "How
very sad," I replied, "when a boy feels that the only power he has
with his mommy is to make her angry and to get her to hurt him,
instead of making her admire and love him and his penis." Randy
now remembered wistfully, "I made a piss on the carpet in the
living room at C-Road and she ran in, looked at me, got mad,
and then came the drag-wipe-dress we talked about." His reference
to C-Road helped us to time this period as taking place in his third
year. Over the next few days his angry tirades persisted, but with
a difference: they invited attention, not anger. "What a big show,"
I commented one day. Randy looked sheepish and protested, "I
am not a big show-off." I suggested that perhaps now we could
understand what had made him piss on the floor: he wanted his
mother to be excited and to admire him like daddy. How disappointed and angry he must have been when he only succeeded in
making her mad. A part of him must still feel that, for he tried
to use the showing of his big excited anger to upset his mother and
me so that we would have to think of him instead of our husbands.

Our reconstructions of Randy's phallic competition with his
sister and father led to a serious intensification of his obsessions.
He was helplessly caught in doing and undoing during dressing
and his incessant doubting paralyzed his actions. His most terrify-
ing recurring thought was that he was Sirhan, the murderer, and
was carried off by the police. I pointed out that this was but an
extension of the dilemma he had shown earlier in holding back,
then letting go, in showing off to impress, then leaning back to be
touched and hurt, in wanting to be a man, then a girl. These ter-

rible doubts were safer for him than the more terrible truth, namely, that he really never had the choice, that he was a little boy who had often felt unloved and unsafe within and without. His doubts and obsessions protected him from this helpless feeling.

Randy's obsessional symptoms subsided. From the subsequent material we learned that his mother had been quite depressed during Randy's third year and that, during the same period, he had witnessed a primal scene a tergo, which further augmented his narcissistic hurt and interfered with appropriate drive fusion and drive control. Randy first linked this primal scene to his early wetting problem by recalling that, "When I pissed on the carpet I was on all fours." When the analysis eventually reached the traumatic events of his fourth year, Randy's symptoms became phobic, a repetition of several months of severe phobic anxieties which had preceded the original onset of his obsessional neurosis.

Summary

The limited period in Randy's analysis which was described above serves to illustrate some of the reconstructive work with him. It does not differ essentially from other analyses. When I viewed it over a period of years, however, and saw it within the wider context of his whole treatment, my attention was drawn to some features which I had not noted so clearly in other patients. These aspects underlined for me some of the problems inherent in reconstructive work with children.

One special set of circumstances centered on the role of the parents, both as informants and as love objects on whom the child depends in the present. Although Randy was only 4½ years old when I began to see his parents, their recollections of his personal history omitted many of those events which to him were the most important. Insofar as the parents did relate the past, their view of it differed drastically from that of the patient's, as we came to understand it in the analysis. It is rare for parents of a very young child to be so utterly lacking in empathy with their child's inner and outer life experiences. This attitude did not change throughout the course of the treatment, although consciously and conscientiously both parents did their utmost to support the analytic

work and to provide a good home and family life. This basic difficulty, an outcome of their own disturbances, made it impossible
for the parents to refrain from repeating some of the inappropriate
handling and situations which had been, and still were, beyond
Randy's mastery. As a result, Randy found it very hard to face
certain feelings, conflicts, and realities. After all, they existed not
only in the past; they threatened him in the present, in his relationship with his most important love objects. Although the difficulties of Randy's parents in these areas were very marked, to some
extent these and other parental personalities play a significant part
in all child analyses and affect the reconstructive work.

The other special set of circumstances focused on the child's
immature personality and individual characteristics. The first few
years of Randy's analysis were taken up with reconstructive work
which was made particularly difficult by his predominant use of
the mechanisms of isolation, undoing, and doubting. These mechanisms overshadowed the importance of repression in his defensive
structure. Gradually he acquired a considerable amount of feelingful awareness of the links between his current behavior and
conflicts and their past determinants. The need for repeated working through was not surprising. It was striking, however, to what
extent the later years of the analytic work centered on his impaired
synthetic function which limited his ability to integrate the past,
on his low frustration tolerance which, along with other factors,
handicapped his decathexis of instinctual investments, and his difficulty in neutralizing large amounts of energy in spite of his excellent intelligence. As was true of his parents, the difficulties inherent in Randy's disturbance and immaturity were unusually
great. Yet, to a lesser extent, they are characteristic of young children and play their part in the course of the reconstructive work
and in its utilization by the patient.

BIBLIOGRAPHY

BORNSTEIN, B. (1931), Phobia in a Two-and-a-Half-Year-Old Child. *Psycho-
anal. Quart.*, 4:93–119, 1935.

— (1946), Hysterical Twilight States in an Eight-Year-Old Child. *This Annual,* 2:229–240.
— (1949), The Analysis of a Phobic Child. *This Annual,* 3/4:181–226.
— (1953), Fragment of an Analysis of an Obsessional Child. *This Annual,* 8:313–332.
BURLINGHAM, D. (1951), Present Trends in Handling the Mother-Child Relationship during the Therapeutic Process. *This Annual,* 6:31–37.
BUXBAUM, E. (1954), Technique of Child Therapy. *This Annual,* 9:297–333.
FREUD, A. (1951), Observations on Child Development. *This Annual,* 6:18–30.
FREUD, S. (1909), Analysis of a Phobia in a Five-Year-Old Boy. *Standard Edition,* 10:3–149. London: Hogarth Press, 1955.
FURMAN, E. (1969), Treatment via the Mother. In: *The Therapeutic Nursery School,* ed. R. A. Furman & A. Katan. New York: International Universities Press, pp. 64–123.
HALL, J. W. (1946), The Analysis of a Case of Night Terror. *This Annual,* 2:189–227.
KATAN, M. (1939), Der psychotherapeutische Wert der Konstruktionen in der Analyse. *Int. Z. Psychoanal.,* 24:172–176.
— (1969), The Link between Freud's Works on Aphasia, Fetishism and Constructions in Analysis. *Int. J. Psycho-Anal.,* 50:547–553.
KENNEDY, H. (1971), Problems in Reconstruction in Child Analysis. *This Annual,* 26:386–402.
KRIS, E. (1956), The Recovery of Childhood Memories in Psychoanalysis. *This Annual,* 11:54–88.
Proceedings of the 6th Annual Scientific Meetings of the American Associa- for Child Psychoanalysis (1971) (in press).

Problems in Reconstruction in Child Analysis

HANNA KENNEDY

IN HIS PAPER "CONSTRUCTIONS IN ANALYSIS" (1937), INTERESTINGLY enough published in the same year as "Analysis Terminable and Interminable," Freud describes the work of analysis as a *search* for a "trustworthy and in all essential respects complete picture

This paper was presented at the Sixth Annual Scientific Meetings of the American Association for Child Psychoanalysis at Williamsburg, Virginia, on March 20, 1971.

The author is on the staff of the Hampstead Child-Therapy Clinic, an organization which at present is maintained by the Field Foundation, Inc., New York; the Foundation for Research in Psychoanalysis, Beverly Hills, Calif.; the Anna Freud Foundation, New York; the Freud Centenary Fund, London; the Grant Foundation, Inc., New York; the National Institute for Mental Health, Bethesda; The New-Land Foundation, New York; the Andrew Mellon Foundation; and a number of private supporters.

I am greatly indebted to Dr. Joseph Sandler for collaborating in the preparation of this paper and for allowing me to include some of his ideas in this presentation.

of the patient's forgotten years." The work of analysis consists of "two quite different portions" and "involves two people, to each of whom a distinct task is assigned. . . . the person who is being analysed has to be induced to remember something that has been experienced by him and repressed; and the dynamic determinants of the process are so interesting that the other portion of the work, the task performed by the analyst, has been pushed into the background. . . . His task is to make out what has been forgotten from the traces which it has left behind or, more correctly, to *construct* it. The time and manner in which he conveys his constructions to the person who is being analysed . . . constitute the link between the two portions of the work of analysis, between his own part and that of the patient" (p. 258f.).

Thus Freud used the term "construction" or "reconstruction" in two senses, namely, *reconstruction as a process in the mind of the analyst, and reconstruction as a type of verbal intervention.* He also introduced the notion that the analyst's reconstructions of aspects of the patient's forgotten past facilitate the recovery of childhood memories. Obviously, this topic is a wide and complicated one, encompassing, in addition to many other aspects, the cognitive and technical facets of Freud's use of the term as well as the processes involved in the recovery of childhood memories.

The main focus of this paper will be on the *technical* aspects of reconstruction. I intend to emphasize the point that the technique of *reconstruction in child analysis and the recovery of memories in the course of psychoanalytic treatment,* although intimately related, are not as close as might be assumed.

We know that some previously forgotten memories arise spontaneously during the work of analysis, some emerge following transference interpretation of what is currently going on in the analytic situation. Indeed, we expect, ideally, that the interpretation of a transference resistance, for example, will be followed by a freeing of material, much of which might include or otherwise relate to past memories. Conversely, some reconstructions are not followed by the recovery of confirmatory memories, but they *do* have an effect on the course of the analysis, as is evident in the material brought subsequently by the patient. It is the problems involved in phenomena such as these, especially as they manifest themselves in child analysis, which I intend to discuss and clarify.

Analysts have generally attributed great significance to the actual recall of forgotten or repressed memories, and even used "recall" as an index of progress in the evaluation of therapeutic results. These notions are deeply rooted in the history of psychoanalytic theory and practice, and can be traced back to the first phase of Freud's thinking when he worked with the traumatogenic theory of hysteria (1893–1895). These ideas still influence our thinking, even though changes in psychoanalysis have occurred with the introduction of the structural theory, advances in ego psychology, and the increasing role played by studies of child development. With these advances in mind, I shall question the tradition-bound importance attached to recall.

Even if we no longer see the recovery of childhood memories as a *sine qua non* of successful treatment, the recovery of memories still has a special significance for both patient and analyst, and we need to re-examine the reasons for this.

It must be obvious to all of us that we are constantly searching for supporting evidence for our reconstructions, in the hope of refining both theory and technique. This too has its historical roots because it was from reconstructions in the analysis of adults that Freud arrived at his discoveries of infantile sexuality and the important part played by childhood development in the neurotic disorders of later life. These reconstructions could later be corroborated and refined through psychoanalytic childhood observation and child analysis, for example, in the Little Hans case.

It is also obvious that in analytic work with our patients, we feel gratified when our reconstructions appear to be validated by the recovery of childhood memories, but as we know this does not always occur.

It seems to me that our search for confirmatory evidence is based upon our equating the effectiveness of our interventions, especially in the realm of reconstruction, with an assumption that what is reconstructed is an exact reflection of what actually occurred. However, there appear to be grounds for questioning this in the light of our knowledge that childhood experience cannot be recovered in the exact original form. This point has been emphasized by Ernst Kris in his illuminating paper on "The Recovery of Childhood Memories in Psychoanalysis" (1956), on which I shall draw substantially. Kris pointed out that we are misled in believing that we are, except in rare circumstances, able to find "the 'events' of the afternoon on the staircase when the seduction happened" (p. 73). He stressed that in analysis we are dealing with a whole period in which a seduction may have played a role *and that the distortions of later developmental conflicts* became superimposed on the original situation.

Whereas reconstructions from the analysis of adults has led to an understanding of the role of "screen" or "cover" memories, direct work with children has focused on the multiplicity of the pathogenic happenings, and the complex distortions and ramifications that occur during development. Anna Freud (1951) pointed out that the analyst's search for *the* traumatic event or experience has led him to underestimate the extent of the "telescopic" nature of memory until he was reminded of it by the results of direct childhood observation. "One traumatic prohibition or punishment, remembered or reconstructed, becomes the representative of hundreds of frustrations which had been imposed on the child; one longer separation from the mother takes over the combined effect of innumerable times when the infant has been left alone in his cot, his room, at bedtime etc." (p. 27).

There is a further complicating aspect with regard to memories, namely, that later events may add special significance to earlier experiences, which may then be recalled *as if* they themselves had been traumatic or of particular psychopathological significance.

Much has been learned about these processes by comparing data obtained from children who were first observed in longitudinal studies and later in analysis. Such studies have opened up a variety of different areas of research. Heinicke (1970) has recently described how this approach can be utilized in the attempt to devise a methodology to validate psychoanalytic reconstruction in child analysis.

I believe that it is important to keep in mind the distinction between what one might call the genetic-reconstructive approach in psychoanalysis and the developmental approach. These have been implicitly equated by child analysts for many years, but we need to consider whether in fact the two are identical. The genetic-reconstructive approach is concerned with the analyst's reconstruction of the patient's past, on the basis of the analytic material brought by the patient. The developmental approach, on the other hand, is much more concerned with internal and external influences in actual ongoing childhood development, especially those leading to a failure to make the crucial transition from one developmental phase to another. We would all like to believe that what we reconstruct in the work of child analysis is identical with the actual developmental processes which have taken place, but Ernst Kris offers much evidence, as does our own clinical experience at Hampstead, that this is not so. We must also keep in mind that in analysis we are dealing with the world as the child sees it —that is, not only the internal world of the child's drives and fantasies, but his own unique perception of the external world. The case reported by Mary Bergen (1958), to take just one example, illustrates this point with particular clarity.

Thus the developmental approach may lean more heavily on child observation and external sources for evidence of what went on, for example, in the child-parent relationship, whereas the genetic-reconstructive approach leans heavily on what the child brings to the analysis. The reconstructions based on what is brought by the child at different points in his analysis may therefore differ from what a psychoanalytic observer may have seen at a specific point in development. The two approaches to the child are not contradictory; rather, I believe they are different but complementary standpoints from which to view the child. It will be evident that in child analysis we constantly move from the developmental approach to the genetic-reconstructive and from the genetic-reconstructive to the developmental, but the assumption that the two points of view are the same may contribute to unclarity in our thinking.

Not all of our child patients have been observed longitudinally; but we usually obtain a detailed developmental history from the parents, the school, the pediatrician, and other sources, and these fragments of information undoubtedly influence our view of the material. In addition, throughout the course of the child's treatment, we frequently obtain external information about both his past and his present. A crucial question is the extent to which we permit such information, often biased, to prompt the formulation of a reconstructive interpretation, without it always being adequately substantiated by the analytic material brought by the child. While we may at times have to rely on such information in child analysis, we may occasionally focus too much on the genetic-reconstructive approach in our thinking. This is particularly evident when we make the assumption that what the child brings or enacts in the present is an exact repetition of what occurred or was experienced in the past. This may lead us at times into analyzing what the child is experiencing predominantly in terms of his defenses, and his projections of wishes, fantasies, and conflicts, without acknowledging sufficiently that, in certain cases, what the child brings is shaped by the fact that he lived in a "crazy world" which has become internalized.

With regard to the function of memories in the course of development, we have the notion of, so to speak, a "two-way traffic"; i.e., early experiences may color and distort later ones, just as later events sometimes add special significance to earlier experiences. The child analyst is confronted by the additional problem of distinguishing between the developmental and the genetic-reconstructive view of the material, a distinction he must keep in mind when he considers how past experiences enter into the analytic process and what part *reconstruction* plays in it.

The developmental age at which a crucial event takes place is of great importance. Events which occur very early in life and give rise to strong affective experiences and somatic reactions are, as we all know, of the highest significance for later development. They have a profound influence on the child's personality development by determining his modes of functioning and by coloring his attitudes and response patterns.

To take a simplified example, experiences of physical overstimulation in the first year may show up in later life in a variety of ways. We may see a child with a heightened excitability which manifests itself in all phases of libidinal development. We may recognize in such a child a tendency to search over and over again for similar exciting experiences, and these general features may or may not become secondarily involved in later psychopathology, as Anna Freud has stressed recently (1971). What we see is a complicated style of approach to the world, spelled out so beautifully by Erikson (1950), in what he calls the "modality of social life." This is determined originally, for instance, by somatic experiences, and can show itself as a characteristic in all developmental phases, even though the child may reach phase dominance in the various phases through which he passes.

It is important to keep in mind that what is created by such early experiences are not conflict situations but *attitudes* which may not have specific fantasy or memory content attached to them. This is often lost sight of in clinical work.

Let me give a brief clinical illustration of a 10-year-old patient who was excessively demanding, yet permanently dissatisfied and always anticipating loss. Oral features dominated the transference and fantasy material and also found expression in behavioral manifestations. We know from his history that he had been exposed to a sudden weaning experience followed by prolonged feeding difficulties which persisted in one form or another through all the developmental phases. Feeding difficulties still played an important part in his present symptomatology. The core of his pathology, however, was in his inappropriate affective responses and severely impaired object relationships, and these were the areas focused on by the analytic work and explored from the very beginning of the analysis. It is natural for the analyst to assume that the unsatisfactory early feeding situation contributed to the disturbances in the mother-child interactions. Having made this obvious assumption, we may have some differences of opinion with regard to specific details: some analysts will attach more importance to the sudden so-called "loss of the breast"; others, to the infant's inability to make adaptive moves and to accept whatever substitute was offered at the time. We may not agree on the significance of such developmental reactions; some will regard them merely as signs that all is not going well now; others will view these experiences as inevitably laying the ground for *later disturbances*. We may differ in our emphasis on whether the major contribution to these mutually unsatisfactory experiences comes from the mother or from the infant. But despite these differences, all of us will naturally construct some sort of mental bridge from

the present pathology to these early experiences. Here a knowledge of the developmental history will certainly color our view of
the child.

The questions we really have to examine are *when* and *why* we
reconstruct such early experiences for the patient, and *how* they
become meaningful for him. First, with regard to the timing of
a reconstruction, I want to quote Ernst Kris (1956): "the analyst
watches a reorganization of forces in the patient's behavior and
guides this reorganization by his interpretations. . . . In the
course of this process the past emerges into the present, and a
readiness, a 'need' for reconstructive interpretation may be noticed" (p. 58f.). These comments refer predominantly to the analysis of adults and older children and are crucial in that context.
Although they also apply to child analysis, we may find that there
is less "readiness and need" for reconstruction, especially with
younger children.

The child patient may *follow us* or *lead us* along the path from
the present to the past experiences. Even children who show little
interest in their past will begin to do so when they become involved in the analysis because they are responding, step by step,
to those of our interventions which lead them in this direction.
Others, and these are more often the more disturbed children,
lead us directly to the past via their material. But which past?

The 10-year-old borderline patient mentioned earlier came to
analysis with a firmly established conviction that the roots of his
current problems were to be found in his distressing childhood
experiences. This enabled him covertly to blame his parents for
causing his distress and misery. There were several early experiences, all on a similar theme, which we may call "childhood memories" and which were constantly reiterated.

A typical memory of this sort related to sitting behind the bars
of a cot, panic-stricken and helplessly immobilized while watching
a fight between his parents, who threw crockery at each other. The
feelings the patient ascribed to this experience afforded the bridge
from the present to the past because the patient could see that
they were identical to the panic states he frequently experienced
in his current life. He constantly referred to experiences in his

daily life which "paralyze me with fear" or made him feel "frozen on the spot," and interpretation could serve to make the link with the past.

From the developmental history we know that violent scenes between the parents prevailed throughout his infancy and early childhood, often leading to prolonged periods during which the parents were separated. In analysis we are, of course, not concerned with whose "fault" it was. What we are concerned with is that the patient re-experienced something which he remembered from the past; and that the reconstruction, which in this case was not difficult, afforded considerable relief to the patient because it enabled him to gain a perspective on his difficulties and this he previously had not had.

While this example illustrates the bridge from the present to the past, the enactments in the transference displayed the past in the present. He re-created a situation in which his unremitting demands could never be satisfied or modified, and which inevitably had to evoke feelings of hopelessness, despair, utter isolation and emptiness. The analytic exploration and interpretation of the patient's current feeling states and defensive maneuvers, and the attempt to understand his current conflicts in terms of the early experiences he remembered, did not diminish his misery and dissatisfaction. Nor did this analytic work lessen the pressure of his demands for supplies from the analyst, but interpretations involving the patient's feeling states helped to crystallize his demands into oral cravings for unlimited and "continuously flowing" supplies of orange juice and sweets (candy).

At this point in treatment an attempt was made to reconstruct the unsatisfactory early feeding situation and the sudden weaning experience. It should be noted that in this reconstruction the therapist *avoided* focusing on the specific traumatic event, i.e., sudden loss of milk or breast, but attempted to catch and verbalize the affective significance and atmosphere of this whole period in his life. This is in keeping with Kris's and Anna Freud's views that experiences are molded into patterns and that the analyst deals with these patterns rather than with specific events.

Before examining the function of reconstructive interpretation in general, I wish to insert some brief comments on the special problems posed by so-called primary repression in relation to the reconstruction of *preverbal* experiences. Discussions of experiences of the preverbal stage always present particular problems because, as Hartmann (1958) has pointed out, the structure of the mental apparatus and the laws governing it are less familiar to us and we do not have enough experiential checks available for verification.

We assume that a child exposed to a traumatic experience will at a later stage in development have formed a memory structure with ideational and affective content, which can (at least theoretically) become "recoverable" as a memory of an experience. According to our classical theory, the recovery of such early forgotten memories mobilizes affects and creates the possibility of assimilating the experience in a different way. The "traumatic" experience which has hitherto found expression in a pathological reaction can now find new solutions. But can similar alterations be achieved with regard to preverbal experiences?

There are analysts (for example, Winnicott, M. Little) who claim to have devised techniques which reach the individual's earliest experiences. It is their belief that by encouraging regressive transference relationships they enable their patients to relive early affective experiences which can then be "corrected." They argue that the regression not only leads to a repetition of the past, but also affords the opportunity to relive the past in a more satisfactory way.

Anna Freud has often pointed out, in discussions of this kind, that classical psychoanalytic technique was devised not to *undo* experiences but to help the individual understand and deal with them internally. At Hampstead we maintain that we cannot change the problems, we can only change the solutions of the problem.

When we consider the aftereffects of an experience which the child had, or is having (and this applies to preverbal experiences as well), we must also take into account the effects that interpretations have on the mental apparatus of the child in the present, because interpretations which reconstruct the past are, after all, also new experiences.

While theoretically every subjective experience (in the sense of the German *Erlebnis*) leaves a memory trace which is in some way recoverable, one might with equal justification say that nothing is recoverable in its original form. The trace itself is, of course, never recoverable. What can be recovered is another experience structured by that memory trace. The recovery of a memory is in a sense like a perception, so that remembering something from the past is like *perceiving it anew*, in exactly the same way as an external perception of the same sort of event is perceived anew by the child when he is older. *Even ordinary remembering is thus a reconstruction of the past rather than a simple reproduction of the past.* In the same way as every percept is a construction, every memory is intrinsically a reconstruction—an achievement of the mental apparatus of the child. This is also in line with the views of Ernst Kris.

It follows from this that in the process of remembering in any form, the material of past experience is reorganized in a new way, albeit slightly. The new memory structures that are created will reflect the maturational and developmental level of the child's mental apparatus. Interpretations and reconstructions by the analyst inevitably enter into this reorganization as well, so that the child, by establishing causal relations in connection with the memory, *changes the content and structure of the memory*. He will be seeing it in a new way. This may be different from cases of traumatic war neuroses in adults, who, when they are treated by abreaction or catharsis, relive essentially the same traumatic experience. From this viewpoint we can say that reconstructions allow a drive derivative or other derivative (e.g., an omnipotent wish) to find new pathways in the form of a thought or a fantasy which acts as an organizer of experience. These new formations will in turn, through being subjected to the analytic process, lead to the emergence of less and less distorted derivatives and will facilitate unconscious content becoming conscious. But, and I want to stress this, repressed memories can never return entirely or exactly in their *original* form. Freud referred to this progressive aspect of the analytic process when he said (1937, p. 260f.): "The analyst finishes a piece of construction and communicates it to the subject of the analysis so that it may work upon him; he then constructs a further piece out of the fresh material pouring in upon him, deals with it in the same way and proceeds in this alternating fashion until the end."

This brings us to another conceptual problem, namely, whether "reconstructions" viewed in this way can be differentiated from other interpretations, except in a descriptive way. Freud (1937) commented that, if, in accounts of analytic technique, little is said about "constructions," it is because "interpretations" and their effects are spoken of instead. He then proceeded to suggest a distinction on the basis that "interpretation" applies to something one does to a single element in the material (such as an association or a parapraxis), whereas in "constructions" one lays before the patient a whole piece of his forgotten past. Hartmann (1958) makes a similar distinction between an interpretation which aims at establishing connections and "another level of cognitive interpretation [where] a great number of data . . . and a considerable amount of hypothetical thinking have to be introduced in order to come to a conclusion" (p. 135). Loewenstein (1951) speaks of dynamic and genetic interpretation, as does Kris (1956), who suggests that genetic interpretations should be depicted as a continuum ranging from archaic impulses related to preverbal and nonverbal ideations embedded in unconscious fantasies to those which establish a historical context and are based on inferences drawn from many sources in the analytic material (e.g., screen memories or recovered memories).

The distinction between interpretations and reconstructions may, as I have suggested, be useful from a descriptive point of view, but all interpretations are essentially reconstructions. Interpretations may be conceptualized as reconstructions of the present, in analogy to "constructions" or "reconstructions" of the past. Kris expresses a similar view when he says, "even the yesterday is part of the past" (p. 56). I would add that even the child's last unexpressed thought is part of the past. Even our interpretation of what is happening in the present session, however exact it may be, structures a previously unorganized experience, aspects of which have usually been unconscious.

The role of verbalization in the efficacy of interpretation and its contribution to the ego's method of adaptation have been much discussed in the psychoanalytic literature. Its importance for child-hood development, especially its function in promoting secondary process thinking, has been emphasized by Anny Katan (1961). Anna Freud (1965) has stressed the special significance of verbalization for children who enter analysis at an early age and for those who have severe delays, arrests or defects of ego development. We may focus here especially on the role that verbalization plays in organizing preverbal experiences into more comprehensible and meaningful ones. *In analysis, the putting of words to unorganized sensations, which might be part of early memories, creates new memory structures that replace the old ones. This is equally true for postverbal experiences.*

Loewald (1960) has given a beautiful description of the organizing role of the analyst's interpretations, which aptly applies to the problems I am discussing. He says:

> . . . the analyst structures and articulates . . . the material and the productions offered by the patient. If an interpretation of unconscious meanings is timely, the words by which this meaning is expressed are recognizable to the patient as expressions of what he experiences. They organize for him what was previously less organized and thus give him the 'distance' from himself which enables him to understand, to see, to put into words and to 'handle' what was previously not visible, understandable, speakable, tangible. . . . The analyst functions as a representative of a higher stage of organization and mediates this to the patient, in so far as the analyst's understanding is attuned to what is, and the way in which it is, in need of organization [p. 24].

Enactments or references to primitive bodily sensations and experiences that appear in the analytic material of children may often indicate to the analyst that such experiences are in need of organization through reconstruction of preverbal experiences.

I have previously stated that no reconstruction corresponds exactly to an experience the child has had, but I have not yet discussed the problem implicit in this statement: whether for this reason our "incorrect" or inexact reconstructions are therapeutically less useful or effective.

A reconstruction may be inexact, but, provided it satisfies certain criteria, it will have a therapeutic effect and further the analysis. In order to examine this problem we must look at the patient's responses to the reconstructions, not so much in terms of their being immediately accepted or rejected or ignored, but in the way in which they affect the subsequent analytic material and the subsequent course of the patient's development, including the resolution of conflicts.

For example, my 10-year-old patient "used" the reconstruction of his unsatisfactory early feeding experiences in a variety of ways: as a sign of my rejection (he brought his own supplies of candy the next day); as a challenge to me that I implied his mother was a bad mother; as an excuse to become even more demanding. But more important than any of these defensive responses was the one significant word he added to my reconstruction. In my attempt to get hold of his affective experiences I had linked his excessive demandingness with his feeling hungry and empty inside, to which he responded with: "You mean all deserted." This ushered in a wealth of material about the more recent past when he felt "all deserted" while waiting for his mother, always convinced that she would never return.

While he was working through this material in the transference and in current experiences outside the treatment, he periodically returned to his childhood memories of watching his parents quarreling and fighting, in a position of helpless panic. One gained the impression that these memories still carried the full impact of the "traumatic experiences" and were therefore constantly impinging on his current experience. This impression, stemming from the developmental approach, temporarily impeded the analyst's understanding of *the new significance* that now emerged in relation to this memory. As soon as his feeling of being "all deserted" by his fighting parents (and of being frightened and immobilized as a result of it) could be reconstructed, the memories decreased in importance and were subsequently only rarely referred to. The analysis entered a new phase.

What I am trying to demonstrate is that reconstructions must have an "intrapsychic fit" at any given point in the analytic work, and this can be achieved by picking up the affective elements (especially anxiety) in the material, so that the child can get a new perspective on something which previously had psychic reality for him.

By drawing the child's attention to previously unconscious feelings and ideas and by establishing links between his present concerns and these feelings or ideas that may have been conscious but isolated, we give the child insight, that is, enlarge his self-awareness. Thus reconstruction in child analysis functions primarily as a means of providing a conceptual framework to the child whereby he can understand his present experiences and dilemmas. Reconstruction also leads to a release of dammed-up impulses and affects and to their abreaction, but this function is relatively less important in children. This may be so because in children dammed-up impulses and affects can find expression in enactment or in some other mode that represents an adaptation the child has made to what has been defended against. It follows from this that the interpretative work with children is much more effective when it deals with the child's current interaction with his parents, his peers, and his feelings about himself. *Although in the transference past object relationships and experiences may be relived in some form, the interpretation of the transference aims at showing the child why he tends to function in a particular manner at the moment, and not at the reconstruction of the past,* but this may be brought in for purposes of adding conviction.

In the face of conflict the child's mental apparatus finds it very difficult to maintain its controls as well as its functioning at the highest level of maturity reached, as Anna Freud (1952) has stressed. She pointed out that in the immature personality the ego often does not stand firm under the pressure of instinctual regression, but regresses simultaneously. The regressed ego then becomes compliant toward the regressed id demands. Anna Freud emphasizes that this compliance mitigates the intensity of the child's internal conflict, but it produces instead arrests in development, infantilisms, failures in adaptation, and so forth.

The "compliant" aspects of the child's ego development may also facilitate a tendency to absorb the affects aroused by traumatic experiences and by other situations as well. Thus we may in child analysis be very much concerned with dissecting the child's adaptation to the pressures which he feels operate on him. The whole of this approach relates to the aim of child analysis, which at the Hampstead Clinic is to restore the child to the path of normal development. We see the child's difficulty and his symptoms as being a present adaptive solution which prevents his taking the next step in development, and the aim of our work is to allow him to take this step.

This approach may give us a basis for taking a pragmatic view of our interpretative interventions, which are aimed at enabling the child to resolve conflicts holding his development back, rather than aimed at giving him a complete and "true" insight into everything that happened in the past. This point is perhaps particularly underscored by the fact that young children, after they have completed their analysis, tend very quickly to forget what insights they have had, even though they have moved forward developmentally in a satisfactory way, and pathological conflicts have disappeared sufficiently for the move forward to take place.

As a final comment I should like to say that although the reader may not agree with what has been said, which I know is to some extent controversial and provocative, the main purpose of the paper really is to encourage us as child analysts to take a new look at the meaning of our technical interventions and the things we have previously taken for granted. I hope that, in spite of all that was said, we will all continue to get that feeling of satisfaction that usually follows a "good" reconstructive interpretation.

BIBLIOGRAPHY

Bergen, M. E. (1958), The Effect of Severe Trauma on a Four-Year-Old Child. *This Annual,* 13:407–429.

Breuer, J. & Freud, S. (1893–1895), Studies on Hysteria. *Standard Edition,* 2. London: Hogarth Press, 1955.

Erikson, E. H. (1950), *Childhood and Society.* New York: Norton.

Freud, A. (1951), Observations on Child Development. *This Annual,* 6:18–30.

— (1952), The Mutual Influences in the Development of Ego and Id: Introduction to the Discussion. *This Annual,* 7:42–50.

— (1965), *Normality and Pathology in Childhood.* New York: International Universities Press.

— (1971), The Infantile Neurosis: Genetic and Dynamic Considerations. *This Annual*, 26:79–90.

FREUD, S. (1937), Constructions in Analysis. *Standard Edition*, 23:255–269. London: Hogarth Press, 1964.

HARTMANN, H. (1958), Comments on the Scientific Aspects of Psychoanalysis. *This Annual*, 13:127–146.

HEINICKE, C. (1970), In Search of Supporting Evidence for Reconstructions Formulated during a Child Psychoanalysis. *Reiss-Davis Clin. Bull.*, 7:92–110.

KATAN, A. (1961), Some Thoughts about the Role of Verbalization in Early Childhood. *This Annual*, 16:184–188.

KRIS, E. (1956), The Recovery of Childhood Memories in Psychoanalysis. *This Annual*, 11:54–88.

LOEWALD, H. W. (1960), On the Therapeutic Action of Psycho-Analysis. *Int. J. Psycho-Anal.*, 41:16–33.

LOEWENSTEIN, R. M. (1951), The Problem of Interpretation. *Psychoanal. Quart.*, 20:1–14.

A Study of the Separation-Individuation Process

And Its Possible Application to Borderline Phenomena in the Psychoanalytic Situation

MARGARET S. MAHLER, M.D., Sc.D. (Med.)

THE QUESTION OF THE KIND OF INFERENCES, IF ANY, THAT CAN BE drawn from preverbal material in and outside the psychoanalytic situation is a most controversial one. It is, I feel, a very interesting issue, yet quite difficult to deal with. Precisely because verbal

This presentation is partly based on that portion of research at the Masters Children's Center, New York, N.Y., which was sponsored by grant #MH 8238 of the N.I.M.H. of the P.H.S.; by the Foundation for Research in Psychoanalysis, Los Angeles, Calif.; the Strick Foundation, Philadelphia, Pa.; and quite recently by the Foundations Fund for Research in Psychiatry, New Haven, Conn. The research study was done in association with John B. McDevitt, M.D. and Mrs. Anni Bergman; with the assistance of Mrs. Emmagene Kamaiko, Laura Salchow, and Margaret Hawkins, and in consultation with Fred Pine, Ph.D., research psychologist.

This paper was presented as the Twentieth Freud Anniversary Lecture on April 14, 1970. Its extended version will be published in The Freud Anniversary Lecture Series of The New York Psychoanalytic Institute by International Universities Press, Inc., New York.

means lend themselves only very poorly to the translation of such material, most researchers have seen fit to create a new language, often filled with metaphors, in order to communicate their findings to others.

Early Development in Observational Research

Psychoanalytic observational research of the first years of life touches on the essence of reconstruction and on the problem of coenesthetic empathy, both so essential for the clinical efficiency of psychoanalysis.

At one end of the spectrum of opinion on these questions stand those who believe in innate, complex oedipal fantasies, those who, like Melanie Klein and her followers, assume and rely on earliest extrauterine (human) mental life. They believe in a quasi-phylogenetic memory, an inborn symbolic process. For them, no phenomenological, behavioral data can have sufficient validity to refute their *a priori* convictions about complex mental positions, such as the schizoid position in the fourth month of life, or the depressive position at 8 months.

At the other end of the spectrum stand those among us Freudian analysts who look with favor on stringent verbal and reconstructive evidence. We organize these on the basis of Freud's metapsychological constructs; yet some of us seem to accord preverbal material no right to serve as the basis for even the most cautious and tentative extension of our main body of hypotheses, unless these, too, be supported by reconstruction, that is to say, by clinical and, of course, predominantly verbal material.

Yet Freud's hope was that his fundamental body of theory—that truly monumental basis of clinical and theoretical work—would remain a *living heritage*. Even his genius could not work out every detail in one lifetime; these, added bit by bit, should eventually coalesce to form a general psychology.

Instead of entering into the controversy on whether or not preverbal infant observation has any validity for drawing inferences about the evolution of *intrapsychic* human life, I would like to present an account of one such effort. I do so in order to show what possible inferences were permitted from some of the repetitive, fairly regularly occurring clusterings of the data, which we accumulated around our tentative working hypotheses.

I will put aside the history of my work and descriptions of our methods and proceed to some observations made, and inferences drawn, from my more recent studies at the Masters Children's Center and in the psychoanalytic situation.

Beyond the conceptualization of the subphases of the separation-individuation[1] process, we have made additional observations relevant to substantive issues of the study. They are repetitive, if not ubiquitous, age-specific clusterings of behavioral sequences and affective reactions found in our children between 5 and 36 months of age. These were polarized by the mother-child interaction during their coenesthetic[2] period of life, and continued in individually more and more differentiated sequences and reactions into the period Spitz has called the "diacritic organization." [3]

First Substantive Issue: We observed the bridge function of mother-related parts of the familiar inanimate surroundings of our nursery of our infants—for example, the chair on which mother habitually sat or her handbag and so on. The infant, within a certain age span, turned to these objects as substitutes for the mother when she left the room, rather than to another adult. This mechanism we recognized as a transitional phenomenon between Kestenberg's (1971) organ-object bridges, Winnicott's (1953) transitional, and Greenacre's (1969, 1970) fetishlike objects.

Second Substantive Issue: We observed in life and on film a differential, truly coenesthetic response to the *warmth* and *turgor,* to the "feel" of the human body (molding phenomena [Mahler and La Perriere, 1965], tactile and visual exploration of the human face and similar behaviors) quite different from their handling of inanimate objects (Mahler and McDevitt, 1968). The inverted

---

[1] I owe the term *separation-individuation* to Dr. Annemarie Weil's suggestion to point out clearly the two aspects of this intrapsychic process (personal communication, 1954).

[2] *Coenesthesia* is defined in Drever's *Dictionary of Psychology* as: common sensibility, the total undifferentiated mass of sensations derived from the body as a whole, but more particularly, the internal organs.

[3] *Diacritic*—from the Greek—is "to distinguish, to separate across" (cf. Spitz, 1945).

and grossly distorted response to the animate and inanimate object world in psychosis was described by Sechehaye (1947), Mahler (1960), Searles (1960), and others.

Third Substantive Issue: Our data have indicated the importance of the "carrying power," as it were, of the young child's "confident expectation" (Benedek, 1938) as contrasted with some children's "basic mistrust," to use Erikson's term (1950). This we saw in some children as early as 6 or 7 months. We observed children of the same mother at comparable ages, one of whom showed minimal stranger anxiety and optimal basic trust; the other, increased stranger anxiety and a lack of basic trust.

One tries to understand these variations by way of the siblings' different endowment on the one hand and, on the other, through the prevalent emotional climate of the particular mother-infant relationship, as observed in their interaction and through interviews with the mother (cf. Weil, 1970).

This phenomenon of "confident expectation," as well as its opposite—more than optimal stranger anxiety and "basic mistrust" —contributes and relates to later attitudes in life, even though intervening drive and defense vicissitudes will, of course, greatly influence and may even change these patterns.

Fourth Substantive Issue: The basic mood, our study indicated, appeared to have its beginning as early as the last half of the second year. It seemed to derive substantially from this very "basic trust" or, in contrast, from "basic mistrust"; as I have described (1966), it also derived from a too sudden deflation of the obligatory infantile belief in the own and the borrowed magic omnipotence (Jacobson, 1953).

Our research design had built into it brief, passive separation experiences, experiments as it were. Once a week, a senior worker assigned to a particular mother-child pair interviewed the mother in a room outside the nursery.

From the infant's reactions to these brief separations I believe that we were able to judge fairly how the infant's "need" became a "wish" in Max Schur's sense (1966). Our data indicated the phenomenological concomitants of the development from an "unspecific craving" to the specific "object-bound" affect of "longing" (Mahler, 1961, 1963). This seemed to occur gradually and had, at first, a "waxing and waning" quality. It had its beginnings at the height of bodily differentiation from the love object and continued into the practicing period of 10 to 15 months. At that age "longing" is indicated by the phenomenon of *"low-keyedness"* during brief separations. This culminates—during the *rapprochement* period at 15 to 25 months—in impressive, individually different reactions to mother's absences, which are much more specific and readable.

The smoothly separating and individuating toddler easily finds solace in his rapidly developing ego functions. The child concentrates on practicing mastery of his own skills and autonomous capacities.

During this practicing subphase of separation-individuation, one can occasionally see with particular clarity that the intrapsychic process of separation and individuation runs on two intertwined, but not always synchronized developmental tracks: one is *individuation*—the evolution of intrapsychic autonomy; the other is the intrapsychic *separation* process, which runs along the track of differentiation, distancing, boundary-structuring, and disengagement from mother.

As I indicated elsewhere, in a study such as ours, one learns most when elements of the process are "out of kilter."

Brief Comparative Developmental Histories of Barney and Sammy

I shall illustrate this with two brief vignettes.

Barney, whose maturational process enabled him to achieve upright locomotion precociously at 9 months of age, had the opportunity, by endowment and by the nature of the mother-child relationship, to take into and integrate in his early ego structure certain patterns of the mother-child relationship, and eject, i.e., externalize, others. He also seemed to have ample opportunity to emulate and eventually to identify with his father, who was very much a hero for him by the last half of the second year. Barney's mother emphasized this again and again.

Barney's early darting away from his mother with the expectation of being chased by her had interesting components of the mother-child as well as of the father-child relationship.

The contrasting mother-child pair, *Sammy* and his mother, had a greatly prolonged symbiotic and—on the mother's part—parasitic relationship. His mother breast-fed Sammy for 1½ years. Both parents kept him in continual dependency. Confined to a small area by his own, partly constitutional, partly environmental, delay in locomotor capacity, Sammy made the most extensive use of his visibly emerging perceptive, cognitive, and prehensile faculties. He occupied and amused himself alone in our playpen for long periods of time when his mother was out of the room. This he did at an age when children of comparable age would vigorously protest against such confinement. He willingly engaged others and accepted their active comforting, which other children would not. He did not show any sign of low-keyedness or of specific longing at the age at which we observed such phenomena in other children. (Such behavior appeared delayed in Sammy.)

The normal child's early defensive struggle against interferences with his autonomy was, however, amply exemplified by Sammy. He valiantly struggled, from an early age, in fact, from the fifth month on and attempted to extricate himself from the smothering grip of his mother (cf. Spock, 1963).

Most of the time children in the practicing period appeared relatively elated and self-sufficient. They became low-keyed only when they became aware that mother was absent from the room. In those instances their gestural and performance motility slowed down, their interest in their surroundings diminished; they appeared to be preoccupied with inwardly concentrated attention, with what Rubinfine (1961) called "imaging." This we were permitted to assume from behavioral evidence: (1) when another person than the mother actively tried to comfort the child, he would lose his intrapsychic balance and burst into tears; and, of course, also from (2) the child's reaction to reunion with the briefly absent mother. The low-keyedness and apparent "imaging" of mother, I tend to interpret as the attempt to hold on to a state of mind that Sandler et al. (1963) have termed "the ideal state of self." This seems to consist of a symbiotic closeness, completeness, a coenesthetically sensed dual unity with mother.

Separation Anxiety

Some children transiently appeared quite overwhelmed by fear of object loss, so that the "ego-filtered affect of longing" was in danger of very abruptly turning into desperate crying. This was the case with Barney for a short time at a period when his "individuation" had not yet caught up with his maturational spurt of locomotion, serving separation. He was unable to cope emotionally, for a while, with the experience of the self-induced separations from mother in space. He was visibly bewildered when he hurt himself and noticed that his mother was not, automatically, close.

Our data, in their rich detail, have unmistakably shown regularly occurring combinations of factors from which we were permitted to conclude that there was a dawning awareness that the still-symbiotic mothering half of the self was missed. The ensuing behavior of low-keyedness had different shadings in individual children compared with each other and with themselves over time. In a paper written with McDevitt (1968) I likened this initial "low-keyedness" with the "conservation-withdrawal" of monkeys as described by Charles Kaufman and L. A. Rosenblum (1967).

This longing for the state of well-being and unity, or closeness, with mother we found peculiarly lacking in children whose symbiotic relationship had been an unduly prolonged or a disturbed one: in Sammy, who had an exaggeratedly close, parasitic symbiosis with his mother; in another child, a little girl (Harriet), in whom the mother-infant relationship was what Robert Fliess (1961) termed *a*-symbiotic. It seemed diminished and irregular in children in whom the symbiotic relationship with mother was marred by the unpredictability and impulsivity of a partly engulfing and partly rejecting mother.

In the course of the practicing period, we were impressed by the tremendously exhilarating, truly dramatic effect that upright locomotion had on the hitherto also very busy quadruped infant's general mood! I became aware of its importance for the achievement of the "psychological birth experience," the "hatching," through unexpected, regularly occurring observations of behavioral sequences, comparing them with Phyllis Greenacre's work (1957) on the childhood of the artist. It seemed to me that most practicing toddlers had a "love affair with the world" as well!

This exhilaration occurred later than usual in those cases where the ascendancy of the child's free locomotor capacity was delayed. Thus, this phenomenon seemed definitely connected with and dependent on the function of free locomotor activity of the ego.

With this acquisition of exhilarating upright, free locomotion and the closely following attainment of that stage of cognitive development that Piaget (1936) regards as the beginning of representational intelligence, the human being had emerged as a separate and autonomous being. These two powerful "organizers" (Spitz, 1959) seem to be the midwives of *psychological birth*. With this "hatching" process the toddler reaches the first level of identity, that of being a separate individual entity (Mahler, 1957).

Now that the child has come to be more aware of his separate self, he has once again an increased need to seek closeness with mother. This had been, so to speak, held in abeyance throughout the practicing period. That is why I gave this subphase the name *rapprochement*.

Importance of the Emotional Availability of Mother and Disengagement from Her in the Rapprochement Subphase

One cannot emphasize too strongly the importance of the optimal emotional availability of the mother during this subphase. The value of the father in this period has been stressed by Loewald (1951), Greenacre (1966), and Abelin (1971).

The refueling type of bodily approach described by Furer,[4] which characterized the practicing infant, was now replaced in the period between 15 and 25 months by interaction of toddler and mother on a much higher level; symbolic language, vocal and other intercommunications, as well as play became increasingly prominent (Galenson, 1971).

[4] Personal communication.

We observed separation reactions in all our children during this rapprochement subphase. And I would venture the hypothesis that it is in those children whose separation reactions are characterized by moderate and ego-filtered affects, in which the libidinal valence—love instead of aggression—predominated, that subsequent development is more likely to be favorable.

Through this rapprochement process, the sense of identity, the self representation as distinct from the object representation, begins to become consolidated.

Two characteristic patterns of behavior—the shadowing of mother and the darting away from her with the expectation of being chased and swept into her arms—indicate the toddler's wish for reunion with the love object, and, side-by-side with this, also a fear of re-engulfment. One can continually observe the warding-off pattern against impingement upon the toddler's recently achieved autonomy. Moreover, the incipient fear of loss of love represents an element of the conflict on the way to internalization. Some toddlers of rapprochement age already seem to be rather sensitive to disapproval. Autonomy is defended by the "no" as well as by the increased aggression and negativism of the anal phase. (One is reminded of Anna Freud's classic paper on negativism and emotional surrender [1951].)

In most mother-toddler pairs, these rapprochement conflicts, which McDevitt calls the *rapprochement crises,* do finally come to an end. This is helped by the developmental spurt of the conflict-free parts of the autonomous ego (Hartmann, 1939). These then, in the third year, help the child in his progress toward the attainment of libidinal object constancy, in Hartmann's sense (1952).

During the time of normal symbiosis, the narcissistically fused object is felt to be "good," i.e., in harmony with the symbiotic self, so that primary identification takes place under a positive valence of love. Later on, after separation, the child may have encountered "bad," frustrating, unpleasurable, even frightening experiences in his interaction with mother and "other," so that the image of the object may have assumed a "negative emotional valence" (Heimann, 1966).

The Role of Aggression and the Defense Mechanism of Splitting the Object World into "Good" and "Bad"

The less gradually the intrapsychic separation-individuation process takes place, and the less the modulating, negotiating function of the ego gains ascendancy, the greater the extent to which the object remains an unassimilated foreign body, a "bad" introject in the intrapsychic emotional economy. In the effort to eject this "bad" introject, derivatives of the aggressive drive come into play and there seems to develop an increased proclivity to identify with, or to confuse, the self representation with the "bad" introject. If this situation prevails during the rapprochement subphase, then aggression may be unleashed in such a way as to inundate or sweep away the "good" object, and with it the "good" self representation. This would be indicated by early, severe temper tantrums, for example, in children in whom the too sudden and painful realization of their helplessness results in the too abrupt deflation of their previous sense of their own and shared magic omnipotence (in Edith Jacobson's sense, 1964).

I observed many of our normal children recoil, or show signs that had to be interpreted as a kind of erotized fear, on being cornered by an adult who wanted to seek, often playfully, bodily contact with the child. This seemed to be felt as overwhelming by the toddler because of the adult's sheer bodily size and strength.

These behaviors remind us of the fear of re-engulfment by the by-then already somehow contaminated, dangerous "mother of separation" in whose omnipotence the child still believes, but who does not seem to let him share in her omnipotence anymore.

There were other early constellations of variables, which may represent fixation points for pathological regression, such as the precocious differentiation of a "false self" (Winnicott, 1965) by a little girl (Heather), who played peek-a-boo with herself when her mother rejected her because she was a late walker; or the narcissistic hypercathexis of the body ego in the case of Harriet, a child whose mother did not seem to have enough tender emotion for her children, but rather overstimulated them. All these constellations of factors are possible contributories to borderline features in personality development.

In incipient infantile neurosis, conflict is indicated by coercive behaviors directed toward the mother, designed to force her to function as the child's omnipotent extension. This alternates with signs of desperate clinging. In other words, in those children with less than optimal development, the ambivalence conflict is discernible during the rapprochement subphase in rapidly alternating clinging and increased negativistic behaviors. This may be in some cases a reflection of the fact that the child has split the object world, more permanently than is optimal, into "good" and "bad." By means of this splitting, the "good" object is defended against the derivatives of the aggressive drive.

These mechanisms, coercion and splitting of the object world, are characteristic in most cases of borderline transference. We were able to study these in the verbal, primary process material of a few children at the end of their second and during their third year of life. These mechanisms, along with the problem of finding what the late Maurice Bouvet (1958) described as the "optimal distance," may prevail as early as in the fourth subphase of separation-individuation at a time when "libidinal object constancy" should have been achieved and separation reactions be receding.

Disturbances during the rapprochement subphase are likely to reappear in much more definite and individually different forms during the final phase of that process in which a unified self representation should become demarcated from a blended and integrated object representation.

The clinical outcome of these rapprochement crises will be determined by: (1) the development toward libidinal object constancy; (2) the quantity and quality of later disappointments (stress traumata); (3) possible shock traumata; (4) the degree of castration anxiety; (5) the fate of the oedipus complex; and (6) the developmental crises of adolescence—all of which function within the context of the individual's constitutional endowment.

Two Important Findings

During the years of our data collection, we classified and sorted the material and ordered it into distinct categories that were relevant to our working hypotheses.

One interesting yield of our data processing was the finding that, from 16 or 17 months on, the data no longer "fit" comfortably into discrete categories. It began to appear increasingly arbitrary to describe any one item of behavior without referring to more and more of the total array of behaviors that were to be seen in the child at a particular period of time. It seemed that the behavior of the child was becoming increasingly integrated.

That also meant that early affectomotor and preverbal sensorimotor patterns had already been integrated by the middle of the second year, solidly enough, so that derivatives could not be reconstructively traced back, step-by-step, by means of deduction. In other words, we learned inductively that in most individuals the derivatives of the early, preverbal, sensorimotor period became integrated into character structure.

The second observation during data processing had to do with sex differences. Until this point, the children often seemed to us to fit into various subgroups from the separation-individuation point of view—subgroups containing both boys and girls. But now while, on the one hand, the complexity of the children made it difficult to group them, on the other hand, those common traits that existed were suggestive of a growing trend toward sexual differentiation and identity formation.

In average development, as I indicated in my Brill Memorial Lecture (1963), the progressive forces of the growing ego are astonishingly successful. Often they tend to even out most of the discrepancies and minor deviations.

It is precisely the deficiencies of integration and internalization which will leave residua and thus may manifest themselves in borderline mechanisms, which indicate a degree of failure of the synthetic function of the ego.

Early Development Reconstructed

I should emphasize, however, as others and I myself have done before, that in terms of reconstruction in the psychoanalytic situation in general, none of the phenomena that can be reconstructed from unintegrated residua will be an equivalent repetition, a replica as it were, of early developmental sequences of the preverbal phase.

One must expect that reconstructions will always contain telescoped screen memories and defense formations that have been altered by subsequent progressive development, as well as by regressive changes in the instinctual drives, in the ego, and in the superego. These may, or may not, make their appearance in the verbal and nonverbal material.

For many borderline phenomena, one can apply what is learned from observation, not so much to content as to general behaviors and attitudes of the patient in the psychoanalytic situation, that is to say, to certain configurations, persistent transference or acting-out patterns which seem to be the outcome of unresolved conflicts of the separation-individuation process.

My intention, at first, was to establish in this paper a linking up, in neat detail, of the described substantive issues with specific aspects of borderline phenomena shown by child and adult patients in the psychoanalytic situation. But I have come to be more and more convinced that there is no "direct line" from the deductive use of borderline phenomena to one or another substantive finding of observational research.

It cannot be accidental, however, that in the literature it is the borderline pathology that authors single out as paradigmatic of fixation or regression, traceable to certain aspects of the formative events of the separation and individuation process (Kohut, 1966; Tartakoff, 1966; Kernberg, 1967; Frijling-Schreuder, 1969).

The literature abounds in papers and symposia dealing with the sequelae of the failure of internalization, increased separation anxiety, and other clinical signs that indicate, for example, the following: that the blending and synthesis of "good" and "bad" self and object images have not been achieved; that ego-filtered affects have become inundated by surplus unneutralized aggression; that delusions of omnipotence alternate with utter dependency and self denigration; that the body image has become or remains suffused with unneutralized id-related erogeneity and aggressive, pent-up body feelings, and so on.

Before I proceed to my case illustration, I would like to single out two main additional propositions which seem to me relevant for the understanding of borderline phenomena in the psychoanalytic situation. One is the importance of reconciliation and thus of integration of the image of the erstwhile "good" symbiotic mother, whom we long for "from the cradle on to the grave," this image to become blended with the representation of the ambivalently loved—dangerous because potentially re-engulfing—"mother after separation."

I also wish to point out my impression—just an impression—gained of the importance of the preoedipal father's role in the sample that we have studied. We gained the impression that he was not only the "awakener from sleep" (Lewin, 1952), but also the protector from the by-then, in so many cases, contaminated (Kris, 1954), potentially overwhelming "mother of separation."

The second proposition refers to the erogeneity of the body image, its suffusion with narcissistic cathexis (Schur, 1955). This seems to be due to a disturbed cathectic balance of libido distribution between the self and the object. I found a group of borderline phenomena which seems to be related to heightened body narcissism, focal and diffuse erogeneity of the body image, prevalent in many borderline features of male and female patients alike.

If there was major failure of integration during the first three subphases of separation-individuation, particularly on the level of gender identity, the child might not have taken autonomous, representationally clearly separated possession of his or her own bodily self, this partly because he or she did not experience the mother's gradual relinquishment of her possession of the toddler's body (Anna Freud, 1952, 1953; Hoffer, 1950a, 1950b; Greenson, 1945). Such male and female patients alike will ever so often act out in the transference and in life, especially in marriage, the unconscious role of a cherished or rejected part of the parent's hypothetical body-self ideal, or treat the spouse's body as a cherished or rejected organ of their own self (Stein, 1956).

Let me cite only one example of borderline phenomena in the psychoanalytic situation.

Mr. A., an unmarried man in his late 20s, and an only child, was one of those patients who demonstrated as well as unconsciously acted out man's eternal search for the "good symbiotic mother," so as to latch on to her, to be united with her, to be "safe" with her. The basic importance of this archaic mechanism has been described by the Hungarian analyst Imre Hermann (1936). In many cases the so-called primordial transference (Stone, 1961) is found to contain this basic longing for reunion with the symbiotic mother—with the search for her in fantasy after intrapsychic separation had severed the tie with her.

My patient, Mr. A., after a period of analysis, during which he occasionally complained bitterly that he could not feel close to or relate to the analyst, or to anybody else, gave vent to his great resentment, and every so often his rage against his superiors, his contemporaries, his father, his mother, and of course also his analyst. They had all "let him down; they just expected too much of him." His mother, in particular, was impossible to please, she was unloving, undemonstrative, and so on. His anger was readily turned back upon the self.

In the midst of these "grievance sessions," in which self-accusations and self-denigration played just as prominent a role as his complaints about people, there were by contrast, but only on rare occasions, hours in which he saw the object world and himself in a rather rosy light. On those days his grandiose fantasies (Kohut, 1968) easily came through, and his transference feelings swung from despondency and self-denigration to childlike admiration for and unqualified overestimation of others—particularly his analyst (Greenacre, 1966). In real life he showed a more adequate evaluation of his real worth and of his truly excellent endowment, but in his transference neurosis his mood swings were extreme, as was his belief in his own magic omnipotence and that of analysis itself, although both collapsed from one day to another (We owe the description of this mechanism to Edith Jacobson, 1953, 1957, 1964, 1967).

During a long stretch of analysis, two screen memories stood out. I believe that these will be better conveyed if they are interwoven with and discussed in the light of the working-through process.

In one of these all-too-rare "good hours" (Kris, 1956), the patient brought out—this time with an amazing array of rather libidinally cathected strong affects dominated by muted anxiety and longing —the helplessness and misery of the episodes that we knew so well as screen memories: his helplessness and lonesome desperation when as a schoolboy he had been wheeled away from his parents into the operating room and another traumatic episode when he had been banished from the parental bed.

The impact of his upsurging affects was connected in the transference with his apprehension about being taken from and thus losing the analyst by the demands of his job.

He indicated that when he was lying on the couch, he would feel himself floating far away into space. He associated this feeling with those he had had when he was anaesthesized and also with man's flight into space away from his safe anchorage on earth. Both groups of associations shook him up considerably. At the end of the hour he seemed to be literally collapsed and miserable. In spite of his tall, imposing stature he became little more than a small heap of misery—an abandoned child. His body narcissism was greatly increased, and counterphobic mechanisms became prominent as a way of fending off his hypochondriacal preoccupations.

In one of the succeeding hours, the patient, in one of his characteristic mood swings, announced that he definitely wanted to sit up; he said this with what was for him unusual determination. "When I lie down, I get this floating feeling again, as if I am floating far away from you into space." The feeling he experienced during anaesthesia, of the stars and rockets overhead falling upon him, piercing his skin, was related to the prickly feeling in his limbs that he had felt before falling asleep at the onset of anaesthesia. He considered man's ambition to land on another planet to be the culmination of his detachment from earth, a demonstration of the possibility that man would never achieve anchorage again.

These fantasies were associated with the other affect-laden screen memory as well: his mother, who had until then allowed him to snuggle up to her and occupy his father's bed, had told him one day that he was now too big a boy for such intimacy. He insisted that this had occurred when he was not yet 3 years old.

The predominant nightly fear of his early childhood had reappeared during his anaesthesia. There was the little dark man of his early nightmares, sitting on his shoulder, grinning unmercifully and thus indicating that "he was about to kidnap me." He desperately wanted his father—not his mother—to come to his rescue with a flashlight, as he had indeed done during the patient's early childhood, so as to dispel his son's night terrors.

During the hour in which he sat up, the patient, with averted gaze, expressed his past longing to throw his arms around his mother's neck and to be told by her that everything will be all right! He now felt the same way about his analyst, and he dreaded, when lying down, the vivid sensation that he was about to float away into space. At times, he said, the distance between the analyst and himself became too threatening.

Fear of the grinning, dark little man, who had perched on his shoulder during anaesthesia, seemed to have originated at the height of the phallic phase; it occurred coincidentally with or subsequently to the time when he had been banned by his mother from his snuggling position beside her. The fear of the little dark man was, of course, overdetermined. The homunculus symbolized his body as a whole, detached—banished—from his anchorage at his mother's body. It also symbolized many other elements.

Ever since that very early occurrence of being banished, the patient felt that he could not approach his mother; she was hard, forbidding, and critical of him. He could not share with her. He had had the urge to run away from home and search—but *for what* and *where?* Until his analysis during his adult life he used to wander aimlessly in the streets or take endless drives without any goal —away from people.

Fixation to the rapprochement subphase of development seemed to be quite obvious and convincing. His splitting of the object world was overdetermined; it consisted basically of searching for the good symbiotic mother as contrasted with the forbidding "bad" mother after separation. The bad castrated and castrating, yet phallic woman's forbidding quality was projected onto the "bad outside world," and his relationships with women were marred by a fear of being engulfed by them. The competitive, but admired, protective, "good" masculine world as represented by his father was pitted against this "bad mother of separation."

After this sequence of analysis he again brought out, but with attenuated guilt feelings, his death wishes concerning the "mother of separation." She was standing in the way of his pallike relationship to his father. This came to the fore with appropriate affective cathexis and could be connected by him with many of the subsequent vicissitudes of his instinctual drives, conflicts around the two levels of his identity, and the adverse fate of his originally quite adequate "basic trust" (Mahler, 1957).

His main primordial transference began to change when, after we had worked through his utter dependency needs, he exclaimed that, for the first time, he felt that the analyst was his friend!

I think these are the instances to which Winnicott (1969) was referring when he spoke of his patients' long-standing inability and then their final ability to use the object, the analyst, in the transference.

It was clear that the patient felt an intense longing for the symbiotic mother—not just the need-satisfying one—the symbiotic half of the self, the longing for the probably still coenesthetically remembered harmony of the dual-unity stage. Side by side with this there was the impotent rage, hatred that the patient felt toward the depreciated, castrated, and castrating "mother of separation." This was connected, of course, with the patient's feeling that sexuality was dirty and that because mother and father had indulged in it, the product would inevitably have to be an anal monster—the little dark homunculus—he himself.

It befits this Freud Anniversary Lecture that I conclude by quoting Freud himself, by citing from *Civilization and Its Discontents* (1930), which bears on his implicit recognition of the importance of the coenesthetic realm of human experiences.[5] He said:

---

[5] I am grateful to Dr. Kestenberg (1971) for drawing my attention to this quotation.

. . . through a deliberate direction of one's sensory activities and through suitable muscular action, one can differentiate between what is internal . . . and . . . what emanates from the outer world. In this way one makes the first step towards the introduction of the reality principle which is to dominate future development. This differentiation, of course, serves the practical purpose of enabling one to defend oneself against sensations of unpleasure which one actually feels or with which one is threatened. In order to fend off certain unpleasurable excitations arising from within, the ego can use no other methods than those which it uses against unpleasure coming from without. . . .

In this way then, the ego detaches itself from the external world. Or, to put it more correctly, originally the ego includes everything, later it separates off an external world from itself. Our present ego-feeling is, therefore, only a shrunken residue of a much more inclusive—indeed, an all-embracing—feeling which corresponded to a more intimate bond between the ego and the world about it. If we may assume that there are many people in whose mental life this primary ego-feeling has persisted to a greater or less degree, it would exist in them side by side with the narrower and more sharply demarcated ego-feeling of maturity, like a kind of counterpart to it. In that case, the ideational contents appropriate to it would be precisely those of limitlessness and of a bond with the universe—the same ideas with which my friend [Romain Rolland] elucidated the 'oceanic' feeling [p. 67f.].

BIBLIOGRAPHY

ABELIN, E. L. (1971), The Role of the Father in the Separation-Individuation Process. In: *Separation-Individuation,* ed. J. B. McDevitt & C. F. Settlage. New York: International Universities Press, pp. 229–252.

BENEDEK, T. (1938), Adaptation to Reality in Early Infancy. *Psychoanal. Quart.,* 7:200–214.

BOUVET, M. (1958), Technical Variations and the Concept of Distance. *Int. J. Psycho-Anal.,* 39:211–221.

ERIKSON, E. H. (1950), *Childhood and Society.* New York: Norton.

FLIESS, R. (1961), *Ego and Body Ego.* New York: Schulte Publishing Co.

FREUD, A. (1951), Notes on a Connection between the States of Negativism and of Emotional Surrender (*Hörigkeit*). *The Writings of Anna Freud*, 4:256–259. New York: International Universities Press, 1968.

— (1952), The Role of Bodily Illness in the Mental Life of Children. *This Annual*, 7:69–81.

— (1953), Some Remarks on Infant Observation. *This Annual*, 8:9–19.

FREUD, S. (1930), Civilization and Its Discontents. *Standard Edition*, 21:59–145. London: Hogarth Press, 1961.

FRIJLING-SCHREUDER, E. C. M. (1969), Borderline States in Children. *This Annual*, 24:307–327.

GALENSON, E. (1971), A Consideration of the Nature of Thought in Childhood Play. In: *Separation-Individuation*, ed. J. B. McDevitt & C. F. Settlage. New York: International Universities Press, pp. 41–59.

GREENACRE, P. (1957), The Childhood of the Artist: Libidinal Phase Development and Giftedness. *This Annual*, 12:47–72.

— (1966), Problems of Overidealization of the Analyst and of Analysis. *This Annual*, 21:193–212.

— (1969), The Fetish and the Transitional Object. *This Annual*, 24:144–164.

— (1970), The Transitional Object and the Fetish: With Special Reference to the Role of Illusion. *Int. J. Psycho-Anal.*, 51:447–456.

GREENSON, R. R. (1954), The Struggle against Identification. *J. Amer. Psychoanal. Assn.*, 2:200–217.

HARTMANN, H. (1939), *Ego Psychology and the Problem of Adaptation*. New York: International Universities Press, 1958.

— (1952), The Mutual Influences in the Development of Ego and Id. *This Annual*, 7:9–30.

HEIMANN, P. (1966), Comment on Dr Kernberg's Paper [Structural Derivatives of Object Relationships]. *Int. J. Psycho-Anal.*, 47:254–260.

HERMANN, I. (1936), *Sich Anklammern, Auf-Suche-Gehen. Int. Z. Psychoanal.*, 20:553–555.

HOFFER, W. (1950a), Oral Aggressiveness and Ego Development. *Int. J. Psycho-Anal.*, 31:156–160.

— (1950b), Development of the Body Ego. *This Annual*, 5:18–24.

JACOBSON, E. (1953), Contribution to the Metapsychology of Cyclothymic Depression. In: *Affective Disorders*, ed. P. Greenacre. New York: International Universities Press, pp. 49–83.

— (1957), On Normal and Pathological Moods: Their Nature and Functions. *This Annual*, 12:73–113.

— (1964), *The Self and the Object World*. New York: International Universities Press.

— (1967), *Psychotic Conflict and Reality*. New York: International Universities Press.

KAUFMAN, I. C. & ROSENBLUM, L. A. (1967), The Reaction to Separation in

Infant Monkeys: Anaclitic Depression and Conservation-Withdrawal. *Psychosom. Med.,* 29:648–675.

KERNBERG, O. (1967), Borderline Personality Organization. *J. Amer. Psychoanal. Assn.,* 15:641–685.

KESTENBERG, J. S. (1971), From Organ-Object Imagery to Self and Object Representation. In: *Separation-Individuation,* ed. J. B. McDevitt & C. F. Settlage. New York: International Universities Press, pp. 75–99.

KOHUT, H. (1966), Forms and Transformations of Narcissism. *J. Amer. Psychoanal. Assn.,* 14:243–272.

— (1968), The Psychoanalytic Treatment of Narcissistic Personality Disorders: Outline of a Systematic Approach. *This Annual,* 23:86–113.

KRIS, E. (1954), Discussion of paper, On Symbiotic Child Psychosis, by M. S. Mahler & B. Gosliner, at the New York Psychoanalytic Society.

— (1956), On Some Vicissitudes of Insight in Psycho-Analysis. *Int. J. Psycho-Anal.,* 37:445–455.

LEWIN, B. D. (1952), Phobic Symptoms and Dream Interpretation. *Psychoanal. Quart.,* 21:295–322.

LOEWALD, H. W. (1951), Ego and Reality. *Int. J. Psycho-Anal.,* 32:10–18.

MAHLER, M. S. (1957), On Two Crucial Phases of Integration of the Sense of Identity: Separation-Individuation and Sexual Identity. Abstr. in: Panel on Problems of Identity, rep. D. L. Rubinfine. *J. Amer. Psychoanal. Assn.,* 6:131–142, 1958.

— (1960), Symposium on Psychotic Object Relationships: III. Perceptual De-Differentiation and Psychotic 'Object Relationship.' *Int. J. Psycho-Anal.,* 41:548–553.

— (1961), On Sadness and Grief in Infancy and Childhood: Loss and Restoration of the Symbiotic Love Object. *This Annual,* 16:332–351.

— (1963), Thoughts about Development and Individuation. *This Annual,* 18:307–324.

— (1966), Notes on the Development of Basic Moods: The Depressive Affect. In: *Psychoanalysis—A General Psychology,* ed. R. M. Loewenstein, L. M. Newman, M. Schur, & A. J. Solnit. New York: International Universities Press, pp. 152–168.

— & LA PERRIERE, K. (1965), Mother-Child Interaction during Separation-Individuation. *Psychoanal. Quart.,* 34:483–498.

— & McDEVITT, J. B. (1968), Observations on Adaptation and Defense *in statu nascendi. Psychoanal. Quart.,* 37:1–21.

PIAGET, J. (1936), *The Origins of Intelligence in Children.* New York: International Universities Press, 1952.

RUBINFINE, D. L. (1961), Perception, Reality Testing, and Symbolism. *This Annual,* 16:73–89.

SANDLER, J., HOLDER, A., & MEERS, D. (1963), The Ego Ideal and the Ideal Self. *This Annual,* 18:139–158.

SCHUR, M. (1955), Comments on the Metapsychology of Somatization. *This Annual,* 10:119–164.

— (1966), *The Id and the Regulatory Principles of Mental Functioning.* New York: International Universities Press.

SEARLES, H. F. (1960), *The Nonhuman Environment.* New York: International Universities Press.

SECHEHAYE, M. A. (1947), *Symbolic Realization: A New Method of Psychotherapy Applied to a Case of Schizophrenia.* New York: International Universities Press, 1951.

SPITZ, R. A. (1945), Diacritic and Coenesthetic Organizations. *Psychoanal. Rev.,* 32:146–162.

— (1959), *A Genetic Field Theory of Ego Formation.* New York: International Universities Press.

SPOCK, B. (1963), The Striving for Autonomy and Regressive Object Relationships. *This Annual,* 18:361–364.

STEIN, M. (1956), The Marriage Bond. *Psychoanal. Quart.,* 25:238–259.

STONE, L. (1961), *The Psychoanalytic Situation.* New York: International Universities Press.

TARTAKOFF, H. H. (1966), The Normal Personality in Our Culture and the Nobel Prize Complex. In: *Psychoanalysis—A General Psychology,* ed. R. M. Loewenstein, L. M. Newman, M. Schur, & A. J. Solnit. New York: International Universities Press, pp. 222–252.

WAELDER, R. (1930), The Principle of Multiple Function. *Psychoanal. Quart.,* 5:45–62, 1936.

— (1963), Psychic Determinism and the Possibility of Predictions. *Psychoanal. Quart.,* 32:15–42.

WEIL, A. P. (1970), The Basic Core. *This Annual,* 25:442–460.

WINNICOTT, D. W. (1953), Transitional Objects and Transitional Phenomena. *Int. J. Psycho-Anal.,* 34:89–97.

— (1965), *The Maturational Processes and the Facilitating Environment.* New York: International Universities Press.

— (1969), The Use of an Object. *Int. J. Psycho-Anal.,* 50:711–716.

The Decision-Making Process

A Contribution from Psychoanalysis

LEO RANGELL, M.D.

IN THE PAST DECADE OR SO THERE HAS COME TO EXIST A VAST BODY
of literature on what is called "decision theory." Its borders are
diffuse and ill defined, the number of titles overwhelming, and
the areas of knowledge which contribute to it are many and scattered. Deriving its original impetus from a motivation of sales-
manship, the theoretical literature on decision has remained intimately attached to hard questions of practical application in
business, commercial, and military life. Until today it is more
abundant in the journals of mathematics, economics, business,
and applied statistics than in the behavioral sciences, is part of

The Fifth Annual Freud Anniversary Lecture of The Psychoanalytic Association
of New York, presented at the New York Academy of Medicine, New York, May
18, 1970.

game theory, but has also found its way into psychology, philosophy, and sociology.

Psychoanalysis, however, is conspicuously not represented. In the author index of a recent survey on decision-making (Edwards and Tversky, 1967), of some 500 listed authors, Freud's name does not appear, nor, to my knowledge, does that of any other psychoanalyst. Although recently lip service has begun to be paid to the need for "a dynamic decision theory," such theory remains "static" and "ahistorical," and "decision theorists look to the current situation, rather than to the past experiences of the decider, for the variables that control decision" (Edwards and Tversky, 1967, p. 8).

This is not to say, however, that we are excluded from without. The same lacuna is curiously evident within the psychoanalytic literature. "Decision" does not appear in the subject indices of our journals, in any of the *Annual Surveys of Psychoanalysis* in the past 20 years, nor is it a familiar title or subject in our scientific panels or discussions. Close in the alphabet to "defense," the latter generally occupies a half page to a page of listings, with no listing of any contribution to "decision-making." Yet the institution of defense requires a decision.

It is obvious that a lag is in evidence and that decision-making has a deep root in the unconscious and the genetic past, which brings it into the center of the domain of psychoanalysis.[1] I would like in this presentation to begin to fill this lacuna and to add the psychoanalytic view to this crucial aspect of human psychic activity.

Thinking about how best to approach this topic, I was reminded of facing similar problems in connection with a psychoanalytic study of "friendship" (Rangell, 1963a). There is an obvious parallel: friendship is to object relations what decision-making is to general psychic activity. Both constitute what I called then "the psychological sea or air around us." Both seem to be everywhere, occupy the very interstices of psychic life, yet are usually looked through rather than at.

To bring the subject into focus, I shall start with a clinical situation. As is often the case in psychoanalysis, psychic functions

---

[1] Mathematicians and engineers call what comes from here "noise" in the system! (Swets, 1967).

come to be best understood by studying instances of their break-down. To understand decision-making I shall therefore turn to a case which is mainly one of indecision. Problems of decision-making occur perhaps in all psychoanalytic cases, but in some they are the central issue. In the case to be presented, indecision raged as the central feature, both in the patient's life and during the psychoanalytic process.

Case Illustration

Mr. A. came to the analyst because his wife, to whom he had been married for 10 years, was pregnant, about which he was in a state of severe anxiety and panic. One of the conditions of the marriage on his part had been an agreement not to have children. This was not merely a matter of preference or predilection, but his aversion to children had a phobic intensity. He took every precaution and watched every movement during the marriage to carry out this prerequisite. His wife, in contrast, used every guile and trick and many ingenuous maneuvers to try to bring a pregnancy about. She had managed, in the most creative ways, to become pregnant three or four times, but each time had conveniently miscarried, probably deliberately and mainly to please him—not out of love and consideration, but out of awe, fear, and a deep respect for the intensity of his fear and determination. Now she was pregnant again, but on this occasion she seemed to be determined to keep it. By this time he was too guilty and ambivalent to stop it. The result was severe anxiety and his move to come into analysis to enable him to face what was to come.

Almost as soon as he started, his wife miscarried again. The patient's anxiety ceased at once, but his analysis continued and settled down to a natural and unhurried course. What gradually unfolded was a chronic, relentless, and paralyzing indecision, present virtually throughout his life, coupled with an incapacity to carry anything through to completion. The pervasiveness of these traits was evident centrally and alternately in the two major areas of psychic activity, the history of his love and work.

Mr. A. had married his wife after going with her for some time when she told him she was pregnant. He did not check or wait, just married her secretly out of town before a Justice of the Peace, because he knew that otherwise he would never decide to marry her or anyone else. He continued, however, to live with his parents for a year without telling them, trying to decide how to do so. He remembered finally telling his father, expecting him to break down at the news of the marriage. Instead, the father seemed happy and said, "We'll have to get you an apartment," at which the patient broke into tears. Similar episodes took place when he successively informed his mother and his brother.

There followed then all the years of his determination not to father a child, for which he gave a host of rationalizations and spurious reasons, all boiling down to a severe anxiety about becoming committed any further. Parenthood would make his choice irreversible. The effect of this attitude on this couple's sexual and object relatedness can easily be imagined. Bitterness, ambivalence, arguments, and chaos ensued, with each chasing and running away from the other. She would chase him and he would run, and then she would walk away and he would chase her. A chronic, mutually teasing and taunting, sadomasochistic relationship developed from which neither would go forward nor retreat. He repeatedly mistreated her, and she railed against him in return, and both were filled alternately with complaints and remorse. His attitudes toward her vacillated, over long periods of time as well as during each individual hour, between: "She's a bitch. She's impossible. She's horrible. She's a monster," to "Poor Joan. It's all my fault. She's a beautiful person. I've wasted the best years of her life. I see her growing old and wrinkled."

The quality and intensity of this marital dilemma were matched only by his occupational history. The patient was trained extensively not in one, but in two related highly skilled professions, either one of which, or both in combination, or any one of the many specialties of each, provided a choice of many remunerative, rewarding, important, and prestigious ways of life. He could not, however, choose any one aspect of the many opportunities available, but vacillated endlessly between all the possibilities, and spent his time occupationally—presumably on a temporary basis, which, however, proved to be permanent—as a menial technician at the lowest rung of the ladder in the lesser of the two fields, ruminating about what he could and should do, finding interminable excuses not to proceed to any of them, and constantly bemoaning his fate. It became apparent, as his past history unfolded and his present behavior became understood, that the goal was always just to be accepted, wanted, chosen, and favored by a father figure—by the dean of the professional school, by the professor, by the president of the business, by the general in the army, by the analyst—to promise them all, and be accepted by and promised to them in return, and never to carry through.

Each opportunity was inexorably and in turn aborted. He never had a plan for what to do after finishing school or a piece of training, except to begin the cycle all over again. While working in one area, he would be full of fantasies concerned with completely alien fields and daydream about dramatic achievements in the stock market, advertising gimmicks, TV, promotion schemes of various sorts, financial deals, and certain spectacular and potentially important research ideas. There was always enough promise, substance, and beginning recognition in some wild, glamorous, exhibitionistic idea to stimulate him to persist and to keep those around him interested and hopeful, to prevent them from giving up on him. He talked his way into every office, never failed to interest a potential benefactor, and never followed through to fruition on any plan.

Theoretical Considerations

From this small thread of a complex case as a base, I turn next to a specific segment of psychoanalytic theory which I believe is relevant to the topic of this paper and which in the past has served as a track for my own interests. In a series of papers (Rangell, 1955, 1963c, 1963d, 1967a, 1968c) I came to delineate a microdynamic sequence of intrapsychic events which could serve as a model for what takes place in the unfolding of "the intrapsychic process" (1969a, 1970). Prior to the experience of signal anxiety, the ego, by permitting a small and controlled amount of instinctual discharge, and sampling the resulting and proportional reaction of the superego, brings about a preliminary, tentative, and experimental signal conflict. It is following this reactive response

of the superego, which depends on which of the store of traumatic memories have been evoked, that signal anxiety, if it is to
occur, takes place. The next step, though often overlooked, is a
crucial one, which I feel illuminates a large segment of derivative
external behavior. I would have us stop the action, as it were, at
this point, to absorb fully an understanding of its theoretical
implications. The resulting anxiety, when it occurs, confronts
the ego with a dilemma between alternatives, with the necessity
for a choice as to what to do next, which of two competing psychic
systems to follow. This introduces into metapsychology a new
concept of the meaning of intrapsychic conflict, an intrapsychic
choice conflict of the ego, which is different from the oppositional
type of ego-id conflict usually meant in descriptions of intrapsychic conflict. In my earlier papers I have elaborated on the
relationships between this specific choice-dilemma type of conflict
and the more general concept of intrasystemic conflict introduced
by Hartmann (1950).

Our interest will trail off here from following the great variety
of subsequent paths and psychic end products, the elaboration of
which constitutes the bulk of the psychoanalytic literature. These
have been laid down in classic contributions, from Freud's original descriptions (1900, 1923, 1926), to the definitive additions by
many of the major subsequent contributors, from the early pioneers through Anna Freud (1936) and Fenichel (1945), to the
many more recent contributors to psychoanalytic theory. What I
have specifically added and referred to above centers mainly on
the initial phases of the intrapsychic sequence: (a) I have extended
Freud's signal theory to include the preliminary experimental
signal conflict *before* signal anxiety takes place. In terms of Freud's
inoculation analogy, this in effect includes a description of the
injection phase of the inoculation prior to the reaction to it,
which is the signal anxiety. (b) From this I subsequently attempted a clarification of the psychoanalytic theory of anxiety,
and suggested a unification of Freud's two historical theories. (c)
Following the anxiety, I believe there occurs an intrapsychic
choice conflict within the ego, in addition to the more usual oppositional type of intersystemic conflict between ego and id (which
may come later as one outcome). (d) Within the inventory of ego

functions I delineated a "decision-making function of the ego," specifically designed to resolve this intrapsychic choice or dilemma conflict.

It is this composite phase of the intrapsychic process with its intrinsic ego sequence of anxiety-choice-decision-action which, I submit, serves as the theoretical model for the psychoanalytic contribution to decision theory. I do not believe that indecision stems from polar and opposite instinctual drives, or drive components, or qualities of drives. Such instinctual dichotomies result in ambivalence but not in indecision. Without an ego dilemma, both drive elements can be discharged and given expression, either simultaneously or successively. Where love and hate are in opposition, one of them, usually love, has made its claim upon the superego, which then succeeds in rendering the ego opposed to the opposite instinct of aggression. The dilemma and indecision follow.

The psychoanalytic process reverses this inner sequence and, starting from outward behavior, gives increasingly clear views of its origins within (Rangell, 1968a). The psychoanalytic process results in an evagination of the intrapsychic process. It is of central interest to this study to trace the connections between the core intrapsychic activity described and the variations and vacillations of decision-making as seen in external behavior—and thereby arrive at an understanding of the history, vicissitudes, and characteristics of the decision-making process itself. Having understood this in the analysis of individual patients, we may hope, as always, to transfer such knowledge to the decision-making process of man in general.

Early Development

In order to pursue this early development, I return to the case of Mr. A. and cite the genetic factors that were associatively connected with his behavior. The patient's father was, we agreed, Willy Loman of *The Death of a Salesman*—full of schemes, promises, and failures. "They wanted me in Alaska" became a meaningful phrase in the analysis. When the father retired with a stroke after faithfully serving his firm for many years, he was presented with a gold watch inscribed "To Joe, a nice guy."

One of the patient's most vivid early memories was of sitting on a bannister, out of sight, watching his parents fighting, in terror that "daddy would kill mommy." There was one particular occasion when, after such a scene, the father sat the patient on his lap and said slowly and deliberately, "Danny, daddy is going away and is never coming back." The patient remembered breaking into inconsolable sobs, feeling shattered, helpless, as if his heart would break. His grief was so extreme that both parents became alarmed, tried desperately to console him, and repeatedly kissed each other, saying, "See, it's all right. Mommy loves daddy. Daddy loves mommy. It's going to be all right." He remembered feeling that somehow he had been bad and was responsible for all this.

The events surrounding this scene and his perception of them became a nodal traumatic memory. For years thereafter—in fact as long as he could remember—his one goal was "not to make waves," "don't do anything." He would "walk on eggs" not to antagonize one against the other, so that they would continue to be nice to each other, so that "mommy and daddy would love each other." He remembered anticipating his father's return home each night; he would check the dinner table to make sure that the knives, spoons, and forks were set exactly right, that the right dishes were used for each of them, so that neither of them would get mad at the other.

Another shattering experience, another determining traumatic incident in his life, occurred at age 11, when his father visited him at summer camp and informed him that his mother had given birth to a baby brother—but again saying that "it's all right, everything is okay. It's all going to be all right." He remembered getting sick in the pit of his stomach, feeling as if the world had come to an end, wandering off alone in the woods to compose himself, and suffering a crucial anxiety attack such as he was to know many more of later. This initial reaction was quickly submerged and replaced by a reactive love and devotion to his brother of exaggerated and maudlin degree. Another memory, recalled with horror and guilt, was of a year or so later: he inserted his penis into the mouth of his baby brother who was standing in the crib. This memory was part of another important line of development and played an equally crucial role in subsequent events.

During the course of years of analysis, many of the unconscious roots were exposed and linkages established between his present alternating anxiety and indecision and the early genetic backgrounds from which they developed. Forward movement in his marital life would both break his existing real oedipal attachments to which he was fixed and committed (his wife was an avowed enemy of his mother) and create new ones in disguised and displaced form. Each of these would result in an intolerable increase in anxiety. On the other hand, he would not sever the marriage and leave his wife, which would mean being wrenched away from the regressed pregenital comfort he derived from his willing wife-mother. She, for her part, took care of his every need, fed him, gave up all her friends and activities to stay with him, coddled him, babied him, masturbated him—and also lost her temper with him, screamed, threatened, and beat at him in her exasperation. The latter only made up for his guilt and made him feel better. The stalemate and only the stalemate suited his every need. His father had died during the analysis, and the patient now had his mother (two of them), his brother and himself as a menage, all of whom depended on him. His brother now was his son. He need not and would not repeat the trauma of his birth by voluntarily having another.

The same gains were forthcoming from his frozen occupational status. His identification with his father in his present situation was clear and became evident. Going forward to a new and advanced position would both betray and dethrone his homosexually loved father and lead to further demands and expectations from his wife-mother, whom he was of no mind to treat better than his father did. "I am watching her being strangled to death," he complained, and continued.

The patient lived on a razor's edge between decisions—actually on two razors, one with regard to the marriage and one to work. And there was another razor between the two: whenever the discussions about either one began to lean him toward moving to one side or the other, he would turn to an endless to and fro concentration on the other issue. Any associations leading in one direction were automatically balanced by bringing up some which pulled in another. This mechanism was further fortified by somatic accompaniments. He developed a head nod so that whenever he was associating about potent reasons for one side of any dilemma, his head would be rhythmically and desperately nodding "no." And whenever he came up with strong reasons for staying with his wife, his face would simultaneously assume an anxious grimace, or he would bare his teeth, and automatically put on record a few reserve associations about some bitchy and impossible episode on her part.

Further Comment

In the sequence of intention-anxiety-choice-decision, the interrelationships between the elements are as complex and varied as is human life itself. The fate of decision-making is not necessarily parallel to the degree of anxiety experienced, neither is it to the benignness or malignancy of the final psychic outcome, but has a specific and individual background of its own. There may be acute and severe anxiety with no faltering of the decisions to be made and, conversely, less severe anxiety may be associated with paralyzing indecision. As a general statement, decision-making is most difficult when the greatest evenness and the most exquisite balance exist between desired gratification on the one hand, and expectant punishment and disapproval on the other—and when a person's life history has not resulted in experiences leading to an undeniable inner advantage and therefore a clear-cut preference of one over the other. This was the case with the patient just described.

At this point in my presentation, I would have wished to describe, as a contrasting example, a patient in a chronic, severe, unremitting anxiety state in whom the decision-making function nevertheless remained intact and efficient. For reasons of space, I shall insert this here, so to speak, by title only, to make the main point without the luxury of the details.

In the face of her severe anxiety which stemmed from a different genetic development than those of Mr. A., Mrs. B. knew decisively, unconsciously what she wanted to do—to withdraw from and deny the noxious stimuli. This mechanism helped but did not suffice. The anxiety continued to rage due to the uncontrollable impulses, the continually pressing traumatic memories, and the relative incapacity of her ego to contain or deal with them. Her decisions were not in question, only her capacities. She displayed no indecisiveness in the small or large decisions of life. It was remarkable, for example, how, when a good husband prospect appeared, she came out of herself long enough to be courted fairly normally and to enter upon what turned out to be an enduring marriage.

Psychoanalytic Decision Theory

Leaving psychopathology, I turn to general theory. The delineation of a psychoanalytic decision theory serves as a link between motivation (Rapaport, 1960) and action, and is en route to a psychoanalytic theory of action, which, as Hartmann (1947) pointed out, we do not yet have. From this point on, in commenting on the normal decision-making process, I shall select only a few of what I consider the most salient and pressing considerations in a voluminous subject.

Decision and indecision, where psychoanalysis has given them direct and specific attention, have been linked historically, from the genetic point of view, with influences and residuals deriving from the anal stage (Freud, 1909, 1918; Abraham, 1921; Jones, 1918). As we look back at this connection, which by continuous usage has become quite automatic, we see a phenomenon that commonly occurs in the development of our science. A historical linkage which, at the time of its origin, was responsible for an important leap in understanding, turns out upon closer inspection to be true and important but somewhat too exclusively specific. To cite an analogous example: I have previously (1959) spoken for a severance of the automatic linkage between conversion and hysteria, and pointed out that conversion occurs over a wider range of etiological foci than in hysteria alone. The same, I submit, obtains with what by now has become an automatic association between doubting and pathological indecision on the one hand, and anal and obsessive psychopathology on the other. Further experience with this psychic phenomenon, as with many others, has repeatedly shown the existence of a more continuous etiological spectrum.

The capacity to decide, to choose among alternatives, and thereby to shape rather than only to suffer one's destiny, has a unique and individually determined ontogenetic history. Arising out of the matrix of physiological reflexes, its precursors, and the necessary equipment with which it will be exercised, begin with the origins of psychic structure, the differentiation of the ego from the undifferentiated ego-id matrix (Hartmann, 1939, 1948), and with the first awakenings of what Greenacre (1945) has aptly called "the dawning ego." Following up Spitz's (1957) description of the origins of the No and Yes gestures, I studied the backgrounds and origins of the No and Yes verbal symbols themselves and showed how these were related to the physiological occurrences within the oral cavity in relation to the incoming supplies of milk (1963b). In the earliest physiological state, the newly born organism either can comply with this incoming flow and move it along its path, in which case the lip-tongue-palate-throat movements effect ingress and swallowing, or it can close the throat and push with the tongue toward the nose, in which case it ejects and spits out what the mother gives. In the first instance, the lapping motion of these organs serving the "come-in" function is the same as that later used phonetically in the "yy," which linguistically develops into the "yes." On the other hand, the opposite motion, with the tongue upward toward the palate and nose, ejecting milk and air, is the same movement that is later used in the "nn" sound, which progresses gradually into the "no." If the infant "chooses" to do neither, i.e., remains truly passive and neither helps the milk in nor pushes it out, the milk of its own accord goes in all directions, down the throat, out the mouth, and out the nose as well.

The acquisition of the no and yes during the toilet-training phase—according to Spitz, "the most spectacular intellectual and semantic achievement in early childhood (p. 99)—demonstrates in a very visible and concrete way the nodal choice between compliance or rejection achieved at this point. In addition to its de-

finitive forerunners and neuromuscular channels, however, subsequent elaboration takes place in a gradual and continuous
transition with every step in development. Child analysts have
recently disputed the existence of a "latency phase" (Maenchen,
1970), of any lag or delay in maturation, in any aspect of instinctual or ego development.

Decision-making, as other psychic functions, increases steadily
in complexity, importance, and scope. I shall again refer by title
only at this point to a section which I can only allude to since to
deal with it comprehensively would require another paper. I am
referring to the problems and agonies of modern youth. One
etiologic aspect is pointed to here which has to do with the fact
that this period is the expected "time for decision," again in the
two major areas of psychic life, love and work.

Just as decision-making can receive increments at any level of
forward development, there may be fixation and regression in
decision-making at each developmental phase. Each may variously
affect the quality, the content, and the scope of this function. The
etiologic connection between pathological indecision, doubting
mania, and the doing and undoing of anal-sadistic impulses,
established by the first major insights into such psychopathology
by Freud, Abraham, Jones, and other psychoanalytic pioneers,
turns out to be but one example—and by no means the only one
—of the psychic background of such conditions. The same type
and degree of ego alternation between id and superego as was
originally shown to exist over anal impulses can rage with equal
intensity at any other stage or level of development. The case of
Mr. A. reported above centered mainly around oedipal, castration,
and separation conflicts. The other patient alluded to, Mrs. B.,
exhibited a wider range of diffuse pregenital conflicts, but the
decision-making function of the ego was not centrally involved.

A person's capacity to make decisions does not by itself speak
for his adaptedness, since decisions can be as characteristically destructive as they can be constructive and psychically economical.
There are also a myriad of decisions which are come to instantly,
impulsively, in much the same way as a counterphobic attitude or
action. These are often predicated basically upon an inability to
tolerate intrapsychic tension, whether of delayed gratification or

of the pain of an unconscious traumatic memory. As a result there is an aversion to expose the ego to the necessary intermediate steps in unconscious decision-making, the anxiety, the uncertainty, and the experimentally induced painful and traumatic tension states upon which more considered opinions and more appropriate decisions would be based.

It is also to be noted in this connection, however, that the secondary effects and sequelae of decisions are not always and automatically to be counted as their original motivations. Hartmann (1956) has pointed out that reality is more than man's unconscious. Man's decisions can set off actions the effects of which from then on can well have an autonomy of their own. The migration to California in the 1940s or to Israel during recent history was motivated on the parts of hundreds of thousands by a combination of surface and rational motives plus a welter of subjective, idiosyncratic, and unconscious factors. The subsequent effects of living in the new land for years, however, took their own course and cannot be forever attributed to the sought-for goals of those who chose them. In şimilar vein, a person marries for a wide variety of reasons, conscious and unconscious, a kaleidoscope of internal motivating forces and external impingements. Not everything that happens thereafter, however, is what he wished, hoped or bargained for.

Central to the willingness to commit oneself to a decision is the capacity to anticipate its consequences. The anxiety signal is not the only outcome of the capacity to anticipate. The nature and quality of decisions result from the same capability. However, included in this capacity is the knowledge of its limitations, of the fact that not all consequences and consequences of consequences can be foreseen. This is part of the developmental task which goes along with the relinquishing of infantile omnipotence. The extent to which this is achieved determines the ability to accept the limitations imposed by reality and the willingness to proceed always to some extent into the unknown. Trust in consequences beyond the foreseeable depends of course on the genetic history of past satisfactions and successes.

Decision-making thus involves planning. Nonanalytic psychologists and other workers in the field of decision theory speak of utility and probability variables, i.e., of the capacity to predict the utility of a particular considered decision and the probability of the utility coming about (Edwards and Tversky, 1967). Psychoanalysis adds the level of unconscious mental functioning, with its scanning for memories of previous psychic traumata, by which the utility of anticipated decisions are judged. The scope and accuracy of predictions are thus enormously amplified by bringing into play previous experience and the entire sweep of the genetic past.

In the sequence of anxiety-choice-decision, both affective and cognitive elements accompany and follow each other and are actively operative at the unconscious level. Various authors have concentrated on specific aspects of these processes, such as Arlow (1969) on unconscious fantasies, Beres (1960), Kohut (1960), and Rosen (1960) on the process of imagination, Schur (1953, 1958, 1963, 1967) on unconscious anxiety and unconscious affects in general, a concept which Freud showed some reluctance to accept. Gehl (1970) questions the relationships between indecision, doubt, and uncertainty. I would say that uncertainty obtains when the cognitive search for the anticipated outcome is incomplete or unsatisfactory; indecision is the unwillingness or inability of the ego to commit itself to a course of action either because of this or even after the cognitive consequences are known; and doubt is the affective state accompanying either or both of these cognitive conditions. Piaget (1970) speaks of the simultaneous operation of "the affective unconscious" and "the cognitive unconscious." Just as secondary elaboration works over a latent dream into an integrated manifest product (Freud, 1900), so does thinking, of elaborate and accurate nature, with the equivalent of secondary process decision-making as a final outcome, take place completely at unconscious levels. Indeed, problem-solving of highly sophisticated degree, on an unconscious or preconscious level (Kris, 1950), is known to take place in acts of discovery and creativity, wherein dreams or reverie states impinge on consciousness.

This brings me to an important consideration that I would like to submit to close inspection. It is one of theoretical, philosophical, and technical interest; might well lead to a new emphasis and orientation; and also serves as a bridge between theory and clinic. The very factor I have stressed—that of active unconscious decision-making, of the exercise of control and of "chosen" direction —also brings with it the opposite side of the coin of ego autonomy, the important and subtle issue of "responsibility." The privilege of autonomous choice brings with it the responsibility for making it. It is in fact this very coexistence which often brings about inhibition, withdrawal, and indecision. Because of its crucial relevance to today's psychosociopolitical human scene, I would like to demonstrate what I mean by examining the role of this factor within both psychoanalytic theory and technique.

As psychoanalytic theory developed, the general thrust of its implications, on an individual and social basis, varied according to which element within it was being described and highlighted at the particular time. Thus during the early period, at the time of the discovery of the unconscious and the emphasis on the role of the instincts, the stress was on psychic determinism, and on the relentlessness and inevitability of the unconscious inner forces which shaped and influenced overt behavior. This was stressed unduly, for a long period of time, to the exclusion of all acknowledgment of freedom of will, of choice, and of responsibility. The next phase in our history balanced this one-sided emphasis by adding the counterforces of defense, control, and adaptation which the ego contributes. The extent of behavior now encompassed and the scope of explanatory power of psychoanalytic theory were enormously widened, and moved psychoanalysis further toward its claim of being a general psychology.

The ego function of decision-making carries psychoanalysis further in this direction. The delineation of an intrapsychic choice conflict spells out a moment in intrapsychic life in which the human psyche is confronted with the opportunity, and the necessity, to exercise its own directive potentials and to determine its own active course. Psychic determinism, which at the time of its inclusion added a dimension then unknown, is now not to be replaced but added to in its turn. Taken by itself psychic determinism is incomplete, unless it is viewed in the context of the role played by the individual himself in controlling and shaping his own destiny. By adding the conflict-free and autonomous aspects of ego functioning, Hartmann (1939) made available to psychoanalytic theory and observation aspects of human life that until then had been less the focus of attention. The close study of the function of decision, I submit, moves the psychoanalyst's interest, concern, and armamentarium further in that direction because it makes explicit the methods by which the patient utilizes his autonomous functions and guides his life toward goals and areas determined by his own decisive ego. Composite external behavior consists of forces passively endured, fused with a spectrum of active, controlling, and deciding elements ranging from unconscious to full conscious control. It is this which makes for the "mutuality" of internal and external, of parent and child interaction, which Erikson (1950), Winnicott (1957), and other clinicians and theoreticians have come to as an inclusive formulation.

Although active ego decision-making, as stressed here, takes place in the unconscious as well as in the conscious and preconscious, analysts have generally tended to assume that responsibility begins to apply only as such activity approaches the border of conscious control. If the "free" of "free will" is limited to conscious freedom, however, the "will" is now seen to have a wider base and to exist in the deepest unconscious elements of ego and drive activity, as much as in their conscious derivatives and additions. Is action which is under conscious control, although there is also a world of unconscious motivation, to be considered fully responsible—and action which is unconsciously planned and premeditated but which, because of its impact, has been separated from external awareness to be considered free of responsibility? Clearly, simplistic criteria in this area of transition and ambiguity have become anachronistic.

The borderland and gray shadings which exist here have long made this an area of discomfort and uncertainty to psychiatrists and psychoanalysts who are in various ways asked to translate "responsibility" into practical and pragmatic terms. There is, or should be, a spectrum of responsibility from none or little through partial to full. It is this spectrum, as contrasted to the duality represented by the poles at either end, which is at the bottom of the dissatisfactions, uncertainties, and debates on the parts of many with regard to the legal aspects of responsibility and the dubious role of psychiatrists and psychoanalysts in the court room. It is from the fact of this spectrum that Szasz (1961) proceeds to his exaggerated position that there is no such entity as mental illness and that psychiatrists are the modern imposers of conformity. On the other hand, it is from these same considerations that Karl Menninger (1966) and others derive the recent more sober and scientific view that since all actions are a combination of less and more responsible elements, psychiatrists should not be called upon to assess right or wrong but should confine themselves to understanding and treatment.

Technical Considerations

This same issue, of a scale of responsibility, and the fact that it is subject to change, is reflected in the psychoanalytic situation as well. Mr. A., in spite of years of reconstruction, interpretation, insight, and reliving, continued to perpetuate the state of suspended indecision to the mounting frustration and exasperation of all about him. His vacillations were such as to exhaust everyone, tried the patience of all, and seemed to have become permanent and structured. His goal was to react, not to act. He invariably waited until others were forced to act, in which case he could react, with opposition and panic, no matter which way they had turned. Yet nobody broke. His wife screamed and stayed. His mother and brother became sicker but remained patient. As ambivalent and erratic as he acted in each position, his employers kept him and never forced an issue. He had a knack of stretching the rubber band longer, tighter, and further, without it breaking, than anyone could imagine.

The analyst, after he too had been stretched to his capacity, was then confronted with the task of dealing with this global resistance, the patient's inability, hesitation, and refusal to decide and act. All three were involved and blended together. The situation was akin to that obtaining in the phobic patient who, after extensive and intensive analysis of the components of the neurosis, hesitates similarly to strike out and be well, to confront and master the phobic object. It was at this one point that Freud (1918) is often quoted as having recommended that activity on the part of the analyst is in order. I should like to submit, however, that while this therapeutic maneuver derives from a piece of insight first noted in a specific clinical situation, its applicability needs to be considered on a more general level. The need for an active ego move toward consolidating the gains of analysis exists not only in a localized phobia, but is present in many other types of cases, including states of more diffuse anxiety. In this context it is of course possible to look at Mr. A. in another way and to characterize him as a person who suffers from phobic anxiety—the phobic element in this case being concerned with the avoidance of choosing and completing a significant task.

At any rate, in such instances, the analyst is confronted with the patient's failure to propel the dynamic process further. Correct interpretation alone is not enough. The analyst's interpretations need to be followed by the patient's absorption of them, integration, and necessary action. What is involved now is the full acknowledgment of the patient's role in the duality of the psychoanalytic process, the operations of the executive segments of the patient's ego which, after analysis, insight, and sufficient working through must decide, test, try, and do. Psychoanalysis dissolves many of the ties which, operating from the unconscious, are strangling the progression to choice and action. After such work is accomplished, voluntarily executed action, by providing examples of safety rather than danger, of mastery rather than trauma, is the final test and the final confirmation of the absence of danger.

Psychoanalysis, by increasing the patient's width of choice (making the unconscious conscious), places the "responsibility" increasingly on him to effect them. This is implicit in Erikson's (1964) title *Insight and Responsibility*. Similar to the phobias, but extending as I suggested to a more general situation, many analyses reach a point where, after extensive loosening of the unconscious soil, the patient's capacity and willingness for experimental action is necessary to carry the analytic process further toward its goals. This is a crucial and often sensitive point in the therapeutic advance, at which faltering, even failure, may take place, and about which more needs to be said than I can say here. One must be alert, of course, to the danger of the analyst misusing this necessity to cover up a host of other reasons for blockage or incompleteness, such as inadequate or insufficient analytic understanding, failure of emotional insight or working through, or a variety of limiting factors stemming from the countertransference.

I wish, however, to add this particular dynamic situation, which I believe is a common occurrence, not only in the instances of "interminable analysis" but also as a transitory resistance during the course of average analyses. When, as in the case of Mr. A., this mechanism becomes a nodal point for interminability, it is to be separated from the repetition compulsion or a negative therapeutic reaction. The compulsion to repeat stems from the id, and the negative therapeutic reaction owes its origin to the superego, while this type of failure to act derives from a specific ego incapacity, a timidity about trying, experimenting, and taking a chance. What is centrally involved in this residual state is neither instinctual pleasure nor superego guilt, but a specific ego insufficiency. Where this particular ego function has been involved, by neurosis, or deficiency, or maturational neglect, it must also be looked into, cared for, and nurtured during the course of the treatment process.

A patient's failure to make such final necessary decisions and to carry out trial actions itself gradually and increasingly causes anxiety to back up and mount. As long as Mr. A.'s indecision went unchallenged and was allowed to remain chronic, anxiety was kept at bay. His own acceptance, via analysis, of the necessity for choice, coupled with his inability or unwillingness to effect it, made for a situation in which anxiety returned in an increasing and spiraling degree. To the extent that he himself as well as his environment felt increasing impatience with his state of inertia, calm ineffectualness was superseded by anxiety and agitation at the necessity but incapacity to act. But this failure itself now needed to be constantly rationalized and defended against, thus augmenting the anxiety which was then used for defensive purposes. When the patient, continuing to fail to choose, instead constantly bombarded the analyst with the physical evidences of his mounting anxiety, to the point of almost a hypochondriacal orgy, the technique was now to interpret to him that it was his own failure to choose, again and still, which determined this inner state. The manifest "I can't" meant the latent "I won't." In his complaint that he could not choose *because of* his anxiety, he was now putting the cart before the horse. Unlike the original intrapsychic sequence as given above, it was now the failure to choose which was causing the anxiety to mount, rather than the other way around. He could not do this or that because he did not want to—which was confirmed by the continued outpouring of contempt for whatever alternative came up for imminent consideration. In the meantime he had indeed chosen—to stay on the fence between both or all worlds, to have the indirect benefit of all. This was concretized in his concoction of a drink consisting of vodka and milk, which he took as a nightly sedative and which he also recommended highly to the analyst.

The steady persistence by the analyst along this line, particularly the insistence within the stream of interpretations that the patient and only the patient must come to face the factor of his own basic choices and of the consequences of his own deepest decision processes, finally produced a felicitous direction of change in the patient. Although the validity of the reasoning and the main points and principles which I am making in this paper do not depend on the therapeutic outcome of a particular case, nor really on therapeutic outcome at all, I am happy to be able to add the following clinical progress note to date.

The condition of the patient has taken such a marked and dramatic turn for the better as is rarely given to us to see in our work. Following a series of events and circumstances, the patient was able to forge for himself a rather new and unique role in his professional life which combined the entire scope of his training and preparation in a creative and integrated way. Unfortunately due to the unusual nature of the particular type of work which has emerged, considerations of discretion prevent a more precise description which would be necessary to impart to the reader the full reality impact of the choices and the subsequent solution. It seems fair to say, however, that opportunities of this type had been within his grasping distance many times before, and that only a psychic readiness, stemming from the resolution and the putting at rest of deep unconscious conflicts, finally enabled him to put together "a winning package."

The patient is scarcely recognizable to his incredulous friends and pinches himself at the change in his life, his demeanor, and his material success. His relationship to his wife has undergone a similar improvement in the direction of increased positive feelings and a lessening of his state of balanced ambivalence. His sexual life has improved concomitantly, and he has spontaneously told her for the first time in years that he loved her.

The patient has changed during the past year from the most abject misery, from a state where a physician who saw him on one occasion at the height of his illness offered "to use his influence" to have him accepted immediately for hospitalization at the Menningers, to a position where he has recently been told that he brings prestige and honor to his profession. With it his physical appearance has changed remarkably, and many psychosomatic symptoms which at the height of his anxiety I had assured him, with some trepidation on my part, were reversible have indeed reversed themselves. He had, for example, been unable to produce tears, and for months would regularly be seen to put drops in his eyes from a supply of artificial tears which had been given him by an ophthalmologist. One day during an outburst of joyful and appropriate laughter in my office, to his great pleasure and surprise his eyes began to tear, and he found himself wiping his wet eyes with a handkerchief.

This description is being written after a long period of steady progress which has never before been the case with this patient, and which includes the overcoming of a number of touchy and disturbing realistic occurrences. After many cautious misgivings, I judge this clinical course now to be on solid and reliable ground.

Another factor which is related to the technical analytic stance as described in this report is the analyst's philosophical attitude to the question of finiteness of a piece of analytic work, whether related to the analysis as a whole or to any specific circumscribed interpretation. Although theoretically the unconscious is more or less infinite, and I myself consider analysis quantitatively comparable to shining a flashlight into the Grand Canyon, operationally and technically speaking analytic work must be looked upon as finite with respect to a particular symptom or a specific interpretation. Although theoretically a dream is never interpreted or understood completely but ultimately dips into "a nexus of obscurity"

(Freud, 1900), for practical and operational purposes its message can be encompassed and utilized. In a symposium on the termination of analysis (1966), I pointed out that the central method of analysis, the resolution of the transference neurosis, must be considered reasonably attainable from a practical and pragmatic point of view because otherwise the possibility of ending an analysis would be inconceivable.

While acting out is generally watched for by vigilant alertness on the part of the analyst, the opposite condition, failure to act in appropriate ways and to an appropriate degree, has been less stressed in analytic literature and technique. I am referring not so much to major decisions and actions as to small ongoing decisions, forward movements, changes in attitudes to spouse, children, or parents, which are often indicative of the status of the analytic work. With regard to acting out it is a technical mistake when the analyst assumes a moralistic or authoritarian attitude; he should adopt as analytic an attitude toward this complication as to all other unconsciously motivated phenomena (Rangell, 1968b). This same point was made by Vanggaard (1968), and affirmed with clinical material by Zetzel (1970), Atkins (1970), and others. The same, however, is also true of the opposite state, an inhibition of action or of the decisions leading to action. The analyst must then adopt and maintain an equally vigilant analytic attitude and vigorously pursue the phenomena of inaction. To this end the relationships between anxiety, decision, and action deserve constant and careful attention, which must extend to the changing order of their sequence and the reciprocal moves of cause and effect. The consequences of failure to observe and to deal with these changing internal relationships lead to a widely held criticism, quoted most recently by Rollo May (1969), that "psychoanalysis is a systematic training in indecision."

Relationship to the Present and Future Role of Psychoanalysis

This brings me to a final point, the relationship of the subject of decision-making to the present and future role of psychoanalysis.

In response to the vicissitudes and pendular swings of psycho-analysis in relation to the outside intellectual world, there are many within and without our field who, believing it necessary to increase its "relevance," emphasize research *on* psychoanalysis and the application of psychoanalytic knowledge to the issues of the day as the most pressing areas for the use of psychoanalytic energy at this moment in our history. While I feel that both of these are necessary as continuing lines of thought and research, I have stated on a number of occasions that continued research *by* psycho-analysis, applied to the psychology and psychopathology current today, continues to be the unique contribution of psychoanalysis to understanding the tenor of our times and the one which only it is capable of providing (Rangell, 1967b). I would like to add at this time that the detailed study of the psychology of the decision-making process not only gives the psychoanalytic method a new dimension but also opens up crucial new areas of its fruitful appli-cation.

Among the areas of increasing interest during this age of chronic crisis is that of the decision-making characteristics of world leaders and policy makers. With physical equipment standing ready which can explode the world, it is the silent as well as the explicit hope of all mankind that those whose fingers can set them off can think, judge, decide, and plan with cool rationality and with no influence, if that is possible, from contaminating idiosyncratic subjective motives which can move a person this or that side of reason. Re-cent psychopolitical studies have demonstrated that this is no mere academic question, and have documented such influences leading to recurrent wars from ancient to modern times. One such study, conducted by the Stanford Studies in International Conflict and Integration (1963), compared the crucial intrapsychic and inter-personal patterns in two international crises of this century, the fateful decisions of the German Kaiser which triggered World War I and the Kennedy-Khrushchev confrontation over the Cuban missile affair in 1962.

Scribbles left by Kaiser Wilhelm in the margins of state docu-ments indicate that he went through a personal crisis. He was seized by attacks of panic resulting in distorted perceptions, loss of control, and irrational judgments which plunged the world into catastrophic war. With two quite different types of leaders at the helm half a century later, the cool though dangerous game which unfolded between them had an opposite outcome. Though close to the brink, but with neither causing the other to have to lose face, the world breathed easier when both men, with calculated risks but unambiguous moves, were able to survive the eyeball-to-eyeball confrontation off the Cuban coast (Robert Kennedy, 1969).

The affective and cognitive reactions of political and military leaders have always been important, but are perhaps only now beginning to receive their full recognition. Events in this country in these past few years have again brought to the fore a deep concern about the psychology of decision-making.[2]

To the growing interest in decision theory to which I have referred, I have added the role which psychoanalysis can play, and indeed which it has already played for many years without this aspect of its functioning having been explicitly studied until now. I do not wish to imply that there can be any greater leap from painstaking psychoanalytic studies of individuals to an effective application to world politics in this any more than in any other aspect of man's psychic functioning. I share Freud's pessimism about psychoanalysis and a Weltanschauung (1926, 1930, 1933), and the sober caution expressed by many subsequent writers up to Waelder (1967). Nor do we often have a chance to analyze decision processes that result in such momentous consequences. But the elucidation of basic psychological principles hammered out from studies of their impact on relatively smaller instances of everyday life is what psychoanalysis has always provided and from 'which lessons and applications have always derived. Decision-making is of central interest in many analyses and of some interest in all. It is also of interest to all of mankind. The findings from psychoanalysis need to be added to those of all other disciplines sharing an interest in human decisions.

---

[2] This lecture was delivered a few weeks after the invasion of Cambodia by American troops and at the height of the national unrest and the general pall which followed this event and the subsequent Kent State shootings.

BIBLIOGRAPHY

ABRAHAM, K. (1921), Contributions to the Theory of the Anal Character. *Selected Papers on Psycho-Analysis.* London: Hogarth Press, 1948, pp. 370–392.

ARLOW, J. A. (1969), Unconscious Fantasy and Disturbances of Conscious Experience. *Psychoanal. Quart.,* 38:1–27.

ATKINS, N. B. (1970), Report of Panel: Action, Acting Out, and the Symptomatic Act. *J. Amer. Psychoanal. Assn.,* 18:631–643.

BERES, D. (1960), The Psychoanalytic Psychology of Imagination. *J. Amer. Psychoanal. Assn.,* 8:252–269.

EDWARDS, W. & TVERSKY, A., Eds. (1967), *Decision Making.* Baltimore: Penguin Books.

ERIKSON, E. H. (1950), *Childhood and Society.* New York: Norton.

— (1964), *Insight and Responsibility.* New York: Norton.

FENICHEL, O. (1945), *The Psychoanalytic Theory of Neurosis.* New York: Norton.

FREUD, A. (1936), The Ego and the Mechanisms of Defense. *The Writings of Anna Freud,* Vol. 2. New York: International Universities Press, 1966.

FREUD, S. (1900), The Interpretation of Dreams. *Standard Edition,* 4 & 5. London: Hogarth Press, 1953.

— (1909), Notes upon a Case of Obsessional Neurosis. *Standard Edition,* 10:153–320. London. Hogarth Press, 1955.

— (1918), From the History of an Infantile Neurosis. *Standard Edition,* 17:3–123. London: Hogarth Press, 1955.

— (1918), Lines of Advance in Psycho-Analytic Therapy. *Standard Edition,* 17:157–168. London: Hogarth Press, 1955.

— (1923), The Ego and the Id. *Standard Edition,* 19:3–66. London: Hogarth Press, 1961.

— (1926), Inhibitions, Symptoms and Anxiety. *Standard Edition,* 20:77–175. London: Hogarth Press, 1959.

— (1930), Civilization and Its Discontents. *Standard Edition,* 21:59–145. London: Hogarth Press, 1961.

— (1933), Lecture 35. New Introductory Lectures on Psycho-Analysis. *Standard Edition,* 22:158–182, London: Hogarth Press, 1964.

GEHL, R. H. (1970), Indecision, Doubt, and Feelings of Uncertainty. Paper presented to New Jersey Psychoanalytic Society.

GREENACRE, P. (1945), The Biological Economy of Birth. *This Annual,* 1:31–51.

HARTMANN, H. (1939), *Ego Psychology and the Problem of Adaptation.* New York: International Universities Press, 1958.

The Decision-Making Process

— (1947), On Rational and Irrational Action. In: *Essays on Ego Psychology*. New York: International Universities Press, 1964, pp. 37–68.

— (1948), Comments on the Psychoanalytic Theory of Instinctual Drives. *Ibid.*, pp. 69–89.

— (1950), Comments on the Psychoanalytic Theory of the Ego. *Ibid.*, pp. 113–141.

— (1956), Notes on the Reality Principle. *Ibid.*, pp. 241–267.

— (1964), *Essays on Ego Psychology*. New York: International Universities Press.

JONES, E. (1918), Anal-Erotic Character Traits. *Papers on Psycho-Analysis*. Baltimore: Williams & Wilkins, 1948, pp. 413–437.

KENNEDY, R. F. (1969), *Thirteen Days: A Memoir of the Cuban Missile Crisis*. New York: Norton.

KOHUT, H. (1960), Report of Panel: The Psychology of Imagination. *J. Amer. Psychoanal. Assn.*, 8:159–166.

KRIS, E. (1950), On Preconscious Mental Processes. *Psychoanal. Quart.*, 19: 540–560.

MAY, R. (1969), *Love and Will*. New York: Norton.

MAENCHEN, A. (1970), On the Technique of Child Analysis in Relation to Stages of Development. *This Annual*, 25:175–208.

MENNINGER, K. A. (1966), *The Crime of Punishment*. New York: Viking Press.

PIAGET, J. (1970), Inconscient affectif et inconscient cognitif. Paper delivered at Fall Meeting of the American Psychoanalytic Association, New York City.

RANGELL, L. (1955), On the Psychoanalytic Theory of Anxiety: A Statement of a Unitary Theory. *J. Amer. Psychoanal. Assn.*, 3:389–414.

— (1959), The Nature of Conversion. *J. Amer. Psychoanal. Assn.*, 7:632–662.

— (1963a), On Friendship. *J. Amer. Psychoanal. Assn.*, 11:3–54.

— (1963b), Beyond and Between the No and the Yes: A Tribute to Dr. René A. Spitz. In: *Counterpoint: Libidinal Object and Subject,* ed. H. S. Gaskill. New York: International Universities Press, pp. 29–74.

— (1963c), The Scope of Intrapsychic Conflict: Microscopic and Macroscopic Considerations. *This Annual*, 18:75–102.

— (1963d), Structural Problems in Intrapsychic Conflict. *This Annual*, 18: 103–138.

— (1966), An Overview of the Ending of an Analysis. In: *Psychoanalysis in the Americas,* ed. R. E. Litman. New York: International Universities Press, pp. 141–165.

— (1967a), The Metapsychology of Psychic Trauma. In: *Psychic Trauma,* ed. S. S. Furst. New York & London: Basic Books, pp. 51–84.

— (1967b), Psychoanalysis: A Current Look. *J. Amer. Psychoanal. Assn.*, 15: 423–431.

— (1968a), The Psychoanalytic Process. *Int. J. Psycho-Anal.*, 49:19–26.

— (1968b), A Point of View on Acting Out. *Int. J. Psycho-Anal.*, 49:195–201.

— (1968c), A Further Attempt to Resolve the "Problem of Anxiety." *J. Amer. Psychoanal. Assn.,* 16:371–404.

— (1969a), The Intrapsychic Process and Its Analysis: A Recent Line of Thought and Its Current Implications. *Int. J. Psycho-Anal.,* 50:65–77.

— (1969b), Choice-Conflict and the Decision-Making Function of the Ego: A Psychoanalytic Contribution to Decision Theory. *Int. J. Psycho-Anal.,* 50:599–602.

— (1970), Discussion of The Intrapsychic Process and Its Analysis: A Recent Line of Thought and Its Current Implications. *Int. J. Psycho-Anal.,* 51: 195–199, 202–209.

RAPAPORT, D. (1960), On the Psychoanalytic Theory of Motivation. In: *Nebraska Symposium on Motivation,* ed. M. R. Jones. Lincoln: University of Nebraska Press, pp. 173–247.

ROSEN, V. H. (1960), Some Aspects of the Role of Imagination in the Analytic Process. *J. Amer. Psychoanal. Assn.,* 8:229–251.

SCHUR, M. (1953), The Ego in Anxiety. In: *Drives, Affects, Behavior,* ed. R. M. Loewenstein. New York: International Universities Press, pp. 67–103.

— (1958), The Ego and the Id in Anxiety. *This Annual,* 13:190–220.

— (1963), Metapsychological Aspects of Phobias in Adults. *Bull. Philadelphia Assn. Psychoanal.,* 13:86–89.

— (1967), Comments on "Unconscious Affects" and "The Signal Concept." Abstr. in Report of Panel: Psychoanalytic Theory of Affects. *J. Amer. Psychoanal. Assn.,* 16:638–650, 1968.

SPITZ, R. A. (1957), *No and Yes: On the Beginnings of Human Communication.* New York: International Universities Press.

Stanford Studies in International Conflict and Integration: Crisis and Crises (1963), *Stanford Today,* Series 1, No. 4.

SWETS, J. A. (1967), Detection Theory and Psychophysics: A Review. In: *Decision Making,* ed. W. Edwards & A. Tversky. Baltimore: Penguin Books, pp. 379–395.

SZASZ, T. (1961), *The Myth of Mental Illness.* New York: Hoeber-Harper.

VANGGAARD, T. (1968), Contribution to Symposium on Acting Out. *Int. J. Psycho-Anal.,* 49:206–210.

WAELDER, R. (1967), *Progress and Revolution.* New York: International Universities Press.

WINNICOTT, D. W. (1957), *Mother and Child: A Primer of First Relationships.* New York: Basic Books.

ZETZEL, E. R. (1970), Introductory Remarks to Panel: Action, Acting Out, and the Symptomatic Act. Abstr. in *J. Amer. Psychoanal. Assn.,* 18:631–643.

An Adolescent Boy's Battle Against Recovery

The Analysis of an Adolescent Whose Ongoing Preoedipal Tie to the Mother Aroused Massive Treatment Resistance and a Terror of Health

MARJORIE P. SPRINCE

OUR INTEREST IN THE TECHNICAL PROBLEMS OF TREATING CHILDREN whose forward moves are held back because of an unconscious interplay between themselves and one or both of their parents is not a new one. This paper sets out to describe the analytic treatment of a 12-year-old boy who at the time of referral was locked in an ongoing preoedipal partnership with his mother which was so intense that therapeutic insight in the patient alone seemed un-

This paper was presented at the Hampstead Child-Therapy Clinic, London, in March, 1971. The author is on the staff of the Hampstead Child-Therapy Clinic which is at present maintained by the Field Foundation, Inc., New York; The Foundation for Research in Psychoanalysis, Beverly Hills, California; the Freud Centenary Fund, London; the Anna Freud Foundation, New York; the Grant Foundation, Inc., New York; the Andrew W. Mellon Foundation, New York; the National Institute for Mental Health, Bethesda, Maryland; the New-Land Foundation, Inc., New York; and a number of private supporters.

likely to counteract the pull exerted by the partnership. In addition, the deep-seated loyalty conflict which was aroused by any attempt to separate Paul emotionally from his mother pervaded all areas of his life and threatened to make treatment impossible. Indeed, he presented a picture which on the surface seemed quite intractable.

During the first weeks of treatment, Paul was so unwilling to attend, even with his mother sitting in the treatment room, that it seemed unlikely that an analysis could be sustained. Insuring his attendance thus became in itself a considerable technical problem.

Our method of choice for such a case, namely, the simultaneous analysis of mother and child as described in previous publications (Levy, 1960; Sprince, 1962), was precluded by this mother's pathology.

A crucial feature in the handling of this case, therefore, lies in the modification of technique that made it possible for Paul to participate in a successful analytic experience in spite of continued, massive, conscious resistance. Early in our contact I decided to adopt the technical device of presenting the necessity for treatment to him so authoritatively that he did not himself have to assume responsibility for his attendance or for getting well. Paul's treatment lasted for a little over 4 years, and finished 3 years ago.[1]

Paul had always been strongly inclined to avoid frightening situations by withdrawal into illness; he had many somatic symptoms, such as headaches, recurring colds, sore throats, stomach trouble, and he made heavy weather of any minor ailments or physical hurt. He was frequently brought home from school because he felt ill. Temper outbursts at home were coupled with regression to whiney, dependent, demanding behavior.

In spite of an above-average IQ (124 on the WISC) and the fact that he had gained a grammar school place, his work was inadequate and he was rapidly developing a school phobia.

[1] When I started to work with Paul some 7 years ago I derived help and encouragement from the members of the Group for the Study of Adolescent Problems (convened by Ilse Hellman) and from discussions with Anna Freud whose technical suggestions are embodied in this paper. More recently I have benefited greatly from discussions with a small group of colleagues (convened by Agi Bene) who meet weekly to consider problems concerned with techniques of child analysis.

At school he was unpopular and a butt for constant teasing and bullying. He had only one boyfriend, whom he had known since he was a small child. In the past he had enjoyed athletics, but now he refused to participate in boyish activities. Paul had been preoccupied with his mother's health ever since his mother had suddenly been hospitalized for 2 weeks with a nervous breakdown when he was 6 years old.

Paul's pathology hinged upon his unconscious conviction that his mother's health and sanity depended upon his remaining a sick and helpless failure. Any move toward emotional separation, personal achievement, or masculinity was felt to constitute an aggressive attack upon his mother and aroused overwhelming anxiety. His analysis was characterized throughout by his denial of any need for treatment, a sullen reluctance to come, and my uncertainty whether he would turn up for the next session.

While my technique ultimately facilitated the development of a transference neurosis and enabled us to work to a successful conclusion, it also relied on those passive features which were at the core of Paul's illness. Thus the analysis started with a basic contradiction—the utilization of the very symptom it set out to cure.

It is my opinion that the use of a device such as that described has repercussions throughout the analysis and must be expected to color the material at each phase of treatment. Moreover, it must be taken into constant consideration in understanding and handling the transference. In addition, an analysis such as Paul's has particular relevance to questions concerning the working alliance and the necessity for such an alliance for a successful outcome. Jack Novick (1970) reported on "The Vicissitudes of the 'Working Alliance' in the Analysis of a Latency Girl" and considered the rational and irrational motives that give impetus to the wish to be cured. Paul was a boy in whom the wish to be cured appeared to be entirely missing.

Background Information

Paul came from a deeply religious family whose somewhat drab home life depended upon the church for entertainment and companionship. He was the youngest of three children and the only boy. One sister, Doris, was 5½ years older than Paul, and Mary, who was married, was 10 years older.

There is little of apparent significance in Paul's early history—pregnancy and birth were normal, Paul was breast-fed for 8 months and weaned gradually. He was believed to have been a contented baby, but was said to have lost confidence at the age of 10 months when he developed his first tooth. He was potted at birth and clean at 2½ years.

Mr. R., aged 52, was a transport supervisor in a large firm. He was a tall, well-built man, slow and ponderous in speech, who though well regarded at work considered himself a failure. As a child he suffered from asthma, was hospitalized frequently, and, like Paul, could not do things that other boys did. His life was dominated by his wife to whom he left all major decisions. Apart from the church, where he was a deacon and Sunday school teacher, he had relatively few interests; he enjoyed reading comics and playing with cars and toy trains. During Paul's treatment he developed a mild angina pectoris, but could not bring himself to ask his doctor about the nature of his illness.

Mrs. R. was 51 years old. She was always neatly but dowdily dressed, obviously making no concession to femininity. A bland vagueness and almost complete inability or unwillingness to recollect incidents and facts were striking in view of Paul's similar characteristics. At times, however, she could be facetiously jocular, using outdated schoolboy jargon, while at other times she was arch and almost birdlike in manner.

Mrs. R. was the youngest of three children and the only girl. Her only wish as a child had been to be as good as her two older brothers and to be accepted as their equal. Cricket had been her primary interest. Initially, my standing as a therapist depended primarily on the fact that I lived and worked near Lord's cricket ground. The many examples of her competitiveness and rivalry with men left me with the impression that her relationship to her two brothers and her sense of injustice that she had been born a girl had an important bearing on her need to subordinate and disparage the male members of her family.

The main feature of Mrs. R.'s personality was what she described as her "cussedness." By this she meant her need to force herself to do things she did not want to do but that her religion taught. She could refuse demands only on the grounds of ill-health, thus often welcoming illness to justify avoiding obligations.

At our initial interview she reiterated how good, thoughtful, and conscientious Paul was. He rarely lost his temper, except to complain of the lack of television which the family did not have because of Mrs. R.'s weak eyes and because the programs were "unsuitable for little boys." On such occasions he always apologized afterward. Fearing that Paul might catch cold or infections and start a routine of staying away from school, she still insisted upon bathing and drying Paul "to make sure he wasn't wet between the crevices." She identified wholly with Paul's night fears since she had suffered similarly as a child but had preferred to lie stiff and terrified rather than let her brothers know of her weakness. When we met she and her husband were unable to sleep with their bedroom door closed. Both mother and Paul shared the same sedatives, taking them night and day.

This picture of a dependent, helpless, and overprotected boy was offset by contradictory features. Paul was encouraged to go off alone for long journeys on his bike, and real illnesses were often ignored or neglected. It seemed that husband and wife did not see. eye to eye on bringing up their children, and Mrs. R. complained of her husband's anxious, overfussy ways, implying that it was not manly to avoid risks.

The details of Mrs. R.'s depressive illness remained unclear, although it was established that it preceded by a matter of weeks or months Paul's own hospitalization for tonsillectomy at the age of 6.

Treatment Material

Technical Difficulties

Paul was a slight boy who did not look his age. His appearance was neat and effeminate. His nails were badly bitten. He sat fully clad in his outdoor clothes, huddled up in his chair in hostile silence. His face was tense and tearful, and his manner of not appearing to hear my overtures was one with which I was to become painfully familiar.

At our first meeting Paul sobbingly clung to Mrs. R. and could be persuaded to come into the treatment room only if she accompanied him. This continued for the first 6 weeks during which time he rarely looked at me or at anything in the room. He gazed rigidly at the floor, but secretly tried to catch his mother's eye with a look that implied that they were united against me. In a whisper he demanded that his mother reply to my questions. At times he would run from the treatment room, dragging his mother with him into the car. Nevertheless, the themes of these initial meetings provided clues to the nature of Paul's conflict. He spoke of his distress at the diagnostic interview because he had been asked whether his parents treated him kindly. He insisted that his only problem was his mother's health and that this had worried him since she had entered a hospital when he was 6 years old. He remembered it clearly because it was the day his dog Jason, who had been with him all his life, had died. Jason was a big dog and he had to be put to sleep because, although his mother loved dogs, her health could not stand up to his wild and messy ways. As he repeated this story sobbing with distress, he insisted that he was crying only because he missed Jason so much and that he had always been better when he had had a pet.

In this early period my interpretations centered on Paul's unhappiness, his need for help, and his belief that his mother felt about her children growing up as he had felt when he lost his dog. When I said that he might feel that if he grew well and independent, his mother might become unhappy and ill, his face lit up with agreement for a brief second. From this period onward I did everything possible to make Paul aware of the two sides of his personality—the infantile regressed part, which could not be relied upon to judge his or other people's needs; and the intelligent developing part, which wanted to be like other boys and did see things as they really were and with which I would ally myself.

Paul permitted his mother to move into the waiting room following a superficially jocular outburst of aggression between them. Paul had teasingly muttered in his mother's presence and between

tears that he had yet to see any order in their household and that
he could never get a word in edgeways against his mother and
sisters. Mrs. R., distressed and embarrassed, described how running the household overwhelmed her. She added that Paul was as
untidy as she, "but you can't flog a dead horse." At this point the
mutuality of their death wishes became obvious, as did their reaction formations of tremendous overprotection and concern for
each other. I interpreted Paul's fear that his angry feelings might
in some way make his mother ill and that he needed to keep her
near to make sure that he had not harmed her.

When Mrs. R. settled into the waiting room with a fire and a
book, she said, "Now I have to go to a little cubby hole and leave
you to the nice big room—it isn't fair." It was characteristic of
Paul's use of denial and distortion that for a whole year he insisted that his mother had not been complaining about the room,
but had used the word "fair" to refer to the inclement weather.
It was equally characteristic of Mrs. R. to greet any sign of independence with a demonstration of illness or martyrdom.

Paul continued to weep throughout his sessions, although he
was at times able to admit that treatment was more helpful than
he had expected it to be. At no time, however, was his mother allowed to know of our more friendly contact. He would leave me
with an amicable if watery smile, but by the time he got to the
waiting room only a few seconds later he was sullen and hostile.
At home he continued to make his parents' life unbearable by insisting that treatment was intolerable. Each day he ordered his
mother to ring and explain that he was really trying hard, but he
could not possibly come again since I, like the consultant, had
asked him questions about his parents. Getting him to his sessions
became so difficult that his parents felt unable to continue, and
the treatment was threatened to terminate before it had got
under way.

At this stage after 6 weeks of contact, the overall pattern of attempts to communicate followed by intense anxiety and resistance
was reviewed from the point of view of technique and the possibility of establishing a working alliance. Anna Freud suggested
that a child with such a loyalty conflict would not be able to

attend voluntarily and that while he should be made increasingly aware of the extent of his illness, other methods of insuring his attendance would have to be considered.

Following this discussion I told Paul that I thought I now knew enough about his difficulties to have formed a clear opinion, which I wanted him to know. I enumerated his many positive qualities and pointed to the worries that stood in the way of his healthy development, including his fear that independence would harm his mother. I said that such a condition must be taken as seriously as a physical illness because it would not get better without help. I had therefore come to the conclusion that it would be wrong to give him the responsibility for deciding whether or not to continue treatment because I was quite sure that his illness would interfere with treatment as it had interfered with everything else. I asked what he would do if he were called to a house on fire and found the owner refusing to leave it, although it seemed likely that the roof would collapse. Paul gave the slightest nod of agreement to my suggestion that he would certainly make sure that the person was taken to safety.

Paul's hostile, angry, and babyish behavior toward his parents continued, but in his sessions the relief that he felt at no longer bearing the responsibility for getting better was discernible.

In the analysis of a late latency or teen-age boy we are accustomed to give ourselves time to listen to the patient's problem, and we can usually bring an open mind to the development of the material as it clusters around the analyst and moves toward a transference neurosis.

After the initial hurdle of ensuring Paul's attendance at sessions had been overcome I approached my work with him with this expectation. Paul's analysis, however, presented further technical difficulties that were rooted not only in the pathology but in the nature of his reluctant working relationship with me. It became evident that for a considerable time I would have to be one step ahead and anticipate which interpretations were likely to relieve anxiety about his mother, only to bring the dangerous affects and distress into the treatment situation, thereby causing a need for further defensive maneuvers or some piece of acting out. For example, my understanding and verbalization of Paul's idea of himself as his mother's dependent pet—and life line—increased his conflict, and especially his fear that he might succumb to the temptation to make use of treatment for masculine and forward moves. While this understanding enabled me to modify my technique and safeguard his attendance, it also forced me to take cognizance of his projective defenses.

A phobiclike response is not unexpected in a boy with such severe conflicts over drive expression. Novick and Kelly (1970) remind us that the work of projection, when the drive is allocated to the therapist, provides no relief but only "the anxiety-driven wish to flee from the situation" (p. 86).

Thus for many months, whenever insight into the affects surrounding drives or their derivatives was imminent, Paul experienced me as intruding, attacking, damaging, and destroying. At such times he became an inaccessible, regressed, whimpering bundle, insisting that I was putting dangerous ideas into his head, that treatment was making him worse, and that he feared he was going mad. His very real terror could not be denied.

Novick and Kelly (1970) have also pointed out that what the child patient projects onto the therapist is likely to have some basis in reality. In Paul's case we were dealing not only with his aggressive drives but also with the reality of his mother's aggressive envy and unconscious impulsion to denigrate the male members of her family.

Another difficulty in the analysis was the central role that the mother's conflict played in Paul's pathology. For the moment, however, I want to emphasize the problem of her unconscious guilt which during the first year impelled her to collude with Paul's acting out, although she had at the same time a genuine wish to cooperate with treatment.

Until I had fully understood this I was "caught out" again and again in situations such as the following one: Paul would leave serenely after what appeared to have been a good session, only to rush to the nearest telephone and ring his mother, saying that treatment had made him ill, that he must be fetched from the station and taken home to bed. He would demand ice cream or sweets and endless attention. These calls were to be kept a secret from me, as were his subsequent school absences. Paul threatened his mother that if she told me, she would be letting him down. She in turn threatened me with the same fate if I betrayed her confidences to Paul.

Eventually, when Paul renewed his threats to end treatment, she was persuaded to let me use this information and I could then show both Paul and Mrs. R. what they were doing. I also adopted other measures to protect the treatment; for example, when I felt that the material discussed in a session would tend to heighten Paul's anxiety and guilt, I warned him in advance that he would probably be tempted to act out his fears in a regressive way in order to make reparations to his mother. At times, with his agreement, I also warned his mother of this possibility.

A third difficulty was Paul's general behavior in the analytic sessions. He tormented me with his sullenness, frustrating me with his bland disinterest, lack of effort, and inability to remember. He controlled and outwitted me with his passive docility, complaints of tiredness, and demands for physical care and attention. He regressed to preoedipal levels whenever he was confronted by conflicts or when he was made aware of aggressive or sexual affects. He would, for example, play with chewing gum with his fingers and tongue or let milk chocolate melt in his mouth and drop from his lips. He would then plead with me to see if his lips were dirty. Thus, in many respects, he related to me as he did to his mother.

His stubborn controlling character, his preoccupation with cleanliness, and his conscious and unconscious withholding and retention were all acted out in relation to me. For a year Paul would arrive late, set the alarm, and draw a time chart so that the best part of every hour would be spent sullenly crossing out each minute as it passed. He used many maneuvers in an attempt to make me threaten him and thereby repeat the toilet situation in which he had been threatened with purgatives. Money played an essential part in our relationship: he handled it in a tantalizing manner, offering me gifts and then withdrawing them.

In this early phase of treatment I worked persistently to demonstrate that I could not be drawn into arguments and battles and that my sole purpose was to understand the meaning of his behavior and the feelings and fantasies behind it. Implicit in my patient but firm attitude was my acknowledgment of Paul as a personality meriting respect in his own right.

In the third year of treatment we were able to uncover his feeling that his internal resources were not his to dispose of at will so that not even his thoughts were his to offer. His rare communications concerned his preoccupation with the morbid—stories of deaths, plane and car crashes, outbreaks of fire, persecution of minorities.

The most striking feature was a passive docile quality which is difficult to pinpoint. Although at times Paul questioned me incessantly, I had the feeling that there was little if any evidence of active curiosity or pleasure in discovery or achievement. He behaved as if treatment was something "done to him." The meaning of this became clearer when I realized that his questioning me became acute at times when he was unable to judge the reality of his bodily sensations; for example, he could not be sure whether he had a pain or whether he felt well or ill until his mother or I had confirmed it. It was as if he had no right to experience his body as belonging to himself.

It was this passivity with its sadomasochistic ramifications which provided a continuous threat to treatment. I told Paul that his need to so determinedly resist all my efforts to understand and work with him pointed to an immense source of strength which at the moment he was using like a wall to block up a dam. For many weeks we spoke of his need to "fight" passively any of the unknown dangers against which his strength was deployed. I likened it to electricity which in its crude form people feared but which once understood could be used to generate life-saving and other devices. It seemed that unleashing his strength was such a danger to him that he had to sacrifice friendships and pleasures in achievement, rather than risk this danger.

Eventually, Paul spoke of a boy in his class who was physically handicapped and who had learned to use cunning to make up for his lack of physical strength. He told me how he had always longed to steer an electric boat and then described the plight of a retired naval pilot who was too old to obtain a license and would have to depend on a younger eligible colleague to go with him.

Gradually he introduced his belief that his mother could not bear to watch him develop physically and mentally while she was aging and daily losing these very qualities. He believed that his mother might commit suicide if he did not constantly demonstrate that far from wishing to steer on her behalf, he was tied to her apron strings. He saw himself as a guide dog who might want to go his own way but had to consider the blind person whose life was entrusted into his hands. At another time he described the gorillas at the zoo who got used to being imprisoned in a confined space because they had been born to it.

We discussed how Paul felt imprisoned by his concern for his mother and frightened of his wish to be free like other boys, but he feared that, like Jason's messy wildness, this wish would make his mother ill. Paul added, "Jason was my dog, so it was the same as if I done it." But at that time Paul did not refer to the fact that Jason had been put to sleep to protect his mother's health and sanity, which he must have perceived as a potent threat of what might happen to him.

Only very much later could we reach the projection of his own death wishes—namely, his admission that he could have borne his mother's death more easily than Jason's and that only if mother were dead could he hope to escape from his bondage and be free to be a man. Ultimately and closely connected with transference thoughts of getting out of treatment as a result of my death, Paul illustrated how any notion of marrying and setting up a family depended upon his parents' demise. He ruminated that if his parents were dead and he were married and living in the parental house, he would alter the lawn—in fact, he would do many things very differently. In this way we discovered that Paul's image of himself as a married man was always in terms of taking over his parents' home. He remarked, "They won't give it to me until they are both dead, so if I ever marry, it will have to be late in life."

Paul's need to protect his objects from his destructive omnipotent power resulted in the suppression of all feelings of rage and anger to the point of something akin to paralysis. He also had to deny that his parents or other people were ever angry with him. The only occasion he remembered seeing his mother angry was on the day of her hospitalization when Paul had forgotten to pass on a message from his father.

Gradually, it became possible to show Paul the aggression behind his clinging dependence and how under the guise of extreme concern for his mother he was keeping her leashed to him as if she were his slave. Paul thought that it might be just this sort of passivity which made him the butt for relentless teasing at school. He admitted how much he admired boys who stood up to authority and how he despised himself for letting me and his parents impose our ideas on him.

This led to a fresh evaluation of what being forced to attend treatment against his will had meant to him. He had experienced it as my ganging up with his parents against him, and he compared this to his present feeling about his school tormentors. The transference revealed the fear of masochistic pleasure at being controlled and forced into submission and was accompanied by anal and phallic fantasies of giving me his thoughts and valuables and thereby becoming part of me. I shall discuss the implications of this for his sexual development in connection with the last phase of his analysis, but here it is relevant that he described how he had been approached in a friendly manner to join a game and had been unexpectedly set upon, stripped, and left naked in the classroom.

It is not surprising that Paul used the couch initially to curl up on and fall asleep. This behavior continued for some weeks during which time he would appear not to hear me and then suddenly awake complaining that he could not move his limbs because they were numb. He himself diagnosed the "deadness" as a safety measure against uncontrolled violence which could harm him as well as others. He spoke of a teacher who, furious at finding his car tire punctured, had kicked it with such force that he dislocated his shoulder.

Paul's inability to tolerate conflicting affects led to the use of primitive defenses such as projection, isolation of affect, obliteration, and a tendency toward a split in the ego. The fact that treatment enabled him gradually to reconcile these opposing affects is illustrated in the story of Dr. Syn, which Paul told me. Dr. Syn was a priest who used his vicarage as a cover for a gang of smugglers. While pretending to be on the side of the law and aiding the search for the gang leader, Dr. Syn was himself the leader of the gang. But whichever role he played, he played it so convincingly that he was able to deny the other role, even to himself. Ultimately Dr. Syn the gangster was killed and his mask fell off.

At this point I shall abandon my focus on the technical difficulties, which in various forms persisted throughout the analysis, in order to discuss the salient features of Paul's development as they appeared in his analytic material.

Conflict over Sexual Identity

The main source of his conflict seemed to me to stem from his mother's narcissistic pathology and her problems over her own sexual identity. In such cases the child finds himself destined to act as a phallic extension of the mother. The mother experiences the child's attempts to separate himself from her as a castration. The child in turn finds himself impelled to protect his mother's needs by remaining psychically attached to her long beyond the stage when it is appropriate, while at the same time taking on the shameful feminine role himself and thus freeing her from her devalued aspects. The mother's intense sexual identity conflicts thus crucially shape the development of the libidinal and aggressive drives in the child, and leave an imprint not only on the child's concept of his own sexual identity but also on his ego and superego functions.

In such mother-child interactions, the conflicts usually become manifest when the child's motor activity or aggressivity begin to threaten the mother's castration fears. In Paul's case, however, there were indications that this had started even earlier.

It is interesting that in the history as well as in her interview with me, Mrs. R. pointed to the growth of Paul's first tooth at 10 months as the moment in his development when he noticeably lost confidence. I have wondered whether this might not be the point when Paul's increased motility differentiated him from his sisters and when his mother's anxiety about his masculinity was first alerted.

Teeth were a prominent feature in Paul's material. Paul told me of his belief that boys and girls were all born alike, but that girls lose their penises earlier than boys. His denial of sex differences is illustrated by the only recollection of his tonsillectomy—namely, that both boys and girls used the same type of bottle to urinate in. He explained that he longed for his teeth to fall out because he had only three grown-up teeth so far. He had verified this fact with his mother, who as usual could not remember but thought that Doris and Mary had lost theirs early while Paul had tended to lose his late and probably still (at 12!) had mainly milk teeth. He showed me his front teeth (which were in fact all second teeth) and after many days of discussion showed them again to his mother who thought she might have been mistaken. Paul could only remember losing one tooth which he had in fact swallowed. I began to see a connection between mother's confusion and vagueness over his and the girls' teeth and Paul's confusion about the difference between himself and his sisters and mother.

Paul first introduced his confusion over sexual identity by questioning me incessantly on how a key worked in a lock. When I remarked that he knew more about mechanical matters than I did and that there was surely some other question he was concerned with, Paul used the word penis for the first time, telling me that the word had never been mentioned at home. Following this he admitted to considerable anxiety over whether the house key was really his or his mother's. He felt she tied him to her through the key and was reluctant to let him grow up by giving him one of his own. But he could not bring himself to mention it to her. Soon a key ring appeared with a plastic tiger, but no key. The tiger was an advertising gimmick from a petrol company which circularized customers with a tiger's tail and a notice saying, "I've got a tiger in my tank." The tail is inserted into a tank so that it sticks out. Paul asked whether I had a tail sticking out of my car tank. In this context he showed me a loose tooth, explaining that the new tooth which was coming up was wearing the old root away.

We could now recognize that it was not only the key that Paul felt belonged to his mother, but also his body and his penis. If mother could not be a boy herself, she could at least possess a penis as long as he remained part of her. To insist upon his independence meant castrating her and taking something from her. This implied destroying her in the way he believed a new tooth destroyed the old one.

Paul brought evidence of his masculine strivings together with his envy of my and my husband's possessions and achievements and his wish to do as well or better than I or his parents. He started to show pride in his clothes and demanded a manly haircut. While he felt that his father might not mind his having a better job or more money than he, Paul was convinced that no mother could really bear her son to do better than she had done. Repeatedly and with some amazement Paul asked whether I knew of any mothers who really wanted their boys to have a better chance than they had had.

Much of all this can be understood as a projection of Paul's own infantile envy and castration fear, but the reality of his mother's intense penis envy and rivalry played into a further belief—that if he showed he possessed a masculine organ, it would be taken from him.

Once Paul arrived in a state of extreme anxiety because the seam of his school cap had become undone. He worried that the slit would show, that it could never be mended properly, and he kept feeling it with his hands and passing it to me for examination. This incident enabled me to speak of his fear that something about him was not right. Paul responded by admiring my water-can with its very long spout, adding, "Mother wants one of these." I said that while mother could have a watering can, the water pipe he was concerned with was something only boys and men had.

There followed material about missing teeth which he feared would never grow properly. He also told me that in the company of boys he felt he was not their equal because he lacked things they had.

We could now see that his feeling of being different from other boys related to his belief that he had to keep pace with the girls, which meant that sooner or later he too would lose his organ. His constant question whether I would let him bring his dog, if he had one, referred to his fear that I too would wish him to keep pace with the girls. Paul's feminine identification was further facilitated by his father's marked preference for his daughters and especially the younger one. Doris was a fragile child who had had many minor ailments, and who did not do well at school. Mr. R.'s protective attitude to Doris outweighed any pride he might have had in Paul's achievements—thus when the letter announcing Paul's grammar school place arrived, the first consideration was how to hide the fact from Doris so that she would not be upset or disappointed. When during the course of Paul's treatment Mr. R. came to see me, his first words were that Doris was in the car and he would like to introduce her to me.

Paul's rivalry with and jealousy of Doris played into his choice of a negative oedipal solution. Many of his passive, whiney, complaining characteristics could be traced to Doris. Work on his envy and jealousy of Doris revealed that his castration fears were balanced by a secondary gain—that he might become a girl and be appreciated as Doris was.

Attempts to link these facts with Paul's preoccupation with wounds, damage to body parts, and loose teeth were followed by the customary resistance and regression. It soon became evident that my old Ford (only slightly less battered than his father's) was safer than my husband's new Vauxhall. Every time he heard the Vauxhall Paul was convinced that the exhaust pipe had a hole in it and would break off, as it had on father's old crock. He remembered that his father had once cut off the tip of his finger, but it had grown again.

Paul's reluctance to participate in sports and athletics was closely tied to his castration fear, as was his general passivity. He believed fervently that the only way to protect your valued possessions—and that included intelligence—was to pretend you hadn't any. Thus he exhibited his weakness and lack to put people off the scent.

As it became possible for him to experience some pride in his masculine achievements Paul became frightened that the "pleasure might go to his head" and that he would show off and court retribution. He told me about the head boy who had thrown his weight about too much and had even started mucking about with the girls, until he had been deprived of his promotion.

One of Paul's rare dreams followed his first shave. "I was using an electric razor, but there was one piece in the center of my beard which I could not remove." It seemed that his penis was becoming more a part of his own body.

Until this point in treatment Paul experienced castration as coming primarily from his mother, with his father acting under her domination. The danger of finally acknowledging his masculine wishes was illustrated in a story he told me just one year before the termination of treatment. It concerned Zorab the son of Rostum. Rostum was a king who went to the wars leaving his wife pregnant. His wife was delivered of a son but dreaded losing him when he reached military age. So she announced to her husband that their child was a girl. When Zorab grew up, he discarded his femininity and joined the army where father and son met in single combat. Zorab recognized his father and rushed to meet him with open arms. But Rostum said, "I have no son" and killed him. Paul commented, "That's my problem—I was brought up as a girl."

It was only with the acknowledgment of his masculine wishes and castration fear that Paul could speak of masturbation. He had previously denied all knowledge of masturbation. The profuse material centering around masturbatory activity, which he both enacted and brought verbally, had little apparent meaning to him until he demonstrated how a run-down dynamo regained strength after a period of rest. He showed me how the slightest touch to the contacting wires would increase the speed of the dynamo until it reached a height which he called a climax. It was at this point that he remembered a recurring dream which he had had as a little boy. It was that he had stroked a tiger which swelled up in 5 seconds. This dream convinced Paul more than anything else that he must in fact have masturbated and had erections as a child. We were able to see that one aspect of his need to sleep with his parents or with his or their door open was his wish to control the temptation to masturbate.

Paul now told me about his lifelong sleeping disturbances and his nightmares of wolves and wild animals coming into his bedroom. He explained that if he did not keep awake at night, a volcano might erupt and lava smother him and his family. He would lie in bed imagining catastrophes and in particular a car driver who fell asleep at the wheel and was thereby responsible for a terrible accident. This story opened the way to a discussion of Paul's need to keep awake to protect his parents from the dangers he believed to be inherent in the sexual act. We began to see that his fantasy of the composite male/female woman who produced her babies alone had the purpose of defending against a greater danger—that of sexual intercourse in which the man *does* play a part.

Paul asked whether I knew that a hatpin dropped from the Empire State Building would fall with such force that it would penetrate the hood of a car and the person inside it. His speculations concerned the danger to the man involved in the act of penetration. Paul believed that if the man was to remain intact and complete, he must insure distance from the woman and remain constantly alert. His concept of sexual intercourse was that of fellatio, which he described as cannibalism since the seed that made the baby was really a section of the man's penis. Thus the man lost a piece of his penis in the making of each new baby. Some of Paul's controlling behavior in the sessions, such as his constant play with the alarm clock, preoccupation with the time chart, and even his sleeping was related to the need to defend against the fantasy which had oedipal significance. Paul had often reported thoughts of making a hole through the consulting room floor which would extend into the roof of my car in the garage below.

This material demonstrates Paul's overwhelming fear of aggressive sexuality, how it distorted his libidinal development, increased his confusion over the sexual roles, and drove him further toward the passive position.

Paul's frightening oral and anal fantasies of sexual intercourse in which he identified with both feminine and masculine roles could now be related to his inhibition of curiosity and learning difficulties. His apparent lack of genuine interest and his inability to take in and remember could be traced back to the time when he shared his parents' bedroom and their bed and later listened to them through the open doors. Although Paul had almost no memories, the analysis of his inhibition of curiosity in the context of his castration anxiety and fear of oral incorporation brought about a gradual change in his capacity to work as well as a considerable extension of his hobbies and social activities. Perhaps more important, this analytic work at last enabled him to express some of his curiosity directly. Paul asked his sister whether she had sexual intercourse for pleasure and what it felt like to be pregnant, and his mother if she could still have a baby. He told me of an Indian child couple aged 13, thereby introducing the question of how far boys and girls of his age were developed. He fully participated in the ensuing discussion, showing amazement and pride when he realized that he really had semen in his testes—he asked whether some boys had more and some boys less. His idea about the interchangeability of sexes must be considered here; his passive identification with his mother and sister has already been mentioned. There were also hints about the wish to have a baby associated with fantasies of swallowing his milk tooth, which I understood as a fellatio fantasy in which he could give himself a baby as he believed his mother could.

More normal fantasies of sexual intercourse appeared only much later when Paul was battling against experiencing his active oedipal wishes in the transference. These fantasies, in which the woman was damaged by intercourse, were clearly associated with his mother's illness and hospitalization.

Oedipal Material

Paul's envy of the "haves" as against the "have nots" and his angry complaints about the exploitation of the underdog referred in the first instance to his view of his own hopeless position in the family. Gradually it became clear that his insistence that even a laborer with very little brains was more valuable to the community than the professional man had relevance to his father onto whom he initially externalized many of the devalued features of his own personality. He moaned incessantly about his father's dirty eating habits, his helpless, fussy, complaining nature, and his critical attitude and explosive outbursts of anger.

It was difficult to separate reality from externalizations, and externalizations from identification with the aggressor. Mr. R., in his own words, was a man "unable to take the man's role in his family." He harbored a constant sense of injustice, was litigious and frequently preoccupied with writing complaining letters (which were never sent) to postal firms whose goods did not come up to standard. Mr. R. reported that he nagged Paul incessantly and saw in him all his own inadequacies. On the other hand, many of Mr. R.'s achievements merited respect, especially his church work, his skill in repairing and handling cars, and his useful hobby of woodwork. The fact that Paul brought so much material via cars has, I think, an oedipal significance since interest in cars was the one area in which Paul could fully identify with his father's masculine qualities. He genuinely admired his father's ability to drive, diagnose faults, and repair the cars he was responsible for. He longed to drive himself, which his father encouraged. In addition, hobbies of bus spotting, plane observing, and constructing model engines and planes were interests Paul began to share with his father.

Paul's sleeping difficulties had already cleared up and he was sleeping alone with the door closed—no mean achievement in this family—when he began to tell me how left out he had felt when his parents were in bed together. He suddenly remembered how when he was small his father would go off for 2 or 3 days for work and Paul would go into his mother's bed to watch father pack. He could not remember whether he slept with his mother while his father was away, but he remembered being disappointed when his father did not go away as he had expected. He thought he enjoyed his father's absences because he brought back cream to eat and also because Paul was left as the man of the family. Surprised at such an admission of rivalry, Paul asked, "Could a boy of 4 really feel like that?"

As Paul increasingly recognized both his rivalry with his father and how much he valued him, his jealousy and anger toward him for preferring his sisters intensified. It seemed to Paul as if once again treatment was running counter to his own interests in that it was siding with his masculinity while in his family girls were more appreciated. I began to notice that any masculine moves were again followed by psychosomatic illness and failure at work. Further understanding of this emerged following the third dream Paul brought to his analysis. In it he was using the down escalator instead of the up one. A specific determinant of the dream related to his headmaster's insistence that Paul was not aiming high enough, that his professional goals were beneath his abilities. Paul's choice of profession at the age of 14 ranged from working with the local garbage disposal authority to police and fire services, which were, unlike his analyst, on the side of the law. It was from this dream that we were able to reach Paul's conflict over competing with and bypassing his father.

The last phase of treatment centered on genitality and Paul's battle to establish himself on the positive oedipal level. This development was in reality aided by Paul's having formed an admiring relationship with his brother-in-law, who had some of the masculine qualities Paul's father lacked.

Both at school and at home Paul's position had changed substantially. He was able to tolerate frustration, to stand up for himself, and to fight back if necessary. He was captain of the school cricket team. He was financially independent of his family, having obtained a Saturday job as well as a paper round. Speaking of the change in himself he observed that to feel easy and confident you have to have a personality of your own.

Paul's behavior in his sessions, however, often made it difficult to believe in these changes. He continued to be whiney, helpless, and stubborn. He appeared to attend reluctantly, absented himself frequently, and often slept during the hour. Interpretations concerning the discrepancy between his outside activities and his behavior in the analysis brought his sexual conflicts into focus and ultimately into the transference.

I discovered for the first time that his school was coeducational when at 15 years of age he complained that the Head was now segregating the girls in the classroom because they were a distraction. He brought a penny into which he had bored a hole with acid and instructed me to feel the hole. It reminded him of a game the boys played together. They would rub each other's hands to magnetize them and then, by putting one of top of the other, make the lower one rise. He wanted me to play this game with him. When we considered the meaning of this game which struck me as highly age-inappropriate, Paul admitted that he avoided the school lavatories because of sexual discussions. This led to the interpretation that Paul behaved as if he were a small child in order to deny the possibility that mother or I could actively excite him. Talking of sexual matters seemed an intimacy similar to being bathed by mother, which he both wanted and dreaded. Paul confirmed this by enacting the danger of having an erection during the hour.

There now followed a phase of what appeared at first to be homosexual play with the prefects and which Paul described as "mucking about." He would provoke these older boys to punish him by calling them "golden-headed" and "blue-eyed" and dare them to cross the barrier between the boys' and the girls' playgrounds. He spoke of "rape" as forcibly stripping someone, usually a girl, and for the first time acknowledged the sexual implication behind his own experience of being stripped. He spoke of the unmarried school dentist, who said, "Don't worry my dear, I won't hurt you," as a queer, and he thought that both the dentist and the Head were frightened of marriage. He thought a homosexual was a man who raped girls.

There was no doubt that a lot of this play was an enactment of his passive fantasies in relation to his father. They were in part based on an identification with his sister Doris and ultimately with his mother. But the play was also an attempt to see whether father could protect his rights in relation to mother and myself.

The most revealing material concerning this issue came up in connection with Paul's 16th birthday and his parents' reluctant agreement to fulfill his almost lifelong ambition to possess an air rifle. I had warned Paul that they might change their minds at the last moment. In the event they gave him a speedometer instead. Paul angrily insisted that he was satisfied with the speedometer, he had not really wanted an air rifle—and fell asleep. We discussed his old pattern of abandoning his masculine interests when he felt his parents could not tolerate them and how he defended against feelings of anger and hopelessness by denial and increased passivity.

Paul then told of a funny incident. His married sister and brother lived in a small country town called Loose. Recently a notice was pinned on to the board outside the Town Hall, headed "The Loose Women's Institute." Paul insisted that it sounded funny, but that it had no particular meaning. I thought that he was "having me on," and said that he certainly knew the word "loose" had a special meaning in connection with women. Paul denied this vehemently and asked whether loose meant being tight with money. If it didn't mean that, what did it mean? He laughed dubiously when I told him that it related to a woman's morals, and he then described his visits to the Institute and their boring jam-making sessions.

This story had its sequel over many weeks. It led to Paul's ability to acknowledge that his mind worked on two levels and that he had defensively refused to make a link between conscious and pre-conscious knowledge. It brought him back to the air rifle and to something that he had forgotten to tell me—namely, that his mother had met his request with the observation that he might damage someone with it and they would have to pay £1000. It really meant, Paul commented, that his parents did not trust him to manage his masculinity and his penis. As we discussed this further it became clear that my belief in his ability to deal with his masculine equipment made me dangerous and put me in conflict with his parents' beliefs. I was, in fact, a seductive and loose woman.

We considered that Paul protected himself from being tempted by me by just not understanding such things. Paul said, "I've never had the chance to understand and now that I've got it here, I daren't use it." In subsequent sessions he confirmed that it was his father who first drew attention to the humorous aspect of the "Loose Woman's Institute." Paul was sure, however, that his father did not understand the sexual connotation because he disapproved of all sexual matters. In this way we at last reached positive oedipal material and castration fears related to father. Simultaneously, Paul admitted sheepishly to having gone out for the first time with a girl.

During the last period of treatment Paul was able to identify more fully with his father's masculinity, but the danger of by-passing him was always prominent. In one of his extremely rare dreams Paul was driving his Mini car. He suddenly realized that he was only a learner and that he was driving at considerable speed. He decided to ask his father to drive with him and slow him down.

Termination

The treatment was terminated as a result of Paul's own request. Nine months previously he had remarked that since I was always interpreting his right to his own opinions, ought I not to prove it by respecting his opinion that there was nothing wrong with him anymore and that his wish for more freedom was justified? Although we were both aware that the freedom he wanted was not freedom from treatment, the fact that he could openly ask for something without moaning merited respect. It must be added that the continued role of jailer has implications for one's own self-esteem and becomes wearing. Paul could rarely risk telling me of his achievements or indicate that he came to treatment with anything but unwillingness, and we now began to work on why this was so. Paul admitted that he felt convinced that I would resent his successes and believe that he was competing with me.

From the point of view of the transference neurosis, therefore, an open acknowledgment of treatment ending successfully was fraught with danger. Succeeding meant for Paul asserting the possession of and right to his penis. But this also implied that he must castrate mother who still wanted a penis. At the same time success meant bypassing father (who had recently been demoted at work) and demolishing him. These problems threatened the adolescent process of severing the tie to the parents, but they also harbored a very real danger that Paul would be impelled to break his infantile ties by moving away from treatment rather than from his family. I therefore feared an abrupt and angry termination in which he would force me as I had initially forced him.

I discussed this danger very openly with Paul and we agreed to reduce sessions gradually. The last 9 months of treatment could thereby be used to consolidate many of the gains. In particular, we clarified the role that speaking in the sessions had for Paul. It symbolized active penetration and the dangers associated with it.

Toward the end of treatment which was to be in December, Paul reported that his mother had said that there were always disasters at Christmas—earthquakes, plane crashes, and assassinations. Paul thought it was really a coincidence, but all the same it was uncanny; as if God were taking revenge. If he were still superstitious, he would think that God was punishing people for being happy. It was during this week that for the very first time Paul burst into free and amused laughter over something I had said, though he quickly checked himself saying, "I am sorry, I just couldn't resist it." Asked why it was so dangerous to be friendly and relaxed in his sessions, Paul suddenly thought how his father and he shared the duty of putting drops into his mother's ears.

During the last weeks of treatment Paul's conflict over being more successful than his father was uppermost, and he was torn between something approaching friendliness and anger with me for confronting him with such conflicts. He spoke about driving a car and imagined his friends seeing him drive—not that there was anything particular in driving, anyone could do it. But he'd be happy if he was half as good a driver as Dad. I wondered whether he would like me to see him drive a powerful car. Paul said he would not like a Mini, although many men drove Minis. I said that Minis were perhaps more of a woman's car and men minded more than women about the sort of car they drove. Paul said, "It's like a horse to a man—a sort of status symbol."

Paul arrived to his final session with a parcel, saying, "This is to say thank you from all of us." The gift was a china horse which he himself had chosen, but attached to the gift was a letter of appreciation from his parents which he had not been given to read.

In the last session the material touched on all the significant aspects of Paul's treatment and finally centered on his feeling that whatever he achieved as a result of treatment, he would somehow always feel he was a disappointment to his parents. We put into words that from the first day of treatment to the last, his wish to achieve independence, masculinity, and the full use of his potentialities had been in conflict with what he believed to be in his parents' interests. Underlying this had been his conviction that he had no right to his penis and that only by hiding it could he hold on to it. Paul now added a small link to the chain which pointed to his confusion about whether the essential organ belonged to the man or to the woman. He referred to the recent heart transplant operations and the danger that the man might reject the heart and die. He added that it was odd, because the man was fitted with a woman's heart.

At the very end of the hour he brought his final communication. It was about Hanratty, who had been sentenced for murdering a man and woman in a car. He couldn't imagine why this had come into his mind just now, but it had suddenly struck him that he was convinced of Hanratty's innocence.

Conclusions

This paper is concerned with the difficulties inherent in the analytic treatment of an adolescent boy who was unconsciously convinced that health and masculinity ran counter to his mother's interests and endangered her life. The treatment was further complicated by the presence of the mother's ongoing pathology which confirmed the internalized conflict by keeping it alive in the external world.

My aim has been twofold. I have tried to illustrate my handling of the technical difficulties involved in gaining an entré into these conflicts by use of measures without which there could have been no analysis at all. I have suggested that these measures had repercussions throughout the treatment and were reflected in the transference and in the ultimate outcome of the analysis. Implicit in this is the likelihood that certain passive features remain embedded in Paul's personality in spite of his analysis. A further aim has been to trace the fate of libidinal and aggressive drives in a boy whose normal developmental moves were impeded by his mother's narcissistic pathology and conflicts over sexual identity, while his father's passivity deprived him of an object for adequate masculine identification.

Paul's treatment material points to an illness, the core of which centers around the need to inhibit drive impulses. While the disturbances became acute at the phallic stage, the drive regression was to the anal-sadistic level where the battle over intake and expulsion provided the first real testing ground. Much of the material, however, had a marked oral coloring pointing to the existence of earlier fixations and indicating that the factors that ultimately determined the illness operated from the beginning. This must be considered from the point of view of predisposing and weakening the developing ego. We have seen that the growth of Paul's first tooth was associated in the mother's mind with the onset of his difficulties and probably with her first anxiety about his masculinity.

Nevertheless, I have the impression that in cases such as Paul's the intense threat to the mother in whom castration anxiety is revived does not become truly malignant until later when motility and signs of aggressivity reach a certain level. During Paul's infancy the mother's pride in her son as her penis seems to have overridden other considerations and to have safeguarded his early development. From the child's point of view it is the threat of losing the love of the object that serves as the main source of narcissistic supplies which appears to be decisive in inducing pathological interference with the process of internalization.

These observations are pertinent to diagnostic considerations and the assessment of treatability. In such cases it seems important to distinguish between the child's prominent drive location and the level of libidinal partnership as it finally crystallizes in the mother-child couple—in Paul's case, in the phallic-oedipal phase. The clinical picture corresponds to Anna Freud's description (1970) of symptoms resulting from undefended regression to anal and oral levels. She includes in this category pseudostupidity, prolonged dependency, and passive feminine traits in boys.

In a personal communication, Anna Freud contrasted children like Paul, whose aggression and masculinity is unacceptable to the mother, with those children who repress aggression because of an overstrict superego. In these children the interference with aggressive masculinity comes solely from within. In reality, the mothers are proud of their son's masculinity, and superego feelings are secondarily displaced onto the mother. In Paul's case the fact that masculine aggressivity was unacceptable from the outset fed into his superego development. Subsequent projections strengthened the inhibition.

Now a brief word on the working alliance. Although it has been established that in Paul's case at least two essential ingredients for a working alliance—a fully internalized conflict and the capacity for self-observation—were available, the alliance as we understand it was lacking. Why then did Paul get better?

If one looks for the factors which aided the therapeutic process, it would seem that treatment relied heavily on Paul's main symptom, namely, his passivity, which he displaced from his mother onto me in the transference. Some modicum of healthy drive toward masculinity must be assumed, but I am inclined to believe that any expression of a conscious working alliance was more in the nature of a need to obtain immediate relief from suffering than a willingness to work toward a distant aim.

Finally, the unexpected support from the mother poses an interesting point for consideration. It would seem to be a mistake to assume that parents whose pathology favors dependence and regression in their children are totally unable to side with healthy forward moves. Perhaps the intolerable reality of the symptomatology outweighs the gain and militates against continued unconscious collusion. In Paul's case at least some of his symptoms increased his mother's anger so that her guilt and need to make reparation could be exploited for the purpose of treatment. It may even be that the mother's initial participation while she was in the treatment room played some part and enabled her to tolerate the changes brought about by treatment. Any such suggestions must, however, be acknowledged as speculations. Only an analysis of the mother as in those cases already described (Levy, 1960; Sprince, 1962; Hellman, 1970) could really answer such questions.

At the time of writing, some 3 years after treatment terminated, Paul visited me to introduce his fiancée. He had left school 2 years previously after a year in the sixth form where his academic gains were somewhat sparse as compared with his athletic achievements. He had been offered a management apprenticeship in the supermarket where he had worked on Saturdays and has remained with this firm. He has a small circle of friends, runs and maintains a car, and plans to marry in a year's time, when he is 21.

To what extent treatment succeeded in bringing about full genital primacy is, of course, still an open question.

BIBLIOGRAPHY

FREUD, A. (1970), The Symptomatology of Childhood: A Preliminary Attempt at Classification. *This Annual,* 25:19–41.

HELLMAN, I. (1970), Simultaneous Analysis of Mother and Child (unpublished).

LEVY, K. (1960), Simultaneous Analysis of a Mother and Her Adolescent Daughter. *This Annual,* 15:378–391.

NOVICK, J. (1970), The Vicissitudes of the "Working Alliance" in the Analysis of a Latency Girl. *This Annual,* 25:231–256.

— & KELLY, K. (1970), Projection and Externalization. *This Annual,* 25:69–95.

SPRINCE, M. (1962), The Development of a Preoedipal Partnership between an Adolescent Girl and Her Mother. *This Annual,* 17:418–450.

APPLIED

PSYCHOANALYSIS

Joseph Conrad
The Conflict of Command

ROBERT M. ARMSTRONG, M.D.

> Every mental state, even madness, has
> its equilibrium based upon self-es-
> teem. Its disturbance causes unhappi-
> ness. . . .
>
> "To-morrow" (1902b, p. 259)

I

ONE OF THE GREATEST IRONIES IN A LIFE FILLED WITH IRONIES IS
that popularity and financial success came to Joseph Conrad only
years after he had written his greatest work. The fiction that came
after the completion of *Under Western Eyes* in 1910 and his subsequent breakdown at the age of 52 is markedly inferior to that
of the enormously productive preceding decade. Only then did
the public take to Conrad. His popularity resting on all the wrong
books, it is not surprising that it declined rapidly following his
death in 1924. Albert Guerard (1958) writes that "it is safe to say

Associate Clinical Professor of Psychiatry, Yale University School of Medicine; Director of Education and Training, Psychiatric Services, West Haven Veteran's Ad-
ministration Hospital.

that in 1947 the large majority of critics in America did not read
Conrad at all" (p. xi). Douglas Hewitt, in the preface to the second
edition of his *Conrad: A Reassessment,* points to the tremendous
change that had occurred between the original publication in 1952
and the second in 1968. He notes a "Selected Checklist" in the
1964 Conrad Number of *Modern Fiction Studies* of some 90 items
dealing with "Heart of Darkness" alone, and quotes F. R. Karl
from *A Reader's Guide to Joseph Conrad* (1960): "In the 1950's,
the centennial anniversary of his birth has increased the flow of
Conrad studies, until, next to Joyce and perhaps Faulkner, he is
at present the most discussed of any modern author writing in
English" (p. viiif.).

This reawakened interest, centered in Conrad's early work, is
attributable to many factors, but among the most important is his
disturbingly prophetic presentation of conflicts which are current
indeed. The studies of colonialism, of politics, pointing to the
violent struggles within Western civilization, seem closer to us
than they possibly could have to his contemporaries. Coupled
with these studies are the startlingly intuitive explorations of the
isolated man at war with himself, divided by impulses he struggles
to integrate, his tragedy springing directly from his failure to do
so. In the short story "An Anarchist" a man speaks of an impulsive
act which has destroyed his life: "It seems I did not know enough
about myself" (p. 145). Living in a world he saw as mechanistic
and controlled by forces impersonal and blind, and in which such
safety as is possible comes from self-knowledge, Conrad, like Freud,
was driven inward; a man knows enough about himself only after
being tested; if he cannot accept and integrate what he learns, he
is destroyed. If untested, he is nothing.

These two themes—the political, man's relationship to the community of man; and the personal, man's need to integrate all
aspects of his personality—come together around issues of authority
and autonomy to a degree not sufficiently recognized. It is here
that a psychoanalytic study can shed more light, both on Conrad
and the conflicts finding expression in his creativity, and on the
insights which he provides into the divided man, insights which
make him seem so contemporary.

The increased interest in Conrad has already led to several psychoanalytic studies. The first of importance is Gustav Morf's *The Polish Heritage of Joseph Conrad* (1930). Edward Bibring was reportedly working on one when he died, and Helene Deutsch in 1959 presented a study of *"Lord Jim* and Depression" in which she wrote that she and Bibring "came to the conclusion that whereas guilt feelings (superego) played a great role in this deeply psychological novel, the most important problem was what we then [early '30s] referred to as *narcissism* and what today we describe as an 'ego-psychological problem' or the 'problem of ego state.'" Jim's belief in his ability to live up to his "highly narcissistic ego ideal" is shattered by his jump from the damaged ship. "His psychological condition corresponded to the 'state of broken-down self-regard'—which Bibring considers to be the basic factor in depression." The rest of the book she sees as a restitution process, even "a state of insanity with delusions of grandeur," whose efficacy in maintaining new sources of narcissistic supplies is dependent upon isolation. When reality again breaks through in the form of visitors from the "outside" world, Jim collapses and goes to his death. Richard Sterba in 1965 presented a paper emphasizing the oedipal significance of Marlow's journey up the Congo to the "center of the earth." Finally, in 1967, Bernard Meyer published his perceptive psychoanalytic biography.

None of these writers, however, has adequately studied the peculiar importance of the theme of "command" in Conrad's greatest work. Unlike the method of literary criticism where a work of art is assumed to stand alone, a psychoanalytic study of such a theme, giving due regard to both conscious and unconscious intentions, has to deal with biographical material and, more difficult, study a number of works as parts in a larger design.

> . . . a novelist [Conrad wrote] lives in his work. He stands there, the only reality in an invented world, among imaginary things, happenings, and people. Writing about them, he is only writing about himself. But the disclosure is not complete. He remains, to a certain extent, a figure behind the veil; a suspected rather than a seen presence—a movement and a voice behind the draperies of fiction [1912, p. xiii].

To clarify the role that "command" plays in his work, it will be necessary to look briefly at some aspects of a very strange life.

II

> Do you see him? Do you see the story? Do you see anything? It seems to me I am trying to tell you a dream—making a vain attempt, because no relation of a dream can convey the dream-sensation, that commingling of absurdity, surprise, and bewilderment in a tremor of struggling revolt, that notion of being captured by the incredible which is of the very essence of dreams. . . .
>
> "Heart of Darkness" (1899, p. 82)

Joseph Conrad was a unique and fascinating man:[1] part of the fascination is related to a series of changing identities; son of a Polish revolutionary honored as a martyr to the cause of his country's independence; adventurous French sailor and gunrunner, the "Young Ulysses"; British seaman and Master Mariner; one of the greatest of English novelists with a striking affinity for the language. The underlying uncertainty in Conrad's sense of identity is no doubt responsible for the break in external ties he seems to have made as he shifted from one identity to another. Leaving Poland at 16, he maintained a meaningful relationship only with his uncle Thaddeus Bobrowski and this mostly by letter (over the next 20 years; until his uncle died, he saw him only four times and one of these was when his uncle came to Marseilles after Conrad's probable suicide attempt). When he departed from Marseilles on an English ship at 20, he severed all the relationships he had formed in France. Again, when at 36 he retired from the Merchant Service and published his first novel, he left behind all those with whom he had served.

---

[1] My biography of Conrad draws on his autobiographical writings (1906a, 1912, 1921, 1926), his letters (Garnett, 1928; Jean-Aubry, 1927; Watts, 1969), as well as numerous biographical accounts. The most useful one is Baines (1960).

Conrad was later (1912) to insist that he had always intended to become a British seaman ("Already the determined resolve, that 'if a seaman, then an English seaman,' was formulated in my head though, of course, in the Polish language" [p. 122]), although this was clearly untrue. In his identity as an English novelist he also made several assertions which are questionable. First, "All I can claim . . . is the right to be believed when I say that if I had not written in English I would not have written at all" (p. vi). He admonished Hugh Walpole, "You may take it from me that if I had not known English I wouldn't have written a line for print, in my life." [2] And, secondly, that he had never wanted to be a writer in the first place: "the ambition of being an author had never turned up amongst these gracious imaginary existences one creates fondly for oneself at times in the stillness and immobility of a day-dream. . . ." Perhaps, he muses whimsically, he had been placed under a spell by an idle and frivolous magician (1912, p. 68). It is not unusual for creative people to deny responsibility for the inspirations which "come" to them unbidden from unknown sources. But taken together, these two statements suggest a strong denial that Joseph Conrad had ever wanted to become a Polish writer.

But he had. Little is known of the period between his father's death when he was not yet 12 and his announcement at 14 that he intended to leave Poland and become a seaman. But that little is significant. He disliked school; in fact, rebelled against any restraints on his freedom. He continued to be sickly with ailments described as extreme nervousness, migraine headaches, and some type of epilepsy. And, like his father, he wrote plays and induced his companions to act them out. His elders were irritated by his boasts that he would become a great writer (Najder, pp. 9–13).

Konrad's relationship with his father was a peculiarly intense one.[3] Apollo Korzeniowski, a minor playwright and poet, and a failure as an estate manager, moved to Warsaw in 1861 when Konrad was 3; supposedly there to start a literary journal, he was

---

[2] Jean-Aubry (1927, 2:206).

[3] He was baptized Józef Teodor Konrad Nałęcz Korzeniowski. The family and friends always called the boy Konrad, a name famous as that of the nationalist hero of Mickiewicz's poetic drama *The Forefather's Eve* (Najder, p. 4).

in fact one of the leaders of the National Central Committee which "virtually controlled Polish opposition to Russia until the crushing of the 1863 insurrection" (Baines, p. 11). In October, Apollo and Konrad's mother, Evelina, were arrested. Apollo was kept in jail until the two were convicted of revolutionary activities, and in May, 1862 the three left for exile in Russia. Outside Moscow Konrad became seriously ill with pneumonia, and after nursing him through the crisis, Evelina began to show evidence of the tuberculosis which would kill her 3 years later when he was 7. In a small Russian village where he was the only child in a foreign group isolated from the hostile inhabitants, he was without playmates or formal schooling except for brief interludes with his mother's family. Her death isolated him even further, as he remained alone with his father. Apollo, himself ill, depressed, and financially dependent, took up the work of translating Shakespeare, Dickens, and Hugo to occupy his time. Thus literature must to some extent have been connected in Konrad's mind with his father's defeat and passive despair. Apollo turned increasingly to a mysticism which combined a preoccupation with Polish destiny and deification of his dead wife. A friend wrote of finding Apollo "sitting motionless in front of his wife's portrait; he did not move and little Conrad, who was coming in behind me, put his fingers on his lips and said: 'Let's go quietly through the room, because father always looks intently at Mother's portrait on the anniversary of her death—all day, saying nothing and eating nothing.'" The two were extremely dependent upon one another, nursing each other through frequent illnesses. "I . . . have limited my efforts to improving my state," Apollo informed a friend, "and caring for Conrad's health. Both wandering exiles, we need each other; he needs me as his miserable guardian and I him as the only power that keeps me alive" (Baines, p. 21ff.). Konrad, who was precocious both in reading and languages, noted years later (1921, p. 168), "I don't know what would have become of me if I had not been a reading boy."

At the end of 1867 Apollo was released from exile because of ill health. Just over a year later, in May, 1869, when Konrad was 11, he died in Cracow. There was an enormous, silent procession at his funeral, the only way the people of Cracow could pay tribute to a man they considered a martyr. Konrad marched at the head of the procession, "in utter, inconsolable despair," his grandmother said (Najder, p. 11). He left his own impression:

> As a child of course I knew very little of my father's activities, for I was not quite twelve when he died. What I saw with my own eyes was the public funeral, the cleared streets, the hushed crowds; but I understood perfectly well that this was a manifestation of the national spirit seizing a worthy occasion. That bareheaded mass of work people, youths of the University, women at the windows, school-boys on the pavement, could have known nothing positive about him except the fame of his fidelity to the one guiding emotion in their hearts. *I had nothing but that knowledge myself;* and this great silent demonstration seemed to me the most natural tribute in the world—not to the man but to the Idea [1912, p. viii; my italics].

But Konrad himself had been dedicated to that "idea" by his parents from birth, both by the implications of name and, explicitly, in a poem Apollo wrote to commemorate his son's baptism: "To My Son born in the 85th year of Muscovite oppression." In part it read, "My child, my son—tell yourself that you are without land, without love, without Fatherland, without humanity—as long as Poland, our Mother, is enslaved" (Najder, pp. 2, 5). Marching in the funeral procession Konrad could not have escaped the implication that he must carry on his father's struggles. His great need and loss were coupled with the profound respect he saw rendered to Apollo's memory. It is not surprising that he idealized his father; yet, his father's idealism had destroyed his family and left Konrad an orphan. Moreover, he could not avoid the image of his father as defeated:

> What had impressed me more intimately than the public funeral was the burning of his manuscripts a fortnight or so before his death. . . . This is the last time I saw him out of bed. His aspect was to me not so much that of a man desperately ill, as mortally weary—a vanquished man. That act of destruction affected me profoundly by its air of surrender [1912, p. viii].

Apollo in fact did *not* destroy all his manuscripts, and Conrad's distortion is important. The inevitable and powerful ambivalence seemingly was apparent to those who knew the boy; it is perhaps best summed up by Zdzislaw Najder, who has evaluated all the primary sources:

> . . . his father's heritage was for Conrad a cause of strong internal conflict. On the one hand he could not escape the powerful appeal of Apollo's fascinating personality and of the heroic fidelity with which he had served to the tragic end the ideals of patriotism as he had conceived them. On the other hand he was by no means sure if these ideals had had any reasonable basis. Conrad's father must have seemed to him at once awe-inspiring and absurd; his attitude towards him was a mixture of admiration and contemptuous pity. And he could never forgive his father the death of his mother [p. 11].

Caught in such a profound ambivalence, Conrad's conflict can be sketched, if in oversimplified form. There would be a strong tendency to deal with the loss by identifying with his father. Dedicated by that father, as well as by the tradition of family, class, and national sentiment to the father's cause, he inevitably would develop fantasies of replacing father. But the father's early death and his idealization would have prevented modification or displacement of superego images prohibiting such a temptation; the passive tendencies resulting from the early and exclusive relationship with the father (and the unsatisfied longings for a mother lost much earlier) would thus be reinforced. To dedicate himself to his father's ideals and goals would be a dedication to hopelessness and self-destruction. But Apollo was also a weak and defeated man; rebelling against him would intensify the son's sense of guilt. To "become like father" thus potentially carries a number of threats: (1) superego guilt over the realization of hostile wishes in the father's early death. Rage over frustrated dependency needs would tend to be projected and would increase the sadism of the superego. (2) Identification with father is identification with a weak and castrated figure. (3) Identification with father also means submission to ideals ultimately self-destructive. The threat of passive submission lies in all directions; but such tendencies would be positively reinforced in that they would lead unconsciously to gratification of the libidinal ties to father and, on a deeper level, the pregenital mother.

It should not come as a surprise that Conrad's life was marked by alternating periods of intense activity and achievement followed by collapse, depression, helplessness. It should come as no surprise either that the identity crisis in adolescence took the form it did. Soon after his father's death his attempts at identification appear in the ambition to become a writer; perhaps also in the illnesses described. But the threat of the submissive attachment to the idealized Apollo was too great. According to Conrad's uncle, he "grew out of his illnesses" at 14 (Najder, p. 11). He was rebellious. All allusions to becoming a writer disappeared, and he announced his decision to become a sailor—a manly profession which no doubt had the added and essential advantage of requiring him to leave Poland, a land-locked country with not even hints of a tradition of the sea. It is fitting, too, that in that year he repudiated his father's religion. "It's strange," he wrote to Garnett in 1902, "how I always, from the age of fourteen, disliked the Christian religion, its doctrines, ceremonies and festivals. Presentiment that some day it will work my undoing, I suppose" (p. 185).

With a tenacity that suggests he was fighting for his life, he held out against all opposition. In 1874, not yet 17, he left Cracow for Marseilles and the sea. If we think of this in Erikson's term (1956), as the moratorium of many creative men, then it was a long one. He did not begin *Almayer's Folly* for 15 years or leave the sea for 20. And all his life he felt compelled to defend himself against charges of desertion.

III

I don't mean to say that a whole country had been convulsed by my desire to go to sea. But for a boy between fifteen and sixteen, sensitive enough, in all conscience, the commotion of his little world had seemed a very considerable thing indeed. So considerable that, absurdly enough, the echoes of it linger to this day. I catch myself in

hours of solitude and retrospect meeting arguments and charges made
thirty-five years ago by voices now for
ever still; finding things to say that an
assailed boy could not have found,
simply because of the mysteriousness
of his impulses to himself. I understood no more than the people who
called upon me to explain myself.
There was no precedent. I verily believe mine was the only case of a boy
of my nationality and antecedents taking a, so to speak, standing jump out
of his racial surroundings and associations.

A Personal Record (1912, p. 120f.)

For the next 4 years Marseilles was his center. He made several
voyages to the West Indies; how he spent the rest of his time is for
the most part a mystery. He may have smuggled guns into Spain,
may have had a disastrous love affair, almost certainly attempted
suicide by shooting himself through the left side of his chest. In
any event, after his wound healed and after his uncle Thaddeus
Bobrowski, his legal guardian, paid his rather large debts, Conrad
signed onto his first English ship. He had "flatly refused" to return
to Poland (Baines, p. 45). He arrived at Lowestoft, England, on
June 18, 1878. For 6 weeks he sailed on a coaster, and by September he had learned enough English to travel to London and secure
help in finding a berth on a wool trader bound for Sydney, Australia. He was not yet 21.

Conrad's achievements over the next 8½ years are indeed remarkable. In 2 years he passed a difficult oral examination, in
English, for second mate papers in the British Merchant Service.
Four and one half years later he passed the first mate's examination.
And, in 1886, at the age of 28, he became a British subject and
earned his Master's Certificate. In February of the following year
he signed on as first mate of the *Highland Forest,* bound for
Samarang, Java. He was sent to Amsterdam to supervise the loading, but the cargo was delayed by a severe winter freeze.

No young man of twenty-four [in fact he was 29] appointed chief mate for the first time in his life would have let that Dutch tenacious winter penetrate into his heart. I think that in those days I never forgot the fact of my elevation for five consecutive minutes. I fancy it kept me warm, even in my slumbers, better than the high pile of blankets, which positively crackled with frost as I threw them off in the morning. *And I would get up early for no reason whatever except that I was in sole charge.* The new captain had not been appointed yet [1906a, p. 50; my italics].

But after Conrad had supervised the stowing of cargo, Captain MacW - - - (to be immortalized in "Typhoon") did arrive. After a brief inspection he announced with "smiling vexation, . . . 'Well, we shall have a lively time of it this passage, I bet.'" He was right; the ship rolled and pitched violently, and Conrad was frequently reminded that his loading was responsible:

It was only poetic justice that the chief mate who had made a mistake—perhaps a half-excusable one—about the distribution of his ship's cargo should pay the penalty. A piece of one of the minor spars that did carry away flew against the chief mate's back, and sent him sliding on his face for quite a considerable distance along the main deck. Thereupon followed various and unpleasant consequences of a physical order—"queer symptoms," as the captain, who treated them, used to say; inexplicable periods of powerlessness, sudden accesses of mysterious pain; and the patient agreed fully with the regretful mutters of his very attentive captain wishing it had been a straight-forward broken leg. Even the Dutch doctor who took the case up in Samarang offered no scientific explanation. All he said was: "Ah, friend, you are young yet; it may be very serious for your whole life. You must leave your ship; you must quite silent be for three months—quite silent."

In the hospital in Singapore Conrad's thoughts went back to Amsterdam, to Hudig, the charterer with whom he had dealt during the long delay:

Hudig, with his warm fire, his armchair, his big cigar, and the never-failing suggestion in his good-natured voice: "I suppose in the end it is you they will appoint captain before the ship

sails?" . . . His enticing suggestions I used to repel modestly by
the assurance that it was extremely unlikely, as I had not
enough experience. . . .

But he had nearly persuaded me that I was fit in every way to
be trusted with a command. There came three months of mental
worry, hard rolling, remorse, and physical pain to drive home
the lesson of insufficient experience [p. 54ff.].

Thus reads the autobiographical account on which Conrad drew
for the background of Jim prior to his taking the "soft berth"
as mate of the *Patna.* The juxtaposition Conrad chooses clearly
links his guilt over wishes to become captain with his "punishment"—his injury with "queer symptoms," "inexplicable periods
of powerlessness, sudden accesses of mysterious pain"—an injury
at least exaggerated, as several writers have noted, by hysterical
overlay. The guilt can be expiated only by passivity, submission.
In the words of the Dutch doctor, he "must quite silent be for
three months—quite silent." And acknowledge that he is not
ready.

Conrad left the hospital to take the "soft" berth as mate on the
Vidar, a small steamship trading in the islands. He held the
position for only 19 weeks, and yet from this period, and the few
days he spent at Berouw, Borneo, came the background and much
of the experience used in *Almayer's Folly, An Outcast of the Islands, The Rescue,* several short stories, and part of *Lord Jim.*
Early in January, 1888 he suddenly resigned for no known reason
except possible fear of the easy life into which he had drifted.
Returning to Singapore with the intention of obtaining passage
for Europe, he was staying in the Sailors Home when he was
suddenly asked to go to Bangkok to take over command of the
Otago, a sailing ship out of Port Adelaide whose master had died.
It must have seemed like fate which had so abruptly and unsought
after placed this opportunity in his path, the test of command. In
Singapore Harbor, as he left for Bangkok, he undoubtedly caught
a glimpse of a steamer that had just arrived. It was named the
Patna.[4]

[4] Sherry (1966, p. 45) assumes that because Conrad undoubtedly saw the *Patna*
and appropriated the name for the ship in *Lord Jim,* therefore any speculation
that he associated the word with *patria* or *Polska* is unjustified. This is, of course,

IV

> Jukes was uncritically glad to have his captain at hand. It relieved him as though that man had, by simply coming on deck, taken most of the gale's weight upon his shoulders. Such is the prestige, the privilege, and the burden of command.
>
> Captain MacWhirr could expect no relief of that sort from any one on earth. Such is the loneliness of command.
>
> "Typhoon" (1902a, p. 39f.)

The evidence suggests that a second major identity crisis began for Conrad with his appointment as captain of the *Otago*. Its resolution, inasmuch as resolution was possible, came only after 6½ more years, when he left the sea and began a struggle for a new identity, as a serious writer of fiction. Those years were filled with crucial events, but the turning point appears in 1889 when he resigned his command abruptly; on the passenger list for his return to England he for the first time signed his name "Joseph Conrad"; once in England he quite suddenly began to write *Almayer's Folly*. The transition was not to be completed for almost 5 years; not until after the Congo; not until he returned to become (and remain) a first mate; not until uncle Thaddeus Bobrowski, his substitute father, had died. But the crisis began with the *Otago*.

Conrad's only command, the high point of his career as a seaman, lasted some 14 months. Again it is a period of his life about which little is known. In his nonfiction he mentions the episode only a few times, and his facts are curiously inaccurate; he made himself younger than he was and claimed the command lasted 2 years and 3 months. He also claimed that his mate distrusted him because

---

an irrelevant assumption. It is not irrelevant, however, that Conrad chose a name for the ship in *Lord Jim* that was associated with his taking command of the *Otago;* nor is it irrelevant that he associated this act with two famous crimes at sea.

"on our first leaving port (I don't see why I should make a secret of the fact that it was Bangkok), a bit of manoeuvering of mine amongst the islands of the Gulf of Siam had given him an unforgettable scare." [5] The only other significant account is of how he inexplicably got permission from the owners to take his ship to Mauritius by way of the dangerous northern route through the Torres Strait at a precarious time of year. There is an unmistakable note of bravado (if not of counterphobia) in his description of the voyage:

> It was not without a certain emotion that, commanding very likely the first, and certainly the last, merchant ship that carried a cargo that way—from Sydney to Mauritius—I put her head at daybreak for Bligh's Entrance, and packed on her every bit of canvas she could carry [1926, p. 20].

A description of Conrad by a man who knew him in Mauritius suggests quite another state of mind:

> Forceful and very mobile features, passing very rapidly from gentleness to an agitation bordering on anger. Big black eyes which were as a rule melancholy and dreamy, and gentle as well, except for fairly frequent moments of annoyance. . . .
>
> As to his moral character: a perfect education; very varied and interesting conversation—on the days when he felt communicative, which wasn't every day. The man who was to acquire fame under the name of Joseph Conrad was quite often taciturn and very excitable. On those days he had a nervous tic in the shoulder and the eyes, and anything the least bit unexpected—an object dropping to the floor, a door banging—would make him jump [Jean-Aubry, 1957, p. 139ff.].

Perhaps this extreme tension in part accounts for Conrad's apparently quite precipitous proposal to a girl he knew so casually that he was unaware she was engaged to be married soon. In any event, he returned to Australia and resigned his command; there is only the statement in one of his fictional stories, "A Smile of

---

[5] *The Mirror of the Sea* (p. 19). Compare "The Secret Sharer," which is discussed in Section VI.

Fortune," for proof of the claim (advanced by a number of biographers) that he did so because the owners refused his request to take the *Otago* into the China Seas and directed him to repeat the voyage to Mauritius. A letter from them does prove that they were pleased with his service and that the resignation was his own desire (Baines, p. 100).

If there was little of the *Otago* in his autobiographical writings, his fiction is another matter, and it suggests that there was more than embarrassment over a girl behind both anxiety and resignation. In addition to the story just mentioned, Conrad wrote three fictional accounts of taking command of the *Otago* over a period of 15 years. There was some compulsion to return to the experience, to rework or revise it, at crucial points in his life. In each story he approached more closely the actual events, and the three contain common elements which clarify the conflict through which he was moving, in erratic and groping manner, toward the old ambition of becoming a great writer. In each story the young captain is unexpectedly appointed to take command of a ship in Bangkok whose old captain has died; usually there is an older mate who resents the young captain, having wanted the command for himself. And in each story, the act of taking command is linked to a crime—cannibalism in "Falk," Leggatt's murder in "The Secret Sharer," the old captain's plundering of medical supplies in *The Shadow Line*. Each story revolves around the narrator's attempts to get his first command to the open sea (i.e., actually to become commander) and in each case the crisis to be overcome is one of threatening passivity. Only by mastering the passive experience does the young captain master his doubts about himself.

In "Falk" it is Falk's refusal with the only tug available to move the ship that brings the narrator close to paranoia and leads to an acceptance of Falk and his great hunger (although at first the captain believes that Falk is going to confess, not to cannibalism, but to the murder of his father). In "The Secret Sharer" it is the captain's identification with the murderer Leggatt which paralyzes him and brings him close to madness; the final danger to be overcome is that of putting his ship in irons to then float helplessly onto the rocks. And, in the third story, *The Shadow Line,* the whole identity crisis takes place in an atmosphere of dead calm;

the young captain almost comes to believe, with his fever-crazed mate, that it is the old captain who lies buried in the Gulf of Siam and who would have preferred to see the ship sunk rather than commanded by another, who will not let the ship pass, who will not release them from the grip of calm and disease. Again the oral-sadistic note is sounded; the narrator's guilt is symbolized in his not having checked the supply of quinine and so discovered that the old captain had sold it and replaced it with worthless powder.

So powerfully did Conrad, writing 28 years after the event, project the spiteful refusal of the evil dead captain to give up his authority that, to his surprise and chagrin, many readers took it as a ghost story. "Strangely enough, you know," he wrote a friend, "I never either meant or 'felt' the supernatural aspect of the story while writing it. It came out somehow and my readers pointed it out to me. I must tell you that it is a piece of as strict autobiography as the form allowed" (Jean-Aubry, 1927, 2:195).

The pattern of these stories, written years later, may be summarized briefly; a young captain achieves his long-standing ambitious dream (which comes to him, however; he does not seek it), and immediately suffers doubts about his ability; his taking command is linked to a crime (including murder and cannibalism); he suffers through a dreaded passivity; finally he breaks free to the open sea with his doubts about himself resolved. The conflict over taking command, with the arousal of active and passive tendencies toward the father, is central to much of Conrad's work, and in his life was not so easily resolved.

Just as he had run from Poland to the sea, he seemed to have left the *Otago*, as if the conflict could be left behind. Paradoxically, back in England with nothing to do, he abruptly and, he claimed, without forethought, began his first novel, *Almayer's Folly*—the story of a man destroyed by ambitions that are largely fantasies and by the emerging sexuality of his only child. But in a few months Conrad again changed course, once more flinging himself into a life of action which objectively made little sense. Although he claimed to be making great efforts to obtain a ship, there is reason to doubt that he did so then, as later, in an effective manner.

Instead he began to push Marguerite Poradowska to help him get command of a river steamer on the Congo. Even if one ignores the fact that Conrad hated steamships, such a move was hardly designed to further his career as master of deep water vessels. It was at best a temporary job, and raises the strong suspicion that Conrad was attempting to work through in this manner the conflict over his profession. If we disregard the use he made of it, the experience was a disaster.

Almost a year after he returned to England, he left Bordeaux for Boma. Although the external events of this venture, as described in "Heart of Darkness," strike some contemporary readers as "romantic" in themselves, they follow the facts very closely, except that Conrad did *not* get command of a riverboat. He was in charge of one for only a short time on the return trip from the attempt to save Klein (Kurtz) when the actual captain was sick. Quarreling with the Belgians in charge, he was denied a command of his own, and, sick with fever and dysentery, he was on his way back to Europe in less than 6 months from the time he set out.

Only 4 of those months were spent in the Congo. But the experience itself must have been profound. His subsequent difficulties cannot be explained away as the result of physical illness. He was frequently depressed, his confidence in himself gone. Except for intermittent work on *Almayer's Folly*, he did little for a year. He *said* he wanted command of a ship, but there is little evidence that he looked for it (the one offer he is known to have had, he refused).[6] When finally he was urged by a friend to become first mate of the famous wool clipper and passenger ship, the *Torrens*, he protested that he might not be able to carry out his duties because of "ill health" and had to be persuaded. He later described his condition as "neurasthenic" (1926, p. 24).

He remained with the *Torrens* for the next 20 months, and while clearly able to function well, his letters indicate that the depression continued. John Galsworthy, who met Conrad on his second voyage between Port Adelaide and England, has left an interesting description (1927, p. 101f.):

[6] Gee and Sturm, p. 24.

It was in March 1893 that I first met Conrad. . . . He was superintending the stowage of cargo. Very dark he looked in the burning sunlight—tanned, with a peaked brown beard, almost black hair, and dark brown eyes, over which the lids were deeply folded. He was thin, not tall, his arms very long, his shoulders broad, his head set rather forward. He spoke to me with a strong foreign accent. He seemed to me strange on an English ship. . . .

The chief mate bears the main burden of a sailing ship. All the first night he was fighting a fire in the hold. None of us seventeen pasengers knew of it till long after. It was he who had most truck with the tail of that hurricane off the Leeuwin, and later with another storm. He was a good seaman, watchful of the weather, quick in handling the ship; considerate with the apprentices. . . .

This is the Conrad who was "convalescing," whose health was "permanently undermined" so that he could not again take the position of captain—a position less arduous in everything but responsibility. In fact his sea life was coming to an end. He left the *Torrens,* probably because of the desire to visit his uncle in the Ukraine:

I took a long look from the quay at that last of ships I ever had under my care, and, stepping round the corner of a tall warehouse, parted from her for ever, and at the same time stepped (in merciful ignorance) out of my sea life altogether [1926, p. 26].

Back in London he continued to complain of depression and idleness. Fitfully he wrote on the novel; he accepted a second mate's position on a steamer, but the venture failed. Once again he requested aid from Marguerite in getting appointed as a Suez pilot. In his next letter he said that steps were being taken to get him a job in the pearl fisheries off the Australian coast.[7] These are not the words of a man vigorously seeking command of a ship.

In February, 1894 an event occurred which seems to have been decisive. Conrad's uncle, his "substitute father," died. He wrote Marguerite a few days later that "it seems as if everything has died in me, as if he has carried away my soul with him." [8] There

---

[7] Gee and Sturm, p. 56f.
[8] *Ibid.,* p. 63.

is no question that he suffered over his uncle's death, and years later he described the essentials of the relationship with the man he saw four times in 20 years; he was "the wisest, the firmest, the most indulgent of guardians, extending over me a paternal care and affection, a moral support which I seemed to feel always near me in the most distant parts of the earth" (1912, p. 31). But there is one startling fact; uncle Thaddeus had urged Conrad several times to write of his experiences for Polish journals, and he never did. But between February and May, with a sudden burst of energy, he finished the English novel he had gradually been adding to for over 4 years. Bernard Meyer (1967) has suggested that Conrad, writing of Almayer's death, was working through his grief. Although it may have had this effect, that cannot be the whole story since Conrad had been working toward Almayer's deterioration and death from the beginning. Moreover, his rewriting that spring most significantly involved working into the opening pages Almayer's incestuous love for his only child, thus intensifying the part played in Almayer's destruction by Nina's awakened sexuality and abandonment of him for her lover (Gordon, 1940).

It thus seems possible that uncle Thaddeus's death was crucial in removing an inhibition on Conrad's turning back to the old ambition identified with his father.[9] After the age of 14 he resisted all suggestions of writing creatively in Polish, but with the uncle's death the drive toward an identity as a writer accelerated. By April the first draft of *Almayer's Folly* was done, and revisions were completed that spring. In August he began *An Outcast of the Islands,* and *Almayer's Folly* was accepted for publication in October. He still insisted that this was an interlude on shore, but in fact the transition from seaman to novelist was complete.

Probably in November he met Jessie George, the 21-year-old girl 16 years his junior to whom he would, a little over a year later, propose and then panic. After disappearing for 3 days, he told her they must marry quickly because he had only a short time to live, and that there would be no children. In fact he lived—and wrote—for 28 years following the marriage and there

[9] Albert Guerard (p. 308) states that Dr. Ernest Kahn of Cambridge, Mass. made a similar suggestion to him.

were two sons he never quite reconciled himself to. The man of action disappears; he became steadily more dependent upon his young wife, and she soon realized she had another child to care for. Activity in one direction was paid for by passivity in another. It is often hard to reconcile the Conrad who now appeared, in many ways seemingly helpless to care for himself, with the man who had arrived in England, not speaking the language and having not a single friend, and who in 10 years reached command of the *Otago*.

The sea life was over; his talk of returning in times of difficulty was, as Jessie realized, not serious. The adventures to come were within himself, "that lonely region of stress and strife. . . ."

V

> . . . you can't, in sound morals, condemn a man for taking care of his own integrity. It is his clear duty. And least of all can you condemn an artist pursuing, however humbly and imperfectly, a creative aim. In that interior world where his thought and his emotions go seeking for the experience of imagined adventures, there are no policemen, no law, no pressure of circumstance or dread of opinion to keep him within bounds. Who then is going to say Nay to his temptations if not his conscience?
>
> *A Personal Record* (1912, p. xviii)

Ernst Kris's research concerning creativity convinced him of this fact: "According to clinical experience, success or failure in these [creative] professions depends, among other factors, . . . on the extent to which the activity itself has for any particular individual become autonomous, i.e., detached from the original conflict which may have turned interest and proclivity into the specific direction" (1952, p. 29). The material I have presented demonstrates that for Conrad the autonomy of the *function* of writing, so closely identified with his father, must have been precarious at best. His need to establish distance between himself and his material is well known; he insisted that he could write creatively only in his third language; he had great difficulty in writing from the vantage point of the omniscient author, i.e., in his own person, and in most of his best fiction he works through a narrator; notoriously awkward in dealing with immediate action, he most often described events that had taken place in the past, even when his manipulations of time did not demand it; and, finally, that impressionistic method itself through which he manipulated chronology and point of view allowed him to approach his material as indirectly as he felt necessary.

Moreover, it is easy to show that even these elaborate precautions were not enough. Throughout his writing life his letters offer abundant evidence of periods of paralysis and creative sterility, periods of days and weeks when he could write nothing or only very slowly with agonizing effort. These were usually periods of depression when he fought against feelings of helplessness and futility, and suffered attacks of hypochondriasis as well as real illness. In October, 1894, while working on his second book, he wrote Marguerite Poradowska:

The other work proceeds very slowly. I am very discouraged. The ideas don't come. I don't *see* either the characters or the incidents. . . . I am in a constant state of irritation which does not allow me to lose myself in my story. Consequently my labors are worthless.

[A few days later he added:] . . . one works hardest when doing nothing. For three days now I have been sitting before a blank sheet of paper—and the sheet is still blank except for a "IV" at the top. To tell the truth, I got off to a bad start. . . . But what can you expect; I don't feel the slightest enthusiasm. And that's fatal.

[After two weeks the pattern which was to become established is suggested:] My work is not advancing, and my health is less good than it was. If I stay ashore much longer, everything will, alas, be spoiled.

[And then:] . . . I am entirely bogged down. For a fortnight now I have not written a single word. It's all over, I'm afraid.

I feel like burning what there is. It is all very bad; yes, too bad! This is my deep conviction and not a cry of stupid modesty. I have been floundering about like this for a long time.

[He complains to her of] the fear of those shades which one himself calls forth and which so often refuse to obey the brain that created them [Gee and Sturm, pp. 82–89].

As Conrad slowly committed himself to the identity of an English author, his difficulties became worse. He started and abandoned a third novel, then began a fourth which was not to be completed for over 20 years.

He wrote Edward Garnett on June 2, 1896:

And every day the Rescuer crawls a page forward—sometimes with cold despair—at times with hot hope. I have long fits of depression, that in a lunatic asylum would be called madness. I do not know what it is. It springs from nothing. It is ghastly. It lasts an hour or a day; and when it departs it leaves a fear.

[On June 19 he wrote again:] Since I sent you that part 1st (on the eleventh of the month) I have written one page. Just one page. I went about thinking and forgetting—sitting down before the blank page to find that I could not put one sentence together. To be able to think and unable to express is a fine torture.

[Almost 2 months later he confessed:] There is 12 pages written and I sit before them every morning, day after day, for the last 2 months and cannot add a sentence, add a word! I am paralyzed by doubt and have just sense enough to feel the agony but am powerless to invent a way out of it. This is sober truth. I had bad moments with the Outcast but never anything so ghastly, nothing half so hopeless. When I face that fatal manuscript it seems to me that I have forgotten how to think—worse! how to write. . . . I ask myself whether I am breaking up mentally. I am afraid of it.

[Two years later he was struggling with the same book:] I am ashamed of myself. I ought to have written to you before, but the fact is I have not written anything at all. When I received your letter together with part II.ᵈ of R[escue] I was in bed—this beastly nervous trouble. Since then I've been better but have been unable to write. . . . I sit down for eight hours every day —and the sitting down is all. In the course of that working day of 8 hours I write 3 sentences which I erase before leaving the table in despair. There's not a single word to send you. Not one!

. . . I want to howl and foam at the mouth but I daren't do it for fear of waking that baby and alarming my wife. It's no joking matter. After such crises of despair I doze for hours still half conscious that there is that story I am unable to write. Then I wake up, try again—and at last go to bed completely done-up. So the days pass and nothing is done. At night I sleep. In the morning I get up with the horror of that powerlessness I must face through a day of vain efforts.

. . . I had a great difficulty in writing the most commonplace note. I seem to have lost all *sense* of style and yet I am haunted, mercilessly haunted by the *necessity* of style. And that story I can't write weaves itself into all I see, into all I speak, into all I think, into the lines of every book I try to read. . . . You know how bad it is when one *feels* one's liver, or lungs. Well I feel my brain. I am distinctly conscious of the contents of my head. My story is there in a fluid—in an evading shape. I can't get hold of it. It is there—to bursting, yet I can't get hold of it no more than you can grasp a handful of water [p. 55f., 59, 64, 134f.].

[While writing *Lord Jim,* he complained:] I am at work, but my mental state is very bad,—and is made worse by a constant gnawing anxiety. One incites the other and vice versa. It is a vicious circle in which the creature struggles.

[Years later, deep in *Nostromo,* one of his greatest novels, he wrote to Galsworthy:] No work done. No spring left to grapple with it. Everything looks black, but I suppose that will wear off, and anyhow, I am trying to keep despair under. Nevertheless I feel myself losing my footing in deep waters. They are lapping about my hips.

My dear fellow, it is not so much the frequency of these gout attacks, but I feel so beastly ill between, ill in body and mind. It has never been so before. Impossible to write,—while the brain riots in incoherent images. It is sometimes quite alarming [Jean-Aubry, 1927, 1:289, 322].

The above examples could be multiplied many times over and from throughout Conrad's writing years. If his complaints seem exaggerated at times, this only enhances the impression that the function of writing itself was endangered by instinctualization, emergence of conflict, and guilt.

Kris's studies of states of inspiration have focused attention on "the importance of pregenital elements in fantasies connected with inspiration." The ego is passive in relation to id material (or better, perhaps, unconscious ego material being shaped by instinctual pressure, often by primary process mechanisms). He points out that "on the level of pregenital meaning creation itself signifies anal production. But the pregenital elements in the fantasies connected with inspiration stand in a special framework. The fantasies—I can speak only of men—are centered around the father and around the conflict between active and passive tendencies. While in autobiographical descriptions of creative states pregenital connotations are frequently implied or even expressed, . . . the relation to the father figure is better hidden." He presents an example which "is the description of a process in which passivity is indeed supreme. In terms of our theory we might say: the path leads from anal activity to homosexual passivity and thus another well-known meaning of creation is evoked—that of giving birth to a child" (p. 300f.). That is, in periods of inspiration and intense creativity, the ego experiences itself as passive in relation to the process itself, and oral, anal, and passive homosexual fantasies may be unrelated to specific conflicts. But if there is too much conflict around passivity, then the autonomy of the function will be threatened, the ego incapacitated in its regulatory function.

Many of Conrad's statements quoted above express his passivity in relation to his material, and the violence of his struggles with that material at times sounds defensive.

> I *never mean* to be slow. The stuff comes out at its own rate. I am always ready to put it down; nothing would induce me to lay down my pen if I *feel* a sentence—or even a word ready to my hand. The trouble is that too often—alas!—I've to wait for the sentence—for the word.
>
> What wonder then that during the long blank hours the doubt creeps into the mind and I ask myself whether I am fitted for that work. The worst is that while I am thus powerless to produce my imagination is extremely active: whole paragraphs, whole pages, whole chapters pass through my mind. Everything is there: descriptions, dialogue, reflexion—everything—every-

thing but the belief, the conviction, the only thing needed to make me put pen to paper. I've thought out a volume in a day till I felt sick in mind and heart and gone to bed, completely done up, without having written a line. . . .

I am impatient of material anxieties and they frighten me too because I feel how mysteriously independent of myself *is my power of expression.* It is there—I believe—and some thought, and a little insight. All this is there; but I am not as the work-men who can take up and lay down their tools. *I am, so to speak, only the agent of an unreliable master* [Baines, p. 213; in last paragraph my italics].

It must be clear from this and previous examples that Conrad is not simply referring to the common feeling expressed by artists of inspiration "coming" to them without conscious effort; he is referring as well to a frequent paralysis of the ego to exert control or mastery over material emerging from deep in his mind. He knew quite well the source of that material. In a rare moment of triumph, after completing his first masterpiece, *The Nigger of the 'Narcissus,'* he stated in the famous preface: "the artist descends within himself, and in that lonely region of stress and strife, if he be deserving and fortunate, he finds the terms of his appeal." He often despaired of controlling the energy he met in that lonely region, and even came to deny that he had ever visited there.

VI

. . . Christianity—is distasteful to me. I am not blind to its services but the absurd oriental fable from which it starts irritates me. Great, improving, softening, compassionate it may be but it has lent itself with amazing facility to cruel distortion and is the only religion which, with its impossible standards, has brought an infinity of anguish to innumerable souls—on this earth.

Letter to Garnett (p. 245)

I have tried to trace the origins of the threats to the autonomy of Conrad's creativity. If, as I am maintaining, Conrad left Poland in an attempt to avoid the conflicts he experienced around the identification with his father, and if he gave up the sea in part because command of the *Otago* aroused these same conflicts, then we might predict that the emergence of these conflicts in the material of his writing would prove particularly threatening. And yet two of his greatest novels, *Lord Jim* and *Under Western Eyes,* deal with just such material. There is not space here to do justice to the conflicts indicated, but certain aspects must be summarized.

Lord Jim is Conrad's best-known book. Jim, recovered from an injury suffered during a storm, takes a berth as first mate on the *Patna,* an old steamer carrying 800 pilgrims from an eastern port to Jeddah. During a night of dead calm the *Patna* strikes some object beneath the surface. Given the rotten condition of the bulkheads, none of the officers believes she can stay afloat more than a few minutes, and there are not enough lifeboats. Jim does what he can, but returning to the bridge he finds the officers preparing to abandon ship. He refuses to help them, watches with contempt their struggle to get a boat over. Finally they succeed and call to the only other officer to jump. Jim alone knows that the engineer has died of a heart attack. At the last moment Jim jumps in his place.

But the *Patna* does not sink. Of all the officers, none but Jim remains to face the court of inquiry, and here he meets Marlow. Jim is stripped of his certificate, and Marlow, an older ship captain, helps him find a position where he can "redeem" himself. Each time Jim is reminded of the *Patna* incident, however, he moves on. Finally, Marlow goes to Stein, a wealthy trader and entomologist, who sends Jim to Patusan, where warring factions have disrupted trade. Allying himself with Doramin, the chief loyal to Stein, Jim conquers all opposition, establishes order, and becomes virtual ruler.

Brown, a marauding pirate, finds his way into Patusan. Trapped with his crew, he confronts Jim with demands for fight or freedom, demands in which run "a vein of subtle reference to their common blood, an assumption of common experience; a sickening suggestion of common guilt, of secret knowledge that was like a bond of their minds and of their hearts" (p. 387). Jim, against all advice, allows Brown to go free, with his own head as surety that no harm will come to Patusan. When Brown and his men kill a number of natives, Jim insists on paying the debt at the hands of Doramin.

There are two major questions in *Lord Jim:* first, why did he jump? And second, does he in fact redeem himself? Jim's reaction to his betrayal of a "fixed standard of conduct" is one of shame, not guilt—a fact which Marlow recognizes with some irritation: "the idea obtrudes itself that he made so much of his disgrace while it is the guilt alone that matters" (p. 177). The betrayal is not of a superego precept but of a narcissistic ego ideal; his fantasies are of triumphant masculinity:

> . . . his thoughts would be full of valorous deeds: he loved these dreams and the success of his imaginary achievements. They were the best parts of life, its secret truth, its hidden reality. They had a gorgeous virility, the charm of vagueness, they passed before him with a heroic tread; they carried his soul away with them and made it drunk with the divine philtre of an unbounded confidence in itself. There was nothing he could not face [p. 20].
>
> [The theme of his fantasies was always rescue:] He saw himself saving people from sinking ships, . . . swimming through a surf with a line. . . . He confronted savages on tropical shores, . . . and in a small boat upon the ocean he kept up the hearts of despairing men—always an example of devotion to duty, and as unflinching as a hero in a book [p. 6].

It is this ideal of himself which Jim has betrayed. But he is not a coward, as the execution of his attack on Sherif Ali's fort, for example, indicates. Why does he jump?

It has often been pointed out that Conrad's heroes do not have fathers; on the other hand he was fascinated by the relationship between father and daughter.[10] But not far beneath the surface

---

[10] This fact has many implications which cannot be detailed here. It should be pointed out, however, that Charles Gould of *Nostromo* and Axel Heyst of *Victory* both deal with *memories* of their fathers, and that in each case the dying father urges passivity on the son. Charles Gould's father has told him to stay away from the mine, and Axel's father has warned him not to get involved in life, to remain a quiet onlooker.

the theme of father and son is very prominent. Jim appeals to a whole succession of fathers for approval. "Didn't I tell you he confessed himself before me as though I had the power to bind and to loose?" Marlow says. "He burrowed deep, deep, in the hope of my absolution, which would have been of no good to him" (p. 97). Jim tells Marlow that he will never leave Patusan because:

> "I must stick to their belief in me to feel safe and to—to" . . .
> He cast about for a word, seemed to look for it on the sea . . .
> "to keep in touch with" . . . His voice sank suddenly to a murmur . . . "with those whom, perhaps, I shall never see any more. With—with—you, for instance" [p. 334].

His achievements are measured by Marlow's approval, whether Marlow is present or not.

In fact, Jim performs for a whole series of father figures—the plantation owner to whom he is first sent by Marlow and who is so pleased by him that he plans to make him son and heir; the succession of ship chandlers for whom he is a daring and successful water-clerk; Stein, for whom, in part, he pacifies Patusan. There is only one moment when Jim *cannot* act for the approval of a substitute father: on the deck of the *Patna* when he is the last living officer aboard and his captain is shouting to him to jump. "I had jumped. . . . It seems" (p. 111). A sudden act he cannot remember. There is a kind of truth in his assertion that it was the doing of the deserting officers "as plainly as if they had reached up with a boathook and pulled me over" (p. 123). *Jim jumps because not to have done so would have left him in command of the Patna.* He feels shame in having betrayed his hypermasculine ego ideal; he does not feel guilt since he has obeyed the superego prohibition against the unconscious wish to replace father.

Albert Guerard (1958) has pointed out that second and third readings of *Lord Jim* leave the reader with more and more doubts concerning Jim's redemption. There can be no doubt that Jim believes his final act does so; the triumph with which he meets death at the hands of Doramin is unmistakable:

> The crowd, which had fallen apart behind Jim as soon as Doramin had raised his hand, rushed tumultuously forward after

the shot. They say that the white man sent right and left at all those faces a proud and unflinching glance. Then with his hand over his lips he fell forward, dead [p. 416].

The discrepancy between Jim's satisfaction and our doubt results in one of the driving ambiguities that forces our participation in creating the novel.[11]

Doramin is Jim's last father; he and Dain Waris, Doramin's son, are blood brothers. The success of Jim's greatest achievement in Patusan, the storming of Sherif Ali's fort which many think impossible, is insured by Doramin having himself carried to a point behind the attackers where, because of his great bulk, he cannot escape in case of defeat. Under Doramin's eyes Jim suffers no doubts.

Inevitably, Brown finds his way in from the outside world. Since the work of Gustav Morf it has been recognized that Jim is paralyzed by the identification Brown weaves so skillfully between them. But it is possible to be more explicit about the points of this identification. "I found a way," the dying Brown gloats, "as broad as a road." Swiftly and surely Conrad creates this savage man whose actions are utterly consistent. He is driven by a violent refusal to tolerate passivity in any form before other men; his whole life has been spent defying all attempts to restrict his activities. Intuitively Brown plays on Jim's moment of panic aboard the *Patna* by acknowledging that he is in his present predicament because *he* was afraid once—of a jail! If a man is going to die, he insinuates, what does he care how many others he takes with him? How can Jim judge when he too has been afraid, has abandoned his duty to save his skin? We are reminded of Brierly, who judged Jim and then committed suicide because his act of judgment forced him to look within himself—at his too easy rise to command, his too easy stepping over those in his way. He has acted out the fantasies of Jim's ego ideal; now for the first time he *judges* his actions, and brings in the verdict of guilty. The three men—Jim, Brierly, and Brown—are interrelated around impulses

[11] See Kris and Kaplan (1948): "In short, ambiguity functions in poetry, not as a carrier of a content which is somehow in itself poetic, but as the instrument by which a content is *made* poetic through the process of re-creation" (see Kris, 1952, p. 258f.).

toward patricide and the opposite, the horror of and fascination with secret passive impulses toward submission, castration, death.

Jim, like Brierly, is asked to judge. It is mentioned once that Brown was known to have been tender on one occasion—to the dying wife of a clergyman he had seduced. One of the few facts we know of Jim's background is that his father, whom he idealized, was a clergyman, and that his refusal to return to England after the trial was based on his refusal to bring shame upon his father. Thus one more point of the identification is forged on oedipal grounds. Brown will not submit, he demands a fight to the death or freedom. Jim is paralyzed. He cannot judge without acknowledging secret wishes to act like Brown. Urged to attack by the people who idealize him, he persuades the reluctant Doramin to let Brown go. He guarantees safety or forfeiture of his life.

Brown is true to himself to the end; while dying he gloatingly describes to Marlow with vicious vitality how he got revenge on Jim for making him feel helpless and trapped. Just as death itself must be turned from a passive to an active experience, so at Patusan he had to have the last word—the wanton slaughter in which Dain Waris is killed.

Jim is once more in the position he was in on the *Patna* just before he jumped; he must take independent action, as urged by Jewel and his loyal followers, or submit to Doramin. But now all the psychological forces lead in one direction. His immolation satisfies his ego ideal, his self-esteem—he sees it as heroic and masculine. The superego prohibition which has prevented him from ever *acting* independently is satisfied, and guilt for patricidal impulses is assuaged. And, deepest and most secret of all perhaps (and most forcefully denied by the act), the passive longings to be penetrated by father are gratified. Nothing now stands between Jim and self-destruction, and he goes triumphantly to his death. Jewel's refusal to forgive him is understandable. She intuitively recognizes that she was never as important to Jim as were his relationships to Doramin, Marlow, the fulfillment of his fantasies. But Marlow's doubts, and the reader's about Jim's "redemption" also become clear: he has *not* acted differently than he did on the *Patna;* he has not been changed by experience; he is the same from beginning to end.

The same conflicts are raised by *Under Western Eyes*, but must be summarized more briefly. Razumov, the hero, is a Russian student, the illegitimate son of a Prince he has met only once, and who supports him on the implicit condition that this relationship never be acknowledged. His mother, daughter of a priest, is dead; his true mother, he feels, is "all Russia." Completely isolated, he is determined to make his way in an academic career, obedient to the system under the Czar, father of all Russians. His plans are destroyed by the sudden appearance in his room of Haldin, a revolutionary student who has just assassinated a hated official and now seeks his help. Razumov at first attempts to make a contact for Haldin's escape, but when this fails he is faced with the prospect of further involvement. He decides to give Haldin up, and his mind leaps to the word "betray."

> A great word [he thinks]. What is betrayal? They talk of a man betraying his country, his friends, his sweetheart. There must be a moral bond first. *All a man can betray is his conscience.* And how is my conscience engaged here; by what bond of common faith, of common conviction, am I obliged to let that fanatical idiot drag me down with him? On the contrary—every obligation of true courage is the other way [p. 37f.; my italics].

In this key passage Razumov protests too much. There is a desperate need to deny a "common bond" in the act of murdering an official of the Czar. As a further denial, Razumov goes to his father for the first and only time to arrange the betrayal. Haldin is trapped and executed.

But Razumov has set in motion a chain of events he cannot escape. Ironically, the radical students believe him to have been an accomplice of Haldin, and he is forced to go to Geneva by the secret police to infiltrate and spy on the anarchists there. He meets Haldin's sister, Natalia, and falls in love with her. Haunted by his double, he confesses to Natalia. He walks home through a thunderstorm, and when his lodgekeeper remarks that he is wet, he mutters, "Yes, I am washed clean" (p. 357). He writes to Natalia, saying in part, "In giving Victor Haldin up, it was myself, after all, whom I have betrayed most basely" (p. 361).

Still he is not satisfied. He goes to the anarchists at the hour on which he betrayed Haldin and confesses to them as well. So that he can "spy" no longer, his eardrums are ruptured by the brutal assassin and double agent, Nikita.

> "Turn his face the other way," the paunchy terrorist directed, in an excited, gleeful squeak.
> Razumov could struggle no longer. He was exhausted; he had to watch passively the heavy open hand of the brute descend again in a degrading blow over his other ear. It seemed to split his head in two, and all at once the men holding him became perfectly silent—soundless as shadows. In silence they pulled him brutally to his feet, rushed with him noiselessly down the staircase, and, opening the door, flung him out into the street [p. 369].

The rape imagery seems unmistakable. Wandering deaf in the streets he is run down by a trolley. He goes off with the peasant woman, Tekla, as Jim goes off with his Eastern bride—and in our last view of him he is helpless, crippled, dying, and tended by the woman "unweariedly with the pure joy of unselfish devotion" (p. 379). He, like Jim, has found a kind of peace.

Razumov is thus destroyed by the denial of identification with Haldin around patricidal impulses. But he finds he cannot escape Haldin (in Conrad's original concept, Razumov was to marry Natalia, and the denouement was to have been brought about by the marked resemblance of their child to Haldin). Expiation once again comes through passive submission.

I suggested earlier that the emergence of such *content* in Conrad's writing, intensifying, so to speak, the passivity of the ego in relation to the creative process, would be particularly threatening. The necessary distance would be lost. If this occurred, one can predict that the erection of more rigid defenses would interfere with the ability to shift psychic levels so necessary in true creativity. While precisely this did occur *after* Conrad completed *Under Western Eyes* and became ill, it did not occur during the writing of these two books. He must have found some other way of defending himself against the threat of being overwhelmed by the conflictual material.

Something unique *did* occur while Conrad was writing these two novels; *in each case he broke off to write a short story intimately connected with the novel.* In each case he wrote with a rapidity of which otherwise he was never capable. In each case the meaning of the story runs opposite to that of the novel on one level, and in each case the *function* of the story was the same.

Conrad originally conceived of *Lord Jim* as a short story ("Jim: a Sketch") which encompassed only the *Patna* episode. When it occurred to him that "the pilgrim ship episode was a good starting-point for a free and wandering tale" (and possibly when he determined to introduce Marlow as a narrator and commentator through whom the events would be observed), he broke off to write "Heart of Darkness"—Marlow's journey within. In other words, when he suddenly conceived of the second half of the book, of Jim's "redemption" at the hands of Doramin, he turned to work through Marlow's test of his strength by reworking his own African experiences. Similarly, a few weeks before completing *Under Western Eyes* (that is, before writing of Razumov's "cleansing" at the hands of Nikita), he broke away and wrote "The Secret Sharer," the second version of his taking command of the *Otago*. These two long short stories are acknowledged as among Conrad's greatest work; both deal with the integration of a personality under stress in terms which seem quite familiar to psychoanalysts. Because of the complexity of "Heart of Darkness," I shall present in some detail "The Secret Sharer," and then draw some parallels with the longer work.

The setting and situation of "The Secret Sharer" are familiar —the young, untested captain taking over his first command in Bangkok. By linking this situation with the famous crime which had taken place on the *Cutty Sark* in 1880, Conrad reverses the central conflict of *Under Western Eyes,* Razumov's betrayal of Haldin—and himself.[12] It is now generally accepted that "The

[12] The abandonment of the *Jeddah* by her officers, the source of the first part of *Lord Jim,* occurred at about the same time in 1880. Moreover, of course, Conrad used part of the *Cutty Sark* incident—the murder of the sailor by the mate—here; the other part, the suicide of the captain 4 days after he allowed the mate to escape, provided the model for Brierly in *Lord Jim.*

Secret Sharer" must be comprehended on more than its literal level, that is represents "the classic night journey and willed descent into the unconscious" (Guerard, p. 26). But it is more than that; it is a beautifully controlled exploration of an identity crisis in which a young man must, to meet the demands made upon him, integrate the struggling components of his personality. The components are presented in terms strikingly similar to those of psychoanalytic structural theory.

The prose, more straightforward and spare than most of Conrad's best, is dense, compact, evocative; unlike "Falk," in "The Secret Sharer" the conflict of taking command is central, and the atmosphere is far less prosaically realistic. The captain's isolation is emphasized, on a dreamlike sea where limits are marked by "lines of fishing-stakes resembling a mysterious system of half-submerged bamboo fences, incomprehensible in its division of the domain of tropical fishes, and crazy of aspect as if abandoned forever." He is alone with his ship, but caught up in a passivity through which the coming experiences will move him:

> She floated at the starting-point of a long journey, *very still in an immense stillness,* the shadows of her spars flung far to the eastward by the setting sun. At that moment, *I was alone on her decks.* There was not a sound in her—and around us *nothing moved, nothing lived,* not a canoe on the water, not a bird in the air, not a cloud in the sky. In this *breathless pause at the threshold of a long passage* we seemed *to be measuring our fitness* for a long and arduous enterprise, the appointed task of both our existences to be carried out, far from human eyes, with only sky and sea for spectators and for judges [my italics].

He must "measure his fitness," and he must do it alone. Since only the sea and the sky will watch and judge, the issue is an intrapsychic one. He is uneasy; he is not just the only stranger on board; "if all the truth must be told, I was somewhat a stranger to myself." He expresses his uneasiness explicitly in terms of the ego ideal: "I wondered how far I should turn out faithful to that ideal conception of one's own personality every man sets up for himself secretly."

In this state of paralysis the descent begins; on impulse the captain gives his first order to the mate for purposes he does not yet understand, and immediately regrets it. "I felt painfully that I—a stranger—was doing something unusual when I directed him to let all hands turn in without setting an anchor-watch." He realizes that, in breaking routine, he is undermining discipline. It is his "strangeness" that has caused him to arrange to be alone on deck "as if I had expected in those solitary hours of the night to get on terms with the ship of which I knew nothing." He attempts to reassure himself; in ego terms, in terms of knowledge and judgment, he is prepared. He reviews the trip ahead; he knows everything:

> All its phases were familiar enough to me, every characteristic, all the alternatives which were likely to face me on the high seas —everything! . . . *except the novel responsibility of command* [my italics].

Again he attempts to reassure himself; all ships and men are alike, and "the sea was not likely to keep any special surprises expressly for my discomfiture." His self-deception continues:

> And suddenly I rejoiced in the great security of the sea as compared with the unrest of the land, in my choice of that untempted life presenting no disquieting problems, invested with an elementary moral beauty by the absolute straightforwardness of its appeal and by the singleness of its purpose.

This attitude of triumph of a young man who has achieved his ambition is immediately shattered; the sea indeed has a "special surprise." But it is a surprise the captain has deliberately, if unconsciously, called forth. *Because* he has dismissed his officers from duty a rope side-ladder has been left hanging overboard. When he attempts to get it in he cannot; "something elongated and pale" floats on the other end, "ghastly, silvery, fish-like," a "headless corpse." It is Leggatt, first mate of a vessel anchored several miles away; he has escaped confinement after having killed a seaman who disobeyed an order during a storm in which his ship was in danger of floundering.

Although the captain reacts to this man "appearing as if he

had risen from the bottom of the sea" with a "horrid frost-bound sensation which gripped me about the chest," an emphasis is placed on the fact that the meeting is not an accident; without the ladder Leggatt would have drowned; "it was as if you had expected me." The captain accepts him immediately, "a mysterious communication was established already between us two." When Leggatt explains that he has committed a murder, the captain sympathizes at once, suggesting it was only a fit of temper. "It was, in the night," he thinks, "as though I had been faced by my own reflection in the depths of a sombre and immense mirror." Leggatt is his double, he insists over and over from this point on, his second self, his gray ghost. Having given Leggatt one of his sleeping-suits, he comments: "He appealed to me as if our experiences had been as identical as our clothes."

It must be clear that Leggatt has come to represent part of the captain, and that he has been called forth in response to the captain's "uneasiness," his uncertain identity in "taking command." Their experiences are "as identical as our clothes," except that Leggatt, in a moment of crisis, has killed a man. Leggatt represents forces or impulses which the captain must master before achieving the integration which will make him one with his function. It is explicit that Leggatt has come for the captain to "see" and "understand" and comprehend in the largest sense. "I didn't mind being looked at," Leggatt says of their meeting, "I—I liked it. And then you speaking to me so quietly—as if you had expected me. . . . I don't know—I wanted to be seen, to talk with somebody, before I went on." Later he will add, "It's a great satisfaction to have got somebody to understand. You seem to have been there on purpose." But comprehension is something else; the identification with what Leggatt represents must be lived through, experienced.

To understand Leggatt's function more fully it is necessary to look closely at the situation aboard the *Sephora* when he killed. She has been running for more than a week in a furious gale, "a sea gone mad! I suppose the end of the world will be something like that; and a man may have the heart to see it coming once and be done with it—but to have to face it day after day——" Captain and crew are in a panic. All the canvas has been blown away, and

the only hope is to set a reefed foresail, the only sail they have
left to maintain control of the ship. Leggatt does it—and it saves
them all. But in the process a seaman, who "wouldn't do his duty
and wouldn't let anybody else do theirs," refuses an order. Leggatt
lashes out, and in the ensuing struggle strangles him.

There is a further point of importance. When Leggatt asks the
captain of the *Sephora* to let him escape, the captain refuses: "This
thing must take its course. I represent the law here." He must
give Leggatt up: "To the law. His obscure tenacity on that point
had in it something incomprehensible and a little awful; something, as it were, mystical, quite apart from his anxiety that he
should not be suspected of 'countenancing any doings of that
sort.' Seven-and-thirty virtuous years at sea, of which over twenty
of immaculate command, and the last fifteen in the *Sephora*,
seemed to have laid him under some pitiless obligation."

The captain of the *Sephora* strikes us as a self-righteous ass. But
just what is being criticized? "I represent the law here"? This is
no more than the truth, and we are reminded that the narrator
has said of himself: "theoretically, I could do what I liked, with no
one to say nay to me within the whole circle of the horizon." Virtuous years at sea, immaculate command, fidelity to a pitiless obligation? Aren't all of these part of the young captain's "ideal
conception of self"?

The answer is soon apparent. The absolute authority of command is justified only by its "fidelity to a pitiless obligation," the
obligation to place the safety and well-being of ship and crew
above all else, to meet every emergency with this singleminded
selfless purpose. The captain of the *Sephora* betrayed that obligation when his nerve went to pieces. He lies when he piously insists that God gave him the strength to order the setting of the
reefed foresail. "I assure you," Leggatt says, "he never gave the
order. He may think he did, but he never gave it. He stood there
with me on the break of the poop after the maintopsail blew away,
and whimpered about our last hope—positively whimpered about
it and nothing else—and the night coming on! To hear one's
skipper go on like that in such weather was enough to drive any
fellow out of his mind." Thus the captain's insistence that he is the
law is offensive because it is not integrated with those qualities

which would justify fidelity. He demands obedience like the irrational and punitive superego which is itself corrupt.

There is one further point. However we may sympathize with Leggatt, we must not overlook his rebelliousness. He heard the captain whimper about their last hope—i.e., the one chance left of setting the reefed foresail. The captain *knew* what should have been done, but from fear could not command. Leggatt *could* have taken this for an order. Instead he *seizes* command, functioning from rage: "It worked me up into a sort of desperation. *I just took it into my own hands* and went away from him, boiling and . . . I don't blame anybody, I was precious little better than the rest. Only—I was an officer of that old coal-wagon, anyhow——" (my italics). In throwing off the captain he becomes a "strung-up force" which does what must be done, but in seizing that force (and all authority must implicitly be backed by force) he destroys the balance which controls it. "The same strung-up force which had given twenty-four men a chance, at least, for their lives, had, in a sort of recoil, crushed an unworthy mutinous existence." This is why Leggatt appears first as a *headless* corpse. He accepts responsibility for what he has done, for the end of his career: "The 'brand of Cain' business, don't you see. That's all right. I was ready enough to go off wandering on the face of the earth—and that was price enough to pay for an Abel of that sort." He will not be judged by the community:

> ". . . you don't see me coming back to explain such things to an old fellow in a wig and twelve respectable tradesmen, do you? What can they know whether I am guilty or not—or of *what* I am guilty, either? That's my affair." ["*My father's a parson in Norfolk,*" he has repeated twice—as does Jim.]

Leggatt and his defiance of authority, his refusal to feel guilty, is a projection of the young captain's guilt over "taking command"; it is as if he is saying, Leggatt is guilty of seizing the position from the old captain, not I. Inasmuch as his task is to acknowledge that the impulses driving Leggatt are within himself, he must accept this guilt as well as that of the force underlying authority. But the situation on the *Sephora* means more than that: a captain whose authority is irrational and unjustified; a mate who has the necessary skill and nerve, but who refuses to submit to authority, who seizes power, and then crushes the first man who challenges it; an unworthy mutinous crewman who wouldn't do his duty and wouldn't let anybody else do theirs. In stress, these components, which must function as one if disaster for all is to be avoided, have turned against one another. The *situation* of disintegration aboard the *Sephora* is the objective correlative of the internal state the young captain fears. The "measure of his fitness" will be his ability to integrate the three—the authority, the ability, the driving force. Only if he can, will he be at one with his ship, one with the function of command.

The captain's test, as he identifies with the "headless" Leggatt and undertakes the internalization of what he represents, is beautifully done. As he undergoes the ordeal of accepting his own depths, the sense of losing his identity is expressed in terms which convey a not unusual psychoanalytic experience. He becomes aware of the uncanny sense of being divided as soon as Leggatt sleeps and he cannot: "I sat there . . . trying to clear my mind of the confused sensation of being in two places at once. . . ." And then "all the time the dual working of my mind distracted me almost to the point of insanity. I was constantly watching myself, my secret self, as dependent on my actions as my own personality. . . . It was very much like being mad, only it was worse because one was aware of it." He comes to feel less torn in two when he is with Leggatt.

But he cannot remain with his double all the time. As soon as the captain has heard the final account of what happened on the *Sephora,* as soon as he assures Leggatt that he "quite understands" the strung-up force which saved the ship and destroyed the mutinous sailor, the test begins in earnest. For at this moment the wind finally comes. He goes on deck "to make the acquaintance of my ship." But he discovers: "I was not wholly alone with my command; for there was that stranger in my cabin. Or rather, I was not completely and wholly with her. Part of me was absent." The immobilization increases; he can no longer count on his instinctive seaman's response, for *"all unconscious alertness had abandoned me"* (my italics). He cannot do without this double yet; when he thinks the steward must have seen Leggatt and yet gives no sign, "Saved," he thinks. "But, no! Lost! Gone! He was gone." For a moment he has the uncanny feeling that only he can see Leggatt. "I think I had come creeping quietly as near insanity as any man who has not actually gone over the border."

We are at the nadir of the descent. Leggatt determines to leave the ship among the islands off the Cambodje shore. It would not do for him to come to life again; he must return to the sea. "As I came at night so I shall go." The captain decides Leggatt will have the best chance off the island of Koh-ring, and determines to go as close as possible, closer than necessary. As he has understood Leggatt, so Leggatt understands him. " 'Be careful,' " he warns, "and I realised suddenly that all my future, the only future for which I was fit, would perhaps go irretrievably to pieces in any mishap to my first command." But that is the point; he must risk *his* future, as Leggatt has, before the identification will be complete.

He gives Leggatt three sovereigns, half of what he has—and, impulsively, his hat. As we are approaching the very gate of Erebus, the gold pieces are no doubt, in part, payment to the guide of this underworld. The hat is a much more condensed symbol and more difficult to define. We feel it is right, and it brings the most complete moment of identification between the two before they separate: "I saw myself wandering barefooted, bareheaded, the sun beating on my dark poll." We are no doubt expected to respond, whether consciously or not, with the memory of our first sight of Leggatt as a headless corpse. The impulse, the captain thinks later, was "the expression of my sudden pity for his mere flesh." What is clear is that such emotions as pity cannot be allowed to interfere with the captain's function: it was the "egoism of pity" which destroyed the unity of the crew of the *Narcissus*. Inasmuch as the hat functions as symbol of authority, of the genitals, it is a dangerous impulse to "complete" the "headless" Leggatt and passively deny the identification, and consequently the responsibility of command.

For the identification is not yet complete; the captain is not free of his "secret sharer." It is not enough to have accepted his guilt, the responsibility of the "strung-up force." The "measure of his fitness" can come only in a situation similar to that of the

Sephora. This is the real reason he takes his ship closer and closer to Koh-ring. "It was now a matter of conscience to shave the land as close as possible—for now he must go overboard whenever the ship was put in stays. Must!" He pushes himself on until the mate begins to break. The land is so close he must shut his own eyes "because the ship must go closer. She must!" Koh-ring hangs overhead and the crew becomes anxious. "I had to go on." This has nothing to do with Leggatt, the powerful swimmer. The young captain is testing himself, ship, crew—his command. "Was she close enough? Already she was . . . gone too close to be recalled, gone from me altogether." But he remains paralyzed, immobilized, still in the grip of unconscious forces, for he has not the feel of his ship. But he increases the pressure. When he orders all hands turned up, he finds they are already nervously there. The ship is gliding now under the very gate of Erebus. The mate cracks: "My God! Where are we?" and again: "Lost!" In despair he cries out, "She will never get out. You have done it, sir. I knew it'd end in something like this. She will never weather, and you are too close now to stay. She'll drift ashore before she's round. O my God!" The mate wails as the captain of the *Sephora* had whimpered, "She's ashore already." The helmsman answers orders "in a frightened, thin, child-like voice."

Thus he has duplicated, in this crisis, the crisis of the *Sephora.* Officers and crew are on the verge of panic. He orders "Hard alee," knowing that Leggatt will step over the side when the ship is in stays. "He was able to hear everything—and perhaps he was able to understand why, on my conscience, it had to be thus close— no less." Like the crucial moment on the *Sephora,* everything depends on his next order. To give it, he must know when the ship has way. And he cannot feel it. He forgets Leggatt, and as at the beginning remembers only that he is a stranger to the ship. "I did not know her." He is still paralyzed.

Then the sign he needs, the saving mark, catches his eye. Leggatt has left his hat on the water, has returned it. He gives the order, the ship comes round. The tension is broken. And thus ends Conrad's story of a man who struggles toward his own integration. "And I was alone with her. Nothing! no one in the world should stand now between us, throwing a shadow on the way of silent knowledge and mute affection, the perfect communion of a seaman with his first command."

He is free. But the dream work, if you will, has been a mutual labor, and Leggatt is free of him. The young captain has one last glimpse of his hat "left behind to mark the spot where the secret sharer of my cabin and of my thoughts, as though he were my second self, had lowered himself into the water to take his punishment: a free man, a proud swimmer striking out for a new destiny."

"Heart of Darkness" served a similar function in dealing with the conflict central to *Lord Jim*. Again, there is general critical agreement that it is the effect of Marlow's journey "to the center of the earth," into the darkness of the unconscious, which changes him and makes it his story, not Kurtz's. And once again, the subject of command is pivotal. Marlow goes to get command of a riverboat; but he projects a sense of uncertainty which will be resolved by "knowing what is in there." One of his first acts is to find the body of the previous commander, whose death in a squabble over a chicken resulted in Marlow's appointment:

> Afterwards nobody seemed to trouble much about Fresleven's remains, till I got out and stepped into his shoes. I couldn't let it rest, though; but when an opportunity offered at last to meet my predecessor, the grass growing through his ribs was tall enough to hide his bones. They were all there. The supernatural being had not been touched after he fell [1899, p. 54].

Marlow gradually identifies with Kurtz, the man who has been there, who knows. Kurtz, he tells us, was a man of ideals, and Marlow's need to know whether those ideals sustained Kurtz under the impact of unconscious impulses grows with his identification. But Kurtz, in his report to the International Society for the Suppression of Savage Customs, began "with the argument that we whites, from the point of development we had arrived at, 'must necessarily appear to them [savages] in the nature of supernatural beings—we approach them with the might as of a deity. . . . By the simple exercise of our will we can exert a power for good practically unbounded' " (p. 118). Later, freed of external regulations and a law unto himself as much or more than any captain at sea, he responds to the temptation to *become* a deity. Throwing off all superego restraints, he discovers that he has no control over the id impulses which overwhelm him. (The id impulses actually suggested are again oral-sadistic; Kurtz has not only become cannibalistic, he would swallow everything if he could.) "The horror" is in part this helplessness of the ego to maintain its integrity; the lack of ego autonomy is part of Kurtz's discovery that he is "hollow at the core."

Marlow has tried to resolve his own uncertainty about the integrity of his identity through an identification with Kurtz. This is why Kurtz's failure is such a threat to him, and why he must master Kurtz's fate, remain loyal to him. The danger of the crippling identification is indicated by a number of passages, such as this, at the climax:

> . . . I had to deal with a being to whom I could not appeal in the name of anything high or low. . . . There was nothing either above or below him, and I knew it. He had kicked himself loose of the earth. Confound the man! he had kicked the very earth to pieces. He was alone, and I before him did not know whether I stood on the ground or floated in the air. I've been telling you what we said—repeating the phrases we pronounced—but what's the good? They were common everyday words—the familiar, vague sounds exchanged on every waking day of life. But what of that? They had behind them, to my mind, the terrific suggestiveness of words heard in dreams, of phrases spoken in nightmares. Soul! If anybody had ever struggled with a soul, I am the man. . . . But his soul was mad. Being alone in the wilderness, it had looked within itself, and, by heavens! I tell you, it had gone mad. I had—for my sins, I suppose—to go through the ordeal of looking into it myself [p. 144f.].

What saves Marlow is clear; he can acknowledge the appeal of the id impulses, acknowledge his kinship with the savages, but maintain the supremacy of quite conscious ego standards concerning work, the necessity of doing one's job well, of maintaining fidelity to the ideals of one's profession. Unlike Jim's, his ego ideal is reality bound and realistic. He does what he can as well as he can, and does not suffer unreasonable guilt about it—as in telling his lie, for example. But this integration does not come easy. The pain of accepting what Kurtz represents again must be experienced passively, in a state of immobilization. During his illness, "a vision of grayness without form filled with physical pain, and a careless contempt for the evanescence of all things—even of this pain itself," it is not his own extremity that impresses him: "No! It is [Kurtz's] extremity that I seem to have lived through" (p. 151). Marlow comes out of the experience a different man, never again to be so comfortable about the reality of man's nature, but he knows himself and controls his own destiny. In any war of conflicting impulses, "I have a voice, too," he says, "and for good or evil mine is the speech that cannot be silenced." The ego is in firm control.

VII

> He appealed to all sides at once—to the side turned perpetually to the light of day, and to that side of us which, like the other hemisphere of the moon, exists stealthily in perpetual darkness, with only a fearful ashy light falling at times on the edge.
>
> *Lord Jim* (1900, p. 93)

It is now possible to demonstrate the interrelationship of the two novels and the two stories:

Lord Jim: Jim exists from first to last in a passive relationship to a series of idealized father figures; his actual father is explicitly idealized, and after the jump Jim must avoid him. This passive relationship he disguises from himself behind the narcissistic, exaggeratedly masculine ego ideal. Presented with the choice of taking command of the *Patna* or betraying his ideal, he jumps. Although consciously motivated by shame to rebuild his self-esteem, he immediately re-establishes himself in the old relationship—submissive (although this is disguised) to an idealized father, thus denying even the suggestion of patricide. He is once again paralyzed by the appearance of Brown. A number of writers (see especially Morf, Guerard, and Meyer) have noted both that Jim suffers more from shame than from guilt, and that the crippling identification with Brown is based on shared guilt, without resolving the paradox. But Jim is not reacting just to the innuendos of desertion (which all of these writers equate with Conrad's desertion of Poland); he is reacting to *Brown*—the defiant, sadistic seducer of the clergyman's wife. The guilt that binds him relates to the unconscious wish to be like Brown.

This impulse is immediately denied by submission to Doramin, and at the same time the situation allows for gratification of self-destructive impulses partially warded off until then.

"Heart of Darkness": Conrad broke off the exploration of Jim's motives to create Marlow, the tested man through whose eyes he could approach the conflict. Marlow associates getting command of the riverboat with Kurtz's seizure of authority over a savage land. And here there is a strong suggestion of what Marlow (and Jim) fears—the throwing off of all superego restraint. With the "idealized father" and the "ideals" overthrown, the sadism contained by the superego and turned against the self is freed and turned outward. Kurtz *becomes* a god whose every lust is gratified; here as elsewhere the sadistic impulses most feared are oral. Marlow can be secure of his self-command only if he can take the position of authority, acknowledge the appeal of primitive impulses, and maintain ego standards of conduct consistent with his self image. He passes through the dreaded experience of passivity, and emerges integrated and certain of his self-knowledge. Only through the screen of such a man could Conrad face Jim's secret, masochistic gratification at the hands of his sadistic superego, projected onto his last father.

Under Western Eyes: Razumov is as isolated from his father as is Jim, and therefore as vulnerable; his father will support him as long as he remains away and does not acknowledge the relationship. Haldin appears after committing a form of patricide. Razumov denies the existence of such impulses in himself by going to his father, betraying Haldin, and writing his conservative creed denying the possibility of any good coming from revolutionary thought or action. But just as Jim's destruction was triggered by the sudden and unexpected command of the *Patna,* so Haldin's appearance is enough to start Razumov on the path toward the masochistic degradation at the hands of Nikita. As with Jim, even association with the breaking of the taboo is enough to awaken the passive impulses.

"The Secret Sharer": Before writing of Razumov's immolation, Conrad again veered away to reverse the conflict. The young captain uneasily approaches his "command" and is immediately brought face to face with Leggatt, with whom he identifies. Leggatt, the first mate, is confronted in a moment of crisis by the weakness of his captain; no idealization of authority is possible at this moment to protect him, as it was not for Jim when his captain abandoned the ship. Leggatt cannot under these circumstances submit to the necessity of maintaining the *structure* of authority even though its weakness has been exposed. If he had, he would have acted *for* the captain. Instead, he *seizes* authority, throws off superego restraints, and acts, like Kurtz, for himself. The consequences are the same; sadism contained is unleashed and turned outward. With the energy of his rage Leggatt saves the ship and strangles the first obstacle to his will.

The young captain must take command, integrate the force which is implicit in authority, and maintain the standards of his profession. Once again, he must pass through the test of passivity. When he does so successfully, he is truly in command of and one with his ship.

As Kris (p. 25f.) noted, Freud described a certain "flexibility of repression" in the artistic personality whereby "a considerable increase in psychic capacity results from a predisposition dangerous in itself." By flexibility of repression he was referring to the same phenomenon which Kris describes as the capacity to shift psychic levels. While Kris emphasizes the ego autonomy necessary for this function, Freud is calling attention to the artist's use of conflictual material in itself dangerous to intrapsychic stability. If the ego can artistically sublimate such material, there may be an increase in psychic capacity to tolerate conflict. But if the impulses loosed from repression are too strong, the ego is in danger of being overwhelmed.

There can be no question that Conrad opened himself to material personally dangerous, that he found it necessary to deal with the passive, submissive impulses explored in the fates of Jim and Razumov. The breaking off of these efforts, however, indicates the danger the ego experienced in dealing both with the passivity of the creative process and with content in which the ego can resolve conflicting demands of superego, ego ideal, and id only by seeking out its own destruction. The artistic function itself, by means of which externalization of the conflict might be achieved, appears threatened by immobilization.

The ego reasserts its mastery in the substituted creative acts. Previous real danger situations it has experienced are reactivated so that a sense of mastery, of integration, can be achieved by a reworking of these experiences. In these substitute situations the ego acts, not passively, but actively in dealing with the same intrapsychic conflicts. Instead of permitting its own destruction, superego and id demands are mastered and the ego emerges whole and triumphant. Specifically, impulses opposed to the passive, masochistic ones in the novels—i.e., the rebellious seizing of superego sadism and turning it outward—are exposed and integrated in the short stories. *In these two stories the ego creates myths of its own mastery over threats to its autonomy.* This sense of mastery permits a return to the original situation with some reassurance that the ego will not be overwhelmed. The "substituted creative task" is a unique and highly creative form of the defense by which a threat passively experienced is converted into an active mastery. Its success in the situations I have described contributes a new kind of support to Ernst Kris's assertion concerning the relationship between creativity and passivity (p. 318): "The integrative functions of the ego include self-regulated regression and permit a combination of the most daring intellectual activity with the experience of passive receptiveness."

BIBLIOGRAPHY

This is a selected bibliography of the works which have been most useful to me. In any paper in which as much material is condensed as in this one, indebtedness to previous studies may not be as clear as it should be. In particular I would point to the following: (1) Thomas Moser was the first who systematically studied the decline of Conrad's fiction after 1910, and related this to his difficulty in dealing with the subject of heterosexual love. Although I would disagree with the emphasis he places upon conscious intention to become a popular writer in Conrad's decline, his work is invaluable. (2) Albert J. Guerard's criticism has consistently been the most balanced, stimulating, and thought provoking for me. (3) The most complete psychoanalytic study is of course that of Bernard C. Meyer. His study of the effect on Conrad of the early loss of his mother, especially as manifested in the later work, is thorough and important. Although the pregenital mother may be discerned behind Conrad's attachment to his father, it seems to me crucial that the active struggle with the father figure is at the heart of Conrad's most successful fiction, and I would differ with Meyer only in this emphasis.

BAINES, J. (1960), *Joseph Conrad: A Critical Biography.* London: Weidenfeld & Nicolson.

CONRAD, JESSIE (1926), *Joseph Conrad As I Knew Him.* New York: Doubleday, Page.

— (1935), *Joseph Conrad and His Circle.* Port Washington, N.Y.: Kennikat Press, 1964.

CONRAD, JOSEPH (1895), *Almayer's Folly.**

— (1896), *An Outcast of the Islands.*

— (1897), *The Nigger of the 'Narcissus.'*

— (1899), "Heart of Darkness." *Youth, Heart of Darkness, The End of the Tether,* 1902.

— (1900), *Lord Jim.*

— (1902a), "Typhoon." *Typhoon and Other Stories,* 1903.

— (1902b), "To-morrow." *Typhoon and Other Stories,* 1903.

* All references to Conrad's writings are to the 21-volume English edition published by J. M. Dent and Sons, Ltd. The pagination is identical to the 26-volume Canterbury Edition published by Doubleday, Page and Company in New York in 1924.

— (1903), "Falk." *Typhoon and Other Stories.*

— (1904), *Nostromo.*

— (1906a), *The Mirror of the Sea.*

— (1906b), "An Anarchist." *A Set of Six,* 1908.

— (1910), "The Secret Sharer." *'Twixt Land and Sea,* 1912.

— (1911a), "A Smile of Fortune." *'Twixt Land and Sea,* 1912.

— (1911b), *Under Western Eyes.*

— (1912), *A Personal Record* (Author's Note written 1919 for Uniform Edition, 1923).

— (1915), *Victory.*

— (1917), *The Shadow Line* (written 1915).

— (1920), *The Rescue.*

— (1921), *Notes on Life and Letters.*

— (1926), *Last Essays.*

DEUTSCH, H. (1959), "*Lord Jim* and Depression." In: *Neuroses and Character Types.* New York: International Universities Press, 1965, pp. 353–357.

ERIKSON, E. H. (1956), The Problem of Ego Identity. *J. Amer. Psychoanal. Assn.,* 4:56–121.

GALSWORTHY, J. (1927), *Castles in Spain.* New York: Scribner's.

GARNETT, E. (1928), *Letters from Joseph Conrad: 1895–1924.* Indianapolis & New York: Charter Books, Bobbs-Merrill, 1962.

GEE, J. A. & STURM, P. J. (1940), *Letters of Joseph Conrad to Marguerite Poradowska.* New Haven: Yale University Press.

GORDON, J. D. (1940), *Joseph Conrad: The Making of a Novelist.* New York: Russell & Russell, 1963.

GUERARD, A. J. (1958), *Conrad the Novelist.* Cambridge: Harvard University Press, 1965.

HEWITT, D. (1952), *Conrad: A Reassessment.* Chester Springs, Penna.: Dufour Editions, 2nd ed., 1968.

JEAN-AUBRY, G. (1927), *Joseph Conrad: Life and Letters,* 2 Vols. Garden City, N.Y.: Doubleday, Page.

— (1957), *The Sea Dreamer.* London: Ruskin House, George Allen & Unwin.

KRIS, E. (1952), *Psychoanalytic Explorations in Art.* New York: International Universities Press.

MEYER, B. C. (1967), *Joseph Conrad: A Psychoanalytic Biography.* Princeton: Princeton University Press.

MORF, G. (1930), *The Polish Heritage of Joseph Conrad.* New York: Haskell House, 1965.

MOSER, T. (1957), *Joseph Conrad: Achievement and Decline.* Hamden, Conn.: Archon Books, 1966.

NAJDER, Z., ed. (1964), *Conrad's Polish Background.* London: Oxford University Press.

(534)   ROBERT ARMSTRONG

(534)   ROBERT ARMSTRONG

(534)   ROBERT ARMSTRONG

Sherry, N. (1966), *Conrad's Eastern World*. Cambridge: Cambridge University Press.

Sterba, R. F. (1965), Remarks on Joseph Conrad's "Heart of Darkness." *J. Amer. Psychoanal. Assn.*, 13:570–583.

Watts, C. T., ed. (1969), *Joseph Conrad's Letters to R. B. Cunninghame Graham*. Cambridge: Cambridge University Press.

Saxa Loquuntur

Artistic Aspects of Freud's "The Aetiology of Hysteria"

ERNEST S. WOLF, M.D.

REVOLUTIONARY ERAS OR EVEN TIMES OF PSEUDOREVOLUTIONARY UN-
rest usually do not present the most propitious moments for
historical retrospective, but perhaps it is precisely then, and therefore now, when renewing one's acquaintance with the wellsprings
of the past is most refreshing. Psychoanalysts, of course, are not
likely to have forgotten this because psychoanalysis is not only
a method or process or a body of data, but is also a new kind of
science whose meaning can be fully encompassed only by seeing
it as a history. It is therefore neither a lack of concern for the

Assistant Professor of Psychiatry, Northwestern University School of Medicine,
Chicago; Faculty Member, Chicago Institute for Psychoanalysis.

I wish to thank Dr. John Gedo for his many helpful suggestions.

This paper was read before the Cincinnati Psychoanalytic Society on May 11,
1971, and before the Chicago Psychoanalytic Society on May 25, 1971.

present nor a sterile impotence in facing the future that leads psychoanalysts again and again to examining the plans of its first master architect who built the fundament upon which the structure is being erected.

Historically oriented studies in psychoanalysis generally fall into two groups. The first of these comprises the tracings of the development of psychoanalytic concepts through the vicissitudes of changing context and meaning, with the purpose of clarifying theory in a developing science. The second group, loosely labeled applied psychoanalysis, attempts to relate biographical and patho-biographical material—and social, cultural, and other historical material in the widest sense—to the growing scientific structure as relevant determinants.

Applied psychoanalysis most generally has addressed itself to the *content* of a work of art or of science and has concerned itself with uncovering latent psychological meanings hidden by the manifest content. Among the numerous examples one might mention Freud's analysis of C. F. Meyer's *Die Richterin,* his discerning dissertation on Jensen's *Gradiva* (1907), and the many other psychoanalytic investigations of literature and drama by Freud's followers.[1] Other researchers have attempted to delineate possible relationships between the psychology of the artist and the product of his creativity. In short, what has been studied has been primarily the "what" and "why" of the creative act. Rarely has the focus of attention been on the *formal aspects,* on the "how." [2]

In contrast to the more traditional applied psychoanalytic investigations of *content,* this inquiry is concerned with studying the *form* of a created work from a psychoanalytic point of view. In this I have been guided by several aims. The first is to demonstrate a method of relating psychoanalysis to the investigation of the

[1] An essay on *Die Richterin* was the first application of psychoanalysis to a work of literature. Freud included it in a letter to Fliess of June 20, 1898 (see Freud, 1950, p. 256f.). See also Niederland (1960). The first published application of analysis to a work of literature was the essay on Jensen's *Gradiva,* while the first psychoanalytic study of the formal aspects of a work of art is contained in Freud's essay on Leonardo (1910).

[2] The formal aspects of Freud's scientific creativity have been highlighted in a series of discerning papers by Gedo et al. (1964), Miller et al. (1969), Sadow et al. (1968), and Schlessinger et al. (1967).

purely formal aspects of a work of science. The formal aspect studied here is the *style* in which a particular scientific work was written. A second aim is to present the finding resulting from this approach, namely, the formal aspects of the created work which was examined are related mainly to the transformations of narcissism, while the content appears to be mainly representative of the vicissitudes of object love. Finally, this paper also aims at making a contribution to the history of psychoanalysis.

I shall focus on Freud as a writer of scientific prose. The recent investigation of Freud's prose style by the philologist, Walter Schönau (1968), has created a basis for further exploration and has provided psychoanalysts with the literary tools needed in this area of mutual interest.

The particular work to be examined here is the lecture Freud delivered to the Viennese Society for Psychiatry and Neurology and subsequently published as "The Aetiology of Hysteria" (1896). According to Strachey, this lecture was given on April 21, 1896, though Jones believes the lecture was given 11 days later.[3] Apparently the paper was not well received and Krafft-Ebing, who was at that time president of the society, commented: "It sounds like a scientific fairy tale" (Jones, 1953, p. 263).

"The Aetiology of Hysteria" is a lecture of about 30 printed pages. In later years Freud gave his lectures without the use of written notes, a practice he probably followed already in 1896. In a letter to Fliess dated May 30, six weeks after the lecture, Freud wrote: "In defiance of my colleagues, I have written out my lecture on the aetiology of hysteria in full for Paschkis."

In general, contemporary witnesses were impressed by Freud's talents as a speaker. Abram Kardiner (1957) thought Freud was the greatest orator he had ever heard and in this respect favored him over Winston Churchill. Wittels (1924) found Freud fascinating and never tiring to his listeners. Jones (1959) was so enthralled that he felt oblivious of the passage of time. One may assume, therefore, that the icy reception that Freud reported in 1896 had little to do with any lack of oratorical talents.

The goal of a scientific lecture is very similar to that of a writer

[3] Strachey's lucid introductory comments (p. 189f.) go far in clarifying the historical significance of this lecture in the development of Freud's thinking.

of scientific prose: to convey his information so that it will be understood and accepted. Notwithstanding the fact that Freud failed to achieve this goal with most of the members of that Vienna society at that particular time, a close study of the published paper reveals it to have been eloquently powerful and worth examining for the style of his approach.

Freud began: "Gentlemen,—when we set out to form an opinion about the causation of a pathological state. . . ." With the word "we" Freud immediately attempted to engage the audience by identifying himself as one of them and as a physician. Then, by picturing a situation of anamnestic investigation, he started his audience off from familiar territory. It is characteristic of good writers or good speakers, and Freud apparently was no exception, to have in mind a clear picture of the audience they are addressing. Freud needed to have a clear image of the reader's expectations, interests, sympathies, level of education, and especially of their prejudices. From previous discouraging experiences with this particular audience, Freud knew that they prejudged him as unscientific. Perhaps in order to counteract this feeling in the audience, he tried to deflect it toward the unscientific patient whom he characterized: "by his lack of scientific understanding of aetiological influences, by the fallacy of *post hoc, propter hoc*,[4] by his reluctance to think about or mention certain noxae and traumas."

It is interesting to note here Freud's use of a Latin citation, though of course physicians of Freud's time generally had a classical education and were familiar with Latin and Greek and occasionally used such citations. Freud did this to a much larger extent and with much greater variety than most. In this particular paper there are one French and three Latin quotations.

In the rest of the paragraph, Freud underlined in some detail the audience's and his own scientific attitude and skepticism in the search for truth. The obstacle was identified to be the patient, whose ignorance prevented him from collaborating in the scientific endeavor.

---

[4] After this, therefore on account of this (an illogical reasoning).

From this basic position, Freud attempted to catch the audience's interest by hinting that perhaps these obstacles could be overcome:

> You will readily admit that it would be a good thing to have a second method of arriving at the aetiology of hysteria, one in which we should feel less dependent on the assertions of the patients themselves.

In simple language he crystallized the painful feelings of frustration of his fellow physicians and held out hope for relief. In so doing he also gave a first definition of the scientific task and took his listeners on the first step toward his goal. Since this gain needed to be consolidated immediately, he proceeded:

> A dermatologist, for instance, is able to recognize a sore as luetic from the character of its margins, . . . and a forensic physician can arrive at the cause of an injury, even if he has to do without any information from the injured person. In hysteria, too, there exists a similar possibility. . . .

In this way two vivid images with which his listeners were thoroughly familiar were used as analogies to clarify and achieve agreement on the goal of the investigation, which was to demonstrate a new investigatory technique that had the merit of being both scientific and able to overcome the difficulties presented by recalcitrant patients.

The use of the word "forensic" may not be accidental. In the first paragraph Freud had used words such as "investigation" and "critical examination" and most importantly, *"agents provocateurs."* The flavor is one of a criminal investigation, of a detective story. This stylistic device also reappears in the structure of the whole essay. Again and again, like Sherlock Holmes, Freud led his listeners on the trail after his elusive antagonist who vanished again and again behind sudden new obstacles, but each time leaving enough of a trace to raise new hopes and expectations in the audience. One can almost feel the excitement of the chase.

But before he could proceed further, Freud had to introduce

the listener to his particular method of investigation. To do this he chose "an analogy taken from an advance that has in fact been made in another field of work."

> Imagine that an explorer arrives in a little-known region where his interest is aroused by an expanse of ruins, with remains of walls, fragments of columns, and tablets with half-effaced and unreadable inscriptions. He may content himself with inspecting what lies exposed to view, with questioning the inhabitants— perhaps semi-barbaric people—who live in the vicinity, about what tradition tells them of the history and meaning of these archaeological remains, and with noting down what they tell him—and he may then proceed on his journey. But he may act differently. He may have brought picks, shovels and spades with him, and he may set the inhabitants to work with these implements. Together with them he may start upon the ruins, clear away the rubbish, and, beginning from the visible remains, uncover what is buried. If his work is crowned with success, the discoveries are self-explanatory: the ruined walls are part of the ramparts of a palace or a treasure-house; the fragments of columns can be filled out into a temple; the numerous inscriptions, which, by good luck, may be bilingual, reveal an alphabet and a language, and, when they have been deciphered and translated, yield undreamed-of information about the events of the remote past, to commemorate which the monuments were built. *Saxa loquuntur!*

With this beautiful metaphorical image Freud succeeded in synthesizing the images of the detective and the scientist. He heightened the interest of his audience who could well remember the skepticism and the excitement surrounding Schliemann's discovery of Troy. He prepared them for the difficulty of the journey and the hard digging work ahead. He warned them of the worthless rubbish that needed to be cleared away. Perhaps he threw a contemptuous look at those who just proceeded on their usual journey without first having done some excavating. But what a reward of riches he promised those who stayed and dug! "Stones talk." What a pithy phrase for an imperative summary.

One of the hallmarks of distinguished literary prose is the frequent and subtle allusion to the literary tradition and heritage of which it is a part. With *saxa loquuntur*[5] Freud reached back to the Bible, to Habakkuk, "For the stone will cry out from the wall"; to Luke, "I tell you if they were silent the very stone would cry out"; to Shakespeare's Macbeth, "The very stones prate of my whereabout"; and to Schiller's poem, *An die Freunde* (To My Friends).

Freud's intimate familiarity with Schiller's works is well known and there are at least 47 references to Schiller in the *Standard Edition*. It is not surprising, therefore, to find that Freud's beautiful metaphor of the undaunted archaeologist contains allusions to a Schiller poem. I shall quote the first stanza in Bowring's translation (1910):

> Yes, my friend!—that happier times have been
> Than the present, none can contravene;
> That a race once liv'd of nobler worth;
> And if ancient chronicles were dumb,
> Countless stones in witness forth would come
> From the deepest entrails of the earth.
> But this highly-favor'd race has gone,
> Gone forever to the realms of night.
> We, *we* live! The moments are our own,
> And the living judge the right.

Schiller not only evokes the scene of ancient ruins and stones but also emanates the stubborn spirit of life asserting itself and making these moments his own. Nothing less can be said about Freud's little story 94 years later.

Yet, one might also speculate what, beyond literary aesthetics and rhetorical eloquence, moved Freud to choose this particular Latin phrase with its allusions. Did he perhaps feel that in the anti-Semitic milieu of Vienna a reminder of the common roots he had with his audience in both the Old and the New Testament might soften their prejudices? Did he, like Macbeth, feel he had to hide some evil? After all he had expressed some rather forceful

[5] "Büchmann's *Geflügelte Worte*" (a widely used compendium of citations, probably also used by Freud) traces *saxa loquuntur* from Habakkuk and Luke to the 13th-century *Legenda aurea* of Iacobus a Voragine and then to L. Th. Kosegarten's Legend *Das Amen der Steine* (1810).

derogatory opinions about his listeners to Fliess and, in an unpublished letter had referred to them as "donkeys" (Freud, 1896, p. 189). Closer to Freud's spirit, however, is the spirit of Schiller's poem, the spirit of youthful defiance, renewal, and affirmation.

It has been suggested that Freud's literary heritage and literary imagination allowed him creatively to form concrete metaphorical images out of vaguely apprehended introspective experiences, and that these images were then harnessed by his scientifically trained ego into scientific concepts (Gedo and Wolf, 1970). Thus the vivid imagery not only serves an aesthetic and rhetorical purpose but may be a necessary step in concept formation itself.[6] The same is suggested by the archaeological metaphor that has just been discussed. At a time when Freud had already begun to appreciate the importance of dreams but had not yet finally formulated his theories, he talked about a yield of "undreamed-of information about the remote past" that could perhaps be "deciphered and translated," that might be "bilingual [and] reveal an alphabet and a language." It was not until 4 years later that he specifically compared the interpretation of dreams to the deciphering of hieroglyphics.

For the purpose of this paper it is not necessary to continue the detailed examination of Freud's style beyond these first few paragraphs. A few more points will suffice. Leading his audience back from the symptom to the scene from which that symptom arose, Freud frequently had to encourage his listeners.

> But the path from the symptoms of hysteria to its aetiology is more laborious and leads through other connections than one would have imagined.
> [Two paragraphs later:] Here we meet with our first great disappointment.
> [Anticipating the objections in the minds of his readers:] The allegedly traumatic experience, though it *does* have a relation to the symptom, proves to be an impression which is normally innocuous and incapable as a rule of producing any effect. . . .

[6] In a similar vein Eissler (1968, p. 151) speculates that "Freud may have discovered the oedipus complex from his study of Shakespeare's tragic hero, as much as from his observation of clinical cases."

[Two paragraphs later:] You can understand how great the temptation is at this point to proceed no further with what is in any case a laborious piece of work.

. Freud used examples from railway accidents, not because they were particularly illuminating, but because he knew his fellow physicians were vitally interested, since in their practices they had to wrestle with cases of suspected malingering and insurance claims. Having used lucid examples to illustrate his points, Freud confessed that he had been obliged to make them up because the real examples were too complicated. Throughout he enlivened the flow of his presentation with vivid analogies, for instance, when he compared chains of associations to a string of pearls, or the interconnections to a genealogical tree. He frequently coined new words or expressions by taking ordinary words, such as *nodal point* or *hysterogenic point* or *neurosis of defense,* and elevating them to the status of a quasi-scientific terminology. Recognizing his audience's deprecatory view of infancy and childhood mentality, he attempted to dignify the memories of the earliest experiences by comparing them to "the most ancient nobility." *Pari passu,* he thereby also struck a blow against the concepts of hereditary degeneracy.

Freud's prodigious literary talents which appear so strikingly in his 1896 lecture were already evident in his adolescent letters (Gedo and Wolf, 1970; Wolf, 1971). They stamp his whole *opus* of writings, scientific as well as personal, with the signature of a *litterateur* of the first rank and earned him the Goethe Prize for literature. Characteristic is his clarity, his vividness of expression, his use of telling aphorisms and beautiful imagery, interlaced with citations and allusions to the great classics, and punctuated by the coinage of memorable new terms. Awareness of his gift as a witty storyteller moved Freud to apologize that his case histories read like novels (Breuer and Freud, 1893–1895). Notable is his craft in drawing the reader into participation by fictive dialogue, and by empathically sensing the resistances Freud was able to refute objections before they obstructed the discussion.

This rhetorical quality of Freud's prose deserves further comment. On the basis of his philologic studies Schönau (1968) has identified Lessing as the most influential model for Freud's *style*.[7]

Lessing not only was a great dramatist and critic, but he is also regarded as the father of German scientific prose. His writings are characterized by many of the same qualities as Freud's, especially the use of fictive dialogue. One also wonders about the influence of Michael Bernays, an uncle of Freud's wife Martha, who as Professor of the History of Literature at the University of Munich had written in 1892 about the specific forms that were demanded by scientific writing and who had recommended Lessing as a standard (Bernays, 1903). Freud himself is reported to have told Wortis (1954) that Lessing was his conscious and deliberate model.

The eloquence Freud manifested in the "Aetiology of Hysteria" is so remarkable that Jones (1953, p. 263) called it a "literary *tour de force*," and one may be reasonably justified in asking whether special circumstances evoked this extraordinary effort.

The months preceding this lecture had indeed been a time of increasing isolation and tension for Freud: the first strains appeared in Freud's relationship with Fliess, and the hostility of the medical community to his ideas surfaced in the publication of a scathing review by Strümpell of the Breuer-Freud *Studies on Hysteria*. On February 6, 1896 Freud complained to Fliess:

> There has been an unconscionable break in our correspondence.
> . . . I am blowing my own trumpet for lack of anyone else to
> blow it for me. . . . Our book had a disgraceful notice by

[7] Many citations testify to Freud's intimate acquaintance with G. E. Lessing's (1729–1781) writings (*Standard Edition*, 2:175; 4:176; 7:309; 8:72; 8:92; 20:62; letters to Martha Bernays [1960, p. 17], to Fliess [1950, pp. 109, 172], and to Pfister [1963, p. 129]). It was Lessing who had in the 18th century broken the bonds of chauvinistic patriotism and narrow theology and who paved the way for the great flowering of German literature in the writings of Goethe and Schiller. At a time when Europe was enthralled by *belles-lettres* Lessing boldly proclaimed the superiority of Shakespeare to Corneille, Racine, and Voltaire. His blank verse play, *Nathan der Weise*, is a dramatization of the idea of religious tolerance, a very meaningful play for Freud from which he paraphrased dialogue in a letter to Martha and whose motto *Introite et hic dii sunt* (Enter for here are gods also) he had planned to use as "the proud words" with which to precede his "Psychology of Hysteria" (1950, p. 172).

Strümpell in the *Deutsche Zeitschrift für Nervenheilkunde*. . . .
[On February 13, he wrote again:] I am so isolated.
[With a kind of forced enthusiasm he encouraged Fliess:]
Criticism will not affect you any more than Strümpell's criticism
affected me. I really do not need to be consoled. . . . [But his
real mood would not be denied:] My health does not deserve to
be asked after. . . . I have grown grey very quickly.

In a letter of March 1, 1896 he advised Fliess on how best to arrange his forthcoming book:

> But one should not provide the public with an opportunity of
> exercising its limited critical faculty, which it generally does to
> its own detriment, in the chapter devoted entirely to facts. . . .
> Otherwise I fear that readers might jump to the conclusion
> that . . .

Surely, here is a writer who is consciously aware of the uses of
rhetoric. Freud always knew well what Michael Bernays had
written a few years earlier about scientific prose (1903): formal
artistic qualities are required to ensure that scientific work en-
dures; otherwise the scientific content is absorbed by science,
while the author and his writings are forgotten.

Fliess seemed to have been unhappy about Freud's comments.
On March 16, 1896 Freud was very apologetic:

> Do not think I am throwing doubt on your period theory. . . .
> I only want to stop you from giving the enemy, the public, some-
> thing on which to exercise its mind—as I unfortunately always
> do—because it usually revenges itself for such a challenge.

In a footnote to this letter Ernst Kris remarked that Fliess's
reaction to Freud's previous letter paved the way to their eventual
estrangement. It seems clear that Freud felt menaced on two
fronts, in his relationship with Fliess and with the public. But
with characteristic humor he was undaunted in stating his secret
ambition and conviction:

> I am met with hostility and live in such isolation that one
> might suppose I had discovered the greatest truths.

On April 2, 1896 Freud was again self-depreciating with Fliess:

> I am delighted to see you are able to substitute realities for my
> incomplete efforts. [But Freud's drive to attain greatness was not
> shaken:] . . . we shall certainly leave behind something which
> will justify our existence. . . . I am convinced that . . . I can
> definitely cure hysteria and obsessional neurosis.

These passages reveal that at the time Freud prepared his lecture, he oscillated between states of depressed self-esteem and
heroic fantasies of eminence. Referring to Freud's relationship to
Fliess, Kohut (1971) believes that at that time Freud needed an
alter ego to mirror his archaic ambitions for greatness as well as
for an idealized self-object as a magnet for his strivings for perfection. Fliess, whose own grandiosity never became transmuted into
a secure self-confidence, must have felt deeply hurt by even the
slightest critical remarks made by Freud and apparently reacted
with the temporary withdrawal of his unconditional acceptance,
thus greatly intensifying Freud's needs. Moreover, the concurrent
publication of Strümpell's contemptuous review together with its
associated reminders of the personally ill-fated collaboration with
Breuer could only have increased the void that Freud felt. In this
emotionally critical situation—many a lesser man's efforts would
have collapsed at this point—Freud marshaled himself, defiantly,
in the spirit of Schiller, into an achievement of superlative beauty
and eloquence. No wonder Jones speaks of a *tour de force*.

Perhaps I am being too speculative in drawing these far-reaching inferences from data which are limited in scope and incomplete. A recent paper by Schur (1966), however, does offer some
support. On the basis of unpublished letters to Fliess, Schur concludes "that while the actual final break in the relationship
between Freud and Fliess did not occur until the last meeting,
during the summer of 1900, the change in Freud's attitude was a
gradual one, *with many ups and downs*" (p. 69; my italics).[8] Fliess's

---

[8] K. R. Eissler (1963, p. 1382) comes to parallel conclusions: "In studying the
lives of some geniuses, such as Dostoevski, one gets the impression that man does
his best creating when he is caught in the pincers of grave dangers that threaten
from within as well as without, whether the outward ones are real or only assumed. . . . one must conclude that suffering, so far from being an obstacle or

mishandling of Emma's nosebleeds which, according to Schur, became in 1895 an important day residue for the pivotal Irma dream, may have been the great and decisive disappointment that started Freud's disillusionment with Fliess.

A brief summary may clarify our thinking before venturing into new territory. I started by taking a new look at a fragment of Freud's *opus* and noted the aesthetic beauty and power. I paid particular attention to some of the formal characteristics which transform prosaic writing into artistic prose; some evidence of the influence of great writers of the past and of the literary tradition was seen. Then, from available historical material, I have reconstructed with reasonable plausibility Freud's psychological state at the time of writing his lecture. But what can one say about creating an admired work of eloquent beauty? Is more involved than merely the wish of an artistically gifted scientist to write in a clear and convincing manner like his admired models?

Let us return to considering Freud's presumable psychological state. Jones (1953, pp. 295, 297, 298) noted he was "drained of the self-confidence he had transferred to his overpowering partner" (that is, to Fliess), whom "he had endowed with all sorts of imaginary qualities" and to whom he had written on July 14, 1894, "Your praise is nectar and ambrosia to me."

Fliess's withdrawal, even if only temporary and vaguely sensed, is likely to have disturbed the "mirror transference" contained in Freud's relationship to Fliess. The gap left in psychological structure by the "absence" of the admired Fliess in whom Freud had been able to mirror himself needed to be filled with another self-object that would restore the former perfection of the self (Kohut, 1966, 1968, 1971). An artistically gifted person, like Freud, is able to fill the gap by creating a work of artistic beauty, which psychologically is experienced as part of the self, and thus the lost beauty and perfection of the self is regained. This creative act is reflected

---

impediment to creativity, is one of its prerequisites." Similarly, Jones (1953, p. 305) reports a self-observation by Freud: "I have come back with a lordly feeling of independence and feel too well; since returning I have been very lazy, because the *moderate misery necessary for intensive work* refuses to appear." This seems to document Freud's awareness of the creatively stimulating power of certain states of psychic tension.

in the *form* of Freud's writing, in its tone, its structure, its artistic beauty which evokes the aesthetic experience. Eissler's (1963) discussion of the vicissitudes of Goethe's relationship to his friends Lavater and Plessing while Goethe's genius was wrestling with writing Book III of *Wilhelm Meister* suggests that Goethe's needs to create artistically were similarly related to his narcissistic transformations.

Returning now to Freud's lecture one need not look very far to see elements of its *content* with which Freud obviously had identified himself. Perhaps the clearest example is the image of the great archaeological explorer who deciphers ancient alphabets. The allusion here is to J. F. Champollion, who had found the key to the decipherment of the Egyptian hieroglyphics on the Rosetta stone. Freud's writings are full of identifications with the great heroes of history, as has been well documented by Jones (1953) and by Schönau (1968). Psychologically, however, such identifications often belong to the developmental line of the cathexes of the functions and actions of objects. In the instance demonstrated here Freud's identification appears to be with the *activity* of the archaeological explorer but not with his *personship,* an inference that is also supported by Freud's omission of Champollion's name. It is interesting to compare this with Freud's mentioning of Hannibal (1900, p. 196f.): "Which of the two, it may be debated, walked up and down his study with the greater impatience after he had formed his plan of going to Rome—Winckelmann, the Vice-Principal, or Hannibal, the Commander-in-Chief?" Freud added, "the wish to go to Rome had become in my dream-life a cloak and a symbol for a number of other passionate wishes. Their realization was to be pursued with all the perseverance and singlemindedness of the Carthaginian." Clearly, among the various determinants Freud seems predominantly to have identified with the tenacious quality of Hannibal's and Winckelmann's actions of conquering new territory. Moreover, the mention of both names in the same breath might be interpreted as de-emphasizing their personship.[9] These findings seem to suggest that two separate

[9] In connection with the allusion to Champollion discussed above, it is doubly interesting to note that J. J. Winckelmann (1717–1768) is generally regarded as the father of classical archaeology and that, like Freud, he also had persevered in his fascination with antiquity through an interlude of medical studies.

developmental lines find separate representation in the product of the artist-scientist's creativity: object relations that are derived from identifications with the actions of others are reflected in the content, while narcissistic transformations shape the form of the created work.[10]

One further comment needs to be made about the public reaction to Freud's paper. Why was this superbly eloquent and beautiful lecture received so icily? Were these sophisticated physicians really so shocked by sexuality even when presented in Freud's circumspect and delicate manner? Perhaps, but I would suggest another and more decisive reason. Freud failed to win acceptance not in spite of his beautifully eloquent presentation but precisely because of its aesthetic qualities. When Krafft-Ebing said, "It sounds like a scientific fairy tale," he was telling a half-truth: this work of science did have the beauty of a fairy tale and, to that audience, beauty in a work of science was suspect and unscientific. One can easily imagine that a more pedestrian and awkwardly embarrassed presentation might have been listened to with more respect. Could it be that Freud, a master of empathic understanding, did not know this? I would suggest that unconsciously the need to create a work of beauty took precedence over the need to persuade. An artistic work of science became a scientific work of art.

Indeed, not only do stones speak, sometimes they also shine.

Although it is useful in common parlance to make a distinction between creative artists and creative scientists, I do not want to raise here again the question whether Freud was more one or more the other. What I am discussing here are aspects of creativity that are shared by both. Freud, especially in his mature years, took vigorous exception to being thought of as an artist. In 1919 Havelock Ellis wrote an essay intended to show Freud as the creator of artistic productions but not of scientific work. Freud (1920, p. 263) replied that "we cannot but regard this view as a fresh turn taken

---

[10] Freud's analysis of tendentious jokes distinguishes two sources of pleasure: an incentive bonus derived from its formal construction, especially its economy of presentation, and a greater amount of pleasure derived from the content by the lifting of repressions (1905b). Similarly, Freud said that writers bribe us by purely formal aesthetic pleasures so as to make possible the release of greater pleasure from deeper sources (1908). Might we discern in Freud's formulation indirect support for the hypothesis being proposed here?

by resistance and as a repudiation of analysis, even though it is disguised in a friendly, indeed in too flattering a manner. We are inclined to meet it with a most decided contradiction." In a letter to Lou Andreas-Salomé he stated it succinctly: "But—in spite of all phrases—I still am not an artist" (1966, p. 213). Yet it is interesting to note that in younger, less guarded moments, Freud did allow himself to flirt with the idea of becoming a great writer, at least in fantasy. As a 17-year-old he reported ironically, though with pride, that his professor compared Freud's style to that of Herder, "a style at once correct and characteristic," and, jokingly, Freud challenged his friend Fluss to preserve his letters—"you never know" (1969). Ten years later he teased his bride, asking her: "Why didn't I become a gardener instead of a doctor or writer?" (1960, p. 40).

In fact, Freud's genius makes it difficult to separate the artist from the scientist, and the attempt to set them apart does violence to a deeper understanding of the creative stream in Freud's personality. It is a false and destructive prejudice of our time that seeks to isolate modern scientific man from that part of himself which cannot be weighed or measured but from which his creative energy flows.

Freud achieved an amalgamation of the artist with the scientist into a harmoniously productive balance such as had not been seen since Leonardo or Goethe. As early as 1896, in a far-seeing review of *Studies on Hysteria,* Alfred von Berger commented that "the attraction constantly exercised on me springs from my artistic sensibility which in manifold ways is stimulated and satisfied by the form and content of this book." With remarkable foresight Berger also discerned "the idea that it may one day become possible to approach the innermost secret of human personality." Freud finally must have felt more secure about the eventual acceptance of his achievement as scientific for he did accept the Goethe Prize for literature "in equal measure to the scholar as to the writer" (Paquet, 1930).

Lest there be any lingering reluctance to acknowledge, even today, the artistic aspects of scientific creativity it might be well to take a brief look at some of the founders of modern theoretical

physics. The British physicist Paul Dirac, who with Erwin Schrödinger shared the 1933 Nobel Prize for their pioneering work in
quantum mechanics, wrote as follows about Schrödinger's discovery of the wave equation of the electron: "Schrödinger got his
equation by pure thought, looking for some beautiful generalization. . . . It seems that if one is working from the point of view
of getting beauty in one's equation, and if one has really a sound
insight, one is on a sure line of progress." Another prominent
physicist, Max Born, is reported to have hailed the advent of
relativity because, he confessed, it made the universe of science
"more beautiful and grander." Poincaré wrote that what guided
him toward new discoveries was "the feeling of mathematical
beauty, of the harmony of numbers and forms, of geometric ele-
gance. This is a true aesthetic feeling that all mathematicians
know." [11]

Scientists often acknowledge a quasi-religious feeling of ecstasy
in the contemplation of the beauty and order of nature. Albert
Einstein (1931) gave eloquent testimony to this "fundamental
emotion which stands at the cradle of true art and true science.
. . . A knowledge of the existence of something we cannot penetrate, our perception of the profoundest reasons and the most
radiant beauty, which only in their most primitive forms are accessible to our minds" (p. 11).

As psychoanalysts we can discern here not only a defensive position derived from the danger situations that menace object-rela-
tional developments but also a striving for participation of the
self in Nature's infinite beauty and goodness derived from archaic
narcissistic disappointments.

For Freud, who was less assured of public acceptance as a scientist than are Nobel laureate physicists, it may have been good
politics publicly to deny the poet inside himself. Perhaps, even
more than by such external pragmatic considerations, he may have
felt persuaded by inner voices to distance himself from the exhibitionism of his illustrious but ill-reputed predecessors, such as
Charcot and the hypnotists. But his *opus* is a monument to the

---

[11] The quotations in this paragraph are from Koestler (1964, pp. 245, 147).

undiminished power of the Muse, "for the words which we use in our everyday speech are nothing other than watered-down magic" (Freud, 1905a, p. 283).

BIBLIOGRAPHY

BERGER, A. (1896), Chirurgie der Seele. *Psychoanal. Beweg*, 4:73–76, 1932.

BERNAYS, M. (1903), Zur Lehre von den Citaten und Noten (1892). In: *Schriften zur Kritik und Litteraturgeschicte*, Vol. 4. Berlin: Behr.

BOWRING, E. A. (1910), *The Poems of Schiller*. London: Geo. Bell.

BREUER, J. & FREUD, S. (1893–1895), Studies on Hysteria. *Standard Edition*, 2. London: Hogarth Press, 1955.

BÜCHMANN, G. (1964), *Geflügelte Worte*. Berlin: Haude und Spenersche Verlagsbuchhandlung, p. 82.

EINSTEIN, A. (1931), The World As I See It. In: *Ideas and Opinions*. New York: Crown Publishers, 1954.

EISSLER, K. R. (1963), *Goethe: A Psychoanalytic Study*. Detroit: Wayne State University Press.

— (1968), The Relation of Explaining and Understanding in Psychoanalysis. *This Annual*, 23:141–177.

ELLIS, H. (1919), Psycho-Analysis in Relation to Sex. *The Philosophy of Conflict and Other Essays in Wartime*, second series. London: Constable.

FREUD, S. (1896), The Aetiology of Hysteria. *Standard Edition*, 3:89–221. London: Hogarth Press, 1962.

— (1900), The Interpretation of Dreams. *Standard Edition*, 4 & 5. London: Hogarth Press, 1953.

— (1905a), Psychical (or Mental) Treatment. *Standard Edition*, 7:283–302. London: Hogarth Press, 1953.

— (1905b), Jokes and Their Relation to the Unconscious. *Standard Edition*, 8. London: Hogarth Press, 1960.

— (1907), Delusions and Dreams in Jensen's *Gradiva*. *Standard Edition*, 9:7–95. London: Hogarth Press, 1959.

— (1908), Creative Writers and Day-Dreaming, *Standard Edition*, 9:141–153. London: Hogarth Press, 1959.

— (1910), Leonardo da Vinci and a Memory of His Childhood. *Standard Edition*, 11:59–137. London: Hogarth Press, 1957.

— (1920), A Note on the Prehistory of the Technique of Analysis. *Standard Edition*, 18:263–265. London: Hogarth Press, 1955.

— (1950), *The Origins of Psychoanalysis: Letters, Drafts and Notes to Wilhelm Fliess (1887–1902)*. New York: Basic Books, 1954.

— (1960), *Letters of Sigmund Freud,* ed. E. L. Freud. New York: Basic Books.
— (1966), *Sigmund Freud—Lou Andreas-Salome Briefwechsel.* Frankfurt: Fischer.
— (1969), Some Early Unpublished Letters of Freud. *Int. J. Psycho-Anal.,* 50:419–427.
— & PFISTER, O. (1963), *Psycho-Analysis and Faith.* London: Hogarth Press.
GEDO, J. E., SABSHIN, M., SADOW, L., & SCHLESSINGER, N. (1964), *Studies on Hysteria:* A Methodological Evaluation. *J. Amer. Psychoanal. Assn.,* 12: 734–751.
— & WOLF, E. (1970), Die Ichthyosaurusbriefe. *Psyche,* 24:785–797.
JONES, E. (1953), *The Life and Work of Sigmund Freud,* Vol. 1. New York: Basic Books.
— (1959), *Free Associations: Memories of a Psycho-Analyst.* London: Hogarth Press.
KARDINER, A. (1957), Freud—The Man I Knew, The Scientist, and His Influence. In: *Freud and the 20th Century,* ed. B. Nelson. New York: Meridian Books, pp. 46–58.
KOESTLER, A. (1964), *The Act of Creation.* New York: Macmillan.
KOHUT, H. (1966), Forms and Transformations of Narcissism. *J. Amer. Psychoanal. Assn.,* 14:243–272.
— (1968), The Psychoanalytic Treatment of Narcissistic Personality Disorders. *This Annual,* 23:86–113.
— (1971), *The Analysis of the Self.* New York: International Universities Press.
MILLER, J. A., SABSHIN, M., GEDO, J. E., POLLOCK, G. H., SADOW, L., & SCHLESSINGER, N. (1969), Some Aspects of Charcot's Influence on Freud. *J. Amer. Psychoanal. Assn.,* 17:608–623.
NIEDERLAND, W. G. (1960), The First Application of Psychoanalysis to a Literary Work. *Psychoanal. Quart.,* 29:228–235.
PAQUET, A. (1930), Brief an S. Freud. In: *Gesammelte Werke,* 14:545 footnote. London: Imago Publ. Co., 1948.
SADOW, L., GEDO, J. E., MILLER, J., POLLOCK, G. H., SABSHIN, M., & SCHLESSINGER, N. (1968), The Process of Hypothesis Change in Three Early Psychoanalytic Concepts. *J. Amer. Psychoanal. Assn.,* 16:245–273.
SCHLESSINGER, N., GEDO, J. E., MILLER, J., POLLOCK, G. H., SABSHIN, M., & SADOW, L. (1967), The Scientific Styles of Breuer and Freud in the Origins of Psychoanalysis. *J. Amer. Psychoanal. Assn.,* 15:404–422.
SCHÖNAU, W. (1968), *Sigmund Freuds Prosa.* Stuttgart: J. B. Metzlersche Verlagsbuchhandlung.
SCHUR, M. (1966), Some Additional Day Residues of "The Specimen Dream of Psychoanalysis." In: *Psychoanalysis—A General Psychology,* ed. R. M. Loewenstein, L. M. Newman, M. Schur, & A. J. Solnit. New York: International Universities Press, pp. 45–85.

WITTELS, F. (1924), *Sigm. Freud: Der Mann, die Lehre, die Schule.* Leipzig: Tal.

WOLF, E. S. (1971), Sigmund Freud: Some Adolescent Transformations of a Future Genius. In: *Adolescent Psychiatry, Vol. 1: Developmental and Clinical Studies.* New York: Basic Books, pp. 51–60.

WORTIS, J. (1954), *Fragment of an Analysis with Freud.* New York: Simon & Schuster.

INDEX

Index

557

Death (*continued*)
  prerequisite of life, 28, 32
  of psychologically deprived infant, 36
    and structuralization, 37
Death instinct (drive)
  biological basis, 26–35
  and constancy-unpleasure principle,
    114
  critique, 112–116
  in Kleinian psychology, 112–116, 134–
    142, 145–149
  in support of, 25–75
Death wishes, 81
  mutual, 459
Décarie, T. Gouin, 358, 371
Decision, 13
  in adolescence, 244
  impact of personality on political,
    448–449
  psychoanalytic theory, 435–442, 449
Decision-making process, 425–449
Defecation, 212
Defense, 7, 18, 174, 244
  aggression as, 56
  against aggression, 67–70
  of artist dealing with conflictual ma-
    terial, 517
  autonomy of, 21–22
  and conscious motivation, 96–97
  conscious vs. unconscious, 96–99
  and creativity, 516
  and decision, 426
  development, 175
  and ego, 142, 144
  exaggerated, 83
  and fantasy, 144–145, 151
  against helplessness, 365
  impact of early sexual discovery on,
    195–215
  intensification in adolescence, 246
  interpretation, 151
  Kleinian concept, 134, 137–139, 145–
    146
  laughter as, 305
  against libidinal wish, 68
  manic, 139–140, 145
  and neurosis, 80–82
  neurotic vs. psychotic, 139
  normal, 9
  obsessional, 377–384
  and postcoital masturbation, 65
  precursors, 189, 297
  and reconstruction, 376–377
  against reorganization, 103
  repetitive, rigid, 21–22
  and repression, 96, 98

  against separation, 166
  splitting into good and bad object,
    135–139, 196, 412–413, 420; *see also*
    Splitting
  "substituted creative task" as, 531
  used repetitively, 21
  vulnerabilities, 20
  see also sub specific mechanisms
Delinquency, 53, 70
Delusion, 225
  of grandeur, 487
  of omnipotence, 416
  see also Body
Dementia senilis, 61
Denial, 52, 63, 69, 207, 265, 305, 312–
    313, 380, 382, 435, 474
  of anxiety and guilt, 56
  of need for treatment, 455–481
  of persecution, 136
  of reality, 140
Dependency, 88, 260, 333, 416, 420, 492–
    493
  anaclitic, 251
  prolonged, 480
Depersonalization, 220
Depression, 15, 84, 163–165, 190, 197,
    219, 223, 243, 257, 383, 487, 493, 502,
    505
Depressive core, 339
Depressive position, 133, 137–140, 146–
    150, 404
Deprivation, 5, 19, 37, 88–89, 253, 331
Despair, 265, 268, 300, 305, 309–313
Destruction, Destructiveness, 38–40, 45–
    47, 58–61, 69, 72, 75
  and food intake, 66
  oral, 62–63; *see also* Food intake
  pleasurable, 53, 64–65
Detachment, 265, 268, 305
Determinism, psychic, 12–15, 440
Deutsch, H., 249, 262, 307, 313, 487,
    533
Development
  arrest in, 89, 400
  assessment of, 179–193
  balance between deprivation and grat-
    ification, 8
  of blind infants, 355–370
  block in, 87
  of body-self experience, 236–239
  change of function in, 7, 9, 21
  cognitive, 410
  of complex nonverbal symbols, 198
  conflict-free, 37
  critical phases, 177
  dating of events, 150

inborn capacities, 84
innate factors in, affecting mother's mothering capacity, 334
intrapsychic life, 404–407
licking and tongue movements, 38–40, 61–62, 436
merging of physiological and psychological phenomena, 174
mimicking mother, 177–178
on mother's knee, 335–337
need satisfaction, 185–186
perception of other people's affects, 190
raised by nonspeaking adult, 36
reactions to feeding, 181–182
response to: maternal care, 191; mother's affective state, 83, 190
see also Child, Neonate
Infant-mother unit
"good enough," 333–334, 337–340, 343, 347
a psychic field, 118–119, 124, 318–319
see also Mother-child relationship, Symbiosis
Infantile amnesia and imaginary companion, 168–170
Infantile neurosis
and component instincts, 85–87
and early psychosomatic events, 82–84
forerunners, 85–87
genetic and dynamic considerations, 79–90
impact on late adolescence, 243–263
incipient, 413
multiple view, 89
Infantile sexuality, 246, 388
Infantilism, 18, 400
Inhibition, 8, 16, 20, 22, 83, 88, 115, 133, 139, 226–227, 447, 471, 479–481
Insight, 13, 401, 442–444
Inspiration, 508–509
Instinct, Instinctual drives (*Trieb*)
ambiguity of concept, 107
and autonomy, 18
biological concept, 100–101, 126
as biological force, 106–115
breakdown, 56
changes in theory, 105–113
clash between, 136, 139, 141, 145, 150
classification, 26, 33–34, 59–60, 99, 112
and cognitive memorial processes, 121
and defense, 11, 109
defusion, 52–54, 62, 99
development: 38–41, 53–54, 62, 66–67, 126, 183–188, 420, 437; early, 85–87
discharge, 121–122

duality, 113, 116
and ego, 10–11, 17, 20, 25, 207–208
fusion of, 36–42, 46, 53–54, 61, 64–66, 99, 383
interaction with environment, 47–48
Kleinian theory of, 146–147
and mental (psychic) representative, 107, 109, 112–113, 119–122, 126, 143–145
and motivation, 109, 115
as motivational force, 118
nonanalytic concepts, 105
and object, 116–126
organization, 118–126
passive and active aims of, 14
psychological concept, 100–101, 116
sexual, 123; *see also* Libido, Sex
somatic concept, 119
and total psychic organization, 104–114
transformation, 100
transmutation of, 104
vicissitudes, 119
see also Aggression, Death instinct, Libido, Life instinct
Instinct psychology, 114
Instinctualization, 6, 9–12, 22–23, 102, 256, 507
Institutional care, *see* Residential nurseries
Integration
failure, 416
of imaginary companion, 170
Integrative function, 5, 531; *see also* Synthetic function
Intellectual defects, 81
Intellectualization, 7
Intelligence, representation of, 410
Intercourse, 43, 134, 141, 471
Internalization, 27, 84, 170, 411, 480
failure, 415
and imaginary companion, 160
transmuting, 316–349
weak, 88
Interpretation, 89, 151
in analysis of resistant adolescent, 458–477
in child analysis, 130–131
cognitive, 397
"complete," 446–447
and confirmatory memory, 387–388
downward and upward, 98
dynamic, 94–95
dynamic-genetic, 397
effect of, 97–98
of failure to choose, 444–445

CONTENTS OF VOLUMES 1–25

CONTENTS OF VOLUMES 1—25